# JavaScript
## Concepts & Techniques
Programming Interactive Web Sites

## Tina Spain McDuffie

*Cuyamaca College*

Franklin, Beedle & Associates, Inc.
8536 SW St. Helens Drive, Suite D
Wilsonville, Oregon 97070
(503) 682-7668
www.fbeedle.com

President and Publisher     Jim Leisy (jimleisy@fbeedle.com)
Production                  Stephanie Welch
                           Tom Sumner
Proofreader                Dean Lake
Cover                      Ian Shadburne
Marketing                  Christine Collier
Order Processing           Krista Brown

Printed in the U.S.A.

Library of Congress Cataloging-in-Publication Data is available from the publisher upon request.

**For Tim:**
  my rock, my anchor,
  and the wind beneath my wings.

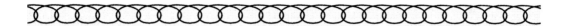

# Contents

## Chapter 3    Data Types, Variables, and Literals    page 75

## Chapter 4    Expressions and Statements    page 107

## Chapter 5    Events and Event Handlers                    page 131

## Chapter 6    Control Structures                            page 161

## Chapter 7     Arrays                                           page 187

## Chapter 8     Functions and Libraries                           page 223

# Chapter 9     Manipulating Strings        page 249

# Chapter 10     Dates and Math        page 291

# Chapter 11     Windows and Frames        page 327

## Chapter 14    Cookies                                     page 471

## Chapter 15    Dynamic HTML                                page 519

# *Preface*

## Who Should Read This Book

This book is appropriate for anyone with a good working knowledge of HTML who wants to add interactivity to a Web site with JavaScript, including Web development students, Web professionals, and Web hobbyists. Written with the novice programmer and non-programmer in mind, *JavaScript Concepts & Techniques: Programming Interactive Web Sites* introduces basic programming concepts in a friendly manner while demonstrating techniques and scripts that you can immediately begin applying to your Web projects. Experienced programmers will find plenty of information on JavaScript's idiosyncrasies, a detailed object reference, and oodles of scripts to begin playing with immediately.

## Supporting Web Site

Because JavaScript is so tightly tied to the Web, I thought it appropriate and essential to create a Web site in direct support of this book. You'll find it at www.javascriptconcepts.com and www.webwomansbooks.com. Features of the Web site include

- **A searchable glossary**, which you can use to quickly look up programming and Web development terms.
- **A sample chapter** and **table of contents**.
- **Errata**, listing all known errors in the book with appropriate correction notes. Should you discover an error, an online form is provided so you can report it. I'll even give you credit for reporting it on the Errata page.

- ✗ The book's **index**, which provides an in-depth look at everything in the book.
- ✗ **FAQ**, a list of frequently asked, and answered, questions.
- ✗ **News and reviews**—you, too, can post your own review of the book.
- ✗ **A connection to WebWoman**, www.webwoman.biz, a Web site dedicated to providing information on a variety of Web development topics in the form of articles and numerous scripting examples.

# Formatting Conventions

## Terms

New terms are listed in bold and defined within the text near the bolded term. These items are also listed in the glossary at the end of the book.

**side note** — Tidbits and notes of general interest appear here and there. They are formatted like this.

## Short Bits of Code

```
All JavaScript and HTML coding is formatted in a monospaced
font and indented as shown here. Single words representing
code are simply written in this monospaced font.
```

Code that wraps to the next line but needs to be entered as one line has gray arrows showing the line continuation.

```
Example of a long snippet of code that should be entered ⟶
⟶ on a single line.
```

## Blocks of Code

Entire blocks of code are displayed as shown below. Lines are numbered in gray so that I can easily explain what a line does without having to repeat the contents of the line. Unnumbered lines of code indicate a continuation of the previous numbered line of code. Do *not* enter a hard return between the numbered and unnumbered lines. You also should *not* number your lines of code. JavaScript does *not* recognize line numbers in its code. I have provided line numbers here only to make explanations simpler and debugging easier. Another reason for showing line numbers here is that error messages usually specify a line number. Most good editors allow you to display line numbers next to your code, so that you can more easily troubleshoot and debug it. While technically a block of HTML code alone does not a script make, I will still refer to all blocks of code as "scripts."

| Script | Sample Block of JavaScript and/or HTML Code |
|---|---|

```
1   Code shown here in monospaced font.
2   Do not type line numbers.
3   They are placed here to simplify explanations and
4   assist with debugging only!
5   Because of formatting constraints, some lines of
        code run over like this.
6   Treat unnumbered lines as part of the previous one.
7   Write the two parts of line 5 on a single line.
```

## Use of Semicolons (or Lack Thereof in This Book)

According to the author of the JavaScript language, Brendan Eich, "requiring a semicolon after each statement when a new line would do, [was] out of the question—scripting for most people is about writing short snippets of code, quickly and without fuss." Thus, the JavaScript language does not require the use of semicolons to terminate statements; a simple line break will do unless you place more than one statement on a single line.

> **programmer's tip**
> Tips and tricks to help you, the programmer, are scattered throughout the book and easily identified by the formatting you see here.

While some JavaScript programmers use semicolons religiously even though they are optional, I have intentionally left them out except where required. Without them the code is simpler. There is one less thing for the novice programmer to worry about. Besides, who am I to argue with the guy who wrote the language in the first place?

> **peek ahead**
> Descriptions of scripts or topics that will be covered in more depth in a future chapter or section appear in boxes like this. They give you something to look forward to.

My personal recommendation is that if you are in the habit of using semicolons because you are currently programming in a language that requires them, such as C, C++, Java, Perl, or PHP, then, by all means, continue to use them, even in your JavaScript programs. Why try to break a habit? You'll just end up with some lines with them and some lines without them, which *can* cause you trouble. Either use them all the time, or skip them altogether, except in those cases when you must use them, like when writing two or more statements on a single line, usually in an event handler.

# CD-ROM

All scripts listed in this book have been provided on the accompanying CD; they are organized by chapter. When a script requires more than one file, it will reside in its own directory. Any images or other files referenced in the HTML or JavaScript code can be found in a subdirectory named "images" with the appropriate script.

# XHTML Compliance

For the most part, the scripts in this book are pretty close to XHTML compliance. You'll generally need to make only a few changes to bring them into XHTML compliance:

1. Change the Doc-Type tag at the beginning of the script. All of the scripts on the CD-ROM include an appropriate Doc-Type tag at the beginning. However, for simplicity's sake, I left them out of the text of the book.
2. Close empty tags. In XHTML all tags must be closed, even those that do not normally have a closing tag. To close a <br> tag, replace the <br> tag with <br />.
3. Place quotation marks around *all* tag attribute values. In HTML, the rule is that any attributes that contain characters other than letters or numbers must be quoted. For the most part, I've quoted all HTML attribute values except in a few cases where not doing so made the JavaScript simpler.
4. Provide values for all tag attributes. For instance, HTML checkboxes and radio buttons may have a checked attribute that causes the field to be checked by default:

   ```
   <input type="checkbox" value="white" checked>
   ```

   XHTML requires that all attributes have a value. Thus, you would fix the <input> tag as follows. (Note: It also needs a closing tag.)

   ```
   <input type="checkbox" value="white" checked="checked" />
   ```

That pretty much covers the changes you're likely to have to make to bring the scripts in this book into compliance. The remaining rules of XHTML are

1. Write all tags in lowercase.
2. Write all attributes in lowercase.
3. Write all attribute values in lowercase.

Perhaps the next version of the book will have scripts in total compliance with XHTML.

# A Note to the Instructor

Teaching JavaScript is different than teaching other programming languages in that most students enrolling in a JavaScript course do not have any prior programming experience. Further, unlike most programming students, they will likely *not* go on to become computer programmers or computer scientists. Most JavaScript students are Web developers or would-be Web developers seeking knowledge and skills they can immediately apply to their own Web projects or use to enhance their employability.

What sets this book apart from others is its coverage of basic programming concepts. Most JavaScript books on the market assume prior programming experience of the reader. I have found that in a college and continuing education environment this is an unreasonable and faulty assumption. At least 75–85% of my JavaScript students have been novice programmers for whom JavaScript was their first programming language. While some found an interest in Web programming, most had no desire to learn another language.

In addition to the programming concepts and language details you expect to find in a programming textbook, I have provided numerous scripting examples that students can deconstruct for enriched understanding, then quickly apply to their existing Web projects. Every chapter ends with a series of review questions, exercises, and scripting exercises. Where appropriate, programming projects have been provided as well.

## Instructor Manual

An instructor manual is available from the publisher. It contains the usual things found in an instructor manual, including

- ✗ Solutions to all of the review questions and exercises in this book
- ✗ Scripted solutions to all scripting exercises in this book
- ✗ Suggested projects and sample solutions to projects
- ✗ A sample class syllabus
- ✗ A sample class schedule of topics (with variations)
- ✗ An archive of test questions, both multiple choice and written

## Online Instructor Resources

In addition to the instructor manual, a Web site has been created to support this book. Besides the usual table of contents, errata, and sample chapter, the Web site is loaded with additional information regarding the book, including

- ✗ **A searchable glossary** students can use to quickly look up programming and Web development terms.
- ✗ The book's **index**, which provides an in-depth look at everything in the book.
- ✗ **FAQ**, a list of frequently asked, and answered, questions.
- ✗ **A "Tips for Teaching JavaScript" discussion forum** where instructors can share tips and problems and otherwise communicate and support each other.

## Chapter Selection for Different Courses

### An 18-week course devoted to JavaScript programming:

Introduction, Chapters 1 through 16, and Appendix D ("Debugging JavaScript"). The course could also use Appendix F ("Cross-Browser Dynamic HTML") to augment Chapter 15.

### A 16-week course devoted to JavaScript programming:

Introduction and Chapters 1 through 16, one chapter per week. The course could replace one of the last two chapters with Appendix D on debugging.

**An eight-week introduction to JavaScript course:**
Introduction and Chapters 1 through 8, one chapter per week.

**An eight-week intermediate JavaScript course:**
Quick review of material in Chapters 1 through 8; focus on Chapters 9 through 16. The course could include Appendix D.

**A 10-week, quarter-session course on JavaScript:**
Chapters 1 through 8 and selected topics or chapters from Chapters 9 through 16. Chapters 11 and 13 are highly recommended.

# *Acknowledgments*

I had a lot of support throughout this project from the planning stages through to the final product. In acknowledgment of that support I now extend many heartfelt thanks to:

- Tim McDuffie. Thank you for your loving support and long patience with my endless hours on the computer writing: during holidays, school breaks, summers, and weekends beyond count when we should've been enjoying our vacation.

- My students. You inspired me to write this book by providing the need and the initial encouragement. Your enthusiastic reception of completed chapters told me I was on the right track. Your pleading for new chapters kept me writing to the end.

- Marilyn Sprechman of the University of Phoenix for giving me confidence in my writing abilities. Were it not for your rigorous instruction, criticism, and praise, I'm not certain I would've attempted this book. That I still don't know how to use a comma is certainly not your fault. Yes, I still split an infinitive now and again. How else can one boldly go where no one has gone before?

- Nicolette Barber for your summer assistance compiling the glossary, entering changes, and performing other assorted word-processing tasks. Your help finishing the draft was invaluable: it bought me a week of relaxation before school started again. Thank you. I desperately needed that little break.

- Lori Beckstrand, Robert Del Valle, Jarod Galm, Gay Farace-Mann, PJ Filia, Jennifer Joe, Scott Kelman, Mel Mann, April McDevitt, Tim McDuffie, Chris Perrine, Mary Perrine, Tom Powell, Sandra Carine Smith, and Adnan Syed, my steadfast friends and former students who helped test my end-of-chapter review questions and exercises. Thank you, thank you, thank you. Without you, the Instructor's Manual would likely still be a work in progress. By the way, Scott, thank you for taking on those extra chapters and suggesting additional entries for the glossary.

✗ PJ Filia and Deanna Thompson for your last-minute word-processing help on the final revision when I was stressed and running against the clock.

✗ Jennifer Joe for your never-ending encouragement and conversations in the wee hours of the morning about lots of things from the latest reviews to choosing a color scheme for the book's Web site. Your friendship and advice are always appreciated.

✗ Again, my heartfelt thanks to my husband, Tim McDuffie, who gave up our Christmas and New Years to help me complete the index. Your patience and willingness to help in any way you could with nary a complaint is just one of the reasons that I love you so much.

Many thanks to the wonderful people at Franklin, Beedle, and Associates whose efforts, support, and expertise made publishing this book possible. My special thanks to

✗ the reviewers Michael Losacco, College of DuPage; Scott Mcleod, Riverside City College; and Dennie Van Tassell, Gavilan College, for helping to identify the strengths and weaknesses in my first draft. While your candidness was sometimes painful to hear, I appreciated it nonetheless. Incorporating many of your suggestions made for a better book.

✗ Ian Shadburne, illustrator. You've created an inviting, "JavaScript, take me away" feel that I like very much.

✗ Stephanie Welch, my editor. Thank you for correcting my creative use of commas and unsnarling those few tangled sentences in which I had trouble expressing myself. Your patience for renumbering lines in the scripts during the proofing stage deserves an award.

✗ Jim Leisy, my publisher. Thank you for believing in this project, and me as a writer. I greatly appreciate your hard work and dedication towards making this the best JavaScript textbook possible. You're good! You've already got me thinking about my next book!

# *Introduction*

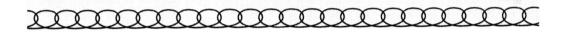

*It would appear that we have reached the limits of what it is possible to achieve with computer technology, although one should be careful with such statements, as they tend to sound pretty silly in 5 years.*

—John von Neumann (circa 1949)

I n the early days of the Web, there was only HTML. HTML was a wonderful invention: it provided us with a simple, yet effective, way to share information, images, etc. with others regardless of their computer or operating system type. However, authors and Web developers soon discovered that HTML had one serious drawback: it is static and unchanging. Once a document loads, it sits there like a bump on a log. HTML alone cannot dynamically respond to a visitor's actions, other than to open a document in response to a click on a link. HTML cannot, for instance, ask for the visitor's name and then greet him or her personally. HTML alone cannot query a visitor's preferences, store them, and retrieve them on the next visit. In short, HTML alone cannot interact with the user or write content dynamically. Enter JavaScript.

JavaScript is an **object-based** scripting language specifically designed to make Web pages dynamic and interactive. Client-Side JavaScript, so named because it runs on the visitor's or *client's* computer, derives most of its objects from the Web page itself. For instance, an image on a Web page is an object that can be manipulated with JavaScript. We can change its source property (src attribute) to display a different image in response to some user event such as the visitor moving the mouse over an image link. This is called an **image rollover**.

JavaScript allows us to obtain information from visitors in several ways. We can even store that information in a cookie and retrieve it on the user's next visit. Suppose the visitor prefers the non-frame version of a Web site. The next time she visits, we check the cookie, see that this person (actually this computer) prefers no frames, and refer the visitor to the appropriate Web document.

JavaScript is also wonderful for form validation. Because JavaScript runs on the client, the visitor's own computing power is used to validate form data, eliminating the need for long waits for a response from a **server-side** program. A server-side program is one that executes on the Web server using the resources and computing power of that computer. Server-side programs are more demanding on a server than client-side programs. The results of using Client-Side JavaScript to validate a form are a faster, perkier response for the user and less strain on the Web server.

**Table 1.1      *Popular Uses for JavaScript***

| | |
|---|---|
| ✗ Rollovers | ✗ Cookies |
| ✗ Status Bar Messages | ✗ Slide Shows |
| ✗ Browser Detection | ✗ Calculations |
| ✗ Redirecting the Visitor | ✗ Plug-in Detection |
| ✗ Random Images and Quotes | ✗ Random Sounds |
| ✗ Pop-Up Windows | ✗ Cycling Banners |
| ✗ Form Validations | ✗ Displaying Current Date |
| ✗ Loading Multiple Frames at Once | ✗ Displaying Last Modified Date |

The table above lists only a smidgen of JavaScript's capabilities. As you work through this book, you will quickly discover that the possibilities are endless, limited only by your imagination.

# Other Approaches to Making Web Pages Dynamic and Interactive

Before the debut of JavaScript (and since), Web developers tried other approaches to creating dynamic Web pages including CGI (Common Gateway Interface) scripts, Java applets, client pull, server push, and a variety of plug-ins. While there are times when each of these methods may be a more appropriate choice than JavaScript, each has its drawbacks for client-side interaction. Let's take a closer look.

## CGI Scripts

**CGI scripts**, often written in Perl (Practical Extraction and Report Language), are programs that run on the server and are capable of interacting with other applications and server resources. CGI scripts can be quite powerful and are often used to provide Web-database interaction, create shopping carts, etc.

Perhaps the two most common ways that CGI scripts have been used to add interactivity to Web pages are through form validations and image maps. However, client-side image maps provide a more responsive alternative to CGI-scripted image maps. While form validations are still regularly performed by CGI scripts, JavaScript form validations typically execute faster and are often easier to implement. Please don't think that this makes CGI scripting useless, far from it. While Client-Side JavaScript can check to see if a zip code *looks* valid, a CGI script can determine if it *is* valid by looking it up in a database of valid zip codes. When it comes to opening, reading, and searching files, CGI scripting is the clear winner. JavaScript, except for the server-side version, is of no help whatsoever; it does not have permission to open, read, and manipulate files.

**programmer's tip**
Use JavaScript to validate a form, but back it up with a call to a CGI script form validator. That way if the visitor's browser doesn't support JavaScript, then the form data still gets validated by the CGI script. If the visitor's browser does support JavaScript, then that's one less form validation the server had to perform and you've lightened its load. Multiply that by thousands or even millions of transactions, and if the server has to perform 50% of the validations (though 5 to 10% is more likely), you've still lightened its load considerably.

## Java Applets

Another approach Web developers have used and continue to use to create interactive Web sites is **Java**. Java is a full-fledged, object-oriented programming language, unlike JavaScript, which is only an **object-based** programming language. Java was developed by Sun Microsystems to provide a **cross-platform** programming language. "Cross-platform" means able to run on a variety of operating systems and computer types. Java can be used to write complex applications as well as small programs, called **applets**, that can be embedded in Web pages and run by a browser.

All Java programs are first compiled into **byte code** and then interpreted by a Java Virtual Machine (JVM). "Byte code" is a term coined by Sun to describe its not-quite-machine-code equivalent. In the case of applets, the Java Virtual Machine is part of a Java-enabled Web browser.

Because Java is a full-fledged, object-oriented programming language, it is much more complicated to use, is not forgiving in the least (one missing semicolon can break your program), is **strongly typed**, and has a much steeper learning curve. Assuming you get past those barriers and successfully write your own applets, applets can still sometimes take a while to load.

Because JavaScript is still often confused with Java, let's take a closer look at their differences:

**Table 1.2    *JavaScript vs. Java***

| JavaScript | Java |
|---|---|
| Object-based scripting language, uses built-in objects, but no classes. | Object-oriented programming language. |
| Developed for the express purpose of enhancing Web pages. | General-purpose language. *One* of its uses is to enhance Web pages through Java applets. Originally developed as a cross-platform language for home electronics. |
| Interpreted. | Compiled into byte code, then interpreted by a Java Virtual Machine. In the case of applets, the JVM is contained in the browser. |
| Loosely typed—don't have to declare a variable's type before using it. Netscape describes JavaScript as "dynamically" typed because a variable's data type can change during program execution. (We'll discuss data types in detail in Chapter 3.) | Strongly typed—must declare a variable's type before using it. (We'll discuss data types in detail in Chapter 3.) |
| Code embedded into HTML. | Applet code is distinct from HTML because it is compiled. The applet itself is a class file, called by an <applet> HTML tag. |
| Forgiving syntax. | Strict syntax. |
| Easy to learn, easy to use. | Difficult to learn, complicated to use. |
| Not fully extensible. Has a limited set of base objects, properties, methods, and data types. | Fully extensible. Programmers can define their own classes. |
| Good for client-side interactivity. | Good for client-side special effects in the form of applets for client-server interaction and stand-alone applications. |
| Developed by Netscape Communications. | Developed by Sun Microsystems. |

## Client Pull

**Client pull** is a dynamic document mechanism whereby a Web page contains a directive, usually in a <meta> tag, that says, "Reload this document in seven seconds." Well, it doesn't use those words exactly, and it doesn't have to be seven seconds per se. The tag looks like this:

```
<meta http-equiv="refresh" content="7">
```

Alternatively, and more often, the directive might say, "Load this other document in seven seconds":

```
<meta http-equiv="refresh" content="7;
url=http://www.someplace.com/otherdoc.html">
```

Cool, huh? Notice that the quotation marks in the second example surround "7; url=http://www.someplace.com/otherdoc.html". This is correct, as the quoted text—including the time period and the URL—is the value for the content attribute.

Client pull is how most Web developers accomplish **splash pages**. Splash pages show a fancy graphic or run a Flash animation, then sweep the visitor on to the main site. Client pull is also excellent for "We've moved" Web pages and auto-running slideshows. The refresh value also works on images and audio files. Imagine using it to continuously update a live image from a camera feed!

## Server Push

**Server push** is client pull's opposite. In this case, the server sends a requested document, but instead of terminating the connection as it normally does after serving a request, it maintains the connection and after some period of time delivers more data. The server has total control over when and how often data is sent. The major drawback of server-push technology is that it is extremely demanding on the server. This can be a problem if the server has few TCP/IP ports. One very cool thing about server push is that you can use it to send a single inline image; that is, the rest of the Web document can stay where it is and just the image changes. There is no need to reload the entire document when only that image changes (for example, a live camera feed) and the visitor won't see any blank screens between updates. Server-push applications are generally created with a CGI-compatible language like Perl or C, though they can be written in shell script as well.

## Plug-ins

**Plug-ins** such as Shockwave, Flash, QuickTime, RealAudio, RealVideo, and Windows Media Player are wonderful ways to add interactivity and animation to Web sites. The major drawback of plug-ins is that the visitor must have the appropriate plug-in installed in order to access the animation, movie, sound file, etc. If the visitor doesn't already have the appropriate plug-in installed, chances are very high that he or she will simply surf on, rather than take the time to download and install the plug-in. The good news is that many newer browsers now have built-in support for Flash; users don't have to download the plug-in separately. Here's a short list of some of the most popular file types and their associated plug-ins:

**Table I.3        Popular Plug-ins**

| | |
|---|---|
| **File Extension:** | .au |
| **File Type:** | Next/Sun audio format |
| **Plug-in:** | Apple QuickTime, Windows Media Player |
| **Where to Get It:** | http://www.apple.com/quicktime/download/ http://windowsmedia.com/ |
| **File Extension:** | .avi |
| **File Type:** | Audio-Video Interleaved (Windows video format) |
| **Plug-in:** | Apple QuickTime, Windows Media Player |
| **Where to Get It:** | http://www.apple.com/quicktime/download/ http://windowsmedia.com/ |
| **File Extension:** | .dcr, .dir, .dxr |
| **File Type:** | Shockwave |
| **Plug-in:** | Macromedia Shockwave Player |
| **Where to Get It:** | http://www.macromedia.com/shockwave/download/ |
| **File Extension:** | .mid, .midi |
| **File Type:** | Musical Instrument Digital Interface |
| **Plug-in:** | Apple QuickTime, Windows Media Player |
| **Where to Get It:** | http://www.apple.com/quicktime/download/ http://windowsmedia.com/ |
| **File Extension:** | .mov, .qt |
| **File Type:** | QuickTime movie |
| **Plug-in:** | Apple QuickTime |
| **Where to Get It:** | http://www.apple.com/quicktime/download/ |
| **File Extension:** | .mp3 |
| **File Type:** | MPEG-1 Layer 3 |
| **Plug-in:** | Apple QuickTime, RealJukebox, Windows Media Player |
| **Where to Get It:** | http://www.apple.com/quicktime/download/ http://www.real.com/jukebox/ http://windowsmedia.com/ |
| **File Extension:** | .mpeg |
| **File Type:** | Moving Pictures Expert Group |
| **Plug-in:** | Apple QuickTime, Windows Media Player |
| **Where to Get It:** | http://www.apple.com/quicktime/download/ http://windowsmedia.com/ |

| File Extension: | .pdf |
|---|---|
| File Type: | Portable Document Format |
| Plug-in: | Adobe Acrobat Reader |
| Where to Get It: | http://www.adobe.com/products/acrobat/readstep.html |

| File Extension: | .ra, .ram |
|---|---|
| File Type: | Real Audio |
| Plug-in: | RealPlayer |
| Where to Get It: | http://www.real.com/player/ |

| File Extension: | .rm, .ram |
|---|---|
| File Type: | Real Video |
| Plug-in: | RealPlayer |
| Where to Get It: | http://www.real.com/player/ |

| File Extension: | .swf |
|---|---|
| File Type: | Flash animation |
| Plug-in: | Macromedia Flash Player |
| Where to Get It: | http://www.macromedia.com |

| File Extension: | .wav |
|---|---|
| File Type: | Waveform (Windows audio format) |
| Plug-in: | Apple QuickTime, Windows Media Player |
| Where to Get It: | http://www.apple.com/quicktime/download/ http://windowsmedia.com/ |

| File Extension: | .wm, .wma, .wmv |
|---|---|
| File Type: | Windows Media, Windows Media Audio, Windows Media Audio/Video |
| Plug-in: | Window Media Player |
| Where to Get It: | http://windowsmedia.com/ |

## Summary

Hopefully this short introduction has given you a better understanding of why JavaScript has become the most popular scripting language on the Internet. As you read and work through this book, you'll learn how to add interactivity to your own Web sites with JavaScript.

## Review Questions

1. What is the major benefit of HTML?
2. How is HTML limiting?
3. List five popular uses of JavaScript in the order of your interest in learning to integrate them into your own Web sites.

4. List three technologies, besides JavaScript, that Web developers have used to create dynamic, interactive Web pages.
5. What is a CGI script?
6. What kinds of functions can a CGI script perform?
7. What is Java?
8. What is a Java applet?
9. What kinds of things is Java good for?
10. What is client pull?
11. What is server push?
12. What are plug-ins?
13. List your three favorite plug-ins in order of preference.
14. What kind of application does JavaScript perform best? Why?
15. How does JavaScript differ from Java? What do they have in common?

## Exercises

1. Make a list of at least three terms that you didn't understand from this chapter. Visit the supporting Web site for this book (http://www.javascriptconcepts.com). Use the searchable glossary to look up those terms.
2. Visit whatis.com. Enter any terms in your list of unknown terms that you didn't find in WebWoman's searchable glossary.
3. Visit the supporting Web site for this book (http://www.javascriptconcepts.com). Check the errata page to see if there have been any corrections/updates to the book and make the appropriate notes in your copy.
4. Visit the supporting Web site for this book (http://www.javascriptconcepts.com). Skim the list of frequently asked questions and read the details of any that you're curious about.
5. Many Web sites use JavaScript to add interactivity to their Web pages and to create special effects. Search the Web for sites (personal, professional, or commercial) that you think use JavaScript. Describe the interactivity or special effect you think was created with JavaScript. Explain whether you think the scripting was effective; that is, was it helpful, fun, useful, or just annoying? Would you use something similar on your Web site?

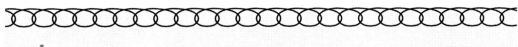

*chapter* **one**

# Introduction to JavaScript

*Any sufficiently advanced technology is indistinguishable from magic.*

—Arthur C. Clarke,
"Technology and the Future"

I n this chapter, we'll discover what makes JavaScript an object-based scripting language and take a look at the language's origins and history. Then we'll sink our teeth into the meat of JavaScript: objects, properties, methods, and events. We'll also

- see where JavaScript objects come from, when they are created, and how to access them.
- take a close look at the Document Object Model (DOM). What is it? And what does it have to do with JavaScript?
- examine the event model and how it makes JavaScript interactive.

## What Is JavaScript?

In the introduction we discussed how JavaScript can be useful. But what *is* JavaScript exactly? JavaScript is an object-based scripting language modeled after C++. Java, too, was modeled after C++, which is one reason they look similar and are often confused as the same language. So while you're learning JavaScript, you're also learning a little of the basic command syntax for Java and C++. Keep in mind, however, that while Java is a full-fledged, object-oriented programming language, developed by Sun Microsystems, complete with all the bells and whistles and complications inherent in object-oriented programming (OOP) languages, JavaScript is simply an **object-based** language. Most of Client-Side JavaScript's objects come from things found in Web pages such as images, forms, and form elements. That's one of the reasons JavaScript is considered an object-based language. More about that later.

*side note*

JavaScript is often said to be a sub-language of Java or derived from Java. That is simply not true. JavaScript is a programming language in its own right, developed by Netscape Communications. It is *not* a sub-language of Java.

OK, so JavaScript is a **scripting language**. "But what's a scripting language?" you ask. Scripting languages are programming languages that are generally easy to learn, easy to use, excellent for small routines and applications, and developed to serve a particular purpose. For instance, Perl (Practical Extraction and Report Language) began its life as a scripting language written for the express purpose of extracting and manipulating data and writing reports. JavaScript was written for the express purpose of adding interactivity to Web pages.

Scripting languages are usually **interpreted** rather than **compiled**. That means that a software routine, an interpreter, must translate a program's statements into **machine code**, code understandable by a particular type of computer, before executing them *every time the program is run*. Compiled languages, on the other hand, are translated into machine code and stored for later execution. When the compiled program is run, it executes immediately without further need of interpretation; it was interpreted into machine code when it was compiled. Because programs written in interpreted languages must be translated into machine code every time they are run, they are typically slower than compiled programs. However, this does not usually present a problem for the small applications for which scripting languages are generally used.

Being interpreted does have its advantages. One is platform independence. Because an interpreter performs the translation, you can write your program once and run it on a variety of platforms. All you need is the correct interpreter. In the case of JavaScript, the interpreter is built into Web browsers. Browsers are available for a variety of platforms and operating systems. Another advantage is that scripting languages are often loosely typed and more forgiving than compiled languages.

As a scripting language, JavaScript is easy to learn and easy to use. You can embed commands directly into your HTML code and the browser will interpret and run them at the appropriate time. JavaScript is also much more forgiving than compiled languages such as Java and C++. Its **syntax**, the special combination of words and symbols used by the language for programming commands, is simple and easy to read.

JavaScript is **loosely typed**. You don't have to declare the type of data that will be stored in a variable before you use it. If you decide to first store a number in a variable, then later store a string in it, JavaScript will neither grumble nor complain, even if doing so *isn't* the best programming practice.

# History

JavaScript was created by Brendan Eich of Netscape Communications and was first made available in 1995 as part of Netscape Navigator 2.0, the first JavaScript-enabled Web browser. Originally called LiveScript, JavaScript owes the Java part of its name to the popularity of Java, the cross-platform, object-oriented programming language created by Sun Microsystems. JavaScript was designed for the specific purpose (remember I said scripting languages are developed for a specific purpose) of extending the capabilities of Web browsers and providing Web developers with an easy means of adding interactivity to their Web sites.

**Table 1.1    Version History and Browser Support of JavaScript**

| Core JavaScript Version | ECMA Script Support | Client-Side JavaScript Version | Equivalent JavaScript Version | Browser Support | | |
|---|---|---|---|---|---|---|
| | | | | **NN** | **IE** | **OP** |
| 1.0 | | 1.0 | 1.0 | 2.0x | 3.0x | — |
| 1.1 | version 1 | 1.1 | 2.0 | 3.0x, | 3.02x* | 3-0x–3.5x* |
| 1.2 | | 1.2* | 3.0** | 4.0x-4.05 | 4.0x** | — |
| 1.3 | version 2 | 1.3 | 5.0-5.1 | 4.06-4.7x | 5.0x–5.1x* | 4.0x–5.0x |
| 1.4 | version 3 | | 5.5 | 5.0 (no release) | 5.5x* | 6.0x |
| 1.5 | version 3 | | 5.6 | 6.0x-7.0x+ | 6.0x* | 6.0x |

ECMA = European Computer Manufacturers Association, NN = Netscape Navigator, IE = Internet Explorer, OP = Opera
* Not fully ECMA-262 compliant (current version listed in chart at that level)
** ECMA-262 version 1 compliant

There are actually three flavors of JavaScript: Core JavaScript, Client-Side JavaScript, and Server-Side JavaScript. **Core JavaScript** is the basic JavaScript language. It includes the operators, control structures, built-in functions, and objects that make JavaScript a programming language (see Table 1.2). **Client-Side JavaScript** (CSJS) extends the JavaScript core to provide access to browser and Web document objects via the Document Object Model (DOM) supported by a particular browser. Client-Side JavaScript is, by far, the most popular form of JavaScript.

**Table 1.2     Core JavaScript**

| Objects | Operators | Functions | Control Statements |
|---------|-----------|-----------|--------------------|
| Array | `+ - * / % ++ -- -n` | `Boolean()` | `?...:` |
| Boolean | `= += -= *= /= %=` | `escape()` | `break` |
| Date | `== != === !== < <= > >=` | `eval()` | `continue` |
| Function | `&& || !` | `isFinite()` | `do...while` |
| global | `& | ^ ~ << >> >>>` | `isNaN()` | `for` |
| Math | `delete` | `Number()` [NN4] | `for...in` |
| Number | `new` | `parseFloat()` | `if` |
| Object | `this` | `parseInt()` | `if...else` |
| RegExp | `typeof` | `String()` [NN4] | `label:` |
| String | `void` | `unescape()` | `switch` |
| | | | `while` |
| | | | `with` |

Another extension to Core JavaScript is **Server-Side JavaScript** (SSJS). A Netscape server-side technology that provides access to databases, SSJS is a bit more complicated than its client-side sibling. SSJS, like CSJS, is embedded directly within HTML documents. However, in order to increase execution speed, an important concern when assembling Web pages on the server before delivering them to the Web browser, HTML documents that contain SSJS must be precompiled into JavaScript byte code. When a Web page that contains Server-Side JavaScript is requested, the server retrieves the document, executes the appropriate byte code on the server, accesses databases and other resources as necessary, and serves up the results as plain vanilla HTML to the browser. Because it returns plain HTML, SSJS can serve any type of Web browser and runs on any SSJS-enabled Web server. Client-Side JavaScript requires a JavaScript-enabled Web browser. Most of today's browsers are JavaScript-enabled.

In June 1997, the European Computer Manufacturers Association (ECMA) announced a new cross-platform scripting language standard for the Internet known as ECMA-262 or **ECMAScript**. The standard is based on Netscape's Core JavaScript 1.1. ECMAScript received International Organization for Standardization (ISO) approval as international standard ISO/IEC 16262 in April 1998. After some small editorial changes, the ECMA General Assembly of June 1998 approved a second edition of ECMA-262 in order to keep it fully aligned with ISO/IEC 16262. A third edition was approved in December 1999; it includes many improvements.

The subject of this book is Client-Side JavaScript, which includes Core JavaScript. However, in this text we'll refer to it simply as "JavaScript."

# Objects, Properties, and Methods, Oh My!

Because JavaScript is an object-based language, we will be working with—you guessed it—**objects**, as well as their properties and methods. So what *is* an object? Well, what's an object in the real world? It's an item, a thing. And as an item or thing, it has attributes or **properties** that describe it and make it unique. An object also has **methods**: actions you can perform with the object or on the object.

For instance, take your writing pen. It's an object. It has a case color on its outside, a particular ink color, and a type such as ballpoint, fountain pen, rollerball, etc. These pen attributes or *properties* describe your particular pen.

Now what is a pen good for? For writing, of course. Writing is an action you can perform *with* your pen. So we could say that your pen has a write *method.* What other actions can be performed with or on your pen? When the ink runs out, you can refill your pen. So we could say that your pen has a refill method. In this case, refilling is an action performed *on* your pen. Methods are, therefore, actions that we can perform with or on an object.

Another way to think of objects and their properties and methods is in terms of the parts of speech. In this case, objects are nouns, properties are adjectives because they describe the noun, and methods are verbs because they specify what the noun does.

JavaScript uses **dot notation** to refer to an object and its associated properties and methods. For instance, in dot notation, we refer to your pen as simply

```
pen
```

To reference your pen's ink color property we use the name of the object followed by a dot (period) and the name of the property. Notice that there are no spaces in the object and property names.

```
pen.inkColor
```

Changing the value of an object's property is often just the simple matter of assigning a new value to it. For instance, to change your pen's ink color, we could use a statement like this:

```
pen.inkColor = "blue"
```

The dot notation for methods is slightly different. While we still reference the name of the object first, followed by a dot and the method name, we end with a set of parentheses. The parentheses are meant to hold any arguments or parameters that provide data to or modify the performance of a method. For example, we need to be able to tell our pen what to write, so we send in an argument representing the text we want to write:

```
pen.write("Hello")
```

Now let's consider a real-world JavaScript example. Remember I said in the introduction that JavaScript derives most of its objects from Web documents? In fact, one of the most important objects in JavaScript is the document object itself.

Many HTML tag attributes can be accessed as object properties with JavaScript. Most, but not all, object properties have the same name as their HTML tag attribute equivalent. For instance, the appropriate attribute of the <body> tag for setting the background color is bgcolor. The equivalent document property name in JavaScript is bgColor (same name, different capitalization). Keep in mind that while HTML is **case insensitive**, JavaScript is **case sensitive**. While to HTML BGCOLOR, bgColor, and bgcolor are all the same, to JavaScript they are not the same at all!

Remember I said, "Most, but not all, object properties have the same name as their HTML tag attribute equivalent." The attribute of the <body> tag that specifies the document's text color is text. The equivalent document property is fgColor, which is short for "foreground color." HTML and JavaScript are referring to the same thing, only HTML uses the term "text," while JavaScript uses the term "fgColor." This happens from time to time. You'll find Appendix A, "JavaScript Object and Language Reference," to be quite useful in figuring out property names.

Let's get back to that real-world example I promised you. To refer to the document object itself in JavaScript dot notation, we simply write

document

To refer to its background color we write

document.bgColor

We can also write directly to the document using the document's write method:

document.write("Hello")

Try it for yourself. Open your favorite HTML editor or text editor and type the following code:

> **side note**
>
> Technically, document is a property of the window object. Its formal dot notation is window.document. However, JavaScript assumes when you use the shorthand, document, that you must be referring to the current window, that is, the window in which the document resides. Using the shorthand saves you a lot of typing, but there are times when it is critical to specify the window formally. We'll discuss those instances in Chapter 11, "Windows and Frames." For now, we'll continue to use the shorthand, document, instead of the formal, window.document, to reference the document object.

**Script 1.1   Using the write Method**

```
1   <html>
2   <head>
3   <title>Script 1.1: Using the Write Method</title>
4   </head>
5   <body bgcolor="white" text="black">
6   <script language="JavaScript" type="text/javascript">
7        document.write("Hello")
```

```
8    </script>
9    </body>
10   </html>
```

Save your document as a text file with an .html extension and open it in your browser. The results should look similar to this:

*Figure 1.1*    **Results of Script 1.1**

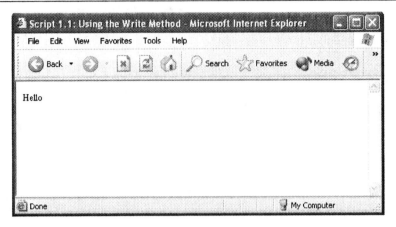

You can even use JavaScript to write HTML. What may seem confusing at first is that you write HTML tags like other strings in JavaScript, delimited by quotation marks. JavaScript doesn't understand HTML codes per se. The way it works is that you can use JavaScript to write the HTML code for you, *then* the HTML interpreter in the browser parses the HTML and applies your markup. You can also use JavaScript to write a <style> tag and stylesheet rules in the <head> of a document. Cool, huh?

To see this in action, let's modify Script 1.1 to write the greeting as a centered heading with the <h1> tag.

*Script 1.2*    **Using the `write` Method to Write HTML**

```
1    <html>
2    <head>
3    <title>Script 1.2: Using the Write Method to Write HTML</title>
4    </head>
5    <body bgcolor="white" text="black">
6    <script language="JavaScript" type="text/javascript">
7         document.write("<h1 align=center>Hello</h1>")
8    </script>
9    </body>
10   </html>
```

Here's what it looks like:

***Figure 1.2*** **Results of Script 1.2**

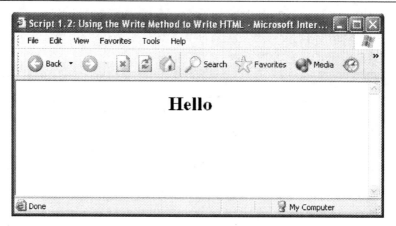

Now let's change the document's background and foreground colors from white and black (as set on the <body> tag) to blue and white. Insert the following lines before line 8 of Script 1.2 and change the title:

```
document.bgColor = "blue"
document.fgColor = "white"
```

Your script should now look like this:

***Script 1.3*** **Changing the Background and Foreground Colors**

```
1    <html>
2    <head>
3    <title>Script 1.3: Changing Background &amp;
         Foreground Colors</title>
4    </head>
5    <body bgcolor="white" text="black">
6    <script language="JavaScript" type="text/javascript">
7         document.write("<h1 align=center>Hello</h1>")
8         document.bgColor = "blue"
9         document.fgColor = "white"
10   </script>
11   </body>
12   </html>
```

Save the changed file with a new name and view it in your browser. This time, the document's background color will change to blue and its foreground color to white, like this:

***Figure 1.3    Results of Script 1.3***

Cool, huh?

Let's modify the script a little more. This time we'll examine the value of the document's `bgColor` and `fgColor` properties before and after our changes. Again, we can have JavaScript write the HTML to mark up the text. The document's `write` method can accept multiple string parameters; we simply have to separate them with commas, like this:

```
document.write(string1, string2, string3, ... stringN)
```

If you have really long strings to write, you can place them on separate lines; just always break at a comma, like this:

```
document.write(reallyReallyReallyReallyLongString1,
               reallyReallyReallyLongString2,
               string3, ... stringN)
```

This way, you can use a single `document.write` statement to write several lines of text.

Insert the following two lines of code after line 6 of Script 1.3:

```
document.write("<i>Original bgcolor: ", document.bgColor,
"</i><br>")
document.write("<i>Original fgcolor: ", document.fgColor,
"</i><br>")
```

Keep in mind, however, that you cannot simply let a string of characters wrap onto more than one line, like this:

```
document.write("<i>A Really Long Word: Supercalifragilistic
expialidocious</i>")
```

This would cause an error. You have two choices to fix it: keep the text all on one line or break the string into two strings, like this:

```
document.write("<i>A Really Long Word: Supercalifragilistic",
"expialidocious</i>")
```

This is perfectly legal and will output exactly as you intended.

Another important thing to keep in mind: Do *not* place quotation marks around object, property, or method references. Script 1.3 shows an example of how they should be written in lines 8 and 9: document.bgColor and document.fgColor. Both are property references and should not be quoted.

Insert the following two lines of code after line 9 of Script 1.3:

```
document.write("<b>New bgcolor: ", document.bgColor,
"</b><br>")
document.write("<b>New fgcolor: ", document.fgColor,
"</b><br>")
```

Your new script should look like this:

**Script 1.4     *Changing the Background and Foreground Colors***

```
1    <html>
2    <head>
3    <title>Script 1.4: Changing Background &amp;
        Foreground Colors</title>
4    </head>
5    <body bgcolor="white" text="black">
6    <script language="JavaScript" type="text/javascript">
7         document.write("<i>Original bgcolor: ",
             document.bgColor, "</i><br>")
8         document.write("<i>Original fgcolor: ",
             document.fgColor, "</i><br>")
9         document.write("<h1 align=center>Hello</h1>")
10        document.bgColor = "blue"
11        document.fgColor = "white"
12        document.write("<b>New bgcolor: ",
             document.bgColor, "</b><br>")
13        document.write("<b>New fgcolor: ",
             document.fgColor, "</b><br>")
14   </script>
15   </body>
16   </html>
```

Notice that each of the new `document.write` statements has three parameters; they are separated by commas. The document's `write` method allows you to send multiple parameters, each representing a piece of text to write to the document. For instance, in line 7 of Script 1.4, the browser is told to write the text `"<i>Original bgcolor: "`, followed by the current (original) value of the `bgColor` property, followed by a closing `</i>` and a `<br>` tag. Without the `<br>` tags, all the text would write on a single line. Remember, HTML ignores white space, so writing the JavaScript statements on different lines doesn't automatically get the content on different lines.

Now save your modified script with a new name and run it. The results should look similar to this:

***Figure 1.4***     ***Results of Script 1.4***

Notice that the colors are listed in hexadecimal: #ffffff is the hexadecimal equivalent of white, #000000 is black, and #0000ff is blue. White was the value initially assigned to the `bgColor` property of the document by the HTML in line 5. The values listed after "Hello" are the values we assigned to the `bgColor` and `fgColor` properties with JavaScript.

Table 1.3 summarizes our discussion of objects, properties, and methods.

***Table 1.3***     ***Summary of Objects, Properties, and Methods***

|  | Description | English Analogy | Real-world Example | JavaScript Example |
|---|---|---|---|---|
| **Object** | An item or thing. | noun | `pen` | `document` |
| **Property** | An attribute that describes an object. | adjective | `pen.inkColor` | `document.bgColor` |
| **Method** | An action that can be performed with or on an object. | verb | `pen.write()` | `document.write()` |

## Where Do JavaScript Objects Come From?

JavaScript objects originate in one of four places. Some are built into the language, like `Math`, `String`, `Date`, and `Array`; remember Core JavaScript? (See Table 1.2.) Most come from Web documents and are made available to Client-Side JavaScript via the Document Object Model (DOM). We've also seen that many object properties come from Web documents, often the attributes of HTML tags. A few objects come from the browser, such as the `navigator`, `location`, and `history` objects also made available to Client-Side JavaScript by the DOM. Lastly, we, as programmers, can create our own custom objects. Because most of JavaScript's objects come from Web documents, let's take a closer look at those first.

When a Web document contains an image, specified by an <img> tag in HTML, that document is said to "contain an `Image` object." If it has a form, specified by a <form> tag, it contains a `Form` object. It also may have paragraphs, headings, blockquotes, divisions, etc., but only the very latest browsers allow us to access or manipulate those objects, and they're still working on doing it the same way in compliance with Web standards. So what determines which objects we can manipulate? The Document Object Model implemented by a particular browser determines which objects we can access and manipulate in that browser.

# The Document Object Model

Think of the **Document Object Model** as a template built into a browser that specifies all of the objects and properties in a Web document that the browser can identify and allow you to access and manipulate, plus all of the methods you can perform with or on those objects. The Document Object Model represents *possibilities*.

Unfortunately, there's currently only a smattering of agreement among the major browser vendors, Netscape, Microsoft, and Opera, as to what possibilities to support and how to access them. The situation *is* improving with each new browser release as the major browser vendors adopt more of the current World Wide Web Consortium (W3C) DOM standard as well as the W3C's HTML and Cascading Style Sheets (CSS) standards. Pressure from standards support groups like The Web Standards Project (WaSP) have helped encourage browser vendors to comply with W3C standards.

**Figure 1.5    Cross-Browser DOM (JavaScript 1.1)**

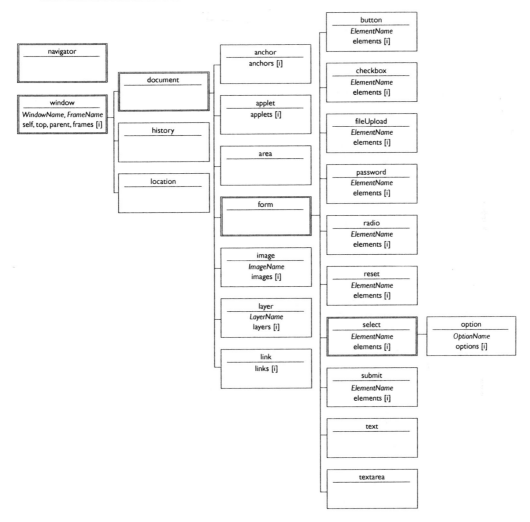

The above DOM illustration represents the DOM common to all three major browsers: Netscape Navigator, Microsoft Internet Explorer, and Opera. The newest browsers each support many more objects than those shown here, but they do so independently of or inconsistently with the other browser companies. See Appendix E, "Evolution of the Document Object Model," for a detailed description.

In the meantime, there are still plenty of objects for us to work with. While it can be frustrating sifting through all the differences and exceptions, there is a set of objects that we can safely rely on support for in all JavaScript-enabled browsers: those listed in Figure 1.5. Our initial focus in this book will be on those objects and their associated properties and methods. As you become more familiar with JavaScript, I will introduce additional objects, properties, and methods and specify which browsers support them. Sound good? Then let's go see how objects are created.

## When Are Objects Created?

The items contained in a Web document become objects in the browser's memory as the browser loads and interprets the HTML code that defines them. Notice that the DOM is arranged in a hierarchical way with `window` as the highest-level object. If you think about it a moment, you'll realize that every Web document is displayed or contained within a browser window. In essence, every object in a Web document is contained within some other object, with the exception of the `window` and `navigator` objects. The `window` object is the topmost or outermost container, and the `navigator` object, which represents the browser, is on the same level. Netscape characterizes this as an "**instance hierarchy.**"

Netscape originally called its DOM an "instance hierarchy" because its objects come into being the *instant* that the HTML code or JavaScript code that defines them is read and interpreted by the browser. Each Web document, therefore, creates a different and unique instance hierarchy. While the Document Object Model supported by a particular browser provides *possibilities*, the instance hierarchy specifies the *actual objects* that are created in the browser's memory when a particular Web document loads. If you stop a Web document's loading halfway through, only those objects already read and interpreted by the browser will be represented in its instance hierarchy.

Let's take a look at a simple HTML document, listed in the first column, and the instance hierarchy the browser creates in memory as it loads the document. We'll use the DOM in Figure 1.5 as our guide.

**Figure 1.6    Illustration of Instance Hierarchy**

| HTML | Instance Hierarchy |
|------|--------------------|
| `<html>`<br>`<head></head>`<br>`<body>`<br>`</body>`<br>`</html>` | 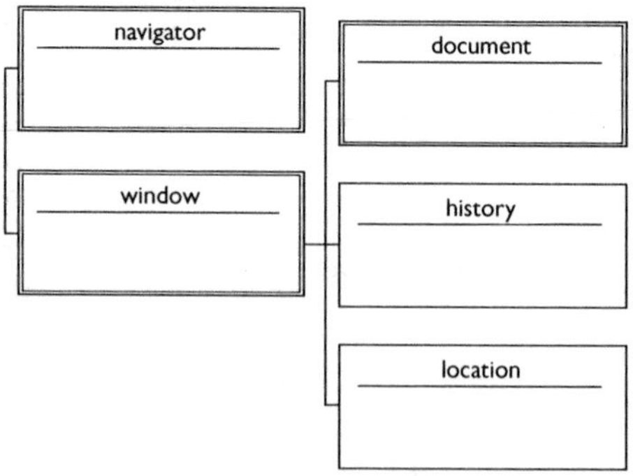 navigator / window / document / history / location |

OK, so this Web document doesn't really contain anything. If you preview it in your browser, you'll see only a blank page. Still, notice that this document does have an instance hierarchy. It's turned on its side to make it easy to see the associated dot notation:

**Figure 1.7    Illustration of Instance Hierarchy with Dot Notation**

| HTML | Instance Hierarchy | JavaScript Dot Notation |
|---|---|---|
| ```<html>```<br>```<head></head>```<br>```<body>```<br>```</body>```<br>```</html>``` | navigator    document<br><br>window    history<br><br>location | ```navigator```<br>```window```<br>```window.document```<br>```window.history```<br>```window.location``` |

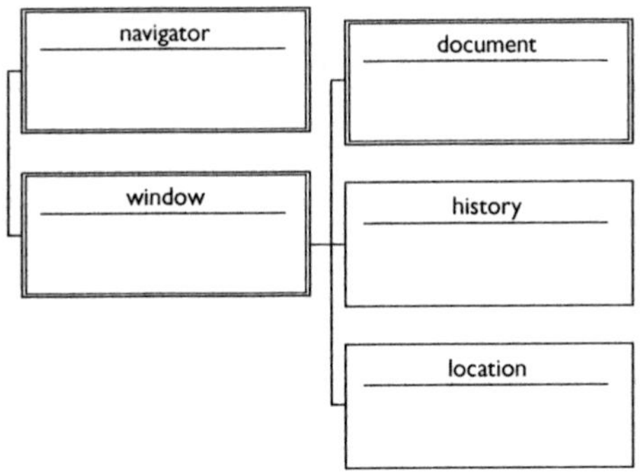

Dot notation dictates that you write the object name, followed by a dot and the object's property. Read the instance object hierarchy diagram above, left to right, inserting dots as needed and you get the dot notation listed in the last column. The `navigator` object represents the browser and is one of two top-level objects. Its name is rather Netscape biased, "browser" would be a non-biased name, but then Netscape was the company that created the JavaScript language, so I think that entitles them to some liberties. The `window` object is the other top-level object.

The `document` object is itself a property of the `window` object. This makes sense, because all documents in a Web browser are displayed in a window. The `history` object, also a property of the `window` object, represents the history list in the window. The history list contains the most recent pages you've visited during the current browser session, those that you can get to with the Back and Forward buttons. The `location` object, also a property of the window, represents the location of the current document (usually shown in the location bar, also known as the address bar) in the browser window.

Remember how we examined the contents of the document's `bgColor` and `fgColor` properties before and after we changed them in Script 1.4 using `document.write` statements? Let's use that same method to examine some of the properties of the objects listed in Figure 1.7 above.

Flip to Appendix A at the back of this book. You'll see a complete JavaScript object reference. You're going to be referring to this frequently, so you might want to stick a bookmark in it. It lists all of the objects, properties, and methods currently supported by the JavaScript language. Look up the `navigator` object. It will be listed in the "Client-Side JavaScript Objects" section.

**Figure 1.8     navigator *Object Listing from Appendix A***

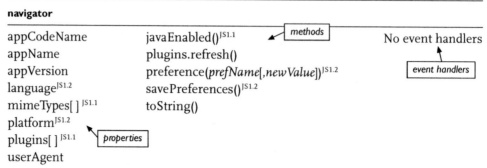

In the client-side section, each object has three columns listed under it. The first column lists all of the properties supported by that object as provided by the JavaScript language itself. The second column lists the methods that apply to that object, and the third lists the event handlers that can be used to handle activity on the object. See Figure 1.8.

We're going to use the document's `write` method (look it up, you'll find it listed in the second column under the document object) to display some of the `navigator` object's properties in Script 1.5, as well as those of the `window`, `history`, and `location` objects. Look up each object yourself and examine its properties. We'll use the dot notation listed in Figure 1.7 as a starting point and append each object with a dot and a property. For instance, to access the `userAgent` property of the `navigator` object, start with

```
navigator
```

and follow with a dot and the property name:

```
navigator.userAgent
```

Watch the case—remember JavaScript is case sensitive. Create a new document and type in the following code, or copy Script 1.5 from your CD-ROM. Typing the code yourself is good experience and highly recommended.

**Script 1.5     *Examining Property Values Using* document.write**

```
1    <html>
2    <head>
3    <title>Script 1.5: Examining Property Values Using
        document.write</title>
4    </head>
5    <body>
6
7    <script language="JavaScript" type="text/javascript">
8       document.write("<h2>Some navigator Properties</h2>")
9       document.write("appName: ", navigator.appName, "<br>")
10      document.write("appVersion: ", navigator.appVersion, "<br>")
11      document.write("userAgent: ", navigator.userAgent, "<br>")
```

```
12
13      document.write("<h2>Some window Properties</h2>")
14      document.write("innerHeight: ", window.innerHeight, "<br>")
15      document.write("innerWidth: ", window.innerWidth, "<br>")
16      document.write("location: ", window.location, "<br>")
17
18      document.write("<h2>Some history Properties</h2>")
19      document.write("length: ", window.history.length, "<br>")
20
21      document.write("<h2>Some location Properties</h2>")
22      document.write("href: ", window.location.href, "<br>")
23      document.write("protocol: ", window.location.protocol, "<br>")
24    </script>
25    </body>
26    </html>
```

Save the file to your floppy or Zip disk and open it in a browser. Your results may differ from those shown below depending on what browser you use and where you saved the file. Lines 9 through 11 of Script 1.5 write three properties of the navigator object to the document: appName, appVersion, and userAgent. The appName property indicates the browser's application name, appVersion indicates the browser's version number, and userAgent represents the user-agent header sent by HTTP from the browser to the Web server. It identifies the browser being used by the client.

**Figure 1.9     *Results of Script 1.5 in Internet Explorer***

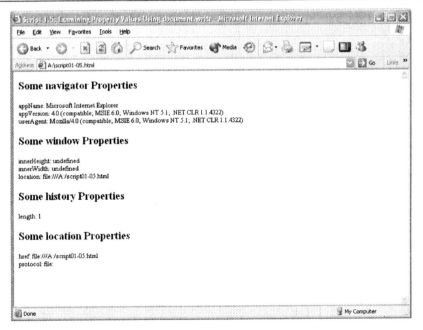

The window properties `innerHeight` and `innerWidth` (lines 14 and 15) are supposed to specify the inner dimensions of the window. Unfortunately, Internet Explorer's DOM doesn't support them and so wrote "undefined." The window's `location` property (line 16) *is* supported by Internet Explorer (IE) and shows the URL to the file currently being displayed in the window. The `history` property, `length`, indicates the total number of items in the history list (line 19). Finally, the `location` properties, `href` and `protocol`, represent the URL of the current document being viewed and its protocol (lines 22 and 23).

Let's see how this same document looks in a different browser. How about Netscape Navigator:

### Figure 1.10    Results of Script 1.5 in Netscape Navigator

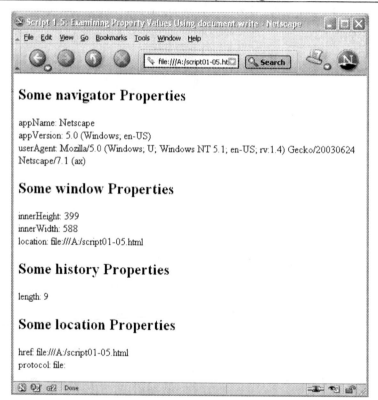

It's strange that this browser shows version 5 as its `appVersion` when we're using Navigator 7.0. It just goes to show that the `appName`, `userAgent`, and `appVersion` properties don't always report what you expect. Still, all three are often used to perform browser detection.

Look at the properties of the `location` object listed in Appendix A. See how you can access any part of a location's URL? Here's what each property that's a part of the URL means:

- ✗ hash—indicates the part of the URL that follows the hash mark or pound sign, that is, a named anchor reference.
- ✗ host—lists the server name, subdomain, and domain name.
- ✗ hostname—provides the full hostname of the server, including the server name, subdomain, domain, and port number.
- ✗ href—the entire URL.
- ✗ pathname—the path part of the URL, including the file name.
- ✗ port—the port number, if specified in the URL. If not, returns nothing.
- ✗ protocol—just the protocol portion of the URL, such as http:, ftp:, or file:.

You can check these out for yourself using Netscape Navigator and the javascript: pseudo-protocol. (This only works with Netscape Navigator, so if you don't have a copy, I highly recommend that you download one now.) Type a URL in the location bar. I'm going to visit Yahoo!, then click on Help and then Shopping so I get a nice long URL that includes a path as well as a domain name in the location bar. You don't have to visit Yahoo!, just visit the interior page of some Web site so you have a URL that has both a domain name and a path showing in the location bar.

*Figure 1.11    Visiting a Web Site's Interior Page*

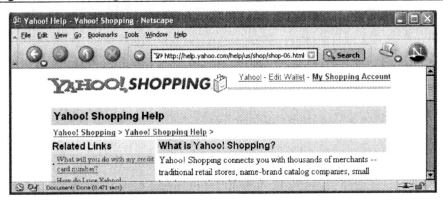

OK, now the fun part begins. Type

```
javascript: location.href
```

in the location bar of your Netscape Navigator browser. The javascript: pseudo-protocol allows you to run a JavaScript statement directly in your browser. You should get something like this after you press the Enter key.

**Figure 1.12    *Using the javascript: Pseudo-Protocol
to Display the Location's `href` Property***

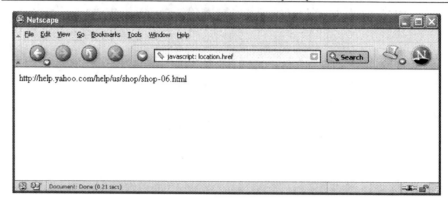

As you can see, the `href` property displays the entire URL. Let's try another. Click on the Back button of your browser to return to the Web page you were viewing. Now type

```
javascript: location.protocol
```

in the location bar and press the Enter key.

**Figure 1.13    *Viewing the `protocol` Property of the `location` Object***

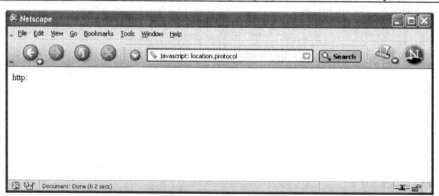

This time only the protocol portion of the location is displayed. Let's look at the hostname. Click on the Back button, then type

```
javascript: location.hostname
```

in the location bar and press Enter.

**Figure 1.14   Viewing the `hostname` Property of the `location` Object**

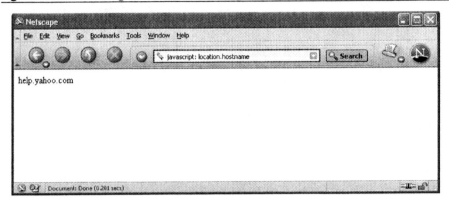

Now one more. Click on the Back button and type the following:

```
javascript: location.pathname
```

Press the Enter key.

**Figure 1.15   Viewing the `pathname` Property of the `location` Object**

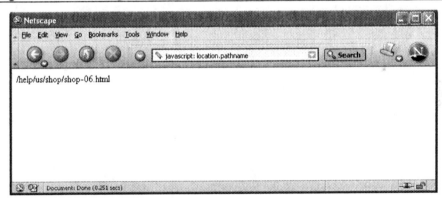

Cool, huh?

You can change the current location, that is, you can open a new location or URL in the current window, by modifying the `location` object's `href` property, like this:

```
location.href = newURL
```

Let's try it. In the location bar, type the following:

```
javascript: location.href = "http://google.com"
```

Press Enter. Navigator should take you to Google.

**Figure 1.16   Changing the Location**

Cool, huh? You'll use this a lot in scripts to open new documents in a window.

**programmer's tip**

You can save JavaScript statements using the javascript: pseudo-protocol as bookmarks and call them at any time to help you examine the results of scripts and assist with debugging. Here's how:

1. Type "javascript:" followed by the statement you'd like to invoke in the location bar.
2. From the Bookmarks menu, choose Add to Bookmarks or File Bookmark. I recommend the latter; then you can file them all in the same folder. I put mine in a bookmark folder named "JavaScript Statements."
3. Now you can access them at any time from your Bookmark list, like this:

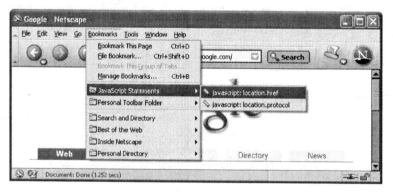

Nice little tool, huh?

OK, let's continue our discussion about the instance object hierarchy and how objects are created with another example. Let's modify the original HTML document shown in Figure 1.7 by adding an image. You can find the image in the images folder under the scripts directory on the CD-ROM that accompanies this book.

### Figure 1.17    Illustration of Instance Hierarchy with Image Added

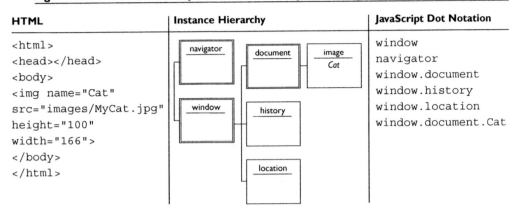

| HTML | Instance Hierarchy | JavaScript Dot Notation |
|---|---|---|
| `<html>`<br>`<head></head>`<br>`<body>`<br>`<img name="Cat"`<br>`src="images/MyCat.jpg"`<br>`height="100"`<br>`width="166">`<br>`</body>`<br>`</html>` | navigator, document, image Cat, window, history, location | `window`<br>`navigator`<br>`window.document`<br>`window.history`<br>`window.location`<br>`window.document.Cat` |

Notice that the instance hierarchy now contains an image; that image object's name is Cat. To see what properties an Image object has, turn to Appendix A, "JavaScript Object and Language Reference," and look up the Image object in the "Client-Side JavaScript Objects" section. Notice how the properties of an Image object roughly correspond to the attributes of an <img> tag?

### Table 1.4    Property Values for image Object Shown in Figure 1.17

| Property | Value |
|---|---|
| `window.document.Cat.name` | Cat |
| `window.document.Cat.src` | images/MyCat.jpg |
| `window.document.Cat.height` | 100 |
| `window.document.Cat.width` | 166 |

Let's write those properties out.

### Script 1.6    Examining Properties of the Cat image Object

```
1    <html>
2    <head>
3    <title>Script 1.6: Examining Properties of the Cat Image
4    Object</title></head>
5    <body>
6    <img name="Cat" src="images/MyCat.jpg" height="100" width="166">
7
8    <script language="JavaScript" type="text/javascript">
9      document.write("<h2>Some Properties of the Cat Image
         Object</h2>")
10     document.write("Name: ", window.document.Cat.name, "<br>")
11     document.write("Src: ", window.document.Cat.src, "<br>")
```

```
12      document.write("Width: ", window.document.Cat.width, "<br>")
13      document.write("Height: ", window.document.Cat.height, "<br>")
14  </script>
15  </body>
16  </html>
```

Lines 10 through 13 print the `name`, `src`, `width`, and `height` properties of the `Cat` image object. Notice that we accessed the `Cat` image object by its name, the name given it with the HTML name attribute on the `<img>` tag. A document can contain many images. The best way to distinguish between them is to give each a name. Then you can use that name to easily access that particular `image` object. I like to capitalize the names of objects I create with HTML so I can easily distinguish them from those I create with JavaScript. Then when I see a capitalized object name, I know immediately to look in the HTML document for that object.

Here's what the script looks like when run in a browser:

**Figure 1.18    Results of Script 1.6**

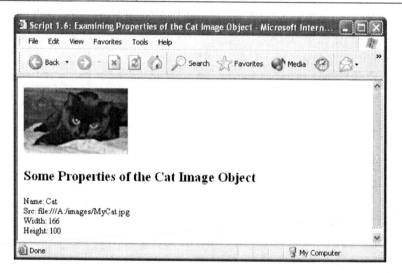

Now let's add a form and a text element to further illustrate this idea of accessing an object by its name as provided by the HTML element's name attribute.

*Figure 1.19     Illustration of Instance Hierarchy with Form and Text Element Added*

| HTML | JavaScript Dot Notation |
|------|------------------------|
| ```html
<html>
<head></head>
<body>
<img name="Cat" src="images/MyCat.jpg"
height="100" width="166">
<form name="MyForm"
method="post"
action="mailto:sam@pooch.com">
Name: <input type="text"
name="Visitor" value="Sam">
</form>
</body>
</html>
``` | ```
window
navigator
window.document
window.history
window.location
window.document.Cat
window.document.MyForm
window.document.MyForm.Visitor
``` |

**Instance Hierarchy**

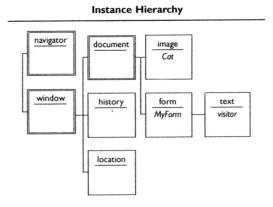

The form has the following properties:

*Table 1.5     Property Values for Form Object Shown in Figure 1.19*

| Property | Value |
|----------|-------|
| window.document.MyForm.name | MyForm |
| window.document.MyForm.method | post |
| window.document.MyForm.action | mailto:sam@pooch.com |

The text box has these properties:

**Table 1.6** **Property Values for Text Object Shown in Figure 1.19**

| Property | Value |
|---|---|
| window.document.MyForm.Visitor.name | Visitor |
| window.document.MyForm.Visitor.type | text |
| window.document.MyForm.Visitor.value | "Sam" or whatever value is typed in the box |

Let's verify the property values listed in Tables 1.5 and 1.6 by writing them with a script. This time we'll dispense with using "window" in the dot notation. When no particular window is specified, the interpreter assumes you are referring to the current window. While Tables 1.5 and 1.6 shows the formal dot notation to access those properties, we can simplify and shorten our code a little by letting the interpreter assume that the current window is the one whose document we want to access, like this:

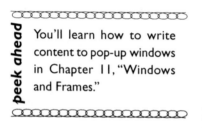

**peek ahead**

You'll learn how to write content to pop-up windows in Chapter 11, "Windows and Frames."

```
document.MyForm.method
document.MyForm.action
document.MyForm.Visitor.name
document.MyForm.Visitor.type
document.MyForm.Visitor.value
```

This saves us some typing. Keep in mind, however, that sometimes it *is* necessary to reference a specific window object by name. For instance, if you wanted to write content to a pop-up window, you'd have to reference that pop-up window by name to call the document.write method for that window.

**Script 1.7** **Examining Properties of the Form and Text Element**

```
1   <html>
2   <head>
3   <title>Script 1.7: Examining Properties of the Form and Text
        Element</title>
4   </head>
5   <body>
6   <img name="Cat" src="MyCat.jpg" height="100" width="166">
7   <form name="MyForm" method="post" action="mailto:sam@pooch.com">
8       Name: <input type="text" name="Visitor" value="Sam">
9   </form>
10  <script language="JavaScript" type="text/javascript">
11      document.write("<h2>Some Properties of the MyForm Form
            Object</h2>")
12      document.write("Name: ", document.MyForm.name, "<br>")
13      document.write("Method: ", document.MyForm.method, "<br>")
14      document.write("Action: ", document.MyForm.action, "<br>")
```

```
15
16              document.write("<h2>Some Properties of the Visitor Text
                   Element</h2>")
17              document.write("Name: ", document.MyForm.Visitor.name,
                   "<br>")
18              document.write("Type: ", document.MyForm.Visitor.type,
                   "<br>")
19              document.write("Value: ", document.MyForm.Visitor.value,
                   "<br>")
20      </script>
21      </body>
22      </html>
```

Save and view your file. The result should look similar to this:

### Figure 1.20    Results of Script 1.7

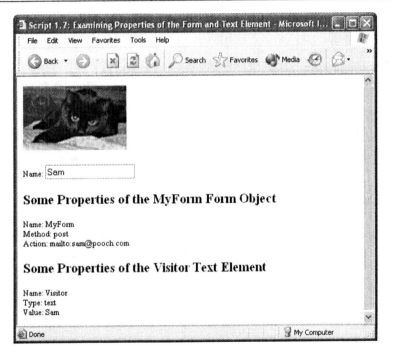

OK, so this may not be the most useful script in the book in terms of use on a Web site. Still, it's good to know how to access and write the values of object properties. When we discuss **debugging**, we'll use a similar technique to periodically check the values of object properties. Debugging is the process of finding and eliminating coding errors. Now on to the event model.

# The Event Model

While the Document Object Model supported by a particular browser specifies the objects and their associated properties and methods that we may manipulate and use, the **event model** specifies the browser and user events to which we, as programmers, may respond.

## Events Are the "Active" in Interactive

**Events** are occurrences generated by the browser, such as loading a document, or by the user, such as moving the mouse. They are the user and browser activities to which we may respond dynamically with a scripting language like JavaScript. Here's a short list of events that Web developers like to capture:

**Table 1.7**     ***Most Popularly Captured Events***

| Event | Description |
| --- | --- |
| Load | Browser finishes loading a Web document |
| Unload | Visitor requests a new document in the browser window |
| Mouseover | Visitor moves the mouse over some object in the document window |
| Mouseout | Visitor moves the mouse off of some object in the document window |
| Click | Visitor clicks the mouse button |
| Focus | Visitor gives focus to or makes active a particular window or form element by clicking on it with a mouse or other pointing device or tabbing to it |
| Blur | Visitor removes focus from a window or form element |
| Change | Visitor changes the data selected or contained in a form element |
| Submit | Visitor submits a form |
| Reset | Visitor resets a form |

There are several more events that we can capture with JavaScript, but the ones listed above are, by far, the most popular.

*side note*

The event model was originally a Netscape extension to HTML incorporated in the Netscape 2.0 browser. It has since been incorporated into the HTML 4.0 specification. HTML 4.0 refers to the event model as "intrinsic events." The HTML 4.0 specification is language neutral. That means that the specification neither recommends nor endorses a particular language for scripting event handlers. Currently, however, JavaScript is the only cross-browser, client-side language available for use in scripting event handlers.

*peek ahead*

We'll take an in-depth look at the complete event model in Chapter 5, "Events and Event Handlers."

## Event Handlers Are the "Inter" in Interactive

While events are the activities we, as Web developers, can respond to, event handlers are the mechanisms that allow us to capture and actually respond to events with JavaScript statements. Event handlers make Web pages *inter*-active. Here are the event handlers that correspond to the above-listed events:

**Table 1.8    Event Handlers Corresponding to Events Listed in Table 1.7**

| Event | Event Handler |
| --- | --- |
| Load | onLoad |
| Unload | onUnload |
| Mouseover | onMouseover |
| Mouseout | onMouseout |
| Click | onClick |
| Focus | onFocus |
| Blur | onBlur |
| Change | onChange |
| Submit | onSubmit |
| Reset | onReset |

Event handlers are written inline with HTML like tag attributes. For instance, to display an alert box that says "Welcome" when a document loads, write the event handler as you would any other HTML tag attribute, complete with quotes around the value associated with the attribute:

```
<body onLoad="alert('Welcome!')">
```

Try it. Type the following in your favorite editor and save it as a text file with an .html extension.

**Script 1.8    An onLoad Event Handler**

```
1    <html>
2    <head>
3    <title>Script 1.8: An onLoad Event Handler</title>
4    </head>
5    <body onLoad="alert('Welcome!')">
6
7    </body>
8    </html>
```

Open the document in your Web browser. An alert box should pop up with the message "Welcome" that looks similar to this:

**Figure 1.21    Results of Script 1.8**

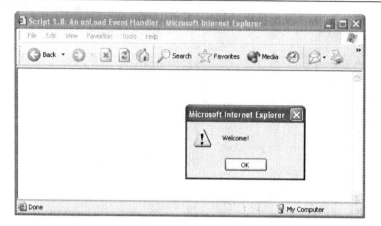

The title and exact appearance of an alert box vary by browser. Don't worry if yours doesn't look exactly like this. The message should be the same, though: "Welcome!"

Once the browser loaded the document, a *load* event occurred. The onLoad event handler in line 5 of Script 1.8 *handled* the event by generating an alert box with the message "Welcome!" Cool, huh? In later chapters, we'll examine how to capture other events and respond to them with JavaScript. For now, how about a recap?

**side note**

alert is a method of the window object. It takes a single string parameter representing the text you want to display in the alert box. Technically, its formal reference is *window.alert("Some Text")*. However, like with document, JavaScript assumes we want to use the current window, so most of the time we can leave off the window designation.

## Summary

JavaScript is an object-based scripting language modeled after C++. As a *scripting language* it is easy to use, easy to learn, is loosely typed, and was created for the express purpose of adding interactivity to Web pages. JavaScript is not Java, nor is it a sub-language of Java. JavaScript was created by Brendan Eich of Netscape and was first made available in 1995 as part of the Netscape Navigator 2.0 browser.

JavaScript comes in three flavors: Core JavaScript, which includes the basic constructs of the language; Client-Side JavaScript, which adds access to browser objects and elements in a Web page; and Server-Side JavaScript, which allows interactivity with server-side databases and other resources. Because JavaScript is an object-based language, it makes extensive use of objects and their inherent properties and methods.

The key to HTML/JavaScript functionality is the Document Object Model. The Document Object Model exposes HTML and browser elements to JavaScript for manipulation. The DOM represents *possibilities*. An instance hierarchy, on the other hand, is a model of a particular Web document in memory. The instance hierarchy and references to the objects modeled within it are created in memory as the Web page loads.

While the Document Object Model supported by a particular browser specifies the Web page and browser objects and their associated properties and methods, the event model specifies the browser and user *events* to which we may respond. Events are the browser and user activities that occur. Event handlers allow us to define how to handle those events with JavaScript.

## Review Questions

1. Who developed JavaScript?
2. List three common features of scripting languages.
3. List and describe the three "flavors" of JavaScript.
4. Is JavaScript a sub-language of Java? Explain.
5. What's the difference between a compiled language and an interpreted language?
6. What advantages do interpreted languages offer?
7. What is a Document Object Model?
8. What is an instance hierarchy as described in this book? When is it created?
9. Who is the World Wide Web Consortium (W3C)?
10. What does the W3C have to do with JavaScript?
11. Who is the European Computer Manufacturer's Association (ECMA)?
12. What does the ECMA have to do with JavaScript?
13. Define each of the following:
    a. object
    b. property
    c. method
14. Where do JavaScript objects come from?
15. What determines which objects in a Web document are accessible in a particular browser?
16. When are objects actually created?
17. What was the first browser to provide support for JavaScript?
18. What was Netscape's original name for the DOM?
19. What's the difference between an event and an event handler?
20. When does a load event occur?

## Challenge Questions

1. Why don't browser vendors adhere to the standards established by the World Wide Web Consortium? Or do they? Explain. (Hint: Read Appendix E, "Evolution of the Document Object Model.")

2. What object, added to the DOM with the release of Netscape Navigator 3, is one of most popular objects used in JavaScript? (Hint: Read Appendix E.)

3. What choices does a Web developer have when endeavoring to write code that works in most browsers? (Hint: Read Appendix E.)

# Exercises

1. Visit Netscape's "JavaScript Documentation" Web site (http://developer .netscape.com/docs/manuals/javascript.html). Check out the latest JavaScript specification. Download the current "Client-Side JavaScript Reference" for use in your scripting. This reference is invaluable.

2. Visit Opera Software's Web site (http://www.opera.com/). Download and install the latest browser. Visit the support page and examine the latest developments and JavaScript support criteria.

3. Visit Netscape's Web site (http://www.netscape.com/). Download and install the latest browser.

4. Visit Microsoft Internet Explorer's Web site (http://www.microsoft.com/ie/). Download and install the latest browser.

5. Suppose you have an object named Rose whose color property was set to pink.
   a. Write the appropriate dot notation to access the Rose object's color property.
   b. Write the appropriate code to change the Rose object's color property to yellow.

6. Draw a diagram describing the instance hierarchy a browser would create associated with the following HTML code:

```
<html>
<head>
        <title>My Document</title>
</head>
<body bgcolor="yellow" text="black" link="blue"
  vlink="purple">
<img name="MailBanner" src="banner.gif" width="600"
  height="100">
<form name="MailingList" method="post">
        Name: <input type="text" name="Visitor"
          value="Devan"><br>
        Email: <input type="text" name="Email"
          value="devan@kitcat.com"><br>
        <input type="submit" name="SubmitButton">
        <input type="reset" name="ResetButton">
</form>
</body>
</html>
```

    a. Write the complete dot notation for each object and property in your diagram.

    b. Modify the Web document to write the values of the Visitor and Email fields at the end of the page.

    c. Add JavaScript statements to change the background color to purple and the text (foreground) color to yellow.

    d. Using the JavaScript object reference in Appendix A, write the complete dot notation to call at least one method for each object in your diagram.

7. Visit the Web site for the W3C (http://www.w3.org). Check out the latest HTML specification.

8. Visit the Web site for the ECMA (http://www.ecma.ch). Check out the latest ECMA script specification.

9. Write the appropriate JavaScript statement to print your name in bold letters and your town in italics on the same line.

10. Write the appropriate JavaScript statement to print your name in bold letters and your town in italics on separate lines.

11. Write two JavaScript statements, one to print your name and one to print ", aka" and your nickname. Your nickname should be written in italics. Both your name and your nickname should appear in the document on the same line like this:

Tina Spain McDuffie, aka WebWoman

12. Many Web sites use JavaScript to add interactivity to their Web pages and to create special effects. Search the Web for sites (personal, professional, or commercial) that you think use JavaScript. Describe the interactivity of a special effect you think was created with JavaScript. Explain whether you think the scripting was effective; that is, was it helpful, fun, useful, or just annoying. Would you use something similar on your Web site?

13. Search the Web for three articles about good Web design. Summarize what you found.

# Scripting Exercises

Create a folder named assignment01 to hold the documents you create during this assignment.

1. Create a document named exploringJOR.html. Using the JavaScript object reference in Appendix A as a guide to the appropriate document properties, write a script to display the following information in a Web browser:

    a. The title of the Web document

    b. The location of the Web document

    c. The date the document was last modified

2. Create a personal home page named home.html with the following content:

    a. Your name written in the <title> and an <h1> tag at the top.

    b. A picture of yourself after or next to the heading. If you don't have a digital picture of yourself, use clip art or a favorite landscape.

    c. Add the following sections using the tags listed:
- i. &lt;h2&gt;My Assignments&lt;/h2&gt;—leave space underneath for later input.
- ii. &lt;h2&gt;About Me&lt;/h2&gt;—again leave space for later input.
- iii. &lt;h2&gt;Bio&lt;/h2&gt;—complete this section with some biographical information in paragraphs &lt;p&gt; . . . &lt;/p&gt;.
- iv. &lt;h2&gt;My Hobbies&lt;/h2&gt;—leave blank for later input.
- v. &lt;h2&gt;My Work/Job&lt;/h2&gt;—leave blank for later input.
- vi. &lt;h2&gt;My Browser&lt;/h2&gt;—leave blank for later input.
- vii. &lt;address&gt;Contact Info&lt;/address&gt;—leave blank for now.
- viii. &lt;p&gt;&lt;b&gt;Last Update:&lt;/b&gt; &lt;/p&gt;—we'll add more later.

3. Create a home page named toyStore.html for a company that sells toys. Include images of balls, jacks, whistles, skateboards, dolls, and other items that the toy company sells. You should be able to find the images you need from an online clip art library.

4. Open the personal home page you created. Insert a script under the My Browser heading that prints the following information about your browser:
   - a. appCodeName
   - b. appName
   - c. appVersion
   - d. platform
   - e. userAgent

5. Open the personal home page you created. Insert a script within the Last Update paragraph right after the words "Last Update:" to write the date when the document was last modified. (Hint: Examine the properties of the document object in Appendix A to find the appropriate property to supply this info.)

6. Open the personal home page you created. Under the image, add a script that writes the `src` property and dimensions of the image. (Hint: Give the image a name with HTML if you haven't already, so you can easily access its properties. Don't put any spaces in the image's `name` attribute.)

7. Open the personal home page you created. In the My Browser section, add a script that displays the current screen resolution, like the following example:

Screen Resolution: 800 x 600

Of course, the numbers should be provided by the appropriate property. (Hint: Check out the screen object in Appendix A.)

8. Open the personal home page you created. In the My Browser section, add a script that displays the current window's dimensions, like this:

Window Dimensions: 452 x 300

where the numbers are provided by the appropriate window properties. (Hint: Look up the `window` object in Appendix A. This may not work in all browsers; experiment with several different properties.)

9. Open the personal home page you created. In the My Browser section, add a script that displays the current document's location. Do not use the `href` property. Instead, write the protocol, host, and path name one after the other to display the document's URL.

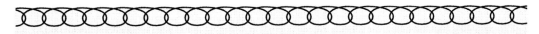

## chapter two

# Writing Scripts with JavaScript

*To do his work well, a*

*workman must first*

*sharpen his tools.*

—Chinese proverb

Before we continue our adventure into the world of JavaScript, we need to gather some tools and learn how to integrate our scripts with HTML.
In this chapter, we'll first look at the tools necessary for writing, testing, and running scripts. I'll even make some recommendations. Then we'll discuss the script development process and the various ways in which we can meld JavaScript with HTML, write non-executing comments within our scripts to describe what our code does, and hide JavaScript from browsers that don't understand it. We'll finish off this chapter by creating a script that dynamically writes content to a Web page about the browser currently being used. In a nutshell, we'll

- explore the tools of the trade: editors and browsers.
- look at the script development process.
- describe the scripting workflow.
- scrutinize the <script> tag.
- learn how to integrate JavaScript into Web documents.
- determine where to place scripts and why.
- discover how to hide scripts from old browsers.

&#9994; study JavaScript's case sensitivity.

&#9994; see how to add comments to our code and learn why we should comment our code.

&#9994; play with the properties of the `navigator` object.

Let's get started.

# Tools of the Trade

JavaScript programmers don't require much in the way of tools. The most basic JavaScript programmer's toolkit need contain only two things:

&#9994; A text editor for writing programs.

&#9994; A Web browser in which to run and test programs.

However, a third tool, while optional, can be particularly useful:

&#9994; A debugger to help identify and correct programming errors.

Let's take a closer look at text editors.

## Text Editors

Every major operating system comes with some sort of text editor. The Windows operating system comes with WordPad and Notepad; Linux operating system installations usually include vi, Pico, or another editor; and Macintosh systems are equipped with Apple's NotePad.

While any text editor will do for writing JavaScript, which is good to know when you're in a pinch and don't have your favorite tools with you, I recommend using a good, non-WYSIWYG (what you see is what you get) HTML editor or an editor designed specifically for programming. Here are some features you should look for in an editor:

&#9994; Line numbering

&#9994; Color coding

&#9994; Search and replace tools

&#9994; HTML coding help

&#9994; HTML validator

&#9994; Debugging capabilities

**Line numbering** is an essential feature you should look for in any editor you consider. When a browser encounters an error in a script it always reports a line number. Being able to turn on line numbers in your editor can help you quickly locate the culprit line and, hopefully, eliminate the pesky bug quickly.

**Color coding** helps you identify errors as you type. For instance, in HomeSite when you type a quotation mark ("), any text that follows the quotation mark displays in red, reminding you that the quote has not yet been closed. Once you type the closing quotation mark, the text settles to a cool blue, indicating that all is well. This is a very useful feature, because one of the most common errors programmers regularly make is to forget to close a quote.

**Search and replace tools** can speed up the process of making global changes to a document, for instance, changing a variable name from Visitor to realname.

**HTML coding help** is a particularly useful feature when you're programming with JavaScript because JavaScript works hand in hand with HTML. You'll also often use JavaScript to write HTML statements. HTML coding help provided by an editor can be in the form of one-click tag insertion, auto completion, tag insight, link checking, or all of the above.

**HTML validators** are wonderful tools that may save your hair! Sometimes a JavaScript program will not run correctly due to an error in your HTML. A good HTML validator can help you locate and eliminate HTML errors quickly and painlessly, saving you from pulling your hair out in frustration.

**Debuggers** are sweet little tools that help you find and eradicate—you guessed it—bugs in your programs. A good debugger will have trace features that allow you to step through your script line by line and watch windows that let you see how variable and property values change as the script executes. Debuggers can save you loads of time and energy, once you learn how to use them. Debugging is discussed in detail in Appendix D.

Now that we've discussed the key features to look for when choosing an editor, let's look at some particular editors and their features.

### Notepad

Many Web developers still use Notepad to create their Web documents. I don't understand why they continue to put themselves to so much work, typing in all the code themselves, when better tools are available, but that's their choice. One good thing about Notepad: it comes with every Windows operating system, so you can always count on a Windows machine having Notepad installed.

Perhaps the best feature of Notepad lies in its simplicity. Because it supports only very basic formatting, you cannot accidentally save special characters or formatting in documents that need to remain pure text. When working with Web documents, this can be especially useful; some special characters or other formatting may not be visible, but still, just by being present, can cause errors.

Notepad has a simple search and replace capability, but it only works within a single open document. It also has **Go to line**, which allows you to jump directly to a specific line in your document. This can be very useful when debugging. A major limitation of Notepad is that it cannot open large documents.

> **Programmer's tip**
>
> Notepad can be very useful for removing special characters and formatting not visible to the naked eye. Simply open theWeb document in Notepad that you suspect has a hidden character or hidden formatting in it, and then save it. Notepad will remove any special characters or formatting contained in your document.

### WordPad

Another basic text editor that ships with Windows, WordPad includes many word-processing features. It can also open large documents that are too big for Notepad. Otherwise, for our purposes, WordPad is little better than Notepad for editing Web documents and writing scripts.

An important thing to keep in mind about WordPad is that, by default, it does not save documents in .txt format. This makes it especially easy to accidentally save special formatting in your Web documents. To avoid this, when saving a Web document, choose *Text Document* or *Text Document - MS DOS Format* in the Save As Type box.

### HomeSite

This is my personal favorite. While not developed specifically for writing JavaScript programs, HomeSite was created with the myriad tasks of Web developers in mind. HomeSite has everything on our list of key features, except debugging capabilities, including the following:

- ⌘ Line numbers. Turn them on and off as needed.
- ⌘ Color coding. This allows you to easily distinguish between text, HTML code, and JavaScript. It indicates when you've forgotten to close a quote or parenthesis. It is completely customizable.
- ⌘ Search and replace within a document and across multiple documents in a directory and its subdirectories.
- ⌘ Loads of HTML help, including
    - ⌘ The ability to insert tags with a click of a mouse button.
    - ⌘ Tag insight.
    - ⌘ A link checker.
    - ⌘ The automatic completion of HTML tags.
    - ⌘ The automatic insertion of closing HTML tags.
- ⌘ HTML validator. You can specify which HTML version your code should conform to and set other restrictions according to your own needs and desires.

In addition to most of the key items on our list, HomeSite also features the following:

- ⌘ The ability to save snippets of code. This is of particular use to JavaScript programmers. With the click of a mouse button, you can insert your tried and proven scripts into new HTML documents instantly. This is one of my favorite HomeSite features.
- ⌘ A customizable user interface.
- ⌘ The ability to preview your document in a variety of resolutions with HomeSite's internal browser. You can even set up HomeSite to preview a document in any browser installed on your computer with a click of a button. This makes switching between editing and browsing fast and simple.
- ⌘ A Cascading Style Sheets editor, TopStyle Lite.
- ⌘ Project management tools.
- ⌘ A built-in deployment system. It allows you to quickly and easily upload your entire site or only those documents that have changed.

I've programmed for years in JavaScript using only HomeSite and a Web browser. It works like a charm. HomeSite is available from Macromedia for a 30-day trial (http://www .macromedia.com/software/homesite/). It is shareware, not freeware. It often comes bundled with Macromedia's Dreamweaver. The two make an awesome team for Web development.

### BBEdit

If you're using a Macintosh computer, my students recommend BBEdit. They claim it is the best general editor for the Mac, hands down. As I don't own a Mac (no groans from the apple bin), I cannot comment on it other than to tell you it was created by Bare Bones Software, hence the BB in the name. A demonstration version is available that works for a limited number of uses (http://www.barebones.com/).

### Freeware and Shareware Text Editors

There are, of course, many other shareware and freeware text editors available for downloading on the Internet. Here are a few of the most popular ones:

✄ TextPad (shareware). A powerful, general-purpose text editor for Windows. You can get the details and download a trial copy at http://www.textpad.com/.

✄ EditPad (freeware and shareware). Another general-purpose text editor for Windows; this one's by JGsoft. The Lite version is free for non-commercial use. The Pro version has many more features; an evaluation version is also available. You can learn more about both and download them at http:// www.editpadpro.com/.

✄ ConTEXT (freeware). ConTEXT bills itself as the "programmer's editor." The author says, "After years and years searching for [a] suitable Windows text editor, I haven't found any of them to completely satisfy my needs, so I wrote my own." One of the features listed is powerful syntax highlighting for JavaScript and HTML, among other languages. You can learn all about it yourself and download it at http://fixedsys.com/context/.

# Web Browsers

A **Web browser** is an essential tool in your JavaScript programmer's toolkit. You need some way to preview your progress and run your scripts. As I discuss each browser, it is not my intent to recommend any one browser over another, but rather to describe the strengths of each. Browser preferences are like computer preferences; there are people who swear by PCs and those who believe Macintosh systems are the only way to compute. While I do have my own browser preference, I think it is important that Web developers have a *variety* of Web browsers at their disposal for testing and previewing their Web documents and JavaScript programs. For instance, on my computer I have a copy of every generation of Netscape Navigator, the latest version of Internet Explorer, and three generations of Opera. This allows me to test my programs and Web pages pretty thoroughly before deploying them to the Web. Ideally, I would also have Macintosh and Unix machines, each with a variety of browsers installed. Someday. For most people, however, multiple computers and operating systems are just not financially feasible. Regardless of which browser you prefer for your own personal use, testing is a crucial part of any programming or Web development undertaking. So load your computer up with as many as you can. Here's a list of the major browsers in use today. You will find copies of each on the CD that accompanies this textbook.

### Netscape Navigator

You would think that the browser that first supported JavaScript would have the best support for JavaScript and contain features for working with JavaScript. You would be right. The latest version of Netscape has, by far, the best and most complete support for the JavaScript programming language. This makes total sense because Netscape, after all, is the company that developed JavaScript in the first place.

As far as special features for working with the language go, Netscape has a built-in JavaScript Console that allows you to test lines of code live and view a list of errors encountered after running a script. For many years, JavaScript Console was the only JavaScript debugging tool available.

You can access JavaScript Console by typing **javascript:** in the location bar of any Netscape browser, version 2 or after.

*Figure 2.1    Netscape's JavaScript Console*

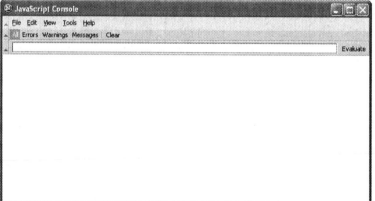

The Netscape browser changed dramatically when it abandoned its 5.0 browser update in order to focus its efforts on Gecko, a Web page "layout engine" that forms the basis of Netscape's 6.0+ browsers. The browser's layout engine handles the display of Web pages. It parses the HTML and applies stylesheet rules.

Mozilla, a Netscape-sponsored, open-source, Web browser project, also uses Gecko as the layout engine. According to The Mozilla Organization, the Mozilla browser was "designed for standards compliance, performance and portability." Gecko itself was designed to support leaner, faster browsers with good support for existing Web standards.

The latest version of Navigator is available at http://www.netscape.com/. You can learn more about Mozilla and download a copy at http://www.mozilla.org/.

### Microsoft Internet Explorer

Microsoft was a latecomer to the Web, but it now has the most widely used browser. Internet Explorer (IE) does a good job of supporting JavaScript, but tends to lag behind Navigator in its support of the *latest* JavaScript features.

If you have a Windows system, you probably already have a copy of Internet Explorer installed on your computer since Microsoft bundles it with the operating system. You can get the latest version at http://www.microsoft.com/windows/ie/default.asp.

### Opera

As the newest major entry to the browser market, Opera is quickly gaining market share. It truly is the fastest browser of the three listed here. Opera's makers seem to be dedicated to supporting and sticking to established Web standards. As such, Opera's support for JavaScript began primarily with support for Core JavaScript only; Opera followed the ECMAScript specification. With each new generation, Opera has increased its support for JavaScript.

Opera comes in both adware (not too obtrusive) and commercial versions. Adware is software you can use freely as long as you're willing to put up with little advertisements displaying as you work. Opera displays the ads across the top right of the browser window. Adware is becoming quite popular. Qualcomm now lets everyone use its Eudora Pro email program as adware for free. Eudora displays its ads in the bottom left corner of the program. If you don't like the ads, you can pay a small fee (like with shareware), receive a registration code, and voilà, no more ads! You can get a copy of Opera at http://www.opera.com/.

# The Script Development Process

The **script development process** is very similar to the program development process:

1. **Requirements Analysis Phase**: determine needs and requirements.
2. **Design Phase**: formulate a plan that will meet the needs and requirements.
3. **Implementation Phase**: write the code, testing regularly as you work; deploy to the server; and test again.
4. **Support and Maintenance Phase**: maintain and support the finished project.

Entire books have been written on the program development process. We can't possibly cover all of the details and approaches to program development here. Instead, we'll just give a brief overview of each phase.

## The Requirements Analysis Phase

Before beginning any project, it's a good idea to first determine the project's requirements. Here are some good questions to ask during this phase:

- ✗ What is the goal? Is there more than one goal?
- ✗ What needs must be addressed or answered? What problems need to be solved?
- ✗ Who is the Web site's audience? What browser(s) will visitors be using? What size of monitors do they have?
- ✗ What constraints must you work under? What technologies does the Web site's Internet service provider (ISP) support or not support?

## The Design Phase

This is where you plan how to solve the problem, answer the needs, and reach the goals determined during the requirements analysis phase. When planning Web sites, you might sketch what the site will look like, create a storyboard, diagram the site architecture with a site map, outline the content, or all of the above. For scripting, you may need to perform some of those same activities, but you'll also definitely want to consider performing activities specific to program design such as flowcharting or writing pseudocode.

Flowcharts let you visually diagram the flow of your program. Programmers have used them for years to great success. Pseudocode is another useful design tool and the method I most often use to design scripts. Pseudocoding is the process of describing the steps of your program in simple English. One really nice thing about pseudocode is that you can type real code in right next to it, commenting out the pseudocode as you go. When you're done, you have a complete program with detailed comments; your pseudocode becomes your comments and program documentation.

## The Implementation Phase

This is where you perform the actual coding, writing JavaScript and HTML as necessary and testing and debugging as you go. When testing, it's a good idea to run your scripts in various browsers and view your pages at different screen resolutions. You'll want to periodically deploy the site and test it online as well.

## The Support and Maintenance Phase

Once your project is complete, tested, deployed, and tested again, your project falls into the support and maintenance phase. You may be asked to make minor modifications, add or change content, etc. to keep the Web site fresh and interesting. This may also be when your part in the project ends, depending on how the project was set up. An important thing to note is that when new needs and goals are found, it is time to begin the cycle again with the requirements analysis phase.

OK, we've looked at the various stages of the script development process, but what about the nitty-gritty details of the day-to-day work during the implementation phase? After all, we're here to learn how to code JavaScript. To address this, let's look at the scripting workflow.

# The Scripting Workflow

The workflow of writing JavaScript is very similar to the workflow of writing plain old HTML: code it, test it, code it, and test it; in other words, regularly switching back and forth between editor and browser.

This process may already be quite familiar to you. However, for the sake of completeness, I think it's a good idea if we review it anyway.

## Code It

Open your text editor. For this example, we'll use Notepad. Create a basic Web page by typing in the following. Do not type the line numbers, just type the code listed in the second column.

**Script 2.1     A Basic Web Page**

```
1    <html>
2    <head>
3          <title>A Basic Web Page</title>
4    </head>
5    <body>
6          <h1>My Web Page</h1>
7    </body>
8    </html>
```

Save your document as index.html and note what directory you saved it in. Leave Notepad open.

## Test It

Do not close Notepad. Start Netscape Navigator and open the document you just created. To do so, choose File from the menu bar and choose Open Page. Browse to index.html. Choose Open. Your Web page should look similar to this:

**Figure 2.2     Results of Script 2.1**

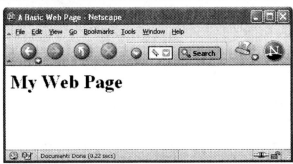

OK, so far so good.

## Code It

Now let's add a little JavaScript. Leave your browser open, and switch to Notepad. You can do this in one of two ways:

- ✄ Press Alt + Tab until you get to the Notepad icon.
- ✄ Click on Notepad in the taskbar.

Modify your code so it looks like the following:

**Script 2.2    Adding Some JavaScript**

```
1    <html>
2    <head>
3          <title>A Basic Web Page</title>
4    </head>
5    <body bgcolor="white" text="black">
6          <h1>My Web Page</h1>
7    <script language="JavaScript" type="text/javascript"><!--
8          document.write("Hello, World!")
9    // -->
10   </script>
11   </body>
12   </html>
```

Save your file.

## Test It

Leaving Notepad open, switch to your browser by clicking on it in the taskbar or pressing Alt + Tab. Click the Reload button on the browser's toolbar. You should see something similar to this:

**Figure 2.3    Results of Script 2.2**

Continue the process of coding, testing, coding, and testing. Add some more HTML or try some simple JavaScript statements.

# The <script> Tag

When Netscape introduced JavaScript in Netscape Navigator 2, it included support for a new tag: the <script> tag. The <script> tag has several attributes, two of which you should *always* set: `language` and `type`.

## The `language` Attribute

The `language` attribute specifies which scripting language you are using. The <script> tag was intended to be programming-language neutral. While JavaScript is the default scripting language supported by most browsers, other languages, including Jscript, VBScript, and PHP can also be used in Web documents within the <script> tag.

The language attribute also lets us specify which version of JavaScript we are using. Here are the possibilities and what each indicates:

*Table 2.1*     **`language` *Attribute Value Meanings***

| `language=` | Result |
|---|---|
| `JavaScript` | Browsers that support JavaScript 1.0 and later will read and interpret the contents. JavaScript 1.0 support corresponds to Netscape Navigator 2+ and roughly to Internet Explorer 3+ and Opera 3+. |
| `JavaScript1.1` | Browsers that support JavaScript 1.1 and later will read and interpret the contents. JavaScript 1.1 support corresponds to Netscape Navigator 3+ and roughly to Opera 3.5+. |
| `JavaScript1.2` | Browsers that support JavaScript 1.2 and later will read and interpret the contents. JavaScript 1.2 support corresponds to Netscape Navigator 4+ and roughly to Internet Explorer 4+. |
| `JavaScript1.3` | Browsers that support JavaScript 1.3 and later will read and interpret the contents. JavaScript 1.3 support corresponds to Netscape Navigator 4.5+ and roughly to Opera 4+. Core JavaScript corresponds roughly to ECMA Script Version 2. |
| `JavaScript1.4` | Browsers that support JavaScript 1.4 and later will read and interpret the contents. JavaScript 1.4 support corresponds to Netscape Navigator 5+ (NN 5 was never released). Core JavaScript corresponds roughly to ECMA Script Version 3. Opera 5 supports most of JavaScript 1.4's functionality. |
| `JavaScript1.5` | Browsers that support JavaScript 1.5 and later will read and interpret the contents. JavaScript 1.5 support corresponds to Netscape Navigator 6+. Opera 6 also supports most of JavaScript 1.5's functionality. Some of JavaScript 1.5 has also been incorporated in the ECMA script version 3 specification. |

## The type Attribute

The type attribute specifies the MIME type of the text contained within the <script> tag or the file referenced by the <script> tag. MIME (multipurpose Internet mail extensions) is an extension of the original Internet email protocol that lets people exchange different types of data files on the Internet. Servers insert the MIME header at the beginning of any Web transmission, and browsers use the MIME type listed in the header to choose the appropriate player application for the type of data specified. Some players are built into browsers, such as those needed to display GIFs, JPEGs, and HTML files; others are plug-ins and have to be downloaded, like Adobe Acrobat Reader.

The first part of a MIME type specifies the general file type of the data file. The second part, after the slash, indicates the specific type of file the data file represents. For instance, here's a list of common MIME types having to do with Web pages:

**Table 2.2     MIME Types for the Web**

| Type of File | MIME Type |
| --- | --- |
| JavaScript | text/javascript |
| HTML | text/html |
| Cascading Style Sheets | text/css |
| GIF image | image/gif |
| JPEG image | image/jpeg |

You should always set the type attribute; however, it is particularly important that you set the type attribute with the appropriate MIME type whenever you reference an external JavaScript file with the src attribute. Otherwise, the browser may not understand what type of file the referenced file is or know what to do with it.

The MIME type and appropriate type attribute for JavaScript (any version) is text/javascript.

## The src Attribute

You'll only need to set this attribute when you attach an external JavaScript file. An external JavaScript file is just a simple text document with a .js extension. However, the external JavaScript file may contain only legal JavaScript statements. <script> tags are unnecessary and moreover not allowed inside an external JavaScript file. The <script> tag is HTML code, not JavaScript. We'll talk more about external JavaScript files later.

You may use either a relative or an absolute path to indicate the location of your external JavaScript file. If you use a relative path, that path is relative to the HTML document to which the external script file is being attached.

# Integrating JavaScript into Your Web Documents

There are basically five ways to integrate JavaScript into HTML documents:

- ✗   In a <script> tag in the <head> of an HTML document.
- ✗   In a <script> tag in the <body> of an HTML document.
- ✗   Inline with HTML as an event handler.
- ✗   In an external JavaScript file.
- ✗   Inline using the javascript pseudo-protocol.

Let's look at each in turn and specify reasons for each placement.

When programming in JavaScript, you will place scripts in all five areas according to the needs of the task at hand. Each placement area has its own benefits, and there are instances in which a particular area is the best choice. There is no one particular area that is best for *all* coding needs. Likely, you will use multiple areas for every one of your applications.

During our discussion of JavaScript placement, we'll mention topics and use terms that may not mean much to you at this point. Don't worry about it. We'll cover every aspect in detail in future chapters. The main thing for you to get from this section is an idea of how to integrate JavaScript into your Web documents. The details will become clear later as we cover each topic. You may want to refer back to this chapter from time to time as you work your way through the book.

# Placing JavaScript Statements in a <script> Tag within the <head>

Why and when should you place scripts in the <head> of an HTML document? The <head> of an HTML document is the perfect place for any statements that need to be read and executed before the contents of your Web document (in the <body> tag) load. This is also a good place to declare **user-defined functions**. A user-defined function is a set of pre-defined, deferred statements that do not execute until the function is **called**. You call a function by invoking its name, followed by an optional set of parameters in parentheses. If the idea of a function seems a little confusing right now, don't worry about it. For now, just file it away in the back of your mind that a <script> tag in the <head> of a document is one good place to write function definitions. By declaring a function in the <head> of an HTML document, you ensure that it is defined and ready to use by the time the <body> of the document loads. The <head> always loads before the <body>.

**peek ahead**  We'll define and discuss functions in much greater detail in Chapters 4 and 8.

Global **variables** are also best declared in the <head> of an HTML document, within a <script> tag, of course. A variable is a temporary holding place in memory in which we can store data for future use. We'll define and discuss variables in detail in Chapter 3.

Statements that preload images for use in rollover effects are also most appropriately placed in the <head> of your HTML document within a <script> tag. Basically, the <head> is the best place to put statements that must execute before the content of your HTML document loads.

Here's an example:

**Script 2.3** **Placing JavaScript Statements in the <head>**

```
1    <html>
2    <head>
3    <title>Placing JavaScript Statements Appropriately</title>
4    <script language="JavaScript" type="text/javascript"><!--
5         var visitor = prompt("What is your name?", "")
6    // -->
7    </script>
8    </head>
9    <body>
10
11   </body>
12   </html>
```

In the above example, we asked the Web site visitor to enter his or her name, and we stored that value in the variable `visitor`. We used the window's `prompt` method, which pops up a prompt dialog box where the question is displayed and a text box is provided for the visitor to enter an answer. Try it for yourself. Type in the above code in your favorite text editor and view it in your browser. You should see the following prompt:

**Figure 2.4** **Results of Script 2.3**

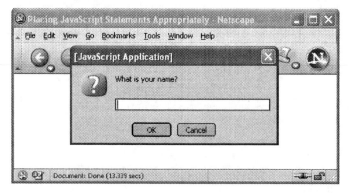

Something to keep in mind when you are writing JavaScript is that you should never place statements that *write* Web page content such as headings, paragraphs of text, tables, lists, etc. in the <head> unless they are part of a function definition. Why? Because Web page content, that is, the text the visitor sees while viewing a Web page, should never be placed in the <head> of an HTML document. Content goes in the <body> of an HTML document. Only titles, meta tags, and other special data such as scripts and stylesheets are appropriately placed in the <head> tag.

To demonstrate this, create a new document and type in the following:

**Script 2.4      Placing `write` Statements in the <head> Illegally**

```
1    <html>
2    <head>
3    <title>Placing JavaScript Statements Illegally</title>
4    <script language="JavaScript" type="text/javascript"><!--
5        document.write("<h1>Hello, I am in the wrong place.</h1>")
6    // -->
7    </script>
8    </head>
9    <body>
10
11    </body>
12    </html>
```

You'll need an old copy of Netscape Navigator (4.7x or prior) to see the problem with this script. When you view the source in an old Netscape Navigator browser, it shows you the *results* of your document.write statements, instead of the write statements themselves. This makes it easy to tell if your script is generating the correct HTML statements, stylesheet code, or any other type of string you might be trying to write with a script.

View your file. You should see a blank page or something like this:

**Figure 2.5      Results of Script 2.4**

Now view the source of the document in Navigator. Navigator shows you the result of your write statements, inappropriately written in the <head> of the document. We'll show you the correct place to put write statements in the next section.

**Figure 2.6**　**Viewing the Source of Script 2.4 in Netscape Navigator 4.75**

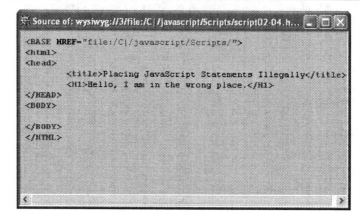

## Placing JavaScript Statements in a <script> Tag within the <body>

Another place you can write JavaScript statements is in a <script> tag within the <body> of an HTML document. This is the best, and only, place to write statements that actually produce content for inclusion in an HTML document. Calls to functions that write content are also best placed here.

Let's expand on our earlier example, the one where we prompted the visitor for his or her name. This time, we'll make use of the information we gathered by writing a custom greeting.

> **peek ahead**
>
> We'll explain function calls in Chapters 4 and 8.

**Script 2.5**　**Placing JavaScript Statements in the <body>**

```
1    <html>
2    <head>
3    <title>Placing JavaScript Statements Appropriately</title>
4    <script language="JavaScript" type="text/javascript"><!--
5         var visitor = prompt("What is your name?", "")
6    // -->
7    </script>
8    </head>
9    <body>
10   <script language="JavaScript" type="text/javascript"><!--
11        document.write("<h1>Welcome, ", visitor, "</h1>")
```

```
12  // -->
13  </script>
14  </body>
15  </html>
```

Try it. You should see something like this:

**Figure 2.7    Prompt for Script 2.5**

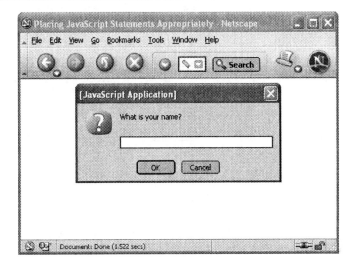

Go ahead and enter your name. Now a custom welcome should appear, similar to this:

**Figure 2.8    Final Results of Script 2.5**

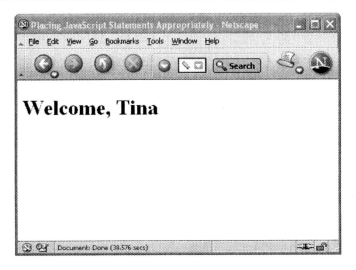

# Writing JavaScript Statements Inline as Event Handlers

Recall from Chapter 1 that an event handler is one or more JavaScript statements called in response to a particular event. Here's an example that pops up an alert box with the message "Welcome" when the Web document loads:

**Script 2.6**     **Writing JavaScript Statements Inline**

```
1    <html>
2    <head><title>Writing JavaScript Inline with HTML</title></head>
3    <body onLoad="alert('Welcome!')">
4    </body>
5    </html>
```

Try it.

# Placing JavaScript Statements in an External JavaScript File

An external JavaScript file is a simple text file containing only JavaScript statements whose name has a .js extension. External JavaScript files are another excellent place to declare functions, especially functions you plan to use again and again with a variety of HTML documents.

**peek ahead** We'll discuss events and event handlers in detail in Chapter 5.

By placing functions used repeatedly in Web pages throughout your Web site in an external JavaScript file and linking that file to those documents, you can reduce the overall loading time of your Web site. The external JavaScript file will have to transfer only once, the first time the visitor requests a page that uses it. Any future pages that use that file can access it from the cache, eliminating the need to transfer it again.

**programmer's tip**

To view the source code of an external JavaScript file, follow these steps:

- ✗ View the HTML document's source.
- ✗ Note the path to the external JavaScript file in the src attribute of the <script> tag, usually found in the <head> of the document.
- ✗ Modify the current URL in your location bar to point to the path and file you noted from the src attribute.
- ✗ Some browsers may require you to add the JavaScript MIME type before allowing you to view the .js file in your Web browser. Internet Explorer will usually let you choose what application to open the file with. Choose Notepad, WordPad, or your favorite HTML editor.
- ✗ You can also get the file from your cache. Look for a new file with a .js extension.

External JavaScript files also help to hide your code from would-be pilferers. While a savvy Web developer can still view its contents, many do not know how and others will simply not go to the trouble. Like how a steering wheel lock deters would-be car thieves, but doesn't completely prevent the determined thief from stealing your car, an external JavaScript file provides one more layer of protection against novice, would-be code stealers.

Using an external JavaScript file, you can begin building a library of frequently used functions and routines. For instance, you might want to gather all of your methods related to form validation into a single formValidation.js library file. Then whenever you need to validate a form, you attach your form-validation library and more than half the battle's won.

**peek ahead** You'll learn more about libraries in Chapter 8 and how to build a form validation library in Chapter 13.

# Writing JavaScript Statements Inline Using the JavaScript Pseudo-Protocol

You can also write JavaScript statements using the javascript: pseudo-protocol in the `href` attribute of an anchor (<a></a>) or area (<area>) tag. The idea is that instead of going right to a document or resource, the JavaScript pseudo-protocol will instead execute one or more JavaScript statements, which may or may not return a URL for the anchor tag to follow.

In the Netscape Navigator browser, typing **javascript:** into the location bar will cause JavaScript Console to pop up. JavaScript Console displays the latest error messages the browser encountered while executing scripts. It can be a big help for light debugging. We can also use it to test and experiment with JavaScript statements.

We'll discuss the JavaScript pseudo-protocol in more detail when we cover the click event in Chapter 5. We won't use this method of JavaScript integration right away. In fact, it isn't often used. But keep it in mind for future reference.

While we've put a lot of details off for future discussion, at this point you should understand that there are reasons to place JavaScripts in particular locations according to need and task. As a JavaScript programmer, you will use each of the five ways of integrating JavaScript at one time or another.

## Hiding Scripts from Old Browsers

If you've ever looked at other people's scripts, you've probably noticed an odd thing: an HTML comment surrounding the contents of the <script> tag. The closing comment tag is usually preceded by two forward slashes. What's with that?

The truth is, the comment is there for a good reason. To discover that reason, you need first to answer a simple question: if you use a tag that a browser does not recognize or support, what happens to the text contained within the unrecognizable or unsupported tag? For instance, say you place some text in a <blink> tag, then view the document in Internet Explorer. But IE doesn't support the <blink> tag. So what happens to the text? Does it even display in the browser? Sure it does. It just doesn't blink.

OK, so now let's say you write a bunch of JavaScript statements inside a <script> tag. Some browser doesn't recognize your script tag. What does it do? It displays all the JavaScript code contained in the <script> tag in the browser window. Uh oh! Not exactly what you intended to have happen.

That's where that HTML comment comes in. To hide the contents of a <script> tag from old browsers that don't recognize it, simply surround the content with an HTML comment.

**Script 2.7    Hiding <script> Content (not quite right)**

```
1    <html>
2    <head>
3         <title>Hiding Scripts from Old Browsers</title>
4         <script language="JavaScript" type="text/javascript"><!--
5             JavaScript statements go here
6         -->
7         </script>
8    </head>
9    <body>
10        <script language="JavaScript" type="text/javascript"><!--
11            JavaScript statements go here
12        -->
13        </script>
14
15   </body>
16   </html>
```

There is only one problem with the above: once we get past the opening <script> tag and the opening HTML comment, we're in JavaScript land. Thus, the JavaScript interpreter in the browser will try to execute every statement it comes across until it encounters the closing <script> tag. When it comes to the -->, it runs into an error. The closing comment, -->, has no meaning to the JavaScript interpreter, so it generates an error. To avoid this error, comment out the closing HTML comment tag with a JavaScript single-line comment: //. Now our corrected code should look like this:

**Script 2.8    Hiding <script> Content the Right Way**

```
1    <html>
2    <head>
3         <title>Hiding Scripts from Old Browsers</title>
4         <script language="JavaScript" type="text/javascript"><!--
5             JavaScript statements go here
6         // -->
7         </script>
8    </head>
```

```
 9    <body>
10         <script language="JavaScript" type="text/javascript"><!--
11              JavaScript statements go here
12         // -->
13         </script>
14
15    </body>
16    </html>
```

Today, most browsers support JavaScript. So is it really necessary to go to all this trouble anymore? For now, I would say yes. Even though most people use newer browsers that support JavaScript, it's really not that much extra work to make sure that your Web page is accessible to everyone, regardless of what browser they're using.

## JavaScript Is Case Sensitive

One important thing you need to know about JavaScript is that it is case sensitive. That means that

```
Document.Write("Hello")
```

and

```
document.write("Hello")
```

are *not* equivalent.

The first means nothing to JavaScript, the second calls the `write` method of the `document` object. This is extremely important to keep in mind. As you continue through this book, you'll see many examples of how JavaScript's case sensitivity affects what you do.

## Commenting Your Code: How and Why

I mentioned in an earlier section, while discussing pseudocode, the concept of commenting your programs. Commenting your scripts as you write them is a good habit to get into, especially any place you use tricky or complex coding. Not only is it helpful to you when you revisit code six months or a year later to clue you in on what you were doing and why you approached it that way, but also it is helpful to anyone else that might have to modify or enhance your code.

In today's Web development world, it is quite common for a team of people to work together on a project. With the high turnover rate in the information technology industry in general, it is also likely that someone else will take over editing and maintaining your code when you move up the ladder. Your well-commented code could win friends and influence people. Well, at least it will make the job of those coming after you easier and they'll think better of you as a programmer.

JavaScript supports two types of comments: single-line comments and multi-line comments.

## Single-line Comments

**Single-line comments** are designated with two slash marks in a row (//). You'll likely use single-line comments the most often because you can place them on the same line as the code on which they comment. For example:

```
var visitor              // Visitor's name
visitor = prompt("Enter your name: ", "")
```

I used a single-line comment above to describe the variable. It is not necessary to comment every line of code. For instance, `document.write` statements are often self-explanatory and need no further comment. However, you should get in the habit of describing each new variable as you declare it and commenting on code that is not self-explanatory at first glance. While learning JavaScript, you might want to consider commenting every line of code until you become more familiar with the language.

## Multi-line Comments

Multi-line comments begin with a slash and an asterisk (/*) and end with an asterisk and a slash (*/). They are most often used to

- ✗ provide reference information for an entire script or library, such as title, author, last update, etc.
- ✗ describe a block of code or user-defined function.
- ✗ list copyright notices and script license information.

For example:

```
/* Form Validation Library
   Author: Tina McDuffie      */
```

You should provide a multi-line comment at the beginning of every external JavaScript file. You should also use multi-line comments to describe each function definition and to list any important notices about code such as copyright.

# To Semicolon or Not to Semicolon

Many programming languages such as C, C++, Java, Perl, and PHP require the use of semicolons as statement terminators. Not JavaScript. According to the author of the JavaScript language, Brendan Eich, "Requiring a semicolon after each statement when a new line would do, [was] out of the question—scripting for most people is about writing short snippets of code, quickly and without fuss."

The only time you are *required* to use a semicolon in JavaScript is when you place more than one statement on a single line. Here's an example:

```
document.write("Hello, "); document.write("World")
```

You could just as easily have written the statements as

```
document.write("Hello,  ")
document.write("World")
```

which, in my opinion, is more readable. Of course, you could've combined the two statements into one, too. The only time you're really likely to want to write two statements on a single line is in an event handler. We'll talk more about event handlers in Chapter 5.

To make the code simpler and give you one less thing to worry over, we've left the semicolons out of the scripts in this book, except where they're required, like in the aforementioned event handlers when you *need* more than one statement on a single line.

# Introducing the **navigator** Object

Let's practice some of what we've learned by using JavaScript to write information about a visitor's browser. To do this, we'll need to make use of the `navigator` object. We worked with it a little in Chapter 1.

The `navigator` object gets its name from the browser that first supported JavaScript: Netscape Navigator. You can think of the `navigator` object as a browser object, as its properties describe the current browser.

Before we begin writing a script, look up the `navigator` object again in Appendix A. What properties are listed? Can you make a guess at what any of them mean? Table 2.3 describes each of them in turn.

*Table 2.3*    **Properties of the navigator Object**

| Property | Description |
| --- | --- |
| appCodeName | The browser's internal code name. |
| appName | The browser's name. |
| appVersion | The browser's version, the platform on which it is running, and the country. |
| language | Specifies which human language the browser supports. |
| mimeTypes[ ] | A list of the MIME types supported by the browser. |
| platform | The platform on which the browser is running. Possible values for PCs and Macs are Win32, Win16, Mac68k, and MacPPC. |
| plugins[ ] | A list of all of the plug-ins currently installed on the browser. |
| userAgent | "User agent" is another name for a browser. This property specifies the user-agent header. Web servers often collect it. |

Let's construct a script to report information about the browser currently being used. To do this we'll use the `document.write` method and the `navigator` properties listed above. Open Notepad or your favorite editor and type in the following script:

**Script 2.9**     **Reporting Browser Information**

```
1    <html>
2    <head>
3        <title>Reporting Browser Information</title>
4    </head>
5    <body>
6    <h1>Your Browser</h1>
7    <script language="JavaScript" type="text/javascript"><!--
8        document.write("<b>appCodeName:</b> ",
             navigator.appCodeName, "<br>")
9        document.write("<b>appName:</b> ", navigator.appName,
             "<br>")
10       document.write("<b>appVersion:</b> ",
             navigator.appVersion, "<br>")
11       document.write("<b>language:</b> ", navigator.language,
             "<br>")
12       document.write("<b>platform:</b> ", navigator.platform,
             "<br>")
13       document.write("<b>userAgent:</b> ", navigator.userAgent,
             "<br>")
14   // -->
15   </script>
16   </body>
17   </html>
```

Save it and view it in as many different browsers as you have installed on your computer. Here's what the results look like when run in Netscape Navigator 7, Netscape Navigator 4.75, Internet Explorer 6.0, and Opera 6.05.

**Figure 2.9**     **Results of Script 2.9 in Netscape Navigator 7**

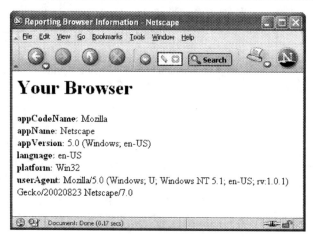

**Figure 2.10    Results of Script 2.9 in Netscape Navigator 4.75**

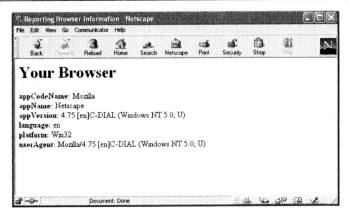

**Figure 2.11    Results of Script 2.9 in Internet Explorer 6.0**

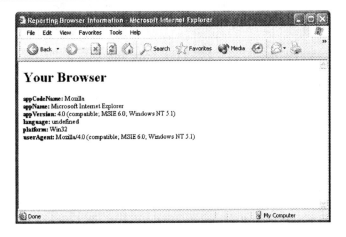

**Figure 2.12    Results of Script 2.9 in Opera 6.05**

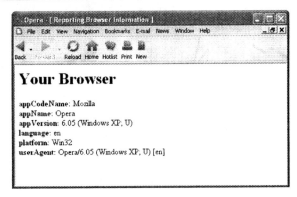

As you can see, all four browsers reported the appCodeName as Mozilla. If we were trying to perform browser detection, appCodeName wouldn't be of much use. However, notice that the appName property does a better job of distinguishing among the browsers, as does userAgent. The "en" reported as the language means English. Netscape 7 further distinguished the language as United States English.

One browser, Opera, has the capability of being able to report one of several different browser identifications, depending on which choice you make in Opera's preferences. Opera has the ability to emulate other browsers. This can make it difficult to determine for certain whether or not a visitor is using Opera.

To change the mode in Opera, choose File on the menu bar and choose Preferences. In Network, choose "Identify as MSIE 5.0" under Browser identification.

**Figure 2.13    Setting the Browser Identification in Opera 6.05**

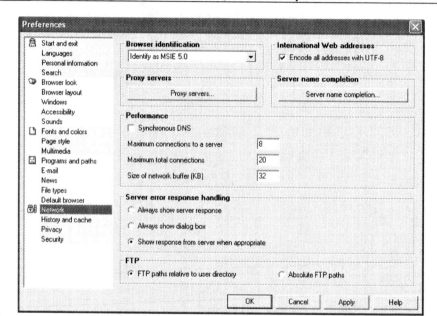

Here's an example of what Opera reports when in Internet Explorer mode.

*Figure 2.14    Results of Script 2.9 in Opera 6.05 in IE Mode*

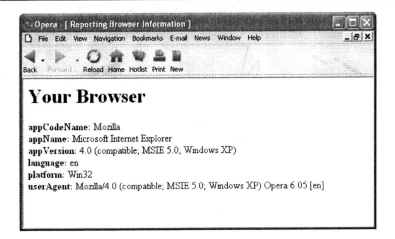

## Summary

In this chapter we looked at the tools of the trade for programming in JavaScript. There aren't many: a simple text editor for writing code and a browser for viewing the results are all that are required. However, there are better alternatives with a little more punch and utility. My personal favorite is HomeSite.

After examining the features of a few editors and browsers, we looked at the script development process, which includes the following phases:

1.  Requirements Analysis Phase: determine needs and requirements.
2.  Design Phase: formulate a plan that will meet the needs and requirements.
3.  Implementation Phase: write the code, testing regularly as you work; deploy to the server; and test again.
4.  Support and Maintenance Phase: maintain and support the finished project.

The workflow for scripting JavaScript is very similar to that of writing plain old HTML: primarily a continuous cycle of coding, testing in the browser, coding, and testing in the browser.

Next we looked at the attributes of the <script> tag and the various places we could put JavaScript statements:

- ✗ In a <script> tag in the <head> of an HTML document. This is the best place to put statements that must execute before the page content displays. This is also a good place to declare functions and global variables and to preload images.
- ✗ In a <script> tag in the <body> of an HTML document. This is the best and only location to place statements that will actually write Web page content.
- ✗ Inline with HTML as an event handler. It is used to call an event handler.

✗ In an external JavaScript file. This is a good place for frequently used functions. It is also a way to help hide your code somewhat.

✗ Inline using the javascript pseudo-protocol. This is used in `href` attributes only.

We discovered how and why to hide the contents of our <script> tags from old browsers. JavaScript, it turns out, is case sensitive, so we need to be conscious of the type case we use when writing scripts. It is also a good idea to comment our scripts as we write them. JavaScript supports two kinds of comments: single-line (//) and multi-line (/* . . . */).

Finally, we put what we've learned to work and wrote a script that displays information about the browser the visitor is using. To test it, we ran our script in several different browsers and noted the differences in each.

## Review Questions

1. At a minimum, what tools does a JavaScript programmer need to code and test a Web page that uses JavaScript?
2. What features does an editor like HomeSite offer that make it a more desirable alternative to Notepad?
3. Why do you need a Web browser for developing scripts?
4. How can JavaScript Console, which comes built into Netscape Navigator, assist a JavaScript programmer?
5. What is Opera?
6. Describe the script development process.
7. Describe the major goal and processes involved in each phase of the script development process.
8. Describe each of the following attributes of the <script> tag:
   a. language
   b. type
   c. src
9. What is MIME?
10. What are the five ways in which you can integrate JavaScript into your Web pages; that is, where can you put JavaScript statements?
11. For each of the places you listed in question 10, list an example of the type of task that makes that particular place the best choice.
12. Why should you hide scripts from old browsers? What happens if you don't?
13. How can you hide scripts from old browsers that don't support the <script> tag?
14. What does it mean to say that JavaScript is case sensitive?
15. What two types of comments does JavaScript support? For each type, explain how to write that type of comment in JavaScript and when you would most likely use that type of comment.
16. Name and describe three properties of the `navigator` object.
17. Why is the `navigator` object called "navigator" and not "browser"?
18. Why does Script 2.9 display different results in different browsers?

19. Which browser reports different results for Script 2.9 depending on the user's preferences?
20. Why is it a good idea to have multiple browsers and multiple versions of each browser?

## Exercises

1. Explain when you should attach an external JavaScript file and when it is better to embed JavaScript in the HTML document.
2. Write a set of empty script tags complete with the appropriate attributes and necessary notation to hide the script's contents from old browsers.
3. Write the appropriate <script> tag to attach an external JavaScript file named myLib.js located in the scripts subdirectory off of the root of the Web site. Assume the document you are attaching the script to is in the root as well.
4. Write the appropriate <script> tag to attach an external JavaScript file named myLib.js located in the scripts subdirectory off of the root of the Web site. Assume the document you are attaching the script to is in a subdirectory named products off of the root.
5. Research text editors on the Web. Find three that look like good ones to you and compare their features. Summarize your findings. How much does each cost? Were you able to find any really good freeware text editors?
6. Research debugging on the Web. What is it? See if you can find any good debugging pointers specifically for JavaScript. Summarize what you've learned.

## Scripting Exercises

Create a folder named assignment02 to hold the documents you create during this assignment. Save a copy of the personal home page you created at the end of Chapter 1 as home.html in the assignment02 folder.

1. Create a simple JavaScript program that writes "Greetings, Earthlings!" in an <h1> tag and an image that displays a picture of an alien, Marvin the Martian, or a spaceship. (You should have no trouble finding one online.) All HTML code within the <body> should be created with JavaScript. At the bottom of the document, write "This document was created with JavaScript." Save the document as aliens.html.
2. Create a Web page named docColors.html with a white background, black text, blue links, purple visited links, and red active links. Insert a script that writes the values of the document's color settings. Acquire the color settings from the corresponding properties of the document object. See Appendix A for a list of document properties.
3. Modify docColors.html so that at the end of the document, the background color is changed to a color of your choice. Save it as docColors2.html.
4. Insert a script into home.html that writes a new section heading and a blockquote, like this:

```
<h2>My Favorite Quote</h2>
<blockquote>your favorite quote goes here</blockquote>
```

Place your favorite quote between the <blockquote> tags.

5. Add a script to home.html that writes a numbered list of your hobbies and interests under the My Hobbies heading. Use JavaScript to write the appropriate <ol> and <li> tags and their content.

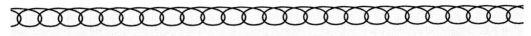

## chapter *three*

# Data Types, Variables, and Literals

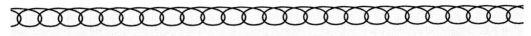

*Too often we forget that*

*genius . . . depends*

*upon the data within*

*its reach, that*

*Archimedes could not*

*have devised Edison's*

*inventions.*

—Ernest Dimnet

E
very programming language needs to be able to handle and manipulate data. JavaScript is no different in this respect. Programmers need a means of inputting data, temporarily storing it, modifying it, and outputting it. It helps if data can be categorized by type as well: this is a number, this is a string (text), etc.

In this chapter, we'll

ℨ look at the various data types and special values that JavaScript recognizes.

ℨ define the terms "literal" and "variable."

ℨ specify how to declare and initialize a variable.

ℨ examine JavaScript's variable-naming rules and establish some acceptable naming conventions.

ℨ define "expression evaluation."

ℨ see how being loosely typed makes it easy for JavaScript to convert one data type to another.

ℨ learn how to convert a variable from one data type to another.

ℨ see how to determine a variable's true data type.

⚡ Examine why number, string, and Boolean are primitive data types, built-in functions, and objects.

Let's get started.

# JavaScript Data Types

JavaScript supports three **primitive data types**—number, string, and Boolean—and one **composite data type**—Object. By "primitive," I mean that they can't get any simpler. By "composite," I mean that it is made up of a combination of data, usually of various types. You know that an object has properties that define and describe it and methods on which it can act. Thus, an object is a composite of the data defined and stored in its properties and the data defining its methods. In addition to these data types, JavaScript recognizes four special values: null, undefined, NaN, and Infinity. Let's examine each of these data types and special values in turn.

## Number

A **number** is any numeric value, be it a floating-point number (float) such as 4.17 or -32.518 or a whole number (integer) like –55 or 187. For the most part, JavaScript does not distinguish between the two, although it is possible to convert a string specifically to an integer or a float. More about that later.

JavaScript represents numbers using the eight-byte, floating-point, numeric format standard established by the Institute of Electrical and Electronics Engineers, Inc. (IEEE). Say that three times fast! What it means is that you can represent very large numbers up to $\pm1.7976931348623157x10^{308}$ and very small numbers down to $\pm5.0x10^{-324}$. "Very large" is a bit of an understatement, we're talking *huge* here; $\pm1.79x10^{308}$ is bigger than a centillion! To better wrap your mind around the size of this number, visit http://mathworld.wolfram.com/LargeNumber.html for a list of large numbers and their English word equivalents. I couldn't find a word to describe a number as small as $\pm5x10^{-324}$, but I can tell you that it is very, very tiny indeed. It is highly unlikely you'll need to reference a number smaller than that.

When it comes to working with numbers in JavaScript, you're not stuck working with the decimal (base 10) number system alone. JavaScript also recognizes and supports the hexadecimal (base 16) and the octal (base 8) number systems and lets you enter integers in those formats, as well as the normal decimal format. Because decimal is the most popular and often used number system, to indicate a number in decimal, you simply write the number as you normally would without a leading zero (0). Hexadecimal and octal numbers are a little different. To enter a number in hexadecimal, precede the number with 0x (zero x). For octal numbers, use a leading zero (0). Here's a summary. The examples in the following table all evaluate to 127 decimal.

*Table 3.1*    **Specifying Integer Bases in JavaScript**

| Number System | Base | Notation | Example |
|---|---|---|---|
| decimal | 10 | Enter the number as a normal integer without a leading 0 (zero). | 127 |
| hexadecimal | 16 | Enter the number as an integer with a leading 0x (zero x) or 0X (zero X). | 0x7F or 0X7F |
| octal | 8 | Enter the number as an integer with a leading 0 (zero). | 0177 |

JavaScript is also flexible about how you designate floating-point numbers. You can write floating-point numbers in the usual way, as an integer followed by a decimal point and a fraction expressed in decimal, or you can write them in scientific notation.

*Table 3.2*    **Specifying Floating-Point Numbers in JavaScript**

| Method | Notation | Examples |
|---|---|---|
| normal | Enter the number as a decimal integer followed by a decimal point (.) and a fraction expressed in decimal. | 12000000 -7.35 .552 |
| scientific notation | Enter the number as a decimal integer followed by an exponent indicator (E) and an integer that can be signed (preceded by a "+" or "-"). | 12E6 -.735E1 .552E0 |

OK, so numbers are simply numbers. That's easy. But what's a string?

## String

A **string** is text, that is, any combination or *string* of letters, numbers, punctuation, etc. Maybe that's where the name came from: it's a *string* of characters. However it got its name, a string is easily recognized because it is always contained within or delimited by quotation marks. JavaScript allows you to use either double quotation marks or single quotation marks, also known as apostrophes, to delimit strings. Here are some examples of strings:

```
"WebWoman"
"3.141592"
'Greetings, Earthling'
"onClick=alert('Hello, World')"
'2, 4, 6, 8, who do we appreciate?'
"What\'s up?"
"Tina says, \"She who laughs, lasts!\""
```

Notice the odd backslashes in the last two examples? Why are they there? Because quotation marks, both double and single, are special characters used by the JavaScript language to delimit strings. You have to **escape** them in order to use them as part of a string; that is, you have to preface each with a backslash character in order to *escape* its special meaning to JavaScript. Look at the next to last example above. The apostrophe (single quotation mark) has been escaped. If you were to write that string out in JavaScript using the document's write method,

```
document.write("What\'s up?")
```

the result would be

```
What's up?
```

The same is true for the last example, that is, the quotation marks in the string have been escaped so that the statement

```
document.write("Tina says, \"She who laughs, lasts!\"")
```

results in

```
Tina says, "She who laughs, lasts!"
```

If you didn't escape the apostrophe and double quotation marks, you could get an error when you run the code. For every opening single or double quotation mark, JavaScript expects a corresponding closing quotation mark.

Many HTML attribute values must be enclosed in quotation marks. In fact, any HTML attribute value that contains any character other than a number or a letter must be delimited with quotation marks. Some older browsers do not recognize single quotation marks, so it is a good habit to only use double quotation marks around HTML attribute values. Because you often use JavaScript to write HTML statements, it is important that you know how to escape quotation marks. Here's another example, this time writing HTML:

```
document.write("<a href=\"http://www.webwoman.biz/\"> ⸻▶
  ⸻▶ WebWoman</a>")
```

The `href` attribute value in the code above contains a colon (:) and several forward slashes (/) so it *must* be delimited by double quotation marks (an HTML requirement). The result of the above statement is that the following HTML code is written to the document:

```
<a href="http://www.webwoman.biz/">WebWoman</a>
```

OK, so both single and double quotation marks have special meaning to JavaScript. Are there any others you need to worry about? As a matter of fact, there are.

## JavaScript Special Characters

The backslash character (\) itself has a special meaning to JavaScript. It escapes a character from its special JavaScript meaning. The backslash, single quotation mark, and double quotation mark are the only characters you need to worry about escaping. However, there's actually a whole list of escape sequences you can use in JavaScript. I've listed the most often used sequences first.

**Table 3.3   *JavaScript Escape Sequences and Special Characters***

| Escape Sequence | Character Represented |
|---|---|
| \ " | Double quotation mark (") |
| \ ' | Single quotation mark or apostrophe (') |
| \\ | Backslash (\) |
| \n | New line—causes following text to begin on a new line. Particularly useful in alert message strings. |
| \x*HH* | The character with the Latin-1 encoding specified by two hexadecimal digits, *HH*. The hexadecimal number must fall between 00 and FF, inclusive. For example, \xA9 is the hexadecimal sequence for the copyright symbol. |
| \u*XXXX* | The Unicode character specified by four hexadecimal digits, *XXXX*. For example, \u00A9 is the Unicode sequence for the copyright symbol. |
| \ *XXX* | The character with the Latin-1 encoding specified by up to three octal digits, *XXX* . The octal number must fall between 0 and 377, inclusive. For instance, \251 is the octal sequence for the copyright symbol. |
| \b | Backspace |
| \f | Form feed |
| \r | Carriage return |
| \t | Tab |

In addition to numbers and strings, JavaScript supports Boolean data values.

## Boolean (Logical)

A **Boolean** value is a truth value that specifies whether something is true or false. While there are an infinite number of possible values for the string and number data types, there are only two possible values for the Boolean data type: true and false. Notice the absence of quotation marks around true and false. Some languages, like C, do not have a specific Boolean or logical data type, as it is often called. Instead, they often use the integers 1 (true) and 0 (false) to represent truth values. JavaScript, however, does recognize Boolean as a distinct data type.

**peek ahead** You'll see how useful the Boolean data type is when you begin working with comparison and logical operators in Chapter 4 and when you learn about control structures in Chapter 6.

## Object

An **Object** is a composite data type, that is, it does not hold just one primitive type of data value, such as number, string, or Boolean. Instead it is *composed* of zero or more pieces of data, each of which may be of a different basic data type. For example, an image's `src` property is a string, whereas its `width` property is a number and its `complete` property is a Boolean. Together with some other information, these properties help make up an `image` object. We'll continue to discuss and use objects throughout this text. For now, just file it away as another data type.

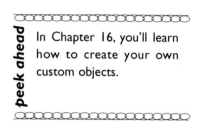

*peek ahead*

In Chapter 16, you'll learn how to create your own custom objects.

## Special Values

In addition to the data types discussed above, JavaScript recognizes four special values: `null`, `undefined`, `Infinity`, and `NaN`.

- ✗ `null` is a special keyword that represents no value, nothing.
- ✗ `undefined` is a special keyword indicating that the value has not been defined. You'll run across this nasty value whenever you try to write out or work with a variable that has been declared, but not initialized, and has never had a value assigned to it. We'll define the terms *variable, declare,* and *initialize* in the next section.
- ✗ `Infinity` is a numeric value representing infinity. You'll usually encounter it when you perform mathematical computations that result in an infinite or undefined value. For instance, divide any number by zero and you'll get `Infinity`. However, in really old browsers, you may get `undefined` or `NaN` instead.
- ✗ `NaN` is a special value indicating that the result is "not a number." We'll look more closely at it a bit later in this chapter.

To summarize, all data handled by JavaScript will be one of the above-listed primitive data types—number, string, or Boolean—or one of the above-listed special values—`null`, `undefined`, `Infinity`, or `NaN`. Every piece of data that you can work with, whether it be a variable, a literal, an object property, or the result of an expression evaluation, is, in its most basic sense, one of the following:

- ✗ a number
- ✗ a string
- ✗ a Boolean
- ✗ `null` (it has no value)
- ✗ `undefined` (it has not yet been declared or its value has not yet been assigned)
- ✗ `Infinity`
- ✗ `NaN` (it is not a number)

# Literal vs. Variable

What do the terms "literal" and "variable" mean? A **literal** is any value that can be expressed verbatim or *literally*, that is, a literal is a fixed value taken in its basic sense, exactly as written. For instance, the number 10 is a numeric literal, whereas the word "Hello" is a string literal. You use literals throughout your programs in calculations, to print words and phrases on the screen, and much more.

While a literal is a fixed value, a **variable** is a symbolic name that represents a value that can, and likely will, change or *vary* during a program's execution. Physically, it is a storage place in memory that you can access using a symbolic name that you choose when you define or *declare* that variable. When you **declare** a variable, the JavaScript interpreter tells the computer to set aside space in memory to hold the value of your variable.

As a real-world analogy, you may think of a variable as a cup. Let's label the cup myCup. Throughout its life, myCup may contain a variety of liquids. For instance, in the summer you may fill myCup with lemonade, ice water, iced tea, or soda, and in the winter with hot tea, cocoa, or coffee. The contents of myCup *vary* according to your needs. Similarly, the contents of a variable can vary according to the needs of your program. Whereas a literal has only one literal, fixed value, a variable's value varies.

# Declaring Variables

In order to use a variable, you should first declare it and, preferably, **initialize** it; that is, you should define its name and, optionally, assign it a starting value. Notice that I said "should." While it is good programming practice to declare and initialize a variable before using it in your program, JavaScript does not require you to do so. By initializing it when you declare it, you avoid the risk of errors that can result from attempting to evaluate an undefined value.

To declare a variable, you simply type the special keyword var, followed by a space and the name of your variable:

```
var myVariable
```

The above variable declaration tells the computer to allocate space for myVariable. It does not specify what type of data you intend to store in myVariable, nor does it place a value in the allocated space. It simply sets aside the space and labels it. At this point, the value of myVariable is undefined.

Here are three more examples:

```
var num1
var firstName
var isOn
```

These too have an initial value of undefined. You can also declare two or more variables at once in a single JavaScript statement: simply separate them with commas. The above example could also be written

```
var num1, firstName, isOn
```

# Initializing Variables

To **initialize** a variable is to assign it a default or starting value. The best time to initialize a variable is when you declare it. So how do you do that? Simple, you follow your declaration with an **assignment statement**. An assignment statement is an operation that *assigns* a value to a variable. The most often used assignment operator is = (equals). Here are some variable initialization examples:

We'll look at more assignment operators in Chapter 4.

```
var num1 = 37
var firstName = "Tina"
var isOn = false
```

To declare and initialize two or more variables in one fell swoop, simply separate them with commas. The above example could also be written as

```
var num1 = 37, firstName = "Tina", isOn = false
```

You can also initialize a variable with the result of a method or function call:

```
var visitor = prompt("What\'s your name?", "")
```

The above example first prompts the user for her name, then assigns the result of the window prompt method to the variable `visitor`.

Not only is it considered good programming practice to initialize your variables when you declare them, it is also good form to place all of your variable declarations at the beginning of your program and to provide a short description for each variable in a comment. For example:

```
var num1 = 37             // first number entered
var firstName = "Tina"    // user's first name
var isOn = false          // indicates whether Java is
                          //    enabled or not
```

Comments not only make your code more readable for other people, they also help you quickly figure out what you did when you revisit your code six months or a year later. Believe me, if you don't insert comments when you write the code in the first place, you'll be cussing yourself later when you have to decipher and modify your code.

Current versions of JavaScript do not *require* you to declare a variable before using it, that is, you can introduce and use variables on the fly throughout your program. For instance, in the middle of your program you could start using a variable called num5, even though you never declared it:

```
num5 = 99
document.write(num5)
```

JavaScript will neither grumble nor complain. It will simply create your new variable, num5, and assign it the value 99. From that point on, you can use that variable in your program. You *can* do it. However, I do *not* recommend that you do it. Declaring your variables before you use them not only shows forethought and helps you plan out your program, but it also makes your code more readable and more easily modifiable. It's much easier and quicker to change variable default values when they're all in one place: at the beginning of your program. Also, when debugging, you won't have to hunt through a ton of code just to discover what values your variables began with.

One more important point to consider: while current versions of JavaScript do not require you to use the keyword `var` to declare a variable, future versions of JavaScript may. So, have I convinced you to follow the conventions I've suggested yet? I hope so.

# Variable-Naming Rules

When it comes to *naming* variables, JavaScript has a few rules that you need to keep in mind:

✗  Variable names may not contain any punctuation, except the underscore (_). Only letters, numbers, and the underscore are valid characters in a variable name.

✗  Variable names may not begin with a number. They must start with a letter or an underscore (_).

✗  Variable names may not contain spaces. Thus if you want to use more than one word as a variable name, then you need to mix the case (lastName), separate the words with an underscore (last_name), or simply string them together eliminating the space (lastname).

✗  Reserved words may not be used as variable names. Reserved words are special words that a programming language sets aside or *reserves* for its own use. Appendix C contains a list of words JavaScript has reserved for its current and future use.

✗  Pre-defined object, property, method, and built-in function names are also off limits, for example, document, window, form, name, src, isNaN, etc. Consider them reserved words. While you may, technically, sometimes be able to implement them successfully, using pre-defined object, property, method, and function names as variable identifiers is asking for trouble. Not only can it create confusion for anyone trying to read your code, it can also cause error messages, generate undesired side effects or unintended results, or have other unforeseen consequences.

*programmer's tip*

Personally, I prefer the first option, mixing cases. I find the underscore character difficult to type correctly: I end up with a dash as often as not. The mixed case is also more readable than all lower case. While mixed case is my personal preference, you should choose a convention that works best for you (within the rules, of course) and stick to it.

**Table 3.4     JavaScript Variable-Naming Rules**

| Rule | Invalid Variable Names | Valid Variable Names |
|---|---|---|
| No punctuation except underscore (_) | first-name<br>last-name! | first_name<br>lastName |
| May not begin with a number | 1stName<br>2be<br>3rdNumber | firstName<br>_2be<br>num3 |
| No spaces allowed | last name | lastName |
| No reserved words | case<br>class<br>package | myCase<br>class2<br>zPackage |
| No object, property, method, or built-in function names | document<br>form | theDocument<br>zForm |

### JavaScript Is Case Sensitive

One last note about naming JavaScript variables: JavaScript is case sensitive. Thus, the names `sitevisitor`, `SITEVISITOR`, `siteVisitor`, `SiteVisitor`, `Sitevisitor`, and `sItevisitor` refer to six *different* variables. Remember this. It's easy to overlook, especially since you're used to HTML being case *insensitive*. For instance, say your program needs to refer to a variable declared as follows:

```
var myVariable = "Greetings!"
```

The correct dot notation to access the variable is

```
myVariable
```

The value of

```
MyVariable
```

on the other hand, is `undefined`. In the above example, there is no such variable named `MyVariable`; we named it `myVariable`, and JavaScript is case sensitive enough to know the difference even if HTML is not.

## Evaluating Expressions: Just What Are You *Really* Saying?

**Expression evaluation** is closely related to data values and variables. To determine the value of a variable, you have to assess, calculate, or *evaluate* the expression that declared it or was later assigned to it. For instance, when you declare and initialize the variable `num1`

```
var num1 = 37
```

num1 evaluates to 37. In JavaScript, a variable always evaluates to its value. The expression on the right side of the equal sign, 37, assesses or evaluates to 37. The expression

```
30 + 7
```

also evaluates to 37.

We're used to making such evaluations without thinking too much about it. In our everyday language, we often use and evaluate expressions. For instance, we evaluate the expressions "kitty," "pussy cat," "kitty cat," "kit kat," and "puddy cat" to mean "cat." They're all *expressions* for cat; they all mean or *evaluate to* cat.

In the next chapter, we'll begin working a lot with expressions as we define the various types of operators that JavaScript supports.

When a variable has not been assigned a value, it is considered **unassigned** and has the value undefined. However, when that variable is *evaluated*, the results of the evaluation vary depending on how the variable was declared, or not declared, as the case may be. If the unassigned variable was never really declared formally using the var keyword, evaluating it results in a runtime error. For instance, consider Script 3.1:

**Script 3.1     Using an Undefined Variable**

```
1    <html>
2    <head>
3         <title>Script 3.1: Using an Undefined Variable</title>
4    </head>
5    <body>
6    <script language="JavaScript" type="text/javascript"><!--
7         document.write(zVar)
8    //-->
9    </script>
10   </body>
11   </html>
```

The variable zVar is never formally declared. Although its value is undefined because it was never declared nor initialized, using it results in a runtime error.

*Figure 3.1* **Results of Script 3.1—Using an Undefined Variable**

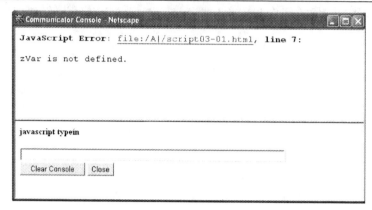

On the other hand, if an unassigned variable were formally declared using the var keyword, an evaluation of that variable would result in undefined or **NaN**. NaN means "not a number." Its use is explained in more detail in a later section of this chapter.

*Script 3.2* **Using a Defined Variable Whose Value Is undefined**

```
1    <html>
2    <head>
3         <title>Script 3.2: Using a Defined Variable Whose
4         Value Is undefined</title>
5    </head>
6    <body>
7    <script language="JavaScript" type="text/javascript"><!--
8         var zVar
9         document.write(zVar)
10   //-->
11   </script>
12   </body>
13   </html>
```

**Figure 3.2      Results of Script 3.2—Using a Defined**
**Variable Whose Value Is undefined**

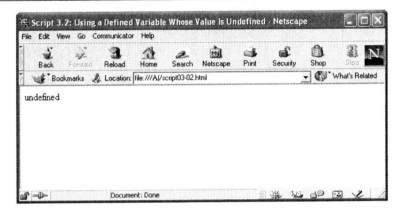

Runtime errors certainly are an unwanted side effect. They are a good argument for always formally declaring variables. However, an evaluation of undefined can be just as devastating to a program. For that reason, among others, it is considered good programming practice to initialize all variables when you declare them.

# Data Type Conversions:
# From Numbers to Strings and Back Again

JavaScript is a **loosely typed** language. That means that you do not have to specify the data type of a variable when you declare it or before you use it. In fact, you can actually initialize a variable as a number, then later assign it a string value and still later a Boolean value. For example, the following code is perfectly legal:

```
var guess = 37          // number
guess = "white"         // string
guess = true            // boolean
guess = "pink"          // string
guess = 22              // number
```

Because of this feature, Netscape describes JavaScript as a "**dynamically typed** language." Being dynamically typed has its advantages. For instance, as the above example shows, it is easy to change the data type of a variable on the fly. Simply assign a value of a different data type to the variable.

It is also easy to convert from one data type to another. When a JavaScript expression involving the plus or concatenation operator contains numbers followed by strings, JavaScript automatically converts the numbers to string values before evaluating the expression. For example:

```
7 + "up"          // result: 7up
"hi" + 5          // result hi5
```

This is good to know. That means converting a number to a string is easy: just add an empty string to it. For example:

```
var num1 = 85        // initialize num1 as a numeric: 85
num1 = num1 + ""     // now num1 is a string: "85"
```

OK, so converting from a number to a string is easy: just add an empty string to the number. But what if you want to go the other direction and convert from a string to a number? Fortunately, JavaScript has that covered by two very useful built-in functions: `parseInt()` and `parseFloat()`.

## parseInt() and parseFloat()

When working with Web pages, programmers often need to convert string values to numbers. For instance, did you ever notice that HTML does not provide a *number* box form element? It's true; HTML only provides a *text* box. Similarly, the `window.prompt()` method, which we discussed in Chapter 2, returns a string. So what if you want to perform calculations on data entered in a prompt or text box? Type in the following code:

### Script 3.3　　*Prompts Return Strings*

```
1   <html>
2   <head>
3       <title>Script 3.3: Prompts Return Strings</title>
4   </head>
5   <body>
6   <script language="JavaScript" type="text/javascript"><!--
7       var qty = prompt("Enter the quantity you want to
            order:", "")
8       var price = prompt("Enter the price:", "")
9       alert("Your total is: " + qty * price)
10  // -->
11  </script>
12  </body>
13  </html>
```

Open the document in your browser and provide a value for quantity and price when prompted:

### Figure 3.3    Prompts for Script 3.3

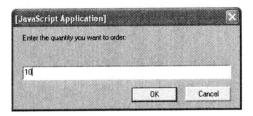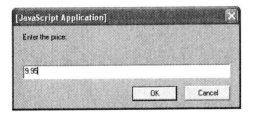

Assuming you didn't make any errors typing in the code, you'll see that, in this case, JavaScript took care of converting the strings you entered in the prompt boxes into numbers before multiplying them.

### Figure 3.4    Final Results of Script 3.3

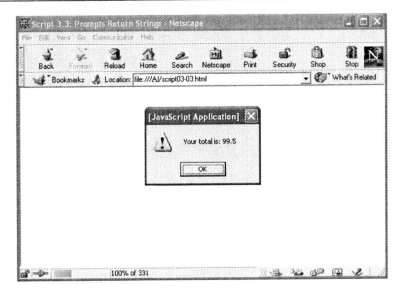

JavaScript recognized that the multiplication operator doesn't apply to strings, so it performed the conversion for you in order to make the expression make sense, in *this* case.

Let's try another example:

### Script 3.4    Prompts Return Strings, Version 2

```
1   <html>
2   <head>
3       <title>Script 3.4: Prompts Return Strings</title>
4   </head>
5   <body>
6   <script language="JavaScript" type="text/javascript"><!--
```

```
 7              var num1 = prompt("Enter a number:", "")
 8              var num2 = prompt("Enter another number:", "")
 9              alert("Sum: " + (num1 + num2))
10   // -->
11   </script>
12   </body>
13   </html>
```

Run the script and enter some numeric values.

**Figure 3.5    Prompts for Script 3.4**

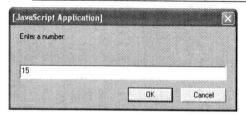 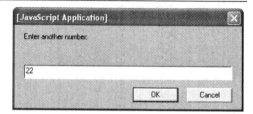

What happened?

**Figure 3.6    Final Results of Script 3.4**

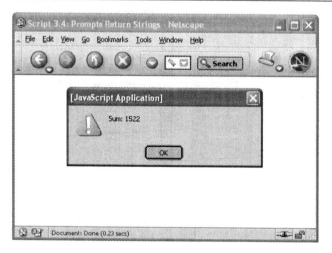

This time JavaScript treated both numbers as strings! Why? Because you used the + operator, a legitimate operator for strings, JavaScript did not convert the strings to numbers. Instead, it concatenated them.

When you used the multiplication (*) operator, JavaScript assumed you wanted to convert the strings to numbers and took care of it for you. After all, you can't multiply strings. However, when you used the + operator, which means addition for numbers and concatenation for strings, JavaScript had no way to tell what you wanted to do. So it treated both strings as the *strings* they were and concatenated them. Remember, you entered the numbers into a prompt *text* box.

So how do you get around that? How do you force JavaScript to treat the text box entries as numbers? The answer is that you deliberately convert them to numbers using `parseInt()` or `parseFloat()` before performing a mathematical operation.

Make the following changes to your script and run it, entering the same numbers as before.

**Script 3.5     Converting Text Entries to Numbers**

```
1    <html>
2    <head>
3       <title>Script 3.5: Converting Text Entries to Numbers</title>
4    </head>
5    <body>
6    <script language="JavaScript" type="text/javascript"><!--
7        var num1 = prompt("Enter a number:", "")
8        var num2 = prompt("Enter another number:", "")
9        alert("Sum: " + (parseFloat(num1) + parseFloat(num2)))
10   // -->
11   </script>
12   </body>
13   </html>
```

Now the program works as originally intended. It adds the entries together instead of concatenating them.

**Figure 3.7     Results of Script 3.5**

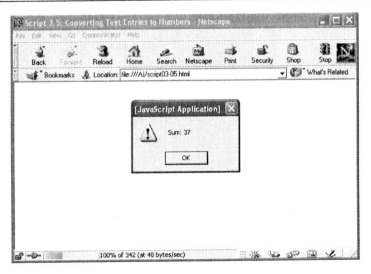

You might also prompt the user for a number and convert it on the spot:

```
var num1 = parseFloat(prompt("Enter a number:", ""))
```

In the above statement, the visitor is first prompted for a number. Remember, prompt receives the entry as a string data type. parseFloat then converts the string into a number. The result is then assigned to num1.

### NaN and isNaN()

What happens if you try to convert a string that does not have a numeric equivalent into a number? For instance, what value would num1 be set to in the previous example if the visitor entered the string "ten"? Let's look at another example and examine the results:

*programmer's tip*

You *cannot* use parseInt to turn a floating-point number into an integer. Neither can you use parseFloat to turn an integer into a floating-point number. parseInt and parseFloat only work on *strings*. Their purpose is to convert strings to numbers.

*Script 3.6     NaN*

```
1    <html>
2    <head>
3         <title>Script 3.6: NaN</title>
4    </head>
5    <body>
6    <script language="JavaScript" type="text/javascript"><!--
7         var guess = "white"
8         document.write(parseFloat(guess))
9    // -->
10   </script>
11   </body>
12   </html>
```

The result:

***Figure 3.8***    ***Results of Script 3.6***

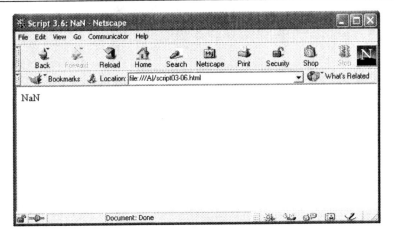

**NaN** is a special keyword that indicates the value is *not a number*. `parseFloat` tried to convert `guess` into a number, but `guess` held the value "white," which is a string with no numeric equivalent, so `parseFloat` returned `NaN` to indicate that it was not a number.

**side note**

Script 3.7 makes use of an `if` statement. We'll cover the `if` control structure thoroughly in Chapter 6. I've included it here only to illustrate the limitations of NaN. For most students, the `if` statement is pretty self-explanatory. After all, you're always making decisions based on some `if` condition. For instance, "If today is Sunday, do the laundry." Should this code confuse you, please feel free to refer back to it after you've read all about control structures in Chapter 6.

Since NaN is a special value, can you use it like the special values `undefined` and `null` in comparisons? Let's try this bit of code and see:

***Script 3.7***    ***Evaluating NaN***

```
1   <html>
2   <head>
3       <title>Script 3.7: Evaluating NaN</title>
4   </head>
5   <body>
6   <script language="JavaScript" type="text/javascript"><!--
7       var guess = "white"
8       guess = parseFloat(guess)
9       document.write("Guess: ", guess, "<br>")
```

```
10        if (guess == NaN)      // is guess equal to NaN?
11              document.write("It is not a number", "<br>")
12 // -->
13 </script>
14 </body>
15 </html>
```

The result:

**Figure 3.9    Results of Script 3.7**

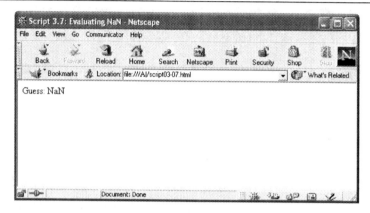

But wait a minute, guess *is* not a number! So why didn't the program write "It is not a number" when it checked to see if guess was equal to NaN  (guess  == NaN)?

Unlike null and undefined, the special keyword NaN cannot be used directly for comparisons. JavaScript does, however, provide a way to see if an expression evaluates to NaN. The built-in function to perform this check is—you guessed it—isNaN(). With this information in mind, let's modify the script and try it again:

**Script 3.8    Using *isNaN***

```
1    <html>
2    <head>
3         <title>Script 3.8: Using isNaN</title>
4    </head>
5    <body>
6    <script language="JavaScript" type="text/javascript"><!--
7         var guess = "white"
8         guess = parseFloat(guess)
9         document.write("Guess: ", guess, "<br>")
10        if (isNaN(guess))        // is guess not a number?
11              document.write("It is not a number", "<br>")
```

```
12  // -->
13  </script>
14  </body>
15  </html>
```

This time it worked as we intended:

**Figure 3.10     Results of Script 3.8**

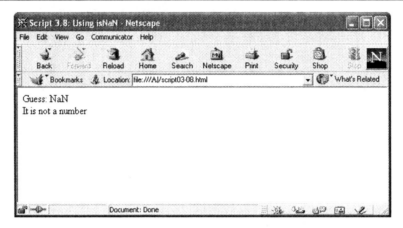

As you work with JavaScript, and especially with forms, you'll find these built-in functions extremely useful.

## Other Built-in Functions for Data Type Conversions

Two other built-in functions, `Number()` and `String()`, can also assist with data type conversions, as can the `toString()` method that is associated with every object.

The `Number` function is not associated with any particular object. It is a built-in function like `parseInt()` and `parseFloat()`. `Number()` attempts to convert any object or string passed to it into a number. If the object sent to it cannot be converted into a number, the function returns NaN.

Like the `Number` function, the `String` function is not associated with any particular object. `String()` converts the value of any object into a string. It returns the same value that the object's `toString()` method would.

## What Data Type Am I? The `typeof` Operator

One more JavaScript feature that needs mentioning while we're discussing data types is the `typeof` operator. The `typeof` operator lets you easily determine the current data type of any variable. The result of a `typeof` operation is one of the following strings. It indicates the data type of the variable.

- ✗ "number"
- ✗ "string"
- ✗ "boolean"
- ✗ "object"
- ✗ "undefined"

The syntax is

```
typeof (operand)
typeof operand
```

operand is the variable, object, object property, literal, or special keyword (null, undefined, etc.) whose type you wish to know.

Note that the parentheses are optional, but it is considered good programming style to use them. For example:

**Script 3.9    typeof**

```
1   <html>
2   <head>
3        <title>Script 3.9: typeof</title>
4   </head>
5   <body>
6   <script language="JavaScript" type="text/javascript"><!--
7        var myVariable = "cat"
8        document.write("myVariable\'s type is: ")
9        document.write(typeof myVariable, "<br>")
10  // -->
11  </script>
12  </body>
13  </html>
```

The result:

*Figure 3.11  Results of Script 3.9*

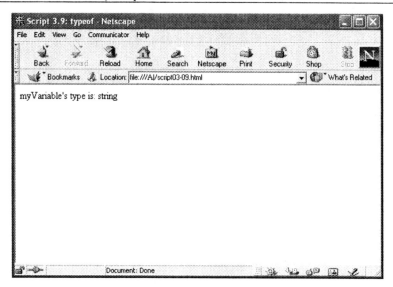

Here's one that's a little more complicated and shows you more of the possible values returned by the typeof operator. You're going to have to take line 10, which creates a Date object, on faith for now and learn the details later in Chapter 10.

*Script 3.10  typeof Operator*

```
1    <html>
2    <head>
3        <title>Script 3.10: typeof Operator</title>
4    </head>
5    <body>
6    <script language="JavaScript" type="text/javascript"><!--
7        var myNum = 7
8        var myWord = "Oh, my!"
9        var answer = false
10       var today = new Date()
11       var notDefined
12       var noValue = ""
13
14       document.write("<b>Variable: typeof</b><br>")
15       document.write("myNum: ", typeof(myNum), "<br>")
16       document.write("myWord: ", typeof(myWord), "<br>")
17       document.write("answer: ", typeof(answer), "<br>")
18       document.write("today: ", typeof(today), "<br>")
19       document.write("document: ", typeof(document), "<br>")
20       document.write("notDefined: ", typeof(notDefined), "<br>")
```

```
21          document.write("noValue: ", typeof(noValue), "<br>")
22
23          document.write("undefined: ", typeof(undefined), "<br>")
24          document.write("null: ", typeof(null), "<br>")
25          document.write("NaN: ", typeof(NaN), "<br>")
26
27          document.write("undeclared: ", typeof(undeclared), "<br>")
28
29          document.write("document.bgColor: ",
                typeof(document.bgColor), "<br>")
30  // -->
31  </script>
32  </body>
33  </html>
```

Here are the results:

**Figure 3.12     Results of Script 3.10**

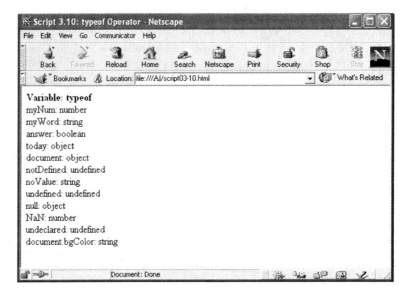

Notice that when a `typeof` operation is performed on a variable that has not yet had a value assigned to it, the operation results in `undefined` (see lines 11 and 20 in Script 3.10). `undefined` is also the result of performing a `typeof` operation on a variable that has not even been declared (line 27). Beware of performing a `typeof` operation on an object that does not exist: the result is a nasty runtime error.

A `typeof` operation on a variable whose value is `null` or on the keyword `null` results in `object` (line 24). It seems like a strange response to me.

Interestingly, a value of NaN causes typeof to return number (line 25). Perhaps the language realizes that you tried to convert the value to a number, and even though it wasn't possible to convert that value to a number, recognizes that you at least *intended* the value to be a number. At least that's my theory.

Clearly, JavaScript makes data type conversions quite easy. Keep in mind, though, that this can also present some potential pitfalls. Here are a few tips that might help you avoid tripping over JavaScript's dynamic data typing:

1. Declare all variables before using them with the keyword var, preferably at the beginning of your program.
2. Use descriptive names when defining your variables.
3. Initialize all variables and try to stick to the initial data type throughout your program. Simply initializing all of your variables will help prevent that nasty undefined value from popping up in your programs.
4. Describe each variable with a brief comment when you declare and initialize it.
5. When in doubt about whether JavaScript will convert a string to a number for you or not, perform the conversion yourself. That way you'll know for certain that it is taken care of, and you will be less likely to encounter side effects when your script is run in different browsers.
6. Always convert form field entries and prompt box responses for which you expect numeric input into numbers with parseInt() or parseFloat() and test the result of these operations with isNaN() before performing any mathematical operations. You could also use Number() to perform the conversion, but it has not been supported as long as parseInt() and parseFloat() have and will not work in older browsers.

# It's an Object, It's a Function, and It's a Primitive Data Type. Huh?

Take a look at your JavaScript object reference in Appendix A. Notice how Number, Boolean, and String are listed as *objects*? But didn't we already say they were *primitive data types*? Didn't we also point out that there are Number() and String() *functions* as well? So which are they? Primitive data types? Functions? Or objects? The answer is all three.

Number, string, and Boolean are indeed primitive data types. Every value of every property, literal, and variable will boil down to one of these data types or the special values null, undefined, Infinity, or NaN. Number() and String() are also *functions* that allow you to convert a string to a number and vice versa. Notice that these function names are capitalized, unlike most built-in JavaScript function and method names.

Finally, Number, String, and Boolean are pseudo-objects. According to Netscape's JavaScript reference, they are **object wrappers**. What this means is that, for the purposes of using methods associated with these pseudo-objects, a variable will temporarily become the appropriate object for the duration of a method call, then the "object" will be discarded from memory. In other words, the object *wraps* around the primitive data type, temporarily making it an object so that you can use a method defined for that object on the primitive data value. After you're done using the method, the object wrapper is stripped off and discarded like a wet suit.

For example, the `String` object, in particular, has many useful methods defined for it that allow you to manipulate, tear apart, put back together, uppercase, lowercase, strike out, and even search strings. JavaScript allows you to use all of these `String` object methods on ordinary strings. For example:

```
var response = "blue"
response = response.toUpperCase()      // result "BLUE"
```

JavaScript automatically converts the string to a temporary `String` object. Then, after calling the `toUpperCase()` method, it discards the temporary `String` object from memory.

Another useful side effect of JavaScript's treating ordinary strings as objects is that you can use the `length` property of the `String` object to determine the length of any string. For example:

```
response.length               // result 4
```

Keep in mind, however, that ordinary strings are not really objects. We can verify that this is true by using the `typeof` operator on the string we created:

```
typeof(response)              // result string
```

If for some reason you need a genuine `String` object, then you can create one using the `new` operator:

```
var genuineString = new String("The real McCoy")
```

The same holds true for creating genuine number and Boolean objects.

## Summary

JavaScript, like any other programming language, has a predefined set of data types and special values that it is able to recognize and manipulate. JavaScript's primitive data types include number, string, and Boolean. The four special data values JavaScript recognizes are `null`, representing no value; `undefined`, representing the value of a variable that has been declared, but not yet initialized, or the value of a variable or property that simply has not been defined; `Infinity`, usually the result of dividing by zero; and `NaN`, which means not a number. JavaScript also supports one composite data type: object.

> **peek ahead**
>
> We'll discuss the new operator in detail in Chapter 10 and string methods in Chapter 9. You can refer back to this section then for a better understanding of what I just said.

JavaScript is a dynamically typed language. A programmer may easily change the data type of a variable. Strongly typed languages like Java and C++ do not allow this. JavaScript further facilitates dynamic typing by providing several built-in functions for converting data types, including `parseInt()`, `parseFloat()`, `String()`, and `Number()`. In addition, every object has a built-in `toString()` method for converting the object into a string. The `typeof` operator lets you determine the data type of any variable, and the `isNaN()` built-in function lets you verify that a string converted to a number did indeed result in a number.

Finally, JavaScript defines Number, String, and Boolean objects that are really object wrappers that allow you to treat variables with primitive data values as objects for the purpose of using the methods and properties associated with those objects.

## Review Questions

1. What does it mean to be a primitive data type?
2. What is a composite data type?
3. What three primitive data types does JavaScript support?
4. What composite data type does JavaScript support?
5. What special values does JavaScript support? List and describe each one.
6. What number bases can JavaScript recognize?
7. How do you differentiate between number bases in your code?
8. What is a string?
9. How does JavaScript recognize strings as strings?
10. What symbols are used to delimit strings in JavaScript?
11. What symbol does HTML prefer to delimit attribute values?
12. What does it mean to "escape a character"? Provide an example.
13. What's the difference between a literal and a variable?
14. What does it mean to initialize a variable?
15. What is an assignment statement?
16. List five rules you must take into consideration when naming variables.
17. Define the term "expression."
18. What does it mean when a programming language is "loosely typed"?
19. How does Netscape describe JavaScript in terms of its typedness?
20. What do the built-in functions `parseInt` and `parseFloat` do?
21. Describe a scenario when converting a string to a number might be necessary.
22. What does NaN mean? When are you likely to encounter it? Can you use it in a comparison? Explain.
23. What does the `typeof` operator do?
24. What is an object wrapper?
25. List three tips that you would give a new programmer to help him avoid problems with JavaScript's dynamic data typing.

## Exercises

1. Which of the following are valid variable declarations or initializations? Explain why each one is or is not valid. If an item is not valid, explain how you could change it so that it is.

a. var bean_count = 39
b. my name = "Sam"
c. var zipCode = document.myForm.zip.value
d. var 1stName = "Sam"
e. his-name = "Devan"
f. var phoneNum = "(619)555-1212"
g. var Tim'sNum = "(619)555-1213"
h. var car make = "Nissan"
i. var num3 = 88
j. var #99 = 99

2. Evaluate each of the following expressions and specify whether the result is a string, numeric, Boolean data type, or some special value.

a. 7 + 5
b. "7" + "5"
c. "7" + 5
d. 7 + "5"
e. "Hi " + 5
f. 5 + 2 + " up"
g. parseInt("7" + "5")
h. parseInt("7") + parseInt("5")
i. parseInt("seven" + 5)
j. parseInt(nine)

3. List the result of each of the following typeof statements. Try to figure them out without running them in a script. Then run each statement and see how you did.

a. typeof (-78)
b. typeof ("Sam")
c. typeof ("50 ways to leave your lover")
d. typeof(parseFloat("50 ways to leave your lover"))
e. typeof (parseInt("7up"))
f. typeof (true)
g. typeof (87 + "")
h. typeof (86 + 99)
i. typeof (count)
j. typeof (null)
k. typeof (parseInt("seven"))
l. typeof ()

4. Write the appropriate code to convert each of the following to a string and then back to a number.

a. 17
b. 181.99
c. -97.56
d. -87
e. 0

5. Write the appropriate JavaScript expression to write each of the following decimal numbers in hexadecimal. (Hint: They correspond to the color values allowed in the browser-safe color palette.)

a. 00
b. 51
c. 102
d. 153
e. 204
f. 255

6. Specify the data type of each of the following. Assume the Web document has the following code defined before the statements:

```
<img name="MyPicture" src="images/me.jpg"
   width=100 height=100>
```

   a. var num = "7"
   b. var num2 = 57.5
   c. var happy
   d. var myPic
   e. MyPicture.src
   f. MyPicture.height
   g. var val = null
   h. var truth = false
   i. var myDoc = window.document
   j. var myImage = document.MyPicture
   k. var num3 = 87
   l. var myNum = parseInt("87")
   m. var zNum = parseInt("eight")

7. Specify whether each of the following is a reserved word, a word currently used by JavaScript, a word currently used by HTML, a word currently used by CSS, or a word that is perfectly safe to use as a variable name.

   a. background
   b. backColor
   c. border
   d. checkBox
   e. client
   f. code
   g. color
   h. count
   i. data
   j. double
   k. email
   l. font
   m. java
   n. leftMargin
   o. location
   p. map
   q. max
   r. myVar
   s. name
   t. number
   u. position
   v. radioButton
   w. selection
   x. single
   y. string
   z. visitor

8. Write two JavaScript statements, one to print your name and one to print your nickname in quotation marks. Both your name and your nickname should appear in the document on the same line, like this:

Tina Spain McDuffie "WebWoman"

9. Write a single JavaScript statement to display your favorite quote in a <blockquote> tag, within quotation marks, and written in italics. Choose a fairly long quote that

spans multiple lines. Preface it with *"Person's name says/said:"*. Here's an example of what the output should look like:

Arthur C. Clarke said:

*"Any sufficiently advanced technology is indistinguishable from magic."*

10. Write the appropriate JavaScript statement to write the following statement to the document:

He said, "It's not whether you win or lose, but how you play the game that counts & don't forget that!"

# Scripting Exercises

Create a folder named assignment03 to hold the documents you create during this assignment. Save a copy of the personal home page you modified at the end of Chapter 2 as home.html in the assignment03 folder.

1. Create a new document named favColor.html. Write a script that
   a. Prompts the visitor for his or her name and assigns it to a variable.
   b. Prompt the user for his or her favorite of the following colors: red, green, blue, magenta, yellow, teal, or silver.
   c. Use those variables to set the background color of the document and to welcome the user by name.
2. Create a new document named sum.html. Write a script that
   a. Prompts the user for two numbers.
   b. Then displays their sum in the following format: 10 + 15 = 25
3. Modify the following script to both declare *and* initialize each variable on a single line. Change the values to suit your own personal tastes.

```
<script language="JavaScript" type="text/javascript"><!--
        var favDrink
        var favSoda
        var favFruit
        var favSalad
        var favDinner
        var favDessert
        var favCandyBar

        favDrink = "Lemonade"
        favSoda = "Dr. Pepper"
        favFruit = "orange"
        favSalad = "Ceasar Salad"
        favDinner = "Chicken-n-Bean Burrito at Teo Leo's"
        favDessert = "Chocolate Fudge Cake Sundae"
        favCandyBar = "Butterfinger"
```

```
// -->
</script>
```

Use the modified script to write the content for the Favorite Foods section in your personal home page.

4. Modify home.html as follows:
   a. In the head of the document, declare and initialize the following variables:
      i.   myName
      ii.  myNickname
      iii. myGender
      iv.  myBirthday
   b. Use these variables and JavaScript to complete the About Me section like this:

      Name: your name here
      Nickname: your nickname here
      Gender: male or female
      Birthday: your birthday here

   c. For an extra challenge, and to make everything line up nicely, write the information in a table. Use JavaScript to write all of the information including the tags necessary to create the table.

5. Modify home.html as follows:
   a. In the head of the document, declare and initialize the following variables:
      i.   myTitle
      ii.  myJobDescription
      iii. myEmployer
      Declare and initialize additional variables if you want.
   b. Use these variables and JavaScript to complete the My Job/Work section like this:

      I'm a(n) <insert myTitle here> at <insert myEmployer here>. My duties include: <insert myJobDescription here>.

      or something similar. The idea is to create some variables and use them to write information to the screen, a very common and important task performed with JavaScript.

   c. For an extra challenge, fancy your content up with HTML in your document.write statements.

6. Modify home.html as follows:
   a. Declare and initialize the following variables:
      i.   myName (if not already created)
      ii.  myEmail
      iii. myPhone
      iv.  myWebsite

b.  Remove the words "Contact Info" from the <address> tag at the bottom of the page and replace them with the following:

This site maintained by: <your name here>
Email: email@address.com  Phone: (123)456-7890
<web site URL here>

or something similar. Use your variables and JavaScript to write the content. Make your email address and the Web site URL links. To do so, you'll need to use the `myEmail` and `myWebsite` variables twice each.

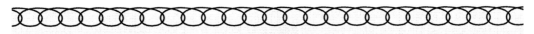

## chapter *four*

# *Expressions and Statements*

I n Chapter 3, we talked about expression evaluation and its close relationship to data values and variables. Most JavaScript statements contain an expression of some kind that requires evaluation. At the heart of these expressions are operators and function calls.

In this chapter, we'll

- ✗ define the terms "expression" and "state-ment."
- ✗ look at the various types of operators you can use in expressions, including
  - ✗ string operators.
  - ✗ arithmetic operators.
  - ✗ assignment operators.
  - ✗ comparison operators.
  - ✗ logical operators.
  - ✗ the conditional operator.
- ✗ introduce functions.
- ✗ learn how to declare a function with and without parameters.

*Sure as*

*one plus one*

*is two . . .*

—Mac Davis

✄ learn how to return a value from a function.

✄ study and apply the established order of operations.

Let's get started by taking a closer look at expressions versus statements.

# What Is an Expression?

Although we should, by now, have a good feeling for what an expression is, we have yet to define it. An **expression** is any valid set of literals, variables, operators, function calls, and expressions that evaluates to a single value. The resulting single value can be a number, a string, a Boolean, or a special value (null, undefined, Infinity, or NaN); that is, the result of any expression is always one of JavaScript's defined data types or special values. Here are some examples:

```
3 + 7
3 + 7 + 10 + ""
"Dr." + " " + "Pepper"
```

The first expression adds the numbers 3 and 7 and *evaluates to* 10.

The second expression adds the numbers 3, 7, and 10 and an empty string and evaluates to "20", which is a string.

The last expression adds three strings together and evaluates to "Dr. Pepper".

# What Is a Statement?

While an expression is any valid set of literals, variables, operators, function calls, and expressions that *evaluates* to a single value, a **statement**, on the other hand, is any set of declarations, method calls, function calls, and expressions that performs some *action*. The possible results of a JavaScript statement are infinite. Here are some examples:

```
var num = 1
document.write("hello")
```

The first statement above declares a variable named num and initializes it to the value of 1. The second statement performs the action of writing "hello" to the document.

# Expressions vs. Statements

Statements often contain expressions that have to be evaluated before the specified action can be performed. For instance:

```
document.write("Sum: ", 3 + 7, "<br>")
```

The *statement* above has to evaluate the *expression* "3 + 7" before it can convert it to a string and write the result between the strings "Sum: " and "<br>". The statement performs several actions:

✄ It evaluates the expression "3 + 7."

✄ It writes the string "Sum : ".

✗ It converts the number 10 to a string and writes it (10 was the result of evaluating the expression "3 + 7").

✗ Finally, it writes the string "<br>".

Here's another example of a statement that has to evaluate an expression before it can perform its intended action:

```
total = 1 + 2
```

This statement first has to evaluate the expression "1 + 2" before it can assign it to `total`.

JavaScript has the following *types* of expressions. Notice that they correspond to the three primitive data types supported by JavaScript that we discussed in Chapter 3:

✗ Number—evaluates to a number, for example, 15, 7.57, or -3.145

✗ String—evaluates to a character string, for example, "Jane", "Hello", or "9455"

✗ Boolean—evaluates to true or false

This makes sense when we consider that every expression evaluates to a single value and that all JavaScript values can be classified as one of the three primitive data types or one of the special values null, undefined, Infinity, or NaN.

# What Is an Operator?

**Operators** are the workers in expressions. They come primarily in two flavors: unary and binary. A unary operator performs work, or operates, on one operand, whereas a binary operator operates on two operands. Table 4.1 provides some examples.

**Table 4.1      Operator Flavors**

| Operator Flavor | Syntax | Examples |
|---|---|---|
| unary | *operand operator* or *operator operand* | -88 count++ !flag |
| binary | *operand operator operand* | 7 + 8 num1 < num2 |

# Types of Operators

The JavaScript language supports many operators. They are easily organized into five categories:

✗ **String operators**—operators that work on strings. There are only two.

✗ **Arithmetic operators, also known as mathematical operators**—operators that perform mathematical computations.

✗ **Assignment operators**—operators that assign a value to a variable, object, or property.

✗ **Comparison operators**—operators that compare two values or expressions and return a Boolean value indicating the truth of the comparison.

✗ **Logical operators, also known as Boolean operators**—operators that take Boolean values as operands and return a Boolean value indicating the truth of the relationship.

In addition to these five categories of operators, JavaScript supports one special operator, the conditional operator. The conditional operator is the only operator that has three operands. We'll discuss it in more detail later. For now, let's start with string operators and work through them all from there.

## Concatenation, the String Operator

There are really only two string operators: the concatenation operator (+) and the concatenation by value operator (+=). The first concatenates two strings together. Thus, the operation

```
"Greetings, " + "Earthlings"
```

evaluates to the string

```
"Greetings, Earthlings"
```

An equivalent operation using variables is

```
var salutation = "Greetings, "
var recipient = "Earthlings"
salutation + recipient
```

The last statement evaluates to

```
"Greetings, Earthlings"
```

*peek ahead* — While there are only two string operators, there are many string methods. We'll look at string methods in detail in Chapter 9.

The second string operator, concatenation by value (+=), concatenates the string on the right side (or the value of a string variable) to the string value stored in the variable on the left side, then assigns the result back to the left operand variable. Here's an example:

```
var greeting = "Greetings, "
greeting += "Earthlings"
```

The first statement declares a variable named `greeting` and initializes it to the string "Greetings, ".

The second statement concatenates "Earthlings" onto the value contained in `greeting`. So the variable `greeting` now evaluates to

```
"Greetings, Earthlings"
```

Cool, huh?

A common use of the concatenation by value operator (+=) is to pile a bunch of HTML statements into a single string variable for easy writing to a pop-up window. While we're not ready to tackle pop-up windows just yet, we can see how easy it is to cram a bunch of HTML into one tiny little variable.

*Script 4.1*    **Using Concatenation by Value**

```
1    <!doctype html public "-//W3C//DTD HTML 4.0 Transitional//EN">
2    <html>
3    <head>
4    <title>Script 4.1: Using Concatenation By Value</title>
5    <script language="JavaScript" type="text/javascript"><!--
6       var docContents = ""
7    //-->
8    </script>
9    </head>
10   <body>
11   <script language="JavaScript" type="text/javascript"><!--
12      // now you generate the custom content, maybe from values of
13      // form fields or other operations performed on the page
14      docContents += "<h1>Dynamically generated page content.</h1>"
15      docContents += "<p>More dynamically generated page content. "
16      docContents += "Still more dynamically generated page
17         content.</p>"
18      docContents += "<p>Yet more dynamically generated page
19         content.</p>"

20      // here you would create a new window,
21      // you'll learn how in Chapter 11

22      document.write(docContents)    // here you write it out
23   //-->
24   </script>
25   </body>
26   </html>
```

Run the code and check out the results:

*Figure 4.1*    **Results of Script 4.1**

*peek ahead*

You'll learn how to create pop-up windows and write to them dynamically in Chapter 11.

JavaScript supports only the two string operators just discussed. Attempts to perform mathematical operations (other than + and +=, which are technically string operators when they're used with strings) on strings that cannot be converted to numbers result in NaN. Let's examine arithmetic operators now.

## Arithmetic (Mathematical) Operators

Arithmetic operators, that is, operators that perform mathematical operations, should be quite familiar to you. After all, you've been using them since grade school. Because they're so self-explanatory, rather than describe each one in detail, here's a handy chart that describes each operator complete with an example and its name.

Note that all arithmetic operators work on numbers and result in a number. Division by zero results in the numeric value Infinity. In some older browsers, division by zero may result in undefined or NaN; it depends on the browser.

**Table 4.2    Arithmetic Operators**

| Operator | Name | What It Does | Flavor | Example | Result |
|---|---|---|---|---|---|
| + | plus | Adds the two operands | binary | 7 + 5 | 12 |
| - | minus | Subtracts the right operand from the left operand | binary | 7 - 5 | 2 |
| * | multiply | Multiplies the two operands | binary | 7 * 5 | 35 |
| / | divide | Divides the left operand by the right operand and returns the quotient | binary | 7/5 | 1.4 |
| % | modulus (remainder) | Divides the left operand by the right operand and returns the remainder | binary | 7%5 | 2 |
| - | negation | Negates the operand | unary | -7 | -7 |
| ++ | increment | Adds 1 to the operand | unary | *assume x=7*<br>++x<br><br>x++ | 8 (before assignment)<br><br>7 (before assignment)<br>8 (after assignment) |

| | | | | assume x=7 | |
|---|---|---|---|---|---|
| -- | decrement | Subtracts 1 from the operand | unary | --x | 6 (before assignment) |
| | | | | x-- | 7 (before assignment) 6 (after assignment) |

OK, so maybe a few of them do need a little explanation. For instance, what is this modulus operator? I don't remember *that* one from grade school.

The modulus operator is a remainder operator, that is, it performs division, throws the quotient away, and keeps the remainder. Thus,

    5 % 3

evaluates to

    2

because 3 goes into 5 one time with a remainder of 2.

   Let's try another:

    9 % 3

evaluates to

    0

because 9 divided by 3 equals 3 with a remainder of 0.

   One more:

    4.5 % 2

evaluates to

    .5

because 2 goes into 4.5 two times with a remainder of .5.

   See how that works? It takes a little braintwisting, but not too much.

   The increment and decrement operators also require special mention. While incrementing and decrementing are simple in themselves—incrementing adds 1, decrementing subtracts 1—these operators can work pre-evaluation or post-evaluation when used in conjunction with an assignment operator.

   Either way, pre- or post-evaluation, the operation is performed, that is, the operand is incremented or decremented. However, if an assignment is involved, the value actually assigned will vary according to which side of the operand the increment or decrement operator is placed. To explain this, let's start with a few variables initialized to zero:

    var countA = 0
    var countB = 0

**programmer's tip** Should you try to perform mathematical operations on strings, other than + and +=, which are legitimate string operators, JavaScript will attempt to convert the strings into numbers before performing the operation. If the conversions are successful, the result is a number. If they are not, the result is NaN.

```
var num1 = 0
var num2 = 0
```

Now let's use a pre-increment operator. You can tell it's a pre-evaluation operator because the operator precedes the operand.

```
num1 = ++countA
```

Because this statement used a pre-evaluation increment operator, countA is incremented *before* the assignment. So num1 gets the value 1:

```
document.write("num1: ", num1, "<br>")
```

Now let's try a post-evaluation increment operator. Post-evaluation operators are placed after the operand. They don't execute until *after* the rest of the statement has executed, just before the next line of code.

```
num2 = countB++
```

Because this statement used a post-evaluation increment operator, countB doesn't get incremented until after the assignment is made to num2. So num2 gets the value 0, but countB holds the value of 1 after the statement is executed:

```
document.write("num2: ", num2, "<br>")
document.write("countB: ", countB, "<br>")
```

If this seems a bit confusing, don't worry. Most of the time, it isn't an issue. Only when an assignment is involved do you need to look closely at it and determine what it is that you want to accomplish. In fact, you may want to avoid using increment and decrement operators in this fashion altogether just because it *is* confusing. It's safer to use them alone, on a line by themselves, to either increment or decrement a variable; *then* perform your assignment on the *next line*. This makes your code easier to read and eliminates the guesswork.

After you've learned more about assignments and assignment operators, reread this section; it may all seem clearer then.

## Assignment Operators

As with arithmetic operators, assignment operators should seem pretty straightforward. In essence, every assignment operation either initializes or changes the contents of the variable listed on the left side of the operator. Remember myCup from Chapter 3? Let's update its contents a few times to get a better picture of how assignment operators work. For instance, the statement

```
myCup = "lemonade"
```

changes the contents of myCup so that myCup now holds lemonade. If myCup had not yet been assigned a value, the above statement would initialize myCup with "lemonade";

otherwise, it replaces myCup's contents with lemonade. Because myCup is a variable, we can also say that myCup *evaluates* to lemonade. Remember, a variable always *evaluates* to its contents.

The statement

```
myCup += " tea"
```

works a little differently. This statement adds tea to myCup of lemonade so that myCup now holds both lemonade and tea—an excellent combination, especially on a hot summer day.

Of course you can, at any time, completely replace the contents of myCup with something else by making a new assignment:

```
myCup = "ice water"
```

This statement replaces the "lemonade tea" in myCup with "ice water".

While we've been using strings to illustrate how assignment operators work, most of the assignment operators listed here, all but equals (=) and add by value (+=), work only on numbers; += also works on strings and = works on any data type. Here's a list of JavaScript's assignment operators:

**Table 4.3    Assignment Operators**

| Operator | Name | Examples | Is Equivalent To | Means | Applies To |
|---|---|---|---|---|---|
| = | equals *or gets* | x = y <br> x = 7 | | x gets the value of y <br> x gets the value of 7 | any data type |
| += | add by value | x += y <br> x += 5 | x = x + y <br> x = x + 5 | x gets the value of x + y <br> x gets the value of x + 5 | numbers and strings |
| -= | subtract by value | x -= y <br> x -= 7 | x = x – y <br> x = x -7 | x gets the value of x – y <br> x gets the value of x - 7 | numbers only |
| *= | multiply by value | x *= y <br> x *= 5 | x = x * y <br> x = x * 5 | x gets the value of x * y <br> x gets the value of x * 5 | numbers only |
| /= | divide by value | x /= y <br> x /= 7 | x = x/y <br> x = x/7 | x gets the value of x/y <br> x gets the value of x/7 | numbers only |
| %= | modulus by value | x %= y <br> x %= 5 | x = x % y <br> x = x % 5 | x gets the value of x % y <br> x gets the value of x % 5 | numbers only |

# Comparison Operators

Comparison operators should also look familiar to you: like arithmetic operators, you've been using them since grade school. Comparison operators allow you to compare two values or two expressions of any data type. Usually, the two items being compared are of the same data type, so we're comparing apples to apples. It doesn't make much sense to compare apples to oranges. The result of a comparison is always a Boolean truth value: true or false.

Here's a list of JavaScript comparison operators:

**Table 4.4      Comparison Operators**

| Operator | Name | Description | Example (assume: x=7, y=5) | Example Result |
|---|---|---|---|---|
| == | is equal to | Returns true if the operands are equal | x == y | false |
| != | is not equal to | Returns true if the operands are not equal | x != y | true |
| > | is greater than | Returns true if the left operand is greater than the right operand | x > y | true |
| >= | is greater than or equal to | Returns true if the left operand is greater than or equal to the right operand | x >= y | true |
| < | is less than | Returns true if the left operand is less than the right operand | x < y | false |
| <= | is less than or equal to | Returns true if the left operand is less than or equal to the right operand | x <= y | false |
| === | is equivalent to | Returns true if the operands are equal and of the same type | x === y | false |
| !== | is not equivalent to | Returns true if the operands are not equal and/or not of the same type | x !== y | true |

JavaScript often performs conversions for you when you do comparisons of strings and numbers. For instance, should you compare the following:

        5 == "5"

the result is true. Why? After all, the left operand is a number and the right a string. In this and all comparisons except "is equivalent to" (===) and "is not equivalent to" (!==), JavaScript assumes you are trying to compare similar data types and performs the conversions for you. In this example, JavaScript converted the string to a number in order to perform a meaningful comparison.

Comparison operators are often used in conjunction with control structures to direct the flow of a program.

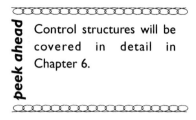

*peek ahead* Control structures will be covered in detail in Chapter 6.

# Logical (Boolean) Operators

Logical operations, also known as Boolean operations, always result in a truth value: `true` or `false`. Perhaps the best way to illustrate logical operators is to use some English expressions and let you evaluate whether each expression is `true` or `false`.

## The && (AND) Operator

Let's first look at the `&&` operator. In order for an `&&` (AND) expression to be `true`, both operands must be `true`. With that in mind, consider this expression. Is it `true` or `false`?

```
You are currently reading Chapter 4 && this book is about ⸺▶
⸺▶ Visual Basic.
```

It's `false`. Why? Because while you are indeed reading Chapter 4, this is *not* a book about Visual Basic. The second part of the expression, the right operand, is `false`, making the AND (`&&`) expression `false`.

Let's try another:

```
The subject of this book is JavaScript && the author is ⸺▶
⸺▶ Tina Spain McDuffie.
```

The result:

```
true
```

Both sides of the AND (`&&`) expression are `true`, thus the expression is `true`.

Now let's take a look at the `||` (OR) operator.

## The || (OR) Operator

In an OR situation, only one side needs to be `true` in order for the expression to evaluate to `true`. If both sides are `true`, the expression is still `true`. Only if both sides are `false` will an OR operation evaluate to `false`. Here's an example:

```
This book is about JavaScript || this book is about ⸺▶
⸺▶ Visual Basic
```

The result:

```
true
```

The first part was `true`; so even though the second part was `false`, the overall expression is `true`. Had we used the AND (`&&`) operator, the result would have been `false`.

## The ! (NOT) Operator

Last but not least, we have the ! (NOT) operator. For example:

```
This book is !Visual Basic.
```

results in

```
true
```

This book is not about Visual Basic, it's about JavaScript, so the expression is `true`.

The NOT operator is often used to see if the value of a variable is `false` or to determine if an object doesn't exist. We'll see several examples of these uses throughout the book, after we've covered control structures.

Following is a table listing each logical operator, its associated truth table, and an example using that operator:

**Table 4.5     Logical Operators**

| Operator | Name | Flavor | Truth Table | | Example (isJS=true, isC3=false) | Result |
|---|---|---|---|---|---|---|
| && | AND | binary | **Expression** | **Result** | isJS && isC3 | false |
| | | | true && true | true | | |
| | | | true && false | false | | |
| | | | false && true | false | | |
| | | | false && false | false | | |
| \|\| | OR | binary | **Expression** | **Result** | isJS \|\| isC3 | true |
| | | | true \|\| true | true | | |
| | | | true \|\| false | true | | |
| | | | false \|\| true | true | | |
| | | | false \|\| false | false | | |
| ! | NOT | unary | **Expression** | **Result** | !isC3 | true |
| | | | !true | false | | |
| | | | !false | true | | |

# The Conditional Operator

The conditional operator is the only JavaScript operator that takes *three* operands. The result of the operation is one of two values, based upon the evaluation of the *condition.* If the condition is true, the first value is the result; if the condition is false, the second value is the result.

The syntax is

```
(condition) ? ValueIfTrue : ValueIfFalse
```

You can use the conditional operator anywhere you would use a standard operator. For example, try the following:

```
var age = 38
status = (age >= 18) ? "adult" : "minor"
```

`status` evaluates to

```
"adult"
```

Because the variable `age` holds the value 38, the condition, `age >= 18`, is `true`. There-fore, the conditional statement evaluates to the first value listed, which is `"adult"`, and that value is assigned to the variable `status`. If the condition evaluates to `false`, then the expression evaluates to the second value, `"minor"`, and that is assigned to `status`. For example:

```
var age = 7
status = (age >= 18) ? "adult" : "minor"
```

`status` evaluates to

```
"minor"
```

Cool, huh? OK, we've covered all the basic operators. Now let's look at JavaScript special operators.

## Special Operators

JavaScript supports several special operators that you should be aware of: `delete`, `new`, `this`, `typeof`, and `void`. Let's look at each of them in turn.

### delete

The `delete` operator allows you to delete an array entry or an object from memory. You need to know more about arrays and objects before you can see a good example of its use. So we'll postpone an example until Chapter 7 when we talk about arrays.

### new

Most JavaScript built-in objects like `Image` and `Array` have a corresponding constructor function already built into the language. **Constructor** is an object-oriented programming (OOP) term that refers to a function that specifies how to initialize a particular type of object when it is created. Constructor functions generally cannot be called directly. Instead, you use the special operator, **new**, in conjunction with the constructor function to create a new object and initialize it with its constructor. For instance, the following JavaScript statement creates and initializes an `Image` object in memory:

**peek ahead**
You'll use the new operator to create images for an automatic slideshow in Chapter 8.

```
var myPic = new Image()
```

Note that, in this case, no parameters were provided to the `Image` constructor func-tion. While many constructor functions require parameters to help define an object, some do not. In the case of the `Image` constructor above, its built-in function definition provides for the case of receiving no parameters. You can also, optionally, pass the image's dimensions, `width` and `height`, as parameters, in that order.

## this

The `this` operator is totally cool and can save you loads of typing, which is always a popular feature with programmers. The special keyword `this` is a shortcut way of referring to the current object. You need to learn more about event handlers, forms, and other objects before looking at a good working example, so we'll save a demonstration of it until that time. For now, just file it away in your brain as a special operator.

> **peek ahead**
> You'll get to use `this` to create a go menu in Chapter 12 and to perform form calculations and validations in Chapter 13.

## typeof

As we saw in Chapter 3, the `typeof` operator lets you easily determine the current data type of any variable.

The result of a `typeof` operation is always a *string* indicating the variable's data type. Thus, possible values are `"number"`, `"string"`, `"boolean"`, `"object"`, and `"undefined"`. See Chapter 3 for a working example of this useful operator.

## void

The `void` operator tells the interpreter to evaluate an expression and return no value. That's kind of weird, huh? Why would you want to evaluate an expression and then return no value? Well, actually it does come in handy when you want to make sure your program takes no action whatsoever in response to an event. In fact, we'll see `void` in action in the very next chapter.

For now, let's get back to our original discussion about expressions and statements. Recall that an expression is any valid set of literals, variables, operators, function calls, and expressions that evaluates to a single value. A statement is any set of declarations, method calls, function calls, and expressions that performs some *action*. Notice that twice we referred to function calls. So what's a function?

> **peek ahead**
> You'll learn how to use the `void` operator in conjunction with the javascript: pseudo-protocol and an `onClick` event handler in Chapter 5.

# What Is a Function?

A **function** is a block of predefined programming statements whose execution is deferred until the function is "called." In other words, a function is a predefined routine that doesn't execute until you "call" it.

You **call a function** by invoking its name with any required or optional parameters. A **function parameter**, also known as an argument, is a data value or data reference that you can pass to the function to work on or use. Parameters make functions more useful and flexible. For instance, you could define a `greetVisitor` function that would greet visitors to a Web site. Here's an example:

```
function greetVisitor() {
    alert("Hello!")
}
```

To call it, you invoke the function's name:

```
greetVisitor()
```

That's pretty easy, huh?

## Passing Parameters to Functions

Wouldn't the `greetVisitor` function be more useful if you could actually greet the visitor by name? That's where function parameters come in. How about you give the visitor's name, as a parameter, to `greetVisitor` so it can use that data when performing its function, which is to greet the visitor by name? Here's what your revised function might look like:

```
function greetVisitor(visitor) {
    alert("Hello, " + visitor + "!")

}
```

To call it, send the visitor's name as an argument to the function. You could've acquired the visitor's name in a variety of ways: from a prompt, a form field, or even a cookie stored during a previous visit. In this example, we'll use a simple string.

```
greetVisitor("WebWoman")
```

When you call `greetVisitor`, the string `"WebWoman"` is passed to the function's `visitor` parameter, which is a variable. Here's a picture of what happens:

```
greetVisitor("WebWoman")
```

passed to `greetVisitor` function

WebWoman

*visitor*

Were the information stored in the `firstName` variable, the call might look like this:

```
greetVisitor(firstName)
```

Here's a picture:

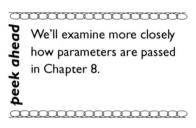

This time the value of `firstName` was assigned to the `visitor` parameter.

### Returning a Value from a Function

Another feature of functions is that they may optionally **return** a value. That is, they can do some processing and spit out (return) a result. This feature makes functions even more useful and flexible. For instance,

We'll examine more closely how parameters are passed in Chapter 8.

let's say we need a function to find the area of a rectangle. We'll provide the width and height; we want the function to return the area:

```
function calcRectangleArea(width, height) {
    var area = width * height
    return area
}
```

Here is one way to call it:

```
alert("The area of an 8x5 rectangle is: " +
    calcRectangleArea(8, 5))
```

The result:

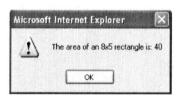

You'll often use functions that return a value in expressions. As you'll see in the next section, the function call usually occurs first, returning some value that is then used in the expression evaluation.

We'll look at functions in much greater detail in Chapter 8. For now, let's move on to the order of operations.

## The Order of Operations

When it comes to expression evaluation, it is essential to know which operations have priority, that is, you need to know who gets to go first. For instance, what does the following statement evaluate to?

```
4 + 10/2 * 3 - (1 + 2) * 4
```

If you evaluated the expression left to right, giving each operator equal precedence,

> 4 + 10 is 14
> divided by 2 is 7
> times 3 is 21
> - 1 is 20
> + 2 is 22
> times 4 is 88

Right? Sure, *if* that's how math really worked. But math doesn't work that way. So 88 is the wrong answer. If you have any math background whatsoever, you're already screaming, "No! No! No! That's not how it's done!" And you're right.

Mathematics has an established order of operations:

1. First you work the expressions within parentheses from the inside out.
2. Then you perform any squares, cubes, or other to-the-*n*th-ofs from left to right.
3. Then you multiply and divide from left to right.
4. Finally, you add and subtract from left to right.

Programming languages also have an order of operations. They must. There has to be some established guideline that determines the order of precedence of each programming construct. We saw how important the order of operations was when we worked with the increment and decrement operators. The order of operations directly affected the results of our assignments.

JavaScript's order of operations table is a little longer and more complex than the basic mathematical outline shown above because it also has to factor function calls and such into the equation. Still, the general concept is the same.

The following table describes JavaScript's order of operations. The bitwise operators have been left out to make it simpler, since we won't be covering them in this book.

**Table 4.6     Order of Operations**

| Order | Description | Operator(s) |
|-------|-------------|-------------|
| 1 | Parentheses (work from the inside out) | `( )` |
| 2 | Member of an object or an array | `. [ ]` |
| 3 | Create instance | `new` |
| 4 | Function call | `function()` |
| 5 | Boolean NOT, negation, positive, increment, decrement, typeof, void, and delete | `! - + ++ -- typeof void delete` |
| 6 | Multiplication, division, and modulus | `* / %` |
| 7 | Addition, concatenation, and subtraction | `+ -` |
| 8 | Relational comparisons | `< <= > >=` |

| 9 | Equality, inequality, equivalency, and non-equivalency | == != === !== |
|---|---|---|
| 10 | Boolean AND | && |
| 11 | Boolean OR | \|\| |
| 12 | Conditional expression | ? : |
| 13 | Assignment | = += -= *= /= %= |

Some of the descriptions in Table 4.6 refer to stuff we haven't covered yet, like arrays. Don't worry, all will become clear later. As you complete each new topic, come back and take a look at Table 4.6 again and see how the new topic fits into JavaScript's order of operations.

In the meantime, let's apply the stuff we've learned so far. Let's go back to the expression we looked at earlier and see if we can arrive at the correct answer, which is 7, by applying the correct order of operations step by step.

Original expression:

```
4 + 10/2 * 3 - (1 + 2) * 4
```

Any parentheses? Yes.

```
4 + 10/2 * 3 -    3    * 4   // evaluate parens
```

There are no arrays, objects, instance creations, or function calls (whatever they are), so we can skip 2 through 4. Any NOTs (!)? No. Any negative or positive signs? No. Any increments or decrements? No.

Next is multiplication, division, and modulus. Any of those? Yes. Let's do them one at a time, left to right:

```
4 +   5 * 3 -    3    * 4   // * and / left to right
4 +      15   -        12
```

Next is addition, concatenation, and subtraction. Any of those? There surely are. Let's do those one at a time, too:

```
    19         -        12     // + and - left to right
                7
```

Looks like we're done. We didn't even get to comparisons, equality and inequality, Boolean AND, Boolean OR, Boolean NOT, conditional expressions, or assignments.

The order of operations can have a dramatic effect on expressions and statements involving both strings and numbers. Let's explore a few expressions to see how.

```
7 + 5 + "dollars"
```

According to Table 4.6, the addition and concatenation operators have equal precedence. So, we evaluate the expression left to right. The result is

```
12  +  "dollars"
   12 dollars               // which is a string
```

Now let's try it the other way:

```
"dollars " + 7 + 5
```

Concatenation and addition have equal precedence, so it's left to right again:

```
"dollars 7" + 5        // add 7 to the string dollars
 dollars 75            // we're still adding to a string
```

Because the first operand, `"dollars "`, is a string, the + operator is the concatenation operator. So instead of adding 7, 7 is converted to a string and concatenated to the string `"dollars "`. The same is true for the 5.

## Summary

An expression is any valid set of literals, variables, operators, and expressions that evaluates to a single value. A statement is any set of declarations, method calls, function calls, and expressions that performs some action.

The JavaScript language is rich with operators that we can use in expressions, including

- ✗ string operators that work on strings.
- ✗ arithmetic operators, used for mathematical operations.
- ✗ assignment operators, used to assign a value to a variable or object property.
- ✗ comparison operators, used to compare two values or expressions.
- ✗ logical operators, used to determine the truth value of a Boolean expression.
- ✗ the conditional operator, used to choose one of two values based upon the result of a condition. The condition can be a comparison, a truth value, or the result of a logical operation.

The JavaScript language also supports several special operators:

- ✗ delete—used to delete an array element or object.
- ✗ new—used to create new objects with a constructor function call.
- ✗ this—used to refer to the current object.
- ✗ typeof—used to determine the data type of a variable, object property, object, or special value.
- ✗ void—used to prevent an expression from returning a value.

Expressions and statements sometimes include function calls. A function is a predefined set of programming statements whose execution is deferred until the function is called. Functions may optionally accept parameters and/or return a value. Those that return a value are often used in expressions.

Like any other programming language or mathematical system, JavaScript has an established order of operations to determine operator precedence. Table 4.6 describes JavaScript's order of operations.

## Review Questions

1. What is an expression?
2. What type(s) of value can an expression evaluate to? Be specific.
3. What's a statement?
4. What's the difference between an expression and a statement?
5. What's an operator?
6. What string operators does JavaScript support?
7. What type of operators performs mathematical computations?
8. What does the % operator do?
9. What's the difference between the pre-increment operator and the post-increment operator? How can using the wrong one affect your program?
10. Does it always make a difference to the result of your program whether you use a pre- or post-increment or decrement operator?
11. Describe assignment operators. Name three assignment operators.
12. What type of value does a comparison operation result in?
13. What's the difference between = and ==?
14. What's the difference between == and ===?
15. List and describe three logical operators.
16. What data type is returned by a logical operation?
17. What operator is the only one that takes three operands?
18. What's a function?
19. How do you call a function?
20. What's a parameter?
21. What does it mean to say that a function can *return* a value?
22. What is the purpose of having an order of operations?
23. Which comes first, multiplication or modulus?
24. Which comes first, a less than or equal to comparison or an inequality comparison?

## Exercises

1. Specify what each of the following expressions evaluates to:

   a. 4 + 9
   b. 4 + 10 - 5 + 2
   c. 4 * 2 + 7 - 1
   d. 7 + 4 * 2 - 1
   e. 3 - 2 * 6
   f. 4%2 * 98
   g. 1 + 4%2 * 75

   h. 6 + 25/5
   i. 4 + 5%3 + 7
   j. 2 * 4 * 8 - 6 * 2
   k. 8/4 %2
   l. 5 * "4"
   m. 2 * 4 +"5"
   n. "4" - 2

2. For each of the statements, *in the following sequence*, specify what myVar evaluates to after the statement executes in JavaScript.

a. var myVar = 5

b. myVar *= 5

c. myVar = myVar % 6

d. myVar += "45"

e. myVar = "Sam"

f. myVar = true

g. myVar = (!myVar && true)

h. myVar = ((5 == 5) || (2 >= 5)) || (!(6 >= 10))

i. myVar = 6 * 2 + 10/5 - 5%2

j. myVar = 6 * ((2 + 10/5) - 5%2)

3. Specify what each of the following expressions evaluates to. Assume that num1=8, num2=7, num3=-5, string1="8", and string2="7".

a. num3 ==num2

b. num1 < 8

c. num1 <= 8

d. num2 > 7

e. num3 < num1

f. num2 != num3

g. string1 == num1

h. string2 === num2

i. string2 < string1

j. num1 < string1

4. Specify what each of the following expressions evaluates to. Assume that flag=false, isEmpty=true, validString=false, and validNum=true.

a. !isEmpty

b. flag

c. isEmpty && flag

d. validNum || validString

e. validString && !isEmpty

f. !isEmpty && validNum

5. Specify what values count and newCount hold after each of the following statements, *in order.*

a. var count = 0

b. count++

c. newCount = count++

d. --count

e. count %= newCount

6. Write a conditional statement that evaluates to "happy" if mouthCurve is less than 180 and "sad" if mouthCurve is greater than or equal to 180.

7. Given the following function:

```
function greet(message, visitor) {
        document.write("<h1>", message, ", ", visitor,
                        "</h1>")
}
```

a. Write the appropriate JavaScript to call the greet function so that it will write "Hullo, Sam."

b. Write the appropriate JavaScript to call the greet function so that it will write "Greetings and Salutations, Wilbur."

c. Write the appropriate JavaScript to call the greet function so that it will write "Greetings, Earthlings."

## Scripting Exercises

Create a folder named assignment04 to hold the documents you create during this assignment. Save a copy of the personal home page you last modified as home.html in the assignment04 folder.

1. Examine the following script:

```
<script language="JavaScript" type="text/javascript"><!--
        var num1 = prompt("Please enter a number: ", 0)
        var num2 = prompt("Please enter a number: ", 0)
        var sum = num1 + num2

        document.write("You entered: ", num1, " and ",
                        num2, "<br>")
        document.write("Sum: ", sum)
//-->
</script>
```

Try running it and enter two numbers when prompted. The script does not do what was intended. Fix it so it does.

2. Write a script that prompts the visitor for two numbers, then displays the two numbers and their sum, difference, product, quotient, and modulus in the document. For instance, if the visitor entered 5 and 2, the results would display as follows:

```
You entered: 5 and 2
Sum:    7
Difference: 3
Product:    10
Quotient: 2.5
Modulus: 1
```

3. Write a script that prompts the visitor for two values, then displays the two entries, their data type, and the truth of some comparisons, including is equal to, is not equal to, is equivalent to, is not equivalent to, is less than, is less than or equal to, is greater than, and is greater than or equal to. For instance, if the visitor entered 5 and "2", the results would display as follows:

```
You entered: 5 (number) and 2 (string)
5 == 2? false
5 != 2? true
5 === 2? false
5 !== 2? true
5 < 2? false
5 <= 2? false
5 > 2? true
5 >= 2? true
```

4. Write a script that prompts the visitor for three numbers, then calculates and displays their average.

5. Write a script that prompts the visitor for the number of hours he or she worked that week and his hourly rate. Calculate and display the visitor's expected gross pay for that week. Don't forget that hours over 40 are paid at time and a half. Here's what the display should look like if the visitor entered 35 hours at $10/hour:

```
Total Hours Worked:   35
Regular Pay:   35 hours @ $10/hour = $350
Overtime Pay:   0 hours @ $15/hour = $0
Total Pay: $350
```

6. Create a new document named currency.html.

   a. Look up the current exchange rates for converting U.S. dollars to three different foreign currencies. You can look exchange rates up at http://www.x-rates.com/.

   b. Write a script that will acquire an amount in U.S. dollars from the visitor and display its equivalent in each of the foreign currencies whose exchange rate you looked up.

   c. Your output should look similar to this:

```
$55.78 in U.S. Currency is equivalent to:
35.9870 GBP (British Pounds)
435.084 HKD (Hong Kong Dollars)
542.516 MXN (Mexican Pesos)
```

## chapter five

# Events and Event Handlers

*There are no mistakes.*

*The events we bring*

*upon ourselves, no*

*matter how unpleasant,*

*are necessary in order to*

*learn what we need to*

*learn; whatever steps we*

*take, they're necessary to*

*reach the places we've*

*chosen to go.*

—Richard Bach,
"The Bridge Across Forever"

O f all the capabilities of JavaScript, event handlers are the most fun to implement because they allow you to script responses to actions taken by visitors to your Web site. That is, you can program a Web site to respond to visitors in various ways depending on what they do while browsing through your site. For instance, you could program your navigation buttons to change whenever the visitor moves the mouse over them.

In this chapter we'll

- define the terms "event" and "event handler."
- look at the intrinsic events recognized by HTML 4.0.
- examine in detail the event handlers supported by JavaScript across all platforms and browsers.
- discover how to use event handlers to dynamically interact with visitors.

Let's get started.

# Event and Event Handler Defined

Recall that an event is an action performed by a visitor, the browser, or sometimes even a script, such as moving the mouse over a link, clicking on a button, or surfing to a new Web page. **Events** are visitor and browser activities. While events are visitor and browser *activities*, **event handlers** are the mechanisms that allow us to capture and actually *respond to* those events with a scripting language. In other words, event handlers *handle the event* with a series of JavaScript statements.

To help clarify this concept, let's look at a real-world analogy.

> Event: the phone rings.
> Event handler: pick up the phone and say, "Hello."

When your phone rings, what do you usually do? Most of us pick it up and say, "Hello." In this analogy, the *event* is the phone ringing. The *event handler* is you picking it up and saying, "Hello." Events and their corresponding event handlers are the key to interactive Web pages.

# Writing Event Handlers

Event handlers are quite easy to implement. They are written inline with HTML, just like an HTML attribute. Perhaps that's why the HTML 4.0 specification calls event handlers **intrinsic event attributes**. The only difference between a normal tag attribute and an event handler (intrinsic event attribute) is that you enter a script or function call as the attribute value in an event handler rather than a simple value such as "2" or "right"; that is, the *value* of an intrinsic event attribute is one or more JavaScript statements.

**Table 5.1    Similarity Between Tag Attributes and Event Handlers**

| Syntax | Example |
|---|---|
| `<tag attribute="value">` | `<p align="right">` |
| `<tag eventHandler="script">` `<tag eventHandler="function call">` | `<body onLoad="alert('Hello')">` `<body onLoad="greetVisitor()">` |

In the first event handler example above, when the document loads, an alert box pops up with the message "Hello." In the second example, when the document loads, the greetVisitor function is called. Note that in each example, the entire script is surrounded by double quotes, just like a regular attribute would be.

Returning to our real-world phone analogy, we would write that event handler as

```
<phone onRing="pickUpPhone(); say('Hello.')">
```

or

```
<phone onRing="answerPhone()">
```

Our answerPhone function could be defined as

```
function answerPhone() {
   pickUpPhone()
   say ("Hello")
}
```

**peek ahead** We'll cover functions and defining functions in depth in Chapter 8.

Notice that I've provided two types of event handler examples. The first executed a two-line script, the second called a function. Both are perfectly legal. However, if the response to the event is going to be more than a single JavaScript statement, it is considered good form to define those statements as a function and call the function in response to the event.

Before going any further, let's take a look at the various events and event handlers supported by HTML 4.0.

## Intrinsic Event Attributes, Also Known As Event Handlers

According to the W3C's Web site, "The HTML 4.0 specification defines the following intrinsic event attributes for exploitation by scripting languages such as JavaScript, Tcl, VBScript, etc." Remember, "intrinsic event attribute" is just a fancy way of saying "event handler." The HTML 4 specification probably uses the name "intrinsic event attributes" because event handlers are written as HTML element attributes.

**Table 5.2    Events and Corresponding Event Handlers**

| Event | Intrinsic Event Attribute (Event Handler) |
|---|---|
| Load | *onLoad* |
| Unload | *onUnload* |
| Click | *onClick* |
| DblClick | onDblClick |
| MouseDown | onMouseDown |
| MouseUp | onMouseUp |
| MouseOver | *onMouseOver* |
| MouseMove | onMouseMove |
| MouseOut | *onMouseOut* |
| Focus | *onFocus* |
| Blur | *onBlur* |
| KeyPress | onKeyPress |

| KeyDown | onKeyDown |
|---------|-----------|
| KeyUp | onKeyUp |
| Submit | ***onSubmit*** |
| Reset | ***onReset*** |
| Select | ***onSelect*** |
| Change | ***onChange*** |

It is important to note that, of the above-listed event handlers, only those listed in bold italics are well-supported both cross-browser and cross-platform. In other words, they're the only ones you can count on working reliably right now. Until the major browsers conform strictly to W3C specifications, it's safer to stick to those listed in bold italics. You'll save yourself a lot of headaches.

In the following sections, we'll look at each event in turn. Each section will specify when the event occurs, list the HTML tags and JavaScript objects its associated event handler can be applied to, describe the usual real-world uses of handling the event, and conclude with an example or two. On to the fun stuff.

## Load and Unload

The **Load event** is associated with windows and images. A Load event occurs on a window when the browser has retrieved all of the content between the <body> tags or all of the frames within a <frameset> tag. A Load event occurs on an image when the image is displayed. **onLoad** event handlers are often used to display alert messages, pop up windows, and call image preload functions or other document-preparation routines.

**peek ahead**
To be really nice to your visitors, you could use cookies and allow visitors to turn off the pop-up windows. You'll learn how in Chapter 14, "Cookies."

Many commercial sites now use pop-up windows to ~~annoy~~ notify visitors with announcements and advertisements. A more useful application would be to display a news update or tip of the day when the document loads.

The **Unload event** is associated only with the window object; its event handler, **onUnload**, is invoked whenever a visitor or the browser requests a new page in the same browser window. Ever visit a Web site that just seemed to not want to let you go? Every time you tried to leave the site, it popped up another window. The site's Web developers accomplished that pop-up prison with the onUnload event handler. When you encounter a site like that, often the only way out is to close your browser completely.

Here's an example of onLoad and onUnload event handlers at work:

*Script 5.1*      **Responding to Load and Unload Events**

```
1    <html>
2    <head>
3    <title>Script 5.1: Responding to Load and Unload Events </title>
4    </head>
5    <body onLoad="alert ('Welcome!')"
6          onUnload="alert('C ya!')">
7    <h1>Load and Unload</h1>
8
9    <p>Load and Unload event handlers that pop up alert boxes should
10   be used sparingly. They can become annoying after a while.</p>
11
12   <p>To see an onUnload event handler in action, try one of the
13   following:</p>
14   <ul>
15       <li>follow this
16           <a href="http://www.webwomansbooks.com/">link</a></li>
17       <li>click the back button</li>
18       <li>type a new URL in the location bar</li>
19   </ul>
20
21   </body>
22   </html>
```

The above example pops up an alert box with the message "Welcome!" when the document loads (line 5). Here's a picture:

*Figure 5.1*      **Results of Script 5.1—onLoad**

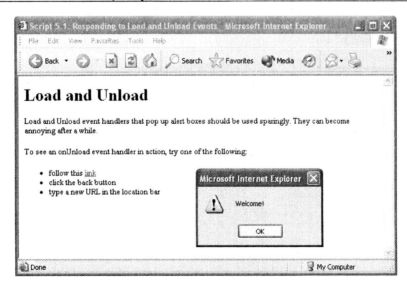

When the document is unloaded, that is, another document is requested, an alert with the message "C ya!" is displayed (line 6). Here's a picture:

**Figure 5.2**     **Results of Script 5.1—onUnload**

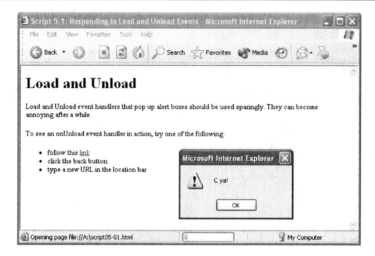

# MouseOver and MouseOut

Theoretically, **MouseOver** and **MouseOut** events can be associated with any element in an HTML document, including headings, paragraphs, links, images, form elements, and tables. Theoretically. In reality, it is best to stick with links and areas of an image map. The most popular uses of the onMouseOver and onMouseOut event handlers are status bar changes and image rollovers.

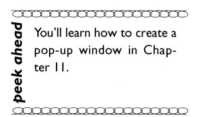

You'll learn how to create a pop-up window in Chapter 11.

A MouseOver event occurs when the visitor places the mouse cursor over a link or an area of an image map. MouseOver's other half, MouseOut, occurs when the visitor moves the mouse off of the link or area of an image map. The two are almost always used in tandem:

**Table 5.3**     **onMouseOver and onMouseOut in Tandem**

| Effect | onMouseOver | onMouseOut |
|---|---|---|
| Status bar message | Display link description in the status bar. | Clear the status bar. |
| Image rollover | Swap in high state image. | Swap back in low state image. |

Here are some examples. *Note:* You'll need the images on the accompanying CD for the second example. They're in the images folder under scripts.

***Script 5.2***        ***Responding to MouseOver and MouseOut Events: Status Bar Change***

```
1    <html>
2    <head>
3    <title>Script 5.2: Responding to MouseOver and MouseOut Events:
4            Status Bar Change</title>
5    </head>
6    <body>
7    <h1>MouseOver and MouseOut: Status Bar Change</h1>
8    <p>A MouseOver event occurs when you move the mouse over a link,
9    MouseOut when you move it off of a link. Move the mouse over
10   <a href="examples.html"
11     onMouseOver="window.status='See a list of event examples';
         return true"
12     onMouseOut="window.status=' '; return true">this link</a>
13   then off of it. Watch the status bar change.</p>
14   </body>
15   </html>
```

Script 5.2 performs a status bar change when the visitor moves the mouse over the link shown in the document (line 11). Notice the use of single quotation marks to delimit the strings inside of the event handler. If we had used double quotation marks instead of the single quotation marks in line 11, for instance, the browser would have thought that the event handler ended after the equals sign.

While normally you can choose which type of quotation mark to use on the outside and which on the inside, you *must* use double quotation marks around HTML tag attributes and event handlers. HTML doesn't always recognize single quotation marks and may generate an error if you use them to delimit an event handler or tag attribute. Also, notice that line 11 used a semicolon to separate the two JavaScript statements. Why couldn't we have just written each statement on a separate line? Because the entire contents of an event handler must be written on a single line. The quoted value may *not* flow over multiple lines.

**Figure 5.3**     **Results of Script 5.2 when Mouse Moved over Link**

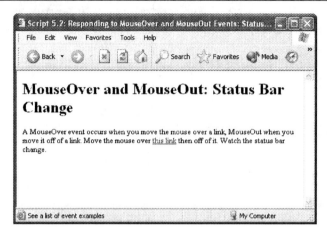

When the visitor moves the mouse off of the link, the status bar clears (line 12). Notice the message in the status bar in Figure 5.3. This is a nice way to provide navigation hints for your navigation buttons.

Notice that each event handler in Script 5.2 actually calls two JavaScript statements, separated by semicolons. Recall that when you write more than one statement on a single line, you must separate them with a semicolon. The first statement in each event handler changes the content of the status bar; the second says "return true." What's this "return true"?

Whenever you attempt to change the status bar in an event handler, you must reassure the browser that you really did intend to change the status bar by telling it `return true`, meaning "yes, I really meant to do that." Remember, the status bar is part of the browser window and normally the browser uses it to display the URL of a link when it is moused over. You're trying to override that default function when you modify the contents of the status bar with a JavaScript statement. You must return true after any status bar change called by an event handler, otherwise the browser will not comply.

Try it yourself. Remove the "return true" statements in lines 11 and 12 of Script 5.2 and run the script. No status bar changes. Reinsert the statements. Everything works as it should.

Now let's look at an image rollover example. You'll find the images in the images folder under scripts on the CD that accompanies this book.

**Script 5.3**     **Responding to MouseOver and MouseOut Events: Image Rollover**

```
1    <html>
2    <head>
3    <title>Script 5.3: Responding to MouseOver and MouseOut Events:
4         Image Rollover</title>
5    </head>
6    <body>
7    <h1>MouseOver and MouseOut: Image Rollover</h1>
```

```
 8   <p>A MouseOver event occurs when you move the mouse over a link,
 9   MouseOut when you move it off of a link. Move the mouse over the
10   image links below.</p>
11
12   <a href="onload.html"
13      onMouseOver="document.goback.src='images/backhi.gif'"
14      onMouseOut="document.goback.src='images/back.gif'"><img
15      name="goback" src="images/back.gif" width="36" height="23"
16      alt="Back" border="0"></a>
17   <a href="onmouseover2.html"
18      onMouseOver="document.goforward.src='images/forwardhi.gif'"
19      onMouseOut="document.goforward.src='images/forward.gif'"><img
20      name="goforward" src="images/forward.gif" width="36"
21      height="24" alt="Forward" border="0"></a>
22   </body>
23
24   </html>
```

You've probably seen this done a thousand times. Perhaps you thought the rollover was accomplished by recoloring the image. What really happens is that the original image is replaced with another image when the visitor moves the mouse over a link. This is accomplished by modifying the image's `src` property (lines 13 and 18). When the visitor moves the mouse off of the link, the original image is restored by changing the image's `src` property back to the path and name of the original image (lines 14 and 19).

Notice that each image is named (lines 15 and 20), making it easier to access it (lines 13, 14, 18, and 19). Figure 5.4 shows the right arrow changed from a pink arrow (original image) to a blue arrow when the mouse is moved over it.

**peek ahead**

You'll learn how to preload images in Chapter 8 so that rollovers appear without delay.

**Figure 5.4    Results of Script 5.3 when Right Arrow Moused Over**

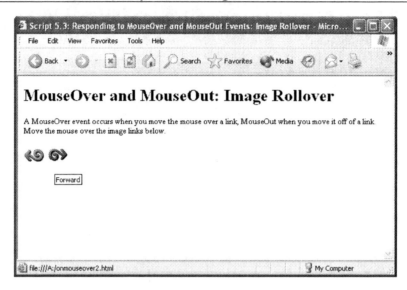

There's one very important thing you need to know about swapping images: each image in a pair of swapped images must have the same dimensions. Swapping images of different sizes can have unpleasant and unpredictable results.

It's also a good idea to preload your images with JavaScript so that there is no delay between the visitor mousing over an image and the browser displaying the replacement image. Normally, replacement images are not downloaded until they are needed, that is, when someone mouses over a link and the script changes the image's source attribute, thus requesting the replacement image.

# Click

A **Click event** occurs when the visitor clicks with a mouse on a link or form button or presses the Enter key when that element has focus. Theoretically, any element visible in an HTML document when it is displayed in a browser can be clicked on, so in theory, a Click event can be associated with almost any HTML element. In practice, however, for cross-browser and cross-platform compatibility, the list of elements for which a Click event can be captured and scripted is much shorter: links, imagemap areas, buttons, checkboxes, radio buttons, reset buttons, and submit buttons.

**onClick event handlers** are commonly used to invoke all sorts of scripts, including

- ✗ pop-up windows
- ✗ alert messages
- ✗ loading a new document in the browser
- ✗ calling a function
- ✗ performing form calculations

Here are some examples:

***Script 5.4     Responding to Click Events***

```
1   <html>
2   <head>
3   <title>Script 5.4: Responding to Click Events</title>
4   </head>
5   <body>
6   <h1>Click</h1>
7   <p>Click on the button and link below to see click event
8   handlers in action.</p>
9
10  <form method="post">
11  <input type="Button" name="" value="Click Me!"
12      onClick="alert('Ouch!')">
13  </form>
14
15  <a href="javascript: void(0)"
16      onClick="alert('Hey! What\'d you do that
17          for?')">Click Here</a><br>
17  <br>
18
19  <a href="http://www.webwoman.biz/"
20      onClick="return confirm('Are you sure you want to go
              there?')">Visit
21      WebWoman</a>
22
23  </body>
24  </html>
```

The first onClick event handler in Script 5.4, line 12, is applied to a button. Plain old form buttons really have no other purpose than to call scripts. In fact, that's why they were added to the HTML specification in the first place: to provide an easy means of calling a script. In line 12, the script is a simple alert box that says "Ouch!" Try it.

**Figure 5.5    Results of Script 5.4 when Button Clicked**

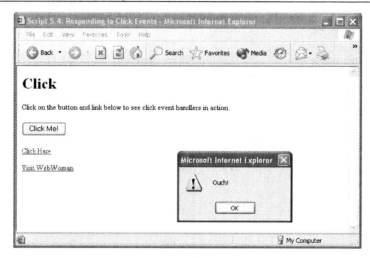

OK, so that wasn't the most useful example. But it was simple and it illustrated the process very well. Let's try the second one (line 16). Click on the link labeled "Click Here."

**Figure 5.6    Results of Script 5.4 when "Click Here" Link Is Clicked**

OK, so this one wasn't very useful either. But it does show you how you can call a script in response to the visitor clicking on a link. It also illustrates something very important about using click event handlers on links. Look closely at lines 15 and 16 of Script 5.4. This link has a conflict: it has an `href` attribute, which indicates a URL that should be followed when the visitor clicks on the link, and an `onClick` event handler that should be performed when the visitor clicks on the link.

When an onClick event handler is applied to an <a> tag, the onClick event handler gets executed first (if JavaScript is supported and turned on) before the href. You can stop the href attribute from executing by having the onClick event handler return false. You can also set the href attribute to "#". <a href="#">____</a> is a link to a named anchor in the current document with no name.

Look closely at the href attribute. It uses the javascript: pseudo-protocol to call the void operator to clear up the confusion. Let's see how.

## The javascript: Pseudo-Protocol

Recall from Chapter 2 that you can also write JavaScript statements using the javascript: pseudo-protocol in the href attribute of an <a> or <area> tag. The idea is that instead of requesting a document, the JavaScript pseudo-protocol will instead execute one or more JavaScript statements, which may or may not return a URL to the href attribute for the <a> or <area> tag to follow.

In this case, the javascript: pseudo-protocol called the void operator.

## The void Operator

The void operator tells the interpreter to evaluate an expression and return no value. You can call the void operator in either of two ways:

```
void (expression)
void expression
```

void is an operator, not a function or method, where expression is an expression to be evaluated. While the parentheses are optional, it is considered good programming style to use them.

You want to make certain that a statement called via the pseudo-protocol does not return a value and provoke the link to load a new document indicated by the returned value. One way to do this is to use the void operator. The void operator will ensure that no value is returned to the hypertext link at all.

In this example, we only want to invoke the onClick event handler in response to the visitor's clicking on the link labeled "Click Here." Having the location change would be an unwanted side effect. By calling the void operator to evaluate zero with the javascript: pseudo-protocol, no value was returned to the href attribute. Because no value was returned to the href attribute, it could not try to load a document, thus solving the conflict between the href attribute and the onClick event handler. Thus the script in the onClick event handler was called and the result was the alert shown in Figure 5.6.

Now let's look at the last onClick event handler in Script 5.4, the "Visit WebWoman" link in lines 19 through 21. This is a useful example. When the visitor clicks on the link, a confirm dialog box pops up asking the visitor to confirm his desire to visit WebWoman. If he chooses OK, his desire is granted and he gets to visit the WebWoman Web site. If he chooses Cancel, the link is not invoked. Try it.

***Figure 5.7*** **Results of Script 5.4 when "Visit WebWoman" Is Clicked**

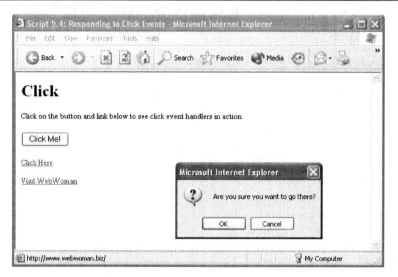

The onClick event handler can return false when used on checkboxes, links, radio buttons, reset buttons, and submit buttons. Remember how we specifically returned true earlier when performing a status bar change to assure the browser that's what we really wanted to do? By returning false, the onClick event handler can cancel the action that usually takes place when the visitor clicks on an element of that type. For example, the usual action when a visitor clicks on a link is to request the Web document specified in the link's href attribute. The usual action when a visitor clicks on a submit button is that the form in which the button resides is submitted. When the onClick event handler returns false, the usual action is canceled, that is, the link will not be followed, the form will not be submitted. In Script 5.4, the former occurred: the link was not followed.

This is very useful, especially when applied to links that leave your Web site altogether, also known as **external links**. Notice the return keyword that precedes the confirm method call in line 20 of Script 5.4. That causes the result of the confirm method to be returned to the event handler so that the event handler can cancel or proceed with the action accordingly. Without it, the link is invoked no matter what the visitor chooses in the confirm dialog box.

Table 5.4 shows each element that an onClick event handler can be applied to and the result by return value.

**Table 5.4**  **Result of `onClick` Event Handler Return Value**

| Element | Result when `true` Returned | Result when `false` Returned |
|---|---|---|
| area | Link followed | Link not followed |
| checkbox | Checkbox gets checked | Checkbox does not get checked |
| link | Link followed | Link not followed |
| radio button | Radio button gets checked | Radio button does not get checked |
| reset button | Form gets cleared | Form does not get cleared |
| submit button | Form is submitted | Form is not submitted |

# Submit

The **Submit event** occurs when a visitor or a script submits a form. A visitor usually generates a Submit event by clicking on a form's submit button or pressing Enter when a submit button has focus. A script can also generate a Submit event by calling a form's `submit` method. The corresponding **onSubmit** event handler can be implemented only on a form.

The onSubmit event handler is most often used to call form validation routines. It can also be used to call functions that perform calculations or set the values of hidden fields before submitting a form to a CGI script or other server-side utility. Here is a simple example of the onSubmit event handler in action.

**programmer's tip**

One common mistake many programmers make is to try to write an onSubmit event handler within a submit button's tag instead of in the <form> tag. One way to keep it straight in your mind is to remember that you submit *forms*, not *buttons*.

**peek ahead**

You'll learn how to write and call form validation routines in Chapter 13.

**Script 5.5**  **Responding to a Submit Event: Giving Thanks**

```html
1    <html>
2    <head>
3    <title>Script 5.5: Responding to a
         Submit Event: Giving Thanks</title>
4    </head>
5    <body>
6    <h1>Submit: Giving Thanks</h1>
7    <p>A Submit event is always associated with a form element,
8    never with a submit button. Here's a simple form. When the form
9    is submitted a thank you message is displayed.</p>
10
11   <form action="" method="post"
12         onSubmit="alert('Thank you!')">
```

```
13              <b>Name: </b><input type="Text"><br>
14     <b>Email: </b><input type="Text"><br>
15     <input type="Submit"> <input type="Reset"><br>
16     </form>
17
18     </body>
19     </html>
```

Line 12 of Script 5.5 uses the onSubmit event handler to pop up an alert dialog box when the visitor submits the form. It looks like this:

*Figure 5.8*     **Results of Script 5.5 when Form Submitted**

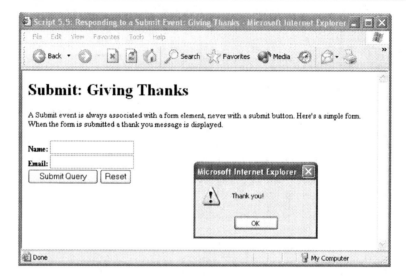

The onSubmit event handler can return a value to tell the browser to proceed with the Submit or to cancel it.

# Reset

Like the Submit event, the **Reset event** is only associated with forms. Both visitors and scripts can generate a Reset event. A visitor generates a Reset event by clicking on a form's reset button or pressing Enter when a reset button has focus. A script generates a Reset event by calling a form's reset method. The corresponding **onReset** event handler can be implemented only on a <form> tag; that is, it doesn't work on the tag for a reset button.

The most popular use of the onReset event handler is to confirm that a visitor really does want to clear a form *before* clearing its contents. Providing visitors with a bail-out option in case they hit the reset button by mistake is always a nice touch. Here's an example:

*Script 5.6*     **Responding to a Reset Event: Providing a Bail-out Option**

```
1    <html>
2    <head>
3    <title>Script 5.6: Responding to a Reset Event: Providing a
4    Bailout Option</title>
5    </head>
6    <body>
7    <h1>Reset</h1>
8    <form action="" method="post"
9     onReset="return confirm('Are you sure you want to clear this
          form?')">
10        <b>Name: </b><input type="Text" name="visitor"><br>
11        <b>Email: </b><input type="Text" name="email"><br>
12        <input type="Submit"> <input type="Reset"><br>
13   </form>
14
15   </body>
16   </html>
```

The onReset event handler can also return a value to tell the browser to proceed with the reset or to cancel it. Notice the return before the confirm method call in line 9 of Script 5.6.

# Focus and Blur

The Focus and Blur events are associated with windows, frames, links, and form elements. A **Focus event** occurs when the visitor or a script gives focus to a window, frame, link, or form element, that is, makes it the current element. A visitor can give focus to an element by selecting, clicking on, or tabbing to that element. A script can give focus to an element by calling that element's focus method.

A **Blur event** occurs when the visitor or a script removes focus from an element that has focus. When a visitor selects, clicks on, or tabs to another element, he or she invokes a Blur event on the element that had focus before his or her action. A script generates a blur event when it calls an object's blur method.

The **onFocus** and **onBlur** event handlers are often used in tandem. The following script displays an instruction in the status bar whenever a link receives focus and clears the instruction when the link loses focus.

*Script 5.7*     **Responding to onFocus and onBlur Events**

```
1    <html>
2    <head>
3    <title>Script 5.7: Responding to onFocus and onBlur
        Events</title>
```

```
4    </head>
5    <body>
6    <h1>Focus and Blur</h1>
7    <p>To make this one work, you're going to have to
8    tab through the links by pressing the Tab key.</p>
9    <br>
10   <br>
11   [ <a href="http://www.excite.com/"
12     onFocus="window.status='Press Enter to visit Excite';
         return true"
13     onBlur="window.status=' '; return true">Excite</a> ]
14   [ <a href="http://www.google.com/"
15     onFocus="window.status='Press Enter to visit Google';
         return true"
16     onBlur="window.status=' '; return true">Google</a> ]
17   [ <a href="http://yahoo.com/"
18     onFocus="window.status='Press Enter to visit Yahoo!';
         return true"
19     onBlur="window.status=' '; return true">Yahoo!</a> ]
20
21   </body>
22   </html>
```

To see this one in action, you're going to have to press the Tab key to tab through the links, giving them focus as you go. Here's what it looks like when the Yahoo! link has focus.

**Figure 5.9     Results of Script 5.7 when Yahoo! Link Has Focus**

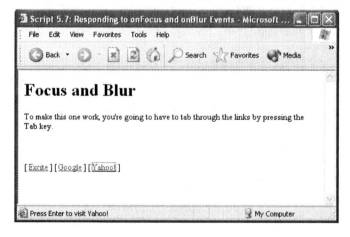

# Change

The Change event is associated with several form elements, including text boxes, text areas, password fields, file uploads, and select lists. A **Change** event occurs when one of the aforementioned form elements blurs and the value of the field changes from the value it had when it first received focus.

*peek ahead*

The onChange event handler is popularly used to perform calculations and to validate field contents whenever a field's value has changed. You'll learn how to use it in Chapters 12 and 13.

The following example uses the **onChange** event handler to display a thank you message whenever the visitor changes the contents of a text area.

### Script 5.8    Responding to a Change Event

```
1    <html>
2    <head>
3         <title>Script 5.8: Responding to a Change Event</title>
4    </head>
5    <body>
6    <h1>Change</h1>
7    <p>A Change event occurs when a form element loses
8    focus <i>and</i> its value has changed from when it received
9    focus. To see an onChange event handler in action, try typing
10   something in the textarea below then tab to the submit
11   button.</p>
12
13   <form action="" method="post">
14        <b>Comments: </b><br>
15        <textarea name="comments" cols="50" rows="3" wrap="soft"
16         onChange="alert('Thank you for your comments')"></textarea>
17        <input type="Submit"><input type="Reset">
18   </form>
19
20   </body>
21   </html>
```

Here's what it looks like:

### Figure 5.10    Results of Script 5.8 when Comments Field Is Changed

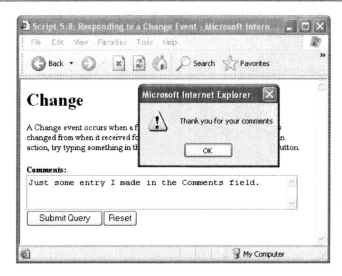

Line 16 of Script 5.8 calls the `alert` method to display the thank you message.

# Select

Select events are associated with text boxes, password fields, and text areas. Usually, visitors generate **Select events** when they select text, that is, when they drag the mouse over text with the left button depressed or hold down the Shift key while moving the left and right arrow keys, thus *selecting* the text. Scripts can also invoke a Select event by calling an object's `select` method.

I can't remember ever seeing an **onSelect event handler** used on a Web site, but here's an example anyway:

### Script 5.9    Responding to a Select Event

```
1    <html>
2    <head>
3    <title>Script 5.9: Responding to a Select Event</title>
4    </head>
5    <body>
6    <h1>Select</h1>
7    <p>A Select event occurs when text in a form element is
8    selected. Select the contents of the textarea below to see an
9    onSelect event handler in action.</p>
10
11   <form action="" method="post">
12           <b>Quote of the Day: </b><br>
```

```
13            <textarea name="comments" cols="50" rows="3" wrap="soft"
14            onSelect="alert('Be mindful of copyright law.')">
15   He who laughs, lasts!
16   </textarea>
17   </form>
18
19   </body>
20   </html>
```

Line 14 of Script 5.9 alerts the visitor to be mindful of copyright laws when he selects the text contained in the text area. Here's what it looks like:

*Figure 5.11    Results of Script 5.9 when Text Selected in Text Area*

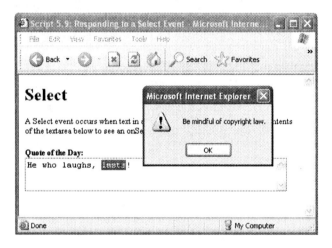

# Abort

The **Abort event** occurs when a visitor aborts loading an image in some way, perhaps by following a link or clicking on the Stop button. Its associated event handler, **onAbort**, can be attached only to an image and is rarely used. For education's sake, here's an example anyway.

You'll need an image from the accompanying CD for this one and you'll have to hit the Stop button fast before the image finishes loading.

*Script 5.10    Responding to an Abort Event*

```
1    <html>
2    <head>
3    <title>Script 5.10: Responding to an Abort Event</title>
4    </head>
5    <body>
```

```
 6   <h1>Abort</h1>
 7   <p>To see this one in action, hit the stop button as fast as
 8   you can, before the picture finishes loading. You may have
 9   to upload the file and view it from a server, the slower the
10   connection the better, to see this work. You can also try
11   replacing this with an even bigger image.</p>
12
13   <img src="images/Sam.jpg" width="640" height="480" border="0"
14       alt="Sammy Sam"
15       onAbort="alert('Hey! You really must see this picture!')">
16
17   </body>
18   </html>
```

Line 15 does all the work. I picked a large image so you'd have time to interrupt the loading process. Today's hard drives are very fast, though, so you may not have much luck running this script locally. If you're having trouble getting it to work, upload it to a Web site and try running it over the Web.

*Figure 5.12*    *Results of Script 5.10 when Image Loading Is Aborted*

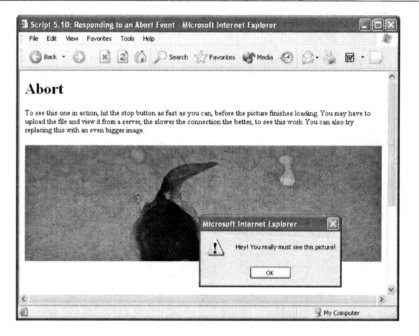

# Error

Like the Abort event, the **Error event** is rarely *handled*. It's associated with both images and windows and occurs when a JavaScript syntax or runtime error is encountered. For instance, an illegal URL in an image's `src` attribute or a corrupted image will generate an Error event. A browser error, such as trying to load an image that simply doesn't exist, will *not* generate an Error event. Here's an example. Note the illegal file name in line 7; it contains an illegal character.

**Script 5.11    Responding to an Error Event**

```
1    <html>
2    <head>
3    <title>Script 5.11: Responding to an Error Event</title>
4    </head>
5    <body>
6    <h1>Error</h1>
7    <img src="images/zIm@ge.jpg"
8         onError="alert('Uh, Oh!')">
9
10   </body>
11   </html>
```

Line 8 of Script 5.11 calls the alert method to display a dialog box with the message "Uh, Oh!" as soon as the error is encountered.

**Figure 5.13    Results of Script 5.11 when Error Encountered**

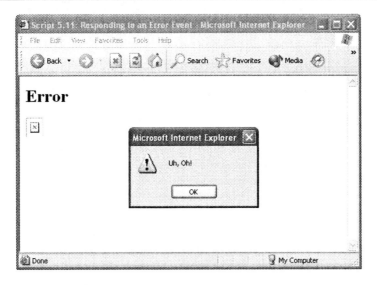

# Cross-Browser Event Handlers—The Safe List

Here's a summary of the commonly used events we just discussed. Table 5.5 describes each event and lists its associated event handler, the HTML tags the event handler can be called on, and the JavaScript objects it can be associated with.

**Table 5.5**    *The Safe List of Events and Event Handlers*

| Event<br>Event Handler | HTML Element(s) | JavaScript Object(s) | Description |
|---|---|---|---|
| Load<br>onLoad | \<body><br>\<frameset><br>\<img>[1] | window<br>Frame<br>Image[1] | The browser has retrieved the content between the \<body> tags or all of the frames within a \<frameset> tag. For an image, a load event occurs when the image is displayed. |
| Unload<br>onUnload | \<body><br>\<frameset> | window<br>Frame | The browser removes a document from a window or frame. It usually occurs when the visitor or browser requests a new page in the same browser window. |
| MouseOver<br>onMouseover<br><br><br><br>MouseOut<br>onMouseout | In reality:<br>\<a href = ""><br>\<area>[1]<br>In theory: all elements *except* \<applet>, \<base>, \<basefont>, \<br>, \<font>, \<frame>, \<frameset>, \<head>, \<html>, \<iframe>, \<meta>, \<param>, \<script>, \<style>, and \<title> | Link<br>Area[1] | The visitor places the mouse pointer *over* a hyperlink, image map area, or other document element.<br><br>The visitor moves the mouse pointer *off* of a hyperlink, image map area, or other document element. |
| Click<br>onClick | In reality:<br>\<a href = ""><br>\<area><br>\<body><br>\<input type=button><br>\<input type=checkbox><br>\<input type=radio><br>\<input type=reset> | Link<br>Area<br>document<br>Button<br>Checkbox<br>Radio<br>Reset | The visitor uses the mouse to click on a form button or a hyperlink or presses the Enter key when a form button or link has focus.<br><br>An onClick event handler can return false to cancel the |

| | | | |
|---|---|---|---|
| | `<input type=submit>` In theory: all elements *except* <applet>, <base>, <basefont>, <br>, <font>, <frame>, <frameset>, <head>, <html>, <iframe>, <meta>, <param>, <script>, <style>, and <title> | Submit | action normally associated with a click event.[1] |
| Submit onSubmit | <form> | Form | The visitor clicks on a form's submit button. An onSubmit event handler can return false to cancel the submit action. |
| Reset onReset | <form> | Form | The visitor clicks on a form's reset button. An onReset event handler can return false to cancel the form reset. |
| Focus onFocus | <body>[1] <frameset>[1] <button>[1] <input type=checkbox>[1] | window[1] Frame[1] Button[1] Checkbox[1] | A window, frame, or form element *receives focus* because the visitor selects, clicks on, or tabs to the element. |
| Blur onBlur | <input type=file>[1] <input type=password>[1] <input type=radio>[1] <input type=reset>[1] <input type=submit>[1] <input type=text> <select> <textarea> | FileUpload[1] Password[1] Radio[1] Reset[1] Submit[1] Text Select Textarea | A window, frame, or form element *loses focus* because the visitor selects, clicks on, or tabs to another element, that is, the visitor leaves an element that has focus. |
| Change onChange | <input type=file> <input type=text> <select> <textarea> | FileUpload[1] Text Select Textarea | A file upload, password, text, select, or text area form element loses focus and its value changes from the value it had when the element received focus. |

| Event<br>Event Handler | HTML Element(s) | JavaScript Object(s) | Description          (continued) |
|---|---|---|---|
| Select<br>onSelect | <input type=text><br><textarea> | Text<br>Textarea | The visitor selects some or all of the text within a text or text area field. |
| Abort<br>onAbort | <img>[1] | Image[1] | The visitor aborts the loading of an image in some way, for instance, by clicking on the Stop button, clicking on the Reload button, or following a link. |
| Error<br>onError | <img><br><body> | Image[1]<br>window[1] | A JavaScript syntax or runtime error occurs. For instance, a bad URL in an image tag or a corrupted image will generate an error event.<br><br>An Error event is not generated by a browser error. For instance, trying to load a file that simply does not exist will not generate an error event. |

[1] Implemented in JavaScript 1.1

## Other Events—The Danger List

OK, we've covered all of the safe and best-supported event handlers in detail. Let's now get a little more description of the not-so-compatible event handlers.

The following event handlers are also defined as "intrinsic event attributes" in the HTML 4.0 specification and may be scripted for with the JavaScript language. However, keep in mind that the three major browsers do not support these event handlers consistently.

**Table 5.6**     **Danger List of Event Handlers Recognized by HTML 4.0**

| Event Handler | Description |
|---|---|
| onDblClick | The visitor double-clicks on an HTML element with the mouse. It is recognized by the latest versions of NN and IE, but not Opera. |
| onMouseDown | The visitor depresses the mouse button. It is recognized by the latest versions of NN and IE, but not Opera. |
| onMouseUp | The visitor lets the mouse button up after depressing it. It is recognized by latest versions of NN and IE, but not Opera. |
| onMouseMove | The visitor moves the mouse. This event handler returns the coordinates of the mouse's position. It is recognized only by IE. |

| onKeyPress | The visitor presses and releases a key on the keyboard. There is no support. |
|---|---|
| onKeyDown | The visitor presses a key. There is no support. |
| onKeyUp | The visitor releases a depressed key. There is no support. |

The JavaScript language recognizes the following additional events:

**Table 5.7**     *Danger List of Event Handlers Recognized by JavaScript Only*

| Event Handler | Description |
|---|---|
| onMouseDrag | The visitor holds the left mouse button down and moves the mouse. |
| onDragDrop | The visitor drags a system item, such as a file or a shortcut, onto the browser window and drops it. |
| onMove | The visitor changes a window's position. |
| onResize | The visitor resizes a window. |

## Summary

Event handling is one of the most fun aspects of JavaScript. Event handling allows you to program your Web site so that it can truly interact with your visitors! Event handlers work by capturing events such as button clicks, mouse movement over links, and form submissions and responding to those events by executing a script.

While some event handlers may theoretically be associated with virtually all elements in an HTML document, the technology—cross-browser and cross-platform—is really not there yet. Even so, there are still many event handlers that you can use to make your Web pages richly interactive. Among the visitor actions you can capture and react to are

- ✗ opening a document (Load)
- ✗ requesting a new document in the current browser window (Unload)
- ✗ moving the mouse over a link (MouseOver)
- ✗ moving the mouse off of a link (MouseOut)
- ✗ clicking on a form field or link (Click)
- ✗ submitting or resetting a form (Submit and Reset)
- ✗ clicking on or tabbing to a form field or window (Focus)
- ✗ leaving a form field or window (Blur)
- ✗ changing the contents of a form field (Change)
- ✗ selecting the text in a form field (Select)
- ✗ hitting the Stop button in the midst of loading an image (Abort)

Eventually, you'll also be able to respond to the following visitor actions in all browsers:

- ✗ dragging and dropping (DragDrop)
- ✗ moving the mouse over plain text (MouseOver)

≋　resizing windows (Resize)
≋　moving windows (Move)
≋　entering data with the keyboard (KeyPress)
≋　depressing and releasing the mouse (MouseDown and MouseUp)

In the meantime, there's still plenty to keep you busy.

## Review Questions

1. What is an event?
2. What is an event handler?
3. Why does HTML refer to event handlers as intrinsic event attributes?
4. How are event handlers similar to HTML attributes?
5. When does a Load event occur on a window?
6. When does a Load event occur on an image?
7. What event handlers are most appropriately used to create a rollover effect?
8. To what objects are the intrinsic event attributes mentioned in Question 7 applied?
9. There are two ways in which a visitor can generate a Click event. Describe them.
10. On what elements can a Click event be captured? (Hint: Refer to Appendix B, "Event Handlers.")
11. What does the `javascript:` pseudo-protocol have to do with click events?
12. What use is the `void` operator? Explain when you would most likely use it.
13. What does the keyword `return` do when used in an `onClick` event handler applied to a link? Applied to a checkbox or radio button?
14. With what HTML element are Submit and Reset events associated?
15. When does the Submit event occur?
16. When does a Focus event occur?
17. On what elements can an `onFocus` event handler be applied?
18. When does a Blur event occur?
19. When does a Change event occur?
20. To what elements can a Change event be applied?
21. When is a Select event generated?
22. What is the Abort event? What element does it apply to?
23. When does an Error event occur?
24. Why should you avoid scripting for DblClick, MouseUp, MouseDown, KeyPress, KeyDown, and KeyUp events? After all, they are defined in the HTML 4 specification.
25. Describe a practical use for each of the following event handlers:
    a. onFocus and onBlur used in tandem
    b. onClick
    c. onReset
    d. onMouseOver and onMouseOut used in tandem
    e. onBlur

f. onSubmit

g. onChange

## Exercises

1. Examine the following code. Specify whether each line represents a valid or invalid event handler. If invalid, explain why.

   a. `<input type="button" onClick="alert("Ouch!")">`

   b. `<img name="Cat"`
      `onMouseover="document.Cat.src='catOver.gif'">`

   c. `<a href="contact.html"`
      `onMouseover="window.status='View contact info'">Contact</a>`

   d. `<body onClick="alert('Greetings, Earthlings!')">`

   e. `<a href="products.html"`
      `onMouseover="document.Cat.src='catOver.gif'"><img`
      `name="Cat" src="cat.gif"></a>`

   f. `<input type="submit"`
      `onSubmit="alert('Thank you for your submission')">`

   g. `<body onUnload="alert('Later, Dude!')">`

   h. `<input type="text"`
      `onFocus="window.status='123 456-7890'; return true"`
      `onBlur="window.status=''; return true">`

   i. `<img src="BigPic.jpg"`
      `onAbort="alert(Hey you really should see this image!">`

   j. `<body onError="alert('Uh oh!')">`

2. Write an appropriate event handler to display the alert "See the Clearance Section for special deals on our toys!" when the document is opened.

3. Write an appropriate event handler to display the alert "Y'all come back now, ya hear?" when the visitor leaves the site.

4. Visit several Web sites. Name five ways that they use event handlers to make their Web sites more interactive.

5. Visit several Web sites. Do any of the sites annoy you with their use of event handlers? If so, how? What would you do differently?

## Scripting Exercises

Create a folder named assignment05 to hold the documents you create during this assignment. Save a copy of the personal home page you last modified as home.html in the assignment05 folder. Save a copy of the toy store home page you last modified as toyStore.html in the assignment05 folder.

1. Develop a Web document named events.html with a white background, black text, blue links, and the following features:

a. A link labeled "Touch Me." When the visitor moves the mouse over this link, the status bar reads "Ooo, that tickles." When the visitor moves the mouse off of the link, the status bar reverts to empty.

b. A button labeled "Click me." When the visitor clicks on the button a box pops up with the message "Ouch!"

c. A line that says "My name is" followed by a text box with "Sam" already entered in it and the message "Go ahead, change my name." When the visitor changes the name in the box, an alert should pop up with the message "Sam I am!" Then the value in the text box should change back to Sam.

d. Create a button labeled "Reload." When it is pressed, the browser should re-request the current document.

2. In your personal home page, try to organize the sections that go best together into pages and break your one long document up into at least four separate documents. Leave the contact and last update info on the home page.

3. Modify your personal home page as follows:

a. In each document, set up a named anchor for each section heading in that document.

b. At the top of each page, create a set of links to the section headings.

c. Set up each link to provide a hint in the status bar when the visitor mouses over it. Don't forget to clear the status bar when the visitor mouses off of the link.

d. Copy each navigation bar and paste it at the bottom of the page it applies to.

4. Create a new document named colorSettings.html.

a. Set up a form with several buttons labeled with the names of 15 of the 16 pre-defined HTML colors. The 16th will have to be your text color. Copying and pasting will make the process easier.

b. Set up each button so that when it is pressed, it changes the background color of the document accordingly.

5. Modify your personal home page Web site as follows:

a. Insert a set of navigation buttons using the <input type=button> tag. Label each one appropriately. Each will link to a page in your Web site.

b. Set up an onClick event handler on each one to change the location to the appropriate document's URL.

6. Modify your toy store home page as follows:

a. Find or create some images for a navigation bar.

b. Use HTML to make the images links.

c. Apply a rollover effect to each link using JavaScript and the appropriate event handlers.

d. In addition to swapping the images, display link descriptions in the status bar whenever they are moused over. Don't forget to clear the status bar on mouse out. Don't worry about preloading the images, we'll learn how to do that later.

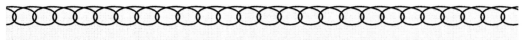

## chapter *six*

# *Control Structures*

*If you don't control*

*your mind, someone*

*else will.*

—John Allston

Programs would be pretty boring and have marginal use if they weren't able to act conditionally or repeat actions as long as necessary. That means that, to be useful, programs need to be able to branch and iterate. Enter control structures.

In this chapter, we'll

- ✗ define the term "control structure."
- ✗ discover the various control structures incorporated into the JavaScript language, including
  - ✗ `if . . . else`
  - ✗ `switch`
  - ✗ `for`
  - ✗ `while`
  - ✗ `do . . . while`
  - ✗ `with`
- ✗ examine each control structure in detail.
- ✗ view some examples of these powerhouses in action.

Let's get started.

# What Is a Control Structure?

**Control structures** let you, the programmer, control the flow of your programs and make your programs capable of reacting dynamically to a variety of conditions. For instance, you might want to set the background color of a Web document to yellow during daylight hours and to black during nighttime hours. Without a control structure, you could not accomplish this.

Remember all of those comparison and logical operators we discussed in Chapter 4? They're going to come in handy when we begin our work with control structures. Most control structures rely on an expression, called a **condition**, that evaluates to a Boolean value: either `true` or `false`. Let's take a closer look at a condition by examining the most popular and often used control structure: the `if` statement.

# Making Decisions with the `if` Control Structure

If you're going to program, you've got to be able to make decisions. The **`if` control structure** lets you do just that. An `if` statement tells your script to perform an action or set of actions only *if* a particular condition is true. Here's the syntax of an `if` statement and an example of its use.

**Syntax:**

```
if (condition)
     statement
```

or

```
if (condition) {
     statements
}
```

The syntax indicates that braces are only required around the statement block if the block contains more than one statement. If there is only one statement, you can omit the braces.

Here's an example of the `if` control structure in action.

### Script 6.1      *`if` Control Structure*

```
1    <html>
2    <head>
3        <title>Script 6.1: If Control Structure</title>
4    </head>
5    <body>
6    <script language="JavaScript" type="text/javascript"><!--
7        var response = parseInt(prompt("What is 100 + 50?", ""))
8        if (response == 150) {
9             alert("That is correct! 100 + 50 = 150")
10        }
11   //-->
12   </script>
13   </body>
14   </html>
```

Notice that in line 9 the contents of the `if` block are indented and that braces are incorporated even though the block contains only one statement. The statement in the `if` block is indented to improve readability. Now anyone reading the script can easily tell that the alert statement is part of the `if` control structure.

But why put braces around the `alert` statement when they're only needed if the block contains more than one statement? Because later you might add more statements to the `if` control structure. By entering them now you don't have to worry that you might forget them later. It's a good habit to get into.

**programmer's tip** Whenever you write a control structure, immediately write the closing brace after writing the opening brace. Then go back and enter the contents of the control structure. That way, you'll rarely have to hassle with syntax errors having to do with mismatched braces.

Here's what it looks like when 150 is entered into the prompt:

**Figure 6.1    Results of Script 6.1**

# Providing a Default Action with `else`

`if`'s cousin, the **`if`...`else` control structure**, lets you instruct your script to perform one of two actions, or sets of actions, depending on some condition. In other words, if the condition is `true`, then the script will perform the set of statements in the `if` block. Otherwise (else), it will invoke the set of statements in the `else` block, that is, it will perform some default action. Following is the syntax and an example:

**Syntax:**

```
if (condition)
      statement
else
      default statement
```

or

```
if (condition) {
     statements
} else {
     default statements
}
```

Here's an example.

**Script 6.2**     **if...else *Control Structure***

```
1     <html>
2     <head>
3          <title>Script 6.2: If...Else Control Structure</title>
4     </head>
5     <body>
6     <script language="JavaScript" type="text/javascript"><!--
7          var response = parseInt(prompt("What is 100 + 50?", ""))
8          if (response == 150) {
9               alert("That is correct! 100 + 50 = 150")
10          } else {
11               alert("Wrong! 100 + 50 = 150")
12          }
13     //-->
14     </script>
15     </body>
16     </html>
```

Notice how in lines 10 and 12 the closing braces line up with the first letter of the if statement. When you line up the braces, at a quick glance you can easily verify that you opened and closed each set of braces. You can also quickly distinguish the contents of each control block from the rest of the regular program flow. That's good programming style!

Try it! Run the script and type 150 in the prompt. You should get this:

*Figure 6.2*    *Results of Script 6.2 when Correct Answer Provided*

Now run it again. This time type in something other than 150. This time you get this:

*Figure 6.3*    *Results of Script 6.2 when Incorrect Answer Provided*

# if...else if...

`if` and `else` can be combined to form a series of `if ... else if ... else if ...` condition evaluations and associated responses.

**Syntax:**

```
if (condition1) {
    statements
} else if (condition2) {
    statements
} else if (condition3) {
    statements
```

```
} else if (condition4) {
    statements


    .

    .

    .

} else if (conditionN) {
    statements
}
```

Here's an example:

**Script 6.3    if...else if... Control Structure**

```
1    <html>
2    <head>
3        <title>Script 6.3 If...Else If... Control Structure</title>
4    </head>
5    <body>
6    <script language="JavaScript" type="text/javascript"><!--
7        var answer = 150
8        var response = parseInt(prompt("What is 100 + 50?", ""))
9        if (response == answer) {
10            alert("That is correct! 100 + 50 = 150")
11        } else if (Math.abs(answer-response) == 1) {
12            alert("You\'re very close!")
13        } else if (Math.abs(answer-response) <= 5) {
14            alert("You\'re sort of close.")
15        }
16    //-->
17    </script>
18    </body>
19    </html>
```

This script delivers one of three alert boxes, depending on what is typed in the prompt. They should look like the screen shots in Figure 6.4.

*Figure 6.4    Possible Responses to Script 6.3*

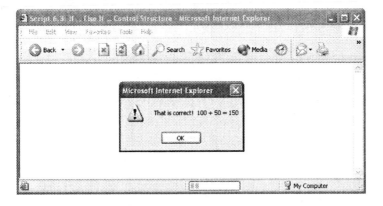

Lines 11 and 13 get the absolute value of the difference between the correct answer and the response so the result can be easily compared to a positive number.

# if...else if...else

To provide a default response should none of the conditions prove true, add an else at the end.

**Syntax:**

```
if (condition) {
     statements
} else if (condition2) {
     statements
} else if (condition2) {
     statements
} else if (condition3) {
     statements


     .

     .

     .

} else if (conditionN) {
     statements
} else {
     default statements
}
```

Here's an example:

**Script 6.4    *if...else if...else* Control Structure**

```
1   <html>
2   <head>
3   <title>Script 6.4: If...Else If...Else Control Structure</title>
4   </head>
5   <body>
6   <script language="JavaScript" type="text/javascript"><!--
7        var answer = 150
8        var response = parseInt(prompt("What is 100 + 50?", ""))
9        if (response == answer) {
10            alert("That is correct! 100 + 50 = 150")
11       } else if (Math.abs(answer-response) == 1) {
12            alert("You\'re very close!")
13       } else if (Math.abs(answer-response) <= 5) {
14            alert("You\'re sort of close.")
15       } else {
16            alert("You\'re way off the mark!")
17       }
18  //-->
19  </script>
```

```
20   </body>
21   </html>
```

Here's what the default response looks like:

***Figure 6.5        Default Response for Script 6.4***

# The switch Statement

Occasionally, instead of evaluating a condition, you simply want to match the result of an expression with several possible cases. While you could construct a series of if...else if...statements to test against the various cases, it's nicer, and sometimes simpler and more readable, to use a **switch statement** and match the value of the expression against various label values.

**Syntax:**

```
switch (expression) {
case label1:
     statements
        [break]
case label2:
     statements
        [break]
case label3:
     statements
        [break]
...
[default:
     statements]
}
```

If a single block of statements applies to more than one label, you can write it as follows:

```
switch (expression) {
case label1:
      statements
        [break]
case label2: label3:
      statements
        [break]
case label4:
      statements
        [break]
...
[default:
      statements]
}
```

The *expression* parameter must be a constant expression that evaluates to any string, numeric, or Boolean value. For example, "apple", "Thursday", and 15 are all constant expressions and legal labels for a switch case. "Thursday" always evaluates to "Thursday". However, the following expressions are not constant and are therefore not legal switch case labels:

```
!= "Wednesday"
<= 15
```

Get the picture? Let's look at a real example.

**Script 6.5      *switch* Control Structure**

```
1    <html>
2    <head>
3         <title>Script 6.5: Switch Control Structure</title>
4    </head>
5    <body>
6    <script language="JavaScript" type="text/javascript"><!--
7    // give the user a hint of how you want the data entered
8    window.status="Monday, Tuesday, Wednesday, Thursday,
        Friday, Saturday, Sunday"
9    var today = prompt("Enter a weekday: ", "")
10
11   // clear the status window
12   window.status = ""
13
14   switch (today) {
15   case "Monday":
```

```
16          alert("It is the beginning of the week, all things
               are possible!")
17          break
18  case "Tuesday": case "Thursday":
19          alert("Go to JavaScript class!")
20          break
21  case "Wednesday":
22          alert("Alas! It\'s humpday!")
23          break
24  case "Friday":
25          alert("Thank goodness! It\'s Friday!")
26          break
27  default:
28          alert("Live it up!")
29  }
30  //-->
31  </script>
32  </body>
33  </html>
```

Why is that break statement in all the blocks? The break statement terminates the current switch or label statement and continues to the statement following the terminated switch statement. It also works on loops, terminating the current loop and transferring program control to the statement following the loop, as you will see later in this chapter.

Try Script 6.5. Depending on what you type in, you'll get one of these five responses:

*Figure 6.6        Possible Results of Script 6.5*

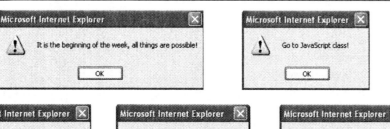

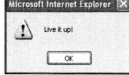

# The for Loop

Sometimes you'll want or need to perform the same action or set of actions repeatedly until some condition is met. Loop statements simplify that process.

The **for loop** is the perfect tool when you know, or your program can determine, exactly how many times you need to perform a particular set of actions. For instance, if you want to know a visitor's three favorite movies, you know in advance that you'll need to prompt the user three times for that information.

Like the if control structure, for needs a condition. The for control block executes until the condition evaluates to false. In addition to a condition, the for loop relies on two other expressions in order to work properly: an initial expression that initializes the loop counter and an update expression that changes the loop counter between iterations.

**Syntax:**

```
for ([initial expression]; [condition]; [update expression]) {
    statements
}
```

Loop counters are commonly named i, j, k, l, etc. starting with i for the outermost loop. In the following example, the loop counter, i, is initialized to 1 the first time through the loop.

```
for (i=1; i<=3; i++) {
    statements
}
```

The process proceeds as follows:

Loop 1:

- ⚡ Loop begins
- ⚡ i is initialized to 1
- ⚡ Condition is evaluated: is i <= 3? yes
- ⚡ Condition evaluated to true, so execute the statements inside the for block
- ⚡ Hit closing brace and execute update expression: i now equals 2

Loop 2:

- ⚡ Evaluate condition: is i <= 3? yes
- ⚡ Condition is true, so execute the statements inside the block
- ⚡ Hit closing brace and execute update expression: i now equals 3

Loop 3:

- ⚡ Evaluate condition: is i <= 3? yes
- ⚡ Condition is true, so execute the statements inside the block
- ⚡ Hit closing brace and execute update expression: i now equals 4

**side note**

The naming of loop counters and array subscripts as i, j, k, l, m, and n hearkens back to the early days of Fortran. In Fortran, variables whose names begin with letters I through N were by default integers, the rest were floats.

**peek ahead**

for loops are particularly useful when working with arrays. In Chapter 7, "Arrays," we'll revisit this powerful control structure.

Loop 4:
- ✗ Evaluate condition: is i <= 3? no
- ✗ Condition is false, so continue program execution at the statement following the closing brace

Ready for a real-world example? Try to walk through the following script's execution like we did above and see if you can figure out exactly what it will do. Then run the code and see if you were right.

**Script 6.6        for Loop—Favorite Movies**

```
1   <html>
2   <head>
3        <title>Script 6.6: For Loop</title>
4   </head>
5   <body>
6   <script language="JavaScript" type="text/javascript"><!--
7   var favMovie = ""
8
9   document.write("<h1>Your Favorite Movies</h1>")
10  for (i=1; i<=3; i++) {
11       favMovie = prompt("Enter your #" + i + " favorite
            movie:", "")
12       document.write(i, ". ", favMovie, "<br>\n")
13  }
14  //-->
15  </script>
16  </body>
17  </html>
```

This is what you should get:

**Figure 6.7        Results of Script 6.6**

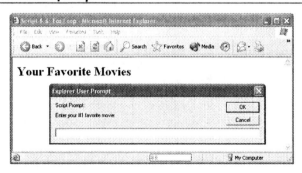

Did you guess right?

# `while` Loops

Sometimes it's impossible to determine exactly how many times a program will need to perform an action. For instance, you could ask a visitor to enter a number and keep asking until he enters a valid number. You don't know how many times you'll have to ask; he might enter a valid number the first time or you might have to prompt him 20 times before he gets it through his thick skull that you want a number and nothing but a number. This is where the **`while` loop** comes in handy.

A `while` loop continues executing a set of statements as long as some condition is `true` or until that condition is `false`.

**Syntax:**

```
while (condition) {
        statements
}
```

Here's an example that will prompt the visitor for a number and keep prompting until the visitor enters a valid number.

*Script 6.7*      *`while` Loop—Get a Valid Number*

```
1    <html>
2    <head>
3    <title>Script 6.7: While Loop - Get a Valid Number</title>
4    </head>
5    <body>
6    <script language="JavaScript" type="text/javascript"><!--
7         var num = parseFloat(prompt("Enter a number:", ""))
8
9         while ( isNaN(num) ) {
10               alert("Error! You did not enter a number!")
11               num = parseFloat(prompt("Enter a number: ", ""))
12         }
13
14         alert("Success! You entered: " + num)
15   //-->
16   </script>
17   </body>
18   </html>
```

Line 7 prompts the visitor for a number and saves the response in the variable num. The `while` control structure, lines 9 through 12, checks to see if the value entered is actually a number. If the value entered is not a number, the statements in the block execute, displaying an error message and prompting the visitor for a number again. The `while` control structure continues checking for a good number, displaying an error message, and prompting for a number as long as the data entered is not a number. Cool, huh?

Give it a try. First enter some letters. You should get this:

***Figure 6.8*** ***Results of Script 6.7 when Non-Number Entered***

Enter letters again the second time around. You can enter numbers too, as long as your entry doesn't *start* with a number. As long as you enter a string that doesn't start with a number you should get the same result as in Figure 6.8.

When you're satisfied that as long as you enter a non-number, you'll keep getting prompted for one, enter a number or a string beginning with a number. Here's what you get:

***Figure 6.9*** ***Results of Script 6.7 when Number Entered***

## do . . . while Loops

**do . . . while** is while's cousin. The major difference between the two is that a while loop's contents may never execute, depending on the condition's evaluation. A do . . . while loop's contents will always execute at least once. For instance, in the while loop in Script 6.7, if the visitor entered a number the first time he was prompted, the condition would have evaluated to `false` and the `while` block would never have executed, not even once.

The contents of a `do...while` loop, on the other hand, *always* execute at least once because the condition is not tested until *after* the statement block. This is called a post-test. `while` uses a pre-test.

**Syntax:**

```
do {
     statements
} while (condition)
```

To illustrate the difference between `while` and `do...while`, let's perform the task from Script 6.7 with a `do...while` loop. We'll get a valid number from the visitor.

**Script 6.8     *do...while Loop—Get a Valid Number***

```
1    <html>
2    <head>
3    <title>Script 6.8: Do...While Loop - Get a Valid Number</title>
4    </head>
5    <body>
6    <script language="JavaScript" type="text/javascript"><!--
7         var num = ""
8         do {
9              num = parseFloat(prompt("Enter a number: ", ""))
10             if ( isNaN(num) ) {
11                  alert("Error! You did not enter a number!")
12             }
13        } while ( isNaN(num) )
14
15        alert("Success! You entered: " + num)
16   //-->
17   </script>
18   </body>
19   </html>
```

`do...while` is an appropriate control structure to use when you know you must always perform some action at least once, like prompting the visitor for an entry. If you didn't want to display an error message, you could eliminate lines 10 through 12 above. The `while` loop would simply prompt for a number and keep reprompting until a valid number were entered.

In a real-world script, you wouldn't notify the user of a proper entry like we did in line 15. Instead, you'd just go on and do whatever it is you needed to do, like perform a calculation.

Before we leave the subject of loops, let's look a little more closely at the `break` statement mentioned earlier; this time we'll use it with a loop. Then we'll look at `break`'s cousin, `continue`.

# Breaking out of a Loop with break

Sometimes a loop is used to perform a task like searching for a desired string. Once the desired item is found, there is no need to continue looping. Fortunately, JavaScript provides a way for us to **break** out of such a loop when our task is accomplished.

In the following example, the plan is to ask the visitor for his seven favorite movies. However, if the visitor enters "Abyss" (my favorite movie), we'll break out of the loop because we now have something we can chat with the visitor about.

**Script 6.9    Using break—Favorite Movies Revisited**

```
1    <html>
2    <head>
3          <title>Script 6.9: Using Break - Fav Movies
             Revisited</title>
4    </head>
5    <body>
6    <script language="JavaScript" type="text/javascript"><!--
7    var favMovie = ""
8    document.write("<h1>Your Favorite Movies</h1>")
9    for (i=1; i<=7; i++) {
10         favMovie = prompt("Enter your #" + i + " favorite
             movie:", "")
11         document.write(i, ". ", favMovie, "<br>\n")
12         if (favMovie == "Abyss") {
13               alert("I love that movie! Let\'s talk!")
14               break
15         }
16   }
17   //-->
18   </script>
19   </body>
20   </html>
```

Run the script and enter "Abyss" as one of your favorites. If you want, you can modify the script so that it checks for *your* favorite movie instead. Just change line 12. Either way, watch what happens when you enter that particular favorite movie at the prompt.

**Figure 6.10    Results of Script 6.9 when Appropriate Favorite Movie Is Entered**

As you can see, the program exits the loop. Execution would then continue after the `for` loop, but we don't have any other statements to execute. One word of caution with regard to break: try not to use it too often. As a rule, loops should terminate normally as often as possible.

Now let's look at break's cousin, `continue`.

# Directing Loop Traffic with `continue`

Sometimes you may want to skip execution of some statements in a `for` loop if a certain condition is met, but still continue looping. JavaScript provides the **`continue` statement** to handle this task.

In this example, if the visitor enters "Seven" (a movie I despise) as a favorite movie, we won't add it to the list, but simply *continue* with the next iteration. Feel free to change the movie to one you despise. Just modify line 12.

**Script 6.10    Using `continue`**

```
1    <html>
2    <head>
3         <title>Script 6.10: Using Continue</title>
4    </head>
5    <body>
6    <script language="JavaScript" type="text/javascript"><!--
7    var favMovie = ""
8    document.write("<h1>Your Favorite Movies</h1>")
9
10   for (i=1; i<=7; i++) {
11        favMovie = prompt("Enter your #" + i + " favorite
            movie:", "")
```

```
12          if (favMovie == "Seven") {
13                  alert("Ugh!  I hate that movie!")
14                  continue
15          }
16          document.write(i, ". ", favMovie, "<br>\n")
17  }
18  //-->
19  </script>
20  </body>
21  </html>
```

Run the script. Enter the despised movie at one of the prompts, but not the last one.

*Figure 6.11     Results of Script 6.10 when Despised Movie Title Is Entered*

Notice how execution of the loop continues, even though the remaining statements of the iteration in which you entered the despised movie are skipped. That's continue in action.

## with

The **with statement** doesn't really let you control program flow depending on a condition, it's more of a typing saver. Instead of typing the entire formal address of each and every property or method in a group of statements that all deal with the same object again and again, you can place that group of statements in a with control block.

**Syntax:**

```
with (object) {
      statements that use same object
}
```

To see how much typing you can save, compare the following two coding examples. Neither is a completed script; neither can be run without a form on the same page.

### Script 6.11     More Typing Without *with*

```
1   for(i=0; i<document.forms.length; i++) {
2       document.write("Form: ", document.forms[i].name, "<ul>")
3       for(j=0; j < document.forms[i].elements.length; j++) {
4           document.write("<li>",
5               document.forms[i].elements[j].name, " = ",
6               document.forms[i].elements[j].value, "</li>")
7       }
8       document.write("</ul>")
9   }
```

Notice how lines 2 through 6 all refer to "document.forms[i]"? Now we'll use `with` to simplify the code a little.

### Script 6.12     *with*, the Typing Saver

```
1   for(i=0; i<document.forms.length; i++) {
2       with (document.forms[i]) {
3           document.write("Form: ", name, "<ul>")
4           for(j=0; j < elements.length; j++) {
5               document.write("<li>",
6                   elements[j].name, " = ",
7                   elements[j].value, "</li>")
8           }
9       }
10      document.write("</ul>")
11  }
```

In this coding example, lines 3 through 8 correspond with lines 2 through 7 of Script 6.11. See how much shorter the lines are when you use `with`?

## Conditional

While the **conditional statement** is not *exactly* a control structure, its function is similar to that of an `if...else` statement. It is also sometimes used as a short replacement for an `if...else` statement.

The conditional statement evaluates an expression and returns one of two values depending on whether the result is `true` or `false`. If the condition evaluates to `true`, the conditional statement returns the first value; if the condition evaluates to `false`, it returns the second value. You can easily use an `if...else` statement to replace any conditional statement.

To clarify the similarity between `if...else` and the conditional statement, let's perform the same task as in Script 6.2.

### Script 6.13    The Conditional Statement Revisited

```
1    <html>
2    <head>
3    <title>Script 6.13: The Conditional Statement Revisited</title>
4    </head>
5    <body>
6    <script language="JavaScript" type="text/javascript"><!--
7         alert(parseInt(prompt("What is 100 + 50?", "")) == 150 ?
             "Correct!" : "Wrong!")
8    //-->
9    </script>
10   </body>
11   </html>
```

Using the conditional statement, we were able to perform the same task in only one line of code instead of six! While doing so much with a single line of code may demonstrate your programming prowess, you may be sacrificing readability. Many programmers may not be familiar with the conditional statement, but any programmer worth her salt can easily recognize an if statement when she sees one.

Still, the conditional statement is quite useful for assigning a value to a variable from among two choices in one short line of code like we did in Script 6.13. The two possible results of Script 6.13 are shown in Figure 6.12.

### Figure 6.12    Two Possible Results of Script 6.13

 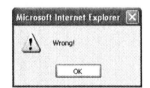

An equivalent if ... else statement would require five lines of code, four if written in short form without braces.

## Summary

Control structures are a very important part of any programming language. Without them, a program would be reduced to a series of executed statements with no branching, repetition, or flexibility whatsoever.

Control structures provide programs the ability to evaluate conditions and follow preset courses of action accordingly. if, if ... else, if ... else if, and if ... else if ... else are examples of this type of program flow control. Using a for loop, you can cause a block of code to iterate a preset number of times. Programs can even be instructed to loop as long as a particular condition is true: while and do ... while.

Using a `switch` statement, you can define a series of cases, such as menu choices, then have your program evaluate an expression and match it against those cases, performing the appropriate set of actions accordingly. Control structures can even save you typing (`with`) and make your code more readable.

In short, control structures give programs necessary power and flexibility. The flexibility and power to execute statements according to current needs and conditions is what programming is all about.

## Review Questions

1. What is a control structure?
2. Why are control structures so important to programming?
3. Describe a good use for an `if ... else` control structure.
4. What do the braces (`{ }`) mean in control structures?
5. What do the parentheses `( )` usually contain in control structures?
6. What is a condition?
7. Why should you indent the contents of a control structure?
8. What control structure can sometimes be used to replace a long `if ... else if` control structure?
9. What is a line label?
10. Does the switch statement make use of a condition or an expression? Explain your answer. (Hint: What's the difference between an expression and a condition?)
11. What does it mean to iterate?
12. Name and describe the three types of expressions required in a `for` statement.
13. Describe a good use for a `for` loop.
14. What's the difference between a `for` loop and a `while` loop?
15. Describe a good use for a `while` loop.
16. What's the difference between a `while` loop and a `do ... while` loop?
17. What's the difference between `break` and `continue`?
18. What is the `with` control structure good for?
19. Name and describe the three parts of a conditional statement.
20. What can you do with an `if ... else` control structure that you can't accomplish with a conditional statement?

## Exercises

1. Convert this `if ... else if ... else` statement to a `switch` statement:

```
if (today == "Monday") {
        alert("It\'s a new week. All things are possible.")
} else if (today == "Tuesday" || today == "Thursday") {
        alert("Don\'t forget to go to JavaScript class ⤏
        ⤏ today.")
```

```
} else if (today == "Wednesday") {
    alert("It\'s hump day! The week is half over!")
} else if (today == "Friday") {
    alert("TGIF!")
} else {
    alert("Seize the day!")
}
```

2.  Convert this switch statement to an if ... else if ... else statement:

```
switch (choice) {
case "magenta" :
    document.bgColor = "magenta"
    break
case "yellow" :
    document.bgColor = "yellow"
    break
case "lime" :
    document.bgColor = "lime"
    break
case "cyan" :
    break
case "purple" :
    document.bgColor = "purple"
    break
default :
    document.bgColor = "white"
}
```

3.  Specify how many times each for loop's block of statements will execute. Then convert each for loop into a while loop.

```
a. for (i=1; i<13; i++) {
       document.write("loop ", i, "<br>")
   }
b. for (i=4; i>0; i--) {
       document.write(i + "<br>")
   }
c. for (i=1; i<=99; i=i*2) {
       i = i/1.5
   }
```

    d.
```
for (i=0; i <= 18; i++) {
    if (i == 5)
        break
}
```

4.   Convert this do ... while loop into a while loop:

```
var num
do {
    num = parseFloat (prompt ("Enter a number:", " "))
} while (isNaN (num))
```

5.   Use a with control structure to simplify the following code:

```
document.write ("Src: ", document.MyPic.src, "<br>",
            "Width: ", document.MyPic.width, "<br>",
            "Height: ", document.MyPic.height, "<br>",
            "Complete? ", document.MyPic.complete, "<br>")
```

6.   Convert the following conditional statement to an if ... else statement:

```
var custName = (login != "" && login != null) ? ⟶
⟶ login : "Guest"
```

# Scripting Exercises

Create a folder named assignment06 to hold the documents you create during this assignment. Save a copy of the personal home page you last modified as home.html in the assign-
ment06 folder. Save a copy of the toy store home page you last modified as toyStore.html in
the assignment06 folder.

1.   Create a document named getNum1to100.html. Write a script to prompt the visitor
for an integer between 1 and 100 and to continue prompting until a valid number is
entered.

2.   Create a new document named favBooks.html. Prompt the visitor for his or her five
favorite books and write them to the screen as an ordered list using a for loop and
the HTML <ol> and <li> tags.

3.   Create a document named getDestination.html. Write a script to prompt the visitor
for one of four destinations. You choose the destinations. (Google, Yahoo!, Excite,
and HotBot would be good ones.) Show a list of the choices in the status bar each
time you prompt the visitor. Keep prompting the visitor for a choice until he or she
chooses one of the four destinations you've decided on. Once a valid destination is
chosen, take the visitor to that site.

4.   Copy the script you wrote in Scripting Exercise 1 as countPrompts.html. Modify it so
that it keeps track of how many times you had to prompt the visitor before you got a
valid number in the range of 1 to 100. Display the count in an alert at the end.

5.   Create a new document named guess.html. Write a number guessing game that prompts the visitor for a number and keeps prompting until the guess matches the target. Keep a count of how many guesses the visitor makes. Display a message after each guess as follows:

   a.   If the guess is within three, either higher or lower, than the target number, display the message "You're Red Hot!"

   b.   If the guess is more than three away, but less than 10 away from the target number, say "You're getting warm."

   c.   If the guess is more than 10 away but less than 20, say "You're getting cold."

   d.   If the guess is more than 20 away, say "You're Ice Cold!"

   e.   If the guess is correct, say "Success! You Win!" in an alert box. On the second line of the alert box, display the appropriate message. If the number of guesses was

      i.   less than five: "You did an awesome job, it only took you ___ tries to guess the number!"

      ii.   less than or equal to 15, but more than five: "Goodness. It took you ___ tries to guess the target number."

      iii.   greater than 15: "Yikes! It took you ___ tries to guess the target number."

6.   Create a new document named ageEntitlements.html.

   a.   Acquire the visitor's age.

   b.   Write the statements that apply to the document under the heading "Being ___ Entitles You To:". Replace the blank space with the visitor's age. If the age is

      i.   less than or equal to five: "Take a nap every day."

      ii.   less than or equal to 13: "Be a child, play and have fun."

      iii.   between 13 and 19, inclusive: "Be a teenager."

      iv.   greater than or equal to 16: "Drive."

      v.   less than 18: "Report to your parents."

      vi.   greater than or equal to 18: "Vote."

      vii.   greater than or equal to 18: "Legally buy cigarettes."

      viii.   greater than or equal to 21: "Legally drink alcohol."

      ix.   greater than or equal to 25: "Get a discount on car insurance from most insurance companies."

      x.   greater than or equal to 65: "Retire."

      xi.   greater than or equal to 65: "Take a nap every day."

7.   Create a new document named table.html. Write a script that does the following:

   a.   Creates a table with a border in HTML.

   b.   Uses variables named `rows` and `cols` to determine the number of rows and columns to create. You should prompt the visitor for this information.

   c.   Uses variables to set the border width and background color of the table.

   d.   Uses appropriate control structures to create the table.

   e.   Prefills each cell with a non-breaking space ( ).

8. The lastModified property of the document object does not always report the last modified date. Some servers simply do not return that information. When no date is reported, lastModified gets set to zero, which indicates January 1, 1970, in JavaScript's date scheme.

   a. Modify home.html so that it writes document.lastModified only if it is not equal to zero.

   b. Otherwise write "not reported," "unknown," or something similar.

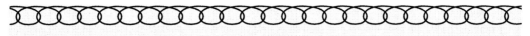

## chapter *seven*

# Arrays

*Captain, I am detect-ing an array of holometric radiation clusters at the edge of sensor range.*

—Worf, *Star Trek: The Next Generation*

While it's handy to have variables in which to store information, sometimes a good variable is just not enough. This is especially true if you want to store a list of values that are related, such as a list of students or the months of the year. Enter arrays.

In this chapter we'll
- define what an array is.
- discover how to declare and populate an array.
- learn how to retrieve data from an array.
- discuss uses for parallel arrays.
- learn how to copy an array.
- use Array methods to sort, reverse, and join arrays.
- look at some real-world examples using arrays.

Let's get started.

# What Is an Array?

Recall from Chapter 3 that a variable is a storage place in memory that you can access using a label that you define. You can think of a variable as a cup whose contents can vary. An **array** is also a storage place in memory. You can also access an array using a label you define. However, whereas a variable holds a single value of some data type, an array holds multiple data values, usually, but not always, of the same data type. You can think of an array as a tray holding multiple cups. Each cup has something in it.

Taking this analogy a step further, envision those cups labeled with numbers, beginning with 0. You can then identify a particular cup on the tray by its **index**. An array element's index is its numbered position in the array. For example, let's declare an array of cups using the new operator. Recall from Chapter 4 that the new operator creates a new instance of an object of the type specified by the constructor function following the operator. In this case, we're going to create a new `Array` object and store the array in a variable named `cups`.

```
var cups = new Array()
```

Let's set the value for the first cup in the array, whose index is 0, to "lemonade":

```
cups[0] = "lemonade"
```

Now the first cup, `cups[0]`, contains "lemonade".

Arrays are particularly useful for storing data that are somehow related to each other, such as student names, days of the week, friends' telephone numbers, the images in a Web document, the elements in a form, the plug-ins supported by a browser, etc. JavaScript always begins numbering array elements at zero.

# Declaring an Array

There are basically three ways to declare an array. The first we saw above: simply declare a variable with the keyword `var`, followed by your chosen name for the array, the equals assignment operator, the keyword `new`, and the object constructor function name. In this case we're constructing an array object, so we use the `Array()` constructor function. Optionally, you can specify how long you expect the array to be by placing a number, indicating the desired length of the array, within the parentheses.

```
var cups = new Array()
```

> **programmer's tip**
> When you declare an array, give it a plural name like `cups` or `students`. That will help alert you to the fact that is an array and contains multiple values.

While strongly typed languages, such as Java and C++, require that you specify both an array's size and its data type when you declare it, JavaScript does not. JavaScript only allows you to specify the length of an array when you declare it. Remember, JavaScript is a dynamically typed language. Even so, it is considered good form to specify an array's length when you declare it.

Because it's good programming practice to specify the expected size of an array when you declare it, we'll modify our example accordingly:

```
var cups = new Array(8)
```

The above statement declares an array of cups with eight elements. This sets aside space in memory for an array of eight cups. Keep in mind that the last element of the array will be cups [7] . Why? Because array elements begin numbering at 0. So 0, 1, 2, 3, 4, 5, 6, and 7 makes eight elements. Thus the index of the last element of an array is always the array's length minus one, commonly written as n-1.

## Populating an Array

To store actual values in an array, use the array name, followed by an index number in brackets and an assignment expression. For example:

```
cups[0]  =  "lemonade"
cups[1]  =  "iced tea"
cups[2]  =  "Pepsi"
cups[3]  =  "margarita"
cups[4]  =  "Dr. Pepper"
cups[5]  =  "lemonade"
cups[6]  =  "Diet Pepsi"
cups[7]  =  "margarita"
```

Now our array is populated. It's just like assigning values to variables, except for the brackets containing an index number, that is.

## Accessing Array Elements

Accessing the values of array elements or referring to array elements is easy. Simply specify the array name followed by the desired element's index number in brackets. Again, this is just like working with a variable. Remember, arrays always begin numbering at zero (0). Thus,

```
cups[0]
```

returns the value

```
lemonade
```

and similarly,

```
cups[6]
```

returns the value

```
Diet Pepsi
```

You can use array elements to make assignments just like they were regular variables. For example:

```
var myFavoriteSoda = cups[4]
```

The above statement assigns the value of the fifth element of the cups array (remember arrays begin numbering at zero) to the variable myFavoriteSoda. You can also do the opposite: assign the value of myFavoriteSoda to cups[4]:

```
cups[4] = myFavoriteSoda
```

# for Loops and Arrays, the Perfect Team

So why didn't we just use regular variables such as cup1, cup2, cup3, etc. What's the big deal about *arrays*?

Remember the for loop from Chapter 6 and how good it is at performing a task repeatedly a known number of times? Now take a look at the properties listed for the Array object in Appendix A. See if you can identify the property that specifies how many elements are contained in the array.

Did you find it? The Array property that specifies the number of elements it contains is the length property. With this information in hand, we can now construct a for loop to do something with an array. The array's length property will provide the appropriate number of iterations for our condition, that is, it will specify how many times to perform the operation. For example:

```
for (i=0; i<cups.length; i++) {
    document.write(i, ". ", cups[i], "<br>")
}
```

The result:

```
0. lemonade
1. iced tea
2. Pepsi
3. margarita
4. Dr. Pepper
5. lemonade
6. Diet Pepsi
7. margarita
```

We can generalize this technique for all arrays as

```
for (i=0; i<arrayName.length; i++) {
    document.write(i, ". ", arrayName[i], "<br>")
}
```

Just fill in the appropriate array name and you have a routine for writing the contents of an array as a numbered list. We'll use this bit of code to examine the contents of our arrays as we create them throughout this chapter.

Here's the script in its entirety from array declaration to writing the array's contents:

**Script 7.1**      *Declaring, Populating, and Printing anArray*

```
1    <html>
2    <head>
3    <title>Script 7.1: Declaring, Populating, and Printing an
4    Array</title>
5    <script language="JavaScript" type="text/javascript"><!--
6            var cups = new Array(8)
7            cups[0] = "lemonade"
8            cups[1] = "iced tea"
9            cups[2] = "Pepsi"
10           cups[3] = "margarita"
11           cups[4] = "Dr. Pepper"
12           cups[5] = "lemonade"
13           cups[6] = "Diet Pepsi"
14           cups[7] = "margarita"
15   //-->
16   </script>
17   </head>
18   <body>
19   <script language="JavaScript" type="text/javascript"><!--
20           for (i=0; i<cups.length; i++) {
21                   document.write(i, ". ", cups[i], "<br>")
22           }
23   //-->
24   </script>
25   </body>
26   </html>
```

**Figure 7.1**      *Results of Script 7.1*

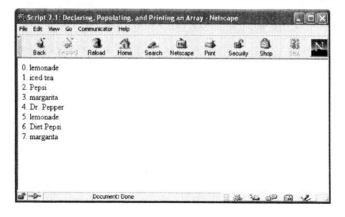

This is just a peek at the power of arrays and `for` loops together. Let's get back now to the various ways in which you can declare an array.

# Dense Arrays

The second way to declare an array is to initialize it when you declare it. An array initialized at declaration is called a **dense array**, perhaps because it is densely packed at the get-go.

For example:

```
var days = new Array("Sun", "Mon", "Tues", "Wed", "Thurs",
   "Fri", "Sat")
```

The above dense array was declared and initialized in one fell swoop. Note: You can list the array elements on multiple lines when declaring a dense array. Simply break each line after a comma:

```
var months = new Array ("January", "February", "March",
                        "April", "May", "June", "July",
                        "August", "September", "October",
                        "November", "December")
```

This is extremely useful, because often all of the array element values will not fit on a single line. It can also improve readability considerably.

# Array Literals

The third way to create an array is to use an **array literal**. An array literal is a list of zero or more expressions enclosed in brackets ( [ ] ). Each expression represents an array element. Here's an example of an array literal:

```
["Friday", "Saturday", "Sunday"]
```

Creating an array using an array literal is similar to declaring a dense array in that you both declare and populate the array in one fell swoop; the syntax is just a little different. As with a dense array declaration, the length of an array created using an array literal is set to the number of arguments listed. Here's an example:

```
var weekendDays = ["Friday", "Saturday", "Sunday"]
```

How do you access elements of an array literal? The same way you access elements of an array declared any other way: with the array name followed by an index number in brackets. For example, to access the second element of weekendDays (index 1), you simply write

```
WeekendDays [1]
```

**side note**

Netscape, Microsoft, and Opera first supported array literals in version 4 of their browsers.

Array literals are `Array` objects. They may contain extra commas as placeholders for uninitialized elements. The extra commas affect the calculated length of the array. For instance, the following script creates an array of three elements. The second element is not initialized (line 5). Using a `for` loop, let's examine the value of each element of the array.

**Script 7.2       Using Placeholders in an Array Literal**

```
1    <html>
2    <head>
3    <title>Script 7.2: Using Placeholders in an Array Literal</title>
4    <script language="JavaScript" type="text/javascript"><!--
5         var flowers = ["rose", , "stargazer"]
6    //-->
7    </script>
8    </head>
9    <body>
10   <script language="JavaScript" type="text/javascript"><!-
11        for (i=0; i<flowers.length; i++) {
12             document.write(i, ". ", flowers[i], "<br>")
13        }
14   //-->
15   </script>
16   </body>
17   </html>
```

**Figure 7.2       Results of Script 7.2**

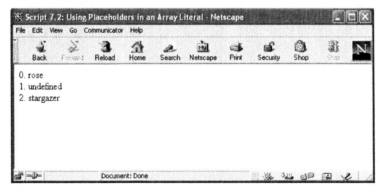

Notice that the uninitialized element's value is undefined. We declared the second array element by using a comma placeholder in our array literal, but since we did not provide an initializing value, its value is undefined. This is similar to declaring a variable, but not initializing it. Its value remains undefined until a value is assigned to it.

All of the browsers seem to handle comma placeholders in the middle of an array literal the same. However, Netscape Navigator, Microsoft Internet Explorer, and Opera handle extra commas listed *at the end* of an array literal differently. Netscape Navigator creates empty elements for each comma at the end of the array, but does not assume an additional element after the last comma; Internet Explorer and Opera create empty elements for each comma, plus one to follow the last comma. Run the following code in Navigator, Internet Explorer, and Opera to see the difference for yourself:

**Script 7.3    Empty Elements at the End of an Array Literal**

```
1    <html>
2    <head>
3    <title>Script 7.3: Empty Elements at the End of an Array
        Literal</title>
4    <script language="JavaScript" type="text/javascript"><!--
5         var lilies = ["Stargazer", "Mona Lisa", "Calla",,,]
6    //-->
7    </script>
8    </head>
9    <body>
10   <script language="JavaScript" type="text/javascript"><!--
11        document.write("lilies contains ", lilies.length,
12                        " elements<br>")
13        for (i=0; i<lilies.length; i++) {
14             document.write(i, ". ", lilies[i], "<br>")
15        }
16
17   //-->
18   </script>
19   </body>
20   </html>
```

*Figure 7.3* **Results of Script 7.3 in Netscape Navigator**

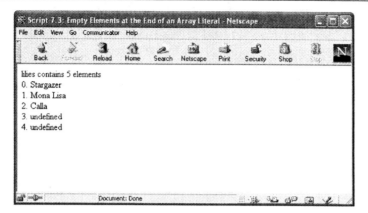

*Figure 7.4* **Results of Script 7.3 in Internet Explorer**

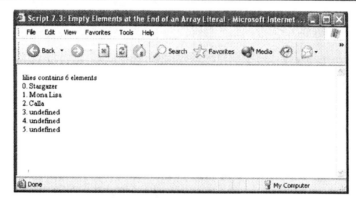

*Figure 7.5* **Results of Script 7.3 in Opera**

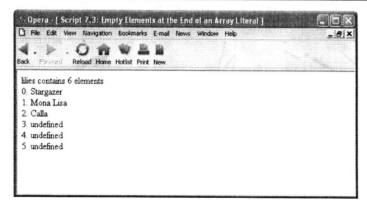

## Associative Arrays

Thus far you have been accessing array elements using their ordinal index numbers. Array elements can also be indexed by their names, if a name has been defined. An array indexed by a word, rather than by an ordinal number, is called an **associative array**.

When working with arrays that are properties of the document object, being able to access an element with its name can come in handy. For example, the following HTML code defines four named images:

```
<body>
        <img src="products.gif" name="products">
        <img src="services.gif" name="services">
        <img src="contact.gif" name="contact">
        <img src="home.gif" name="home">
</body>
```

Using JavaScript, you can access those images with their ordinal index numbers as follows:

```
document.images[0]
document.images[1]
document.images[2]
document.images[3]
```

or by their names:

```
document.images["products"]
document.images["services"]
document.images["contact"]
document.images["home"]
```

Thus, document.images[2] and document.images[contact] refer to the same image in the document's images array.

When working with images and other objects in a document, it is often much easier to access the object via its name rather than its index number. Support for associative arrays is a nice feature of JavaScript. It particularly comes in handy for accessing absolutely positioned elements by their id name.

You can also create your own associative arrays. For instance, you could create an array of your friends' and family members' birthdays, indexed by their names.

**peek ahead**

You'll learn how to access objects by their id name from an associative array when we talk about Dynamic HTML in Chapter 15 and Appendix F.

```
var birthdays = new Array()

birthdays["Tim"] = "May 15"
birthdays["Mom"] = "March 22"
```

```
birthdays["Jana"]  =  "February 18"
birthdays["Electra"]  =  "April 25"
birthdays["Philip"]  =  "January 25"
birthdays["Mary"]  =  "January 31"
birthdays["Jennifer"]  =  "January 5"
birthdays["Adnan"]  =  "October 1"
```

Then if you wanted to write Tim's birthday, you could use

```
document.write("Tim\'s birthday is ", birthdays["Tim"],
"<br>")
```

Purty cool, huh?

## Dynamic Array Lengths in JavaScript

In a strongly typed language such as Java or C++, array lengths are fixed; that is, once you declare the length of the array you cannot add elements beyond that length on the fly. You usually have to jump through several hoops to reallocate space for it first. Not so with JavaScript. JavaScript, being a dynamically typed language, lets you modify the length of an array dynamically. To make an array longer, simply add more elements to it. Let's look at an example:

```
var colors = new Array(3)
colors[0]  =  "white"
colors[1]  =  "fuchsia"
colors[2]  =  "electric blue"
```

Here we've declared an array called colors with an initial length of three and set the values of those three elements. We can verify its length by writing its length property:

```
document.write("colors length: ", colors.length, "<br>\n")
```

The result:

```
colors length: 3
```

Now let's add a color at the eighth position, index number seven (remember, arrays begin numbering at zero) and reexamine the length property.

```
colors [7] = "pink"
document.write("colors length: ", colors.length, "<br>\n")
```

This is perfectly legal in JavaScript. It results in

```
colors length: 8
```

Now the array's length is eight. A strongly typed language like Java would not allow you to do this. JavaScript, however, simply expands the array's length to encompass the newly added element. The elements at indices 3, 4, 5, and 6 have no value; they are undefined. Let's verify that by running the following code:

```
for (i=0; i<colors.length; i++) {
      document.write(i, ". ", colors[i], "<br>")
}
```

The result:

```
0. white
1. fuchsia
2. electric blue
3. undefined
4. undefined
5. undefined
6. undefined
7. pink
```

Here's the script in its entirety.

**Script 7.4      Dynamic Array Lengths**

```
1    <html>
2    <head>
3    <title>Script 7.4: Dynamic Array Lengths</title>
4    </head>
5    <body>
6    <script language="JavaScript" type="text/javascript"><!--
7          var colors = new Array(3)
8          colors[0] = "white"
9          colors[1] = "fuchsia"
10         colors[2] = "electric blue"
11         document.write("colors length: ", colors.length, "<br>\n")
12         document.write("colors contents: <br>")
13         for (i=0; i<colors.length; i++) {
14               document.write(i, ". ", colors[i], "<br>")
15         }
16         document.write("<br>")
17         document.write("Now let\'s add a color at the 8th
              position<br>")
18         colors [7] = "pink"
19         document.write("colors length: ", colors.length, "<br>\n")
20         document.write("colors contents: <br>")
21         for (i=0; i<colors.length; i++) {
22               document.write(i, ". ", colors[i], "<br>")
23         }
24   //-->
```

```
25    </script>
26    </body>
27    </html>
```

Run it to see the results yourself.

**Figure 7.6      Results of Script 7.4**

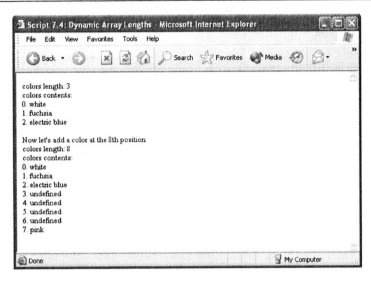

## Array Methods

JavaScript provides several methods that you can use to manipulate arrays. While some work well cross-browser and cross-platform, the rest work reliably only in the newest browsers. We'll look closely at those that are the most reliable. The syntax and a description for each `Array` method is listed in Table 7.1 at the end of this section.

### toString()

**Syntax:** *arrayName*.toString()

This method joins the elements of an array together and returns the resulting string. It does not affect the array itself. Every object in JavaScript has a `toString` method. An object's `toString` method is automatically called whenever you try to represent the object as text or concatenate it to text. For instance, try the following code:

```
var pets = new Array("Sam", "Devan", "Daisy")
document.write("Using pets: ", pets)
```

The result:

```
Using pets: Sam,Devan,Daisy
```

If you think about it, this perhaps should not have worked. We just called the `write` method to write out an object. The `write` method requires string parameters. However, JavaScript took care of it for us by calling the array's `toString` method, which converted the array to a string and returned that string's value to the `write` method. You can also call an object's `toString` method implicitly in your own code to quickly convert it to a string. The latter is the preferred method. Here are two examples:

```
document.write("Using pets.toString(): ", pets.toString())
var myPets = pets.toString()
```

The first line has the same results as our last example. The second line assigns the string returned by the `toString` method to the variable `myPets`.

Here's the whole thing together so you can test it yourself.

**Script 7.5    Using the *toStringArray* Method**

```
1    <html>
2    <head>
3    <title>Script 7.5: Using the toString Array Method</title>
4    </head>
5    <body>
6    <script language="JavaScript" type="text/javascript"><!--
7         var pets = new Array("Sam", "Devan", "Daisy")
8         document.write("Using pets: ", pets, "<br>")
9         document.write("Using pets.toString(): ",
10                         pets.toString(), "<br>")
11        var myPets = pets.toString()
12        document.write("Using myPets.toString(): ",
13                         myPets.toString(), "<br>")
14   //-->
15   </script>
16   </body>
17   </html>
```

Here are the results:

*Figure 7.7*     ***Results of Script 7.5***

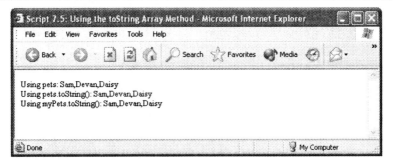

We'll use the toString method in future examples to quickly show the contents of our arrays after calling various methods.

## concat( )

**Syntax:**

*firstArrayName*.concat(*arrayToAdd1*[, *arrayToAdd2*, *arrayToAdd3*, ...])

It's often handy to be able to combine two or more arrays together into one, that is, to concatenate one or more arrays on to the end of another array. The concat method allows you to do just that. It does not change the array whose method you call.

To see how this works, let's create two arrays, concatenate the second array on to the first, and assign the result to a new array. Finally, we'll write the results.

```
var oldFriends = ["Janine", "Electra", "Mary", "Shellie"]
var newFriends = new Array("Adnan", "Jennifer", "April",
  "Scott")
var partyInvites = oldFriends.concat(newFriends)

document.write("partyInvites:<br>")
for(i=0; i<partyInvites.length; i++) {
      document.write(i, ". ", partyInvites[i], "<br>")
}
```

The results:

```
partyInvites:
0. Janine
1. Electra
2. Mary
3. Shellie
4. Adnan
5. Jennifer
6. April
7. Scott
```

Try writing the contents of oldFriends to verify that the array remains unchanged by the concat method call.

```
document.write("oldFriends: ", oldFriends.toString())
```

The result:

```
oldFriends:  Janine,Electra,Mary,Shellie
```

## join()

**Syntax:** *arrayName*.join([*separator*])
The join method is similar to the toString method. The main difference is that the join method allows you to optionally specify the delimiter or separator you want to appear between elements. If no separator is specified, the array elements are separated by a comma.

For example, let's use our oldFriends array defined previously and a few different delimiters:

```
document.write("join(\" \"): ", oldFriends.join(" "), "<br>")
document.write("join(\" and \"): ", oldFriends.join(" and "),
   "<br>")
document.write("join(): ", oldFriends.join(), "<br>")
```

The result:

```
join(" "): Janine Electra Mary Shellie
join(" and "): Janine and Electra and Mary and Shellie
join():  Janine,Electra,Mary,Shellie
```

We used a space as our separator in the first line of code and the word "and" with a space on each side in the second. In the third statement we did not specify a separator so the default, a comma, was used. One common use of the join method is to create a string of an array's contents by assigning the result of the join operation to a variable.

## reverse()

**Syntax:** *arrayName*.reverse()
This method reverses the order of the elements in an array. Be careful, because it actually modifies the array itself.

For example, using our oldFriends array again:

```
document.write("oldFriends originally: ",
   oldFriends.toString(), "<br>")
oldFriends.reverse()
document.write("oldFriends reversed: ",
   oldFriends.toString(), "<br>")
```

The result:

```
oldFriends originally: Janine,Electra,Mary,Shellie
oldFriends reversed: Shellie,Mary,Electra,Janine
```

Here is a script that incorporates the statements from concat, join, and reverse so you can test them for yourself:

***Script 7.6***   ***Using the Array Methods concat, join, and reverse***

```
1   <html>
2   <head>
3   <title>Script 7.6: Using Array Methods: concat, join, and
       reverse </title>
4   </head>
5   <body>
6   <script language="JavaScript" type="text/javascript"><!--
7       var oldFriends = ["Janine", "Electra", "Mary", "Shellie"]
8       var newFriends = new Array("Adnan", "Jennifer", "April",
          "Scott")
9
10      document.write("<h1>Using Array Methods</h1>")
11
12      document.write("<h2>concat</h2>")
13      var partyInvites = oldFriends.concat(newFriends)
14      document.write("partyInvites:<br>")
15      for(i=0; i<partyInvites.length; i++) {
16          document.write(i, ". ", partyInvites[i], "<br>")
17      }
18      document.write("<br>oldFriends: ", oldFriends.toString())
19
20      document.write("<h2>join</h2>")
21      document.write("join(\" \"): ", oldFriends.join(" "),
          "<br>")
22      document.write("join(\" and \"): ",
          oldFriends.join(" and "), "<br>")
23      document.write("join( ): ", oldFriends.join(), "<br>")
24      document.write("join(\" \"): ", newFriends.join(" "),
          "<br>")
25      document.write("join(\" and \"): ",
          newFriends.join(" and "), "<br>")
26      document.write("join( ): ", newFriends.join(), "<br>")
27
28      document.write("<h2>reverse</h2>")
29      document.write("oldFriends originally: ",
          oldFriends.toString(), "<br>")
30      oldFriends.reverse()
```

```
31      document.write("oldFriends reversed: ",
          oldFriends.toString(), "<br>")
32      document.write("newFriends originally: ",
          newFriends.toString(), "<br>")
33      newFriends.reverse()
34      document.write("newFriends reversed: ",
          newFriends.toString(), "<br>")
35  //-->
36  </script>
37  </body>
38  </html>
```

Here's what you should see:

**Figure 7.8    Results of Script 7.6**

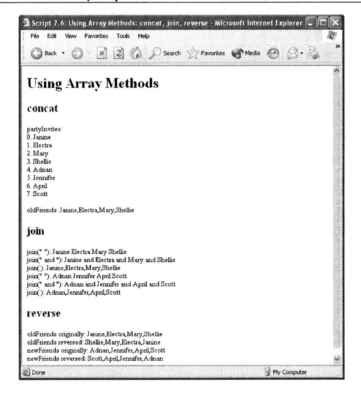

### sort()

**Syntax:** *arrayName*.sort([*compareFunction*])

By default, this method sorts the elements of an array lexicographically if no compare function is specified. **Lexicographically** means that elements are sorted alphabetically in "dictionary" or "telephone book" order by comparing them *as strings*. For instance, "50" comes before "6". Be careful, this method permanently changes the order of the array.

To show this, let's create a new array of mixed data types and a new array of numbers and sort each.

```
var mixedArray = new Array("hi", "Hi", "HI", -1.5, 9, 700.5,
                           700, 1, -1)
var numArray = new Array(9.75, -4, 1, 7.5, 3, 2, 9, -4.25,
                         11, 3, 8, 900)
mixedArray.sort()
numArray.sort()
document.write("mixedArray after sort: ",
   mixedArray.toString(), "<br>")
document.write("numArray after sort: ", numArray.toString(),
   "<br><br>")
```

The result:

```
mixedArray after sort: -1,-1.5,1,700,700.5,9,HI,Hi,hi
numArray after sort: -4,-4.25,1,11,2,3,3,7.5,8,9,9.75,900
```

That's nice, *if* you want to sort in dictionary order. But what if you want to sort numbers in numerical order? Don't worry, you're not stuck with lexicographic order, that's just the default. You can define your own custom compare function.

When a user-defined compare function is specified in the sort method call, the method orders elements according to the value returned by the compare function. Let's look at this more closely. Assume that a and b are two elements being compared, then:

- ✗ If *compareFunction*(a, b) returns a number less than 0, sort b to a lower index than a.
- ✗ If *compareFunction*(a, b) returns 0, leave a and b alone with respect to each other, but sorted with respect to all different elements.
- ✗ If *compareFunction*(a, b) returns a number greater than 0, sort b to a higher index than a.

In other words, any user-defined compare function should have the following form, where a and b are two values to compare:

```
function compareFunction(a, b) {
       if (a<b)                 // by some ordering criteria
             return -1
     if (a==b)
             return 0
     if (a>b)                 // by some ordering criteria
             return 1
}
```

The user-defined compare function's job is simple: it must accept two values, a and b, compare them, and then return a value that specifies which one, a or b, comes first. A value of -1 should be returned if a comes before b; a value of 0 should be returned if a and b are equal, that is, neither clearly comes before the other; and the function should return 1 if b comes first in the ordering.

When the compare function is called with an `Array`'s `sort` method, the `sort` method calls the user-defined compare function repeatedly to compare each adjacent pair in the array. This process is repeated until the array is completely sorted.

Allowing programmers to provide their own compare function to an `Array`'s `sort` method is pure genius. It allows programmers, like you, to perform infinite kinds of sorts.

Here's a simple example that lets you compare numbers instead of strings:

```
function compareNumbers(a, b) {
       return a - b
}
```

That seems too simple, huh? Let's look at it more closely.

Assume a = 8, b=10. Then 8 - 10 = -2, which is a number less than 0. So according to the rules of the compare function, b should be sorted to a lower index than a. In other words, b should come after a in the sorted list. Hey, it works!

Let's use our custom compare function, `compareNumbers`, on the lexicographically sorted `numArray` from above.

```
numArray.sort(compareNumbers)
document.write("numArray after sort(compareNumbers): <br>",
               numArray.toString(), "<br>")
```

The result:

```
numArray after sort(compareNumbers): -4.25,-4,1,2,3,3, ⟶
⟶  7.5,8,9,9.75,11,900
```

Ta da!—a successful numeric sort. It also works on strings that can be converted to numbers. Give it a try.

Here's the whole script:

**Script 7.7    Using the sort Method with Arrays**

```
1    <html>
2    <head>
3    <title>Script 7.7: Using the sort Method on Arrays</title>
4    <script language="JavaScript" type="text/javascript"><!--
5        var mixedArray = new Array("hi", "Hi", "HI", -1.5, 9, 700.5,
               700, 1, -1)
6        var numArray = new Array(9.75, -4, 1, 7.5, 3, 2, 9, -4.25,
               11, 3, 8, 900)
7
```

```
 8          function compareNumbers(a, b) {
 9              return a - b
10          }
11  //-->
12  </script>
13  </head>
14  <body>
15  <script language="JavaScript" type="text/javascript"><!--
16      document.write("mixedArray original: ",
17          mixedArray.toString(), "<br>")
       document.write("numArray original: ", numArray.toString(),
18          "<br><br>")

19      mixedArray.sort()
20      numArray.sort()
21      document.write("mixedArray after sort: ",
           mixedArray.toString(), "<br>")
22      document.write("numArray after sort: ", numArray.toString(),
           "<br><br>")

24      numArray.sort(compareNumbers)
25      document.write("numArray after sort(compareNumbers): <br>",
26      numArray.toString(), "<br>")
27  //-->
28  </script>
29  </body>
30  </html>
```

Here's what it should look like when you run it:

**Figure 7.9      Results of Script 7.7**

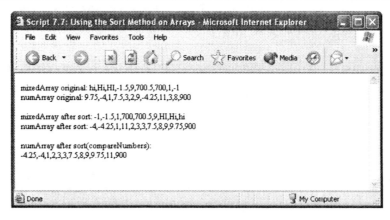

## slice()

**Syntax:** *arrayName*.slice(*beginIndex*[, *endIndex*])
The slice method returns an extracted segment of an array as a new array. It does not modify the original array. slice begins at the beginning index specified and extracts up to, but not including, the end index specified. If no end index is specified, slice extracts the elements from the beginning index to the end of the array. If the end index specified is negative, it indicates the offset from the end of the array.

For example:

```
var zList = new Array("item0", "item1", "item2", "item3",
                      "item4", "item5", "item6", "item7")
document.write("slice(2,4) = ", zList.slice(2,4), "<br>")
document.write("slice(2,-1) = ", zList.slice(2,-1), "<br>")
document.write("slice(2) = ", zList.slice(2), "<br>")
```

The result:

```
slice(2,4) = item2,item3
slice(2,-1) = item2,item3,item4,item5,item6
slice(2) = item2,item3,item4,item5,item6,item7
```

## A Summary of Array Methods

The following table summarizes JavaScript's currently defined array methods.

**Table 7.1        Array Methods**

| Method | Description |
| --- | --- |
| concat(*array2* [, *array3*,...]) | Concatenates two or more arrays and returns the result as a new array. |
| join([*separator*]) | Returns all of the elements of an array joined together in a single string delimited by an optional separator; if no separator is specified, a comma is inserted between elements. |
| pop( ) | Removes and returns the last element of an array. |
| push(*element1* [, *element2*, . . . ] ) | Appends one or more elements on to the end of an array and returns the array's new length. |
| reverse( ) | Reverses the order of an array. This method actually modifies the array. |
| shift( ) | Removes and returns the first element of an array. |
| slice(*beginIndex* [, *endIndex*] ) | Returns an extracted segment of an array as a new array. |

| | |
|---|---|
| sort ( [*compareFn*] ) | Sorts the elements of an array. This method actually modifies the array. |
| splice (*startIndex*, *howMany* [, *element1*, . . . ] ) | Modifies the contents of an array by adding and/or removing elements. It returns the items removed. This method is quite powerful. |
| toString ( ) | Returns the array converted to a string; elements are delimited by a comma. |
| unshift (*element1* [, *element2*, . . . ]) | Inserts one or more elements at the front of the array and returns the new length. Note: IE 5.5 does not return the new length. |

## A String Method That Is Useful for Arrays

While we're on the subject of arrays and their methods, it's a good time to talk about a String method that can come in handy when working with arrays: split.

### split ("*delimiter*"[, *maxElements*])

The split method works in the opposite way of an Array's join method. Remember that join returns a string containing the elements of an array delimited by a delimiter of the programmer's choice. The split method, on the other hand, starts with a string of delimited values and returns an array. You do not have to use the new Array() constructor, simply declare a variable, and split takes care of the rest. Here's an example:

```
var friends = "Rosemarie,Jana,April,Shellie"
var friendsArray = friends.split(",")
document.write("friends: ", friends, "<br>")
document.write("friendsArray: <br>")
for(i=0; i<friendsArray.length; i++) {
    document.write(i, ". ", friendsArray[i], "<br>")
}
```

The result:

```
friends: Rosemarie,Jana,April,Shellie
friendsArray:
0. Rosemarie
1. Jana
2. April
3. Shellie
```

Pretty cool, huh? You can also specify a second parameter: the maximum number of elements the generated array may contain a regular expression to use

**peek ahead**
You'll get to see regular expressions in action in Chapter 9, "Manipulating Strings."

to split up the string. A **regular expression** is a pattern-matching device that defines a pattern of text via a series of characters and symbols. Web programmers often use them when working with Perl and PHP to process and sometimes format strings of data. They're also quite useful for performing form validations with JavaScript.

# Parallel Arrays

You can easily define parallel arrays in JavaScript to solve many problems. **Parallel arrays** are two or more arrays whose elements are related to each other by their respective positions.

For example, you could define a set of parallel arrays containing the names, identification numbers, and grades of students in a class:

```
var students = new Array("Adnan", "Deanna", "Robert", "Tom")
var ids = new Array(178, 122, 107, 155)
var grades = new Array("C", "A", "A", "B")
```

In the above set of arrays, ids [2] represents the ID number for Robert (students [2]), and grades [2] represents Robert's grade. Let's write out the contents of the arrays to a table using a for loop:

```
document.write("<h1>Student Grade Report</h1>")
document.write("<table border=1>")
document.write("<tr><th>Student</th><th>ID</th>",
                "<th>Grade</th></tr>")
for (i=0; i<students.length; i++) {
        document.write("<tr><td>", students[i], "</td>",
                        "<td>", ids[i], "</td>",
                        "<td>", grades[i], "</td></tr>")
}
document.write("</table>")
```

Figure 7.10 shows the result of this script:

In Chapter 16, we'll see how we can create a custom object to achieve the same objective as that achieved with parallel arrays.

*peek ahead*

***Figure 7.10*** ***Results of the Parallel Arrays Script***

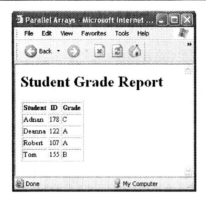

## Copying Arrays

There are times when you'll want to copy an array. For instance, before you sort an array, which changes the array permanently, you might first want to make a copy of it and sort the copy instead, especially if the array you want to sort is one of a set of parallel arrays. So how do you copy an array?

Copying values from one variable to another is simply a matter of assignment:

```
variable1 = variable2
```

No biggie. The value of `variable2` is copied to `variable1`. If you change the value of `variable1`, `variable2` is not affected and vice versa. Each is an independent value.

With arrays, however, it is not quite so simple. When you assign an array to another array, you actually create another reference to the original array, rather than a copy of it. For example:

```
var cups = new Array("lemonade", "orange juice", "iced tea")
var glasses = new Array()

glasses = cups
document.write("cups array: ", cups.toString(), "<br>")
document.write("glasses array: ", glasses.toString(), "<br>")
```

The result:

```
cups array: lemonade,orange juice,iced tea
glasses array: lemonade,orange juice,iced tea
```

It *appears* that we were successful in creating a copy of the cups array in `glasses`. Not so. We've actually only created another reference to the cups array. Watch what happens when we modify an element of the cups array.

```
cups[2] = "Dr. Pepper"
document.write("cups array: ", cups.toString(), "<br>")
document.write("glasses array: ", glasses.toString(), "<br>")
```

The result:

```
cups array: lemonade,orange juice,Dr. Pepper
glasses array: lemonade,orange juice,Dr. Pepper
```

See how glasses reported the change too? That's because glasses is just another name for the cups array. Let's see what happens when we make a change to glasses:

```
glasses[0] = "7-up"
document.write("cups array: ", cups.toString(), "<br>")
document.write("glasses array: ", glasses.toString(), "<br>")
```

The result:

```
cups array: 7-up,orange juice,Dr. Pepper
glasses array: 7-up,orange juice,Dr. Pepper
```

See how cups changed? glasses and cups refer to the same array.

So how *do* you make a real copy of an array? The answer is to copy the contents of the original array element by element to a new array. A for loop comes in very handy. Here's the general form:

```
var originalArray = new Array("item1", "item2", "item3",...)
var copyArray = new Array(originalArray.length)


for (i=0; i<originalArray.length; i++) {
    copyArray[i] = originalArray[i]
}
```

Here's a script that copies the contents of the cups array to the glasses array element by element.

**Script 7.8     CopyingArrays**

```
1    <html>
2    <head>
3    <title>Script 7.8: Copying Arrays</title>
4    <script language="JavaScript" type="text/javascript"><!--
5        var cups = new Array("lemonade", "orange juice", "iced tea")
6        var glasses = new Array(cups.length)
7
8        for (i=0; i<cups.length; i++) {
9            glasses[i] = cups[i]
10           }
```

```
11   //-->
12   </script>
13   </head>
14   <body>
15   <script language="JavaScript" type="text/javascript"><!--
16       document.write("cups array: ", cups.toString(), "<br>")
17       document.write("glasses array: ", glasses.toString(),
            "<br><br>")
18
19       cups[2] = "Dr. Pepper"
20       document.write("cups array: ", cups.toString(), "<br>")
21       document.write("glasses array: ", glasses.toString(),
            "<br><br>")
22   //-->
23   </script>
24   </body>
25   </html>
```

Let's test it.

**Figure 7.11    Results of Script 7.8**

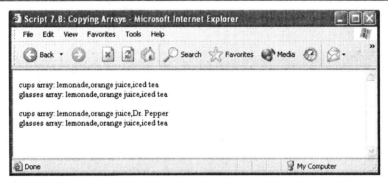

This time glasses didn't change after the modification to cups. This is exactly what we wanted in the first place.

When an array element is assigned to another array element or a variable, the value is assigned. When an array *object* is assigned to a variable, the variable becomes a reference to the original object.

# Client-Side JavaScript Predefined Arrays

Before we leave the topic of arrays, let's look at a list of the predefined arrays in Client-Side JavaScript. Most of Client-Side JavaScript's power comes from its ability to access objects in the browser and Web documents, many of which get stored in the following arrays.

**Table 7.2    *Predefined Arrays in Client-Side JavaScript***

| Array | Description |
| --- | --- |
| document.anchors | Reflects all of the <a name=> tags in a document in source order. |
| document.applets | Reflects all of the <applet> tags in a document in source order. |
| Function.arguments | Reflects all of the arguments to a function. |
| *form*.elements | Reflects a form's elements in source order, for example radio buttons, checkboxes, text fields, etc. |
| document.embeds | Reflects a document's <embed> tags in source order. |
| document.forms | Reflects a document's <form> tags in source order. |
| *window*.frames | Reflects all the <frame> tags in a window containing a <frameset> tag in source order. |
| history | Reflects a window's history entries. Note: This is the short history list used by the Back and Forward buttons, not the full history list. |
| document.images | Reflects a document's <img> tags in source order. Does not include images created with the Image() constructor. |
| document.links | Reflects a document's <a href="..."> tags and <area href="..."> tags in source order. Link objects created with the link method are also included. |
| navigator.mimeTypes | Reflects all the MIME types supported by the client, including those supported via plug-ins, helper applications, or the browser. |
| *form.select*.options | Reflects all the options in a select as a tag element (<option> tags) in source order. |
| document.plugins navigator.plugins | Reflects all the plug-ins installed on the client in source order. |

As you can see, most of the arrays are properties of the document object.

**peek ahead**

We'll make use of many of these arrays in the next section and future chapters. Script 7.9 uses the document.links array. In Chapter 10, we'll use the frames array to access individual frames. In Chapters 12 and 13, we'll use the forms, elements, and options arrays to perform calculations and data validations.

## The Links Array

### Creating a Reference List

To demonstrate how we might use these predefined arrays, let's write a script that will print a reference list of all of the links in a document at the bottom of the page in a reference section. Here goes:

*Script 7.9     Creating a Reference List*

```
1    <html>
2    <head>
3    <title>Script 7.9: Creating a Reference List</title>
4    </head>
5    <body>
6    <h1>Directories and Search Engines</h1>
7    Directories and search engines are excellent tools that can help
8    you find information quickly on the Internet. The oldest and
9    largest directory by far is
        <a href="http:/www.yahoo.com/">Yahoo!</a>. One
10   of the most popular search engines today is
11   <a href="http://www.google.com/">Google</a>. Google ranks pages by
12   popularity, that is, how often people have clicked on a particular
13   hit. <a href="http://www.askjeeves.com/">Ask Jeeves</a> allows
14   visitors to enter their queries as normal English sentences and
        questions.
15
16   <h2>References:</h2>
17   <ul>
18   <script language="JavaScript" type="text/javascript"><!--
19       numLinks = document.links.length
20       for (i=0; i<numLinks; i++) {
21           document.write("<li><a href=\"",
               document.links[i].href, "\">",
22               document.links[i].text, "</a></li>")
23       }
24   //-->
25   </script>
26   </ul>
27   </body>
28   </html>
```

This is what you should get in Netscape and Opera:

**Figure 7.12   Results of Script 7.9**

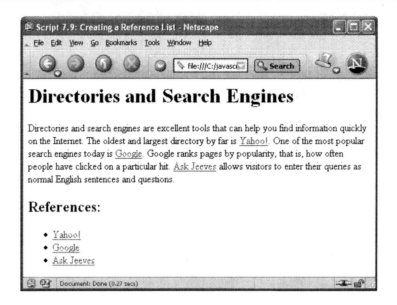

Unfortunately, Internet Explorer doesn't support the `text` property of the `link` object, which allows access to the clickable text. For IE, you can modify the script slightly and use the `href` property as the clickable part of the link written in the reference section as well as the `href` attribute for the link. Then the script will work in all three browsers.

Before we leave the subject of arrays, we need to look at one last item: the `delete` operator.

# The `delete` Operator

The **delete** operator applies only to arrays and objects. It allows you to completely remove an element from an array and to delete entire arrays.

When you remove an element from an array with the `delete` operator, JavaScript *does not* collapse the array over the missing element and renumber the elements accordingly. Instead, that array element becomes `undefined`; any attempt to evaluate that element results in `undefined`. Let's look at an example and see if we can clarify this further.

**Script 7.10   Using the `delete` Operator**

```
1    <html>
2    <head>
3    <title>Script 7.10: Using the delete Operator</title>
4    <script language="JavaScript" type="text/javascript"><!--
5        var cups = new Array("lemonade", "orange juice", "iced tea",
6                             "Dr. Pepper", "Pepsi")
7    //-->
```

```
8   </script>
9   </head>
10  <body>
11  <script language="JavaScript" type="text/javascript"><!--
12       document.write("Original cups Array: <br>")
13       document.write("Length: ", cups.length, "<br>")
14       for(i=0; i<cups.length; i++) {
15            document.write(i, ". ", cups[i], "<br>")
16        }
17
18        delete cups[1]
19
20        document.write("<br>Array After Deleting cups[1]: <br>")
21        document.write("Length: ", cups.length, "<br>")
22        for(i=0; i<cups.length; i++) {
23            document.write(i, ". ", cups[i], "<br>")
24        }
25  //-->
26  </script>
27  </body>
28  </html>
```

Run Script 7.10. This is what you should get:

**Figure 7.13     Results of Script 7.10**

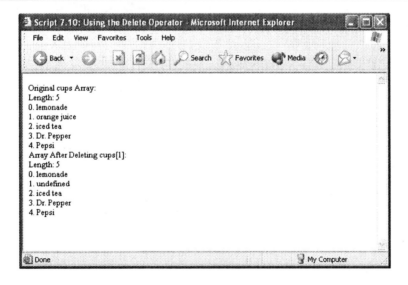

Notice that the array's length remains unchanged. An array's length is not affected by a `delete` operation, even if the element deleted is at the end of the array. Associative array index names can also be used to indicate an array element to delete.

To delete an entire array, simply use the `delete` operator followed by the array's name. For example:

```
delete cups
```

## Summary

Arrays are similar to variables in that they are holding places in memory. However, whereas a variable holds a single data value, an array can hold multiple data values, usually related and of the same data type. An `Array` can be declared in three ways: by simply declaring it, using the `new` operator and the `Array()` constructor function and, usually, specifying the array's length as a parameter; by creating a dense array, that is, declaring and initializing the array in one fell swoop, also with the `Array()` constructor function; or by assigning an array literal to a variable. It is considered good form to give arrays plural names.

A particular array element can be accessed and set via the array's name, followed by an index number that represents the element's place in the array enclosed in brackets: `cups[2]`. Arrays and `for` loops work hand in hand with each other. A `for` loop's ability to iterate a set number of times, which number can be provided by an array's `length` property, allows programmers to perform a task, repetitively working through an entire array, for instance, printing out a list of array elements.

Associative arrays provide a means to access array elements by their textual name. Array lengths in JavaScript are dynamic. It is quite easy to add additional elements to an array.

JavaScript supports several useful `Array` methods that allow programmers to convert arrays to strings, slice and dice them, join two or more arrays together, push elements on to the beginning or end of an array, pop elements off of the end or beginning of an array, and to sort, reverse, and even delete array elements. Copying arrays is a little more complicated than copying the values of variables: array elements must be copied one at a time to the new array.

Client-Side JavaScript supports many predefined arrays, including those that represent the links in a Web page, the images in a Web page, the frames in a window, the arguments of a function, and the elements of a form. Using these predefined arrays, programmers can perform many useful tasks and add interactivity to their Web sites.

## Review Questions

1.  What's an array?
2.  How is an array different from, yet like, a variable?
3.  What is an array index?
4.  What does it mean to "declare an array"?
5.  What does it mean to "populate an array"?
6.  How do you access individual array elements?

7. Why are `for` loops and arrays the perfect team?
8. What property of an Array object returns the number of elements contained within the array?
9. What is a dense array?
10. How do you create a dense array?
11. What is an array literal?
12. How do you create an array literal?
13. What is an associative array?
14. Describe an instance when accessing an array element using its name might be easier or preferred over accessing it via its ordinal index number.
15. Are array lengths static in JavaScript? Explain your answer.
16. How is the `toString` method useful with arrays?
17. What's the difference between the `toString` and `join` methods?
18. What does the `concat` array method do? Does it change the original array?
19. Do any array methods modify the original array? If so, name two.
20. Why must you be careful when using methods that modify an array itself?
21. What does the `slice` method do?
22. What string method can be very useful for turning a string into an array?
23. List and describe three array methods you think you might use.
24. What are parallel arrays? Give an example when you might find them useful.
25. Why can't you copy an array like this:

$$arrayCopy = originalArray$$

Explain your answer.
26. What does the `delete` operator do? When used, does it change the length of an array? Explain.
27. Create two lists. The first should list the array methods that actually change the array on which the method is called. The second should list the methods that do not modify the original array on which the method is called.

## Exercises

1. Write a JavaScript statement to declare an array that will contain seven elements.
2. Declare the same array in Exercise 1 in another way.
3. Write a statement to assign a value to the fifth element of the array you declared in Exercise 1.
4. Write a statement to write the value of the fifth element of the array declared in Exercise 1 to a Web page.
5. Write a JavaScript statement to declare a dense array called `cats` with the following elements: Piwacket, Frisky, Tomasina, Aradia, Daphne, Cassiopia, Devan, and Daisy.
6. Write an example of an array literal.
7. Write a statement to declare the array described in Exercise 5, this time using an array literal.

8. Write a short script to prove that array lengths are dynamic in JavaScript.
9. Write a statement to access an image named Sam from the document's images array.
10. Write a statement to write the name of the image named Sam. Use its index name in the document's images associative array to access the image.
11. Assume that Sam, an image, is the third image in the current document. Write a statement to access its `src` property using its ordinal array index.
12. The `splice` array method is quite powerful. Using one of the arrays you declared in a previous exercise, experiment with the `splice` method. Try to replace two or three elements in the middle of the array.
13. Declare two arrays of your choice and populate them. Using an appropriate array method, join the two arrays into one.
14. Using one of the arrays you declared earlier, make a copy of that array and sort it alphabetically.
15. Using one of the arrays you declared earlier, write a script to join the array elements into a string, such that when that string is printed to a Web document it will print an unordered list of items. You can use a `write` statement before and after the statement that writes the joined array string to start and end the unordered list (<ul>).

## Scripting Exercises

Create a folder named assignment07 to hold the documents you create during this assignment. Save a copy of the personal home page you last modified as home.html in the assignment07 folder. Save a copy of the toy store home page you last modified as toyStore.html in the assignment07 folder.

1. Create a new document named books.html.
   a. Create and populate an array of your seven most favorite books in order. The first book listed should be your most favorite.
   b. Write a `for` loop to display your favorite books, in order, beginning with number one in the document. Do not modify the array. Your list should look similar to this:
      1. *Daughter of the Empire*
      2. *We the Living*
      3. *JavaScript Concepts & Techniques*
2. Add a parallel array to books.html that contains the names of the authors that correspond with the books array you created in Scripting Exercise 1.
   a. Write a `for` loop to display your favorite books and their authors, in order, beginning with number one in the document. Your list should look similar to this:
      1. *Daughter of the Empire* by Raymond Feist and Janny Wurts
      2. *We the Living* by Ayn Rand
      3. *JavaScript Concepts & Techniques* by Tina Spain McDuffie

    b. Add a section to one of the documents in your personal home page named "Favorite Books."

    c. Copy your script and arrays there to display your favorite books.

3. Create a new document named planets.html.

    a. Create a set of parallel arrays representing

        i. the names of the planets in our solar system in order of distance from the sun, starting with Mercury

        ii. their associated masses

        iii. their diameters

        iv. any other properties you think appropriate or of interest

    b. Write a script that uses a `for` loop to write each planet name in a heading tag followed by a paragraph of text that describes the planet. Utilize the parallel arrays you created to write the descriptive information for each planet.

4. Create a new document named products.html.

    a. Create a string of at least 10 toy names using the delimiter of your choice.

    b. Using the split string method, convert the string of values to an array.

    c. Write a script to display the list of toys in the document as a bulleted list. Make each toy name a link to a Web document of the same name that provides more information on that toy.

5. Create a new document named sitemap.html.

    a. Create an array of at least 10 toys in order of their popularity. You decide which are the best-sellers.

    b. Under the heading "Most Popular Toys," write a script that displays the toys in a numbered list (use HTML <ol> and <li> tags).

    c. Make a copy of the array.

    d. Sort the copy alphabetically.

    e. Add another section to the document, this one named "Toys, A-Z."

    f. Write a script to display the toys in alphabetical order. Do not preface each toy name with bullets or numbers, just list each on its own line.

6. Create a new document named sortingNumbers.html.

    a. Declare and populate an array of numbers.

    b. Write a script to sort the array in ascending numeric order.

    c. Write a script to sort the array in descending numeric order.

7. Create a Web page with at least five images in it. You can download them from an online clip-art library. Develop a script that will write the `alt` attribute of each image followed by the image's source in a bulleted reference list at the end of the document. For example:

**Illustrations**

    ✗ Map to our house: images/map.gif

    ✗ Me and my hubby, Tim: images/tNt.jpg

    ✗ Sam, my dog: images/sam.jpg

✗ Me lounging by the pool: images/mePool.jpg

✗ Sam and Levi: images/samNlevi.jpg

8.  Create a new document named students.html.

    a.  Discover the names of five students in your class.

    b.  Declare an array and populate it with their names.

    c.  Create another array, this time an associative array that contains each student's phone number and is indexed by the students' names.

    d.  Sort the students array in alphabetical order.

    e.  Using a `for` loop, write the students' names and their phone numbers in alphabetical order by student name, one student per line.

9.  Copy the script you wrote in Scripting Exercise 5 in Chapter 6, guess.html, as youGuessed.html.

    a.  Create an empty array named guesses.

    b.  Modify the script so that it keeps track of each guess the visitor makes in the guesses array.

    c.  When the visitor finally guesses successfully, display or write to the document a list of the guesses the visitor made and the total count.

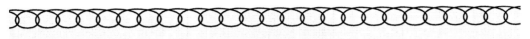

## chapter **eight**

# *Functions and Libraries*

*program - A set of instruc-tions, given to the com-puter, describing the sequence of steps the computer performs in order to accomplish a specific task. The task must be specific, such as balanc-ing your checkbook or editing your text. A gen-eral task, such as working for world peace, is some-thing we can all do, but not something we can currently write programs to do.*

—From *Unix User's Manual, Supplementary Documents*

Throughout this book, we've developed many routines that you are likely to use again and again. Wouldn't it be nice to be able to write them once, debug them, and then use them over and over again in different scripts without having to make any modifications? Sort of like plug-and-play scripts? Well, you can! That's where functions and libraries come in.

While we introduced functions in Chapter 4, we haven't really gotten into the nitty-gritty details of functions. In this chapter, we'll

- review what a function is, how to define a function, and how to call it.
- look at function parameters and how they can make our functions more reusable.
- look closer at returning a value from a func-tion.
- discuss the difference between global and local variables.
- see where to place functions for optimal performance.
- look at the window methods set Timeout and set Interval.

❧ look more closely at the Image object.

❧ learn how to preload images so they're immediately available for rollover effects.

❧ learn how to create an Image object and assign its src in one line of code.

Let's begin with a quick review of what a function is, how you declare one, and how you call one.

# Review: What Is a Function?

Recall from Chapter 4 that a function is a block of predefined programming statements whose execution is deferred until the function is "called." You call a function by invoking its name, along with any required or optional parameters. Function parameters, also known as arguments, are data values or data references that you pass to a function; the function then uses and/or modifies those data values or references during its execution. Parameters make functions more versatile. We saw an example of this in the greetVisitor function that accepted a string argument representing a visitor's name and used that name to pop up an alert with a custom greeting.

Another feature that makes functions versatile is their ability to optionally return a value or a reference to a value, that is, they can do some processing and give back a result. In Chapter 4, we saw a function named calcRectangleArea that accepted the width and height of a rectangle and then calculated and returned the area.

JavaScript supports several *types* of function. Let's take a look at them.

# Types of Functions

In JavaScript, there are basically four types of functions:

1.  **Predefined functions**: functions predefined by the JavaScript language but not associated with any particular object. Examples: parseInt(), isNaN(), and eval().

2.  **Predefined methods**: functions predefined by the JavaScript language and associated with objects that have also been predefined by the language. Examples: window.open(), document.write(), and someDate.getDate().

3.  **User-defined functions, really user-defined window methods**: functions defined by a programmer, often called user-defined functions. However, when a programmer declares a function in JavaScript, he or she is actually defining a method of the window object. So, technically, a user-defined function is really a user-defined window method. Examples: helloWorld(), greetVisitor(), calcAreaRectangle(), and SurfWin.hello().

4.  **User-defined methods**: functions defined by a programmer and associated with a particular object, usually a user-defined object. Example: student.setGrade().

In this chapter, we'll focus on user-defined functions, which technically are user-defined window methods. After all, we have no control over JavaScript's predefined functions and methods, and we need to learn how to write functions to suit our own needs and purposes.

We'll save our discussion of declaring user-defined methods for objects other than the `window` object until Chapter 16.

Keep in mind that all functions have two optional characteristics. They may or may not accept parameters and they may or may not return a value. Some languages, such as Visual Basic, differentiate between a *procedure*, a block of deferred statements that performs some task, and a *function*, a block of deferred statements that performs some task *and* returns a value. In JavaScript, like C, a procedure and a function are one and the same: a function.

**peek ahead**

We'll discuss the association of our user-defined `window` methods with a particular window in detail in Chapter 11, "Windows and Frames."

We'll cover defining methods for user-defined objects in Chapter 16.

# The Best Function-Programming Practices

Before we get into more detail about defining and calling functions, there are a few rules you should keep in mind. While these rules are not set in stone, they are considered good programming practices:

1.  A well-written function performs one task and one task alone.
2.  A well-written function stands on its own and causes no side effects to variables or objects outside its scope.
3.  A well-written function is well documented with comments, including what the function does, what input it requires, and what output, if any, it returns.

# Defining and Calling Functions

So how do we define a function? Before defining a function you first need to answer three questions:

1.  What task is the function to perform?
2.  Does the function require any outside data (parameters) to perform its task?
3.  Does the function need to return a value or should it just execute some statements?

## Defining a FunctionWithout Parameters

Once you've answered the above questions, defining the function is pretty simple and straightforward: use the function keyword, followed by the function's name, followed by a set of parentheses and a set of braces containing the function's deferred statements.

```
function functionName() {
    statements
}
```

The naming rules for functions are the same as those for naming variables:

✗ Function names may not contain any punctuation, except the underscore (_). Only letters, numbers, and the underscore are valid characters in a function name.

✕ Function names may not begin with a number. They must start with a letter or an underscore (_).

✕ Function names may not contain spaces.

✕ Reserved words may not be used as function names.

✕ Predefined object, property, method, and built-in function names are also off limits.

Here's the requisite "Hello, World" example:

```
function helloWorld() {
        document.write("Hello, World!")
}
```

The `helloWorld` function above does not accept any parameters, nor does it return a value. Its task is to simply write the message "Hello, World!" to the document when called. It is important to note that where you place this and all function definitions matters.

## The Appropriate Placement of Function Definitions

Function definition placement is crucial. A function definition needs to be placed such that the function gets defined and read into memory *before* it is called to work. Can you think of a good place that meets that criterion? Here's a hint: it's the part of a Web document that always loads *before* the <body>. You guessed it: the <head>.

So to make certain your functions are defined and ready for use, always declare them in the <head> of the HTML document. You can also put them in an external script, just make sure the <script> tag that links them to the document is in the <head> and before any statements that call the function.

## Calling a Simple Function

To call a function that has no parameters, simply invoke its name:

```
functionName()
```

Don't forget the parentheses at the end! You can always tell functions and methods from variables and objects because they always end in a set of parentheses.

You can call `helloWorld` by invoking its name:

```
helloWorld()
```

Keep in mind that where you *call* a function also matters. For instance, if your function will execute any `document.write` statements, then it must be called within the <body> of an HTML document; it is illegal to write content in the <head> of an HTML document. From what section of the HTML document should `helloWorld` be called? Yep, you guessed it, the <body>, because it contains a `document.write` statement and any Web page content must be placed in the <body> of an HTML document.

## Defining and Calling a Function with Parameters

As we discussed earlier, the original `greetVisitor` function is pretty limited in what it can do. Because we don't know exactly whom we'll need to greet when we define the function, we'll need a variable to act as a placeholder for the visitor's name in our function. This variable will be a *parameter* of our function.

Now that we've decided we need to send a value to the function, in this case visitor, we need to know the proper syntax for declaring a function with one or more parameters. Here's the general form:

```
function functionName([param1, param2, param3, ... paramN]) {
    statements
}
```

Notice that the variable names of the parameters are placed within the parentheses and are separated by commas. It is considered good programming practice to use descriptive parameter names that give the programmer and any future programmers a clear idea of the type and nature of any function parameters.

Let's now declare a `greetByName` function that will accept `visitorName` as a parameter. `visitorName` is a good name because it clearly describes the type of data needed by the function: a visitor's name.

```
function greetByName(visitorName) {
    alert("Hello, " + visitorName + "!")
}
```

To see if it works, let's call it. When we call it, we must send in an argument that will be stored in the `visitorName` placeholder variable:

```
greetByName("Sam")
```

If we typed everything correctly, an alert should pop up with the message "Hello, Sam!" Cool, huh?

Let's try calling our function again, this time using a different argument:

```
greetByName("Devan")
```

Try it for yourself. Now our function greets Devan.

There are a variety of ways that we can acquire the visitor's name. For instance, we could prompt the visitor for his name. Here's a complete script that does just that:

**Script 8.1**   *Defining and Calling a Function with Parameters*

```
1   <html>
2   <head>
3   <title>Script 8.1: Defining &amp; Calling a Function with
4   Parameters </title>
5   <script language="JavaScript" type="text/javascript"><!--
```

```
6          function greetByName(visitorName) {
7                  alert("Hello, " + visitorName + "!")
8          }
9   //-->
10  </script>
11  </head>
12  <body>
13  <script language="JavaScript" type="text/javascript"><!--
14          var visitor = prompt("What\'s your name?", "")
15          greetByName(visitor)
16  //-->
17  </script>
18  </body>
19  </html>
```

Here's what it looks like when you run it.

**Figure 8.1     Prompting the Visitor in Script 8.1**

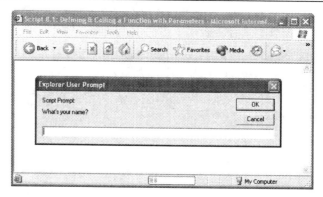

**Figure 8.2     Results of Function Call in Script 8.1**

In this example, we first defined the greetByName function in the <head> of the document (lines 6 through 8). We stored the result of the prompt in the variable visitor (line 14), then used visitor as an argument to the greetByName function call (line 15).

When greetByName was called, the value of visitor was assigned to visitorName, a parameter of the greetByName function. The greetByName function then used visitorName to perform its greeting function. Let's examine this more closely.

## Passing by Value (primitive data types)

Thus far, we've passed arguments to our functions only by value. When we called greetByName("Sam"), the argument "Sam" was passed to the greetByName parameter visitorName. It might be easier to think of this as an assignment, in which case the value "Sam" was assigned to the variable visitorName. Here's a picture of what happened:

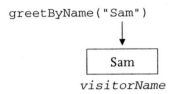

When we use the variable, visitor, as an argument, we again pass by value. Let's say the visitor enters "Tim":

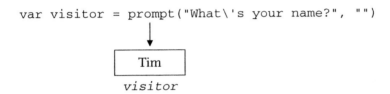

Now we call greetByName:

greetByName(visitor)

Whenever primitive data types are used as arguments to function calls, those arguments are passed *by value*, that is, the function receives the actual value of the argument and stores that value in its parameter variable. The value of the variable used as an argument remains unchanged by the function call. Here's an illustration of this concept:

**Script 8.2      Passing by Value**

```
1    <html>
2    <head>
3    <title>Script 8.2: Passing By Value</title>
4    <script language="JavaScript" type="text/javascript"><!--
5         function greetByProgrammerName(firstName) {
6              firstName = "Programmer " + firstName
7              alert("Hello, " + firstName)
8         }
9    //-->
10   </script>
11   </head>
12   <body>
13   <script language="JavaScript" type="text/javascript"><!--
14        var visitor = prompt("What\'s your name?", "")
15        greetByProgrammerName(visitor)
16        document.write("Visitor is unchanged: ", visitor)
17        document.write("firstName\'s value: ", firstName)
18   //-->
19   </script>
20   </body>
21   </html>
```

This isn't the best example of a function, but it does illustrate an important point. The argument `visitor` passed to the function remains unchanged after the function call. Only the function's `firstName` variable changed, as you can see here:

**Figure 8.3      Results of Script 8.2**

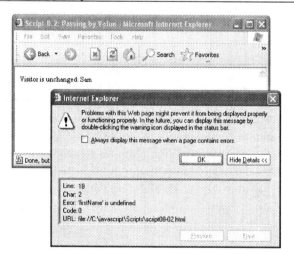

The reason `visitor` remained unchanged is because its *value* was passed to the `firstName` parameter of the `greetByProgrammerName` function. The `firstName` parameter acts as a local variable. A local variable is a variable that can only be affected, and only *works*, in a particular area of the program, usually within the block of the function for which it is a parameter or declared as a variable. In this case, that area is within the `greetByProgrammerName` function block, within the braces. Outside of the function, `firstName` is undefined, which is why we received the runtime error shown in Figure 8.3. In line 17, `firstName` is undefined because it is a local variable for the `greetByProgrammerName` function; `firstName` has meaning only within the function, lines 5 through 8.

Primitive data types *always* pass by value. However, composite data types such as arrays and other objects do not. Composite data types pass by reference.

## Passing by Reference (composite data types)

An important concept to understand—and to be careful of—about functions is that whenever you pass composite data types such as objects as arguments to a function, you pass the actual object itself. The parameter name becomes another *reference* to the object passed; that is, the parameter name becomes another name by which the object can be referred to. Anything you do to the parameter in the function affects the original object.

Remember in Chapter 7 when we tried to copy an array simply by assigning it to another variable? Instead of making a copy, we created another reference to the original array. When we modified the contents using the newly created reference, we modified the original array. Same idea here. The parameter name simply becomes another reference to the object passed. This can have some nasty side effects.

**peek ahead** We'll see an example of a function returning a reference to an object in Script 8.7 later in this chapter.

Please don't get the idea that passing by reference is always a bad thing. It's not. In fact, passing by reference is a valuable and necessary capability of any sophisticated programming language. Not only does it save memory and time by eliminating the need to copy large amounts of data, it can also be empowering. For instance, you could pass an array to a function and have the function fill the array with data without resorting to global variables or wasting precious memory space needlessly with a copy of the array. Cool, huh?

## Declaring a Function to Return a Value

If a function needs to return a value, you need to include a `return` statement in your function, usually as the last line. A function can have more than one `return` statement, each defined for a particular condition, but only one `return` statement can execute and only one value or object can be returned.

```
function functionName(param1, param2, param3) {
    statements
    return someValue
}
```

Here's a real-world example that will return the maximum of two values:

**Script 8.3     *Returning a Value***

```
1    <html>
2    <head>
3    <title>Script 8.3: Returning a Value</title>
4    <script language="JavaScript" type="text/javascript"><!--
5          function getMax(num1, num2) {
6              if(num1 >= num2) {
7                  return num1
8              } else {
9                  return num2
10             }
11         }
12   //-->
13   </script>
14   </head>
15   <body>
16   <script language="JavaScript" type="text/javascript"><!--
17         document.write("The max of 8 and 15 is: ",
              getMax(8, 15), "<br>")
18         document.write("The max of 8 and 7 is: ",
              getMax(8, 7), "<br>")
19         document.write("The max of -9 and 17 is: ",
              getMax(-9, 17), "<br>")
20         document.write("The max of 1.1 and 1 is: ",
              getMax(1.1, 1), "<br>")
21   //-->
22   </script>
23   </body>
24   </html>
```

Lines 5 through 11 define the function. Notice that there are two `return` statements. However, by the logic of the program, only one can execute. Lines 17 through 20 are example calls of the function. You can see the results here:

**Figure 8.4     Results of Script 8.3**

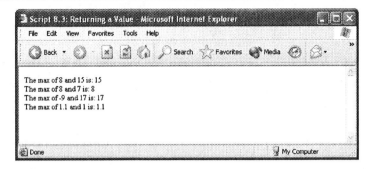

Try adding a few calls yourself and rerun the script.

## Variable Scope (Global vs. Local)

We defined the term "local variable" earlier when discussing arguments and function calls. This subject, however, deserves a closer look and we need a definition for global variables. A **global variable**, usually declared in the <head> of a document within a <script> tag, is any variable defined outside of a function. Variables defined inside of a function, using the var keyword, are **local variables**.

In most programming languages, global variables can be accessed anywhere in a program. JavaScript is a little different in this respect. JavaScript defines "anywhere," that is, the scope of a global variable, as the current document in the current window or frame. All statements in the current page in the current window or frame, including those inside function definitions and event handlers, can access a global variable directly by name. However, other documents in other windows or frames will have to reference the variable through the variable's parent window object.

It is considered better programming practice to return a value from a function and assign it to a global variable rather than to modify the global variable directly from within a function.

**peek ahead**
In Chapter 11, we'll learn how to share variables and functions across windows and frames.

## Creating Libraries in External JavaScript Files

We mentioned earlier that a function definition can be placed in an external JavaScript file and linked to a document with a script tag in the <head> of the HTML document. This is a very useful concept. Place a bunch of regularly used function definitions in one external JavaScript file and you've got yourself a library.

A **library** is a group of reusable function definitions, usually related to each other in some way. For instance, you might create a library of functions for form validation or working with strings. You'll build your own libraries as we continue through the remaining material of this book.

Before adding a function to a library, write it and test it independently. Only when you're certain it works as intended, without error, should you add it to a library. Before you add a function to a library, write a description for it in a multi-line comment. The description should

- describe the purpose of the function.
- specify what arguments, if any, are required by the function and the data type of each argument.
- specify what the function returns, if anything, including the return value's data type.

You can place the comment/description right before the function or as the first few lines inside of the function. I prefer reading the description *before* the function.

It is also a good idea to document the code of the function if you haven't already. At the very least, describe each variable as you declare it with a single line comment. Any code you have to read twice in order to understand what it's doing should also be documented. If you did anything special that may appear odd to a casual reader or that you might forget six months from now, explain it and give your reasoning.

Once you've finished describing and otherwise documenting and commenting your code, test your function again to make certain your comments didn't cause any errors. If all is well, now you can safely add the new function to a library.

## setTimeOut() and setInterval()

While we're on the subject of program flow and calling functions, we should examine the window methods setTimeOut() and setInterval() because they also can affect program flow by calling functions after a specified amount of time.

### setTimeout()

The window method setTimeout lets you call a function after a specified number of milliseconds have elapsed. In essence, it allows you to set a timer that calls a JavaScript statement or function after a certain period of time.

**Syntax:**

```
setTimeout("statement", numMilliseconds)
```

or

```
setTimeout("functionName", numMilliseconds)
```

To see it in action, open the following HTML document in your browser.

### Script 8.4    Using setTimeout

```
1    <html>
2    <head>
3    <title>Script 8.4: Using setTimeout</title>
4    <script language="JavaScript" type="text/javascript"><!--
```

```
 5          function displayAlert() {
 6              alert("5 seconds have elapsed.")
 7          }
 8   //-->
 9   </script>
10   </head>
11   <body>
12   <form>
13   <p>Click the button on the left for a reminder in 5 seconds;
14   click the button on the right to cancel the reminder before
15   it is displayed.</p>
16   <input type="button" value="Set 5-Second Reminder"
17          onClick="reminder=setTimeout('displayAlert()',5000)">
18   <input type="button" value="Clear Reminder"
19          onClick="clearTimeout(reminder)">
20   </form>
21   </body>
22   </html>
```

Press the "Set 5-Second Reminder" button to call the button's onClick event handler (lines 16 and 17) to start the time-out. Begin counting: one thousand one, one thousand two, one thousand three . . . or watch the second hand on your watch. After five seconds, an alert should pop up that looks like this:

**Figure 8.5    Results of Script 8.4**

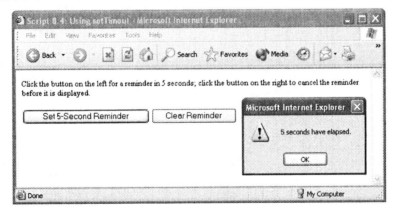

Cool, huh? Is your brain churning with all kinds of ideas of how you might use setTimeout? I know mine was when I first discovered it.

Look a little closer at the script. What's that clearTimeout associated with the "Clear Reminder" button in lines 18 and 19? The creator of JavaScript anticipated that you might want to turn off a setTimeout after you started it, that is, that you might want to stop it before it executed. So he created setTimeout to return an integer representing the time-out's unique identification. By assigning the returned ID to a variable, you can control the time-out, stopping it if necessary. Line 17 of Script 8.4 shows an example of such an assignment to a variable named reminder. Line 19 uses the reminder variable to turn off the time-out when the button is clicked.

If you don't assign the value returned by setTimeout to a variable when it is called, you'll have no way to identify the time-out so you can tell it to stop; it will execute no matter what.

**Syntax for saving a time-out's unique ID:**

```
timerName = setTimeout ("functionName" , numMilliseconds)
```

**Syntax for using clearTimeout:**

```
clearTimeout ("timerName")
```

Let's see this in action. Click on the "Set 5-Second Reminder" button again and start counting, but this time click the "Clear Reminder" button *before* five seconds have elapsed, say at two seconds. Continue counting or watching the second hand on your watch until five seconds has passed. This time the time-out never executes because you turned it off.

## setInterval()

The window method, setInterval differs from its cousin and predecessor setTimeout in that it *repeatedly* calls a statement or function every so many milliseconds.

**Syntax:**

```
setInterval ("statement", numMilliseconds)
```

or

```
setInterval ("functionName", numMilliseconds)
```

To see it in action, open the following HTML document in your browser.

**Script 8.5**    **Using setInterval**

```
1    <html>
2    <head>
3    <title>Script 8.5: Using setInterval</title>
4    <script language="JavaScript" type="text/javascript"><!--
5         function displayAlert() {
6             alert("5 seconds have elapsed.")
7         }
8    //-->
9    </script>
10   </head>
11   <body>
12   <form>
13   <p>Click the button on the left for a repeated reminder every 5
14   seconds; click the button on the right to cancel the reminder.</p>
```

```
15    <input type="button" value="Set Repeating 5-Second Reminder"
16         onClick="reminder=setInterval('displayAlert()',5000)">
17    <input type="button" value="Clear Reminder"
18         onClick="clearInterval(reminder)">
19    </form>
20    </body>
21    </html>
```

Press the "Set Repeating 5-Second Reminder" button; five seconds later an alert should pop up. Click the OK button in the alert and another one should pop up in five seconds, and so on. Press the "Clear Reminder" button to turn it off. Like clearTimeout, clearInterval turns off the named timer. Again, you save the interval's unique ID, returned when setInterval is called, by assigning it to a variable (*timerName*). Line 16 shows an example of such an assignment and line 18 of a call to clear the interval.

**Syntax for saving an interval's unique ID:**

```
timerName = setInterval("functionName", numMilliseconds)
```

**Syntax for using clearInterval:**

```
clearInterval("timerName")
```

Just like with a time-out, if you don't assign the unique ID returned by setInterval to a variable, you'll have no way to turn it off short of closing your browser. It is especially critical to be able to turn off an interval created with the setInterval window method, because otherwise, it will run forever.

OK, so the above examples may demonstrate how setTimeout and setInterval work, but they aren't of much practical use as they are. How about a script that uses setInterval to create an automatic slideshow? That would be cool, huh?

# Using setInterval to Create an Automatic Slideshow

Here we go. You'll need the image files provided on the CD accompanying this book to make it work. You can also replace the images with some of your own, but wait until you get this one working.

**Script 8.6    Slideshow Using setInterval**

```
1    <html>
2    <head>
3    <title>Script 8.6: Slideshow Using setInterval</title>
4    <script language="JavaScript" type="text/javascript"><!--
5         var currentSlide = 0
6
7         if (document.images) {
8         // if images are supported by the browser, create an array
9         // of images and preload them.
```

```
10                var slides = new Array()
11
12                slides[0] = new Image()
13                slides[0].src = "images/img0.jpg"
14
15                slides[1] = new Image()
16                slides[1].src = "images/img1.jpg"
17
18                slides[2] = new Image()
19                slides[2].src = "images/img2.jpg"
20
21                slides[3] = new Image()
22                slides[3].src = "images/img3.jpg"
23
24                slides[4] = new Image()
25                slides[4].src = "images/img4.jpg"
26            }
27
28        function nextImage() {
29            if(document.images && document.slideshow.complete) {
30                if (currentSlide == slides.length) {
31                    currentSlide = 0
32                }
33                document.slideshow.src=slides[currentSlide].src
34                currentSlide++
35            }
36        }
37  //-->
38  </script>
39  </head>
40  <body>
41  <form><table align="center" border=2>
42      <tr><td><img src="images/img0.jpg" name="slideshow"
43            width=240 height=180 alt="My Slideshow"></td></tr>
44      <tr><td align=center>
45          <input type="button" value="Stop Slideshow"
46                onClick="clearInterval(mySlideShow)">
47      </td></tr>
48  </table></form>
49  <script language="JavaScript" type="text/javascript"><!--
50      mySlideShow = setInterval("nextImage()", 2000)
51  //-->
52  </script>
53  </body>
54  </html>
```

Let's look at the script line by line.

Line 5 creates a new variable to hold the current slide position and initializes it to zero, so the slideshow will start with the first slide.

Line 7 checks to see if the `Image` object is supported by the browser. If it is, line 10 creates an array to hold the slides and lines 12 through 25 create `Image` objects and store them in the array.

---

**Programmer's tip**

**Object Detection**

The following statement is an example of object detection:

    if(document.images)

It returns `true` if the current browser supports the `images` property of the `document` object and `false` if it does not. Object detection is frequently used to determine if a browser supports a particular object or property *before* actually accessing that object or property. Should you try to use an object or property *not supported* by a browser, a runtime error is generated. Runtime errors are not a pretty sight; they are often confusing to visitors. However, simply testing to see if an object or property is supported by a browser in an if statement like the one shown above *will not* generate an error.

---

## Preloading Images

When you assign a source to the `src` property of an `Image` object, you cause that `Image` object to be requested from the server and loaded into memory. When you do it in the <head> of a document so that the image is requested before the <body> of the document loads, it is called **preloading** an image. Let's talk about preloading images for a moment.

When you preload an image, you make that image available immediately. When a visitor mouses over a link and the link executes an event handler that changes the image's `src` property to that of a preloaded image, the image displays immediately. Otherwise, as we saw in our example in Chapter 5, if you don't use a preloaded image, the replacement image is not requested from the server until the event handler changes the `src` property of the original image. This results in a lag in the rollover response; a broken image is displayed until the replacement finishes transferring. That is not exactly what you want to have happen.

Now let's get back to our automatic slideshow. Line 29 not only performs an object detection to make certain the `Image` object is supported before trying to access an `Image` object's `src` property, it also verifies that the image named `slideshow` has completely loaded before trying to swap it with the next image in the slideshow. After all, you don't want to show the next image until the current one is `complete`. Because all of the slideshow's images have been preloaded, they will display immediately when called upon by the `nextImage` function (lines 28 through 36). Here's what the first slide looks like:

**Figure 8.6** **Results of Script 8.6**

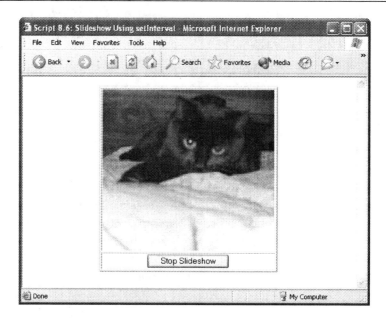

Lines 41 through 48 create a table to hold the slideshow image and a button that, when clicked, stops the slideshow.

Line 50 starts the slideshow. Pretty cool, huh?

**programmer's tip**

Notice that all of the images in the slideshow have the same dimensions. It is extremely important that swapped images have the same dimension. Swapping images of different dimensions can have unpredictable results. Some browsers will squish or expand images to correspond to the original image's size; others will simply not show the image at all or corrupt the entire display.

**side note**

For years, before `setInterval()` was introduced, innovative programmers implemented their own `setInterval()` functions. In order to achieve the effect of a setInterval type of function, these programmers had to resort to *recursion*. **Recursion** is the process of a function calling itself. They created a recursive, setInterval-type function by having the last statement of the function recall the function after a specified interval using `setTimeout()`.

## Creating Image Objects with a Function Call

Before we leave the slideshow script completely, let's make one improvement. Instead of having to write two lines of code to create each image object, let's write a function to do it in one.

***Script 8.7    Creating Image Objects with a Function Call***

```
1      <html>
2      <head>
3      <title>Script 8.7: Creating Image Objects with a Function
          Call</title>
4      <script language="JavaScript" type="text/javascript"><!--
5           function newImg (sourceURL) {
6                zImage = new Image()
7                zImage.src = sourceURL
8                return zImage
9           }
10
11          var currentSlide = 0
12
13          if (document.images) {
14          // if images are supported by the browser, create an
15          // array of images and preload them
16               slides = new Array()
17
18               slides[0] = newImg("images/img0.jpg")
19               slides[1] = newImg("images/img1.jpg")
20               slides[2] = newImg("images/img2.jpg")
21               slides[3] = newImg("images/img3.jpg")
22               slides[4] = newImg("images/img4.jpg")
23          }
```

Our function accepts a string that represents a URL to an image (line 5), calls the Image () constructor function to create a new Image object (line 6), sets the image's src property to the URL passed as an argument (line 7), and returns the image (line 8). Then you need only make a single function call to create each image (lines 18 through 22). That is much slicker and quicker than the way we've been doing it. Script 8.7 shows the modified portion of the script.

# Functions as Objects

One special thing about JavaScript is that it recognizes functions as objects. As objects, functions have properties we can access and manipulate. Look up the Function object in the JavaScript object reference in Appendix A. It is a Core Object. What properties are listed?

Do you see one that might hold a function's parameters? Ah yes, the arguments property, which is an array containing all of the arguments passed to the function when it was called. And because the arguments property is an array, it has a length property, so we can always tell how many arguments were passed.

With the arguments array and length in hand, you can write a function that can accept a variable number of parameters. For instance, wouldn't it be nice to have a rollover function that could work on one, two, three, or even more images, all in one function call? Or perhaps you might want to write a function that would create a list in HTML and be able to vary the number of list items sent to the function. JavaScript's function properties allow you to do both of these tasks and more.

Let's look at the list-writing example.

### Script 8.8    *Writing a Dynamically Sized List*

```
1    <html>
2    <head>
3    <title>Script 8.8: Writing a Dynamically Sized List</title>
4    <script language="JavaScript" type="text/javascript"><!--
5         function writeList() {
6              // first check that at least one argument was passed
7              if (arguments.length < 1) {    //basically do nothing
8                   return
9              } else {                          // write the list
10                  document.writeln("<ul>")
11                  for(i=0; i<arguments.length; i++) {
12                       document.writeln("<li>", arguments[i],
                              "</li>")
13                  }
14                  document.writeln("</ul>")
15             }
16        }
17   //-->
18   </script>
19   </head>
20   <body>
21   <script language="JavaScript" type="text/javascript"><!--
22        writeList("orange", "apple", "pear")
23        writeList("Aradia", "Daphne", "Devan", "Sam", "Daisy")
24        writeList()
25        writeList("pineapple", "kiwi", "orange", "guava", "lemon",
                 "lime")
26   //-->
27   </script>
28   </body>
29   </html>
```

Keep in mind that JavaScript functions must always be defined with a fixed number of parameters. However, you can pass any number of arguments when you call the function. In the above case, we defined the function without any parameters, but passed it a varying number of arguments when we called it. Look at the different results we got by varying the number of arguments passed to the writeList function:

*Figure 8.7*     *Results of Script 8.8*

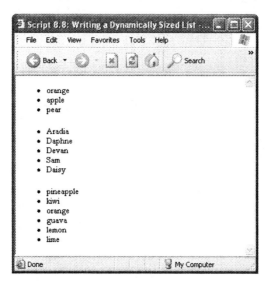

In Script 8.8, writeln statements were used so that the HTML list item output would write neatly on separate lines.

## Summary

A function is a block of predefined programming statements whose execution is deferred until the function is called. The function may optionally accept parameters and/or return a value to the calling statement. You call a function by invoking its name followed by a list of arguments, to match up with its parameters, in parentheses.

In JavaScript, there are four types of functions: (1) predefined functions that are part of the JavaScript language, but not associated with any particular objects; (2) predefined methods, also part of the JavaScript language and associated with predefined objects; (3) user-defined functions, which are really user-defined window methods; and (4) user-defined methods that can be associated with custom objects or any predefined object.

It is considered good programming practice to write functions that perform one task only and cause no side effects outside of their scope.

Proper placement of function definitions and function calls is crucial to program performance. Function definitions should be placed in the <head> of an HTML document or in an external script. A group of often-used function definitions can be placed in an external JavaScript file to form a library. When function definitions are placed in an external JavaScript file, that file should be linked via a <script> tag in the <head> of the document. This is necessary to ensure that the functions are defined before any possible call to them. Function calls that cause writes to the document must always be placed in the <body>. A function call that relies on an object in a Web page must appear *after* the object is created.

The ability to accept parameters and/or return a value makes functions more flexible and reusable. Primitive data types always pass by value, whereas composite data types pass by reference. Functions that return a value may contain more than one return statement, but only one may execute.

In addition to the basic control structures, JavaScript provides two window methods that allow you to alter program flow: setTimeout and setInterval. The setTimeout method calls a function after a specified number of milliseconds have elapsed. The setInterval method calls a function repeatedly every so many milliseconds.

When an Image object is created in the <head> of a document and assigned a src property, it is known as preloading an image. Preloading images is an important task. When an image is preloaded into memory, it is then immediately available to event handlers and makes for better responses. Because image preloading is a common and often-used task, we wrote a function to expedite the creation of a new Image object. With the function, Image object creation can be accomplished with one line of code rather than two for each Image object created.

JavaScript considers functions objects in themselves. As such they have properties associated with them; the most notable is the arguments property. The arguments property is an array containing the arguments passed to the function when it was called. As an array, it has an associated length property. With the arguments array and its length property in hand, programmers can write functions in JavaScript that can accept a variable number of parameters. This does not change the fact that a JavaScript function must be defined with a set number of parameters, it just means that the function can be called with more than that number of arguments. Programmers can access any unnamed arguments by their array index.

## Review Questions

1. What is a function?
2. What does it mean to say that a function contains *deferred* statements?
3. What does it mean to "call a function"?
4. What is a function parameter?
5. What is an argument?
6. What four types of functions does JavaScript support? Describe each.
7. List three good programming practices that have to do with functions.
8. What three things do you need to know before you can write a function definition?

9. Why is a function definition's placement in an HTML document important? How can it affect your program's execution?
10. What's the difference between passing by value and passing by reference?
11. How do primitive data types pass?
12. How do composite data types such as objects pass?
13. How many values can a function return?
14. Define and contrast local and global variables.
15. How do you define a local variable? Provide an example.
16. Where does a local variable have scope?
17. How do you define a global variable?
18. Where does a global variable have scope?
19. What is a library?
20. What two `window` methods allow you to call a function after a specified amount of time has elapsed?
21. Compare and contrast `setTimeout()` and `setInterval()`.
22. Once set, is it possible to turn off a time-out before it executes? If so, how?
23. What should you always do when you call `setInterval()` to ensure you'll have a means of turning it off?
24. What does it mean to "preload" an image? How can you accomplish this?
25. Why should you preload images used in rollover effects?
26. How does JavaScript's treatment of functions as objects assist programmers?
27. What function property contains an array of parameters passed to the function when it was called?
28. Do JavaScript statements placed in the <head> of a document within a function automatically execute when the browser reads them as it loads the page? Explain your answer.
29. When do statements contained in an external JavaScript document execute? Explain your answer.
30. Why would a programmer want to create a library? What advantages does a library offer?

## Exercises

1. Write a function, `areaTriangle()`, that takes two parameters, `base` and `height`, calculates the area of a triangle, and returns the calculated area.
2. Test `areaTriangle` with a few function calls.
3. Write a function definition that utilizes two local variables and one passed parameter.
4. Write a statement to call the function you wrote in Exercise 3.
5. Write a function definition that utilizes two local variables and one passed parameter and returns a value.
6. Write a statement to call the function you wrote in Exercise 5 and assign the value returned to a variable.

# Scripting Exercises

Create a folder named assignment08 to hold the documents you create during this assignment. Save a copy of your most recent toy store documents in a directory named toyStore.

1. Create a document named functions.html.

   a. Write a function, `calcSquare()`, that accepts a numeric value and returns its square. (The square of 2 is 4.)

   b. Write a function, `getNum()`, to get a valid number from the user. The function should accept a message to display as a prompt. Whenever the user enters an invalid value, respond appropriately and then prompt again. Test the function with a few function calls.

   c. Write a function, `swapImg()`, with three parameters: the image to be swapped, the image to swap in, and a blurb to display in the status bar. Test it.

   d. Write a function, `writeList()`, that will accept a variable number of list items and write a numbered list to the document. Provide two or three sample function calls to demonstrate that it works.

2. Copy the document colorSettings.html that you created in Scripting Exercise 4 for Chapter 5.

   a. Write a function named `setColors()` that accepts a `color` (string) as a parameter. Using the color passed to it, the function should change the background color of the document.

   b. Set up each button so that when pressed, it calls the function you wrote to change the background color of the document accordingly.

3. Save a copy of colorSettings.html from Exercise 2 as colorSettings2.html.

   a. Add one more button to the document, labeled with the name of the missing color, the one you used for the foreground color.

   b. Write a function `getColor()` that accepts a `message` parameter and prompts the visitor for a valid color value using the message passed to the function. Only the 16 colors defined by HTML should be allowed: aqua, black, blue, fuchsia, gray, green, lime, maroon, navy, olive, purple, red, silver, teal, white, and yellow.

   c. Modify the `setColors()` function to accept a foreground color as well as a background color.

   d. Modify your event handlers such that whenever visitors press a button, they are prompted for a foreground color and both changes are made to the document. (Hint: The event handler for the button that sets the background color to black should look like this: `setColors("black", getColor() )`.)

4. Write functions to start and end an HTML document.

   a. The `startDoc()` function should accept parameters that will set the title, background color, text color, link color, visited link color, and active link color for the document and write

      ```
      <html><head><title>custom title</title></head>
      ```

followed by an opening <body> tag with the appropriate color settings if passed to the function. Don't forget to write the custom title.

b. In `startDoc()`, the `title` parameter should be required, but the other parameters should be optional. If only the `title` is sent to the function, write the body statement without any color attributes; otherwise, include the color settings provided.

c. The `endDoc()` function should write </body></html>.

5. Create a new document named myLib.js. Place it in a scripts directory off of the root of your Web site.

a. Write a multi-line JavaScript comment at the top naming the library you're about to create and listing your name as the author and the last update date.

b. Copy the functions you wrote in Scripting Exercise 1 without the <script> tag to myLib.js, an external JavaScript file.

c. Before each function, insert a multi-line comment describing
   i.    what the function does
   ii.   what parameters it requires and their data type(s)
   iii.  what the function returns, if anything

d. Add single-line comments as needed to
   i.    describe each local variable
   ii.   describe any tricky lines of code

6. Create a new document named numberPlay.html.

a. Link myLib.js to the document.

b. Using the appropriate functions from your library, write a script that prompts the visitor for a number and then displays that number's square in an alert dialog box as follows:

```
You entered: 5.
The square of 5 is 25.
```

7. Create a new document named toyNav.html.

a. Link myLib.js to the document.

b. Create or acquire a series of navigation buttons for your toy store (at least five). You can use the same images you created or acquired for Scripting Exercise 6 in Chapter 5.

c. In the <head> of your document, use JavaScript to create a series of `Image` objects with names like `contactLo`, `contactHi`, `productsLo`, `productsHi`, etc. and set the appropriate source property for each.

d. Insert the low images into your document and name them appropriately: `contact`, `products`, etc.

e. Make each image a link to the appropriate Web document: contact.html, products.html, etc.

      f. Apply a rollover effect to each navigation button using the appropriate event handler to call the `swapImg()` function. Include an appropriate blurb in the status bar.

8. Create a new document named manualSlideshow.html.

      a. Copy Script 8.7 from the CD to the new document. (Your book only shows a partial listing of Script 8.7; the complete script is on the CD that accompanies the book.)

      b. Remove lines 47 through 50, which start the automatic slideshow.

      c. Add a new function named `previousImage()`, similar to `nextImage()`, that displays the previous image instead of the next.

      d. Remove the Stop Slideshow button and replace it with two buttons labeled Next Slide and Previous Slide.

      e. Apply appropriate event handlers to each button to make the slideshow work manually.

9. Create a new document named multiRollover.html.

      a. Write an image rollover function that will accept a variable number of arguments representing the images to replace and the source to replace each with. The function should be able to perform a rollover effect on one or more images.

      b. Provide one or two examples in which you call the function as an event handler.

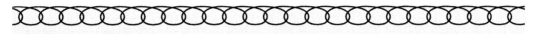

## chapter nine

# *Manipulating Strings*

I n Chapter 4, we looked at a variety of operators supported by JavaScript. Only two applied to strings. Programmers often need to work with and manipulate strings. To support this need, the JavaScript language includes many built-in String methods. JavaScript also supports regular expressions for pattern matching.

*After all, all he did was string together a lot of old, well-known quotations.*

—H. L. Mencken on Shakespeare

In this chapter, we'll

- discuss and describe String methods for changing case.
- examine the many String methods that create HTML markup in order to change the appearance of text in a document.
- play with methods that slice, dice, and reassemble strings.
- look at methods that convert strings to and from Unicode and to and from URL-encoding.
- learn about a String method that can convert a string to an array.
- play with some String methods that allow you to search strings backwards and forwards.
- introduce regular expressions and the methods that can use them.

⚹ discover what regular expression literals, flags, and metacharacters are.

⚹ see how you can use regular expressions to perform complex pattern matching on strings in order to validate the data contained within them.

# String Methods

Think of String **methods** as operations that can be performed on strings or as string operators. JavaScript provides a whole slew of them, allowing you to change a string's case; slice, dice, and reassemble strings; search strings; and more.

One particularly cool thing about JavaScript is that it allows you to call String methods on any string-like object; that is, you can call String methods on all of the following:

**Table 9.1    Candidates for *String Method Calls***

| String-like Object | Example Method Call |
| --- | --- |
| variable whose data type is string | `myName.toUpperCase()` |
| string literal | `"Tina".toUpperCase()` |
| object property whose data type is string | `document.bgColor.toUpperCase()` |

The term "string literal" requires a little explanation. A **string literal** is any string, that is, a series of characters delimited by quotation marks.

For many of our examples in this chapter, we'll use string literals. While most of the time you're more likely to call String methods on string *variables*, it's often easier to see exactly what's going on with a string that is right in front of you, as a literal, rather than one that is hidden, behind a variable name. For example, while you will normally call String methods on variables such as the following,

```
var visitor = "Scott Kelman"
visitor.charAt(6)                        // returns K
```

to understand what the charAt method is doing, you have to do some work: Hmm, charAt(6) on visitor? OK, what's visitor holding? Oh, I see, "Scott Kelman". So I want charAt(6) on "Scott Kelman". The charAt method is supposed to return the character at a particular index in the string: 0 is S, 1 is c ... 6 is K. Now I get it!

Rather than constantly doing lookups like "What's the variable holding?" in order to figure out what the method is doing, it would be easier for you to see what's going on by using string literals. Isn't this example more immediately clear?

```
"Scott Kelman".charAt(6)                 // returns K
```

In this example the string being worked on is right in front of you. Just keep in mind that you can run these String methods on *any* string, whether it's a literal, a variable whose data type is string, or an object property whose data type is string.

Let's get started on our exploration of String methods by looking at two methods that allow you to adjust a string's case.

# Methods for Changing Case:
## `toLowerCase()` and `toUpperCase()`

There are many occasions when you might want to change the case of a variable. For instance, it is much easier to verify that a string entry from a prompt or form field matches a desired entry if you only have to check one possible way of entering that string. For example, you ask for one of two colors, white or black. You get `White`. You could have also received `WHITE`, `wHite`, etc. Who wants to check all the possible case entries? Not me. By first converting the entry to all lowercase, you have to perform only one comparison; against `white`. Cool, huh? The methods `toLowerCase` and `toUpperCase` each return a string whose case has been modified as necessary. `toLowerCase` returns a string in all lowercase characters, and `toUpperCase` returns a string in all uppercase characters. *Neither method actually modifies the string on which it is called.* To see one in action, try typing and running the following code:

```
var myName = "Tina"
document.write(myName.toUpperCase(),  "<BR>")
document.write(myName,  "<BR>")
```

The result should be

```
TINA
Tina
```

Notice that calling the `toUpperCase` method on `myName` did not change the value of `myName`? That's because `String` methods generally do not change the strings on which they are called. A `String` method simply *returns* a modified value. In the above example, the modified value returned by `toUpperCase` was the value contained in `myName` converted to uppercase text.

To specifically change the string itself, you need to make an assignment. Try the following:

```
myName = myName.toUpperCase()
document.write(myName,  "<BR>")
```

The result should be

```
TINA
```

because this time we assigned the value returned by `toUpperCase` back to the variable, `myName`. `myName` now holds the value `"TINA"`.

Now let's see `toLowerCase` in action:

```
"Sammy Sam".toLowerCase()
```

returns

```
sammy sam
```

Now let's look at some methods that mark up strings with HTML.

# Methods for Changing Text Appearance with HTML Markup

As we've seen throughout this book, programmers often use JavaScript to write HTML. To support this custom of using JavaScript to write HTML code, Netscape included many methods in its JavaScript language definition that make marking up your strings with HTML easy and painless. *These methods do not modify the actual string on which they are called.*

Table 9.2 shows a list of the String methods in the JavaScript language that accept a string and return it marked up with the appropriate HTML. These methods may be applied to any property or variable whose data type is string, any string literal, and any String object. The method names are pretty descriptive, in that they describe the type of markup that will be applied. For example:

```
"Hello".big()
```

returns

```
<big>Hello</big>
```

Of course you'll usually want to call these functions inside of a document.write statement so that their result is written to the document, like this:

```
document.write("Hello".big())
```

writes

```
Hello
```

to the document in larger than normal letters; that is, Hello is marked up with the <big> tag.

**Table 9.2     HTML Markup String Methods**

| String Method | Example (zStr = "some text") | Returned String |
|---|---|---|
| anchor("*name*") | zStr.anchor("myAnchor") | <a name="myAnchor">some text</a> |
| big() | zStr.big() | <big>some text</big> |
| blink() | zStr.blink() | <blink>some text</blink> |
| bold() | zStr.bold() | some text |
| fixed() | zStr.fixed() | <tt>some text</tt> |
| fontcolor("*color*") | zStr.fontcolor("#00ff00") | <font color="#00ff00">some text</font> |
| fontsize(*n*) (where n is a number from 1 to 7) | zStr.fontsize(4) | font size=4>some text</font> |

| italics() | zStr.italics() | \<i>some text\</i> |
|---|---|---|
| link("*URL*") | zStr.link("script1.html") | \<a href="script1.html"> some text\</a> |
| small() | zStr.small() | \<small>some text\</small> |
| strike() | zStr.strike() | \<strike>some text \</strike> |
| sub() | zStr.sub() | \<sub>some text\</sub> |
| sup() | zStr.sup() | \<sup>some text\</sup> |

To get a good feel for how the above-listed `String` methods work, type in the following script then open your document in an early version of Netscape Navigator (pre-6.0).

### Script 9.1    HTML Markup String Methods

```
1    <html>
2    <head>
3        <title>Script 9.1: HTML Markup String Methods</title>
4    </head>
5    <body>
6    <script language="JavaScript" type="text/javascript"><!--
7        document.writeln("this is an anchor".anchor('myAnchor'),
            "<br>")
8        document.writeln("big text".big(), "<br>")
9        document.writeln("blinking text".blink(), "<br>")
10        document.writeln("bold text".bold(), "<br>")
11        document.writeln("monospaced text, aka fixed".fixed(),
            "<br>")
12        document.writeln("font colored red".fontcolor('#ff0000'),
            "<br>")
13        document.writeln("font size 5".fontsize(5), "<br>")
14        document.writeln("italicized text".italics(), "<br>")
15        document.writeln("WebWoman".link('http://www.webwoman.biz/'),
            "<br>")
16        document.writeln("small text".small(), "<br>")
17        document.writeln("struck out text".strike(), "<br>")
18        document.writeln("sub".sub(), "script text", "<br>")
19        document.writeln("sup".sup(), "erscript text", "<br>")
20    //-->
21    </script>
22    </body>
23    </html>
```

After looking at the display results, view the source code in an old version of Netscape Navigator (pre-6.0) to see the code JavaScript actually spat out in response to the method calls.

***Figure 9.1      Results of Script 9.1***

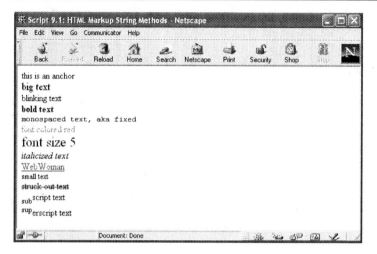

You should use a version of Netscape Navigator prior to version 6 because the View Source command shows you the HTML results of your script. Internet Explorer, Opera, and later versions of Navigator, on the other hand, show you the script itself, which, in this case, is of little help. For this reason, among others, I recommend that you have multiple browsers installed on your system when you're Web developing or scripting and, especially, keep an old version of Navigator on hand.

***Figure 9.2      Source of Script 9.1 as Shown in Netscape Navigator 4.78***

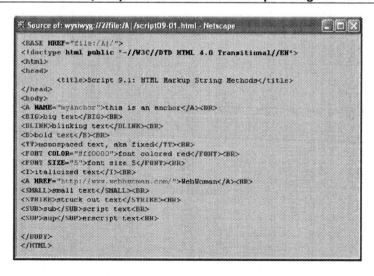

# Methods for Slicing, Dicing, and Reassembling Strings

Programmers often need to slice, dice, reassemble, and otherwise manipulate strings. Luckily, JavaScript provides several `String` methods to assist you with these tasks. For instance, the `charAt` method lets you retrieve any single character within a string by its index number. String character numbering always starts at 0.

Don't forget that the `length` property specifies how long a particular string is and can be used on any string variable, string literal, or `String` object. For example:

```
var myString = "That is just the way it is."
myString.length                         // result 27
```

Remember, JavaScript allows you to access the `length` property and to call `String` methods with string literals. So you could also have determined the above string's length with this code:

```
"That is just the way it is.".length    // result 27
```

Here's a list of the slice and dice `String` methods. *Keep in mind that none of these slice and dice `String` methods actually modify the original string.* They simply return a new string as requested. If you want to modify the original string with the result, you'll have to assign the result of the method call to back to the original string like this:

```
var myString = "Some string"
myString = myString.someMethod(param1, param2)
```

## charAt (*index*)

The `charAt` method allows you to retrieve a particular character in a string using its index number. Valid index numbers are 0 through the string's `length` - 1. For example:

```
"my string".charAt(5)
```

returns

```
r
```

Remember, indexing begins at 0. If the index number specified is beyond the length of the string, JavaScript returns an empty string.

```
"my string".charAt(10)
```

returns

```
                        // an empty string
```

## concat (*secondString*[, *thirdString*, ..., *nthString*])

The `concat` method is equivalent to the concatenation operator (+). The string sent as a parameter is concatenated to the `String` object. For example:

```
"my string".concat(" is now a little longer")
```

returns

```
my string is now a little longer
```

The concat method does not modify the original string, it simply returns the result of the concatenation as a new string.

## slice(*startIndex*[, *endIndex*])

Just like the name implies, slice lets you retrieve a *slice* of a string. Personally, I'd rather have a slice of chocolate cream pie. The slice begins at the start index and ends at the character *before* the end index. For instance:

```
"my string".slice(3,5)
```

returns

```
st
```

Remember, index numbers begin with 0. If the second parameter is omitted, slice continues to the end of the string. For example:

```
"my string".slice(5)
```

returns

```
ring
```

You can also use a negative number for the end index to indicate an offset from the end of the string. For example:

```
"my string".slice(1, -1)
```

returns

```
y strin
```

## substring(*startIndex*[, *endIndex*])

The substring method, as its name implies, lets you extract a substring. The extraction begins at the start index and continues up to, but does not include, the character at the end index. Omit the end index parameter, and the extraction continues to the end of the string. Don't forget, indexing begins at 0.

To see how substring differs from slice, let's call the method so that the return values are the same as those in the examples for slice. For instance:

```
"my string".substring(3,5)
```

returns

```
st
```

In this example, substring and slice worked the same way.

Here's another example:

```
"my string".substring(5)
```

The returned result:

```
ring
```

When we eliminated the second parameter, `substring` worked the same as `slice`.
  One more example:

```
"my string".substring(1, ("my string".length-2))
```

returns

```
y stri
```

Here's where `slice` shows its stuff: by making it easier to specify an offset from the end of the string. As you can see, the process is a bit more cumbersome with `substring`.

### substr(*startIndex[, length]*)

The `substr` method, like `substring`, also allows you to extract a substring from a string. However, when calling this method, you specify the start index and *the number of characters* to extract from that point. Again, remember that indexing begins at 0.
  This example grabs the first four characters:

```
"my string".substr(0, 4)
```

and returns

```
my s
```

As usual, if you do not specify a second parameter, extraction proceeds to the end of the string. The same is true if the `length` parameter is too big, indicating an end point beyond the end of the string. Now that we know how to slice, dice, and reassemble strings, let's learn a little bit about character sets and converting strings to and from Unicode.

## Methods for Converting to and from Unicode

So what's Unicode? Ever heard of the ASCII character set? **ASCII** (American Standard Code for Information Interchange) represents each alphabetic, numeric, or special character as a seven-bit binary number (a string of seven 0s and 1s). That's actually how the computer stores characters. The ASCII character set defines only 128 characters. While this is enough to represent the English alphabet, the numbers 0 through 9, and some symbols and special characters, it is not adequate to represent all of the letters used in the alphabets of the world.
  The **ISO 8859-1 (Latin-1) character set** (from the International Organization for Standardization) is a little better than ASCII; it represents each character as an eight-bit (one byte) binary number and supports 256 values. The first 128 are a direct match of the ASCII character set. While the ISO 8859 character sets were adopted for use on the Internet (MIME) and the Web (HTML and HTTP), they still don't come close to covering all of the character's used in the world. Hence the need for Unicode.

**Unicode** is short for Unicode Worldwide Character Standard. It covers the languages of the Americas, Europe, Middle East, Africa, India, Asia, and Pacifica, as well as some historic scripts and technical symbols. Unicode values range from 0 to 65,535. Its first 128 values match the ASCII character set. Now that you know what Unicode is, let's look at some methods for converting to and from that character set.

### charCodeAt(*index*)

The charCodeAt method allows you to retrieve the Unicode value of a particular character in a string using its index number.

Valid index numbers are 0 through the string's length - 1. For example:

```
"my string".charCodeAt(5)
```

returns

```
114
```

because the Unicode for r is 114.

### fromCharCode(*unicode1[, unicode2, ..., unicodeN]*)

The fromCharCode method accepts a series of Unicode values and returns a string in English. For example:

```
String.fromCharCode(109, 121, 32, 115, 116, 114, 105, ⟶
⟶ 110, 103)
```

returns

```
my string
```

See Appendix G for a list of Unicode values and their corresponding Latin-1 characters. While you may not need to convert to and from Unicode very often, it is quite likely you will need to work with URL-encoded data at some point in time.

## Methods for URL-Encoding and UnURL-Encoding

**URL-encoding** is the format used by the browser when packaging form input data to send to the server or a mailto address. Here's how it works:

1. The browser gets all the names (specified by each form element's name attribute) and values (usually entered or chosen by the visitor) and encodes them as name-value pairs.

   a. Each name-value pair is separated by an equals sign (=). For example:

      ```
      Email=js@javascriptconcepts.com
      ```

   b. Pairs are separated by an ampersand (&). For example:

      ```
      Email=js@javascriptconcepts.com&Gender
      =f&Married=true
      ```

2.   Any spaces in the input are replaced with a plus sign (+). For example:

```
Name=Tina+McDuffie
```

3.   Any special characters are translated into their ASCII hexadecimal equivalent and preceded by a % sign. For example, ® would be encoded as %AE.

Any time you send data from the client to the server or vice versa, it must be URL-encoded. That's a requirement of the HTTP protocol. With JavaScript, there are three cases when you will likely need to send a string to the server: (1) when sending form data, (2) when writing a cookie, and (3) when sending data as part of a URL.

> **peek ahead**
> You'll learn all about forms and JavaScript in Chapters 12 and 13 and how to bake cookies in Chapter 14.

A form's submit method takes care of URL-encoding the form's data when the form is submitted. However, the other two tasks you, the programmer, must perform yourself. Luckily you have the built-in escape and unescape methods to help. The escape and unescape methods aren't String methods like the others we've discussed in this chapter; they're global methods, also known as built-in functions.

## escape("*string*")

escape is a global method that URL-encodes a string. Here's an example:

**Script 9.2     *escape in Action***

```
1    <html>
2    <head>
3        <title>Script 9.2: Escape In Action</title>
4    </head>
5    <body>
6    <script language="JavaScript" type="text/javascript"><!--
7      var myString = "He said, \"Hmmm, T-n-T, huh? Together, we\'re
         dynamite.\""
8      document.write("<b>Original string:</b> ", myString, "<br><br>")
9
10     var newString = escape(myString)
11     document.write("<b>Escaped string:</b> ", newString, "<br>")
12
13   //-->
14   </script>
15   </body>
16   </html>
```

The result:

### Figure 9.3    Results of Script 9.2

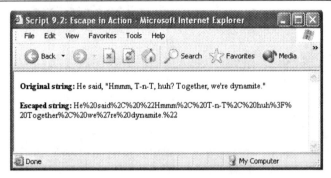

Examine the result carefully, character by character. You can refer to Appendix G for a list of each special character's ASCII code in hexadecimal. Hexadecimal codes are always two digits in length. Now let's see how to unescape a URL-encoded string.

### unescape ("*string*")

The unescape global method turns a URL-encoded string back into a normal string. Here's an example:

### Script 9.3    *unescape inAction*

```
1    <html>
2    <head>
3         <title>Script 9.3: Unescape In Action</title>
4    </head>
5    <body>
6    <script language="JavaScript" type="text/javascript"><!--
7         var ueString = "Hmmm%2C%20T-n-T%2C%20huh%3F"
8         document.write("<b>Original string:</b> ", ueString,
           "<br><br>")
9
10        var newString = unescape(ueString)
11        document.write("<b>Escaped string:</b> ", newString, "<br>")
12
13   //-->
14   </script>
15   </body>
16   </html>
```

The result:

**Figure 9.4**     **Results of Script 9.3**

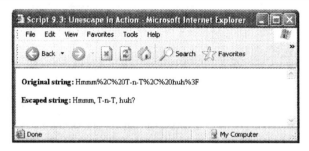

The results of escape and unescape may not seem very impressive to you now, but I assure you, you'll come to love them when you work with cookies or need to send data via the location bar.

# A Method That Converts a String into an Array

**peek ahead**

We'll work with cookies in Chapter 13.

## split("*delimiter*"[, *maxElements*])

In Chapter 7, "Arrays," we showed you how split works in the opposite way of an array's join method. While an array's join method returns a string containing the elements of an array separated by a delimiter of the programmer's choice, the split String method returns an array of strings, each split from the original string at the delimiter specified. The delimiter can be one or more characters. In Script 9.4, we'll use two characters, a comma and a space, as the delimiter (line 8).

You don't have to use the new Array() constructor before performing the split. Just declare a variable and assign the result of split to that variable. The split method takes care of the rest (line 8). Here's an example:

**Script 9.4**     **split *in* Action**

```
1    <html>
2    <head>
3        <title>Script 9.4: Split in Action</title>
4    </head>
5    <body>
6    <script language="JavaScript" type="text/javascript"><!--
7        var flowers = "rose, stargazer lily, gardenia, daffodil"
8        var flowersArray = flowers.split(", ")
9
10       document.write("<b>flowers string: </b>", flowers,
            "<br><br>")
11
12       document.write("<b>flowersArray</b>: <br>")
```

```
13                     for(i=0;  i<flowersArray.length;  i++)  {
14            document.write(i, ". ", flowersArray[i], "<br>")
15      }
16
17  //-->
18  </script>
19  </body>
20  </html>
```

The result:

**Figure 9.5     Results of Script 9.4**

You can also specify a second parameter: the maximum number of elements the gener-ated array may contain or a regular expression to use as a delimiter to split up the string. We'll learn about regular expressions in a bit. For now, let's look at some methods for searching strings.

## Methods for Searching Strings

Ah, the age-old search methods. There will be many times in your life as a programmer when you will need to search a string for a particular character or sequence of characters. For instance, you'll search the `navigator.appName` property to determine what browser a visitor is using. This is easily accomplished using the `String` methods `indexOf` and `lastIndexOf`.

### indexOf("searchString" [, startIndex])

The `indexOf` method begins its search at the beginning of a string (index 0) or the start index specified as the optional second parameter. If the search string is not found, `indexOf` returns `-1`; otherwise, it returns the index of the first character of the first occurrence of the search string within the calling string. For example,

```
"Sammy Sam".indexOf("S")          // returns 0
"Sammy Sam".indexOf("a")          // returns 1
"Sammy Sam".indexOf("am")         // returns 1
```

Here are some examples using the optional second parameter:

```
"Sammy Sam".indexOf("a", 3)            // returns 7
"Sammy Sam".indexOf("mm", 2)           // returns 2
```

Here's a script you can try to determine which browser a visitor is using. It uses the indexOf method, on lines 9, 11, and 13, to check for each browser's name.

**Script 9.5     Browser Detection**

```
1    <html>
2    <head>
3        <title>Script 9.5: Browser Detection</title>
4    </head>
5    <body>
6    <script language="JavaScript" type="text/javascript"><!--
7        var zBrowser = "unknown"
8
9        if (navigator.appName.indexOf("Microsoft") != -1) {
10            zBrowser = "Internet Explorer"
11        } else if (navigator.appName.indexOf("Netscape") != -1) {
12            zBrowser = "Netscape Navigator"
13        } else if (navigator.userAgent.indexOf("Opera") != -1) {
14            zBrowser = "Opera"
15        }
16        document.write("You\'re using: ", zBrowser, "<br>")
17    //-->
18    </script>
19    </body>
20    </html>
```

Figure 9.6 shows one possible result:

**Figure 9.6     A Result of Script 9.5**

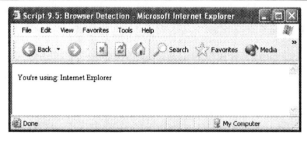

One important note: `indexOf` can blow up on you if you try to search an empty string. Instead of returning `-1`, it will return an empty string. To avoid this unexpected side effect, you might want to verify that the string you plan to search has a `length` of at least 1 before performing the `indexOf` method, like this:

```
if (stringName.length > 0) {
    stringName.indexOf("searchString")
}
```

Better safe than sorry.

### lastIndexOf("*searchString*" [, *startIndex*])

The `lastIndexOf` method is the same as `indexOf` in all ways *except* it begins its search at the *end* of the string and works backwards. It still returns the index number counting from the beginning of the string, where 0 is the index of the first character in the string. Compare the following results with those of `indexOf` above:

```
"Sammy Sam".lastIndexOf("S")          // returns 6
"Sammy Sam".lastIndexOf("a")          // returns 7
"Sammy Sam".lastIndexOf("m")          // returns 8
```

When using the second parameter, the search starts at that index number and proceeds *backwards* to the beginning of the string. Here are some examples:

```
"Sammy Sam".lastIndexOf("a", 3)   // returns 1
"Sammy Sam".lastIndexOf("m", 2)   // returns 2
```

Both `indexOf` and `lastIndexOf` are pretty handy methods you'll use again and again.

While `indexOf` and `lastIndexOf` are handy for searching for a character or string inside of a string, they cannot perform pattern matching. For instance, say you want to see if a string ends with a numeric digit like these do: "num1", "book3", and "script5". While you could do it with `indexOf` or `lastIndexOf`, it would take some work. You'd have to check for "0" in the string, then "1", then "2", and so on. Neither can `indexOf` and `lastIndexOf` determine if a string matches the following pattern: an opening parenthesis, three numeric digits, a closing parenthesis, a space, three more digits, a dash, and four more digits (a possible format of a telephone number).

That's where regular expressions come in.

> **side note**
>
> JavaScript modeled its support for regular expressions after Perl.

## Regular Expressions

A **regular expression** is simply a pattern that you can use to match against character combinations in strings. In JavaScript, regular expressions are also objects like Strings and Numbers; their object name is `RegExp`. As objects, they have properties and methods. The two methods you'll use most often are `exec()` and `test()`, which are similar to the String methods `match()` and `search()` respectively.

In addition to a its own methods, a regular expression can also be used with the `String` methods `match()`, `search()`, `replace()`, and `split()`. Table 9.3 summarizes these methods.

**Table 9.3    Methods That Can Use Regular Expressions**

| Method | Description |
|---|---|
| `exec(string)` | A `RegExp` method that looks for a match in a string and returns the results in an array. It also updates properties of the `RegExp` object. |
| `test(string)` | A `RegExp` method that searches for a match in a string and returns `true` if a match was found and `false` if it was not. |
| `match(regExp)` | A `String` method that attempts to match a regular expression against a string and returns the results in an array. |
| `replace(regExp, newSubstring)` | A `String` method that uses a regular expression to look for a match within a string and replace it with the specified substring. It does not modify the original string, it just returns a string with the replacement(s) made. |
| `search(regExp)` | A `String` method that uses a regular expression to search a string for a match. If a match is found, it returns the index number of the match's position. If a match is not found, it returns `-1`. |
| `split(regExpDelimiter, [maxElements])` | A `String` method that breaks a string up into an array at the specified delimiter(s). You can use a regular expression as a delimiter as well as a plain string. The second parameter, which is optional, specifies the maximum number of array entries to create. |

## Regular Expression Literals

There are two ways to create a regular expression. You can simply use a regular expression literal like this:

```
/num/
```

In this example, `/num/` is the regular expression literal. This is similar to how num is a string literal. Notice that regular expressions are naturally delimited by slashes (/), while strings are delimited by double quotation marks (") or single quotation marks (').

You can first assign the regular expression literal to a variable like this:

```
var myRegExp = /num/
```

When you assign a regular expression literal to a variable, JavaScript calls the `RegExp` constructor function behind the scenes. You don't have to assign a regular expression literal to a variable in order to use it, though programmers often do, like this:

```
var myRegExp = /num/
"Some number".search(myRegExp)
```

returns

> 5

You can also use a regular expression literal directly like this:

```
"Some number".search(/num/)
```

returns

> 5

The results are the same. Keep in mind, however, that regular expressions can get quite long and complicated. Rather than write a complicated regular expression multiple times, you'll find it much easier to write it once when you assign to a variable. Then use the variable from then on.

You may have noticed that the regular expression `search` method, when used on a very simple regular expression like the one above, returns the same result as

```
"Some number".indexOf("num")
```

This is a very simple regular expression. They get much more complicated, as you'll soon see.

## Regular Expression Flags

Three flags, `g`, `i`, and `m`, can be added to a regular expression to modify how a method uses the regular expression to find matches. In a regular expression literal, flags are added after the closing slash (/).

**Table 9.4**    **Regular Expression Flags**

| Flag | Description |
| --- | --- |
| g | The g stands for "global match." When added to a regular expression, the global flag causes methods that use the regular expression to search the entire string for all matches rather than until a single match is found. |
| i | The i stands for "ignore case." When added to a regular expression, the ignore case flag causes methods to ignore case in the search. For example, `/The/i` would match The, the, THE, tHe, etc. |
| m | The m stands for "match over multiple lines." When added to a regular expression, this flag causes methods to look for a match over multiple lines. |

Here's an example of the i flag in action:

```
"Some number".search(/num/i)          // returns 5
"some Number".search(/num/i)          // returns 5
"SOME NUMBER".search(/num/i)          // returns 5
```

Using the i flag causes the method to ignore case. So all three of the method calls above achieve a match.

Let's try another, this time using the match String method. Recall that the match String method returns any matches in an array.

```
results = "Some Mean number".match(/m/i)
document.write(results, "<br>")
```

The result:

```
m
```

which refers to the m in Some. Though we performed a case-insensitive match, using the i flag, only the first match was returned and written to the results array. Why? Because, by default, methods that use regular expressions return only the first match. You must use the g flag to perform a global match on the string and return all results. To demonstrate this, let's use both the g and i flags to perform a global, case-insensitive search. Remember, flags are added after the closing slash of the regular expression.

```
results = "Some Mean number".match(/m/gi)
document.write(results, "<br>")
```

writes

```
m,M,m
```

where the first m is the m in Some; the second, the M in Mean; and the third, the m in number.

## Using the RegExp Constructor

The second way you can create a regular expression is by using the RegExp constructor function with the new operator. Here is the syntax:

```
var regExpName = new RegExp(regExp, [flags])
```

An example:

```
var myRegExp = new RegExp("num")
```

When you create a regular expression using the RegExp constructor function, you must delimit the regular expression with quotation marks. You can also provide a set of flags as a second parameter in quotation marks. You can then use the regular expression the same way you use a regular expression literal assigned to a variable:

```
"Some number".search(myRegExp)
```

returns

    5

Here is an example that uses the g and i flags:

```
var myRegExp2 = new RegExp("m", "gi")
results = "Some Mean number".match(myRegExp2)
```

results contains m, M, m.

## RegExp.test(*string*) vs. String.search(*regExp*)

Reading Table 9.3, you probably noticed that the RegExp test method is pretty similar to the String search method. Let's illuminate the differences. We'll start by declaring a string and a regular expression.

```
var myStr = "A rose by any other name is still a rose."
var myRegExp = /rose/g
```

I'm getting tired of typing "<br>" all the time, so I'm going to declare a variable for it, too:

```
var br = "<br>"
```

Now let's call both methods and write the results to the document:

```
document.write("Result of test: ", myRegExp.test(myStr), br)
document.write("Result of search: ", ⸺▶
⸺▶ myStr.search(myRegExp), br)
```

The result:

```
Result of test: true
Result of search: 2
```

Notice that test returned a Boolean value indicating whether the test was successful, while search returned a number indicating the index where the match was found. Despite the global flag, both methods returned only one value.

Now let's change the value of the regular expression and run both methods again:

```
myRegExp = /lily/g
document.write("Result of test: ", myRegExp.test(myStr), br)
document.write("Result of search: ", ⸺▶
⸺▶ myStr.search(myRegExp), br)
```

The result:

```
Result of test: false
Result of search: -1
```

Again test returned a Boolean value, this time false, and search returned a number, this time -1 to indicate that no match was found. The test method works particularly well as a condition. For instance,

```
if(myRegExp.test(myStr)) {
     // do something
}
```

Keep in mind that `test` is a `RegExp` method and `search` is a `String` method. The `test` method accepts a string argument, while `search` expects an argument that is a regular expression. It's easy to confuse the two so watch your syntax carefully.

Now let's compare the `RegExp` `exec` method and the `String` `match` method.

## `RegExp.exec(`*`string`*`)` vs. `String.match(`*`regExp`*`)`

The `RegExp` `exec` method and the `String` `match` method both return more information than their `test` and `search` counterparts. Both return an array containing the results of the search or `null` if no match is found. The array returned by the `exec` method is a little different than that returned by `match`. The `exec` method reports additional information, as we'll see shortly.

Let's use the same string and regular expression we used earlier.

*Script 9.6     `RegExp.exec( )` vs. `String.match( )`*

```
1    <html>
2    <head>
3    <title>Script 9.6: RegExp.exec() vs. String.match()</title>
4    </head>
5    <body>
6    <script language="JavaScript" type="text/javascript"><!--
7    var br = "<br>"
8
9    var myStr = "A rose by any other name is still a <i>Rose</i>."
10   var myRegExp = /rose/ig
11
12   document.write("<b>Declarations</b>", br)
13   document.write("myStr: ", myStr, br)
14   document.write("myRegExp: ", myRegExp, br)
15
16   var execResults = myRegExp.exec(myStr)
17   var matchResults = myStr.match(myRegExp)
18
19   document.write(br, "<b>Result of RegExp.exec( ):</b>", br)
20   if (execResults != null) {
21        for (i=0; i<execResults.length; i++) {
22             document.write(i, ". ", execResults[i], br)
23        }
24   } else {
25        document.write("none", br)
26   }
```

```
27
28  document.write(br, "<b>Result of String.match( ):</b>", br)
29  if (matchResults != null) {
30      for (i=0; i<matchResults.length; i++) {
31          document.write(i, ". ", matchResults[i], br)
32      }
33  } else {
34      document.write("none", br)
35  }
36
37  myRegExp = /lily/ig
38
39  document.write(br, br, br, "<b>Declarations</b>", br)
40  document.write("myStr: ", myStr, br)
41  document.write("myRegExp: ", myRegExp, br)
42
43  var execResults = myRegExp.exec(myStr)
44  var matchResults = myStr.match(myRegExp)
45
46  document.write(br, "<b>Result of RegExp.exec( ):</b>", br)
47  if (execResults != null) {
48      for (i=0; i<execResults.length; i++) {
49          document.write(i, ". ", execResults[i], br)
50      }
51  } else {
52      document.write("none", br)
53  }
54
55  document.write(br, "<b>Result of String.match( ):</b>", br)
56  if (matchResults != null) {
57      for (i=0; i<matchResults.length; i++) {
58          document.write(i, ". ", matchResults[i], br)
59      }
60  } else {
61      document.write("none", br)
62  }
63
64  //-->
65  </script>
66
67  </body>
68  </html>
```

The results:

*Figure 9.7*        **Results of Script 9.6**

Notice that the arrays of results returned by `match` and `exec` are different. The `exec` method returned only the first match, while the `match` method returned both matches. Why is that? After all, the regular expression, `myRegExp`, had the global flag set, why didn't `exec` return all of the matches?

The answer is that while `exec` does return an array of results, its results are different than those returned by `match`. The `exec` method returns an array whose first element holds the last matched characters; the remaining elements hold any parenthesized substring matches.

Parentheses that surround a part of a regular expression are called "capturing parentheses" and cause the `exec` method to remember any matches with the substring in the capturing parentheses. The matches can be recalled from the resulting array's elements `[1] ... [n]`. To see this in action, let's modify the regular expression in Script 9.6 slightly:

```
var myRegExp = /(rose)/ig
```

Notice the capturing parentheses around `rose`. Let's rerun the script. Here are the results:

**Figure 9.8**     **Results of Using Capturing Parentheses in the Regular Expression**

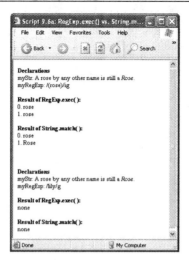

Capturing parentheses are a very useful feature of regular expressions, particularly when you're trying to find and replace text. By knowing exactly what you've matched, you can use the `replace` method to change what you need accordingly.

If what you want as a result is an array of all matches, the `String match` method is the best way to go. However, `exec` provides more than just an array. It also sets the regular expression's properties with values that describe the regular expression and its results. Here's what the properties of myRegExp look like after the first time `exec` is called.

**Figure 9.9**     **myRegExp's Properties after `myRegExp.exec ( )` Call**

Table 9.5 summarizes the properties of a regular expression.

*Table 9.5*      *Regular Expression Properties*

| Object | Property | Description |
|---|---|---|
| *resultsArray* | index | A 0-based index of the first match in a string. |
| | input | The original string against which the regular expression was matched. |
| | [0] | The last matched characters. |
| | [1],...[n] | The parenthesized substring matches, if any. |
| *regExpName* | global | Specifies whether or not the global flag was used. |
| | ignoreCase | Specifies whether or not the ignore case flag was used. |
| | lastIndex | The index at which to start the next match. |
| | multiline | Specifies whether or not the multiline flag was used. |
| | source | The regular expression itself without delimiters or flags. |
| RegExp | $1...$9 | The parenthesized substring matches, if any. |
| | lastMatch | The last matched characters. |
| | lastParen | The last parenthesized substring match, if any. |
| | leftContext | The substring preceding the most recent match. |
| | rightContext | The substring following the most recent match. |

As you can see, some properties belong to the resulting array after an exec call, some to the instance of the regular expression itself, and the rest to the RegExp object. Regular expressions are very complicated (and confusing). One could write a whole book on the subject. So let's leave the nitty-gritty details of regular expression for such a book and keep our discussions here as simple as possible (if anything about regular expressions can be considered simple).

OK, this brings us to the complicated subject of metacharacters (which we're going to keep as simple as possible). The capturing parentheses mentioned earlier are just one of the many metacharacters you can use in regular expressions.

## So What Is a Metacharacter?

The key to the real power of regular expressions is their list of **metacharacters**. Metacharacters are pattern-matching devices. A metacharacter is a character or character combination that is used to specify a pattern, a modifier, or how to process the characters that follow it. For instance, since the early chapters of this book, we've used the backslash character to indicate that the character that follows it should be treated in a special way: \n means to treat it as a new line, \" means to treat it as a literal quotation mark, \' means to treat it as a literal single quote or apostrophe, etc.

The metacharacters listed in Table 9.6 can be used to modify the way a regular expression works.

**Table 9.6    Regular Expression Metacharacters**

**Metacharacters That Specify Text Position**

| Metacharacter | Location | Example |
|---|---|---|
| ^ | Beginning of the string or line. | /^h/ matches *h* in *happy* <br> /^h/ does not match *h* in *catchy* <br> /^h/ does not match *h* in *pooch* |
| $ | End of string or line. | /h$/ does not match *h* in *happy* <br> /h$/ does not match *h* in *catchy* <br> /h$/ matches *h* in *pooch* |
| \b*char* | At the beginning of a word. | /\bl/ matches *l* in *laugh often* <br> /\bl/ matches *l* in *sing loud* <br> /\bl/ does not match *play strong* |
| *char*\b | At the end of a word. | /g\b/ does not match *laugh often* <br> /g\b/ matches *g* in *sing loud* <br> /g\b/ matches *g* in *play strong* |
| \B | Not at a word boundary (the beginning or ending of a word). | /g\B/ matches *g* in *laugh often* <br> /g\B/ does not match *sing loud* <br> /g\B/ does not match *play strong* |

**Metacharacters That Indicate Special Groups of Characters**

| Metacharacter | Character or Group of Characters | Example |
|---|---|---|
| . | Any single character, except a new line (\n). | /h./ matches *ha* in *happy* <br> /h./ matches *hy* in *catchy* <br> /h./ does not match *pooch* |
| \ | Escapes a special character so it is treated as a literal or makes a non-special character special, usually to become a metacharacter. | \" escapes the quotation mark <br> \\ escapes the backslash <br> \/ escapes the slash <br> \n inserts a new line character |
| [*charSet*] | A character in the specified character set. You can indicate a | /[abc]/ matches *a* in *happy* <br> /[abc]/ matches *c* in *catchy* |

| | range of characters by placing a dash between them, for example 0-9, a-z, A-Z, etc. | and matches *c,a,c* in *catchy* if g flag set<br>/ [abc] / matches *c* in *pooch* |
|---|---|---|
| [^*charSet*] | A character that is not in the specified character set. | / [^abchy] / matches *p* in *happy* and matches *p,p* if g flag set<br>/ [^abchy] / matches *t* in *catchy*<br>/ [^abchy] / match *p* in *pooch* and matches *p,o,o* if g flag set |
| \d | A numeric digit, 0 through 9. | /num\d/ matches *num2* in *num2*<br>/num\d/ does not match *number*<br>/num\d/ matches *num4* in *num44* |
| \D | A non-numeric character. | /num\D/ does not match *num2*<br>/num\D/ matches *numb* in *number*<br>/num\D/ does not match *num44* |
| \s | A single white space, such as a space, a new line, or a tab. | /g\so/ matches *g o* in *lag often*<br>/g\so/ matches *g o* in *sing one*<br>/g\so/ does not match *play one* |
| \S | A single non-white space character. | /play\S/ matches *playe* in *player*<br>/play\S/ matches *playw* in *playwright*<br>/play\S/ does not match *play ball* |
| \w | Any letter, number, or underscore. | /play\w/ matches *playe* in *player*<br>/play\w/ matches *play7* in *play7*<br>/play\w/ matches *play_* in *play_ball*<br>/play\w/ does not match *play ball* |
| \W | Any character other than a letter, number, or underscore. | /\W/ matches *@* in *sam@pooch.com* and *@,.* if g flag set<br>/\W/ matches *.* in *webwoman.biz*<br>/\W/ does not match *Hi* |

### Metacharacters That Specify the Number of Times the Preceding Character May Occur

| Metacharacter | Matches Last Character | Example |
|---|---|---|
| * | Zero or more times. | /at*/ matches *a* in *happy*<br>/at*/ matches *at* in *catchy*<br>/at*/ does not match in *pooch* |
| ? | Zero times or one time. | /p?y/ matches *py* in *happy*<br>/p?y/ matches *y* in *catchy*<br>/p?y/ does not match *pooch* |
| + | One or more times. | /p+/ matches *pp* in *happy*<br>/p+/ does not match *catchy*<br>/p+/ matches *p* in *pooch* |
| {n} | Exactly *n* times. | /p{2}/ matches *pp* in *happy*<br>/p{2}/ does not match *patchy*<br>/p{2}/ matches *pp* in *pppooch* |
| {n, } | At least *n* times. | /p{2,}/ matches *pp* in *happy*<br>/p{2,}/ does not match *patchy*<br>/p{2,}/ matches *ppp* in *pppooch* |
| {n,m} | Between *n* and *m* times | /p{2,3}/ matches *pp* in *happy*<br>/p{2,3}/ does not match *patchy*<br>/p{2,3}/ matches *ppp* in *pppooch* |

### Logical Operations

| Metacharacter | Description | Example |
|---|---|---|
| x\|y | Matches either x or y. | /och\|tch/ does not match *happy*<br>/och\|tch/ matches *tch* in *catchy*<br>/och\|tch/ matches *och* in *pooch* |
| (chars) | Capturing parentheses. Matches and remembers the match so it can be recalled from the result array. Also, it is used to group regular expression characters together. | (Sam) matches *Sam* in *Sammy Sam* and *Sam, Sam* if g flag set<br>(Sam) matches *Sam* in *Sam I am*<br>(Sam) does not match *sam* but matches *sam* if i flag set |

| (?:*chars*) | Non-capturing parentheses. Matches but does not remember the match. | same as (*chars*) |
|---|---|---|
| x(?=*y*) | Matches x only if x is followed by y. | /a(?=p)/ matches *a* in *happy* <br> /a(?=p)/ does not match *patchy* |
| x(?!*y*) | Matches x only if x is not followed by y. | /a(?!p)/ does not match *happy* <br> /a(?!p)/ matches *a* in *patchy* <br> /a(?!p)/ matches *a* in *sam* |

Learning how regular expressions work is not an easy task. But don't think all the work of learning regular expression metacharacters applies only to JavaScript. JavaScript followed the lead of Perl when it comes to regular expressions, as did many other languages, like PHP. So what you learn about regular expressions here also applies to regular expressions in Perl.

To understand what's going on, it helps if you can test a regular expression against several strings at once and immediately see the results. With this in mind, let's look at a script that accepts three strings, a regular expression, and optional flags in text boxes. When you press the Test It button, the results of the RegExp test method and of the two String methods search and match are displayed for each string. Sound like it might be helpful? Here's the script.

**Script 9.7    Regular Expression Tester**

```
1    <html>
2    <head>
3    <title>Script 9.7: Regular Expression Tester</title>
4    <script language="JavaScript" type="text/javascript"><!--
5    function testRegExp() {
6        zString1 = document.Testor.TheString1.value
7        zString2 = document.Testor.TheString2.value
8        zString3 = document.Testor.TheString3.value
9        zRegExp = new RegExp(document.Testor.TheRegExp.value,
10                            document.Testor.Flags.value)
11
12       document.Testor.TestResult1.value = zRegExp.test(zString1)
13       document.Testor.SearchResult1.value = zString1.search(zRegExp)
14       document.Testor.MatchArray1.value = zString1.match(zRegExp)
15
16       document.Testor.TestResult2.value = zRegExp.test(zString2)
17       document.Testor.SearchResult2.value = zString2.search(zRegExp)
18       document.Testor.MatchArray2.value = zString2.match(zRegExp)
19
20       document.Testor.TestResult3.value = zRegExp.test(zString3)
21       document.Testor.SearchResult3.value = zString3.search(zRegExp)
```

```
22        document.Testor.MatchArray3.value = zString3.match(zRegExp)
23    }
24    //-->
25    </script>
26    </head>
27    <body bgcolor="Lime">
28    <form name="Testor">
29        <b>String 1:</b><br>
30        <input type="text" name="TheString1" size=80><br>
31                  
32        <b>Test Result:</b> <input type="text" name="TestResult1"
33            onFocus="this.blur()">
34                
35        <b>Search Result:</b> <input type="text" name="SearchResult1"
36            onFocus="this.blur()"><br>
37        <b>Array of Matches:</b> <input type="text" name="MatchArray1"
38            size=63 onFocus="this.blur()"><br>
39        <br>
40        <br>
41        <b>String 2:</b><br>
42        <input type="text" name="TheString2" size=80><br>
43                  
44        <b>Test Result:</b> <input type="text" name="TestResult2"
45            onFocus="this.blur()">
46                
47        <b>Search Result:</b> <input type="text" name="SearchResult2"
48            onFocus="this.blur()"><br>
49        <b>Array of Matches:</b> <input type="text" name="MatchArray2"
50            size=63 onFocus="this.blur()"><br>
51        <br>
52        <br>
53        <b>String 3:</b><br>
54        <input type="text" name="TheString3" size=80><br>
55                  
56        <b>Test Result:</b> <input type="text" name="TestResult3"
57            onFocus="this.blur()">
58                
59        <b>Search Result:</b> <input type="text" name="SearchResult3"
60            onFocus="this.blur()"><br>
61        <b>Array of Matches:</b> <input type="text" name="MatchArray3"
62            size=63 onFocus="this.blur()"><br>
63        <br>
64        <br>
65        <big><b>Enter a Regular Expression Here:</b></big><br>
66        <input type="text" name="TheRegExp" size=50>
```

```
67            
68        <b>Flag(s):</b> <input type="text" name="Flags" size=5> 
69        <input type="button" value="Test It" onClick="testRegExp()">
70    </form>
71    </body>
72    </html>
```

There's nothing very complicated in this script. Lines 30, 42, and 54 create the form fields to hold the three test strings. The subsequent lines under each of those text boxes hold the values returned by method calls in the `testRegExp` function, which is what does all the work (lines 5 through 23).

The first thing `testRegExp` does is declare three variables, one for each string, and initialize each with the value entered in its corresponding text box (lines 6 through 8). Next, the function creates a `RegExp` object (lines 9 and 10) and initializes it with the entry in the text box at the bottom of the form (line 66) and any flag entered in the Flags field (line 68).

Lines 12 through 14 call the `test`, `search`, and `match` methods on the first string respectively and display the results of each method call in the appropriate form fields. Lines 16 through 22 do the same for the other two strings.

Give it a try. Enter one of the examples from Table 9.6 or make up one of your own. Here's a screen shot of the Regular Expression Tester in action using the strings in the first example from Table 9.6. Don't enter the slash delimiters around the regular expression, just enter the text for it.

**Figure 9.10    Results of Script 9.7, the Regular Expression Tester**

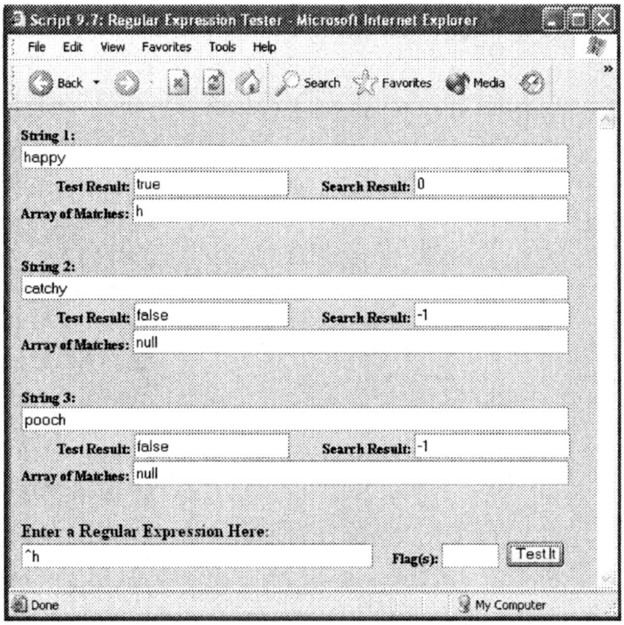

Keep using the Regular Expression Tester to try out various regular expressions until you get a good feel for how they work and can reliably predict the results that will be returned. When you feel comfortable with some simple regular expressions, move on to the next section, where we'll introduce some more complicated ones.

# More Complicated Pattern Matching

One common task programmers around the world use regular expressions for is to validate data. The following sections will walk you through the process of building some more complicated regular expressions for the purpose of validating data.

## Validating a Zip Code

Let's see if we can come up with a regular expression that when tested will return true if it is a valid U.S. zip code and false otherwise. What makes a U.S. zip code valid? U.S. zip codes are made up of five numeric characters, optionally followed by a dash and four more numeric characters. Because the second half is optional (the dash and four digits), let's look at the zip code in two parts. Let's first concentrate on creating a pattern that will match five numeric digits.

Hmm, didn't we see a metacharacter on the list that matches numeric characters? Yepper doodle, it's the \d metacharacter. Wasn't there also a metacharacter that let us specify how many times a particular character or type of character could occur? Yep again, it's the {n} metacharacters, where *n* is the number of times the character must appear.

OK, so that should take care of the first half of the zip code:

```
/\d{5}/
```

Let's try it in the Tester. Type in any five numeric digits in one string field, type a mixture of numbers and letters in the second, and type in numbers and some kind of special character in the third. Type the regular expression we just developed in the appropriate field as well, without the slash delimiters. No flags are needed for this one, so leave that field blank. Press the Test It button. Only the first string should match. Here's what I got:

**Figure 9.11    Results of Regular Expression to Match Five-Digit Zip Code**

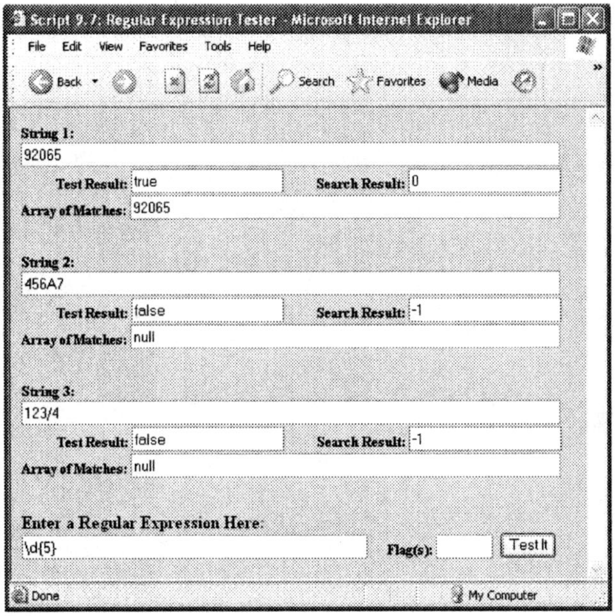

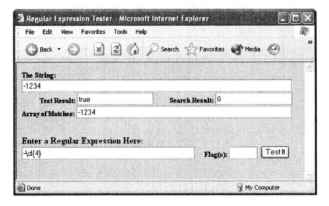

OK, now we need to come up with a pattern for the second half, a dash followed by four digits. How about

`/-\d{4}/`

Let's try it in the Tester. In the interest of smaller screen shots, from now on I'm going to use my mini-tester. It is the same as the regular tester, except it tests one string at a time. Here's what I got when I entered a dash and four numeric digits. You should always try something you don't think will match, too, so you might want to continue using the regular tester.

**Figure 9.12    Results of Testing Second Half of a Zip Code**

A U.S. zip code has two parts: five numeric digits followed by an optional dash and four more digits. We've come up with regular expressions for each half, so now let's put them together. Here's what we've got so far:

```
\d{5}-\d{4}
```

Let's try it. Enter a complete zip code.

**Figure 9.13     Results of Combined Regular Expressions for Matching Full Zip Codes**

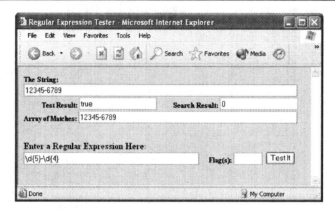

It works! Now try a short zip code.

Unfortunately, that didn't work. OK, so now we have to find some way to specify that the second half is optional. The parentheses should work to group each half together. Then follow the first grouped expression with {1} to indicate that it must appear once and the second grouped expression with ? to indicate that it should appear zero or one times. Let's try it.

**Figure 9.14     Results of Regular Expression That Tests Long and Short Zip Codes**

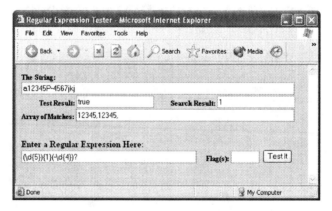

Success! It works with both long and short zip codes. Uh oh, it also works if you precede either the first or second half with one or more characters or put characters after the second half. Looks like it needs a little more work.

Somehow we need to tell it that the string must begin with the first half and end with the second half. Look over the list of metacharacters and see if you can find something that will work.

Let's try placing ^ before the first half to indicate that the string should begin with that pattern. Then let's enclose the entire second half in another set of parentheses so that the ? mark is grouped with it and place $ after the second half to indicate that the string should end with that. Do you begin to see how quickly regular expressions can get complicated?

**Figure 9.15     The FinalWorking Regular Expression toVerify Zip Codes**

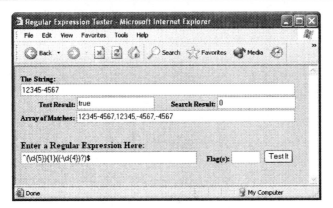

True success at last! Now how do you put that to work in a function, you ask? Here goes:

**Script 9.8        validZip function**

```
1    <html>
2    <head>
3    <title>Script 9.8: validZip function</title>
4    <script language="JavaScript" type="text/javascript"><!--
5         function validZip(zip) {
6              var zipRegExp = /^(\d{5}){1}((-\d{4})?)$/
7              if (zipRegExp.test(zip)) {
8                   return true
9              } else {
10                  return false
11             }
12        }
13   //-->
14   </script>
15   </head>
16   <body>
17   <script language="JavaScript" type="text/javascript"><!--
```

```
18     document.write("12345-6789? ",
          validZip('12345-6789'), "<br>")
19     document.write("12345? ", validZip('12345'), "<br>")
20     document.write("-6789? ", validZip('-6789'), "<br>")
21     document.write("12345-67A9? ",
          validZip('12345-67A9'), "<br>")
22     document.write("12345P-6789? ",
          validZip('12345-67A9'), "<br>")
23     document.write("B12345-6789? ",
          validZip('B12345-6789'), "<br>")
24
25  //-->
26  </script>
27  </body>
28  </html>
```

The `validZip` function in lines 5 through 12 returns `true` if the value passed to it represents a valid zip code and `false` if it does not. Lines 18 through 23 simply test the function to see that it works.

## Validating an Email Address

Now let's see if we can come up with a regular expression for an email address. Let's break it down. An email address consists of

1. one or more letters, numbers, and underscores
2. followed by an @ sign
3. followed by two or more letters, numbers, or dashes for the domain name
4. followed by a dot
5. followed by two or more characters for the top-level domain name

Actually, valid email addresses are more complicated than that, but we're trying to keep this simple, not write a whole book on the subject of regular expressions. So we'll stick to this simple five-point scenario. Part 1:

```
/\w/i
```

takes care of the letters, numbers, and underscores. We can have one or more of those characters, followed by an @ symbol:

```
/\w+@/i
```

Now for the second half. Two or more characters followed by a dot:

```
/[a-z0-9\-]{2,}./i
```

and two or more letters at the end:

```
/[a-z0-9\-]{2,}.[a-z]{2,}/i
```

I don't know of any top-level domain names that contain numbers. Now let's put the two parts together as groups:

```
/^(\w+@)([a-z0-9\-]{2,}.[a-z]{2,})$/i
```

That should do it. Pop that in the Tester and try several email addresses, good and bad, with it. A bad email address should fail like this:

**Figure 9.16**    **Results of Email Validation Tested with Bad Email Address**

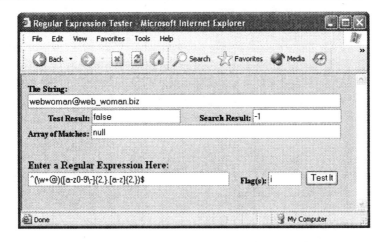

**Figure 9.17**    **Results of Email Validation Tested with Good Email Address**

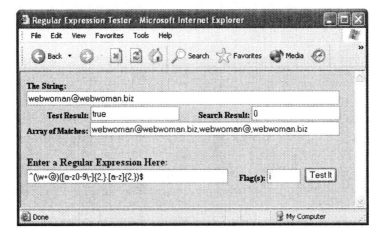

We'll leave it to you to put this in a function, but keep in mind that this email validation routine is not completely ready for prime time. It will reject valid email addresses such as tgmcduff@cuyamaca.cc.ca.us. Unfortunately, a complete, industrial-strength email validation routine is beyond the scope of this book.

# Summary

You can think of String methods as operations that can be performed on strings. JavaScript supports a whole slew of String methods that you can use on any string variable, string literal, or string object. The general categories are

- ✗ Methods for changing the case of a string (toUpperCase and toLowerCase).
- ✗ Methods for changing text appearance by marking up strings with HTML tags, including anchor, big, blink, bold, fixed, fontcolor, fontsize, italics, link, small, strike, sub, and sup.
- ✗ Methods for slicing, dicing, and reassembling strings, including charAt to get a character at a particular index in a string, concat to concatenate strings, slice and substring to retrieve a slice of a string from one index to another, and substr to get a substring of a particular length beginning at the specified index.
- ✗ Methods for converting to and from Unicode (charCodeAt and fromCharCode, respectively). Unicode is a universal character set in the making.
- ✗ A method that converts a string into an array (split).
- ✗ Methods for searching strings (indexOf and lastIndexOf).

Two global methods also work on strings: escape for URL-encoding strings and unescape for unURL-encoding. In addition to all these methods, JavaScript supports regular expressions.

A regular expression is a pattern that you can use to match against character combinations in strings. Regular expressions are commonly used to search strings for a matching pattern or to validate that a string matches a particular pattern.

JavaScript supports a RegExp object. You can create a regular expression object by assigning a regular expression literal to a variable or by calling the RegExp() constructor function in conjunction with the new operator. Regular expression literals are delimited by slashes (/), contain a series of characters and metacharacters, and may end with one or more flags.

JavaScript supports three regular expression flags: g, i, and m for global, ignore case, and multiline, respectively. These flags modify the way the methods that work on regular expressions work. When the global flag is applied, some methods will search for all matches in the string. When the ignore case flag is applied, methods will ignore case while looking for matches.

The RegExp object supports two methods, test and exec, that are similar to two String methods that work on regular expressions, search and match. The RegExp.test() method searches a string and returns true if the string or a substring match the regular expression on which the method was called and false otherwise. The String.search() method does the same thing, except that it returns the index of the matching substring when a match is found and -1 if no match is found.

The RegExp.exec() method also searches a string for matches, but returns an array of results. The String.match() method also returns an array of results after attempting to find matches. The match method's results array is much more useful and thorough than is the exec method's results array. The exec method, however, also sets several properties of the RegExp object and the regular expression instance on which an exec method was called after executing the method. The properties set describe the original regular expression, its flags, the last match made, the last parenthesized substring match, and the substrings to the left and right of the last matched substring.

The power of regular expressions lies in its metacharacters. A metacharacter is a character or character combination that specifies a pattern, a modifier, or how to process the characters that follow it. JavaScript follows Perl's lead in its regular expression support and includes metacharacters that specify the location of text within a string, particular groups of characters, the number of times a character or combination of characters should appear successively, and logical rules to apply.

## Review Questions

1. What is a String method?
2. To what types of elements can String methods be applied?
3. Describe the kinds of operations that can be performed on strings using String methods.
4. What methods allow you to change the case of a string?
5. List and describe three String methods that return a string marked up with HTML.
6. How can you see that a string has been marked up with HTML?
7. What does the method charAt do?
8. How many strings can you concatenate together with the concat method?
9. What's are the differences among slice, substring, and substr?
10. What is Unicode?
11. What methods allow you to convert to Unicode and back?
12. What is the ISO 8859-1 character set and what does it have to do with the Web?
13. What is URL-encoding?
14. Name two global methods that work on strings.
15. What method allows you to create an array from a string?
16. What is the difference between indexOf and lastIndexOf?
17. What is a regular expression?
18. How can you create a regular expression?
19. What do regular expression flags do?
20. What RegExp and String methods search a string and return false and -1 respectively if a match is not found?
21. What RegExp and String methods search a string and return an array of results?
22. What is a metacharacter?
23. List and describe five metacharacters supported by JavaScript.
24. What language did JavaScript model its support for regular expressions after?

25. Create two lists. The first should list all of the String methods that modify the string on which they are called. The second should list all of the String methods that *do not* modify the string on which they are called.

# Exercises

1. For each of the following statements, specify what the expression evaluates to, given
   ```
   var myQuote="He who laughs, lasts."
   ```
   a. myQuote.toUpperCase()
   b. myQuote.indexOf("a")
   c. myQuote.indexOf("@", 1)
   d. myQuote.indexOf("who")
   e. myQuote.indexOf("a", 10)
   f. myQuote.lastIndexOf("a")
   g. myQuote.lastIndexOf("a", 7)
   h. myQuote.lastIndexOf("a", 10)
   i. myQuote.charAt(7)
   j. myQuote.charAt(myQuote.length)
   k. myQuote.charAt(myQuote.length - 3)

2. For each of the following statements, specify what the expression evaluates to or returns, given var myQuote="He who laughs, lasts".
   a. myQuote.concat("forever")
   b. myQuote.concat("forever", " and ", "a day!")
   c. myQuote.slice("7, 13")
   d. myQuote.slice(15)
   e. myQuote.slice(3, -3)
   f. myQuote.substring(7, 13)
   g. myQuote.substring(3, 4)
   h. myQuote.substr(3, 4)
   i. myQuote.substr(7, 6)
   j. var myStr = ""; myStr.concat("S", myQuote.slice(1))

3. Write a JavaScript statement that uses String methods to write

   My big, **bold**, green string.

   to the document marked up appropriately with HTML. The word *green* should be displayed in green.

4. Write a statement to search the navigator's appName property for the word Opera.

5. Write a statement to search Mississippi for the index number of the last s.

6. Write a statement to search Mississippi for the index number of the first s.

7. Write a single JavaScript statement to combine two strings, "Sam" and "Sammy", into one string with a space in between the two.

8. Write a regular expression to match the following strings: num1, num2, num3, etc. The string should start with num followed by a numeric digit.

9. List three strings that each of the following regular expressions would match:

    a. `/[a-z]{3}/`
    b. `/(^[0-9]{2})([A-C])$/`
    c. `/^([0-9]{2})([A-C])$/i`
    d. `/^(\d{2})([abc])$/i`
    e. `/\w{1,}\s\w{1,}/i`

10. Write a regular expression to perform each of the following types of matches:
    a. a combination of the letters `sam` within a word.
    b. any word that starts with `T`.
    c. the substring `match`.
    d. any word like `hat` that starts with the letter `h` and ends with the letter `t` and contains a vowel in between.
    e. a string or line with `.com` at the end.

# Scripting Exercises

Create a folder named assignment09 to hold the documents you create during this assignment. Save a copy of your latest toy store documents in a toyStore subfolder.

1. Write a function, `capitalize()`, that will accept a string parameter and capitalize any word sent to it, in any case, mixed or otherwise. It will make the first letter a capital and the remaining letters lowercase. Test it. Once you're certain it works correctly without error, add it to myLib.js along with the appropriate comments and description.

2. Write a function, `charAppears()`, that accepts a character and a string as parameters, then searches the string for the number of times that character appears within it. The function should return the count. If the character is not in the string at all, return 0.

3. Create a new document named getDestination.html.
    a. Scripting Exercise 3 in Chapter 6 asked you to write a script to prompt the visitor for one of four destinations. You chose the destinations. The script showed a list of the choices in the status bar each time it prompted the visitor. It kept prompting the visitor for a choice until he chose one of the four destinations. Once a valid destination was chosen, the script took the visitor to that site.
    b. Modify the script so that the visitor can enter the destination's name in any case. For instance, if the visitor types in Google, GooGle, google, or any other version of the word "google," he will be transported to that destination without further ado.

4. Modify the `validZip()` function in Script 9.8 to accept two parameters: the zip code to test as a string and a country code. If the country code is "ca" for Canada, return `true` if the string represents a validly formed Canadian zip code and `false` if it does not. Canada uses a six-digit postal code of the form `ANA NAN`, where `A` represents a letter and `N` represents a numeric digit. Use regular expressions.

   Modify your function further to also test for valid zip codes for at least two other countries. You choose the countries. This site can help you figure out the rules:

http://www.freesearching.com/zip_codes_intl.htm. It provides links to looking up international postal codes. You can view a list of two-letter country codes (ccTLDs) at http://www.ccregistrars.com/countries.html.

Add the tested function to myLib.js with an appropriate description and comments.

5. Write a function, `isValidPhone()`, that accepts a string as a parameter and returns `true` if the string represents a validly formed phone number and `false` if it does not. Use regular expressions. The following formats represent valid U.S. phone numbers:

```
123-456-7890
(123)456-7890
(123) 456-7890
```

Pick three countries and test for valid phone numbers for those countries as well. This "Phone Numbers" site can help you determine the appropriate form: http://www.phonenumbers.net/.

Add the tested function to myLib.js with an appropriate description and comments.

6. Write a function, `isValidEmail()`, that accepts a string as a parameter and returns `true` if the string represents a validly formed email address and `false` if it does not. Use regular expressions. Email addresses
   a. may not contain the characters slash (/), colon (:), comma (,), or semicolon (;).
   b. may contain spaces only in the first half of the email address, before the @ symbol, if the first half is delimited by quotation marks.
   c. must contain an @ symbol, but only one and it cannot be the first character in the address.
   d. must contain at least one dot after the @ symbol, but not directly after the @ symbol. There must be at least one character between the dot and the @ symbol.
   e. must have at least two characters after the last dot to represent one of the generic top-level domain names (gTLDs) or a country top-level domain name (ccTLD).

   Add the tested function to myLib.js with an appropriate description and comments.

7. Write a function that will take a phone number in any valid phone format (you can choose a particular country to limit it to), convert it to a particular format, and return the result. You choose the format you want to convert it to.

   For instance, you might want to list all U.S. phone numbers in a database in the following format: `(123) 456-7890`. So if you received a phone number in the format `123-456-7890` or `(123)456-7890` or `1234567890`, your function should convert the phone number to `(123) 456-7890`.

   Add the tested function to myLib.js with an appropriate description and comments.

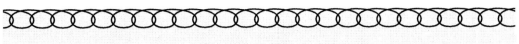

## chapter *ten*

# *Dates and Math*

*I haven't failed. I've found 10,000 ways that don't work.*

—Thomas Edison

B oth the Date and Math objects are defined in Core JavaScript. The Date object supports many methods for working with dates. When used in conjunction with arrays, it allows you to write dates in virtually any type of custom format you desire. The Math object contains many often-used mathematical constants, such as pi, as well as methods for performing popular mathematical operations.

In this chapter we'll

- ✗ examine the Date object.
- ✗ learn various ways to initialize a Date object.
- ✗ use arrays and Date methods to write custom date formats.
- ✗ learn how to write the current date to a Web page and calculate a countdown.
- ✗ examine the Math object and its various properties.
- ✗ use Math methods to write functions that get a random number and a random index number.
- ✗ create the user-defined getRandNdx function to display a random quote when a document opens.

Let's begin with a look at the Date object.

# The Date Object

Face it, in terms of data types, dates just don't fit one of the primitive molds. They're more than simple strings; they have numeric properties, too. For instance, today succeeds yesterday and precedes tomorrow, so there's an order to dates like with numbers. However, you don't normally represent a date just as a number either. It's usually a set of numbers, such as 07/04/1776 or 07-04-1776, or a combination of words and numbers, such as July 4, 1776, or Thursday 4 July 1776.

Because dates are a special kind of data type unto themselves, JavaScript includes a Date object. JavaScript represents a date as a number: the number of milliseconds between January 1, 1970, at 00:00:00:00 hours and the date to be referenced. Dates before January 1, 1970, at 00:00:00:00 are represented as negative numbers, those after as positive numbers. Thus, it is possible to represent dates before Unix time.

## Creating a Date Object

The first, and simplest, way of creating a Date object is to use the new operator and call the Date constructor function without any parameters. This will create a Date object and initialize it with the client's current date and time.

```
var dateName = new Date()
```

For example:

```
var today = new Date()
```

While initializing a `Date` object with the client machine's current system date and time is very useful for some purposes, there are times when you want to work with specific dates and need to initialize a `Date` object accordingly. Fortunately, JavaScript provides four ways of accomplishing this:

1.  Provide a single string argument describing the date and time. The string must be in a format recognized by the `Date.parse` method.

```
var dateName = new Date("month day, ⋯⋯➤
⋯⋯➤ year hours:minutes:seconds")
var dateName = new Date("weekday, month day, ⋯⋯➤
⋯⋯➤ year hours:minutes:seconds")
```

Examples:

```
var independenceDay = new Date("July 4, 1776")
var independenceDay = new Date("July 4, 1776 19:05:20")
var independenceDay = new Date("Thursday, July 4, ⋯⋯➤
⋯⋯➤ 1776 19:05:20")
```

This option is quite useful because a number of properties, such as `document.lastModified`, store the date as a string in this long format recognized by the `Date.parse` method. You can then use the property's value to create a `Date` object:

```
var lastUpdate = new Date(document.lastModified)
```

Cool, huh? Let's look at the second option.

2.  Simply specify the date by providing three numeric arguments representing the year, month, and day.

```
var dateName = new Date(year, month, day)
```

Example:

```
var independenceDay = new Date(1776, 6, 4)
```

This is by far the simplest. Notice that July is represented as a 6. This is not a mistake. JavaScript numbers months beginning at 0. We'll shortly see that JavaScript has other idiosyncrasies when it comes to numbering dates. For now, let's look at the third way of declaring a date.

3.  Specify the date and time down to the millisecond by providing seven arguments representing the year, month, day, hours, minutes, seconds, and milliseconds.

```
var dateName = new Date(year, month, day, hours, minutes, ⋯⋯➤
⋯⋯➤ seconds, milliseconds)
```

Example:

```
var independenceDay = new Date(1776, 6, 4, 19, 5, 20)
```

This is just a longer version of the second option. You can get as detailed as you like, anywhere between options 2 and 3. For instance, if you don't want to worry about seconds and milliseconds, leave them off. They'll get set to 0 and your date will be initialized down to the minute instead of the millisecond. Now let's look at the fourth option.

4. Specify the exact date in milliseconds since January 1, 1970, 00:00:00:00.

```
var dateName = new Date(milliseconds)
```

Example:

```
var independenceDay = new Date(-6106035600000)
```

JavaScript stores dates internally as the number of milliseconds since January 1, 1970, 00:00:00:00. Dates before January 1, 1970, are represented as negative numbers. That's why the Independence Day example above is such a large negative number.

The `Date` object has quite a few methods, mostly for getting and setting parts of the date. Table 10.1 lists each of the basic `Date` methods included in JavaScript with a short description of the type and range of values returned by or used by the method.

**Table 10.1    Date Methods**

| Method | Description | Value Range/Type |
|---|---|---|
| getDate()<br>getUTCDate() | Returns the date's day of the month according to local or UTC time. | 1 to 31, where 1 is the first day of the month. |
| getDay()<br>getUTCDay() | Returns the date's day of the week according to local or UTC time. | 0 to 6, where 0 is Sunday, 1 is Monday, . . . 6 is Saturday. |
| getFullYear()<br>getUTCFullYear() | Returns the date's full, four-digit year according to local or UTC time. | Four-digit year. |
| getHours()<br>getUTCHours() | Returns the date's hour according to local or UTC time. | 0 to 23, where 0 is midnight (12 a.m.), 1 is 1 a.m., . . . 23 is 11 p.m. |
| getMilliseconds()<br>getUTCMilliseconds() | Returns the date's milliseconds according to local or UTC time. | 0 to 99. |
| getMinutes()<br>getUTCMinutes() | Returns the date's minutes according to local or UTC time. | 0 to 59. |

| | | |
|---|---|---|
| `getMonth()`<br>`getUTCMonth()` | Returns the date's month according to local or UTC time. | 0 to 11, where 0 is January, 1 is February, . . . 11 is December. |
| `getSeconds()`<br>`getUTCSeconds()` | Returns the date's seconds according to local or UTC time. | 0 to 59. |
| `getTime()` | Returns the date's value as the number of milliseconds since January 1, 1970, 00:00:00:00 according to local time. | For the specified date, the number of milliseconds since January 1, 1970, 00:00:00:00 local time. |
| `getTimezoneOffset()` | Returns the date's time-zone offset in minutes for the current locale. | 0 to 59. |
| `getYear()` | Returns the date's year according to local time. Because of the idiosyncrasies and inconsistencies of this method, it is better to use getFullYear whenever possible. | Before 1900, four-digit year; in 1900s, two-digit year; in 2000s, four-digit year, except some browsers return 100 for the year 2000, 101 for 2001, etc. |
| `parse("dateString")` | Returns the date value of a date string. | The number of milliseconds since January 1, 1970, 00:00:00:00. |
| `setDate()`<br>`setUTCDate()` | Sets the date's day of the month according to local or UTC time. | 1 to 31, where 1 is the first day of the month. |
| `setFullYear()`<br>`setUTCFullYear()` | Sets the date's full, four-digit year according to local or UTC time. | Four-digit year. |
| `setHours()`<br>`setUTCHours()` | Sets the date's hour according to local or UTC time. | 0 to 23, where 0 is midnight (12 a.m.), 1 is 1 a.m., . . . 23 is 11 p.m. |
| `setMilliseconds()`<br>`setUTCMilliseconds()` | Sets the date's milliseconds according to local or UTC time. | 0 to 99. |

| Method | Description | Value Range/Type *(continued)* |
|---|---|---|
| setMinutes()<br>setUTCMinutes() | Sets the date's minutes according to local or UTC time. | 0 to 59. |
| setMonth()<br>setUTCMonth() | Sets the date's month according to local or UTC time. | 0 to 11, where 0 is January, 1 is February, . . . 11 is December. |
| setSeconds()<br>setUTCSeconds() | Sets the date's seconds according to local or UTC time. | 0 to 59. |
| setTime() | Sets the date's value as the number of milliseconds since January 1, 1970, 00:00:00:00 according to local time. | For the specified date, the number of milliseconds since January 1, 1970, 00:00:00:00 local time. |
| setYear() | Sets the date's year according to local time. Because of the idiosyncrasies and inconsistencies of this method, it is better to use setFullYear whenever possible. | Before 1900, four-digit year; in 1900s, two-digit year; in 2000s, four-digit year, except some browsers return 100 for the year 2000, 101 for 2001, etc. |
| toGMTString() | Converts the date to a string according to the time standard common to every place in the world, known as GMT, World Time, and UTC. toGMTString is deprecated, replaced by toUTCString. | A string representing the date and time in the time standard common to every place in the world, known as GMT, World Time, and UTC. |
| toLocaleString() | Converts the date to a string according to the conventions of the current locale. | A string representing the local date and time. |
| toString() | Returns a string representing the date according to local time. | A string representing the date in local time. |

| toUTCString() | Converts the date to a string according to the universal time convention. | A string representing the date and time in UTC format. |
|---|---|---|
| UTC(*year, month, day* [ *,hrs, min, sec,ms*] ) | Returns the date value in the number of milliseconds since January 1, 1970, 00:00:00:00 universal time. | For the specified date, the number of milliseconds since January 1, 1970, 00:00:00:00 UTC. |
| valueOf() | Returns the primitive value of a Date object. | For the specified date, the number of milliseconds since January 1, 1970, 00:00:00:00. |

Coordinated Universal Time, often written as both Universal Coordinated Time and Universal Time Coordinated (hence the acronym UTC) is the standard time common to every place in the world. You may be more familiar with the terms Greenwich Mean Time (GMT) or World Time; they are the same thing.

Each UTC method works the same way as its non-UTC equivalent, except that it returns a value according to universal time instead of local time. Note that the toUTCString method replaces and deprecates the toGMTString method.

## Formatting Dates

As you can see, JavaScript doesn't provide very many methods for writing date formats, only toString, toLocaleString, and toUTCString. All of them write the date in long format. While this may at times be quite useful, most of the time you'll want to write dates in a more abbreviated or custom format, such as

1. 7/4/1776
2. 7-4-1776
3. 7/4/76
4. 7-4-76
5. 4 July 1776
6. Thursday, July 4, 1776
7. Thurs., Jul. 4, 1776
8. Thursday 4 July 1776

Using the Date methods provided by JavaScript, you can write a date in pretty much any *numeric* format you choose. Using *arrays* with JavaScript's Date methods, you can easily write dates in just about any custom format you desire. How? Most Date methods return a number that can be used as an index into an array of month or day names created by you, the programmer.

Be careful, though. To write the *appropriate* date, you need to be aware of JavaScript's idiosyncrasies in date-related numbering. Table 10.2 sums them up for you.

**Table 10.2     JavaScript's Idiosyncratic Date Numbering**

| Date Element | Method Used In | Idiosyncrasy |
|---|---|---|
| Months of the year | `getMonth()` `getUTCMonth()` `setMonth()` `setUTCMonth()` | Numbered 0 to 11, where 0 is January and 11 is December. |
| Days of the month | `getDate()` `getUTCDate()` `setDate()` `setUTCDate()` | Numbered 1 to 31 as normal. |
| Days of the week | `getDay()` `getUTCDay()` `setDay()` `setUTCDay()` | Numbered 0 to 6, where 0 is Sunday, 1 is Monday, ..., and 6 is Saturday. |
| Time | `getTime()` `setTime()` | Measured as the number of milliseconds since January 1, 1970, at 00:00:00:00. |
| Year | `getFullYear()` `getUTCFullYear()` `setFullYear()` `setUTCFullYear()` | Four-digit year. |
| Year | `getYear()` `setYear()` | Before 1900, four-digit year; in 1900s, two-digit year; in 2000s, four-digit year, except some browsers return 100 for the year 2000, 101 for 2001, etc. |

**Writing Numeric Date Formats**

Notice that months begin numbering at 0, so if you want to write a month's numeric equivalent the way you usually do, you'll need to add 1 to it. Thus, to write Independence Day, July 4, 1776, in the first format in our list (7/4/1776), use

```
var independenceDay = new Date(1776, 6, 4)
document.write(independenceDay.getMonth() + 1, "/",
            independenceDay.getDate(), "/",
            independenceDay.getFullYear())
```

When you initialize the date, you must take into account that July is month 6 in JavaScript time: January is 0. When you *write* the date, you must add 1 to the month because humans count months from 1, where 1 is January.

Despite the millennium bug and all the trouble it caused, humans are still in the habit of writing years as a two-digit abbreviation (see the third (7/4/76) and fourth (7-4-76) date format examples above). Because we often write years as two digits, you'd better learn how to do it in JavaScript. One of JavaScript's string methods should come in handy for this task. The following script demonstrates both the four-digit year format as well as the two-digit year format.

**Script 10.1    Writing Custom Numerical Date Formats**

```
1    <html>
2    <head>
3    <title>Script 10.1: Custom Numerical Date Formats</title>
4    <script language="JavaScript" type="text/javascript"><!--
5        var independenceDay = new Date(1776, 6, 4)
6    //-->
7    </script>
8    </head>
9    <body>
10   <script language="JavaScript" type="text/javascript"><!--
11       // Format:  7/4/1776
12       document.write(independenceDay.getMonth() + 1, "/",
13                   independenceDay.getDate(), "/",
14                   independenceDay.getFullYear(), "<br><br>")
15
16       // Format: 7/4/76
17       var theYear = independenceDay.getFullYear()
18       theYear += ""                             // turn it into a string
19       theYear = theYear.substring(theYear.length-2,
20          theYear.length)
20       document.write(independenceDay.getMonth() + 1, "/",
21                   independenceDay.getDate(), "/", theYear)
22   //-->
23   </script>
24   </body>
25   </html>
```

In line 5, we declare a new `Date` object, and lines 12 through 14 write the date with a four-digit year. The result is

```
07/4/1776
```

To get a two-digit year, you have to assign the full year to a temporary variable (line 17). Then convert `theYear` to a string by adding an empty string to it (line 18). You could also use the `toString` method, like this:

```
theYear = theYear.toString()
```

Line 19 extracts the last two characters of the string, using the `substring` string method. `substring` returns—you guessed it—a substring of the string it is called on. It takes two parameters; the first specifies the index of the starting point, the second the ending point.

`substring` extracts from the starting point up to, but not including, the ending point. We used the string's `length` property to specify two characters from the end as the start (`length-2`) and the `length` as the end.

The `substring` method is just one of several you could have used to get the last two digits of the year. However you extract the last two digits, line 21 writes the date with a two-digit year as in format 3.

The result:

```
7/4/76
```

Be careful of using two-digit years. Most people would probably assume the above date indicates July 4, 1976, or maybe July 4, 2076, instead of the year 1776 that we intended.

Here's a screen shot of the script's results:

### Figure 10.1    Results of Script 10.1

### Writing Textual Date Formats

Using numbers is fine, but what if you want to write out a month's name in full or as an abbreviation rather than a number? Same with days of the week? Where are the methods to do that? The answer is there aren't any. However, using arrays in conjunction with the `Date` methods provided by JavaScript, you can write a date in pretty much any format you desire.

In this script, we'll use the eighth date format from above: Thursday 4 July 1776.

### Script 10.2    Writing Custom Textual Date Formats

```
1    <html>
2    <head>
3    <title>Script 10.2: Writing Custom Textual Date Formats</title>
4    <script language="JavaScript" type="text/javascript"><!--
5         var months = new Array("January", "February", "March",
6                                "April", "May", "June", "July",
7                                "August", "September", "October",
8                                "November", "December")
```

```
9            var weekdays = new Array("Sunday", "Monday", "Tuesday",
10                              "Wednesday", "Thursday",
11                              "Friday", "Saturday")
12
13           var independenceDay = new Date(1776, 6, 4)
14    //-->
15    </script>
16    </head>
17    <body>
18    <script language="JavaScript" type="text/javascript"><!--
19        // Format:  Thursday 4 July 1776
20        document.write(weekdays[independenceDay.getDay()], " ",
21                   independenceDay.getDate(), " ",
22                   months[independenceDay.getMonth()], " ",
23                   independenceDay.getFullYear(), "<br><br>")
24    //-->
25    </script>
26    </body>
27    </html>
```

Here's what the output looks like:

**Figure 10.2    Results of Script 10.2**

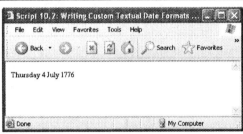

You first must define two dense arrays, one with the names of the months of the year in order beginning with January (lines 5 through 8) and the other with the names of the days of the week, also in order (lines 9 through 11).

To write out the weekday name (line 20), reference the weekdays array and call the getDay method on independenceDay to supply the index number. The same is true for writing the appropriate month name (line 22). The getMonth method supplies the index number so you can access the appropriate element in the months array. Cool, huh?

This same technique can be used to write any other custom date format. Simply load an array according to your output needs. For example, if you wanted to write abbreviated month names, like Jan, Feb, Mar, etc., you would declare the following dense array:

```
var mos = new Array("Jan", "Feb", "Mar", "Apr", "May", "Jun",
                "Jul", "Aug", "Sep", "Oct", "Nov", "Dec")
```

**Writing the Current Date and Time in Web Pages**

Thus far, we've stuck to writing dates. There are times, no pun intended, when you want to write the time as well. Writing time works just like writing numerical dates, you just need to call the appropriate Date methods. To demonstrate this, let's get the current date and time and write it to a Web page.

**Script 10.3     *Writing the Current Date and Time (Military)***

```
1    <html>
2    <head>
3    <title>Script 10.3: Writing the Current Date and Time
       (Military)</title>
4    <script language="JavaScript" type="text/javascript"><!--
5         var months = new Array("January", "February", "March",
6                               "April", "May", "June", "July",
7                               "August", "September", "October",
8                               "November", "December")
9        var weekdays = new Array("Sunday", "Monday", "Tuesday",
10                               "Wednesday", "Thursday",
11                               "Friday", "Saturday")
12
13        var today = new Date()
14   //-->
15   </script>
16   </head>
17   <body>
18   <script language="JavaScript" type="text/javascript"><!--
19        // Today is Weekday, Month Day, Year.
20        document.write("Today is: ",
21                       weekdays[today.getDay()], ", ",
22                       months[today.getMonth()], " ",
23                       today.getDate(), ", ",
24                       today.getFullYear(), ".  ")
25
26        // The time is: Hours:Minutes
27        document.write("The time is: ",
28                       today.getHours(), ":",
29                       today.getMinutes(), ".")
30   //-->
31   </script>
32   </body>
33   </html>
```

Notice in line 13 that we did not initialize the Date object with a particular date. Remember, when the Date constructor function is called without any parameters, the Date object is initialized with the client's current system date and time, which is very convenient for us. Lines 19 through 24 should need no explanation; we're using the same process described in Script 10.2, only the format is a little different.

Lines 27 through 29 write out the time by calling two more Date methods: getHours and getMinutes. The results should look something like Figure 10.3.

*Figure 10.3* **Results of Script 10.3**

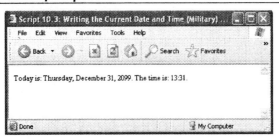

OK, OK. So your results probably show a year well before the end of this century. I set my system's clock way ahead.

### Writing the Time in Terms of a.m./p.m.

Notice that JavaScript reported the hour in military time, using the 24-hour format. I don't know about you, but I find military time a bit confusing, even though I've been married to a Navy man for more than 10 years. The 12-hour format using a.m. and p.m. is much friendlier. A simple if statement should be able to fix it for us.

**Programmer's tip**

**Caution:** The browser's (client's) current date and time may not be correct. It depends on whether or not the visitor keeps the current date and time set on his computer. He may be behind the times, or even years ahead of the rest of us.

*Script 10.4* **Converting Military Time to a.m./p.m.**

```
1    <html>
2    <head>
3    <title>Script 10.4: Converting Military Time to AM/PM</title>
4    <script language="JavaScript" type="text/javascript"><!--
5         var today = new Date()
6         var hour = ""
7         var ext = ""
8         if (today.getHours() == 0) {
9              hour = 12
10             ext = "a.m."
11        } else if (today.getHours() < 12) {
12                hour = today.getHours()
13             ext = "a.m."
```

```
14          } else if (today.getHours() == 12) {
15              hour = 12
16              ext = "p.m."
17          } else {
18              hour = today.getHours() - 12
19              ext = "p.m."
20          }
21  //-->
22  </script>
23  </head>
24  <body>
25  <script language="JavaScript" type="text/javascript"><!--
26      // The time is: Hours:Minutes
27      document.write("The time is: ", hour, ":",
28                      today.getMinutes(), " ", ext)
29  //-->
30  </script>
31  </body>
32  </html>
```

Here's the result:

**Figure 10.4     Results of Script 10.4**

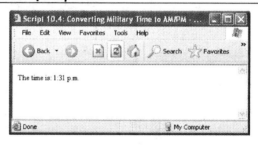

That's much better. Now let's put it all together in one script:

**Script 10.5     *Writing the Current Date and Time (AM/PM)***

```
1   <html>
2   <head>
3   <title>Script 10.5: Writing the Current Date and Time
    (AM/PM)</title>
4   <script language="JavaScript" type="text/javascript"><!--
5       var months = new Array("January", "February", "March",
6                              "April", "May", "June", "July",
7                              "August", "September", "October",
8                              "November", "December")
```

```
 9          var weekdays = new Array("Sunday", "Monday", "Tuesday",
10                                   "Wednesday", "Thursday",
11                                   "Friday", "Saturday")
12
13          var today = new Date()
14          var hour = ""
15          var ext = ""
16          if (today.getHours() == 0) {
17                  hour = 12
18                  ext = "a.m."
19          } else if (today.getHours() < 12) {
20                  hour = today.getHours()
21                  ext = "a.m."
22          } else if (today.getHours() == 12) {
23                  hour = 12
24                  ext = "p.m."
25          } else {
26                  hour = today.getHours() - 12
27                  ext = "p.m."
28          }
29  //-->
30  </script>
31  </head>
32  <body>
33  <script language="JavaScript" type="text/javascript"><!--
34          // Today is Weekday, Month Day, Year.
35          document.write("Today is: ",
36                         weekdays[today.getDay()], ", ",
37                         months[today.getMonth()], " ",
38                         today.getDate(), ", ",
39                         today.getFullYear(), ".   ")
40
41          // The time is: Hours:Minutes
42          document.write("The time is: ", hour, ":",
43                         today.getMinutes(), " ", ext)
44  //-->
45  </script>
46  </body>
47  </html>
```

Here's what the final result looks like on my system:

***Figure 10.5    Results of Script 10.5***

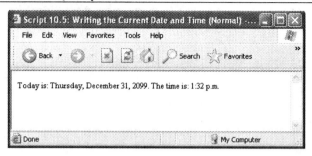

## Countdowns

Countdowns are a nice way to tell the visitor how many days, hours, or even minutes until a particular event occurs. Do you have some date you're looking forward to? Your next birthday perhaps? A particular holiday? Let's see how to put a countdown in a Web page so you can keep track of how fast time is flying to that long-awaited day.

For our example, we'll count down to my dog's next birthday and the 4th of July. Here's the script in its entirety:

***Script 10.6    Countdown***

```
1    <html>
2    <head>
3    <title>Script 10.6: Countdown</title>
4    <script language="JavaScript" type="text/javascript"><!--
5    // Remember getTime is in milliseconds. To calculate a day
6    // in terms of days, we need to divide by 1000 to get time in
7    // seconds, divide by 60 to get time in minutes, divide by 60
8    // again to get time in hours, divide by 24 to get time in days.
9    function dateToDays(zDate) {
10       var time = zDate.getTime()
11       var msPerDay = (1000 * 60 * 60 * 24)
12       var numDays = (time - (time % msPerDay)) / msPerDay
13       return numDays
14   }
15
16   function daysUntil(startDate, targetDate) {
17       var numDays = dateToDays(targetDate) - dateToDays(startDate)
18       return numDays
19   }
20
21   var today = new Date()
22   // set extraneous hours, minutes, seconds, and ms to 0
23   today.setHours(0); today.setMinutes(0)
```

```
24   today.setSeconds(0); today.setMilliseconds(0)
25
26   var thisYear = today.getFullYear()
27   var nextYear = thisYear + 1
28   var birthday = new Date(thisYear, 1, 1)          // Feb. 1
29   var july4th = new Date(thisYear, 6, 4)           // July 4
30
31   // make certain years are set to next year if target date has
32   // already passed this year
33   if (today.getTime() > birthday.getTime()) {
34       birthday.setFullYear(nextYear)
35   }
36   if (today.getTime() > july4th.getTime()) {
37       july4th.setFullYear(nextYear)
38   }
39
40   //-->
41   </script>
42   </head>
43   <body>
44   <script language="JavaScript" type="text/javascript"><!--
45   if (daysUntil(today, birthday) == 0) {
46       document.writeln("<img src=\"images/balloonsAnim.gif\" ",
47           "align=left width=128 height=128 alt=\"Balloons\">")
48       document.writeln("<img src=\"images/redAnimBalloon.gif\" ",
49           "align=right width=128 height=128 alt=\"Red Balloon\">")
50       document.writeln("<h1 align=center>It\'s Sam\'s
                Birthday!</h1>")
51       document.writeln("<div align=center>",
52           "<img src=\"images/birthdayCakeAnim.gif\" ",
53           "width=128 height=128 alt=\"Cake\"></div>" )
54   } else if (daysUntil(today, birthday) == 1) {
55       document.write("<h2 align=center>It\'s only ",
56           daysUntil(today, birthday),
57           " day until Sam\'s birthday.</h2>")
58   } else {
59       document.write("<h2 align=center>It\'s only ",
60           daysUntil(today, birthday),
61           " days until Sam\'s birthday.</h2>")
62   }
63
64   if (daysUntil(today, july4th) == 0) {
65       document.writeln("<img src=\"images/flagAnim.gif\" ",
66           "align=left width=128 height=128 alt=\"American Flag\">")
67       document.writeln("<img src=\"images/july4th.gif\" ",
```

```
68        "align=right width=128 height=128 alt=\"Red Balloon\">")
69      document.writeln("<h1 align=center>It\'s Independence
           Day!</h1>")
70      document.writeln("<div align=center>",
71          "<img src=\"images/july4th1.gif\" width=128 height=128 ",
72          "alt=\"4th of July\"></div>" )
73    } else if (daysUntil(today, july4th) == 1) {
74      document.write("<h2 align=center>Only ", daysUntil(today,
75          july4th), " day until the 4th of July!</h2>")
76    } else {
77      document.write("<h2 align=center>Only ", daysUntil(today,
78          july4th), " days until the 4th of July!</h2>")
79    }
80
81    //-->
82    </script>
83    </body>
84    </html>
```

Let's dissect the script. Lines 9 through 19 define two functions that will perform the actual calculations: dateToDays and daysUntil. The dateToDays function, shown again here,

```
function dateToDays(zDate) {
    var time = zDate.getTime()
    var msPerDay = (1000 * 60 * 60 * 24)
    var numDays = (time - (time % msPerDay)) / msPerDay
    return numDays
}
```

accepts a date object, converts it to JavaScript time in days (remember that JavaScript time is normally measured in milliseconds since midnight January 1, 1970), and returns the number of days since January 1, 1970, that the date equates to.

The daysUntil function, shown again here,

```
function daysUntil(startDate, targetDate) {
    var numDays = dateToDays(targetDate) -
        dateToDays(startDate)
    return numDays
}
```

takes two date objects, a start date and a target date; converts each date to a date in terms of days rather than milliseconds by calling dateToDays; and then returns the difference, in days, between the two dates.

At least two `Date` objects need to be declared for the countdown to work. We've declared three. Line 21 declares a `Date` object for the day from which to count down (`today`), in this case, the current system date. Lines 23 and 24 clear the excess hours, minutes, seconds, and milliseconds from `today` so that we don't have to worry about partial days screwing up the calculation. Lines 28 and 29 declare the other two `Date` objects, one for each special day or event to count down to (`birthday` and `july4th`). Lines 33 through 38 ensure that each special day is in the future. If the event has already passed this year, the event's year is set to next year so the script can perform an appropriate countdown.

That takes care of the set-up, now to writing the results (lines 45 through 81). You can modify this part to your heart's content in order to get the output you desire. The `if...else if...else` statements check for days until the event to be equal to zero (lines 45 and 64), in which case some special message or image is displayed to mark the event. The `else if` and `else` blocks simply write the number of days left until the special event. Lines 54 and 73 account for the need to write "day" when there is only one day left until the event instead of "days."

Whew! And the results are the following:

### Figure 10.6     Results of Script 10.6 on January 1

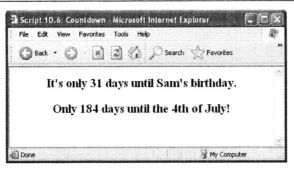

Your results will, of course, vary depending on your current date and time settings. I ran mine with the current system date set to January 1.

So how can you test the darn thing—wait around until the special day has passed and see if it works? No, of course not. If you're running a Windows system, you can easily change the date and time setting on your computer. The time shows in the system tray in the bottom right corner of the screen:

### Figure 10.7     Sample System Tray

Yours may not have all of the icons mine has, it may even have more, but it should have a time showing at the far right. Double-click the time. A calendar similar to the one below should pop up. Use the drop-down menus provided to set the date. You can also modify the time from this dialog box. Type in the appropriate numbers or use the up and down arrows.

**Figure 10.8    Setting the System Date and Time in Windows**

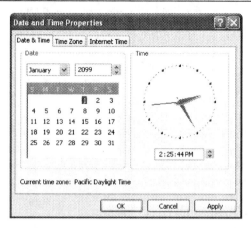

You should try several date settings to test the countdown. In general, you always want to test a number, the date in this case, before the boundary; a number *directly* before the boundary; the boundary itself; a number *directly* after the boundary; and a number a ways after the boundary. The boundary is the target number or date.

For countdowns, January 1 makes a good testing date because you can easily calculate the number of days from January 1 until the special date. Just add up the number of days in each month up to the month your special day is in. In case you always have to look at a calendar to remember how many days there are in each month, here's a list:

**Table 10.3    Number of Days in Each Month**

| January | 31 | April | 30 | July | 31 | October | 31 |
|---|---|---|---|---|---|---|---|
| February | 28/29 | May | 31 | August | 31 | November | 30 |
| March | 31 | June | 30 | September | 30 | December | 31 |

If you've set your system clock to January 1 and the target is the 4th of July, then add 31 + 28 + 31 + 30 + 31 + 30 + 4 = 185. Now subtract 1 for the current day: 185 - 1 = 184.

To test Sam's birthday, add 31 + 1 - 1 = 31. Run the program if you haven't already to see if it works. See Figure 10.6 above for our results, which match the values we calculated manually. Now set your calendar to next February 1.

**Figure 10.9    System Date and Time Set to February 1**

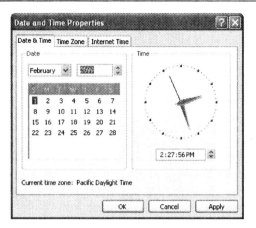

Run the script again. Clicking Reload or Refresh doesn't always work to rerun this script. You may have to reopen the document.

**Figure 10.10    Results of Script 10.6 on February 1**

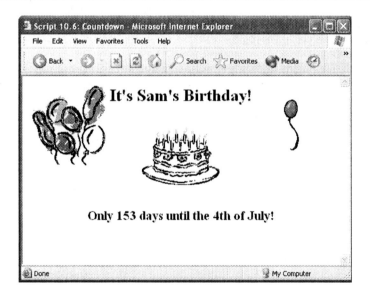

## lastModified

Good Web developers and writers often date their articles and the information they provide so that the reader can place it in the proper context and know how current or applicable the information is. Unfortunately, it's easy to forget to change the date when you update a document. JavaScript, however, has provided a solution: the lastModified property of the document object. The lastModified property of the document object is a string rather than a Date object. Here's what it looks like to write it out:

```
document.write("Last update: ", document.lastModified)
```

The result:

```
Last update: Thursday, December 31, 2099 14:54:49
```

That's pretty easy, huh? The only trouble is that not all servers *report* the date that a document was last modified. An unreported date causes the document's lastModified property to be set to 0, which equals—you guessed it—January 1, 1970, 00:00:00. Rather than mislead your audience into thinking that you last updated your Web page back in 1970, before the Web even existed, the above script should be modified to reflect an unreported date.

Notice that lastModified reported the date in one of JavaScript's standard date formats: *weekday, month day, year hour:minutes:seconds*. You can take advantage of this and create a real Date object and initialize it with the value of lastModified.

```
var lastUpdate = new Date(document.lastModified)
```

This gives you the ability to write the last modified date in a custom date format like you did earlier. For this example, we'll simply write the plain lastModified string.

```
document.write("Last update: ")
if (lastUpdate.getTime() == 0) {
        document.write("unreported")
} else {
        document.write(document.lastModified)
}
```

The result if the server does not report the date:

```
Last update: unreported
```

We'll leave writing lastModified in a custom date format as an exercise for you to do later. Now let's turn our attention to JavaScript's Math object.

## The Math Object

JavaScript provides plenty of mathematical support in the form of its Math object, far more, in fact, than most JavaScript programmers will ever need, let alone use. The Math object's methods perform a variety of mathematical and trigonometric calculations, such as taking the square root of a number or calculating the sine in radians. The Math object's properties are really constants for special, often-used mathematical values such as pi. Let's look a little closer at the Math object and its properties and methods.

## Math Properties

The Math object is a little different than other Core JavaScript objects. Its properties are actually mathematical constants, such as pi, and cannot be modified.

A **constant** is the opposite of a variable. Remember the definition of a variable? A variable is a symbolic name that represents a value that can, and likely will, change or *vary* during a program's execution. A constant is a symbolic name that represents a value that *does not change* during a program's execution. Its value remains *constant*.

To clearly differentiate between a variable and a constant, programmers usually write constant names in all uppercase letters. Netscape used this same convention when choosing names for its mathematical constants, which are properties of the Math object.

Here's a list of the Math object's properties and the constant value each represents.

**Table 10.4    Math Constants**

| Constant | Description | Value |
| --- | --- | --- |
| E | e, Euler's constant | 2.718281828459045091 |
| LN10 | natural log of 10 | 2.302585092994045901 |
| LN2 | natural log of 2 | 0.6931471805599452862 |
| LOG10E | base-10 log of e | 0.4342944819032518167 |
| LOG2E | base-2 log of e | 1.442695040888963387 |
| PI | pi | 3.141592653589793116 |
| SQRT1_2 | square root of ½ | 0.7071067811865475727 |
| SQRT2 | square root of 2 | 1.414213562373095145 |

Let's use PI to write a function that calculates the area of a circle. The formula for the area of a circle is $\pi r^2$, that is, pi * radius². Keep in mind that these constants are properties of the Math object. Thus, if you want to use PI, you must type Math.PI. If you want to use E, you must type Math.E. Watch the case; it matters!

**Script 10.7    Calculating the Area of a Circle with PI**

```
1    <html>
2    <head>
3    <title>Script 10.7: Calculating the Area of a Circle with
       PI</title>
4    <script language="JavaScript" type="text/javascript"><!--
5         function areaCircle(radius) {
6              var area = Math.PI * radius * radius
7              return area
8         }
9    // -->
```

```
10  </script>
11  </head>
12  <body>
13  <h2>Calculated Area of Some Circles</h2>
14  <script language="JavaScript" type="text/javascript"><!--
15      document.write("radius: 1 in  Area: ", areaCircle(1),
16          " in<sup>2</sup><br>")
17      document.write("radius: 5 cm Area: ", areaCircle(5),
18          " cm<sup>2</sup><br>")
19      document.write("radius: 7 ft  Area: ", areaCircle(7),
20          " ft<sup>2</sup><br>")
21      document.write("radius: 11.5 miles  Area: ",
          areaCircle(11.5),
22          " miles<sup>2</sup><br>")
23  // -->
24  </script>
25  </body>
26  </html>
```

Line 6 shows how to access the PI constant as a property of the Math object. Note the capitalization: it is crucial. Lines 15 through 22 show some sample function calls.

Here's what the script looks like when run:

**Figure 10.11    Results of Script 10.7**

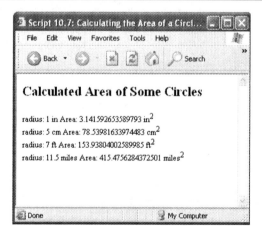

## Math Methods

The Math object's methods perform a variety of mathematical and trigonometric calculations, such as taking the square root of a number or calculating the sine in radians.

Table 10.5 describes the Math object's methods, organized by type.

**Table 10.5     Math Methods**

| Trigonometric Methods | Return Value |
| --- | --- |
| cos(*num*) | Cosine of *num* in radians. |
| acos(*num*) | Arc cosine of *num* in radians. |
| sin(*num*) | Sine of *num* in radians. |
| asin(*num*) | Arc sine of *num* in radians. |
| tan(*num*) | Tangent of *num* in radians. |
| atan(*num*) | Arc tangent of *num* in radians. |
| atan2(*y,x*) | Angle of polar coordinates *y* and *x*. |
| **Maximum/Minimum Methods** | **Return Value** |
| max(*num1, num2*) | Greater value of *num1* and *num2*. |
| min(*num1, num2*) | Lessor value of *num1* and *num2*. |
| **Logarithms and Powers** | **Return Value** |
| exp(*num*) | e (Euler's constant) to the power of *num*. |
| log(*num*) | Natural logarithm (base e) of *num*. |
| pow(*base, exponent*) | Value of *base* to the power of *exponent* ($base^{exponent}$). |
| **Miscellaneous Functions** | **Return Value** |
| abs(*num*) | Absolute value. |
| ceil(*num*) | Integer greater than or equal to *num*. |
| floor(*num*) | Integer less than or equal to *num*. |
| random() | Random floating-point number between 0 and 1. |
| round(*num*) | *num* rounded to an integer. |
| sqrt(*num*) | Square root of *num*. |

Script 10.7 used `radius * radius` to calculate radius². That's OK, but as you can see from Table 10.5, the `Math` object has a method for raising a number to a power. Let's modify Script 10.7 to make use of this helpful method. We'll show only a partial listing of the script as everything else remains the same.

**Script 10.8     Calculating the Area of a Circle**

```
1    <html>
2    <head>
3    <title>Script 10.8: Calculating the Area of a Circle</title>
```

```
4    <script language="JavaScript" type="text/javascript"><!--
5        function areaCircle(radius) {
6            var area = Math.PI * Math.pow(radius, 2)
7            return area
8        }
9    // -->
10   </script>
11   </head>
```

Let's see if the results varied by using the pow method. They shouldn't.

**Figure 10.12    Results of Script 10.8**

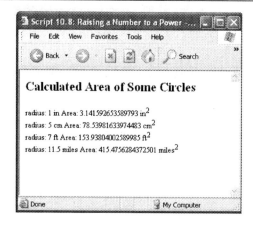

Voilà! The results are identical.

# Randomizing

Scripts that display random quotes, images, tips, etc. rely on the ability to generate a random number. Usually the random number represents an index in an array and thus must be an integer. To illustrate the mathematical methods commonly used to acquire a random number that is an appropriate index into an array, in Script 10.9 we'll break the process down into individual lines and print the results as we go. Usually, you'll combine the lines, excluding the write statements, into one involved calculation. We'll even declare an array and use its length property to determine the appropriate range of values from which to choose the random number so you can see how that's done.

**Script 10.9    Get Random Number**

```
1    <html>
2    <head>
3    <title>Script 10.9: Get Random Number</title>
4    <script language="JavaScript" type="text/javascript"><!--
```

```
5          var zArray = new Array("whatever", "something", "anything",
6                            "gizmo", "jeepers", "creepers", "eyes")
7    //-->
8    </script>
9    </head>
10   <body>
11   <script language="JavaScript" type="text/javascript"><!--
12        var randNum = Math.random()
13        document.write("The original random number: ", randNum,
            "<br>")
14
15        randNum = randNum * zArray.length
16        document.write("Random number in a range: ", randNum,
            "<br>")
17
18        randNum = Math.floor(randNum)
19        document.write("Random index number: ", randNum, "<br>")
20   //-->
21   </script>
22   </body>
23   </html>
```

In Line 12, the script acquires a random number by calling the random Math method. However, this random number is a floating-point number between 0 and 1, not much use for indexing into an array. While it's possible that random will return 0, it will never return 1. By multiplying the random number the script acquired in line 12 by the array's length (line 15), we'll get a floating-point number between 0 and the array's length (line 16).

That's good, but we need an *integer* to index into the array. Line 18 uses the Math object's floor method to reduce the number to an integer. Rounding would be inappropriate, because if the floating-point number were rounded up, we could end up with a number that is the length of the array. The index number of the last element in an array is the array's length-1.

Run it a few times; the results should vary.

*Figure 10.13    Several Runs of Script 10.9*

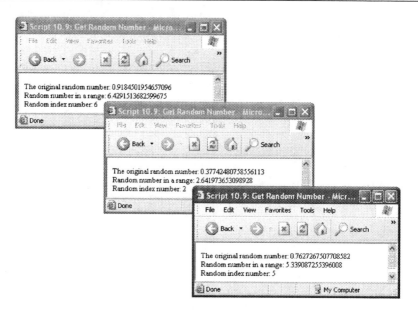

Let's turn this routine into a function that will return a random index number. Then we can use the function to write a random quote, image, tip of the day, sound, etc. This function will come in handy for lots of uses. So you'll probably want to add it to your library.

**Script 10.10    Random Quote**

```
1    <html>
2    <head>
3    <title>Script 10.10: Random Quote</title>
4    <script language="JavaScript" type="text/javascript"><!--
5    function getRandNdx(arrayLength) {
6         var randNum = Math.random()
7         randNum = randNum * arrayLength
8         randNum = Math.floor(randNum)
9         return randNum
10   }
11
12   var quotes = new Array("He who laughs, lasts!",
13        "If a window of opportunity appears, don\'t pull down the
               shade.",
14        "Any sufficiently advanced technology is indistinguishable
               from magic.",
15        "I haven\'t failed. I\'ve found 10,000 ways that don\'t
               work.",
```

```
16        "Warning: The light at the end of tunnel may be an oncoming
             dragon.",
17        "Warning: Objects in mirror may be closer than they appear.",
18        "The eyes are the window of the soul.",
19        "You are in a twisty little passage of standards, all
             conflicting.",
20        "Life is too short to be taken seriously.",
21        "A conclusion is simply the place where someone got tired of
             thinking.",
22        "Experience is something you don\'t get until just after you
             need it.",
23        "Experience is what you get when you were expecting something
             else.",
24        "I\'m sorry, if you were right, I\'d agree with you.",
25        "An expert is a person who never makes small mistakes.",
26        "Faith is believing what you know ain\'t so.",
27        "Faith means not wanting to know the truth.",
28        "Never check for an error condition you don't know how to
             handle.",
29        "Silence is text easy to misread.",
30        "I hear and I forget; I see and I remember; I do and I
             understand.",
31        "Cleverness often defeats itself.")
32   // -->
33   </script>
34   </head>
35   <body>
36   <table width="250" border="0" cellpadding="5" align="center"
37   bgcolor="Yellow">
38   <tr><th>And I Quote:</th></tr>
39   <tr><td>
40   <script language="JavaScript" type="text/javascript"><!--
41        document.write(quotes[getRandNdx(quotes.length)].italics())
42   // -->
43   </script>
44   </td></tr>
45   </table>
46   </body>
47   </html>
```

The get RandNdx function is what does all the work (lines 5 through 10). It should not require any explanation because it is identical to the routine in Script 10.9, minus the intermittent document.write statements, of course. Lines 12 through 31 declare a dense array of quotes. If you wish to display a random image or play a random sound, create an array containing the URLs for those files.

The document.write statement in line 41 calls the getRandNdx function and uses it to generate an index in the quotes array and display a random quote. Notice that we also called the italics String method to write the quote in italics.

Try running Script 10.10 a few times and watch the results. A few runs might look like this:

**Figure 10.14    Results of Script 10.10**

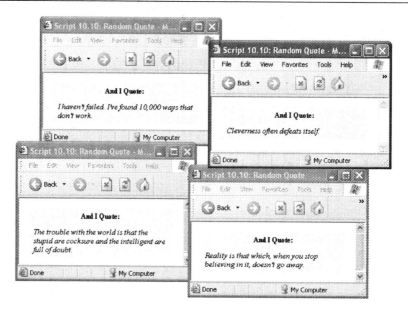

Your results will vary, of course. After all, it's *supposed* to pick quotes randomly.

# Summary

JavaScript supports a Date object with many associated methods for retrieving the parts of a date, such as the day of the week, the day of the month, the month, the year, and the time. JavaScript's numbering scheme for date parts is inconsistent and needs close study to avoid any mishaps. For instance, months begin numbering at 0, while days of a month begin numbering at 1. This, combined with JavaScript's tracking dates in milliseconds from January 1, 1970, 00:00:00:00, can make dates a little confusing to work with.

JavaScript provides only three methods for writing date formats, with little difference among them. However, by using arrays in conjunction with the Date methods JavaScript does provide to retrieve parts of a date, a savvy programmer can easily write any custom date format desired.

The JavaScript Math object is rather different than the objects we're used to working with. Its properties are really mathematical constants for frequently used mathematical values, such as pi. Its methods perform a variety of mathematical computations, including

- ⚡ the trigonometric functions sine, cosine, etc.
- ⚡ comparing two or more numbers and returning the maximum or minimum.
- ⚡ raising a number to a power.
- ⚡ calculating the absolute value, ceiling, floor, or square root of a number.
- ⚡ rounding a floating-point number to an integer.
- ⚡ selecting a floating-point number between 0 and 1 at random.

With these Math constants and methods in hand, you can perform a variety of tasks. In this chapter, we demonstrated how Math constants and methods could be used to calculate the area of a circle and choose a random quote for display in a document.

## Review Questions

1. How does JavaScript measure dates?
2. Describe the four ways of creating a Date object.
3. If you create a Date object using the new operator and the Date constructor function without any parameters, what date does the Date object created hold?
4. Can you count on accuracy in the date described in question 3? Why or why not?
5. On whom does the client system's current date and time depend?
6. What range of values does the getDay method return?
7. What range of values does the getDate method return?
8. What range of values does the getMonth method return?
9. What value does the getYear method return? Be specific.
10. What method has replaced the getYear method? Why?
11. What kind of value does the getTime method return?
12. Does JavaScript support a method for writing a date in the following format: 15 August 2099?
13. How can you write custom date formats with JavaScript? Explain the steps involved.
14. What does the document's lastModified property report? Does it always work? Explain.
15. What's strange about the Math object's properties?
16. List and describe three of the Math object's properties. Choose those you think you are most likely to use at some time or another.
17. What does Math.random() do? Be specific.
18. What does the Math.abs() method do?
19. What Math method returns the integer less than or equal to the number passed to it?
20. What does the Math.pow() method do?

# Exercises

1. If today.getDay() returns the number 5, what does the 5 represent? Be specific.
2. If today.getMonth() returns the number 7, what month does that represent?
3. Declare a new Date object to hold your birthday. If you know what time you were born, specify the time as well.
4. What does your birthday evaluate to in JavaScript? (Hint: Use getTime().) Why is it such a big number?
5. Write a statement to convert your birthday from a measurement in milliseconds to a measurement in minutes.
6. Write a short script that displays a custom message, dependent on the time of day. For instance, it should display "Good Morning" if it is run before noon, "Good Afternoon" in the afternoon, and "Good Evening" in the evening.
7. Write a JavaScript function that will calculate the circumference of a circle and return the result. (Hint: $c = \pi d$ or $c = \pi 2r$—the formula for the circumference of a circle is pi times the diameter or pi times 2 times the radius.)
8. Write a JavaScript statement that calculates $57^8$. Verify your results with a calculator.
9. Write the appropriate JavaScript statements to create a table that shows each of the following numbers and the result of rounding each to an integer, calculating the ceiling of each and calculating the floor of each.
   a. 189.56
   b. -14.325
   c. 266
   d. 1.33333
   e. -175.66

   Does JavaScript seem to be rounding the way you've always known rounding to work? Explain. How about determining the ceiling and the floor?
10. Write a JavaScript statement that calls the appropriate Math method to determine the maximum of two values from the list in Exercise 9.
11. Write a JavaScript statement that calls the appropriate Math method to determine the minimum of two values from the list in Exercise 9.
12. Write the appropriate JavaScript statements to calculate the absolute values of the numbers listed in Exercise 9.
13. Write the appropriate JavaScript statements to calculate the square root of each of the following:
   a. 64
   b. 9
   c. 37
   d. 25
   e. 1
14. Write a short script that writes the current time as follows: 1:09 pm.

15. Write a JavaScript statement that assigns a random number between 0 and 1 to a variable.

16. Write a JavaScript statement that assigns a random number between 0 and 13 to a variable.

17. Write a JavaScript statement that assigns a random number between 1 and 13 to a variable.

## Scripting Exercises

Create a folder named assignment10 to hold the documents you create during this assignment. Save a copy of your latest toy store documents in a toyStore subfolder.

1. Create a new document named timeFunctions.html.
    a. Write a function, `getCurrentTime`, that gets the current system time and returns a string in the format 5:15:16 pm.
    b. Write a function, `getCurrentDate`, that gets the current system date and returns a string in a date format that you use regularly or in the format 4 July 1776.
    c. Test and debug each function. When you're satisfied that a function works as intended, add it to myLib.js along with an appropriate description and comments.

2. Create a new document named dateFunctions.html.
    a. Add the `dateToDays` and `daysUntil` functions to myLib.js.
    b. Write a function, `dateToMinutes`, that will convert a date in milliseconds to a date in minutes and return the value.
    c. Write a function, `dateToHours`, that will convert a date in milliseconds to a date in hours and return the value.
    d. Write a function, `dateToWeeks`, that will convert a date in milliseconds to a date in weeks and return the value.
    e. Write a function, `dateToMonths`, that will convert a date in milliseconds to a date in months and return the value.
    f. Test and debug each function. When you're satisfied that a function works as intended, add it to myLib.js along with an appropriate description and comments.

3. Create a new document named mathFunctions.html.
    a. Write a function, `getAvg`, that will accept a *variable* number of numeric arguments and return their average.
    b. Write a function, `getMax`, that will accept a *variable* number of numeric arguments and return the maximum value passed to it.
    c. Write a function, `getMin`, that will accept a *variable* number of numeric arguments and return the minimum value passed to it.

    d. Test and debug each function. When you're satisfied that a function works as intended, add it to myLib.js along with an appropriate description and comments.

4. Modify your toy store home page.

    a. Add a last update statement at the bottom, with the date supplied by the document's `lastModified` property. (Hint: Convert the string to a `Date` object.)

    b. Write it in the following format:

        Last Update: *Day Month Year* at *hour*:*minutes* am/pm.

5. Modify your toy store home page.

    a. Attach myLib.js to the document. (It must contain the functions you wrote in Scripting Exercise 1, parts a and b.)

    b. Write the current date and time at the top using the `getCurrentDate` and `getCurrentTime` functions you wrote earlier in Scripting Exercise 1.

6. Create a new document named clock.html.

    a. Link myLib.js to the document.

    b. Insert a form with a single text field. Label the field Current Time and name it `clock`.

    c. Using `setInterval` or `setTimeout`, call your `getCurrentTime` function periodically (you determine the period) to update the contents of the clock field.

    d. You now have a working clock!

7. Modify the products.html page of your toy store Web site or create one if you don't have one as yet.

    a. Attach myLib.js to the document.

    b. Using `getRandNdx`, write a script to display a random image of a toy in the Web document.

8. Create a new document named countdown.html.

    a. Attach myLib.js to the document.

    b. Write a script that will get a countdown date from the visitor and then count down the number of months until that target date.

    c. When the result is less than one month, display the countdown in weeks until the target date.

    d. When the result is less than one week, display the countdown in days.

    e. When the result is less than one day, display the countdown in hours.

    f . When the result is less than one hour, display the countdown in minutes.

    g. Use the functions you wrote in Scripting Exercise 2 to assist with your task, and write any additional functions required.

9. Create a new document named jukeBox.html.

    a. Attach myLib.js to the document.

b. Using getRandNdx, write a script to play a random sound file in the Web document.

10. Modify one of the documents in your toy store Web site as follows:

a. Attach myLib.js to the document.

b. Create a new external JavaScript document named specials.js and attach it to the Web document.

c. Using getRandNdx, write a script to display a random special from a list of 10. The array of specials should be defined in specials.js so it can be easily updated without fear of affecting the rest of your Web document. List each special on its own line for easy editing.

d. The special should display in a division or table with a background color and a border around it.

11. Scripts 10.3 through 10.5 all share one minor bug: If the time involves minutes that are less than 10, the time displays in a less than perfect way—8:3 instead of the preferred 8:03. Rewrite Script 10.5 to fix the bug.

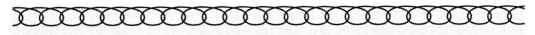

## chapter *eleven*

# *Windows and Frames*

*People are like stained-glass windows. They sparkle and shine when the sun is out, but when the darkness sets in, their true beauty is revealed only if there is a light from within.*

—Elisabeth Kübler-Ross,
*To Live Until We Say Good-Bye*

Pop-up windows have become quite popular on many commercial Web sites for notifying visitors of sales, news, and special offers. Frames, initially invented by Netscape, allow you to break up the browser window into discrete areas, each holding a separate HTML document. This allows you to set up a navigation system that is always present and visible, no matter how much the visitor scrolls through the content of your Web site; you have to modify only one document to update the navigation for the entire site. Frames are also useful for making a company name, logo, copyright, trademark, or other information always present.

While both windows and frames can be initiated and targeted with HTML alone, it takes JavaScript to be able to create pop-up windows of a custom size, at a specific location, and with selected window attributes. JavaScript is also necessary if you want to load new documents in two or more frames at once or write dynamically to a window.

In this chapter we'll

- target windows and frames.
- create pop-up windows.
- set window attributes and position windows.

✗ give focus to, close, and print windows.
✗ create a framed Web site.
✗ write new pages dynamically.
✗ change multiple frames at once.
✗ share variables and functions among frames.
✗ prevent a site from being framed or losing its frame of reference.

Before you can begin to use JavaScript to work with windows and frames, you need to have a good understanding of targeting and window names. So let's start with that.

# The Ins and Outs of Targeting

## Targeting Windows

Unless you have worked with frames before, you may not know that the anchor tag (<a>), used to create links with the href attribute, has a target attribute. The **target attribute** specifies into which window or frame to load the document specified in the href attribute. By default, an anchor tag's target attribute is set to "_self", whether you specify it or not. "_self" refers to the window the link itself resides in.

When you write

```
<a href="somePage.html">Some Page</a>
```

the browser understands it as

```
<a href="somePage.html" target="_self">Some Page</a>
```

It opens the document specified in the href attribute in the same window that the link is in unless you have overridden the default. You can override the default target, _self, by specifying a base target in the <head> of the document, like this:

```
<head>
     <base target="SurfWin">
</head>
```

SurfWin is a custom window name I made up. Now when you write this in the document:

```
<a href="somePage.html">Some Page</a>
```

with the base target set to SurfWin, the browser understands it as

```
<a href="somePage.html" target="SurfWin">Some Page</a>
```

With HTML alone, you can open a document in a new, named window at any time. You can even load other documents into that same window. Open the following document in your browser:

---

**Script 11.1    Targeting a Custom-Named Window**

```
1    <html>
2    <head>
3         <title>Script 11.1: Targeting a Custom-Named Window</title>
```

```
 4        <base target="SurfWin">
 5    </head>
 6    <body>
 7        <a href="somepage.html">Some Page</a><br>
 8        <a href="anotherpage.html">Another Page</a><br>
 9        <a href="yetanother.html">Yet Another</a><br>
10    </body>
11    </html>
```

**Figure 11.1    Results of Script 11.1**

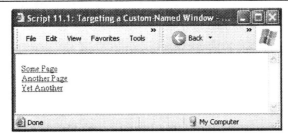

Click on a link.

**Figure 11.2    Results of Script 11.1 when First Link Is Clicked**

What happened? A new window, whose target name is SurfWin, opened with the requested document loaded into it. You can't see the name anywhere, but the browser now knows that particular window as SurfWin. Because it was a new window, that is, it wasn't already open, the browser gave it focus. In other words, the browser brought it to the top and made it the current window.

What caused the document to load into SurfWin instead of the current window? Look at the code. In line 4 of Script 11.1, the base target HTML element changed the default target to SurfWin.

Leave the new window open and click on another link.

**Figure 11.3    Results of Script 11.1 when Another Link Is Clicked Without Closing SurfWin**

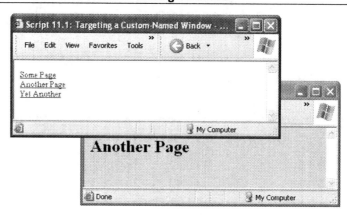

This time the requested document was loaded in the already open SurfWin. Look at the taskbar; it shows the titles of the pages loaded in each window. You'll probably have to click on the minimized button on the taskbar to see that it contains the document on whose link you clicked, because this time SurfWin did not receive focus.

Leave SurfWin open and click on another link. The same thing happens. Close SurfWin so it no longer exists. Click on a link. Once again SurfWin opens and receives focus, but only because it is new.

As you can see, by using target names with HTML links, you can open a document in a new, named window any time, no scripting needed. You can even reuse the window. The catch is that you have no control over the window's size or position and you can't give it focus.

> **web developer's tip**
>
> It's a good idea to open documents that are not part of your site in another window. That way when the visitor finishes with that other site and closes the window, your site is still there, open and ready for another look.

## Magic Target Names

Besides _self, there are three other "**magic target names**," as Netscape calls them. They are _blank, _parent, and _top. Each is described in detail in Table 11.1. The last target name described in the table is a custom name. We've already tried a custom target name, SurfWin. A custom target name is simply one that you make up.

**Table 11.1    Magic Target Names**

| Target Name | Description |
|---|---|
| _self | This is the default if no target is specified and no base target has been specified. The file listed in the href attribute loads into the window it was requested from. |
| _blank | This loads the file listed in the href attribute into a new, unnamed browser window. This window cannot be targeted again for future documents. |
| _parent | This loads the file designated in the href attribute file into the parent frame or window. |
| _top | This loads the file specified in the href attribute into the entire current window, above all framesets. |
| *WindowName* or *FrameName* | This loads the file listed in the href attribute into the window or frame with the specified target name. If no window or frame exists with that name, it opens a new window and assigns it that name. You cannot see the window name. The window is simply known by that name in memory. When the window is initially opened by this method, it will receive focus (come to the top). As long as the window remains open, documents targeted to that window will load there, but the window will not automatically receive focus. |

Let's see how _blank differs from a custom named window like the one used in Script 11.1. Here's the same code as in Script 11.1, with the base target modified to _blank. Otherwise the document remains unchanged.

**Script 11.2    Targeting _blank**

```
1    <html>
2    <head>
3        <title>Script 11.2: Targeting _blank</title>
4        <base target="_blank">
5    </head>
6    <body>
7            <a href="somepage.html">Some Page</a><br>
8            <a href="anotherpage.html">Another Page</a><br>
9            <a href="yetanother.html">Yet Another</a><br>
10   </body>
11   </html>
```

Click on a link.

**Figure 11.4    Results of Script 11.2 when a Link Is Clicked**

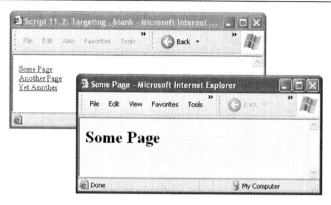

As you can see in Figure 11.4, the results look the same. Leave the window open and click on another link. What happened? Another window opened. The browser didn't reuse the first window that opened. Click on another link. Yet another window opened.

**Figure 11.5    Results of Script 11.2 after Multiple Links Clicked**

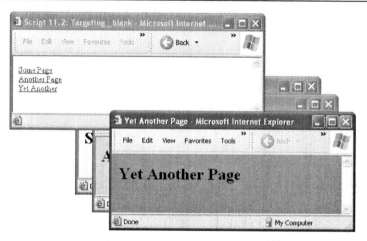

Why did all those new windows open? Because the magic target name, _blank, creates a new, *unnamed* window. Since the new window has no target name, it cannot be reused. See how messy using _blank can get?

**web developer's tip**

Be careful of using _blank too much, for instance, as a base target. It's easy for the visitor to end up with a zillion pages open at once, which is both annoying and confusing.

## Targeting Frames

Normally when working with frames, one frame provides navigation links and another frame holds the documents for viewing.

*Figure 11.6*    **Navigation and Viewing Frames**

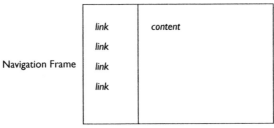

Viewing Frame

Whenever a visitor clicks on a link in the navigation frame, the document loads in the viewing frame. There are two ways you can set that up.

1.  Override the default `_self` by setting a base target to the name of the viewing frame in the <head> of the navigation document. For example:

```
<head>
    <title>My Simple Frameset - Navigation</title>
    <base target="MainFrame">
</head>
```

2.  Set the `target` attribute on each and every link in the navigation document to the name of the viewing frame. For example:

```
<body>
    <a href="catalog.html" target="MainFrame">
    Catalog</a><br>
    <a href="support.html" target="MainFrame">
    Support</a><br>
    <a href="contact.html" target="MainFrame">
    Contact Us</a><br>
    <a href="home.html" target="MainFrame">Home</a><br>
</body>
```

I don't know about you, but the first option looks easier to me! Certainly it's less typing. To see this in action, you first need to set up a simple frameset and related documents.

## Creating a Framed Web Site

Creating a framed Web site requires three general steps:

1.  Create a frameset.
2.  Create the HTML documents that will initially load into the frames.
3.  Create the rest of the HTML documents for the site.

## Creating the Frameset Document

### Organizing by Rows or Columns and Specifying Sizes

Frameset documents do not have a <body> element, they instead have a <frameset> element. The <**frameset**> HTML element allows you to organize the frames in a set by either rows or columns. You can declare the size of each frame in pixels or percentages or with *, which means "Give that frame whatever space is left over" or "Let each frame with * divide equally whatever space is left over." If you know how wide a frame should be, specify that width in pixels. Leave the rest of the frames declared with *. I rarely use percentages for frames; it just never makes much sense. For instance, if the navigation frame is supposed to contain buttons, those buttons are of a fixed width, so set the frame size to a slightly larger fixed width. The same is true of a logo or banner. Don't use percentages for those frames; they'll shrink and grow as the resolution does and may produce undesired results.

> **Programmer's tip**
>
> **Naming Windows and Frames:**
> Window and frame names have the same rules as variable names: no spaces; no special characters except underscore (_); no reserved words; and no function, method, or object names. Only letters, numbers, and underscores are allowed.

### Naming Each Frame and Specifying Initial Sources

Next, you need to name and specify the initial source document for each frame. Order is important; list each frame in the same order you defined each column or row. It is essential that each frame have a specified initial source document, as well as a name. The name will be used for targeting purposes. If a frame has no name, you *cannot* direct documents to load into it.

Here are some frameset definitions and illustrations of the framesets they create.

### Figure 11.7    Sample Frameset Definitions and Illustrations

```
<frameset cols="150, *">
        <frame name="NavFrame"
        src="nav.html">
        <frame name="MainFrame"
        src="home.html">
</frameset>
```

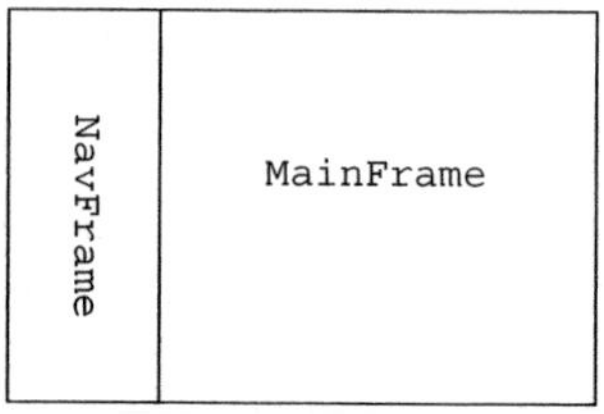

```
<frameset rows="60, *, 40">
        <frame name="NavFrame"
        src="nav.html">
        <frame name="MainFrame"
        src="home.html">
        <frame name="NoticeFrame"
        src="copyright.html">
</frameset>
```

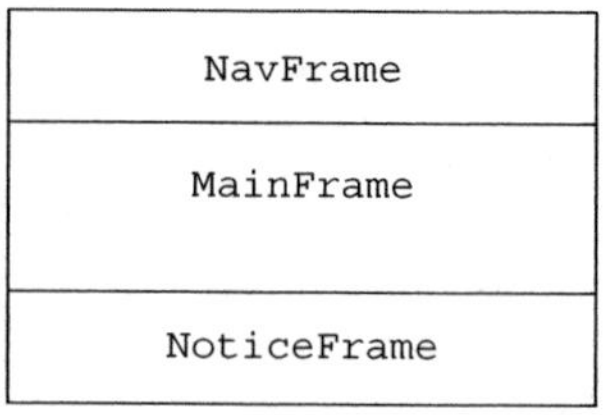

```
<frameset rows="60, *">
        <frame name="BannerFrame" ——▶
        ——▶ src="banner.html">
        <frameset cols="150, *">
                <frame name="NavFrame" ——▶
                ——▶ src="nav.html">
                <frame name="MainFrame" ——▶
                ——▶ src="home.html">
        </frameset>
</frameset>
```

The first example above defines a two-column frameset. The left column is 150 pixels wide, and the right gets whatever space is left over. The HTML document nav.html initially loads in `NavFrame`, the 150-pixel frame. The home.html document loads into `MainFrame`.

The second example creates a three-row frameset.

The third example is a little more complicated, but is also a frequently used layout. First it defines the frame for the 60-pixels-wide row at the top. Then, instead of defining a frame for the leftover space, it defines a frameset made up of two columns. Cool, huh?

### Giving the Frameset a Title

It is very important that you title the frameset document, as its <title> is the one that will appear in the browser window when the frameset and its subdocuments are loaded. The titles in the subdocuments appear in the title bar of the browser only when they are opened alone, outside of the frameset.

A complete frameset document should look like this:

***Script 11.3    Sample Frameset Document***

```
1   <html>
2   <head>
3           <title>Script 11.3: Sample Frameset Document</title>
4   </head>
5   <frameset cols="150, *">
6           <frame name="NavFrame" src="nav.html">
7           <frame name="MainFrame" src="home.html">
8   </frameset>
9   </html>
```

This frameset document looks like the first one in Figure 11.7.

## Creating Initial HTML Source Documents

For the frameset defined in Script 11.3, you need to create at least two HTML documents: nav.html and home.html. These are the documents that will load initially into the defined frames when the frameset is opened in a browser. They are normal HTML documents, that is, each has a <body> element, as is usual. One special thing that needs to be addressed, however, is the targeting for the links in these documents.

### Setting Up Targeting

For our purposes, whenever a visitor clicks on a link in NavFrame, we want that document to load in MainFrame. Let's use a base target element in the head of nav.html to make all links in that document load in MainFrame by default. Here's a sample nav.html:

*Script 11.4    Sample nav.html*

```
1    <html>
2    <head>
3        <title>Script 11.4: Sample nav.html</title>
4        <base target="MainFrame">
5    </head>
6    <body>
7        <a href="catalog.html">Catalog</a><br>
8        <a href="support.html">Support</a><br>
9        <a href="contact.html">Contact Us</a><br>
10        <a href="home.html">Home</a><br>
11    </body>
12    </html>
```

Creating home.html is no sweat. There is nothing special about home.html, unless you want to open documents in a window other than MainFrame.

*Script 11.5    Sample home.html*

```
1    <html>
2    <head>
3    <title>Script 11.5: Sample home.html</title>
4    </head>
5    <body>
6        <h1>Sample home.html</h1>
7        <p>Welcome! Blah, blah, blah, blah, blah, blah,
8        blah, blah, blah, blah, blah, blah, blah, blah,
9        blah, blah, blah, blah, blah, blah, blah, blah,
10        blah, blah, blah, blah, blah, blah, blah.</p>
11    </body>
12    </html>
```

## Creating the Remaining HTML Documents

For the above example, you'll need to create catalog.html, support.html, and contact.html (they're listed as links in nav.html). Now we're ready to test the base target we set up in nav.html (Script 11.4). Open the frameset document index.html, located in the Chapter11Frameset1 folder on the CD accompanying this book. You should see something similar to this:

**Figure 11.8     Sample Frameset Results of Scripts 11.3, 11.4, and 11.5**

Try clicking on a few links. Voilà! The documents load in `MainFrame`.
Let's modify nav.html to see how `_parent` and `_top` work (lines 8 and 9 of Script 11.6).

**Script 11.6     Modified nav.html**

```
 1    <html>
 2    <head>
 3        <title>Script 11.6: Modified nav.html</title>
 4        <base target="MainFrame">
 5    </head>
 6    <body>
 7        <a href="catalog.html">Catalog</a><br>
 8        <a href="support.html" target="_top">Support</a><br>
 9        <a href="contact.html" target="_parent">Contact Us</a><br>
10        <a href="home.html">Home</a><br>
11    </body>
12    </html>
```

Let's try the new nav.html. This time open the index.html file located in the Chapter11Frameset2 folder. Initially it should look the same as the first index.html we tried, Figure 11.8.

Click on Catalog, whose target has not changed.

*Figure 11.9* **Results of Script 11.6 in NavFrame when Catalog Is Clicked**

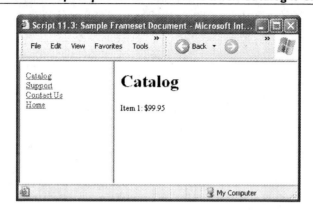

What happened? The document opened in `MainFrame` because `MainFrame` is the default, set in the base target element (line 4 of Script 11.6).

Now click on the link for Support.

*Figure 11.10* **Results of Script 11.6 when Support Is Clicked**

What happened? support.html opened in the current window, but outside of the frameset. In other words, it opened at the *top* of the frameset (line 8 of Script 11.6).

Hit the Back button and try the Contact Us link. What happens? It looks the same. But it isn't. The target for contact.html is `_parent` (line 9 of Script 11.6), which means that it loads in the parent of nav.html. The parent of nav.html is the window that nav.html's frameset loads into, which in this case just happens to be the entire current window, that is, the *top*.

Let's modify nav.html once again and include a link for Downloads (Script 11.9). Instead of creating a regular Web page for Downloads, let's create a frameset, downloadsSet.html, that will load into `MainFrame` (Script 11.7). Thus, `MainFrame` will contain two frames: `ViewFrame` and `BottomNavFrame`.

**Figure 11.11    downloadsSet.html Loading into `MainFrame`**

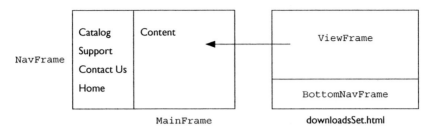

**Script 11.7    downloadsSet.html**

```
1    <html>
2    <head>
3        <title>Script 11.7: Sample Frameset Document</title>
4    </head>
5    <frameset rows="*, 60">
6        <frame name="ViewFrame" src="downloads.html">
7        <frame name="BottomNavFrame" src="downloadsNav.html">
8    </frameset>
9    </html>
```

downloadsSet.html requires two initial Web documents: downloads.html, which will be just a simple Web page, and downloadsNav.html (Script 11.8), which will contain links with various targets. Here's downloadsNav.html and the modified nav.html with the Downloads link added. You'll want to refer to them when you try the links.

**Script 11.8    downloadsNav.html**

```
1    <html>
2    <head>
3        <title>Script 11.8: downloadsNav.html</title>
4        <base target="ViewFrame">
5    </head>
6    <body>
7        <a href="games.html">Games</a>
8        <a href="utils.html">Utils</a><br>
9        <a href="contact.html" target="_parent">Contact Us</a><br>
10       <a href="index.html" target="_top">Home</a><br>
11   </body>
12   </html>
```

Notice the base target set in line 4 of downloadsNav.html.

### Script 11.9  Modified nav.html

```
1    <html>
2    <head>
3        <title>Script 11.9: Modified nav.html</title>
4        <base target="MainFrame">
5    </head>
6    <body>
7        <a href="catalog.html">Catalog</a><br>
8        <a href="support.html" target="_top">Support</a><br>
9        <a href="contact.html" target="_parent">Contact Us</a><br>
10       <a href="downloadsSet.html">Downloads</a><br>
11       <a href="home.html">Home</a><br>
12   </body>
13   </html>
```

To try it out, open the index.html document located in the Chapter11Frameset3 folder. Click on Downloads. It loads a frameset (downloadsSet.html), creating two frames in MainFrame: ViewFrame, which initially contains downloads.html, and BottomNavFrame, which contains downloadsNav.html.

### Figure 11.12  Results of Clicking on Downloads

Let's look at the relationships of the frames now displayed.

*Figure 11.13    Relationship of Frames in Figure 11.12*

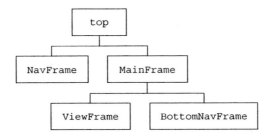

The parent of NavFrame and MainFrame is *top*. The parent of ViewFrame and BottomNavFrame is MainFrame.

Now try the Games and Utils links in downloadsNav.html.

*Figure 11.14    Results of Script 11.8 when Games Is Clicked*

The links for Games and Utils do not have a target specified (lines 7 and 8 of Script 11.8). So why do they load in ViewFrame? Because the base target was set to ViewFrame in downloadsNav.html (line 4 of Script 11.8).

Now try the Contact Us and Home links.

*Figure 11.15    Results of Script 11.8 when Contact Us Is Clicked*

*Figure 11.16   Results of Script 11.8 when Home Is Clicked*

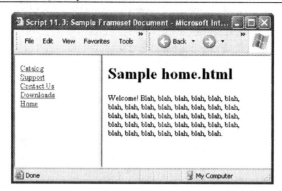

See the difference between _parent and _top now? The Contact Us link (line 9 of Script 11.9) has a target of _parent. Which frame is the parent of BottomNavFrame? MainFrame is the parent of BottomNavFrame, thus the target _parent loads the document in MainFrame. The Home link in downloadsNav.html, on the other hand, has a target of _top (line 11 of Script 11.9). Thus, it loads the original frameset, index.html, at the top of all framesets.

While we're on the subject of frames, let's see how to make them borderless.

# Making Frames Borderless

Borderless frames have become quite popular. In fact, most frame implementations use borderless frames. Let's take a few minutes to see what attributes you need to set on the <frameset> and <frame> tags to create borderless frames.

On the <frameset> tag, set border="0", frameborder="0", and framespacing="0". For example:

```
<frameset cols="150,*" border="0" frameborder="0"
    framespacing="0">
```

On each <frame> tag, set frameborder="0". Here's an example:

```
<frame src="whatever.html" name="SomeName" frameborder="0">
```

---

**programmer's tip**

Technically, frameborder usually takes an attribute value of yes or no, but 1 and 0 are the equivalent of yes and no. Rather than try to remember which statements use yes/no and which use 1/0, just use the 1/0 scheme for all of them. In our case, for borderless frames, we want them all off, so we set them all to 0.

---

Just in case you want to play with any other <frameset> or <frame> attributes, they have been listed here in Tables 11.2 and 11.3, respectively.

*Table 11.2* **<frameset> Attributes**

| Attribute | Description |
|---|---|
| cols="*columnWidthList*" | Specifies the width of each column of the frameset in pixels. Entries are separated by commas. An asterisk (*) indicates "as much space as possible," which means whatever space is left over. If an asterisk is used to designate the size of more than one column, the available space is divided equally among them. |
| rows="*rowWidthList*" | Specifies the width of each row of the frameset in pixels. Entries are separated by commas. An asterisk (*) indicates "as much space as possible," which means whatever space is left over. If an asterisk is used to designate the size of more than one row, the available space is divided equally among them. |
| border="*pixWidth*" | Indicates the thickness, in pixels, of all frame borders in the outermost frameset. It is set to zero to create borderless frames. |
| bordercolor="*color*" | Specifies the color of the frame border. Use one of the 16 color names recognized by HTML or any hexadecimal color value. |
| frameborder="yes/no" frameborder="1/0" | Sets the default border for all frames in the frameset. If the border is set to yes or 1, the frames will have a visible border; if no or 0, they won't. This may be overridden by the frameborder set on <frame> tags. |

*Table 11.3* **<frame> Attributes**

| Attribute | Description |
|---|---|
| bordercolor="*color*" | Sets the color of the frame border. Use one of the 16 color names recognized by HTML or any hexadecimal color value. |
| frameborder="yes/no" frameborder="1/0" | If the border is set to yes or 1, the frame will have a visible border; if no or 0, it will not. This overrides the frameborder value set on the <frameset> tag. |
| marginheight="*numPixels*" | The margin, in pixels, between the top edge of the frame and the content and the bottom edge of the frame and the content. |

| `marginwidth="numPixels"` | The margin, in pixels, between the left edge of the frame and the content and the right edge of the frame and the content. |
|---|---|
| `name="frameName"` | Provides a target name for the frame. The name must begin with a letter or number, may contain no spaces, and may contain no special characters other than underscore. |
| `noresize` | Prevents the user from resizing the frame. |
| `scrolling="auto/yes/no"` | The default is `auto`, which provides scrollbars on a frame only if needed. `yes` shows scrollbars always, whether needed or not. `no` never provides scrollbars, even if needed. Caution: Never set navigation frames `scrolling="no"`. If the user is viewing at a very small resolution, she will be unable to scroll to see the navigation. |
| `src="URL"` | Specifies the document to load into the frame initially, when the frameset is first opened. |

OK, you've seen that you can do quite a lot, as far as targeting windows and frames, with HTML alone. You've probably also noticed that there are several things you *can't* do with HTML alone, including the following:

- ◢ Open a window of specific dimensions.
- ◢ Position a window in a specific place.
- ◢ Give a window focus.
- ◢ Write to a window dynamically.
- ◢ Load more than one frame at once.
- ◢ Share variables and functions across frames and windows.
- ◢ Prevent your Web documents and framesets from loading in other people's frames.
- ◢ Prevent your framed documents from loading without your frameset.

Let's start with number 1.

# Opening and Closing Windows

With JavaScript, you can open and close pop-up windows. *You* determine the dimensions, the features, and even the position of any window you open.

## Opening a Pop-up Window

To create a new window, use the `window` object's open method. It takes three arguments.

**Syntax:**

```
[windowObjectName =] [window.]open("URL", ⟶
⟶ "targetName"[, "features"])
```

*windowObjectName* specifies the name of the `window` object variable. It is very important that you give the `window` a name, as it is used to call methods on the `window` and access the `window`'s properties. The `window`'s object name is not the same as its target name. The target name is simply used in HTML for window or frame targeting purposes.

*URL* specifies the URL of the file to open in the new window. If you want to write to the new window dynamically, do not specify a URL, just provide empy quotes (" ").

*targetName* is the name to use in the `target` attribute of an <a>, <base>, or <form> tag. It can contain only alphanumeric or underscore characters.

*features* is a comma-separated list (without spaces) of any of the options and values listed in Table 11.4. This is how you specify a particular size for the window (`width` and `height`) and position it initially (`screenX` and `screenY`). You cannot change any of a window's features once it has been opened.

**Table 11.4    Window Features**

| Option/Values | Description |
| --- | --- |
| `toolbar[=yes\|no]` \| `[=1\|0]` | Toolbar with buttons such as Back and Forward. |
| `location[=yes\|no]` \| `[=1\|0]` | Location bar where a URL can be entered. |
| `directories[=yes\|no]` \| `[=1\|0]` | Standard browser directory buttons. The browser determines which directory buttons appear. |
| `status[=yes\|no]` \| `[=1\|0]` | Status bar at the bottom of the window where messages, download status, and link URLs typically display. |
| `menubar[=yes\|no]` \| `[=1\|0]` | Browser menu bar with items such as File, Edit, View, and Help. |
| `scrollbars[=yes\|no]` \| `[=1\|0]` | When set to `yes`, provides scrollbars if the content is too large for the window. When set to `no`, scrollbars will not be displayed even if they are needed. |
| `resizable[=yes\|no]` \| `[=1\|0]` | Determines whether the user is allowed to resize the window or not. |
| `width=pixels` | The window's width in pixels. This is still supported, but is replaced by `innerWidth` in JavaScript 1.2. |
| `height=pixels` | The window's height in pixels. This is still supported, but is replaced by `innerHeight` in JavaScript 1.2. |

| `innerWidth=pixels` | The width of the window's content area in pixels. This replaces `width`. It may not be smaller than 100-by-100 pixels unless set in a signed script. |
|---|---|
| `innerHeight=pixels` | The height of the window's content area in pixels. This replaces `height`. It may not be smaller than 100-by-100 pixels unless set in a signed script. |
| `outerWidth=pixels` | The horizontal dimension of the window's outside boundary, in pixels. It may not be smaller than 100-by-100 pixels unless set in a signed script. |
| `outerHeight=pixels` | The vertical dimension of the window's outside boundary, in pixels. It may not be smaller than 100-by-100 pixels unless set in a signed script. |
| `left=pixels` | The position of the top left corner of the window measured in pixels from the left side of the screen. |
| `top=pixels` | The position of the top left corner of the window measured in pixels from the top of the screen. |
| `screenX=pixels` | The position of the top left corner of the window measured in pixels from the left side of the screen. This is not supported in IE. |
| `screenY=pixels` | The position of the top left corner of the window measured in pixels from the top of the screen. This is not supported in IE. |
| `titlebar[=yes|no] | [=1|0]` | The title bar across the top of the browser window, which displays a document's title. To set to no, use a signed script. |

You can set an option as on by simply listing it or by setting its value to `yes` or `1`. The following are equivalent:

```
myWin = window.open("test.html", "TestWin",
    "height=100,width=100,status")
myWin = window.open("test.html", "TestWin",
    "height=100,width=100,status=yes")
```

```
myWin = window.open("test.html", "TestWin", ⟶
⟶ "height=100,width=100,status=1")
```

The following code creates a new window object, map, that loads the document map.html and has a target name of MapWin, dimensions of 150-by-150 pixels, a toolbar, and a status bar.

```
map = window.open("map.html", "MapWin", ⟶
⟶ "width=150,height=150,toolbar,status")
```

## The screen Object

Before we leave the subject of window features, let's also examine the properties of the screen object. The screen object represents the entire viewing screen the visitor sees; it is what's on the visitor's monitor. The screen object has several properties that are similar to, but not the same as, those of windows. The primary value of the screen object is that it tells us the current viewing resolution and the number of colors on the visitor's monitor. Cool, huh?

**peek ahead**  Script 11.13 makes use of some screen object properties to center a pop-up window on the screen.

Knowing the visitor's viewing resolution comes in handy when you want to center a window on the screen or choose an appropriately sized picture to display. Here's a quick rundown of the screen object's properties:

**Table 11.5**    **Properties of the screen Object**

| Property | Description |
| --- | --- |
| availHeight | Refers to the height of the screen, in pixels, less any permanent or semi-permanent GUI (graphical user interface) features displayed by the operating system, such as the taskbar in Windows. |
| availLeft | Indicates the x-coordinate of the first pixel that is not allocated to permanent or semi-permanent GUI features. |
| availTop | Indicates the y-coordinate of the first pixel that is not allocated to permanent or semi-permanent GUI features. |
| availWidth | Refers to the width of the screen, in pixels, less any permanent or semi-permanent GUI features displayed by the operating system, such as the taskbar in Windows. |
| colorDepth | If a color palette is in use, refers to the bit depth of that color palette. If a color palette is not in use, refers to the value of the pixelDepth property. |
| height | Refers to the entire display screen's height. |

| pixelDepth | Refers to the color resolution (bits per pixel) of the display screen. |
| width | Refers to the entire display screen's width. |

## Closing a Window

Closing a window is simple in comparison to opening one. Simply call the `close` method with the window's name. To close map, write

```
map.close()
```

I told you it was simple.

# Window Synonyms

The `window` object has several properties, which are used as synonyms to identify the current `window` object and its related objects. These window synonyms should look familiar. See Table 11.1, "Magic Target Names," if you need to refresh your memory. The only thing missing is the underscore character at the beginning.

**Table 11.6    Window Synonyms**

| Property/Synonym | Description |
|---|---|
| self | Refers to the current window. Equivalent to `window`. |
| parent | Refers to the window that contains a particular window. |
| top | Used with framed windows. Refers to the topmost window containing a particular window. |
| window | Yes, the `window` object has a `window` property, which identifies the current window being referenced. `self` is equivalent to `window`. |
| opener | Refers to the window from which a particular window was opened. |

The window synonyms `self`, `parent`, and `top` work the same as their equivalent magic target names `_self`, `_parent`, and `_top`. Keep in mind, though, that they are window names, not target names. The window name `window` is a synonym for `self` and refers to the current window.

The window synonym `opener` needs additional explanation. If window1 opens window2, then in window2, `opener` refers to the window that opened window2, which is window1.

### Figure 11.17 The *opener* Window Synonym

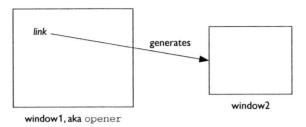

To show this in action, we'll need to create a document that will open a pop-up window and do some scripting in the document that loads into the pop-up window. Let's create a document that opens a pop-up window and displays a map.

### Script 11.10 Opening and Closing a Pop-up Window

```
1    <html>
2    <head>
3    <title>Script 11.10: Opening &amp; Closing a Pop-Up Window</title>
4    <script language="JavaScript" type="text/javascript"><!--
5        var map = null
6        function showMap() {
7            var features = "width=220,height=250"
8            features += ",left=50,top=50,status"
9
10           map = window.open("map.html", "MapWin", features)
11           map.focus()
12       }
13       function closeMap() {
14           if(map != null) {
15               map.close()
16               map = null
17           }
18       }
19   //-->
20   </script>
21   </head>
22   <body>
23       <h1>Contact Us</h1>
24       <p>5052 Map Place<br>
25       San Diego, CA 00000<br>
26       (760)000-0000</p>
27       <p><a href="javascript: void(0)" onClick="showMap()">View
           Map</a> |
28       <a href="directions.html" target="MapWin">View Driving
           Directions</a> |
```

```
29          <a href="javascript: void(0)" onClick="closeMap()">Close
            Map</a></p>
30     </body>
31     </html>
```

In Line 11, to give focus to map (the pop-up window), focus is called using the window's variable name, not its target name. The same is true in line 15 when the close method is called.

There are links at the bottom of Script 11.10:

- ✗ The first link, View Map (line 27), calls showMap (lines 6–12) to create a 220-by-250 window named map with a status bar, positions it 50 pixels from the left and 50 pixels from the top, and gives it focus.

- ✗ The second link, View Driving Directions (line 28), simply opens directions.html in a window with the target name MapWin, which just happens to be the target name assigned to map.

- ✗ The third link, Close Map (line 29), calls the closeMap function (lines 13–18) to close the map window from the window that opened it. So that a visitor would not receive an error if he clicked on the Close Map link when map wasn't open, line 5 creates a global variable named map. This global variable becomes a reference to a window object when the showMap function is called; otherwise, it simply holds its initial value of null.

Now let's create map.html (Script 11.11), complete with Print, Return, and Close buttons to illustrate the window, opener, and self window synonyms. You'll see that window and self are pretty much interchangeable. The Print button (line 11) will print the contents of the map window; the Return button (line 12) will return focus to opener, the window that opened map; and the Close button (line 13) will close map.

**Script 11.11   map.html**

```
1     <html>
2     <head>
3          <title>Script 11.11: map.html</title>
4     </head>
5     <body>
6     <div align=center>
7       <h2>Map to WebWorld</h2>
8       <img src="images/map.gif" border="0" alt="Map to WebWorld"
9       width="200" height="119">
10      <form>
11          <input type="button" value="Print" onClick="window.print()">
12          <input type="button" value="Return"
               onClick="opener.focus()">
13          <input type="button" value="Close" onClick="self.close()">
14      </form>
```

```
15   </div>
16   </body>
17   </html>
```

Script 11.11 shows three labeled buttons: Print, Return, and Close (lines 11, 12, and 13, respectively). Each button has an onClick event handler defined, which will call a corresponding window method when the button is clicked. Close closes the map window; Print prints the contents of the map window; and Return gives focus to the window that opened map. Notice the window synonyms used with each method to reference the appropriate window object.

Run Script 11.10 and click on the View Map link.

*Figure 11.18   Results of Script 11.10 when View Map Is Clicked*

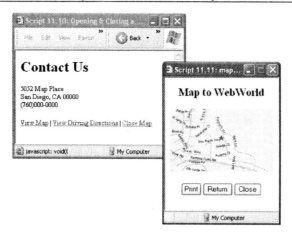

A window named map with a target name of MapWin pops up and displays a map. Now click on the View Driving Directions link.

*Figure 11.19   Results of Script 11.10 when View Driving*
*Directions Is Clicked after View Map*

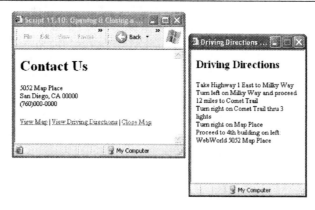

Notice how the driving directions are loaded in MapWin? The `target` attribute setting (line 28 of Script 11.10) does that. If MapWin is not already open, the browser will open a window of no particular size, give it a target name of `MapWin`, and load the directions into it. Using only HTML like this, you cannot give the window focus.

Now try the buttons in the `map` window. Cool, huh?

Table 11.7 lists the current `window` methods, complete with descriptions, that are at your disposal so you can play with them to your heart's content.

**Table 11.7    Window Methods**

| Method | Description |
| --- | --- |
| `alert(text)` | Displays an alert dialog box containing the *text* specified and an OK button. |
| `back()` | Is equivalent to the visitor pressing the Back button. |
| `blur()` | Removes focus from the window. |
| `clearInterval(intervalID)` | Clears an interval. |
| `clearTimeout(timeoutID)` | Clears a timeout. |
| `close()` | Closes the window. If you call `close` alone, without specifying a `windowObjectName`, JavaScript assumes that you mean the current window and closes it.<br><br>    The `close` method only closes windows you've opened using the `open` method. Should you try to close any other window, the user will be asked to confirm whether to close the window or not.<br><br>    In an event handler, you must specify `windowObjectName.close()` instead of simply using `close()`. Calling `close()` in an event handler without specifying a `window` object name is equivalent to calling `document.close()`. |
| `confirm(text)` | Displays a confirm dialog box containing the *text* specified and options for the user to choose OK or CANCEL. If OK is pressed, `confirm` returns `true`; if CANCEL is pressed, `confirm` returns `false`. |

| | |
|---|---|
| `find([targetString[,`<br>`caseSensitive[, backward]])` | Searches for the *targetString* in the contents of the specified window. `caseSensitive` is a Boolean value that is `true` if listed, `false` if not; it specifies that the search be case sensitive. `backward` is also a Boolean value and causes find to search backward instead of forward. If you use either `caseSensitive` or `backward`, you must also use the other. |
| `focus()` | Gives focus to a window, that is, it brings the window to the top and makes it the current window. |
| `forward()` | Is equivalent to the visitor pressing the Forward button. |
| `home()` | Is equivalent to the visitor pressing the Home button. |
| `moveBy(x, y)` | Moves the window *x* pixels horizontally and *y* pixels vertically from its current position. |
| `moveTo(x, y)` | Moves the window to the specified *x-y* coordinates. |
| `open(url, name,`<br>`[windowFeatures])` | Opens a window, loads the document at the specified URL, and gives the window the provided target name and listed features. Details are provided above. |
| `print()` | Prints the contents of a window or frame. |
| `prompt(request, defaultInput)` | Displays a prompt dialog box with the specified request for input from the user. If *defaultInput* is not supplied, `undefined` appears in the dialog box (not very pretty). |
| `resizeBy(x, y)` | Resizes the window *x* pixels horizontally and *y* pixels vertically by moving the bottom right corner. |
| `resizeTo(x, y)` | Resizes the window to the specified *x-y* dimensions. |
| `scroll(x, y)` | Scrolls the window to the specified *x-y* coordinates (deprecated in JavaScript 1.2, replaced by `scrollTo`). |

| | |
|---|---|
| `scrollBy(x, y)` | Scrolls the window contents *x* pixels horizontally and *y* pixels vertically. |
| `scrollTo(x, y)` | Scrolls the window contents to the specified *x-y* coordinates (replaces `scroll`). |
| `setInterval("expression", msec)`<br>`setInterval(function, msec[,`<br>`arg1[, ..., argN]])` | Evaluates an expression or calls a function repeatedly, every so many milliseconds (*msec*). The calls continue to fire until the interval is canceled using the `clearInterval` method (ideally); or until the associated window or frame is destroyed by overload, closing the browser; or until the program crashes (undesired). The expression must be quoted. |
| `setTimeout("expression", msec)`<br>`setTimeout(function, msec[,`<br>`arg1[, ..., argN]])` | Evaluates an expression or calls a function after a specified amount of time. It does not act repeatedly. For example, if a `setTimeout` method specifies 5,000 milliseconds, the expression is evaluated or the function is called *once* after 5,000 milliseconds have passed, not every 5,000 milliseconds like with `setInterval`.<br>    `setTimeout` does not stall the script. The script continues execution immediately after the call, which simply schedules some future event. |
| `stop()` | Stops the current document download. Equivalent to the visitor pressing the Stop button. |

Notice `alert`, `confirm`, and `prompt`; we've used all three quite frequently throughout this book.

`focus` and `blur` make a nice pair; they allow you to give focus to a window or remove focus from it. `focus` is used much more often, while `blur` is rarely used. After all, simply giving a window focus automatically creates a blur on the window that originally had focus.

`close` is often used as an event handler in conjunction with a button, as is `print`, to make it easy for a visitor to close or print a window.

`moveBy`, `moveTo`, `resizeBy`, and `resizeTo` allow you to resize and reposition a window after it has been created. These methods come in handy because JavaScript does not allow you to change a window's features after it has been opened.

scroll, scrollBy, and scrollTo can be used to create fancy scrolling effects in windows and frames. Use them sparingly. Scrolling window contents can be like too many animated GIFs: distracting and annoying.

The window methods back, forward, home, print, and find work just like their browser button equivalents. However, only print seems to work reliably cross-browser and cross-platform. You can, however, also use

```
[window].history.go(1)
```

to go forward one page or

```
[window].history.go(-1)
```

to go back one page. These history methods sometimes work more reliably cross-browser. The window methods setTimeout, clearTimeout, setInterval, and clearInterval allow you to call a function after a specified amount of time. For more details, see the explanation and examples in Chapter 8, "Functions and Libraries."

Many commercial sites now use setInterval in conjunction with pop-up windows to reopen an announcement window that has been closed, annoying as that may be to the visitor. For a friendlier touch, let's use setTimeout to close an announcement window after a bit of time.

***Script 11.12  A Visitor-Friendly Pop-up Announcement***

```
1   <html>
2   <head>
3   <title>Script 11.12: A Visitor Friendly Announcement
       Window</title>
4   <script language="JavaScript" type="text/javascript"><!--
5   function showNews() {
6         news = window.open("news.html", "NewsWin",
              "width=200,height=220")
7         newsTimer = setTimeout("news.close()", "20000")
8   }
9   //-->
10  </script>
11  </head>
12  <body onLoad="showNews()">
13        <h1>Home Page of Some Web Site</h1>
14
15  </body>
16  </html>
```

Lines 5 through 8 define the showNews function, which opens a news window, then sets a timeout to close the window after 20 seconds (20 seconds = 20,000 milliseconds). The pop-up window is called when the document is loaded, as is usual with commercial pop-up announcements. Here's what it looks like:

**Figure 11.20   Results of Script 11.12**

Keep in mind that many Web surfers are coming to loathe pop-up windows. Use them sparingly and kindly close them after a bit so the visitor doesn't have to.

# Writing to Windows Dynamically

Thus far, you've only been opening windows and loading pre-created Web documents. What if you want to create the content for a window on the fly and display it in a pop-up window? For instance, you could display the results of a questionnaire completed by a visitor, choose a random tip of the day, or simply select and display a daily quote. Let's try the last one: a daily quote.

**Script 11.13   Daily Quote**

```
1    <html>
2    <head>
3    <title>Script 11.13: Daily Quote</title>
4    <script language="JavaScript" type="text/javascript"><!--
5    var today = new Date()
6
7    var quotations = new Array(7)
8    quotations[0] = "Stop and smell the roses."
9    quotations[1] = "Just another manic Monday!"
10   quotations[2] = "He who laughs, lasts."
11   quotations[3] = "Ahhhh! It\'s hump day!"
12   quotations[4] = "I haven\'t failed, I\'ve found 10,000 ways that
        don\'t work"
13   quotations[5] = "Thank goodness it\'s finally Friday!"
14   quotations[6] = "Dance the night away, tomorrow\'s only Sunday!"
```

```
15
16    function displayQuote(quotation, width, height) {
17         var startDoc = "<html><head><title>Daily Quote</title>
              </head>"
18         startDoc += "<body bgcolor=yellow text=black>"
19         var endDoc = "</body></html>"
20         var xPos = screen.availWidth > width ? screen.availWidth/2
              - width/2 : 0
21         var yPos = screen.availHeight>height ? screen.availHeight/2
              - height/2 : 0
22
23         var features = "width=" + width + ",height=" + height
24         features += ",screenX=" + xPos + ",screenY=" + yPos
25
26         dailyQuote = window.open("", "QuoteWin", features)
27
28         dailyQuote.document.writeln(startDoc,
              "<h2>Daily Quote</h2>")
29         dailyQuote.document.writeln(quotation)
30         dailyQuote.document.writeln("<div align=right><form>",
31                      "<input type=button value=Close ",
32                      "onClick=\"self.close()\"></form></div>")
33                      dailyQuote.document.writeln(endDoc)
34    }
35    //-->
36    </script>
37    </head>
38    <body onLoad="displayQuote(quotations[today.getDay()], 200, 150)">
39         <h1>Home Page of Some Web Site</h1>
40
41    </body>
42    </html>
```

Look closely at the `displayQuote` function (lines 16–34). See if you can figure out what each and every line does. The two lines that might throw you for a loop are lines 20 and 21. Using properties of the `screen` object, `availWidth` and `availHeight`, you can determine the width and height of the current browser window.

Line 20 says, "If the width of the current browser window (`screen.availWidth`) is larger than the width desired for the daily quote window (`width`), then set `xPos` so that the daily quote window will be centered on the screen." To calculate the x coordinate, the browser window's width (`screen.availWidth`) is

> **Peek ahead**
>
> In Chapter 14, "Cookies," we'll revisit daily quote and provide visitors a means to disable it so that it will not appear on their next visit.

divided by two and half of the size of the daily quote window (`width`) is subtracted from that. Line 21 works the same way, only using the browser window's height and the height desired for the daily quote window.

To choose the appropriate quotation, in line 38 we simply use the `getDay` method of `today` to index into the quotations array. Notice that the name of the window to write to is implicitly specified in lines 28, 29, and 30 when calling the `document.writeln` method. This is important. If a `dailyQuote` window's name were not used, the content would be written to the current window, the home page.

### Figure 11.21    One Possible Result of Script 11.13

## Loading More Than One Frame at a Time

One of the cool things about using JavaScript in conjunction with frames is that you can load more than one frame at a time. Let's use a new frameset with three frames in it (Script 11.14).

### Script 11.14    Three-Frame Frameset

```
1    <html>
2    <head>
3         <title>Script 11.14: 3-Frame Frameset</title>
4    </head>
5    <frameset rows="110, *, 40">
6         <frame name="NavFrame" src="nav.html">
7         <frame name="MainFrame" src="home.html">
8         <frame name="NoticeFrame" src="copyright.html">
9    </frameset>
10   </html>
```

The key document is nav.html (Script 11.15), as it will do all the work.

### Script 11.15    ChangingTwo Frames at Once (nav.html)

```
1    <html>
2    <head>
```

```
 3    <title>Script 11.15: Changing Two Frames At Once
        (nav.html)</title>
 4    <script language="JavaScript" type="text/javascript"><!--
 5         function loadFrames(mainSrc, noticeSrc) {
 6              parent.MainFrame.location.replace(mainSrc);
 7              parent.NoticeFrame.location.replace(noticeSrc);
 8         }
 9    //-->
10    </script>
11    </head>
12    <body>
13    <h1 align="left">WebWorld</h1>
14    <table width="320" border="3" cellpadding="2" align="center"><tr>
15    <th><a href="javascript: void(0);"
16         onClick="loadFrames('catalog.html',
              'special.html')">Catalog</a>
17    </th>
18    <th><a href="javascript: void(0);"
19         onClick="loadFrames('support.html',
              'copyright.html')">Support</a>
20    </th>
21    <th><a href="javascript: void(0);"
22         onClick="loadFrames('contact.html',
              'special.html')">Contact Us</a>
23    </th>
24    <th><a href="javascript: void(0);"
25         onClick="loadFrames('home.html',
              'copyright.html')">Home</a>
26    </th>
27    </tr></table>
28    </body>
29    </html>
```

To view the new frameset and test the links, open index.html, located in the Chapter11Frameset5 folder. Figure 11.22 shows the initial view. Figure 11.23 shows what

---

**programmer's tip**

**Remove Base Target when Targeting Multiple Frames**

Notice that no base target is specified in Script 11.15. In Opera and Internet Explorer, retaining the base target statement prevents the frame named in the base target element from reloading. Netscape Navigator, however, handles it fine.

happens when you click on the Catalog link (line 16 of Script 11.15). The contents of both
`MainFrame` and `NoticeFrame` change with one click.

***Figure 11.22 Changing Two Frames at Once***

***Figure 11.23 Results of Script 11.15 when Catalog Is Clicked***

The secret to accessing the frames is to get to each frame through its parent frameset.
Thus, a frame can be referred to as

`parent.`*FrameName*

See lines 6 and 7 of Script 11.15. You can change the document loaded in a particular frame either by calling the `replace` method of the `location` object or by modifying the `href` property of the `location` object.

Calling the `location` object's `replace` method:

```
parent.FrameName.location.replace(newSource)
```

Modifying the `location` object's `href` property:

```
parent.FrameName.location.href = newSource
```

There is no limit to the number of frames you can change at once. In Script 11.15, we called the `location` object's `replace` method (lines 6 and 7).

# Sharing Variables and Functions across Frames

In addition to loading multiple frames at once using JavaScript, you can also store variables and functions in a document loaded in a static frame and access those variables and functions from documents in other frames. A **static frame** is one whose contents do not change after the frameset is loaded. Generally, you would not want to store data in a dynamic frame, because that data would disappear as soon as a new document was loaded in that frame. A frame that holds your navigation, banner, or logo is usually static and is a good place to store variables and functions.

The ability to store data in a static frame is one way you can use JavaScript to **save state**. To save state is to preserve information about the current session as the user browses through documents on your site. In this case, a **session** begins when a user enters your Web site and ends when he leaves your Web site. In contrast, a **browser session** begins when the user opens his browser and ends when he closes his browser. Right now, we're not concerned about browser sessions. We're only interested in knowing what a visitor does during his visit, i.e., his viewing session.

For this task, we'll use the same frameset as before, Script 11.14. We'll store the visitor's name in nav.html (line 6 of Script 11.16), as it is the one frame that remains static. We'll also make slight modifications to the other documents, customizing each one's message to the current visitor.

**peek ahead**
JavaScript programmers can also maintain state using cookies. Chapter 14 will show you how.

**Script 11.16  *Saving State with Frame Variables (nav.html)***

```
1    <html>
2    <head>
3    <title>Script 11.16: Saving State with Frame Variables
        (nav.html)</title>
4    <base target="MainFrame">
5    <script language="JavaScript" type="text/javascript"><!--
6         var visitor = null
```

```
7
8     //-->
9     </script>
10    </head>
11    <body>
12    <h1 align="left">WebWorld</h1>
13    <table width="320" border="3" cellpadding="2" align="center"><tr>
14        <th><a href="catalog.html">Catalog</a></th>
15        <th><a href="support.html">Support</a></th>
16        <th><a href="contact.html">Contact Us</a></th>
17        <th><a href="home.html">Home</a></th>
18    </tr></table>
19    </body>
20    </html>
```

In nav.html (Script 11.16), we've created a variable named `visitor` to hold the visitor's name (line 6).

### Script 11.17    Saving State with Frame Variables (home.html)

```
1     <html>
2     <head>
3     <title>Script 11.17: Saving State with Frame Variables
          (home.html)</title>
4     <script language="JavaScript" type="text/javascript"><!--
5         function getName() {
6             if (parent.NavFrame.visitor == null) {
7                 parent.NavFrame.visitor = prompt("What\'s your
                      name?", "")
8             }
9             return parent.NavFrame.visitor
10        }
11
12    //-->
13    </script>
14    </head>
15    <body>
16    <script language="JavaScript" type="text/javascript"><!--
17        document.write("<h1>Welcome, ", getName(), "</h1>")
18    //-->
19    </script>
20
21        <p>Welcome! Blah, blah, blah, blah, blah, blah, blah,
22        blah, blah, blah, blah, blah, blah, blah, blah, blah,
23        blah, blah, blah, blah, blah, blah, blah, blah, blah,
24        blah, blah, blah, blah, blah, blah, blah, blah, blah,</p>
```

```
25    </body>
26    </html>
```

The above document, home.html (Script 11.17), actually acquires the visitor's name the first time it loads (line 17), by calling the getName function, called in lines 5–10. After that, it retrieves the visitor's name from the visitor variable in NavFrame (line 9).

The rest of the documents, catalog.html, support.html, and contact.html, just retrieve the visitor's name from NavFrame to customize their messages (lines 11, 9, and 10 of Scripts 11.18, 11.19, and 11.20, respectively).

**Script 11.18    catalog.html**

```
1     <html>
2     <head>
3         <title>Script 11.18: catalog.html</title>
4     </head>
5     <body>
6         <h1>Catalog</h1>
7         <p>Item 1: $99.95</p>
8         <br><br><br>
9         <p><font color="red">Don't miss out on these great sales,
10        <script language="JavaScript" type="text/javascript"><!--
11            document.write(parent.NavFrame.visitor)
12        //-->
13        </script>!</font></p>
14    </body>
15    </html>
```

**Script 11.19    support.html**

```
1     <html>
2     <head>
3         <title>Script 11.19: support.html</title>
4     </head>
5     <body>
6         <h1>Support</h1>
7         <p>How can we help you,
8         <script language="JavaScript" type="text/javascript"><!--
9             document.write(parent.NavFrame.visitor)
10        //-->
11        </script>?</p>
12    </body>
13    </html>
```

**Script 11.20** **contact.html**

```
1    <html>
2    <head>
3        <title>Script 11.20: contact.html</title>
4    </head>
5    <body>
6        <h1>How to Contact Us</h1>
7        <p>Phone: (555) 555-1212</p>
8        <p>
9        <script language="JavaScript" type="text/javascript"><!--
10           document.write(parent.NavFrame.visitor)
11       //-->
12       </script>, we're available 24 hours a day, seven days a
13       week to help you. Just give us a call!</p>
14   </body>
15   </html>
```

Open index.html in the Chapter11Frameset6 folder.

**Figure 11.24** **Saving State with Frames**

Click on a link and watch the results.

You can also store functions and variables in the <head> of your frameset document. Then it's even easier to refer to functions and variables declared in the frameset. Just reference

    parent.*variableName*

or

```
parent.functionName()
```

from any frame in the frameset.

**Figure 11.25    Results when Support Is Clicked**

While frames are cool, two things can happen involving frames that aren't so cool. Let's take a look at them.

# Don't Get Framed

The first not-so-cool thing that involves frames is that your site could get framed; that is, another Web developer could like your content so much that he presents it within his own frameset. It could also be that he just doesn't know about `target` attributes and innocently linked to your site without using an appropriate target, thus framing your site within his own.

At any rate, whether the intent was innocent or not, it's not nice to be framed by someone else's frameset. It makes your content look like it belongs to someone else. Also, it's quite likely that some of your most important content won't be immediately visible because it will be squished unnaturally into someone else's frameset. That's why **framing**, as this practice is called, has become a complicated issue with many legal ramifications.

The best practice is to *not* frame anyone else's site within your own. To avoid *being* framed, simply implement Script 11.21 in all of your Web pages.

**Script 11.21    Don't Frame Me**

```
1    <html>
2    <head>
3        <title>Script 11.21: Don't Frame Me</title>
4        <script language="JavaScript" type="text/javascript"><!--
5            if (self.location != top.location) {
6                top.location = self.location
```

```
7                    }
8           //-->
9           </script>
10  </head>
11  <body>
12          <h1>Don't Frame Me!</h1>
13
14  </body>
15  </html>
```

Notice that line 5 checks to see if the `location` of your document is equivalent to `top`. Recall that `top` is a window synonym that refers to the top of all framesets. If for some reason your document isn't at the top, then line 6 moves it there.

Figure 11.26 shows a framed Web site with a link to Script 11.21 in the bottom frame. No target has been specified on that link, so by default, Script 11.21 should load in the bottom frame.

**Figure 11.26    Attempting to Frame Script 11.21**

Script 11.21 won't allow itself to be framed, resulting in Figure 11.27.

**Figure 11.27    Results of Framing Attempt**

Now that's cool, huh?

# Don't Lose Your Frame of Reference

The second not-so-cool thing that involves frames is that a search engine or a savvy Internet surfer could open one of your framed pages, or link to it, so that it loads *outside* of your frameset. The major problem with this is that without your frameset, your lone page is an orphan, naked to the world, without navigation, copyright notices, or the other important resources usually provided in the other frames.

This practice of opening a page outside of its frameset can also have some legal ramifications. The best practice is don't link to an orphan page, link to the frameset.

To make certain *your* Web pages don't become orphans, you can insert Script 11.22 in the <head> of all of your framed pages.

### Script 11.22 Need My Frame

```
1   <html>
2   <head>
3       <title>Script 11.22: Need My Frame</title>
4       <script language="JavaScript" type="text/javascript"><!--
5           if(self.location == top.location){
6               top.location.href = "myFrameset.html"
7           }
8       //-->
9       </script>
10  </head>
11  <body>
12      <p><strong>I <i>need</i> my frame!</strong></p>
13
14  </body>
15  </html>
```

Figure 11.28 shows what happens when you try to open Script 11.22 itself, instead of its frameset document.

### Figure 11.28 Results of Script 11.22

As you can see, Script 11.22 refuses to be an orphan and loads in its frameset anyway. Line 5 checks to see if the Web page is being loaded in the top window. If it is, then line 6 opens the frameset document, which includes Script 11.22, in the top window instead. Purty cool, huh?

# Summary

Many commercial Web sites use pop-up windows to notify visitors of sales, news, and special offers. The ability to break a browser window into multiple frames was introduced by Netscape. Frames have since become a popular means of providing always-present navigation or notices.

Using HTML alone, it is possible to open a document in a new, named window, reuse that named window, and create framed Web sites. However, HTML alone cannot size a window, position it, give it focus, close it, or print its contents. Nor can HTML alone load documents in more than one frame at a time. Thankfully with JavaScript, all this can be accomplished and more.

As part of its frame technology, Netscape defined several "magic target names": `_self`, which refers to the current window; `_blank`, which refers to a new, unnamed window; `_parent`, which refers to the parent frame or window of the current frame; and `_top`, which refers to the top of the current window, outside of any framesets. These magic target names were incorporated in the HTML 4.0 specification. Creating a framed Web site requires three general steps: (1) create a frameset, (2) create the HTML documents that will initially load into the frames, and (3) create the rest of the HTML documents needed in the site.

To open a pop-up window, use the `open` method of the `window` object. When opening a window, it is a good idea to assign it a `window` object name, as that name is required to make any method calls—such as `close`, `print`, and `focus`—on that window. Without a `window` object name, you cannot call a `window`'s methods.

When you open a window, you can specify the URL of a document to load into the window. If you don't specify a URL, you can write to the window dynamically using *windowName*`.document.write` or *windowName*`.document.writeln`. You can also provide a target name for the window, as well as a set of features. The feature set can specify the window's dimensions, its initial position on the screen, which bars and menus to include, etc.

JavaScript supports several window synonyms that can be used to reference the current window and windows related to it. They are `self` and `window`, which are pretty interchangeable and refer to the current window; `parent` and `top`, which act like their target name equivalents; and `opener`, which refers to the window that opened the current window.

JavaScript supports a variety of `window` methods, including some that allow you to perform functions equivalent to the visitor pressing a button on the browser, such as `back`, `forward`, `home`, `stop`, and `print`. The language also supports methods for giving focus to and removing focus from (blurring) a window. Several methods allow you to change the dimensions and position of a window once it is loaded, as well as scroll the window's contents. Using the setTimeout method, you can cause a pop-up window to close after a certain period of time. If you want to annoy a visitor, you can use setInterval to reopen an announcement window periodically.

The same addressing in JavaScript that allows you to load multiple frames at once also lets you share variables and functions among frames. This provides a primitive method of saving state. It is best to store data and functions used across frames in a static frame, whose contents do not change or in the <head> of the frameset document.

Two not-so-nice things can happen to your Web site that involve frames: a Web site could try to frame your Web documents by opening them in its own frameset or orphan your Web documents by opening them outside of *your* frameset. Scripts 11.21 and 11.22 can prevent both occurrences from happening.

## Review Questions

1. What target name, by default, is automatically set on any link unless overridden?
2. How can you override the default target name for all links in a Web page? Provide an example.
3. How can you override the default target name on a single link? Provide an example.
4. Provide an example of a link that targets a custom-named window.
5. List and describe four magic target names.
6. Why should you be careful using _blank?
7. List the three general steps necessary to create a framed Web site.
8. How are framesets organized?
9. Draw a picture of the frameset created by each of the following frameset definitions:

   a. ```
   <frameset cols="*, 150">
       <frame>
       <frame>
   </frameset>
   ```
   b. ```
   <frameset rows="*, 100">
       <frame>
       <frame>
   </frameset>
   ```
   c. ```
   <frameset cols="150, *">
       <frame>
       <frameset rows="100, *, 40">
           <frame>
           <frame>
           <frame>
       </frameset>
   </frameset>
   ```
10. Why is it essential to name each frame in a frameset?
11. Why must you provide a src attribute for each frame in a frameset?
   ```

12. What happens if you don't title your frameset document? What appears in the title bar?
13. In which document in a frameset is it most essential to set up targeting?
14. Can you load a frameset document into an existing frame? Explain.
15. Which frame attribute determines whether a visitor has the right to resize a frame or not?
16. Which frame attribute determines whether scrollbars appear or not?
17. What attributes must you set on a frameset and each frame in order to create borderless frames? Provide an example.
18. List and describe the three parameters of a window's open method.
19. Why is it essential to give a window an object name when you open it?
20. How do you give a window an object name when you open it? Provide an example.
21. How do you close a window?
22. What is a window synonym?
23. List and describe five window synonyms supported in JavaScript.
24. List three window methods that emulate the action of a visitor clicking a button on the browser toolbar.
25. Name a method that allows you to change a window's position once it is open.
26. Name a method that allows you to resize a window after it is open.
27. Is it possible to write to a window on the fly, instead of loading a pre-created document into it? Explain.
28. What technology is necessary to load more than one frame at once?
29. What does it mean to "save state"?
30. What is a static frame?
31. What does the term "framing" refer to?
32. Why should you avoid framing other people's Web pages?
33. How does a Web page become orphaned?
34. When linking to a framed Web site, why should you always link to its frameset document, rather than to individual content pages?

## Exercises

1. Write the appropriate HTML code to open the file map.html
   a. in a new, unnamed window.
   b. in a custom-named window (you choose the name).
   c. in the current window, outside of all framesets.
2. Create a frameset with two frames and associated documents.
3. Create a frameset that looks like the following diagram. Create the appropriate initial documents and test it.

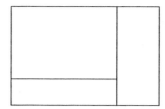

4. Write an appropriate JavaScript statement to create a pop-up window with dimensions of 300 by 150, an initial position at coordinates 70, 85, a status bar, and a location bar.

5. Write an appropriate JavaScript statement to create a pop-up window that can be written to dynamically after it is open.

6. Assume that you are in the window that opened the pop-up described in Exercise 4. Write a statement to
   a. close that window.
   b. print the window's contents.

7. Assume that you are in the document in the pop-up window described in Exercise 4. Write a statement to
   a. give focus to the window that opened the current window.
   b. print the contents of the current window.
   c. print the contents of the window that opened the current window.
   d. close the current window.

8. Assume the frameset below has been defined.

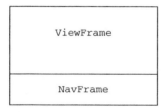

   Write the appropriate JavaScript statements to
   a. access a variable named `password` stored in `NavFrame` from `ViewFrame`.
   b. load map.html in `ViewFrame` from a link in `NavFrame` (use JavaScript, not just HTML).
   c. load newNav.html in `NavFrame` from a link in `ViewFrame` (use JavaScript, not just HTML).
   d. access a variable named `visitor` stored in the frameset from `ViewFrame`.

9. Write appropriate JavaScript statements to
   a. move a window named `surf` 10 pixels to the right of its current position.
   b. move a window named `surf` 15 pixels left and 11 pixels up from its current position.

      c. move a window named `surf` 10 pixels to the right of its current position every 10 seconds. When it is has disappeared off the right side of the screen, it should reappear on the left side of the screen and move from there.

10. List and describe three `window` properties not mentioned in this chapter.

# Scripting Exercises

Create a folder named assignment11 to hold the documents you create during this assignment. Save a copy of your latest toy store documents in a toyStore subfolder.

1. Modify the home page of your toy store Web site as follows:
   a. Add a pop-up window that displays current specials or sales when the document is first opened.
   b. Make the content flashy and attention-grabbing.
2. Modify the contact Web page of your toy store Web site as follows:
   a. Acquire or create a map to your toy store. MapQuest (http://mapquest.com) is a good place to get street maps to specific locations.
   b. Add a button or a link labeled "Directions" or "Map". When clicked, the link or button should generate a pop-up window to display the map.
   c. The window should be sized to hold the map, without scroll bars showing, and two buttons underneath the map. One button should be labeled "Close," the other "Return to Contact Info."
   d. When clicked, the Close button should close the map window and return focus to the window that opened it.
   e. When clicked, the Return to Contact Info button, should return focus to the window that opened the map window, but should not close the map window itself.
3. Create a new document named tips.html.
   a. Modify the daily quote script or start over from scratch, but create a script that displays a random tip about a toy listed on your toy store Web site in a pop-up window every five minutes. For testing purposes, you might want to use one minute.
   b. If the pop-up tip is already open, close it and pop it up again with a new random tip. Set the window to close automatically after 30 seconds or so. Choose an appropriate time depending on the length of your tips. Remember, you've got to give the visitor enough time to read the tip.
   c. Write the tips to the window dynamically from an array of tips located in tips.js.
   d. When you're satisfied that the script is working as planned, add it to the catalog or products page of the toy store Web site.
4. Write a function, `openWin`, that opens a window named `zWindow` and gives it focus.
   a. Its target name should be `zWin`.
   b. The function should have parameters for specifying the width and height of `zWindow`, the optional document to initially load into it, the initial x-coordinate

and y-coordinate positions, and a list of other features desired, such as status bar, toolbar, etc.

   c. Once you have tested and debugged it, add this function to myLib.js.

5. Create a new document named popupNews.html.

   a. Write a script that will create a pop-up window to display news from news.html.

   b. The script should check for a new news.html document every minute and only pop up or refresh the open window if news.html has been updated.

6. Write a script that prevents another Web site from loading your Web site within it.

7. Create a simple framed Web site. Include a script in every framed page to prevent the document from becoming an orphan without its frameset.

# Projects

## Project 1: Tic-Tac-Toe Game

Write a tic-tac-toe game that uses frames. The frameset should contain at least one static frame in which to display the score and store the functions and variables required to play the game. You'll need controls for X and O and a scoreboard.

## Project 2: Planets of Our Solar System

Create a Web site that displays data about the planets in our solar system. Use parallel arrays to store the information. Planet information should at least include name, position, diameter, and mass. You can acquire information about the planets from "The Nine Planets: A Multimedia Tour of the Solar System," located at http://seds.lpl.arizona.edu/nineplanets/nineplanets/nineplanets.html.

You may let the visitor choose a planet from a form, an image map, or a link or prompt her for that information. However the visitor makes her choice, the script should call a function to write the data, including a picture of the planet, in a pop-up window. The content of the pop-up window *must* be generated dynamically.

Once you've got your script working well, decorate your document and make it interesting. Look for pretty pictures of planets and starry backgrounds.

Upload and test your project. Turn in a print-out of your code.

## Project 3: Color-Chooser Utility

Using what you've learned about event handlers, arrays, control structures, functions, and dynamically writing to windows, create a Web presentation that is a color-selector tool.

The visitor should be able to choose from several background images, background colors, text colors, and link colors. Ideally, the visitor can choose any of the 216 browser-safe colors. Using the choices selected by the visitor, pop up a window that displays a sample of how the color choices look together, like in Figure 11.29.

Your presentation should contain at least two documents. The home page should introduce and explain the use of the tool. Use frames if you like.

*Figure 11.29   Sample Pop-up Window for Project 3*

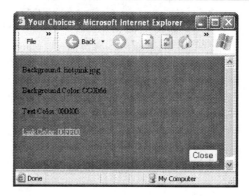

Write a function to create the pop-up window. The function should accept parameters for setting the color choices. The content of the pop-up window should be written dynamically. Include a close button in the window content.

Choose how to acquire the user's choices. I recommend that you make use of forms. The numbers for browser-safe colors are 00, 33, 66, 99, CC, and FF. For instance, #CC0066 makes a hot pink.

Provide clear navigation. Use images and a rollover effect on the main navigation area. Upload and test your project. Turn in a print-out of your code.

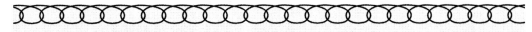

## chapter *twelve*

# *HTML Forms and JavaScript*

*And as imagination*

*bodies forth,*

*The forms of*

*things unknown,*

*the poet's pen,*

*Turns them*

*to shapes, and gives*

*to airy nothing,*

*A local habitation*

*and a name.*

—William Shakespeare,
*A Midsummer Night's Dream*

F orms are an excellent way to collect data from Web site visitors. Because forms are part of standard HTML, virtually every browser on the market supports them. Besides being used to acquire data from visitors, forms can be used to display data as well.

In this chapter we'll

- ⚂ examine forms and the various types of form elements supported by HTML.
- ⚂ discuss how forms are processed.
- ⚂ define the process of URL-encoding.
- ⚂ create forms and form elements with HTML.
- ⚂ learn how to access the properties and value of each type of form element with JavaScript.
- ⚂ see which event handlers work with which form elements.
- ⚂ examine the various form arrays and how to access them.
- ⚂ use the special keyword `this` when appropriate to shorten object and property references.

⊠ create a pull-down navigation menu.

⊠ create a set of navigation buttons using HTML form buttons.

Let's get started.

# HTML Forms

HTML provides many interesting input elements for forms, including hidden data fields, single-line text boxes for plain-text and password entry, multi-line textareas, drop-down selection lists, radio buttons, checkboxes, reset buttons for clearing forms, and submit buttons for sending completed forms to server-side scripts or mailto addresses. Let's look at each in turn, beginning with the form itself. As we introduce the form and each type of form element, concentrate on learning

⊠ the HTML to create it.

⊠ the JavaScript required to access it and its properties and methods.

⊠ the event handlers that are most often used with it.

⊠ the most common tasks performed on or with that particular form element.

Why isn't validation in the list? Because you really need a good foundation of the above before you can tackle form validation. So hold your horses, we'll cover form validation in detail in the next chapter.

# The `form` Object

All forms must begin with a <form> tag. Even if you want to use only a single button for an onClick event handler and nothing more, you still must place that button in a <form>. Them's the rules.

To create a **form** with HTML, use the <form> tag.

```
<form name="FormName" action="someAction" method="get|post">
</form>
```

As you can see, the <form> tag has several attributes. name, action, and method are the ones most often used and of the most importance, so let's look at them in more detail.

### The `name` Attribute

The **name attribute** provides an easy means of accessing a form with JavaScript.

```
document.FormName
```

Without a name, you're forced to access a form via the forms array with its array index, as you'll see shortly.

### The `action` Attribute

The **action attribute** is used to specify a URL to take action when a form is submitted. The action could be a mailto URL or a URL referencing a server-side script.

### Mailto vs. Server-side Scripts

A **mailto URL** causes form data to be sent to an email address. The SMTP server specified in the browser or in the email client that intercepts the mailto is used to email the form. This makes mailto URLs less reliable than server-side scripts. For instance, if the visitor hasn't set up his browser appropriately so that it can send email messages, then you'll never receive the form data.

Also, depending on the security configurations the visitor has set on his computer in both his browser and email client, he may receive one or more warning messages that would allow him to cancel the sending of the message. It's quite possible, perhaps even likely, that a newbie would simply cancel the email. Again, the result is that you never get to see the form data you wanted to collect. The main advantage of mailto URLs for processing form data is that no server-side scripting is required at all, just plain HTML. This makes them a great way to test the output of your forms without having to involve complicated server-side scripts. Consider mailto URLs a last-ditch alternative to server-side scripting.

Here's how to set the `action` attribute with a mailto URL:

```
<form action="mailto:emailaddress@somewhere.com">
```

This example causes the browser to email the form results to emailaddress@somewhere.com.

**Server-side scripts**, on the other hand, are a more reliable means of processing form data. They come in many flavors, including CGI scripts written in a variety of languages, such as Perl, and technologies such as PHP, ASP (Active Server Pages), and ColdFusion. The simplest server-side script will take form data, put it in a nice, readable format, and email it to you. FormMail is an example of such a script and is provided by many ISPs free of charge. Besides formatting the data in a nice, readable form, scripts such as FormMail use utilities on the Web server to email the data, so you're virtually guaranteed to get the data no matter what.

Of course, server-side scripts don't *have* to email anything. They can write the data to a database, begin an order process, or perform just about any type of operation you desire. Here's an example of an `action` attribute set with a URL to call a CGI script to process the form.

**side note**

You can also preset the subject, cc, and bcc fields of an email message when you use mailto: by appending them to the email address, like this: mailto:emailaddress @somewhere.com?subject =*topic*&cc=*addressToCc*&bcc =*addressToBcc*.

You don't have to set all of them; just place a question mark between the email address the message is to and the first or only field setting. Separate multiple field settings with an ampersand.

```
<form action="/cgi-bin/handleForm.cgi">
```

When the visitor clicks the submit button, a script named handleForm.cgi located in the cgi-bin directory off the root of the server is called.

Whether you send a form to a server-side script or a mailto address, the form's contents will be packaged up and sent in URL-encoded format.

## URL-Encoding

**URL-encoding** is the format used by the browser when packaging up form input data to send to the server or a mailto address. Here's how it works:

1. The browser gets all the names (specified by each form element's name attribute) and values (usually entered or chosen by the visitor) and encodes them as name-value pairs.

   a. Each name-value pair is separated by an equals sign (=). For example:
      `Email=js@javascriptconcepts.com`

   b. Pairs are separated by an ampersand (&). For example:
      `Email=js@javascriptconcepts.com&Gender=f&Married=true`

2. Any spaces in the input are replaced with a plus sign (+). For example:
   `Name=Tina+McDuffie`

3. Any special characters are translated into their ASCII hexadecimal equivalent and preceded by a percent sign (%). For example: ® would be encoded as %AE.

Here's the script that creates the form we'll be working with throughout this chapter. We'll excerpt lines as needed to explain how everything works.

### Script 12.1    Customer Data Form

```
1    <html>
2    <head>
3        <title>Script 12.1: Javabilaya - Customer Data</title>
4    <style type="text/css" media="all"><!--
5        body {
6           background-color: #663333;
7           color: #ffcc99;
8           background-image: url(images/javaBeans.jpg);
9        }
10       body, table {
11          font-size: 12pt;
12          font-family: Arial, Helvetica, sans-serif;
13       }
14       h1 {
15          color: #ffcc99;
16       }
17       h2, h3 {
18          color: #ffcc99;
19          margin-bottom: 0px;
20          font-weight: bold;
21          font-variant: small-caps;
22       }
```

```
23        h3 {
24           margin-top: 10px;
25        }
26   -->
27   </style>
28   </head>
29   <body bgcolor="#663333" text="#FFCC99"
30     background="images/javaBeans.jpg">
31   <h1>Javabilaya</h1>
32   <form action="mailto:js@javascriptconcepts.com" method="POST"
33       name="CustomerData"
34       onReset="return confirm('Are you sure you want to clear
                   the form?')">
35     <input type="hidden" name="recipient"
36     value="js@javascriptconcepts.com">
37     <table border=0>
38     <tr>
39        <th width="150" align="right" valign="bottom">
40           <h2>Customer</h2></th>
41        <th colspan="5" align="left" valign="bottom"><h2>
              Data</h2></th>
42     </tr>
43     <tr>
44        <th width="150" align="right">Name:</th>
45        <td colspan="5">
46          <input name="Customer" type="text" size="27"
                maxlength="40"
47                  onFocus="window.status='First Last'; return true"
48                  onBlur="window.status=''; return true"></td>
49     </tr>
50     <tr>
51        <th width="150" align="right">Address:</th>
52        <td colspan="5">
53          <input name="Address" type="text" size="45"
                maxlength="64"></td>
54     </tr>
55     <tr>
56        <th width="150" align="right">City:</th>
57        <td><input name="City" type="text" size="12"
              maxlength="12"></td>
58        <th align="right">State:</th>
59        <td>
60          <select name="State">
61             <option value="" selected></option>
62             <option value="AL">AL</option>
```

```
63                 <option value="AK">AK</option>
64                 <option value="AZ">AZ</option>
65                 <option value="AR">AR</option>
66                 <option value="CA">CA</option>
67                 <option value="CO">CO</option>
68                 <option value="CT">CT</option>
69                 <option value="DC">DC</option>
70                 <option value="DE">DE</option>
71                 <option value="FL">FL</option>
72                 <option value="GA">GA</option>
73                 <option value="HI">HI</option>
74                 <option value="ID">ID</option>
75                 <option value="IL">IL</option>
76                 <option value="IN">IN</option>
77                 <option value="IA">IO</option>
78                 <option value="KS">KS</option>
79                 <option value="KY">KY</option>
80                 <option value="LA">LA</option>
81                 <option value="MA">MA</option>
82                 <option value="MD">MD</option>
83                 <option value="ME">ME</option>
84                 <option value="MI">MI</option>
85                 <option value="MN">MN</option>
86                 <option value="MO">MO</option>
87                 <option value="MS">MS</option>
88                 <option value="MT">MT</option>
89                 <option value="NC">NC</option>
90                 <option value="ND">ND</option>
91                 <option value="NE">NE</option>
92                 <option value="NH">NH</option>
93                 <option value="NJ">NJ</option>
94                 <option value="NM">NM</option>
95                 <option value="NV">NV</option>
96                 <option value="NY">NY</option>
97                 <option value="OH">OH</option>
98                 <option value="OK">OK</option>
99                 <option value="OR">OR</option>
100                <option value="PA">PA</option>
101                <option value="RI">RI</option>
102                <option value="SC">SC</option>
103                <option value="SD">SD</option>
104                <option value="TN">TN</option>
105                <option value="TX">TX</option>
106                <option value="UT">UT</option>
107                <option value="VA">VA</option>
```

```
108          <option value="VT">VT</option>
109          <option value="WA">WA</option>
110          <option value="WI">WI</option>
111          <option value="WV">WV</option>
112          <option value="WY">WY</option>
113        </select>
114      </td>
115      <th align="right"><b>Zip:</b></th>
116      <td>
117        <input name="Zip" type="text" size="9" maxlength="10"
118              onFocus="window.status='12345-6789'; return true"
119              onBlur="window.status=''; return true"></td>
120    </tr>
121    <tr>
122      <th width="150" align="right">Phone:</th>
123      <td>
124        <input name="Phone" type="text" size="12" maxlength="12"
125              onFocus="window.status='123-555-1212'; return true"
126              onBlur="window.status=''; return true"></td>
127      <th align="right"><b>Ext:</b></th>
128      <td colspan="3">
129        <input name="PhoneExt" type="text" size="5" maxlength="10"
130              onFocus="window.status='1234'; return true"
131              onBlur="window.status=''; return true"></td>
132    </tr>
133    <tr>
134      <th width="150" align="right">Email:</th>
135      <td colspan="5">
136        <input name="Email" type="text" size="45" maxlength="64"
137              onFocus="window.status='me@somewhere.com';
                    return true"
138              onBlur="window.status=''; return true"></td>
139    </tr>
140 </table>
141
142 <table border=0>
143    <tr>
144      <th width="150" align="right" valign="bottom">
145        <h3>Payment Info</h3></th>
146      <th colspan="5" align="left" valign="bottom"> </th>
147    </tr>
148    <tr>
149      <th width="150" align="right">Credit Card Type:</th>
150      <td colspan="4">
151        <input type="radio" name="CCtype" value="Visa">Visa
```

```
152             
153           <input type="radio" name="CCtype" value="MC">MasterCard
154             
155           <input type="radio" name="CCtype"
                value="Discover">Discover
156             
157           <input type="radio" name="CCtype"
158             value="AmerEx">American Express
159         </td>
160       </tr>
161       <tr>
162         <th width="150" align="right">Card Number:</th>
163         <td>
164           <input name="CCnum" type="text" size="25" maxlength="20"
165                 onFocus="window.status='1234567890123456';
                          return true"
166                 onBlur="window.status=''; return true"></td>
167         <th align="right"><b>Expires:</b></th>
168         <td>
169           <select name="CCexpMo">
170                   <option value="">Month</option>
171                   <option value="01">01</option>
172                   <option value="02">02</option>
173                   <option value="03">03</option>
174                   <option value="04">04</option>
175                   <option value="05">05</option>
176                   <option value="06">06</option>
177                   <option value="07">07</option>
178                   <option value="08">08</option>
179                   <option value="09">09</option>
180                   <option value="10">10</option>
181                   <option value="11">11</option>
182                   <option value="12">12</option>
183           </select>
184           <select name="CCexpYr">
185                   <option value="">Year</option>
186                   <option value="2005">2005</option>
187                   <option value="2006">2006</option>
188                   <option value="2007">2007</option>
189                   <option value="2008">2008</option>
190                   <option value="2009">2009</option>
191                   <option value="2010">2010</option>
192                   <option value="2011">2011</option>
193                   <option value="2012">2012</option>
194                   <option value="2013">2013</option>
```

```
195              </select></td>
196   </tr>
197 </table>
198
199 <table>
200      <tr>
201        <th width="150" align="right" valign="bottom">
202              <h3>Login Info</h3></th>
203        <th colspan="5" align="left" valign="bottom"> </th>
204      </tr>
205      <tr>
206       <th width="150" align="right">Username:
207           </th>
208        <td>
209          <input type="text" name="Username" size="10"
210                 maxlength="10"
210              onFocus="window.status='Min: 6 char, Max: 10';
                     return true"
211              onBlur="window.status=''; return true">  
212        </td>
213        <th align="right">Password:
214        </th>
215        <td>
216          <input type="password" name="Password" size="5"
                 maxlength="8">
217        </td>
218        <td align="right"><b>Confirm:</b></td>
219        <td>
220          <input type="password" name="PasswordConfirm"
221            size="5" maxlength="8">
222        </td>
223        <td>
224          <small>6 - 8<br>char</small>
225        </td>
226      </tr>
227 </table>
228 <table>
229      <tr>
230        <th width="150" align="right" valign="bottom"><h3>
               Other</h3></th>
231        <th colspan="5" align="left" valign="bottom"> </th>
232      </tr>
233      <tr>
234        <th width="150" align="right" valign="top">How You Heard<br>
235            About Us:<br>
```

```
236              <small>(check all that apply)</small></th>
237          <td valign="top">
238            <input type="checkbox" name="ReferredBy"
239                    value="Web Site">Web Site<br>
240            <input type="checkbox" name="ReferredBy"
                       value="Email">Email<br>
241            <input type="checkbox" name="ReferredBy"
242                    value="Newsgroup">Newsgroup<br>
243          </td>
244          <td valign="top">
245            <input type="checkbox" name="ReferredBy" value="TV">TV<br>
246            <input type="checkbox" name="ReferredBy"
                       value="Radio">Radio<br>
247            <input type="checkbox" name="ReferredBy"
                       value="Store">Store<br>
248          </td>
249          <td valign="top">
250            <input type="checkbox" name="ReferredBy"
251                    value="Newspaper">Newspaper<br>
252            <input type="checkbox" name="ReferredBy"
253                    value="Magazine">Magazine<br>
254            <input type="checkbox" name="ReferredBy"
255                    value="Catalog">Catalog<br>
256          </td>
257          <td valign="top">
258            <input type="checkbox" name="ReferredBy"
259                    value="Family">Family<br>
260            <input type="checkbox" name="ReferredBy"
261                    value="Friend">Friend<br>
262            <input type="checkbox" name="ReferredBy" value="Other"
263                    onChange="if (this.checked)
                           this.form.ReferredByOther.disabled=false">
264          Other
265            <input type="text" name="ReferredByOther" size="7"
266                    maxlength="15" disabled>
267          </td>
268        </tr>
269        <tr>
270          <th width="150" align="right" valign="top">Comments:</th>
271          <td colspan="4">
272            <textarea name="Comments" cols="40" rows="3" wrap="soft"
273                      onChange="alert('Thank you for your comments!')">
274            </textarea>
275          </td>
276        </tr>
```

```
277    <tr>
278      <th width="150"> </th>
279      <td colspan="4" align="left"><br>
280        <input type="submit" value="Send Data">
281        <input type="reset" value="Clear Form">
282      </td>
283    </tr>
284  </table>
285 </form>
286
287 </body>
288 </html>
```

**Figure 12.1    Results of Script 12.1's Customer Data Form (with entries)**

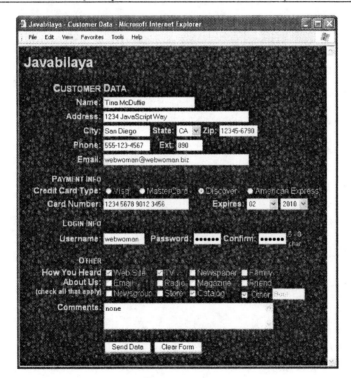

Here's the URL-encoded result of the form shown in Figure 12.1.

```
recipient=js@javascriptconcepts.com&Customer=Tina+McDuffie&
Address=1234+JavaScript+Way&City=San+Diego&State=CA&Zip=12345-
6790&Phone=555-123-4567&PhoneExt=890&Email=webwoman@webwoman
```

```
.biz&CCtype=Discover&CCnum=1234+5678+9012+3456&CCexpMo=
02&CCexpYr=2010&Username=webwoman&Password=shhhhh&
PasswordConfirm=shhhhh&ReferredBy=Web+Site&ReferredBy=
TV&ReferredBy=Catalog&ReferredBy=Other&ReferredByOther=
Book&Comments=none
```

Try it for yourself. Open script 12-1.html and change the email address in the `action` attribute to your own email address. Open the document in your Web browser, modify the entries as you please, and then click the Send Data button. Check your email. Sometimes the form data appears in the body of the email message, sometimes it comes as an attachment. If it's an attachment, you can open it with Notepad or any other text editor. Voilà!—the URL-encoded data.

Should you ever need to convert a string to or from URL-encoding, JavaScript has you covered: `escape("`*`string`*`")` and `unescape("`*`string`*`")`. `escape` and `unescape` are `global` methods. Give `escape` a regular string and it will give you back a URL-encoded string. Give `unescape` a URL-encoded string and it will give you back a regular string. Cool, huh?

Now that you know all about URL-encoding, let's look at the two methods by which the URL-encoded data can be sent.

## The method Attribute

The **method attribute** specifies how the form data is sent. The only options are `get` and `post`. `post` is the preferred method.

### Post vs. Get

With the **post method**, the form data is sent separately from the actual call to the server-side script. Because the form data is sent under separate cover, there is no limit to the amount of data that can be sent. This may be why `post` is the preferred method: no worries about important data getting cut off. Unix servers receive the data through standard input, which makes it extremely easy to access and use the data. Other servers may store the data in a temporary file, which is still easy to access.

With the **get method**, the form data is appended to the end of the URL that calls a server-side script like this:

```
http://somedomain.com/cgi-bin/ ⸺▶
    ⸺▶ somescript.cgi?name=Sam&gender=m
```

In the above example, the form has two form fields: `name` and `gender`. All data after the question mark, the form data, is stored in the `QUERY_STRING` environment variable. Because the data is stored in an environment variable, the amount of data that can be sent is limited by the available environment space on the server, which makes it possible, even likely, that the data will be truncated, that is, part of the data could be cut off.

One advantage of using the `get` method is that visitors can save the whole call as a bookmark for use again later. `get` is also a useful testing tool for beginning Web developers because they can easily see what their data forms are sending. The `get` method is also often used to pass data from one page to another in server-side scripting and JavaScript. JavaScript can access the passed data by passing the location. Other than that, there isn't much else to recommend `get` as a good method for sending form data. As `post` is the preferred form method, we'll use it in all of our examples.

## Accessing Forms with JavaScript

Accessing a form with JavaScript is extremely easy if you assigned the form a name with the name attribute when you created it using the <form> tag.

```
document.ElementName
```

Here's the <form> tag we used in Script 12.1, minus any event handlers:

```
<form name="CustomerData"
    action="mailto:js@javascriptconcepts.com" method="post">
</form>
```

To access the corresponding form object, write

```
document.CustomerData
```

where `CustomerData` is the name of the form. It's also easy to access the form's `action` and `method` properties using the form's name:

```
document.CustomerData.action
document.CustomerData.method
```

No sweat *if* you named the form. Like I said, accessing the form and its properties is no sweat if you named the form. But what if you forgot to name the form? All is not lost. Remember the predefined arrays we discussed in Chapter 7? The `forms` array, a property of the `document` object, was one of them. Any forms loaded in a document are stored in memory within the `forms` array in the order they are loaded into the document. You need only know the form's index number. Remember, arrays begin numbering at zero. Thus, the general form to access a form by its index number is

```
document.forms[i]
```

where *i* is the form's index reference. Let's assume that the following is the first form in the document:

```
<form  action="mailto:js@javascriptconcepts.com"
        method="post">
</form>
```

To access it with JavaScript even though it has no name, you can use its array reference:

```
document.forms[0]
```

You can access its action and method properties as well:

```
document.forms[0].action
document.forms[0].method
```

Cool, huh? So even if you forgot to name a form, you can still access it with JavaScript. Still, it's a good idea to stay in the habit of naming your forms; for most things it's easier to use a form's name to access it. The same is true for all form elements.

Another good reason to name form elements is that the names identify each piece of data. Look at the URL-encoded data for the form in Script 12.1. If no name had been entered on each form field, the data would have little meaning. URL-encoded, it would look like this:

```
=js@javascriptconcepts.com&=Tina+McDuffie&=1234+JavaScript
+Way&=San+Diego&=CA&=12345-6790&=555-123-4567&=890&=web
woman@webwoman.biz&=Discover&=1234+5678+9012+3456&=02&=2010&
=webwoman&=shhhhh&=shhhhh&=Web+Site&=TV&=Catalog&=Other
&=Book&=none
```

As you can see, the data has little meaning without labels. Sure, we as humans can make educated guesses at what each piece of data is supposed to represent, but a database would have no clue. Nor would a server-side script. The point is that it's best, for many reasons, to name all form elements. Now let's look at the event handlers that you can use with a form.

## Appropriate Event Handlers to Use with Forms

There are two event handlers that work hand in hand with forms: onSubmit and onReset.

### onSubmit

Usually onSubmit is used to call a form validation routine to verify that all required fields have been completed or that the information provided is in the appropriate format. We'll look closely at form validation in the next chapter. For now, we'll perform a very simple form validation just to show you how to call a validate function in an onSubmit event handler.

### Script 12.2   *Very Simple Form Validation*

```
1    <html>
2    <head>
3    <title>Script 12.2: Very Simple Form Validation</title>
4    <script language="JavaScript" type="text/javascript"><!--
5    function isEmpty(str) {
6          var empty = (str == null || str == "") ? true : false
7          return empty
8    }
9
10   function validate(zForm) {
11         if (isEmpty(zForm.Visitor.value)) {
12               alert ("Error! Please enter your name.")
13               zForm.Visitor.focus()
14               return false
```

```
15              }
16          return true
17      }
18  //-->
19  </script>
20  </head>
21  <body>
22  <form action="mailto:js@javascriptconcepts.com" method="POST"
23          name="SimpleValidation" onSubmit="return validate(this)">
24  <table border=0>
25      <tr>
26        <th width="150" valign="bottom"> </th>
27        <th colspan="3" align="left">
28              <h2>Simple Validation</h2></th>
29      </tr>
30      <tr>
31        <th width="150" align="right">Name:</th>
32        <td colspan="3">
33              <input name="Visitor" type="text" size="40"
                      maxlength="40">
34        </td>
35      </tr>
36      <tr>
37        <th width="150"> </th>
38        <td colspan="3" align="left">
39          <input type="submit" value="Send Survey">
40          <input type="reset" value="Clear Form">
41        </td>
42      </tr>
43    </table>
44  </form>
45  </body>
46  </html>
```

This example verifies that the visitor entered something in the name field (line 11). If no entry was made, the routine pops up an error message (line 12), gives focus to the empty field (line13), and aborts the sending of the form (line 14).

**Figure 12.2    Results of Script 12.2 when No Entry Made**

If everything is fine, it goes ahead and sends the form (line 16).

# `this` Revisited

The keyword `this` was used as an argument in the validate function call. What is `this`? The special keyword **this** always refers to the current object, wherever `this` happens to be. In the case of line 23, `this` happens to be the `CustomerData` form's event handler, so `this` refers to the `CustomerData` form object. We'll see `this` used in many different places to refer to many different types of objects. The primary reasons for using it are to be succinct, to be clear, and to save typing. If we hadn't utilized `this`, we would've had to write our function call as

```
return  validate(document.SimpleValidation)
```

or as

```
return  validate(document.forms[0])
```

While in this case neither line is very long, in other cases, using `this` is much more succinct and clear and saves you a lot of typing.

# `return`

Another important thing to notice in the `onSubmit` event handler in line 23 is that the `validate` function call is preceded by the keyword `return`. `return` causes the data returned by the `validate` function—`true` if all is well (line 16), `false` if there is an error in the form (line 14)—to be, in turn, returned to the event handler. The event handler can then abort the submission of the form data if it receives `false` or continue with its submission action if it receives `true`. Figure 12.2 shows an example of the submission being aborted because of an error.

The `return` keyword is also commonly used in conjunction with confirm dialog boxes. A good place to see confirm dialog boxes in action is in an `onReset` event handler.

## onReset

The onReset event handler can be used to verify that the visitor really intended to hit the reset button and clear the form's contents *before* clearing the form's contents. How many times have you accidentally hit a reset button when you meant to click the submit button? I know I've done it many times. With a simple onReset event handler, you can save your visitors from frustration and time-consuming data reentry by confirming that they want to clear the form before doing so.

### Figure 12.3     Excerpt from Script 12.1—Confirm before Reset

```
32    <form action="mailto:js@javascriptconcepts.com" method="POST"
33        name="CustomerData"
34        onReset="return confirm('Are you sure you want to clear the
              form?')">
```

In Script 12.1, line 34, we've called a confirm method in response to a reset event. When the visitor clicks the reset button, a confirm dialog pops up and asks, "Are you sure you want to clear the form?" (See Figure 12.4.)

### Figure 12.4     Confirm before Clearing Form Contents

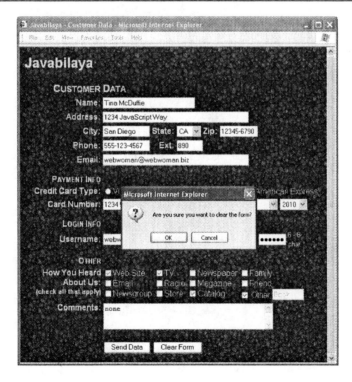

If the visitor clicks OK, the `confirm` method returns `true` and the contents of the form are cleared. If the visitor clicks Cancel, `confirm` returns `false` and the form's contents remain intact. Now let's test what you've learned: what mechanism forwards the result returned by the `confirm` method to the event handler so that the reset is aborted if the visitor's response is Cancel? Need a hint? Look closely at line 34. That's it: `return`! Without the keyword `return` preceding the `confirm` method call, the contents of the form would get cleared no matter what. Try it for yourself. Remove the word `return` from line 34, open the document, type some information in the form, and click the reset button. You still get the confirm dialog, but even when you hit Cancel, the form gets cleared anyway. That's because, with the keyword `return` preceding the method call missing, the result of the `confirm` method never gets back to the event handler.

Now that we've explored the form object itself, let's look at the elements of a form. **Form elements** are the fields and controls in a form.

## The Hidden Form Element

Before we get too far away from the subject of server-side scripts and forms, let's look at the hidden form element. A **hidden** form element is a form element, like any other. It can have a name and hold a text value. Its name and value are URL-encoded along with the rest of the form elements when the form is submitted. However, a hidden form element is just that, hidden. It does not appear in the browser window as part of the form. It is hidden from the visitor's view. So what good is a hidden form element, you might ask.

Remember that the action attribute of a form element accepts a URL. The URL usually points to a server-side script you want to handle the form. There are three very popular CGI scripts that most Internet service providers (ISPs) install on their servers and give their clients access to: FormMail, Guestbook, and Counter. Each of these CGI scripts can be used by multiple people (everyone who uses the ISP that has it installed). FormMail, for instance, parses the URL-encoded data sent to it and creates a nicely formatted, reader-friendly email message displaying the form's contents. FormMail then sends the formatted email message to some recipient. How does the script know whom to email the form data to? How can one copy of FormMail serve all of an ISP's customers?

The answer to both questions is hidden form elements. In the case of FormMail, the author of the form—that's you—must include a form field whose name is `recipient` and whose value is the email address where you want the form data sent. You wouldn't

**side note**

**Hidden Fields and CGI Scripts**

Read the directions. If your ISP provides access to FormMail, Guestbook, or Counter, it'll usually have a FAQ posted on how to use it. `recipient` is just one of the many fields most form-mail CGI scripts will accept and that have special meaning to that script. Keep in mind that the field names are often case sensitive.

want to make your visitors enter that data; you probably don't even want them to see it. So use a form element visitors can't see: hidden.

## Creating a Hidden Field with HTML

The syntax to create a hidden field with HTML is

```
<input type="hidden" name="HiddenFieldName" value="someValue">
```

To create a hidden field to hold the recipient's email address for a form that will be sent to FormMail for processing, you would write something like this:

```
<input type="hidden" name="recipient"
    value="js@javascriptconcepts.com">
```

Unfortunately, I can't show you what a hidden field looks like in the browser, because hidden fields are, by nature, hidden from view. You can, however, see the HTML that creates it in lines 35–36 of Script 12.1. Keep in mind that visitors too can see your hidden fields simply by viewing the source code.

## Accessing a Hidden Field with JavaScript

Accessing a hidden field and its value with JavaScript is quite easy. Here's the general form:

```
document.FormName.HiddenFieldName
```

In our form, the field labeled "recipient" is accessed as

```
document.CustomerData.recipient
```

Should you desire, you can use JavaScript to preset the hidden field's value:

```
document.FormName.HiddenFieldName.value = SomeValue
```

To set the value of recipient with JavaScript, write

```
document.CustomerData.recipient.value =
    "js@javascriptconcepts.com"
```

**Programmer's tip**

Don't use FormMail scripts to collect and send private information, such as credit card numbers, from customers to yourself. Email is insecure and susceptible to prying eyes. It has none of the legal protections regarding interception, privacy, or tampering provided to snail mail.

## Appropriate Event Handlers to Use with Hidden Fields

There really aren't any good event handlers for use with hidden fields, because the fields are not seen.

# Text Boxes

Text boxes are created using the <input> tag and setting its `type` attribute to `text`. You'll shortly see that most form elements are created using the <input> tag, including password fields, radio buttons, checkboxes, submit buttons, reset buttons, regular buttons, and images. The `type` attribute is what makes the difference.

So what's a text box? A **text box** allows visitors to enter a single-line text entry. The box labeled "Name" in Figure 12.1 is a text box, as are those labeled "Address," "City," "Zip," "Phone," "Ext.," "Email," "Card Number," "Username," and "Other" (next to the checkbox). Now let's look at the code that creates the text box itself.

## Creating a Text Box with HTML

```
<input name="TextboxName" type="text" size="numChar" ⎯▶
⎯▶  maxlength="numChar">
```

The `name` attribute identifies the form element and makes it easy to reference that object with JavaScript.

The `size` attribute determines the physical display size of the text box, in terms of the number of characters it appears to be able to hold. The `maxlength` attribute specifies the true maximum number of characters the field can accept. Here's the HTML that creates the one we put in our form (lines 44–48 of Script 12.1):

```
Name: <input name="Customer" type="text" size="27" ⎯▶
⎯▶  maxlength="40">
```

Notice the text label preceding the HTML that creates the text box (line 44 of Script 12.1). You have to manually label most form fields with text. The <input> tag only creates the box or other form element. It doesn't label the form element.

If you so desire, you can enter a default value to prefill the text box by setting the `value` attribute:

```
<input name="Customer" type="text" size="27" ⎯▶
⎯▶  maxlength="40" value="Tina McDuffie">
```

See Figure 12.1 for an idea of what it looks like when you first open the form.

Being able to prefill a text box comes in handy. For instance, when a form requests a URL, you can gently remind the visitor to provide a fully qualified URL beginning with the protocol by prefilling the box with "http://", like so:

```
<input name="URL" type="text" value="http://">
```

## Accessing a Text Box with JavaScript

Accessing a text box with JavaScript requires the usual dot notation:

```
document.FormName.TextboxName
```

In our form, the field labeled "Name" is accessed thus:

```
document.CustomerData.Customer
```

You can also access a form element via the `elements` array, which is a property of the form element. Because the visitor field is the second element entered in the `CustomerData` form (the first was the hidden field `recipient`), it is elements[1] in the form's `elements` array. You can access the form itself by either its name or its index in the document's `forms` array. Thus, you can also access the Customer field by any of the following references:

```
document.CustomerData.elements[1]
document.forms[0].elements[1]
document.forms[0].Customer
```

You can use JavaScript to preset the text box's value too:

```
document.FormName.TextboxName.value
```

In our form, you can set a default value for `Customer` with any of the following statements:

```
document.CustomerData.Customer.value = "Sammy Sam"
document.CustomerData.elements[1].value = "Sammy Sam"
document.forms[0].Customer.value = "Sammy Sam"
document.forms[0].elements[1].value = "Sammy Sam"
```

The important thing to keep in mind is that you cannot access the form or any of its elements until *after* it has been created with HTML. So any script that prefills a form's fields must be called *after* the HTML that creates the form. That usually means placing statements that prefill the form in a <script> tag *after* the form or calling a function to do so in a <script> tag after the form. We'll show you an example of this towards the end of the chapter.

## Appropriate Event Handlers to Use with Text Boxes

### Providing Data Entry Hints for Text Boxes

Text boxes, by themselves, give no hint whatsoever as to the type or format of the data you want to gather. Labels help. They at least give the visitor a clue as to what kind of data you want: a name, an email address, a phone number, etc. However, when it comes to data like phone numbers, zip codes, or credit card numbers, there are lots of ways to enter them. For instance, how do you tell the visitor you want the phone number entered as 10 digits: the three-digit area code, a hyphen, the three-digit exchange, a hyphen, and the last four digits? That's where the `onFocus` and `onBlur` event handlers come in handy. When the text box receives focus, you can display the preferred data format in the status bar. When the text box is blurred—when the visitor leaves that field—clear the status bar.

Lines 125 and 126 of Script 12.1 (see the figure below) show how it's done:

**Figure 12.5    Using onFocus and onBlur to Display Entry Hints**

```
121    <tr>
122      <th width="150" align="right">Phone:</th>
123      <td>
124        <input name="Phone" type="text" size="12" maxlength="12"
125            onFocus="window.status='619-555-1212'; return true"
126            onBlur="window.status=''; return true"></td>
127      <th align="right"><b>Ext:</b></th>
128      <td colspan="3">
129        <input name="PhoneExt" type="text" size="5" maxlength="10"
130            onFocus="window.status='1234'; return true"
131            onBlur="window.status=''; return true"></td>
132    </tr>
```

Try it for yourself. Open Script 12.1 in your browser. Click in or tab to the Phone field. Notice the status bar message.

**Figure 12.6    Using onFocus and onBlur to Display Data Entry Hints**

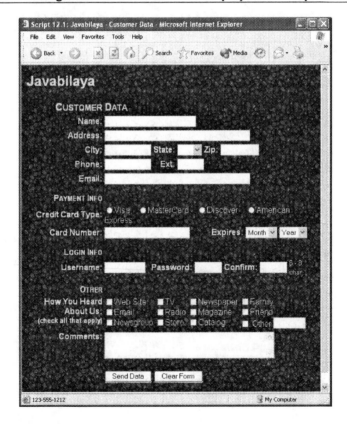

Tab to the next field. Notice that the status bar clears and shows a new message. Tab to or click in the other text boxes and look at the status bar. All but the Other field show a hint. Now examine the code for those fields in Script 12.1.

### Preventing Modification of a Text Box Entry

Sometimes you may want to prevent visitors from modifying the contents of a text box. For instance, you may wish to display the total of an order or a sales tax calculation. Performing the calculations with JavaScript is no sweat. The easiest way to display the results of a calculation is in a form field. Unfortunately, a customer might try to modify the form field displaying the calculation before submitting her order in the hopes of getting the goods at a discounted price.

You can prevent such modification with JavaScript by attaching an onFocus event handler to the field that calls the blur method whenever the field receives focus. This prevents manual changes to the field. You can still modify the field's value with JavaScript, but the field's value cannot be changed by a customer. Lines 145, 157, 169, 181, and 193 of Script 12.3 demonstrate this technique:

**Script 12.3**    *Javabilaya Order Form*

```
1    <html>
2    <head>
3    <title>Script 12.3: Your Javabilaya Order Form</title>
4    <style type="text/css" media="all"><!--
5         body {
6             background-color: #663333;
7             color: #ffcc99;
8             background-image: url(images/javaBeans.jpg);
9         }
10        body, table, td {
11            font-size: 12pt;
12            font-family: Arial, Helvetica, sans-serif;
13        }
14        table {
15            margin-left: 20px;
16        }
17        h1 {
18            color: #ffcc99;
19        }
20        h2, h3 {
21            color: #ffcc99;
22            margin-bottom: 0px;
23            font-weight: bold;
24            font-variant: small-caps;
25        }
26        h3 {
```

```
27          margin-top: 10px;
28        }
29      th {
30          font-variant: small-caps;
31        }
32      input {
33          text-align: right;
34        }
35      input.normal {
36          text-align: center;
37        }
38  -->
39  </style>
40  <script language="JavaScript" type="text/javascript"><!--
41   // converts num to Currency format
42   // set showDollarSign to true if you want a
43   // leading $, otherwise set it to false
44   function toCurrency(num, showDollarSign) {
45          if(showDollarSign) {
46                  return "$" + roundFloat(num, 2)
47          } else {
48                  return roundFloat(num, 2)
49          }
50   }
51
52   // rounds a floating-point number to the
53   // specified number of decimal places
54   // returns the value in string format
55   // to hold the decimal places if decimal
56   // value is 0
57   function roundFloat(num, decimalPlaces) {
58          // convert num to a number if not already
59          if (isNaN(num)) {
60                  num = parseFloat(num)
61          }
62
63          // multiply num by 10 to the x power,
64          // where x = number of decimalPlaces desired
65          var temp = num * Math.pow(10, decimalPlaces)
66
67          // now round to an integer to get rid of
68          // excess digits
69          temp = Math.round(temp)
70
71          // convert to a string
```

```
72          temp = temp.toString()
73
74          // pad numbers that are shorter than the number
75          // of decimal points desired with leading zeros
76          while (temp.length <= decimalPlaces) {
77                  temp = "0" + temp
78          }
79
80          // determine the index number where the decimal
81          // point needs to be inserted and insert it
82          var decNdx = temp.length - decimalPlaces
83          temp = temp.substring(0, decNdx) + "." +
84                  temp.substring(decNdx)
85          return temp
86      }
87
88   // totals the order form
89   function totalOrder(zForm) {
90          var total = 0
91          for (i=1; i<zForm.length-3; i+=2) {
92                  amt = parseFloat(zForm.elements[i].value)
93                  if (isNaN(amt)) {
94                          amt = 0
95                  }
96                  total += amt
97          }
98          zForm.Total.value = toCurrency(total, false)
99      }
100
101  // calculates the extended value and
102  // updates the total
103  function extend(zForm, itemID, price) {
104          var itemQty = zForm[itemID + "qty"].value
105          if (isNaN(itemQty)) {
106                  itemQty = parseFloat(itemQty)
107          }
108          if (isNaN(price)) {
109                  price = parseFloat(price)
110          }
111          var ext = itemQty * price
112
113          zForm[itemID + "qty"].value = toCurrency(itemQty, false)
114          zForm[itemID + "ext"].value = toCurrency(ext, false)
115          totalOrder(zForm)
116      }
```

```
117 //-->
118 </script>
119 </head>
120 <body bgcolor="#663333" text="#FFCC99"
      background="images/javaBeans.jpg">
121 <h1>Javabilaya</h1>
122
123 <form name="OrderForm" method="post"
      action="mailto:js@javascriptconcepts.com"
124      onReset="return confirm('Are you sure you want to clear the
             form?')">
125   <table border="0">
126     <tr>
127       <th align="left"><h2>Order Form</h2></th>
128       <th> </th>
129     </tr>
130     <tr align="left">
131       <th align="left">Java Beans</th>
132       <th>Quantity</th>
133       <th>Price</th>
134       <th align="right">Ext. Price</th>
135     </tr>
136     <tr class=odd>
137       <td>Blue Mountain Blast</td>
138       <td>
139         <input type="text" name="BMBqty" size="7" tabindex="1"
140                onChange="extend(this.form, 'BMB', 6.95)">
141         lbs @</td>
142       <td>$6.95 per lb</td>
143       <td>
144         $<input type="text" name="BMBext" size="11"
145                onFocus="this.blur()">
146       </td>
147     </tr>
148     <tr class=even>
149       <td>French Vanilla</td>
150       <td>
151         <input type="text" name="FVqty" size="7" tabindex="2"
152                onChange="extend(this.form, 'FV', 7.59)">
153         lbs @</td>
154       <td>$7.59 per lb</td>
155       <td>
156         $<input type="text" name="FVext" size="11"
157                onFocus="this.blur()">
158       </td>
```

```
159        </tr>
160        <tr class=odd>
161          <td>German Chocolate Mint</td>
162          <td>
163            <input type="text" name="GCMqty" size="7" tabindex="3"
164                   onChange="extend(this.form, 'GCM', 9.50)">
165            lbs @</td>
166          <td>$9.50 per lb</td>
167          <td>
168            $<input type="text" name="GCMext" size="11"
169                    onFocus="this.blur()">
170          </td>
171        </tr>
172        <tr class=even>
173          <td>Hawaiian Kona</td>
174          <td>
175            <input type="text" name="HKqty" size="7" tabindex="4"
176                   onChange="extend(this.form, 'HK', 8.49)">
177            lbs @</td>
178          <td>$8.49 per lb</td>
179          <td>
180            $<input type="text" name="HKext" size="11"
181                    onFocus="this.blur()">
182          </td>
183        </tr>
184        <tr class=odd>
185          <td>JavaBrosia (House Blend)</td>
186          <td>
187            <input type="text" name="JBqty" size="7" tabindex="5"
188                   onChange="extend(this.form, 'JB', 5.00)">
189            lbs @</td>
190          <td>$5.00 per lb</td>
191          <td align="right">
192            $<input type="text" name="JBext" size="11"
193                    onFocus="this.blur()">
194          </td>
195        </tr>
196        <tr>
197          <th colspan=3 align="right"><b>Order Total:</b></th>
198          <th align=left>
199            $<input type="text" name="Total" size="11"
200                    onFocus="this.blur()">
201          </th>
202        </tr>
203        <tr>
```

```
204          <td colspan=4 align="center">
205             <input class=normal type="submit" value="Send Order"
206                     tabindex="6">
207             <input class= normal type="reset" value="Clear Form"
208                     tabindex="7">
209          </td>
210       </tr>
211    </table>
212 </form>
213
214 </body>
215 </html>
```

Notice the use of the keyword `this`. In the `onFocus` event handlers on the extended total fields, `this` refers to the current field. So

`this.blur()`

says to blur this field, the field on which the event handler resides.

Try it for yourself. Enter some quantities. The extended total will automatically be entered. (We'll learn how this is done a bit later.) Now try to change the extended value. Try changing the total. Your efforts should prove unsuccessful . . . unless you modify the script!

Of course, you can also prevent a field from being modified with the `disabled` attribute. We'll discuss the pros and cons of disabling form fields later in this chapter.

**Figure 12.7    Results of Script 12.3**

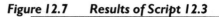

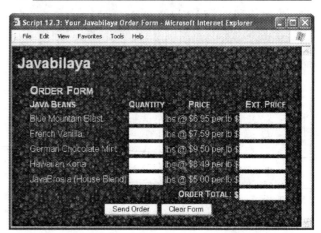

**programmer's tip**

Some older browsers such as Opera 5.02 do not support the `blur` method. One way you can work around this and still prevent the extended price field from being modified is to give focus to, and select, the quantity field on that line. This solution also lets the visitor know in a friendly way that the extended price may only be changed by changing the quantity ordered.

**Using `onChange` to Perform Calculations**

The last section mentions performing calculations, a very common task of order forms. One way to perform calculations, so that the form always shows a running total, is with the onChange event handler. Script 12.3 creates the short order form shown in Figure 12.7. The onChange event handlers attached to the quantity fields (lines 140, 152, 164, 176, and 188) call the extend function (lines 103–116) to perform the calculations and total the form. Let's look at the extend function in more detail.

```
function extend(zForm, itemID, price) {
        var itemQty = zForm[itemID + "qty"].value
        if (isNaN(itemQty)) {
                itemQty = parseFloat(itemQty)
        }
        if (isNaN(price)) {
                price = parseFloat(price)
        }
        var ext = itemQty * price

        zForm[itemID + "qty"].value = toCurrency(itemQty, false)
        zForm[itemID + "ext"].value = toCurrency(ext, false)
        totalOrder(zForm)
}
```

Three arguments are passed to the extend function: the order form, the ID of the item whose quantity changes, and the price.

```
extend(this.form, 'BMB', 6.95)
```

The form passes by reference, that is, the actual form object itself is passed to the extend function. The other two arguments pass by value. The first is a string; the second is a number.

This is really important: look at the keyword this followed by the property form used to pass the current form object to the extend function. Look at the JavaScript object reference in Appendix A and take a look at the text object. Look closely at the text object's properties. See the form property? Now look at the properties of some other form elements. They, too, have a form property.

A form property belonging to a form element object refers to the form in which the element resides. This comes in handy as you can see in the extend function calls. Instead of having to know the name of the form the qty field is in

```
extend(document.OrderForm, 'BMB', 6.95)
```

**Programmer's tip**

By pressing the Tab key, visitors can move through the fields of a form. The default tabbing order is the order in which the form fields appear in your HTML document. You can override this by setting the tab order yourself using the tabindex attribute on each form field. See lines 139, 151, 163, 175, 187, 206, and 208 in Script 12.3 for examples.

we can simply refer to the form with

```
this.form
```

Purty cool, huh? When you're reading the code, you don't have to wonder which form `OrderForm` is. Using `this.form` to refer to the form, you can immediately tell that you're passing the form in which the field resides. I told you `this` was going to come in handy! Now let's look at the rest of the function.

To make our references shorter, we first assign the value of the quantity field to a new variable called `itemQty`, then we make certain it's a number. If it's not, we turn it into a number. Next we check the price and turn it into a number if it isn't already.

We then calculate the extended price and assign it to a new variable called `ext`. The next two lines call a function before assigning values to the `qty` and `ext` fields in the form.

```
zForm[itemID + "qty"].value = toCurrency(itemQty, false)
zForm[itemID + "ext"].value = toCurrency(ext, false)
```

Both lines call some function named `toCurrency`. Guess we'd better look at `toCurrency`:

```
function toCurrency(num, showDollarSign) {
    if(showDollarSign) {
        return "$" + roundFloat(num, 2)
    } else {
        return roundFloat(num, 2)
    }
}
```

It's awfully short. It takes two arguments; the first is a number and the second is a Boolean specifying whether or not we want a leading dollar sign ($). Otherwise, all `toCurrency` does is call `roundFloat`. Let's look at `roundFloat`:

```
function roundFloat(num, decimalPlaces) {
    // convert num to a number if not already
    if (isNaN(num)) {
        num = parseFloat(num)
    }

    // multiply num by 10 to the x power,
    // where x = number of decimalPlaces desired
    var temp = num * Math.pow(10, decimalPlaces)

    // now round to an integer to get rid of
    // excess digits
    temp = Math.round(temp)

    // convert to a string
```

```
temp = temp.toString()

// pad numbers that are shorter than the number
// of decimal points desired with leading zeros
while (temp.length <= decimalPlaces) {
      temp = "0" + temp
}

// determine the index number where the decimal
// point needs to be inserted and insert it
var decNdx = temp.length - decimalPlaces
temp = temp.substring(0, decNdx) + "." +
          temp.substring(decNdx)
return temp
}
```

By reading the comments, you can pretty much tell how it all works. Basically, roundFloat takes a number and turns it into a string formatted with the number of decimal places specified by the decimalPlaces argument. JavaScript has no built-in function or predefined method for rounding numbers to a specific number of decimal places, let alone for displaying numbers in a dollar and cents format. This handy little function, roundFloat, does the trick. The toCurrency function expands on it, by allowing you to choose whether or not you want a leading dollar sign.

The last thing the extend function does is call the totalOrder function:

```
function totalOrder(zForm) {
    var total = 0
    for (i=1; i<zForm.length-3; i+=2) {
          amt = parseFloat(zForm.elements[i].value)
          if (isNaN(amt)) {
                amt = 0
          }
          total += amt
    }
    zForm.Total.value = toCurrency(total, false)
}
```

The totalOrder function was written specifically for the type of field arrangement in the Javabilaya order form. It expects the first extended total field to be the second field in the form and then expects every other field after that to be an extended total field. It also expects the total field be named "Total" and to be the third from the last field.

You can insert additional lines of products without having to modify the totalOrder function. However, if you change the overall organization of the form, you will, of course, have to modify `totalOrder` to compensate. For instance, if you insert fields before the initial quantity field, you'll have to modify the start index number in the `for` loop accordingly. If you insert fields after the total field and before the submit and reset buttons, you'll have to modify the stop condition in the `for` loop. Finally, if you insert fields between the quantity and extended total fields, you'll have to modify the update expression in the `for` loop. Get the idea?

Notice that `totalOrder` calls `toCurrency` to format the resulting total.

What's the secret to the right-aligned data in the text fields? A bit of CSS (Cascading Style Sheets) code right-aligns the contents of the text fields for us (lines 32–34 of Script 12.3).

The `onSelect` event handler also works with text boxes, though it isn't often used.

We've learned how to do all kinds of things with text boxes. Now let's take a look at another type of form element, one that is very similar to the text box: the password field.

# Passwords

Sometimes you need to acquire confidential information, information best not seen by someone looking over the visitor's shoulder, such as a password. For this specific purpose, HTML supports a **password** form element. It is essentially like a text box in its appearance and attributes. However, instead of showing the actual characters entered, it shows asterisks, so anyone looking over your shoulder cannot tell what you entered by looking at the screen. People can still watch what keys you press on the keyboard, though, so beware.

## Creating a Password Field with HTML

```
<input name="PasswordBoxName" type="password"
    size="numChar" maxlength="numChar">
```

It's difficult to tell what you've typed into a password box. That's why it's so common during a registration process to ask the visitor to confirm his password entry by entering it again in a second password box. The theory is that you're unlikely to mistype the password the same way twice. With this in mind, we've added not one, but two password fields to our form in Script 12.1 (lines 213–217 and 218–222).

**Figure 12.8    HTML Used to Create Password Fields**

```
213     <th align="right">Password:
214       </th>
215     <td>
216       <input type="password" name="Password"
                size="5" maxlength="8">
217       </td>
218     <td align="right"><b>Confirm:</b></td>
219     <td>
220           <input type="password" name="PasswordConfirm"
221           size="5" maxlength="8">
222       </td>
223     <td>
224         <small>6 - 8<br>char</small>
225       </td>
```

Here's what the password fields look like with some data typed in:

**Figure 12.9    Password Fields with Data Typed In**

## Accessing a Password Field with JavaScript

You can access a password field just like you do a text box:

```
document.FormName.PasswordFieldName
```

Its value is also accessed in the same way you access the value of a text box:

```
document.FormName.PasswordFieldName.value
```

## Appropriate Event Handlers to Use with Password Fields

The same event handlers that work on text boxes can be used on password fields, but rarely are.

Thus far, we've only looked at form fields that allow a single-line text entry. There are times when a single-line text entry is just not enough, such as when you need to solicit a visitor's comments. That's where the textarea form element comes in handy.

# Textarea

A **textarea** is a multi-line text box, often with a scrollbar down the right side. Other than being able to accept multiple lines of text and being created with a different HTML tag, textareas are pretty much like text boxes; they certainly are the same as far as JavaScript is concerned. You access the value contained in a textarea the same way you do a text box. You even validate textareas the same way, as you'll see in the next chapter.

## Creating a Textarea with HTML

```
<textarea name="TextareaName" cols="numCharAcross"
       rows="numRows">default content</textarea>
```

Here's the code we used in Script 12.1 to create the textarea labeled "Comments" in the CustomerData form.

**Figure 12.10    HTML Used to Create Comments Textarea**

```
269      <tr>
270        <th width="150" align="right"
             valign="top">Comments:</th>
271        <td colspan="4">
272          <textarea name="Comments" cols="40" rows="3"
273                    wrap="soft" onChange="alert('Thank you
                        for your comments!')">
274          </textarea>
275        </td>
276      </tr>
```

Here's what a textarea looks like:

**Figure 12.11    Textarea Field for Comments**

Should you desire to prefill a textarea with content, simply enter the text between the opening and closing tags.

```
<textarea name="Comments" cols="30" rows="5">Enter the
      content you want to appear in the box here.</textarea>
```

If you want a blank textarea, don't put any text between the opening and closing tags.

```
<textarea name="Comments" cols="30" rows="5"></textarea>
```

It's always a nice touch to set the wrap attribute so that the text doesn't scroll past the width of the textarea. The wrap attribute is not part of the HTML 4 specification; it is a browser extension. The options are wrap=soft and wrap=hard.

The soft option makes typing in the textarea similar to typing in a word processor. The text automatically wraps to the next line; no carriage return or line feed becomes part of the text unless the visitor actually presses the Enter key. The soft option is usually the best choice and is the default in Internet Explorer. In Netscape browsers, the default is to not wrap at all.

```
<textarea name="Comments" cols="30" rows="5" wrap="soft">
</textarea>
```

The `hard` option actually enters carriage return/line feed characters at the end of each line. Rarely do you want to use the `hard` option.

```
<textarea name="Comments" cols="30" rows="5" wrap="hard">
 </textarea>
```

### Accessing a Textarea with JavaScript

Accessing a `textarea` with JavaScript is just like accessing a text box:

```
document.TextareaName
```

### Appropriate Event Handlers to Use with Textareas

Textareas are often used to solicit comments or feedback from visitors. It's always a nice touch to thank visitors for taking the time to give you their valuable feedback. You can accomplish this with an `onChange` event handler like the one shown in line 273 of Script 12.1 and Figure 12.10.

## Select Lists and Options

**Select lists** are essentially pull-down menus. They provide an excellent means of listing a lot of data in a very small space.

### Creating a Select List with HTML

Creating a select list requires two tags: the <select> tag and the <option> tag.

```
<select name="SelectListName">
    <option name="Option1Name" value="value1">Option 1</option>
    <option name="Option2Name" value="value2">Option 2</option>
    <option name="Option3Name" value="value3">Option 3</option>
    . . .
    <option name="OptionNName" value="valueN">Option N</option>
</select>
```

The following excerpt from Script 12.1 shows one of the three select lists.

### *Figure 12.12    HTML to Create Select List*

```
169      <select name="CCexpMo">
170             <option value="">Month</option>
171        <option value="01">01</option>
172        <option value="02">02</option>
173        <option value="03">03</option>
174        <option value="04">04</option>
175        <option value="05">05</option>
176        <option value="06">06</option>
177        <option value="07">07</option>
178        <option value="08">08</option>
179        <option value="09">09</option>
180        <option value="10">10</option>
181        <option value="11">11</option>
182        <option value="12">12</option>
183 </select>
```

Here's what the list looks like initially:

### *Figure 12.13    Collapsed Select List*

Here's what it looks like when you click on the down arrow:

### *Figure 12.14    Open Select List*

Usually only one option shows when the list is collapsed, but you can display more of the list by setting the `size` attribute:

```
<select name="SelectListName" size="numOptionsToDisplay">
```

Here's what the Month select list looks like with the `size` attribute set to 3.

**Figure 12.15    Select List of Size 3**

By default, only one selection can be made from a select list. However, you can override this setting and allow multiple entries to be selected by setting the `multiple` attribute.

```
<select name="SelectListName" size="numOptionsToDisplayAtOnce" ⟶
⟶ multiple>
```

The visitor must hold down the Ctrl key while clicking to select multiple options.

## Accessing a Select List and Its Options with JavaScript

One of the nicest things about select lists is how simple it is to determine whether a value has been selected or not. Turn back to the handy-dandy JavaScript object reference in Appendix A and look up the `select` object. Notice that select list has an `options` property, which is an array. See if you can figure out which property tells you which option was selected. You got it—`selectedIndex`. The `selectedIndex` property holds the index number of the currently selected option.

Here's how you would access the value of the currently selected option:

```
document.FormName.SelectListName.
   options[document.FormName.
   SelectListName.selectedIndex].value
```

*Programmer's tip*

It's a good idea to provide directions if you're allowing multiple choices from a select list. Many people don't know how to select multiple options. Also, it helps if you increase the size of the option list with the `size` attribute. It will make it easier for visitors to choose multiple entries.

Note: If multiple options are allowed to be selected, `selectedIndex` returns the index number of the first option chosen in list order, not the first option clicked.

## Appropriate Event Handlers to Use with Select Lists

The event handlers `onChange`, `onBlur`, and `onFocus` all work with select lists. The `onChange` event handler is, by far, used the most.

Perhaps because of their compact size, select lists have become quite popular as drop-down menus, also known as Go Menus. Script 12.4 shows an example.

**Script 12.4    Go Menu**

```
1    <html>
2    <head>
3        <title>Script 12.4: Go Menu</title>
4    </head>
```

```
 5    <body>
 6    <form>
 7          <b>Where would you like to go today?</b>
 8          <select name="GoMenu"
 9          onChange=
              "location.href=this.options[this.selectedIndex].value">
10              <option value="script12-04.html">Choose a Destination
11               </option>
12              <option value="http://javascriptconcepts.com/">
13              JavaScript Concepts</option>
14              <option value="http://www.webwoman.biz/">WebWoman
                  </option>
15              <option value="http://www.webwomansbooks.com/">
16              WebWoman's Books</option>
17              <option value="http://yahoo.com/">Yahoo!</option>
18              <option value="http://google.com/">Google</option>
19              <option value="http://whatis.com/">What Is</option>
20              <option value="http://metacrawler.com/">Metacrawler
                  </option>
21          </select>
22    </form>
23    </body>
24    </html>
```

Line 9 does all the work. When a change in the option chosen in the select list is detected, the event handler sets the hypertext reference in the location bar to the `value` of the `option` selected. In the Go Menu, all of the values are URLs. Cool, huh?

The first option reloads the current document and serves to show how you can reference a relative path. The rest are absolute paths.

Open Script 12.4 and give it a whirl. When you click on the down arrow, the list should look like this:

**Figure 12.16 Go Menu Created by Script 12.4**

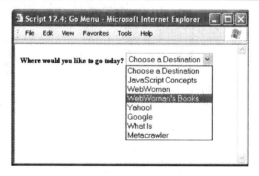

# Radio Buttons

**Radio buttons** are useful when you need the visitor to choose one answer from several choices. With radio buttons, one answer and one answer only will do. Visitors are not allowed to choose more than one. If they click on another radio button, the one already checked turns off. The secret to making a set of radio buttons function in this manner is to give all of the buttons in the set the same name. They can, of course, have different values, and should, but they *must* all share the same name.

## Creating Radio Buttons with HTML

```
Label: <input type="radio" name="RadioSetName" value="value1">
       <input type="radio" name="RadioSetName" value="value2">
```

Script 12.1 shows a set of radio buttons named CCtype (lines 146 through 158).

*Figure 12.17   HTML to Create Radio Buttons*

```
148          <tr>
149            <th width="150" align="right">Credit Card
                 Type:</th>
150            <td colspan="4">
151              <input type="radio" name="CCtype"
152                      value="Visa">Visa   
153              <input type="radio" name="CCtype"
154                      value="MC">MasterCard   
155              <input type="radio" name="CCtype"
156                      value="Discover">Discover   
157              <input type="radio" name="CCtype"
158                      value="AmerEx">American Express
159            </td>
160          </tr>
```

Here's what they look like:

*Figure 12.18   Radio Buttons*

Run the script and try it for yourself. Click on one radio button to select it, then click on another. Notice how the first gets unselected. Only one button may be selected at any one time.

If you want, you can preset a radio button as checked by adding the checked attribute:

```
<input type="radio" name="RadioSetName" value="Value1" checked>
```

Here's what it looks like with Discover checked:

*Figure 12.19 Radio Buttons—One Checked*

## Accessing a Radio Button with JavaScript

Accessing the value of the selected radio button is not nearly as easy as accessing the value of a text box, textarea, or even the selected option in a select list. Take a look at your JavaScript object reference in Appendix A. Find radio buttons as a property of the `form` object. Notice anything interesting? The `radio` property of the `form` object is an array. That means that you have to access radio buttons by their array entries. For instance, to access the first radio button, labeled "Visa," you would type

```
document.CustomerData.CCtype[0].value
```

To access the button labeled "Discover," the third button, type

```
document.CustomerData.CCtype[2].value
```

Remember, arrays begin numbering at zero.

The next problem is determining which radio button is checked. Once you figure that out, you can access that button's value like just shown.

The `checked` property of a radio button returns the value `true` if the button is currently checked and `false` if it is not currently checked. To determine which radio button, if any, has been checked, a `for` loop comes in handy. Here's the general form:

```
var checkedButton = -1
for(i=0; i<radioSet.length; i++) {
    if(radioSet[i].checked) {
        checkedButton = i
        break
    }
}
```

If no button was checked, the variable `checkedButton` still holds the value -1. Otherwise, `checkedButton` holds the index number of the checked entry.

## Appropriate Event Handlers to Use with Radio Buttons

Several event handlers work with radio buttons, including `onFocus`, `onBlur`, and `onClick`. You could use the `onClick` event handler with radio buttons to launch a script or open a document if you so desire. `onFocus` and `onBlur` can be used in tandem to display and erase a message in the status bar as we did earlier with the text box.

# Checkboxes

Checkboxes are similar to radio buttons. The important difference is that radio buttons allow the visitor to check only one choice in a group and **checkboxes** allow the visitor to check all the choices that apply in a group. In other words, radio buttons are "choose one" and checkboxes are "check all that apply."

## Creating Checkboxes with HTML

As with radio buttons, checkboxes in the same group should have the same name. Here's the general form:

```
Label:
<input type="checkbox" name="CheckboxSetName"
       value="value1"><br>
<input type="checkbox" name="CheckboxSetName"
       value="value2"><br>
<input type="checkbox" name="CheckboxSetName"
       value="value3"><br>
<input type="checkbox" name="CheckboxSetName"
       value="value4"><br>
<input type="checkbox" name="CheckboxSetName"
       value="value5"><br>
```

In Script 12.1, lines 233 through 268 show an example of a series of checkboxes.

**Figure 12.20    HTML to Create Checkboxes**

```
233        <tr>
234          <th width="150" align="right" valign="top">How You
235            Heard<br>About Us:<br>
236            <small>(check all that apply)</small></th>
237          <td valign="top">
238            <input type="checkbox" name="ReferredBy"
239                  value="Web Site">Web Site<br>
240            <input type="checkbox" name="ReferredBy"
                 value="Email">Email<br>
241          <input type="checkbox" name="ReferredBy"
242                  value="Newsgroup">Newsgroup<br>
243          </td>
244          <td valign="top">
245            <input type="checkbox" name="ReferredBy"
                 value="TV">TV<br>
246            <input type="checkbox" name="ReferredBy"
                 value="Radio">Radio<br>
```

```
247        <input type="checkbox" name="ReferredBy"
                    value="Store">Store<br>
248          </td>
249          <td valign="top">
250            <input type="checkbox" name="ReferredBy"
251                     value="Newspaper">Newspaper<br>
252      <input type="checkbox" name="ReferredBy"
253          value="Magazine">Magazine<br>
254      <input type="checkbox" name="ReferredBy"
255          value="Catalog">Catalog<br>
256    </td>
257    <td valign="top">
258      <input type="checkbox" name="ReferredBy"
259          value="Family">Family<br>
260      <input type="checkbox" name="ReferredBy"
261          value="Friend">Friend<br>
262      <input type="checkbox" name="ReferredBy"
263          value="Other" onChange = if
                      (this.checked)
                          this.form.ReferredByOther.disabled
                          =false">
264           Other
265           <input type="Text" name="ReferredByOther"
266                     size="7" maxlength="15" disabled>
267        </td>
268      </tr>
```

Here's what they look like:

### Figure 12.21   Checkboxes

Now go ahead and try them. You should be able to choose as many of them as you like. If you want, you can preset one or more checkboxes as checked by adding the `checked` attribute:

```
<input type="checkbox" name="CheckboxSetName"
      value="value1" checked>
```

You can also give each checkbox its own individual name. This is a good idea if you only have a few checkboxes. It makes accessing them a little easier too as we'll see in a few minutes.

## Accessing a Checkbox with JavaScript

In Appendix A, notice that the `checkbox` property of the `form` object is an array. Accessing a checkbox is just like accessing a radio button. To get the values of any of those that are checked, you must first determine which ones are checked, if any.

As with radio buttons, the `checked` property of a checkbox returns the value `true` if the button is currently checked and `false` if it is not currently checked. This `for` loop will create an array containing the index numbers of the values that are checked.

```
var checkedButtons  = new Array()
var j = 0                                    // current index
for(i=0; i<checkboxSet.length; i++) {
    if(checkboxSet[i].checked) {
            checkedButtons[j++] = i
    }
}
```

After running this script, the `length` property of the `checkedButtons` array reports the number of checkboxes that are checked. The index numbers of the checked values are contained in the `checkedButtons` array. This `for` loop writes the values that are checked.

```
for(i=0; i<checkedButtons.length; i++) {
    document.write("Value " + i + ": " +
    checkboxSet[checkedButtons[i].value])
}
```

You can modify it to serve your needs.

If you give each checkbox its own unique name, accessing the value of each checkbox becomes simpler as you no longer have to use an array reference to access it.

### Appropriate Event Handlers to Use with Checkboxes

The same event handlers that work with radio buttons can be used with checkboxes: `onFocus`, `onBlur`, and `onClick`.

# Buttons

Buttons are handy gadgets to which you can easily attach `onClick` event handlers in order to run scripts. They were included in the HTML 4 specification expressly with scripting in mind. The idea is that a button has an associated script that executes when the button is clicked.

### Creating a Button with HTML

To create a button with HTML, use the input element, setting the type to `button`.

```
<input type="button" name="ButtonName" value="buttonLabel"
    onClick="someScript()">
```

The value attribute specifies the button's label. By default, a button has no label. You don't have to name buttons. Even if you do name a button, no name-value pair will be sent when the form is submitted.

## Accessing a Button with JavaScript

You rarely need to access a button with JavaScript unless you want to change its label:

```
document.ButtonName.value = "New Label"
```

## Appropriate Event Handlers to Use with Buttons

The most often used event handler for buttons is onClick. The variety of scripts you can execute in response to a button being pressed is limited only by your imagination and scripting ability. Following is an example of one popular use of buttons: navigation buttons.

### Script 12.5    Navigation Buttons

```
1    <html>
2    <head>
3         <title>Script 12.5: Navigation Buttons</title>
4    </head>
5    <body>
6    <h1>Script 12.5: Navigation Buttons</h1>
7    <p>Click on a button to see it work.</p>
8    <br><br><br><br><br><br><br><br><br><br><br><br><br>
9
10   <form>
11        <input type="button" name="Products" value="Products"
12             onClick="location.href='products.html'">
13        <input type="button" name="Support" value="Support"
14             onClick="location.href='support.html'">
15        <input type="button" name="About Us" value="About Us"
16             onClick="location.href='aboutUs.html'">
17        <input type="button" name="Contact Us" value="Contact Us"
18             onClick="location.href='contactUs.html'">
19        <input type="button" name="Home" value="Home"
20             onClick="location.href='home.html'">
21   </form>
22   </body>
23   </html>
```

Go ahead and give it a whirl. The HTML documents referenced have already been created, so the script is ready to go. The necessary HTML documents are products.html, support.html, aboutUs.html, contactUs.html, and home.html. Here's what the initial script looks like with all its buttons in glorious display.

**Figure 12.22    Navigation Buttons Created with HTML**

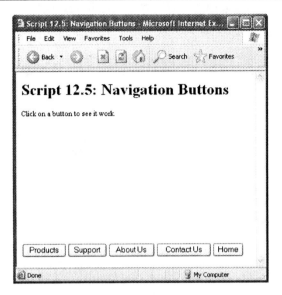

Clicking on the Products button opens this page:

**Figure 12.23    Current Page's Navigation Button Grayed Out**

Notice that on each page the current button is grayed out. The disabled attribute caused that. The disabled attribute can be applied to all form elements. We'll look at it in more detail a little later on. For now, suffice it to say that in the code for the document shown in Figure 12.23, the Products button's tag has the disabled attribute set.

```
<input type="button" name="Products" value="Products"
    onClick="location.href='products.html'" disabled>
```

The onFocus, onBlur, onMouseDown, and onMouseUp event handlers can also be used with buttons. Now let's look at some special types of buttons: submit and reset.

# Submit and Reset Buttons

A **submit button** is a special type of button in HTML. When pressed, it causes the data of the form in which it resides to be submitted to the URL specified in the action attribute of the <form> tag. A **reset button** is also a special type of button in HTML. When activated, it causes the contents of the form to clear, or reset.

An image can be used in place of a submit button, in which case it is known as an **active image**. When activated, an active image not only submits the form data to the URL specified in the form's action attribute, it also sends the current mouse coordinates as two name-value pairs labeled *ImageName*.x and *ImageName*.y, where *ImageName* is the value set in the image's name attribute. Generally, you use an active image in place of a submit button. A form can have more than one submit button, but only one reset button.

## Creating Submit and Reset Buttons with HTML

```
<input type="submit" value="ButtonLabel">
<input type="reset" value="ButtonLabel">
```

By default, submit buttons are labeled "Submit Query" and Reset buttons are labeled "Reset." You can change the default label by setting the value attribute.

Lines 280 and 281 in Script 12.1 show an example of custom-labeled submit and reset buttons.

**Figure 12.24**    *HTML to Create Submit and Reset Buttons*

```
277        <tr>
278          <th width="150"> </th>
279          <td colspan="4" align="left"><br>
280            <input type="submit" value="Send Data">
281            <input type="reset" value="Clear Form">
282          </td>
283        </tr>
```

Here's what they look like with their custom labels:

**Figure 12.25**    *Submit and Reset Buttons with Custom Labels*

The name-value pair for a submit or reset button will only be sent if you name the button by setting its name attribute. Rarely will you want to set the name attribute on a submit or reset button; the data is generally useless and redundant. About the only time naming submit buttons comes in handy is when you need multiple submit buttons, each to perform a different function. You would then program your server-side script to perform the appropriate function according to the name of the submit button that was pressed.

It is also possible to use an image as a submit button.

## Creating an Image Submit Button with HTML

```
<input type="image" name="ImageName" src="imageURL">
```

The image button's name attribute is used to send two name-value pairs, *ImageName*.*x* and *ImageName*.*y*, along with the rest of the form data, indicating the current mouse coordinates when the image was clicked. Therefore, setting the value attribute on an image button has no effect; the coordinates will override any value set.

## Accessing Submit and Reset Buttons with JavaScript

There is rarely a reason to access submit and reset buttons with JavaScript. The only reason I can think of is to change a button's label.

```
document.ButtonName.value = newLabel
```

**programmer's tip** Because clicking on an image button will submit all of the elements in the form, it is a good idea to place the image button at the end of the form, after all other form elements. It doesn't hurt to also explain how it works or label it appropriately.

At this time, active images are not recognized by JavaScript at all.

## Appropriate Event Handlers to Use with Submit and Reset Buttons

Keep in mind that the event handlers onSubmit and onReset do *not* work on their respectively named buttons. *The event handlers onSubmit and onReset work on <form> tags only.* Many novice programmers often confuse this issue.

Event handlers are rarely used directly on submit and reset buttons. However, onFocus, onBlur, onClick, onMouseDown, and onMouseUp are allowed. The last three, especially, do not seem to work very well with submit and reset buttons, perhaps because of the need to submit or reset the form. The submit and reset actions seem to take precedence, causing the onClick, onMouseDown, and onMouseUp event handlers to not function as intended and sometimes not work at all.

# Using the `disabled` Attribute to Prevent Field Modification

Earlier, we showed you how you could prevent a text box's contents from being modified by a visitor. You can also prevent a field from being modified by the visitor by setting the `disabled` attribute.

```
<input type="text" name="TextboxName" disabled>
```

While scripts can still access and modify the field, the contents of the field appear grayed out and the field itself cannot receive focus. The field will also be skipped during tabbing. The `disabled` attribute works on all form elements. To disable a field with JavaScript, type

```
document.FormName.ElementName.disabled = true
```

*Warning: The contents of a disabled field are not sent when the form is submitted.* You can initially disable a field with the `disabled` attribute and later enable it with a line of JavaScript code. As long as you enable the field before the data is submitted, the data will be sent. If, however, at the time the form is submitted, the field is still disabled, then the field's value will not be sent to the URL in the `action` attribute of the form.

To enable a field, type

```
document.FormName.ElementName.disabled = false
```

Look at lines 264–266 of Script 12.1. Notice that the Other text field is disabled.

### Figure 12.26    Disabling and Enabling a Form Field

```
262    <input type="Checkbox" name="ReferredBy" value="Other"
263           onChange="if(this.checked)
                  this.form.ReferredByOther.disabled=false">
264    Other
265    <input type="Text" name="ReferredByOther"
266           size="7" maxlength="15" disabled>
```

The text field cannot be modified unless its corresponding checkbox is checked. Line 263 shows how the `onChange` event handler enables the Other text box when the associated checkbox is checked.

# Prefilling a Form with JavaScript

It's often helpful to be able to preset the values of a form, whether for the visitor's convenience from retrieved cookie values or to make a coding job easier. For instance, who wants to keep filling out a form again and again just to test a validation program you're writing when a few lines of JavaScript at the end of the document can save you from repeated and tedious data entry.

Insert the following script at line 286 of Script 12.1 to prefill the fields with the values shown in Figure 12.1.

**Script 12.6    Prefilling a Form with JavaScript**

```
1    <script language="JavaScript"><!--
2         // Preset all form fields
3         document.CustomerData.Customer.value="Tina McDuffie"
4         document.CustomerData.Address.value="1234 JavaScript Way"
5         document.CustomerData.City.value="San Diego"
6         document.CustomerData.State.selectedIndex=5
7         document.CustomerData.Zip.value="12345-6790"
8         document.CustomerData.Phone.value="555-123-4567"
9         document.CustomerData.PhoneExt.value="890"
10        document.CustomerData.Email.value="webwoman@webwoman.biz"
11
12        document.CustomerData.CCtype[2].checked = true
13        document.CustomerData.CCnum.value = "1234 5678 9012 3456"
14        document.CustomerData.CCexpMo.selectedIndex = 2
15        document.CustomerData.CCexpYr.selectedIndex = 6
16
17        document.CustomerData.Username.value="webwoman"
18        document.CustomerData.Password.value="shhhhh"
19        document.CustomerData.PasswordConfirm.value="shhhhh"
20
21        document.CustomerData.ReferredBy[0].checked=true
22        document.CustomerData.ReferredBy[3].checked=true
23        document.CustomerData.ReferredBy[8].checked=true
24        document.CustomerData.ReferredBy[11].checked=true
25        document.CustomerData.ReferredByOther.value="Book"
26        document.CustomerData.Comments.value="none"
27    // -->
28    </script>
```

The prefilled form will look just like Figure 12.1.

# Summary

HTML supports a variety of form elements for input, including hidden fields, text boxes, password fields, textareas, select lists, radio buttons, checkboxes, submit buttons, reset buttons, and simple buttons. All form elements must be contained within a <form> tag. The <form> tag has three important attributes:

- ✗ name, which identifies the form and makes it easy to access it with JavaScript.
- ✗ action, which specifies the URL to send the form data to when the submit button is pressed. This could be a mailto URL or a server-side script.

⚡ method, which specifies how the form data is sent to the URL specified in the action attribute. The two options are get and post. Post is the preferred method.

Regardless of how and where form data is sent, the form data is first URL-encoded by the browser.

A form can be accessed with JavaScript either by its name, as specified in its name attribute, or by its index reference in the forms array, a property of the document object. It's a good idea to name your forms and especially all form elements. Labels make the associated data meaningful.

Two event handlers often used on forms are onSubmit and onReset. The onSubmit event handler is most often used to call a validation routine before submitting form data. The onReset event handler is most often used to ask the visitor to confirm his desire to clear the form's contents before actually clearing the form.

The keyword this is frequently used in association with forms and form elements. this always refers to the current object, wherever this happens to be. The keyword return must precede a function call whenever the data returned by the function needs to be returned to the event handler that called the function. We saw examples of return at work in both the onSubmit and onReset examples provided in this chapter.

Hidden fields are good for including data in a form that is not visible to the visitor. The data in hidden fields can be used by server-side scripts. A hidden field can be accessed with JavaScript either by its name, as specified in its name attribute, or by its index reference in the elements array, a property of the form object. Event handlers cannot be applied to hidden fields because the fields cannot be seen by the visitor.

Text boxes are excellent for single-line data entry. Like hidden fields, they can be accessed by their name or their index entry in the elements array. The onFocus and onBlur event handlers are often used in tandem on text boxes to provide data entry hints in the status bar. To prevent modification of a field, an event handler can be applied that calls the blur method whenever a field receives focus. Text boxes are often used in order forms to collect order quantities and display calculations.

A simple relative of the text box is the password field. Password fields are good for acquiring confidential information such as, well, passwords. Instead of showing the text typed into the field, password fields show only an asterisk or a dot for each character typed. They are accessed with JavaScript the same way as a text box. The event handlers that work on text boxes also work on password fields.

Textareas are multi-line text boxes. Other than being able to hold multiple lines of data, which is good for comments, they work like text boxes as far as JavaScript is concerned. The most common event handler used with textareas is the onChange event handler to thank visitors for their comments.

Select lists, essentially pull-down menus, are nice for providing many options in a very small space. We used them in Script 12.1 to allow the visitor to choose from a list of 50 states, the 12 months of the year, and several years that a credit card could expire. Accessing the value of the selected option in a select list is quite easy when you use its selectedIndex property. One of the most popular uses of select lists is as Go Menus for navigation on a Web site. The onChange event handler makes it work.

Radio buttons allow the visitor to choose one and only one from several options. Accessing the value of the currently checked radio button is more difficult than accessing the value of the text boxes, passwords, textareas, and select lists. You must first determine which button is checked with a for loop, then access that button's value via its radio array index.

Checkboxes allow visitors to "check all that apply." As far as accessing them with JavaScript, they work just like radio buttons.

Buttons were included in the HTML 4 specification expressly with scripting in mind. Using a button, labeled as you choose, you can call a variety of scripts. What you call is limited only by your imagination and your programming skill. About the only times you're likely to access a button directly with JavaScript are when you want to modify its label, disable it, or enable it.

Submit buttons are special in that they are used to send form data to the URL specified in the form's action attribute. Reset buttons also have a special task: clearing a form's fields. You can give submit and reset buttons a custom label by setting their value attributes. While you can access submit and reset buttons with JavaScript just like you would a regular button or a text box, rarely is this done. Rarely, too, are event handlers associated with these two buttons.

The disabled attribute can be applied to all form elements to prevent visitors from modifying the field or even giving it focus, gray out the field and its contents, and cause the field to be skipped when tabbing. If a form element is still disabled when the submit button is pressed, that element's name-value pair will not get sent.

## Review Questions

1. List five types of form elements supported by HTML and describe each.
2. Why is it helpful to set the name attribute on a form?
3. Why is it essential to set the name attribute on a form element?
4. What does the action attribute of a form do?
5. What is a mailto URL?
6. What is a server-side script?
7. What advantage does a server-side script such as FormMail have over a simple mailto URL when it comes to processing form data?
8. Describe the URL-encoding process.
9. What does the method attribute of a form specify?
10. Describe the differences between the get and post methods. Which is preferred? Why?
11. What is the onSubmit event handler most often used for?
12. What is the onReset event handler most often used for?
13. Explain how the special keyword this works.
14. Explain how the special keyword return works.

15. What is a hidden form element? What good is it if visitors can't see it?
16. What's the difference between a text box and a textarea? Do you use the same tag to create each? If not, what tags do you use for each?
17. What are some useful tasks you can perform on text boxes with event handlers?
18. Name two ways you can prevent a field from being modified by a visitor.
19. Does JavaScript have a built-in method or function for rounding numbers to a specific number of decimal places? If so, what's it called?
20. When you're completing a registration form, why are you usually asked to confirm your desired password?
21. What property of a select object can tell you whether or not an option has been selected? What, specifically, does that property return?
22. What's a Go Menu? How does it work?
23. What must you first do before you can get the value of the currently checked radio button in a set of radio buttons?
24. How do you ensure that a set of radio buttons functions as a set, allowing only one button to be checked at any one time?
25. What's the good of buttons? After all, they can't accept an entry from the visitor. What did the good folks at the W3C have in mind when they created them in the first place?
26. On what element is the onSubmit event handler called? onReset?
27. What additional data is sent with a form when an image button is used to submit its data?
28. What four things does setting the disabled attribute on a form field accomplish?

# Exercises

1. Write the appropriate dot notation to set the action attribute of a form named CustomerOrder in the current document to mailto:*youremailaddress*. Replace *youremailaddress* with your own email address.
2. Write the dot notation to access the method attribute of the third form in a document.
3. Write the HTML necessary to create a five-row textarea that is approximately 40 characters wide. Set it to wrap such that no line feeds or carriage returns will be recorded unless the visitor presses the Enter key.
4. Write the dot notation to access the value of a text box that is the fifth element in the only form in a document.
5. Write the dot notation to access the value of a textarea named Message, which is in a form named Guestbook.
6. Write the dot notation to access the currently selected value in a select list named Size in a form named Order.
7. Write a statement to check the second radio button in a set named PoliticalParty in a form named PoliticalSurvey.

8.  Write a statement to see if the last box in a set of checkboxes named `Movies` in a form named `Survey` has been checked.
9.  Write a statement to give focus to a text field named `Email` in a document named `CustomerInfo`.
10. Write a statement to select the contents of and give focus to a text box named `Email` in a document named `CustomerInfo`.

## Scripting Exercises

Create a folder named assignment12 to hold the documents you create during this assignment. Save a copy of your latest toy store documents in a toyStore subfolder.

1.  Create a new document named formEvents.html.
    a.  Write the appropriate HTML and JavaScript code to create a set of radio buttons named `MailingList` with the values `"Opt In"` and `"Opt Out"`. Label them "I'll pass" and "Sign me up." When the visitor clicks either of the radio buttons, a confirm dialog should pop up verifying that the visitor really intended to make that choice. If the visitor clicks Cancel, don't set the button; if the visitor clicks OK, set the button.
    b.  Create a form with two sets of fields for Name, Address, City, State, and Zip under the headings "Billing Address" and "Shipping Address." Write the appropriate HTML and JavaScript code to create a checkbox labeled "Ship To Billing." When the visitor clicks on the checkbox to check it, confirm that he does indeed wish to ship to the billing address provided. If he confirms by clicking OK, copy the billing data to the appropriate shipping fields. If he clicks Cancel, do nothing. When the visitor clicks on the checkbox to clear the field, that is, removes the check, confirm that he wants to ship to an address other than the billing address. If he confirms, clear the shipping address fields; otherwise leave them be.
2.  Create a new document named order.html to accept a toy order.
    a.  Create a short order form listing a variety of toys (at least five).
    b.  Set it up so that whenever a quantity is entered, the extended total for that line item is calculated and entered into the appropriate field and the entire form is totaled and its total displayed in a SubTotal text field at the bottom.
    c.  Do what you must to make certain that visitors cannot modify the extended totals or SubTotal.
3.  Create a new document named go.html.
    a.  Insert a Go Menu to your favorite Web sites.
    b.  Place the document in a folder on your computer.
    c.  Place a shortcut to the file on your desktop.
    d.  Add a bookmark to it in your browser.
4.  Create a set of navigation buttons using HTML and JavaScript.
5.  Create a Web page containing a form that asks for
    ✄    the visitor's name

- the visitor's email address
- comments
- a field that automatically updates the number of seconds the visitor has spent viewing the form
- whatever other information you desire

Set the form up as a mailto form or, if you have access to a form mail program, use that. The recipient of the form should receive the contents of all fields, including the number of seconds the visitor spent on the form.

6. Modify order.html as follows:

   a. Add a drop-down select list named `TaxingState` near the bottom of the form with two text boxes adjacent to it. Name the first text box `TaxRate` and the second `SalesTax`. The second text box should line up under the extended total fields.

   b. The select list should contain a list of states for whom you must collect sales tax and a "None of the Above" option.

   c. When a state is chosen, enter the appropriate tax rate in the TaxRate field as a decimal. If "None of the Above" is chosen, leave TaxRate blank.

   d. Modify the function that totals the form such that it also calculates the sales tax on SubTotal, if applicable, displays it in the SalesTax field, and writes the grand total in a Total field.

   e. Do what you must to make certain that visitors cannot modify the TaxRate, SalesTax, and Total fields.

7. Modify Scripting Exercise 6. At the top of the order form, request the usual customer data. Include a select list from which the visitor can choose her state of residence. When a state is chosen, set the TaxRate field appropriately.

# Projects

Write a self-scoring quiz program. Arrays will come in handy. To make the program easily reusable, place the questions and answers in one external JavaScript file and the functions that do all the work in another external JavaScript file. Include functions to

- write the quiz to the document from the questions stored in the first external JavaScript file.
- score the quiz and display the results in some way.

Add any other functions you determine that you need. Choose the type of form fields you want to use to gather the answers from the visitor. Text boxes, radio buttons, checkboxes, or select lists are probably your best bets.

*chapter* **thirteen**

# Validating
# Forms

*What is required is simply a little trust and even that only for a little while, for the sooner a man begins to verify all he hears the better it is for him.*

—George Gurdjieff

When you ask visitors for data, it's important that they provide that data in a valid format. For instance, an email address without an @ symbol cannot possibly be a valid email address. Enter form validation.

Form validation is a very important task that can be performed client-side quickly and efficiently with JavaScript. By performing form validations client-side you can reduce the overall load on your Web server and provide more responsive error messages to your visitors.

In this chapter we'll

- ✗ compare the benefits of client-side vs. server-side validation.
- ✗ define the two approaches to form validation: batch and real-time.
- ✗ build a form validation library containing functions to validate each type of form element and to validate email addresses, phone numbers, zip codes, and credit card numbers.
- ✗ use the special keyword this when appropriate to shorten object and property references.

> ✗ write real-time validation functions that can be called as event handlers.
> ✗ write some batch form validation routines using the functions we created.
> ✗ write a script that displays error messages inline, rather than by alert dialog boxes.

# What Is Form Validation?

**Form validation** is the process of checking the data entered into a form to make certain that all required data has been provided and that the data submitted is of the proper format and length. Some typical things that you might want to check during a form validation include the following:

> ✗ Are all of the required fields completed?
> ✗ Is the proposed password of the proper length?
> ✗ Does the confirmation password match the proposed password?
> ✗ Does the email address entered conform with the appropriate format for a valid email address?
> ✗ Does the phone number entered appear to be a valid phone number?
> ✗ Does the zip code field contain five digits or five digits, followed by a hyphen, followed by four more digits?
> ✗ Does the credit card number appear to be valid according to the length and the appropriate prefix for the card type specified?
> ✗ Does the credit card number pass the LUHN formula algorithm, also known as the modulus 10 test?
> ✗ Is the credit card still good according to its expiration date?

# Client-side vs. Server-side Validation

Form validation can be performed by the client, the server, or both.

**Client-side form validation** requires some type of client-side scripting language, such as JavaScript. The major advantage of client-side validation is that all of the processing is done by the client machine. This makes the process fast and responsive. However, if the Web browser does not support JavaScript (most browsers do support it nowadays) or if the visitor has turned off JavaScript support in his browser, the form validation will not be run, so you could receive invalid or missing data.

**Server-side form validation** requires some type of server-side scripting such as PHP, CGI scripting with Perl, or Active Server Pages (ASP) or a technology like ColdFusion. Server-side validation is typically slower and less responsive than client-side validation. The major advantage is that the browser does not need to support client-side scripting or have it turned on. The down side, besides being slow and unresponsive, is that every validation requires running a program on the server, thereby increasing the load on the server and leaving it less free to handle other requests quickly.

The best option is to use both. First validate the form client-side, using JavaScript of course. Then validate it server-side. Most of the work to validate the form will be performed by the client, reducing the server's overall load. Those few forms that cannot be processed client-side still get processed by the server. You are always assured of receiving valid data.

For the rest of this chapter, we'll concentrate on client-side form validation using JavaScript.

## Batch Validation vs. Real-time Validation

There are two approaches you can take to validate forms client-side with JavaScript: batch and real-time. Most server-side form validation is done by batch validation.

**Batch validation** is performed *when the form is submitted.* In one fell swoop, the entire form is checked to be certain required fields have been completed, data is of the proper format, etc. Depending on how the routine is written, it could stop as soon as it encounters an error by reporting the error in an alert or via some other method. Usually the validation routine will select the bad data or give focus to the empty field so the problem is ready for the visitor to correct. The validation routine could also create a list of all errors encountered and report them all at once. Either way, with the batch approach, no validation occurs until the form is submitted.

**Real-time validation** is performed *in real-time upon completion of a field entry.* Whenever a field's entry is changed, an `onChange` event handler on the field calls the appropriate validation function to verify that the entry meets your needs. The advantage of real-time validation is that the visitor is alerted as soon as an error is made. The only problem is that it's easy to bypass correcting the problem. So real-time validation alone is not the best approach.

A combination of real-time and batch validation is an excellent way to go. If you don't feel you have the time to implement both, then stick with batch validation. It's more reliable.

## Calling a Batch, Client-side Form Validation with `onSubmit`

Client-side form validation routines of the batch type are usually called in an `onSubmit` event handler. A typical batch validation routine at least verifies that all required fields have been completed. More complete routines also verify that any data entered is of the proper format.

For instance, you might want to require that the visitor enter an email address. Realizing that some people might just enter a few useless characters to quickly bypass the required field, you might add a function that verifies that the email address entry at least *looks* like a valid email address. It should have an @ symbol in the appropriate place, the minimum number of dots, etc. We learned how to validate a basic email address with regular expressions in Chapter 9. We'll revisit the subject later in this chapter.

We saw a very simple batch validation routine in the previous chapter (Script 12.1). The form of the call looked like this:

```
<form name="CustomerData" action="mailto:me@webwoman.biz"
      method="POST" onSubmit="return validate(this)">
```

Note two important things about the `validate` function call in the `onSubmit` event handler:

1. The presence of the keyword `return`.
2. The use of the keyword `this`.

Recall that `return` causes the data returned by the `validate` function to be returned to the event handler. It allows the event handler to abort the submission of the form data if it receives `false` and to submit the form if it receives `true`. Remember that the special keyword **this** always refers to the current object. In the `onSubmit` event handler shown above, `this` refers to the `CustomerData` form.

We'll see `this` used in many different places to refer to a variety of objects throughout this chapter. For more discussion about `return` and `this`, see Chapter 12.

## Creating Your Own Form Validation Library

Throughout this chapter, we'll be developing reusable validation functions. Some will simply check to see if a form element has an entry. Others will verify whether or not data is of an appropriate format. I recommend that you begin building a form validation library. The functions presented in this chapter will get you off to a good start. You can add others as you develop them.

Our two major tasks in building a form validation library in this chapter involve writing functions that will

1. Check to see if a particular type of form element *has* an entry.
2. Verify whether or not an entry is *correctly formatted.*

You would think the first task could be taken care of with a single function. After all, all you need to know is if each field has a value. However, having read the previous chapter, you probably realize it isn't that simple. While checking whether or not a text box has a value is easy, verifying that at least one checkbox has been checked takes a little more work.

Our first task is to come up with functions that can check each type of form field and determine whether or not a value has been entered or set. Let's start with the easiest, checking to see if a text box, password field, or textarea is empty, and then proceed from there.

## Verifying That Required Fields Each Have an Entry

### isEmpty

As you learned in the previous chapter, accessing the value of a text box, password field, or textarea is pretty straightforward:

```
document.FormName.Fieldname.value
```

You need only check to see if the value is `null` or empty ( " " ). This little function, `isEmpty`, will do the trick (lines 5 through 8 of Script 13.1).

*Script 13.1*    `isEmpty`

```
1    <html>
2    <head>
3        <title>Script 13.1: isEmpty</title>
4    <script language="JavaScript" type="text/javascript"><!--
5    function isEmpty(str) {
6        var empty = (str == null || str == "") ? true : false
7        return empty
8    }
9
10   function validate(zForm) {
11       if (isEmpty(zForm.Customer.value)) {
12           alert ("Error!  Please enter your name.")
13           zForm.Customer.focus()
14           return false
15       }
16       return true
17   }
18   //-->
19   </script>
20   </head>
21   <body>
22   <h1>Testing isEmpty( )</h1>
23   <form name="CustomerData" onSubmit="return validate(this)">
24      <table border=0>
25       <tr>
26         <th width="150" align="right" valign="bottom">
27           <h2>Customer</h2></th>
28         <th colspan="5" align="left" valign="bottom">
29           <h2> Data</h2></th>
30       </tr>
31       <tr>
32         <th width="150" align="right">Name:</th>
33         <td colspan="5">
34           <input name="Customer" type="text" size="27"
35                   maxlength="40"
36                   onFocus="window.status='First Last'; return true"
37                   onBlur="window.status=''; return true"></td>
38       </tr>
39      </table>
40
41      <table>
42       <tr>
43         <th width="150"> </th>
```

```
44          <td colspan="4" align="left"><br>
45             <input type="submit" value="Send Data">
46             <input type="reset" value="Clear Form">
47          </td>
48        </tr>
49      </table>
50    </form>
51
52    </body>
53    </html>
```

Let's call the script in a batch validation routine, called `validate`, and see if it works. Try it. If you leave the field labeled "Name:" blank and press the submit button, you should receive the following error message:

**Figure 13.1    Results of Script 13.1**

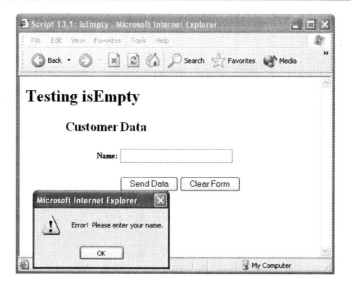

When an entry is required but none is provided, it's always a nice touch to give focus to the empty field after displaying an appropriate error message. That way the visitor can just start typing. Line 13 of Script 13.1 does just that.

### noneSelected

Select lists are also pretty easy to check for an entry. The `selectedIndex` property of the `select` object returns -1 if no value has been selected. If a selection has been made, it returns the index number of the selected option (indexing begins at 0). If multiple selections are allowed, it returns the index number of the first option selected (in index order, not selection order). To verify that some option has been selected, just make certain that the value of `selectedIndex` is not equal to -1.

Keep in mind that the latest browsers consider the first option selected by default, even if you have not specified it to be selected with HTML. For that reason, many programmers like to use the first option of a select list to provide instructions such as "Choose a State:" or a label such as "Month." When the first option is utilized in this way, you must make certain that the value of `selectedIndex` is not equal to 0 as well as not equal to -1.

The `noneSelected` function, shown in lines 5 through 15 of Script 13.2, accepts two parameters: the select list you want to check and a Boolean value indicating whether to check the first option as well. The second parameter is optional. You'll want to check the first option if you use it as a label, that is, if it is not a valid option with a valid value.

**Script 13.2    `noneSelected`**

```
1    <html>
2    <head>
3        <title>Script 13.2: noneSelected</title>
4    <script language="JavaScript" type="text/javascript"><!--
5    function noneSelected(zSelectList, ckFirst) {
6        if(noneSelected.arguments.length == 1) {
7            var ckFirst = false
8        }
9        if(zSelectList.selectedIndex == -1 ||
10            (zSelectList.selectedIndex == 0 && ckFirst)) {
11            return true
12        } else {
13            return false
14        }
15    }
16
17    function validate(zForm) {
18        if(noneSelected(zForm.CCexpMo, true)) {
19            alert ("Error! Please specify the month your card
                    expires.")
20            zForm.CCexpMo.focus()
21            return false
22        }
23        if(noneSelected(zForm.CCexpYr, true)) {
24            alert ("Error! Please specify the year your card
                    expires.")
25            zForm.CCexpYr.focus()
26            return false
27        }
28        return true
29    }
```

```
30  //-->
31  </script>
32  </head>
33  <body>
34  <h1>Testing noneSelected</h1>
35  <form name="CustomerData" onSubmit="return validate(this)">
36  <table border=0>
37      <tr>
38        <th width="150" align="right" valign="bottom">
39          <h3>Payment Info</h3></th>
40          <th colspan="2" align="left" valign="bottom"> </th>
41      </tr>
42      <tr>
43       <th align="right"><b>Expires:</b></th>
44       <td>
45         <select name="CCexpMo">
46                  <option value="">Month</option>
47                  <option value="01">01</option>
48                  <option value="02">02</option>
49                  <option value="03">03</option>
50                  <option value="04">04</option>
51                  <option value="05">05</option>
52                  <option value="06">06</option>
53                  <option value="07">07</option>
54                  <option value="08">08</option>
55                  <option value="09">09</option>
56                  <option value="10">10</option>
57                  <option value="11">11</option>
58                  <option value="12">12</option>
59         </select>
60         <select name="CCexpYr">
61                  <option value="">Year</option>
62                  <option value="2005">2005</option>
63                  <option value="2006">2006</option>
64                  <option value="2007">2007</option>
65                  <option value="2008">2008</option>
66                  <option value="2009">2009</option>
67                  <option value="2010">2010</option>
68                  <option value="2011">2011</option>
69                  <option value="2012">2012</option>
70                  <option value="2013">2013</option>
71      </select></td>
72      </tr>
73  </table>
74  <table>
```

```
75        <tr>
76          <th width="150"> </th>
77          <td colspan="4" align="left"><br>
78            <input type="submit" value="Send Data">
79            <input type="reset" value="Clear Form"><br>
80          </td>
81        </tr>
82    </table>
83    </form>
84    </body>
85    </html>
```

How's it work? First the script checks to see if two arguments were passed to noneSelected (line 6). If the ckFirst argument wasn't provided, then the function sets ckFirst to false (line 7). Only if ckFirst evaluates to true will it matter if selectedIndex==0, which is determined in the second if statement (lines 9 through 14), which checks to see if no selection was made at all (selectedIndex==-1).

The script contains two select lists (lines 43 through 71). Both have labels requiring the visitor to make a choice. Give it a try. Initially, try submitting the form as is. You should receive an error message similar to this:

### Figure 13.2    Results of Script 13.2

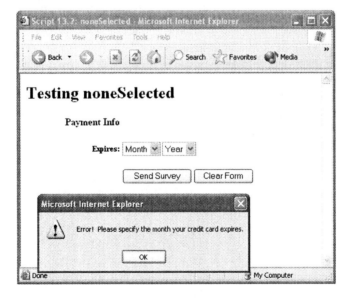

## noneChecked

The most common type of validation performed on a set of radio buttons and checkboxes is simply to verify that at least one button has been checked. There is no need to validate the value of any radio button or checkbox because you, the programmer, entered the values to begin with.

The `checked` property of both a radio button and a checkbox returns the value `true` if the button or box is currently checked and `false` if it is not currently checked. To verify whether or not one of a set of radio buttons or checkboxes has been checked, a `for` loop comes in handy. Script 13.3, in lines 5 through 12, shows the general form.

**Script 13.3 noneChecked**

```
1    <html>
2    <head>
3         <title>Script 13.3: noneChecked</title>
4    <script language="JavaScript" type="text/javascript"><!--
5    function noneChecked(zButtonSet) {
6         for(i=0; i<zButtonSet.length; i++) {
7              if(zButtonSet[i].checked) {
8                   return false
9              }
10        }
11        return true
12   }
13
14   function validate(zForm) {
15        if (noneChecked(zForm.CCtype)) {
16             alert ("Error! Please specify credit card type.")
17             return false
18        }
19        return true
20   }
21   //-->
22   </script>
23   </head>
24   <body>
25   <h1>Testing noneChecked</h1>
26   <form name="CustomerData" onSubmit="return validate(this)">
27        <table border=0>
28         <tr>
29          <th width="150" align="right" valign="bottom">
30            <h3>Payment Info</h3></th>
31          <th colspan="5" align="left" valign="bottom"> </th>
32         </tr>
33         <tr>
```

```
34      <th width="150" align="right">Credit Card Type:</th>
35      <td colspan="4">
36        <input type="Radio" name="CCtype" value="Visa">Visa
37          
38        <input type="Radio" name="CCtype" value="MC">MasterCard
39          
40        <input type="Radio" name="CCtype"
41              value="Discover">Discover
42          
43        <input type="Radio" name="CCtype"
44              value="AmerEx">American Express
45      </td>
46    </tr>
47    </table>
48
49    <table>
50      <tr>
51        <th width="150"> </th>
52        <td colspan="4" align="left"><br>
53          <input type="submit" value="Send Data">
54          <input type="reset" value="Clear Form">
55        </td>
56      </tr>
57    </table>
58  </form>
59
60  </body>
61  </html>
```

This function will return `false` as soon as it encounters a button that is checked. If it gets through all of the buttons without finding one that is checked, it returns `true`, indicating that none were checked.

Try submitting the form without first checking a button. You should receive an error message similar to this:

*Figure 13.3    Results of Script 13.3*

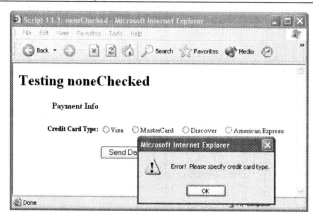

Keep in mind that you do not need to use noneChecked on every set of radio buttons or checkboxes in your form. Only use it if you *require* that at least one choice be checked. There are often times when it is perfectly acceptable for you to allow a visitor to leave all checkboxes or radio buttons unchecked. For instance, consider a series of checkboxes labeled like this

```
Check any or all of the following email newsletters that you
want to fill up your mailbox for the rest of your life:
```

Personally, I'd leave them all unchecked because I get enough junk in my email already. Unless the owner of the Web site is a spammer, he'll let you leave them all unchecked.

The same is true of radio buttons; you don't always *need* to require a choice. For instance, consider a series of radio buttons labeled like this

```
If your order is a gift, choose your preferred wrapping paper
color:
```

In this case, the visitor need choose a wrapping paper color only *if* her order is a gift. Of course, you might want to call noneSelected on the radio button set if a checkbox labeled "This order is a gift" is checked.

Now that you know how to make certain each *type* of field has an entry, let's write some functions to make certain the entries you receive are of a valid format. Entries that need to be of a certain format are usually entered in text boxes, so our primary job will be to see if a string value is of a valid format. This will require the use of some String methods and regular expressions. Please review Chapter 9 as needed.

# Validating Passwords

There are several things you need to consider when validating passwords, including the follwing:

   ✗  Do the password and the password confirmation match?
   ✗  Is the password of the right length?

- Does the password contain illegal characters?
- Does it pass the "security strictness" test?

In this section, we'll write some functions to answer those questions. Then we'll put them together in a function that will report if the password entry supplied is a valid password.

### noMatch

One of the most common validation routines for password fields is to verify that two password entries match. To verify that the password entries match, simply check to see if their values are equal. The function shown in lines 10 through 16 of Script 13.4 does just that. It's written as a stand-alone function because it could be used to see if any two strings match; they don't have to be passwords.

When the entries don't match, you display an error message (line 77). However, it's always a nice touch to clear the confirmation entry and select the contents of the password field for the visitor as well. Lines 78 and 79 provide this courtesy.

**Script 13.4    Validating Passwords**

```
1    <html>
2    <head>
3        <title>Script 13.4: Validating Passwords </title>
4    <script language="JavaScript" type="text/javascript"><!--
5    function isEmpty(str) {
6            var empty = (str == null || str == "") ? true : false
7            return empty
8    }
9
10   function noMatch(str1, str2) {
11           if (str2 != str1) {
12                   return true
13           } else {
14                   return false
15           }
16   }
17
18   function validLength(str, minLen, maxLen) {
19           if(typeof(str) != "string") {
20                   str = str.toString()
21           }
22           if (str.length < minLen || str.length > maxLen) {
23                   return false
24           } else {
25                   return true
26           }
```

```
27  }
28
29  function onlyLettersNnums(str) {
30        var illegalChars = /[^a-zA-Z0-9]/
31
32        if (str.match(illegalChars)) {
33              return false
34        } else {
35              return true
36        }
37  }
38
39  // strict is a Boolean value specifying password must have at
40  // least one lowercase letter, one uppercase letter, and one
41  // number. Set to false if you don't want strict passwords.
42  function validPassword(pwd, pwdConfirm, strict) {
43        var error = false
44        var errorMsg = "Error!\n"
45        if (isEmpty(pwd.value) || isEmpty(pwd.value)) {
46              alert ("Error! You must enter a password and confirm
                        it.")
47              pwd.focus()
48              return false
49        }
50        if (noMatch(pwd.value, pwdConfirm.value)) {
51              error = true
52              errorMsg += "Password entries do not match.\n"
53        }
54        if (!validLength(pwd.value, 6, 8)) {
55              error = true
56              errorMsg += "Password must be 6 to 8 characters
                        long.\n"
57        }
58        if (!onlyLettersNnums(pwd.value) ){
59              error = true
60              errorMsg += "Password contains illegal
                        characters.\n"
61        }
62        if (strict) {
63              if (pwd.value.search(/[a-z]+/g) == -1 ||
64                    pwd.value.search(/[A-Z]+/g) == -1 ||
65                    pwd.value.search(/[0-9]+/g) == -1)  {
66                  error = true
67                  errorMsg += "Password must contain at least one "
```

```
68              errorMsg +=  "lowercase letter, one uppercase
                letter, "
69              errorMsg +=  "and one numeric digit."
70          }
71      }
72      if (error) {
73              alert(errorMsg)
74              pwdConfirm.value = ""
75              pwd.select()
76              return false
77      }
78      return true                        // everything's ok
79  }
80
81  function validate(zForm) {
82      if (!validPassword(zForm.Password, zForm.PasswordConfirm,
83          true)) {
84              return false
85      }
86
87      return true
88  }
89  //-->
90  </script>
91  </head>
92  <body>
93  <h1>Validating Passwords</h1>
94  <form action="" method="post" name="CustomerData"
95      onSubmit="return validate(this)">
96    <table>
97     <tr>
98      <th width="150" align="right" valign="bottom">
99       <h3>Login Info</h3></th>
100      <th colspan="3" align="left" valign="bottom"> </th>
101     </tr>
102     <tr>
103      <th align="right">Password:
104      </th>
105      <td>
106        <input type="Password" name="Password" size="5"
107                maxlength="8">
108      </td>
109     <td align="right"><b>Confirm:</b></td>
110      <td>
```

```
111              <input type="Password" name="PasswordConfirm" size="5"
112                   maxlength="8"
113                   onChange="validPassword(this.form.Password,
                      this, false)">
114         </td>
115         <td>
116           <small>6 - 8<br>char</small>
117         </td>
118       </tr>
119     </table>
120
121     <table>
122       <tr>
123         <th width="150"> </th>
124         <td colspan="4" align="left"><br>
125           <input type="submit" value="Send Data">
126           <input type="reset" value="Clear Form">
127         </td>
128       </tr>
129     </table>
130 </form>
131
132 </body>
133 </html>
```

Try the script for yourself. Enter some characters in the Password field and something different in the Confirm field. Press Send Data. You should receive an error message like this:

**Figure 13.4    Results of Script 13.4 when Password Entries Don't Match**

You may receive additional error messages depending on what you entered. We'll explain the functions that generate those in the following sections. Notice that after you click OK, the contents of the `Confirm` field are cleared (line 74) and the contents of the `Password` field are selected (line 75).

## validLength

The `validLength` function, defined in lines 18 through 27 of Script 13.4, can test the length of a password entry, proposed user name, etc. The `length` property of strings comes in handy for this. Remember, text box entries and password entries are strings, so they have a `length` property. To make this function usable for other data types, lines 19 through 21 first determine the argument's data type and turn it into a string if it's not one already.

To see it in action, rerun Script 13.4. This time type in matching passwords with less than six or more than eight characters to generate the error message seen here:

**Figure 13.5    Results of Script 13.4 when Password Entry Has Illegal Length**

That's pretty straightforward, huh?

## onlyLettersNnums

You may want to disallow the use of special characters in passwords; you almost certainly will want to in user names. You may want to allow only letters and numbers. The `onlyLettersNnums` function defined in lines 29 through 37 in Script 13.4 uses a regular expression to make certain the string sent to the function contains only the lowercase letters a–z, the uppercase letters A–Z, and the digits 0–9. All other characters are considered illegal, as specified by this regular expression declaration from line 30:

```
illegalChars = /[^a-zA-Z0-9]/
```

Recall from our discussion of regular expressions in Chapter 9 that the forward slashes (/) delimit the regular expression and the square brackets enclose the only possible choices. Notice the caret (^) inside the brackets; that reverses the choices, indicating that illegalChars are those characters that are *not* the lowercase letters a–z, the uppercase letters A–Z, or the digits 0–9. In other words, everything but those characters is considered an illegal character.

Try it out for yourself. Run Script 13.4 again, this time entering something that isn't a letter or a number, that is, enter at least one illegal character. An error message should pop up either when you tab out of the confirm box (real-time validation, line 113) or when you press the submit button (batch validation).

**Figure 13.6    Results of Script 13.4 when Illegal Characters Are Entered**

## Is the Password Strict Enough?

While we're on the subject of passwords, there's one more thing you might want to validate. Then again, you might not, so it is written as an optional choice. It's a good idea not to let your visitors choose passwords that are easy for intruders to guess, like a word from the dictionary, their significant other's name, or their kid's birthday. To prevent visitors from choosing easy-to-break passwords, you could require a more strict password entry. For instance, you could require that a password contain at least one uppercase letter, one lowercase letter, and one numeric digit.

Because this restriction applies only to passwords, we simply included it as an optional routine in the `validPassword` function that calls the other functions we talked about in this section. All of the other functions could be used for other purposes; this routine's rather specific (lines 62 through 71). It will only execute if the strict parameter is set to `true` (line 42). So you can see it run both ways, we called `validPassword` with strict set to `false` on the real-time validation (line 113), and strict set to `true` on the batch validation (lines 82 through 83).

## Validating an Email Address Entry

Perhaps the most requested piece of data on the Web is your email address. Many sites don't even ask for your name, they just want your email address so they can add you to their mailing list. Validating an email address can be very simple or very involved. The most simple function to validate an email address simply checks to see if the entry contains an @ symbol. That's certainly better than nothing, but I think we can do better. The W3C recognizes two valid options for the prefix of an email address (before the @ symbol) and two valid options for the suffix of an email address (after the @ symbol).

**Table 13.1     W3C Email Address Options**

| Email Prefixes | @ | Email Suffixes |
|---|---|---|
| `username` | | `somedomain.com` |
| `"name with spaces"` | @ | `[123.123.123.123]` |

According to the W3C, email addresses can start with either a user name, without spaces, or a user name that contains spaces and is delimited by quotation marks. An email address can end with a domain name followed by a TLD (top-level domain) or an IP address delimited by square brackets.

Keep in mind that a TLD can be either a generic top-level domain (gTLD), such as "com" for commercial, "org" for organization, or "biz" for business, or a country code top-level domain (ccTLD), such as "fr" for France, "au" for Australia, or "es" for Spain.

See Chapter 9 for a routine that validates email addresses. Your job, should you choose to accept it, is to turn that routine into a reusable function and place it in your form validation library. You'll need to expand on it in order to support all of the email address formats supported by the W3C (Table 13.1).

*programmer's tip*

Be careful of using email validation routines from script archives. Many of them assume a TLD is made up of only two or three characters and have not been updated to support the new gTLDs: aero, biz, coop, info, museum, name, and pro.

## Validating a Phone Number Entry

In the U.S., legitimate phone numbers are made up of a three-digit area code, a three-digit exchange code, and a four-digit number. The entire length of a complete phone number, not counting any extension, is 10 digits. The difficulty is that visitors are used to entering phone numbers in a variety of ways:

- ✗ (123)456-7890
- ✗ (123) 456-7890
- ✗ 123-456-7890

While data entry hints can help encourage the visitor to enter a phone number in the format you want, you might want to ensure the entry is valid yourself. To accomplish this, just strip all spaces, dashes, and parentheses from the entry and then check to see if it is a valid number and has 10 digits.

For non-U.S. phone numbers, the rules are different and vary by country. To validate an international phone number, you could use the following validation criteria:

- ✗ Allow the entry to begin with an optional plus sign (+).
- ✗ Strip all spaces, dashes, and parentheses and make certain that, otherwise, the entry contains only numeric digits.
- ✗ Allow the entry to be of any length.

See Chapter 9 for a routine that uses regular expressions to determine if a string represents a valid U.S. phone number. You can easily modify it to allow for international phone numbers as well, so we'll leave it as an exercise for you to turn that routine into a reusable function for your function library.

## Validating a Zip Code

This routine should also be easy to turn into a reusable function; we did just that in Chapter 9. Keep in mind that valid U.S. zip codes can be written either as five digits or as five digits, a hyphen, and four more digits: 12345 or 12345-6789. Canadian zip codes have six digits in the form of ANA NAN, where A represents a letter and N represents a numeric digit. Other countries have their own rules.

Using what you learned in Chapter 9, writing a validation routine for zip codes should be no sweat, so we'll leave it as an exercise.

*side note*

Internationalized domain names, that is, domain names in 39 different character sets for over 350 languages, are in the works. VeriSign Global Registry Services is conducting a test permitting registrants to submit internationalized domain names to the Registry. You are no longer limited to English-language character names when creating your Web identity. Cool, huh? Of course, validation just got more difficult.

# Validating a Credit Card Entry

With all the e-business going on nowadays, validating credit card entries has become an important task. While a client-side validation routine cannot possibly verify that a credit card is active and has available credit, it can verify that the number entered is at least of a valid form. So that's what we'll be concentrating on: verifying that the number entered is of a valid form and that the numbers form a valid combination.

Here are the basic rules for validating a few of the major credit cards:

**Table 13.2    Rules for Validating Credit Cards by Type**

| Card Type | Prefix | Length | Check-Digit Algorithm |
|-----------|--------|--------|------------------------|
| American Express | 34 or 37 | 15 digits | modulus 10 |
| Discover | 6011 | 16 digits | modulus 10 |
| MasterCard | 51 to 55 | 16 digits | modulus 10 |
| Visa | 4 | 13 to 16 digits | modulus 10 |

The prefix specifies the card type. The last digit of a credit card number is its check digit. The numbers in the middle identify the bank and the customer. What's a check digit?

A **check digit** is a digit added to a number that validates the authenticity of the number. To check the authenticity of a number, you run a simple algorithm on the digits of the number, excluding the check digit, which is either at the end or the beginning of the number. In the case of credit card numbers, the check digit is at the end. You then compare the result of the algorithm with the check digit; they should match. The algorithm preferred by most major credit card companies is **modulus 10**, also known as the LUHN formula.

The **LUHN formula** was created by a group of mathematicians in the 1960s and is in the public domain, so anyone can use it. It is a simple algorithm used to validate the number on a credit card. To illustrate each step as it is described, we'll try to validate the number 550000000004. Here's how it works:

1. Beginning with the second digit from the end (the last digit on the right is the end) and working right to left, take every other digit and multiply it by two.

   ```
    5    5    0    0    0    0    0    0    0    0    0    4
   x2        x2        x2        x2        x2        x2
   10         0         0         0         0         0
   ```

2. Proceeding from right to left, take each of the digits skipped in step 1, excluding the check digit, and add them to the *digits* that resulted from step 1.

   The digits that resulted from step 1 are listed in parentheses.

   ```
   (0)+0 + (0)+0 + (0)+0 + (0)+0 + (0)+5 + (1+0) = 6
   ```

Alternative method: Proceeding from right to left, take each of the digits skipped in step 1, including the check digit, and add them to the *digits* that resulted from step 1.

```
4 + (0)+0 + (0)+0 + (0)+0 + (0)+0 + (0)+5 + (1+0) = 10
```

3. Subtract the result obtained in step 2 from the next higher number that ends in 0. The result must agree with the check digit.

In this case, the result of step 2 was 6. The next higher number ending in zero is 10.

```
10 - 6 = 4
the check digit = 4 so they agree and the number is valid
```

Alternative method (works only if you used alternative method in step 2): If the sum of the digits is evenly divisible by 10, the number passes the modulus 10 test and is valid, that is, if the result modulus 10 = 0, then the number is valid.

In this case (the alternative method), the result of step 2 was 10.

```
10 % 10 = 0
the number is valid
```

Now you're probably wishing you'd never asked what a check digit was. But now that you know and at least have an inkling how the LUHN algorithm works, we can write a function to perform the credit card number test. Lines 42 through 76 of Script 13.5 define the passMod10 function.

Lines 50 through 60 correspond roughly with step 1 described above, beginning with the next to last digit and multiplying every other digit by 2. The primary difference is that the function goes ahead and adds up the digits resulting from the multiplication, since their sum will be used in the next step. Lines 62 through 66 take care of adding the skipped digits to the check sum. Lines 68 through 75 verify that the check sum passes the modulus 10 test: the check sum mod10 must equal 0 (line 69).

### Script 13.5    *Validating Credit Cards*

```
1    <html>
2    <head>
3        <title>Script 13.5: Validating Credit Cards</title>
4    <script language="JavaScript" type="text/javascript"><!--
5    function whichRadioChecked(radioSet) {
6        var checkedButton = -1
7        for(i=0; i<radioSet.length; i++) {
8            if(radioSet[i].checked) {
9                checkedButton = i
10               break
11           }
12       }
```

```
13          return checkedButton
14      }
15
16      function isEmpty(str) {
17          var empty = (str == null || str == "") ? true : false
18          return empty
19      }
20
21      function noneSelected(zSelectList, ckFirst) {
22          if(noneSelected.arguments.length == 1) {
23              var ckFirst = false
24          }
25          if(zSelectList.selectedIndex == -1 ||
26             zSelectList.selectedIndex == 0 && ckFirst) {
27              return true
28          } else {
29              return false
30          }
31      }
32
33      function noneChecked(zButtonSet) {
34          for(i=0; i<zButtonSet.length; i++) {
35              if(zButtonSet[i].checked) {
36                  return false
37              }
38          }
39          return true
40      }
41
42      function passMod10(ccNum) {
43          if(typeof(ccNum) != "string") {
44              ccNum = ccNum.toString()
45          }
46          var checkDigit = parseInt(ccNum.charAt(ccNum.length - 1))
47          var checkSum = 0
48          var currDigit = 0
49
50          // Step 1: start with next to last digit and work left,
51          // multiplying every other digit by 2, add results to
             checkSum
52          for (i=ccNum.length -2; i>=0; i-=2) {
53              currDigit = parseInt(ccNum.charAt(i)) * 2
54              if(currDigit < 10) {
55                  checkSum += currDigit
56              } else {
```

```
57                              checkSum += currDigit - 10
58                              checkSum += 1                    // for 10's place
59                      }
60              }
61
62              // Step 2: add skipped digits to checkSum
63              for (i=ccNum.length - 1; i>=0; i-=2) {
64                      currDigit = parseInt(ccNum.charAt(i))
65                      checkSum += currDigit
66              }
67
68              // Step 3: verify passes modulus 10 test
69              if (checkSum % 10 == 0) {
70                      // passes
71                      return true
72              } else {
73                      // doesn't pass
74                      return false
75              }
76      }
77
78      function cardExpired(ccExpMo, ccExpYr) {
79              var today = new Date()
80              var currYr = today.getFullYear()
81
82              ccExpYr = parseInt(ccExpYr)
83              if(currYr < ccExpYr) {
84                      return false
85              } else if (ccExpYr == currYr) {
86                      var currMo = today.getMonth()
87                      ccExpMo = parseInt(ccExpMo) - 1
88                      if (currMo <= ccExpMo) {
89                              return false
90                      }
91              }
92              return true
93      }
94
95      function validCC(ccNum, ccType) {
96              var valid = false
97              switch (ccType) {
98              case "AmerEx":
99                      if (ccNum.length == 15 &&
100                     (ccNum.substring(0,2) == "34" ||
101                      ccNum.substring(0,2) == "37")) {
```

```
102                     valid = passMod10(ccNum)
103                 }
104             break
105     case "Discover":
106             if (ccNum.length == 16 &&
107                 ccNum.substring(0,4) == "6011") {
108                     valid = passMod10(ccNum)
109             }
110             break
111     case "MC":
112             if ((ccNum.length == 16 && ccNum.chatAt(0) == "5")
                    &&
113                 (parseInt(ccNum.charAt(1)) >=1 &&
114                 parseInt(ccNum.charAt(1) <=5))) {
115                     valid = passMod10(ccNum)
116             }
117             break
118     case "Visa":
119             if ((ccNum.length >= 13 && ccNum.length <= 16) &&
120                 ccNum.substring(0,1) == "4") {
121                     valid = passMod10(ccNum)
122             }
123             break
124     }
125     return valid
126 }
127
128 function validate(zForm) {
129     if (noneChecked(zForm.CCtype)) {
130             alert ("Error! Please specify credit card type.")
131             return false
132     }
133
134     if (noneSelected(zForm.CCexpMo, true) ||
135         noneSelected(zForm.CCexpYr, true)) {
136         alert ("Error! Please specify an expiration date.")
137             return false
138     }
139
140     if (cardExpired(zForm.CCexpMo[zForm.CCexpMo.
            selectedIndex].value,
141         zForm.CCexpYr[zForm.CCexpYr.selectedIndex].value)) {
142             alert ("Error! Credit card has expired.")
143             return false
144     }
```

```
145
146        if (!validCC(zForm.CCnum.value,
147            zForm.CCtype[whichRadioChecked
                  (zForm.CCtype)].value)) {
148            alert("Error! Invalid card number.")
149            return false
150        }
151        return true
152 }
153 //-->
154 </script>
155 </head>
156 <body>
157 <h1>Validating Credit Cards</h1>
158 <form action="" method="post" name="CustomerData"
159        onSubmit="return validate(this)">
160    <table border=0>
161      <tr>
162        <th width="150" align="right" valign="bottom">
163          <h3>Payment Info</h3></th>
164        <th colspan="5" align="left" valign="bottom"> </th>
165      </tr>
166      <tr>
167        <th width="150" align="right">Credit Card Type:</th>
168        <td colspan="4">
169          <input type="Radio" name="CCtype" value="Visa">Visa
170            
171          <input type="Radio" name="CCtype" value="MC">MasterCard
172            
173          <input type="Radio" name="CCtype"
                 value="Discover">Discover
174            
175          <input type="Radio" name="CCtype"
                 value="AmerEx">American
176          Express
177        </td>
178      </tr>
179      <tr>
180        <th width="150" align="right">Card Number:</th>
181        <td>
182          <input name="CCnum" type="text" size="25" maxlength="20"
183                 onFocus="window.status='1234567890123456';
                        return true"
184                 onBlur="window.status=''; return true"></td>
185        <th align="right"><b>Expires:</b></th>
```

```
186          <td>
187            <select name="CCexpMo">
188                    <option value="">Month</option>
189                    <option value="01">01</option>
190                    <option value="02">02</option>
191                    <option value="03">03</option>
192                    <option value="04">04</option>
193                    <option value="05">05</option>
194                    <option value="06">06</option>
195                    <option value="07">07</option>
196                    <option value="08">08</option>
197                    <option value="09">09</option>
198                    <option value="10">10</option>
199                    <option value="11">11</option>
200                    <option value="12">12</option>
201          </select>
202          <select name="CCexpYr">
203                    <option value="">Year</option>
204                    <option value="2005">2005</option>
205                    <option value="2006">2006</option>
206                    <option value="2007">2007</option>
207                    <option value="2008">2008</option>
208                    <option value="2009">2009</option>
209                    <option value="2010">2010</option>
210                    <option value="2011">2011</option>
211                    <option value="2012">2012</option>
212                    <option value="2013">2013</option>
213          </select></td>
214          </tr>
215 </table>
216
217 <table>
218      <tr>
219        <th width="150"> </th>
220        <td colspan="4" align="left"><br>
221          <input type="submit" value="Send Data">
222          <input type="reset" value="Clear Form">
223        </td>
224      </tr>
225 </table>
226 </form>
227
228 </body>
229 </html>
```

Of course, we should first perform two other checks on a credit card number before doing the modulus 10 test: verify that the card number begins with the proper prefix for the card type specified and make certain the card number is of the proper length for the card type specified. If the card number doesn't have the right prefix or length, why bother running the modulus 10 test?

The function `validCC`, defined in lines 95 through 126, performs the overall credit card validation and calls the `passMod10` function only after first verifying that the card has the proper prefix for the card type specified and is of the proper length (lines 97 through 124). The `validCC` function is called in lines 146–147 of the `validate` function.

Here's what the error message looks like if an invalid card number is entered.

**Figure 13.7    Results of Script 13.5 if Invalid Card Number Entered**

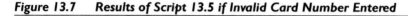

Keep in mind that a card number could be invalid because (1) it had an inappropriate length for the card type specified, (2) it did not have the correct prefix, or (3) it did not pass the modulus 10 test.

Come to think of it, we probably should first check to see if the card has expired before doing *anything* else. The function `cardExpired`, defined in lines 78 through 93 and called in lines 140–141, takes care of that. Here's the type of error generated by an expired credit card:

**Figure 13.8 Results of Script 13.5 when Credit Card Has Expired**

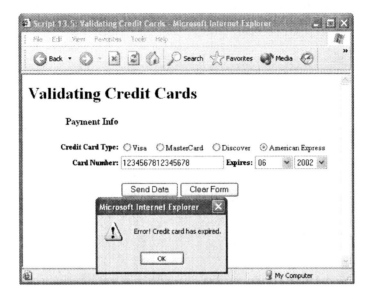

# Using Images to Display Error Messages Inline

Some visitors find alert dialog boxes annoying. Besides startling them by beeping when they least expect it, the dialog boxes also require them to click on the OK button before they can proceed. Fortunately, there is another way to display error messages: inline as images. Here's an example:

**Script 13.6 Using Images to Display Error Messages Inline**

```
1   <!doctype html public "-//W3C//DTD HTML 4.0 Frameset//EN">
2   <html>
3   <head>
4   <title>Script 13.6: Using Images to Display Error Messages
5        Inline</title>
6   <script language="JavaScript" type="text/javascript"><!--
7   function isEmpty(str) {
8        var empty = (str == null || str == "") ? true : false
9        return empty
10  }
11
12  function noneChecked(zButtonSet) {
13       for(i=0; i<zButtonSet.length; i++) {
14            if(zButtonSet[i].checked) {
15                 return false
16            }
```

```
17          }
18          return true
19   }
20
21   // Preload images
22   var noError = new Image()
23   noError.src = "images/blank.gif"
24   var emptyName = new Image()
25   emptyName.src = "images/emptyName.gif"
26   var emptyEmail = new Image()
27   emptyEmail.src = "images/emptyEmail.gif"
28   var noGender = new Image()
29   noGender.src = "images/noGender.gif"
30   var noColor = new Image()
31   noColor.src = "images/noColor.gif"
32
33   var haveError = false
34
35   function swapImage(img, newSrc, error) {
36          img.src = newSrc
37          if (!haveError && error) {
38                 haveError = error
39          }
40   }
41
42   function clearForm() {
43          var clearIt = confirm("Are you sure you want to clear the
             form?")
44          if (clearIt) {
45                 swapImage(document.NameError, noError.src, false)
46                 swapImage(document.EmailError, noError.src, false)
47                 swapImage(document.GenderError, noError.src, false)
48                 swapImage(document.FavColorsError, noError.src,
                    false)
49          }
50          return clearIt
51   }
52
53   function validate(zForm) {
54          haveError = false
55
56          if (isEmpty(zForm.Visitor.value)) {
57                 swapImage(document.NameError, emptyName.src, true)
58          } else {
```

```
59              swapImage(document.NameError, noError.src, false)
60          }
61
62      if (isEmpty(zForm.Email.value)) {
63              swapImage(document.EmailError, emptyEmail.src, true)
64      } else {
65              swapImage(document.EmailError, noError.src, false)
66      }
67
68      if (noneChecked(zForm.Gender)) {
69              swapImage(document.GenderError, noGender.src, true)
70      } else {
71              swapImage(document.GenderError, noError.src, false)
72      }
73
74      if (noneChecked(zForm.FavColors)) {
75              swapImage(document.FavColorsError, noColor.src,
                true)
76      } else {
77              swapImage(document.FavColorsError, noError.src,
                false)
78      }
79
80      return (!haveError)
81  }
82  //-->
83  </script>
84
85  </head>
86  <body>
87  <h1>Trivial Survey</h1>
88  <form action="" method="POST" name="TrivialSurvey"
89      onSubmit="return validate(this)"
90      onReset="return clearForm()">
91    <table border=0>
92      <tr>
93        <th width="150" align="right">Name:</th>
94        <td colspan="3">
95          <input name="Visitor" type="text" size="40"
96                maxlength="40">
97          <font color="#ff0000">*</font><br>
98          <img name="NameError" src="images/blank.gif"
99                width=350 height=10 border=0></td>
100     </tr>
```

```
101        <tr>
102          <th width="150" align="right">Email:</th>
103          <td colspan="3">
104            <input name="Email" type="text" size="40"
105                 maxlength="64">
106          <font color="#ff0000">*</font><br>
107          <img name="EmailError" src="images/blank.gif"
108               width=350 height=10 border=0></td>
109        </tr>
110        <tr>
111          <th width="150" align="right">Gender:</th>
112          <td colspan="3">
113            <input type="Radio" name="Gender" value="female">
114          Female  
115            <input type="Radio" name="Gender" value="male">Male
116            <font color="#ff0000">*</font></td>
117        </tr>
118        <tr>
119          <th width="150" align="right">
120            <img src="images/blankSm.gif" width=10 height=10
121                 border=0></th>
122          <td colspan="3">
123            <img name="GenderError" src="images/blank.gif"
124                 width=350 height=10 border=0>
125          </td>
126        </tr>
127        <tr>
128          <th width="150" align="right"
129              valign="top">Favorite Colors:<br>
130          <small>(check all that apply)</small></th>
131          <td valign="top">
132            <input type="Checkbox" name="FavColors" value="Black">
133            <font color="#000000">Black</font><br>
134            <input type="Checkbox" name="FavColors" value="Gray">
135            <font color="#666666">Gray</font><br>
136            <input type="Checkbox" name="FavColors" value="Red">
137            <font color="#FF0000">Red</font><br>
138            <input type="Checkbox" name="FavColors" value="Pink">
139            <font color="#FF3399">Pink</font><br> </td>
140          <td valign="top">
141            <input type="Checkbox" name="FavColors" value="Orange">
142            <font color="#FF8000">Orange</font><br>
143            <input type="Checkbox" name="FavColors" value="Yellow">
```

```
144         <font color="#F0F000">Yellow</font> <br>
145         <input type="Checkbox" name="FavColors" value="Green">
146         <font color="#008000">Green</font> <br>
147         <input type="Checkbox" name="FavColors" value="Blue">
148         <font color="#0000FF">Blue</font> </td>
149       <td valign="top">
150         <input type="Checkbox" name="FavColors" value="Violet">
151         <font color="#800080">Violet</font>  
152         <font color="#ff0000">*</font><br>
153         <input type="Checkbox" name="FavColors" value="White">
154         White <br>
155         <input type="Checkbox" name="FavColors" value="Other">
156         Other
157         <input type="Text" name="FavColorOther" size="7"
158             maxlength="15">
159         <br><br> </td>
160     </tr>
161     <tr>
162       <th width="150" align="right">
163         <img src="images/blankSm.gif" width=10 height=10
164             border=0></th>
165       <td colspan="3">
166         <img name="FavColorsError" src="images/blank.gif"
167             width=350 height=10 border=0>
168       </td>
169     </tr>
170     <tr>
171       <th width="150"> </th>
172       <td colspan="3" align="left">
173         <small><font color="#ff0000"><sup>*</sup>
174         </font> denotes required field.</small>
175       </td>
176     </tr>
177
178     <tr>
179       <th width="150"> </th>
180       <td colspan="3" align="left">
181         <input type="submit" value="Send Survey">
182         <input type="reset" value="Clear Form">
183       </td>
184     </tr>
185   </table>
186 </form>
```

```
187 </body>
188 </html>
```

Blank images are inserted at lines 98–99, 107–108, 123–125, and 166–167. These images act as placeholders. During the batch validation, if an error is encountered, the blank image is replaced with an image displaying the appropriate error message (lines 56 through 78). You'll find the images for this example on the CD that accompanies this book. Look in the images folder under scripts. You'll want to create your own images to match your own validation needs. They're pretty easy to create, because they contain only text.

**Figure 13.9** **Results of Script 13.6 when Required Fields Not Completed**

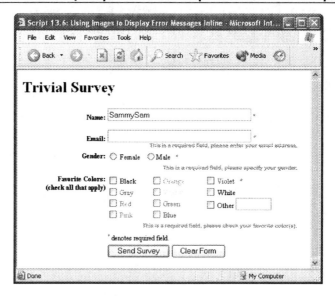

If an error is corrected, the image is replaced with a blank image (lines 59, 65, 69, and 71). Here's the same form showing two of the initial errors corrected. A valid email address has now been entered and a gender has been chosen.

### Figure 13.10    Results of Script 13.6 after Correcting Some Errors

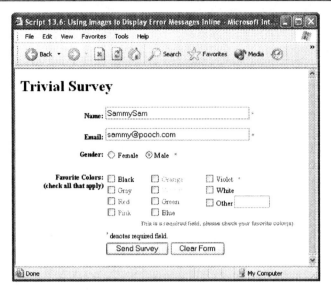

As you can see in Figure 13.10, now only the "Favorite Colors" area needs an entry, as indicated by the image that says "This is a required field . . . ."

If the visitor clears the form, the original blank images must be restored. The clearForm function (lines 42 to 51) takes care of that. Figure 13.11 shows how the form would look after the visitor clicked the Clear Form button.

### Figure 13.11    The Cleared Form

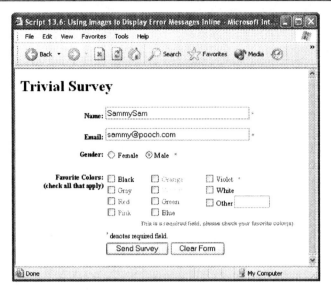

All in all, I like this method of displaying errors the best. It does require some extra work, though. You have to create an image for every error message.

# Summary

Form validation is the process of checking the data entered into a form to verify that all required data has been provided and that the data submitted is of the proper format. Form validation can be performed client-side or server-side. While client-side validation is fast and responsive, if the visitor's browser has scripting turned off, the data will not be validated. Server-side scripting is less responsive and can place heavy demands on the server, but it *is* guaranteed to be executed, regardless of the visitor's browser settings. A combination of the two is the best way to go.

There are two methods by which client-side validation can be performed: batch and real-time. Batch validation is performed all at once when the form is submitted. Real-time validation is performed on a particular field as soon as the visitor changes the field.

Batch validation functions are called using the onSubmit event handler. Preceding the validate function call with the keyword return is essential. Without return, the result of the validation routine cannot get back to the event handler and cancel or continue the form's submission. The special keyword this also plays an important role in client-side form validation. It always refers to the current object and can make passing form objects, form elements, and field values clear-cut and concise.

As you develop new functions for form validation, it's a good idea to begin a form validation library. Before adding any function to a library, you should test it thoroughly, comment it, and provide a detailed description. Then test it again.

In general, there are two types of form validation tasks: those that verify that a particular form element has an entry and those that verify whether an entry is of a valid format. In this chapter, we developed three functions that can be used to verify that a particular type of form element has an entry:

- ⬦ isEmpty, for testing text boxes, password fields, and textareas.
- ⬦ noneSelected, for testing select lists to verify that at least one option has been selected.
- ⬦ noneChecked, for testing sets of radio buttons and checkboxes.

When validating passwords, there are several criteria to consider. We looked at each criterion and developed an appropriate function to test it:

- ⬦ Do the password and the confirming password match? Function: noMatch.
- ⬦ Is the password of the right length? Function: validLength.
- ⬦ Does the password contain illegal characters? Function: onlyLettersNnums.
- ⬦ Is the password strict enough? Part of the validPassword function.

Validating email addresses is a little more complicated. The W3C recognizes two valid options for the prefix (a user name with no spaces or a user name with spaces, delimited by quotation marks) and two for the suffix (a domain name followed by a TLD or an IP address delimited by square brackets) of an email address. These criteria need to be taken into account when developing routines that validate email addresses.

Validating credit card entries has become an important task. While client-side scripting cannot verify that a credit card is active and has available credit, it can verify that the card number is at least of a valid form. Two rules and one algorithm can validate whether or not a credit card number is valid. Each card type has a particular prefix and a particular length or range of lengths. In addition, the LUHN formula, developed by mathematicians in the 1960s, placed in the public domain, and adopted by most of the major credit card companies, can validate the authenticity of the credit card number.

The LUHN formula relies on a check digit, the last number of a credit card, and a simple algorithm that creates a check sum that must match the check digit in order for the card number to be valid. We developed a function called `passMod10` based on this algorithm. The LUHN formula is also known as the modulus 10 test.

In addition, we developed a function named `validCC` to validate credit cards according to the three criteria mentioned above. We also developed a routine to verify whether or not a card had expired: `cardExpired`.

While alert dialog boxes are effective for displaying error messages during form validation, some visitors find them annoying and intrusive. An alternative to alert dialog boxes is error messages that are inserted inline as images. Script 13.6 demonstrates how to accomplish this task.

## Review Questions

1. What is form validation?
2. List five things one might test for in a batch form validation routine.
3. What advantage does client-side validation have over server-side validation?
4. What advantage does server-side validation have over client-side validation?
5. Which is better, client-side or server-side validation? Explain your reasoning.
6. What's the difference between batch and real-time validation?
7. How are batch validation routines usually called?
8. How are real-time validation routines usually called?
9. Before adding a function to a library, you should comment the code and provide a description. What three things should you include in your description?
10. What property of a select object tells you whether or not an option has been selected? What returned value indicates that no selection was made?
11. What property of a checkbox is a Boolean value indicating whether or not the box has been checked?
12. Why ask a visitor to confirm a password request?
13. Can you check the length of a number directly? If so, how? If not, what could you do to find out how many digits a number contains?
14. Why are passwords and user names usually of some particular length?
15. What advantage do longer passwords have?

16. Should you use your significant other's name as a password? Why or why not?
17. What are some criteria for a secure password?
18. Why should you consider requiring more strict passwords, such as passwords that contain both letters and numbers?
19. What is a check digit?
20. What is the LUHN formula? Why is it also known as the modulus 10 test?

# Exercises

1. Write an HTML tag with an appropriate event handler to call a `VerifyForm` function when a document is submitted. If `VerifyForm` returns `true` the form should be submitted, if `false` it should be aborted. Pass the form object to the function.
2. Write an HTML tag with an appropriate event handler to call a `validPhone` function when a field is modified. Pass the field's entry as an argument to the `validPhone` function.
3. Write the opening tag of a select list and apply an event handler to call a `setTaxRate` function when an option is selected from the list.
4. Write an HTML tag with an appropriate event handler to create a button that when clicked calls a function named `popupMap`. The name of the button should be passed to the `popupMap` function as an argument.
5. Create two password fields with HTML. Name and label them as you see fit. Add an appropriate event handler to the second password field that calls a `comparePasswords` function to compare the two values once an entry has been made in the second box. Pass the values of both password fields to the function. You are not given the form's name. You don't even know which form in the document the fields are in, so write your event handler accordingly. You do not have to write the function.

# Scripting Exercises

Create a folder named assignment13 to hold the documents you create during this assignment. Save a copy of your latest toy store documents in a toyStore subfolder. Create a document named validationLib.js and save it in the scripts folder off of the root of your Web site.

1. Write a `validInternationalPhone` function that returns true if the value passed to it appears to be a valid phone number entry, as far as its format goes, and false if not.

   You may use regular expressions if you wish to validate the entry. Test and debug the function. When you're satisfied that it works as needed, add it to validationLib.js along with an appropriate description and comments.
2. Write a `validCAzip` function that returns true if the value passed to it appears, by format, to be a valid Canadian zip code. You may choose to write a zip code

validation function for some other country, other than the U.S. or Canada, if you wish. If so, change the function's name accordingly.

Use regular expressions to validate the entry. Test and debug the function. When you're satisfied that it works as needed, add it to validationLib.js along with an appropriate description and comments.

3. Write a `validFullName` function that verifies that an entry is at least two words, separated by a space. It's OK if the entry contains more than two words. No special characters except those usually used in names, such as spaces, hyphens, apostrophes, commas, and periods, should be allowed. Here are some examples demonstrating when these characters might be used:

- ≩ John von Neumann
- ≩ Maria Sklodowska-Curie
- ≩ Sandra Day O'Connor
- ≩ Martin Luther King, Jr.

Test and debug the function. When you're satisfied that it works as needed, add it to validationLib.js along with an appropriate description and comments.

4. Create a Customer Data form for your Toy Store Web site to collect the following data:

- ≩ First name
- ≩ Last name
- ≩ Individual or Company?
- ≩ Company name
- ≩ Billing address (address, city, state, and zip)
- ≩ Ship to billing address?
- ≩ Shipping address (address, city, state, and zip)

Using JavaScript, set up the appropriate functionality as listed below.

- ≩ If not an individual, require that company name be provided.
- ≩ If ship to billing address is checked, copy data into shipping address fields.
- ≩ If ship to billing address is not checked, require that shipping address fields be completed.

Test and debug your program.

5. Rewrite Script 13.6 to include real-time validation.

# Projects

## Project 1: Putting It All Together

Throughout this and the previous chapter, we've written functions to perform the various tasks needed to validate the Javabilaya Customer Data form. Now it's your turn to put them all together into a batch validation routine. Use the `CustomerData` form from the previous chapter.

**Figure 13.12    Customer Data Form to Validate for Project 13.1**

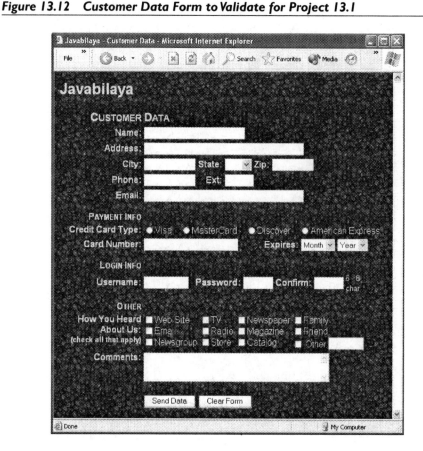

You can attach your form validation library as an external JavaScript, but embed your `validate` function in the <head> of the document as it applies only to this particular form. Don't forget to add real-time validations to the appropriate fields as well.

Consider every field required data and make certain any text box entries are of the proper format for the data requested. You're going to have to write a few more functions to get the job done. If the functions are totally reusable, add them to your library; if not, embed them in the <head> of the document.

Upload and test your project. Turn in a print-out of your code.

## Project 2: Amazing Exercise Ball Order Form

Write a program to validate and total the order form shown below for the The Amazing Exercise Ball. Use the order form provided (Figure 13.13), but change the mailto to your own email address or use a URL to a functioning FormMail program.

*Figure 13.13   Form for Project 13.2*

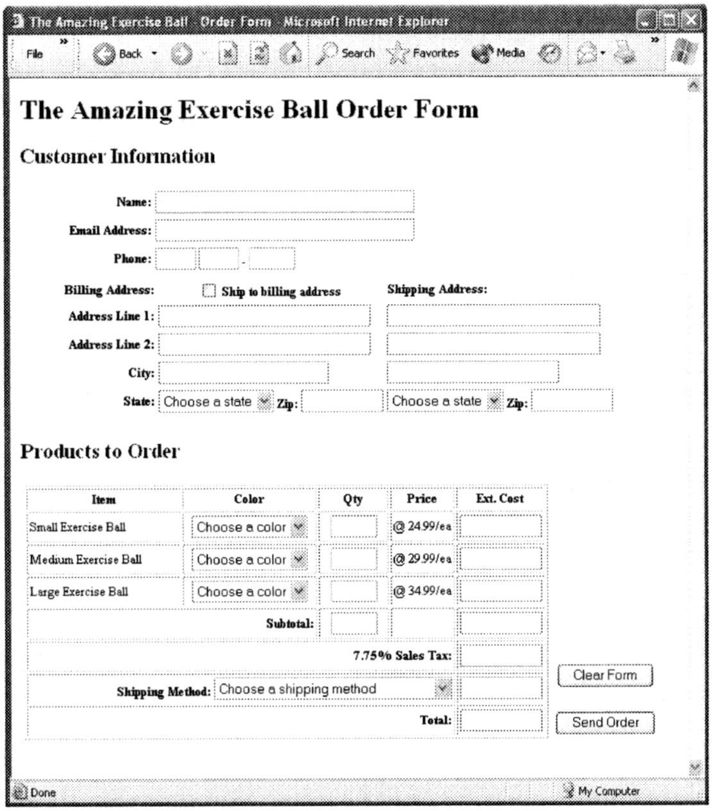

Your program should verify the following:

⚡ A customer name has been entered.

⚡ The form of the email address is valid.

    ⚡ If an invalid email address has been entered, return focus to the email field.

    ⚡ Select (highlight) the contents of the field.

⚡ Only numbers have been entered in the phone number fields.

⚡ If "Ship to billing address" has been checked, no shipping address is required. If it has *not* been checked, require a shipping address.

⚡ At least Line 1 of the billing address has been provided. Line 2 is optional.

⚡ A city has been entered.

⚡ A state has been chosen.

⚡ A valid zip code has been provided. The zip code may also include a dash and four digits, for example, 92102-1317.

⚡ At least one product has been ordered.

⚡ Only integers are entered in the quantity fields.

✄ For each item ordered, a color is chosen.

✄ A valid shipping method has been chosen for the quantity of items ordered. If the customer chooses an invalid shipping method, you should suggest either the correct priority method, UPS, or free shipping, whichever is appropriate for the number of items ordered. Then automatically select that shipping method for the customer.

Additionally, your program should perform the following:

✄ Calculate the extended cost of a line item after a quantity has been entered.

✄ Subtotal the quantity and extended cost columns after each change.

✄ Calculate the sales tax after each change.

✄ Enter the shipping amount in the extended cost column when a shipping method is chosen.

✄ Total the order.

✄ Confirm that the user does indeed wish to clear the form before clearing its contents.

Upload and test your project. Turn in a print-out of your code.

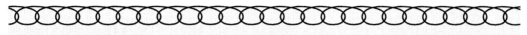

## chapter *fourteen*

# Cookies

In Chapter 11, we saw one way to save state: store data in a static frame variable. While this technique is good for storing data during one session, it does not allow you to save data between visits. Enter cookies.

In this chapter we'll

- review what it means to save state.
- define the term "cookies."
- debunk cookie rumors with a taste of reality.
- discuss the limitations of cookies.
- learn where various browsers hide the cookie jar.
- see how to manage cookies in the latest browsers.
- write functions to create, read, modify, and delete cookies.
- use cookies to save information between visits.
- implement a simple shopping cart.

Grab a cookie and a glass of milk and we'll get started.

# Saving State

Before discussing the concept of cookies, it helps to have a good understanding of the concept of saving state. In Chapter 11, we defined **saving state** as preserving information about the current session as a visitor browses through documents on a Web site. Recall that a **session** begins when a visitor enters a particular Web site and ends when he or she leaves that particular Web site. A **browser session**, on the other hand, begins when a person opens his or her Web browser and ends when he or she closes the browser. An understanding of the distinction between the two types of sessions is important to our discussion of cookies, as you'll see shortly. For now, file their respective definitions away in the back of your mind for retrieval later in this chapter.

Storing data in variables defined in a static frame, as demonstrated in Chapter 11, and storing data in hidden form fields are just two of four ways of saving state. The other two are server-side scripting and cookies.

## Saving State with Server-side Scripting

Server-side scripting is complex and beyond the scope of this book. Suffice it to say that most server-side technologies, including CGI scripting with Perl, ASP, PHP, and Server-Side JavaScript, can track session information and easily write data about the current session to a database for retrieval at the next visit.

Cookies can be generated by either server-side scripts or client-side scripts. Because this book is about Client-Side JavaScript, we'll, of course, focus on the latter.

# What Are Cookies?

The term **cookie** is not an acronym. The term has been around for a long time in the computing world. According to Lou Montulli, who wrote the cookie specification for Netscape Navigator 1.0, the first Web browser to use cookie technology,

> *A cookie is a well-known computer science term that is used when describing an opaque piece of data held by an intermediary. The term fits the usage precisely; it's just not a well-known term outside of computer science circles.*

In the case of cookies on the Web, the *intermediary* is the hard drive on the visitor's computer.

Netscape's formal name for a browser cookie is **Persistent Client-Side HTTP Object**. By breaking apart this lofty title, we can gain a clearer insight into what a cookie is and how it works. So let's dissect the name.

## Persistent

Cookies are persistent in that they are often stored on a Web site visitor's hard drive, rather than solely in memory. HTML alone does not provide any way to save state between Web document requests, let alone between sessions. HTML alone cannot perform shopping cart functions or remember user preferences between visits. Cookies can, however, by writing that information to memory temporarily and eventually to the visitor's hard drive permanently. In the case of a shopping cart, the information may be stored for only a few hours or until the visitor closes the browser. In the case of storing user preferences, the cookie's expiration date likely is set to a year or more in the future. Whether cookies last for years, months, or merely hours, they "persist." They save state.

## Client-side

Cookies exist only on the client side, that is, on the client computer, the computer making requests of a Web server. It is important to remember that. Because cookies are stored on visitor computers, we, as programmers, have little real control of the information. The visitor is free to delete our cookies at any time and even to refuse to accept them in the first place.

## HTTP

Cookies are associated with Web pages and created according to HTTP (Hypertext Transfer Protocol). Technically, a cookie is an HTTP header that contains a string of data to be stored by the client machine in browser memory and, in the case of longer-lasting cookies, eventually on the client's hard drive for later retrieval. The data is usually retrieved when another page in the current Web site is requested (shopping cart) or when the visitor next visits the Web site (user preferences).

**side note**

**Turning off the Cookie Function**

*In Netscape:* Edit → Preferences → Advanced → Cookies → Disable Cookies.
*In Internet Explorer:* Tools → Internet Options → Security → Custom Level button → scroll down to Cookies → Disable Cookies.
*In Opera:* File → Preferences → Privacy → from Cookies drop-down list, choose "Do not accept cookies."

Here's how it works:

1. The user types a URL in the location bar of the browser or clicks on a link to request a Web document.
2. Before contacting the Web server to request the specified document, the browser checks its list of cookies. Does the URL in the location bar match any of the cookies in the list?
3. If it does, then a header is added to the HTTP request containing the name-value pairs of all cookies that match the requested URL. In other words, the browser passes a line of text comprised of the name and value of each cookie from the browser's cookie list that matched the requested URL along with the requested URL. Here's what the header (line of text) looks like:

```
Cookie: cookieName1=someValue; cookieName2=someValue
```

4. If the server desires to write a cookie, then it adds a header to the HTTP response containing the name and value of the cookie, a path, the expiration date, etc. Here's what the header might look like:

```
Set-Cookie: cookieName=someValue; path=/; expires=someDate
```

This system allows server-side scripts, as well as client-side scripts, to access cookie information and write cookies. A server-side script might use the information stored in the cookie to generate a custom Web page based on past interactions with that visitor and send it back to the browser.

## Objects

Cookies are objects. In Client-Side JavaScript, the `cookie` property of the `document` object, `document.cookie`, handles cookie function. It is an object containing all valid cookies for the current Web page. Whenever you assign a value to the `document.cookie` object, a cookie is created. Here's an example:

```
document.cookie = "tipsPref=false; path=/; expires=Fri, ⇢
    ⇢ 01-Jan-2100 00:00:00 GMT"
```

`tipsPref` is the name of the cookie and `false` is the value of the cookie.

You can retrieve all of the cookies valid for the current Web page by reading the `document.cookie` object.

So cookies are Persistent Client-Side HTTP Objects because they are objects that persist on the client's hard drive and are written and transferred from browser to server and vice versa according to HTTP.

## Uses for Cookies

So what's all the hoopla about? What good are cookies anyway? As it turns out, there are many excellent and well-meaning uses for cookies, including

- ✗ saving visitor preferences between visits.
- ✗ storing a visitor's user name and password between visits so he doesn't have to reenter it every time.
- ✗ personalizing the information that's displayed, like on My Yahoo!, My Netscape, or Excite.
- ✗ automatically displaying content relevant to a visitor's previous choices.
- ✗ assisting with online sales (shopping carts).
- ✗ helping with back-end processing, such as interactions with databases.

There are also some not-so-well-meaning uses of cookies, including

- ✗ collecting detailed information about your Web surfing habits.
- ✗ tracking the demographics of visitors by the links they click on.
- ✗ tracking the popularity of various Web sites.

We'll discuss these abuses of cookies in more detail a little later on when we talk about cookies and privacy. For now, let's examine the ingredients of a cookie.

# Cookie Ingredients

All cookies must be baked to specification (the HTTP protocol). Only two ingredients are required to bake a cookie: name and value. However, you can spice up a cookie with an expiration date, a path, and a domain for which it is valid. You can even make a cookie accessible only via a secure server connection. Let's look at each ingredient in turn.

## name

The name ingredient specifies the name of the cookie entry. It labels the information you want to store. When a cookie is set, its name is followed by an equals sign and the value of the cookie. A cookie's name is similar to a variable name in that it is the label you use to access the stored data. The same naming rules that apply to variables apply to cookies. Name and value are the only required ingredients to bake a cookie.

One more thing: always give your cookies *unique* names. If you create a new cookie using the same name and path as an existing cookie, the original cookie is overwritten.

## value

The value ingredient specifies the value of the cookie entry. It is the information you wish to save during or between sessions. A cookie's value can be set to null to clear it. Here's an example of setting a cookie's name and value in JavaScript:

```
document.cookie = "tipPref=false"
```

where tipPref is the name of the cookie and false is the value of the cookie. This cookie would keep track of whether the visitor wants to see pop-up tips displayed.

Here's an example of clearing the tipPref cookie's value:

```
document.cookie = "tipPref=null"
```

Now that we've looked at the basic ingredients, name and value, let's move on to the spices.

## expires

The expires ingredient defines the lifespan of a cookie. It must be supplied in GMT format, also known as UTC format (Wdy, DD-MON-YYYY HH:MM:SS GMT). If an expiration date is not supplied, it defaults to *end-of-browser-session*; that is, the cookie expires when the browser is shut down. During the browser session in which the cookie is created, the cookie remains in memory for easy retrieval. A cookie without an expiration date, which expires at the end of the browser session, is known as a **session cookie** or **transient cookie**.

If an expiration date is specified and is some date and time in the future, then the browser writes the cookie to a cookie file on the client's hard drive at the end of the browser session. When a cookie's expiration date and time has passed, the cookie is immediately deleted from the client's hard drive and memory.

## path

The `path` ingredient specifies the URL path the cookie is valid within, that is, it specifies the path name of URLs allowed to access the cookie. Any Web pages in that path *or directories below it* have full rights to the cookie. Web pages outside of that path have no rights to the cookie, that is, they cannot read, modify, or delete the cookie. If a path is not specified, it defaults to the URL path of the document that created the cookie in the first place. Here are some examples of how `path` would be set by default:

- ⚡ If the document that creates the cookie is located in the root directory of a Web site, by default, `path` is set to `/`. Any Web documents in the Web site can access the cookie.
- ⚡ If the document that creates the cookie is located in the products subdirectory, by default, `path` is set to `/products`. Only Web documents in the products directory and its subdirectories can access the cookie. Documents in the root or any other directory cannot access a cookie whose path is `/products`.
- ⚡ If the document that creates the cookie is located in the widget subdirectory of the products subdirectory, by default, `path` is set to `/products/widgets`. Only Web documents in the widgets subdirectory of products and in subdirectories of widgets can access the cookie. Documents in the root, in products, or in any other directory cannot access the cookie.

The most common `path` setting is `/`, because it makes the cookie accessible by documents in the root and all subdirectories of the Web site. So to make a cookie visible throughout your Web site, set

```
path=/
```

Then every page in your Web site can access it.

## domain

The `domain` ingredient specifies the valid domain for a cookie. By default, `domain` is set to the full domain name of the server that generated the cookie. If a Web site uses multiple servers, however, you may want to make a cookie accessible by all of those servers. Usually, the setting

```
domain=.mydomainname.com
```

will get the job done. In this example, any servers in the mydomainname.com domain can access the cookie, including www.mydomainname.com, machine1.mydomainname.com, studentweb.mydomainname.com, etc.

The domain value must *always* contain at least two dots. For example, for the top-level domains, you should use

```
.mydomainname.com
```

not

```
mydomainname.com
```

For extended domains, use three or more dots:

```
.cuyamaca.cc.ca.us
```

not

```
cuyamaca.cc.ca.us
```

For security reasons, the server that issues a cookie has to be a member of the domain that it attempts to set as the cookie's `domain`. In other words, a server called www.mydomain.com cannot set a cookie to have a domain of www.yourdomain.com.

### secure

The `secure` ingredient is a flag that indicates whether you need a secure HTTP connection to access the cookie. If `secure` is set, a cookie transmits only if the connection between the server and the browser is a secure one. If `secure` is not set, which is the default since most Web documents do not require secure connections, a cookie can be transmitted across any HTTP connection.

# Where's the Cookie Jar?

Depending on the browser, cookies are stored as individual files (with a maximum size of 4KB) or in a single long text file.

Netscape stores cookies by user name. Each user of the Netscape Navigator browser on a particular machine has her own cookie file, called cookies.txt on PCs and MagicCookie on Macs, located in her own user directory. In Windows XP, the cookie file is located in

c:\Documents and Settings\\*username*\Application Data\
Mozilla\Profiles\default\\*someName*.slt\cookies.txt

To view this directory, you'll first have to show hidden files. In Windows Explorer, choose Tools → Folder Options. Click the View tab. Check Show hidden files and folders. Click OK.

In Windows 95/98/X, its default location is

c:\Program Files\Netscape\Users\\*username*\cookies.txt

If Netscape Navigator was installed in a directory other than the default assigned by the installation program, the Users subdirectory is in that directory. Netscape limits the total cookie count to 300.

Opera also stores cookies in a single file: cookies.dat. It is located, by default, at

c:\Program Files\Opera\cookies.dat

If Opera was installed in a different directory, the file will be in that directory.

Microsoft Internet Explorer stores each cookie as a separate, individual file in the Cookies subfolder. In Windows XP, the cookie folder is located in

c:\Documents and Settings\\*username*\Cookies

In Windows 95/98, the cookies subfolder can be found in the Windows folder or a user's Profiles folder. You can also often find IE cookies in the Temporary Internet Files folder.

**Figure 14.1 Location of Cookies in Internet Explorer**

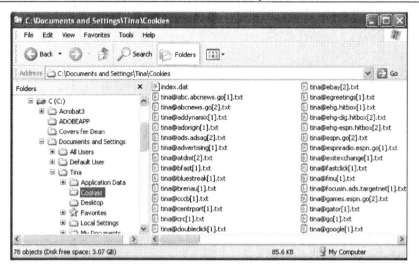

The nice thing about storing cookies as individual files is that you can easily delete individual cookies without losing the rest. The negative side is that the individual cookies, while still limited to 4KB each, take up more space on your hard drive.

## What's in Your Cookie Jar?

Now that we know where the cookie jar is, we can actually view some cookies and see what they look like. Since Netscape invented Web cookies, let's look in the Netscape cookie jar first.

To view Netscape's cookie file, you'll need a simple text editor, such as Notepad. Open your text editor. If you're on a PC, open cookies.txt. If you're on a Mac, open the

**side note** When a hard drive is formatted, it gets divided up into blocks of a uniform size. When a file is written to the hard drive, it must start at the beginning of a block. If the block size of your formatted hard disk is 32KB, then every file written to your hard disk will automatically have at least a 32KB-block of space set aside for it. The file may use only 4KB of the block, but since the next file must start at the beginning of a block, no additional files can use the 4KB-file's extra space. So in effect, the file uses 32KB of hard drive space. Today storage is quite inexpensive, so this little amount of extra space is usually of no concern. Still, this fact could be the source of the unfounded rumor that cookies eat up large amounts of hard drive space.

magiccookie file. Caution: you may not modify this file! Should you do so (if you try it, make a backup copy before you do), Netscape will abandon the modified file and replace it with a brand new cookie file. Somehow the browser will know you messed around with the file and will start over from scratch rather than touch the file you tainted.

The previous section describes each file's location. Here's a sample Netscape cookie file:

**Figure 14.2    Sample Netscape Cookie File**

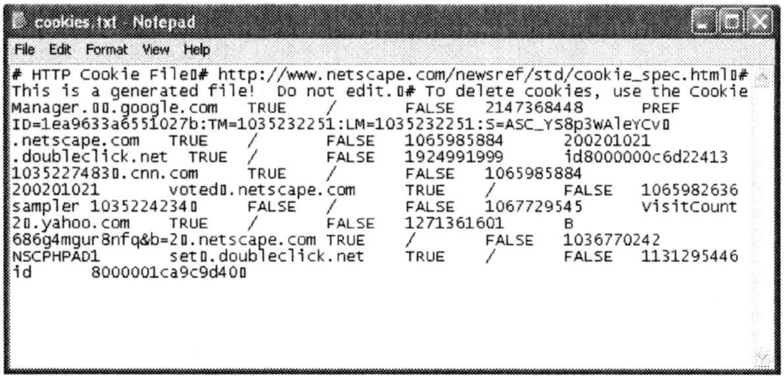

Each line after the first description line and the warning (Do not edit) represents a cookie. Here's one.

```
.doubleclick.net   TRUE   /   FALSE   1924991999 id
8000000c6d22413
```

Let's dissect this cookie into its individual ingredients, from left to right.

⚡ domain—the domain that created and is allowed to read the cookie. In this case the domain is .doubleclick.net.

⚡ flag—a `true` or `false` value indicating whether all machines within a given domain can access the cookie. The browser, depending on the value set for the domain, sets this value automatically. In this case it is `true`.

⚡ path—the path within which the cookie is valid. In this case, / indicates that the cookie is valid for the entire Web site whose domain is doubleclick.net, including the Web site's root directory and all subdirectories.

⚡ secure—a `true` or `false` value indicating whether a secure connection is required to access the cookie. In this case it is `FALSE`; a secure connection is not required.

⚡ expires—the cookie's expiration date and time, specified in Unix time. Unix time is the number of milliseconds since January 1, 1970, 00:00:00:00 GMT. In this case the expiration date in Unix time is 1924991999, which translates to a normal date.

⚡ name—the cookie's name. In this case, the cookie's name is `id`.

⊠ value—the value of the cookie. In this case, the cookie's value is
8000000c6d22413.

You can view your Netscape cookies more easily in Netscape Navigator 6 and above:
Edit → Preferences → Privacy & Security → Cookies. Click "View Stored Cookies." You can
individually remove cookies (click "Remove Cookie") and never allow a cookie back by
checking "Don't allow removed cookies to be reaccepted later" before clicking "Remove
Cookie."

Now let's dissect an Internet Explorer cookie file. Recall that IE stores each cookie in a
separate file. Again, we can use a simple text editor to view the cookie.

**Figure 14.3   Sample Internet Explorer Cookie File**

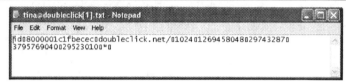

The order of the cookie data is a little different in an IE cookie file: name, value,
domain, path, and expires. IE also allows you to accept or reject cookies by Web site:
Tools → Internet Options → Privacy → Edit button → enter address and click Block or
Allow.

To view Opera's cookie file you need OFE (Opera File Explorer), a freeware program
created by Josef W. Segur that allows users of the Opera Web browser to view and maintain
its cache, cookies, global history, and visited links. You can download it at
http://www.westelcom.com/users/jsegur/#ofe. Here's a screen shot of a cookie file as
shown in OFE:

**Figure 14.4   Sample Opera Cookie File**

| Expires | (GMT) | Used | (GMT) | Status | Site |
|---|---|---|---|---|---|
| 01/14/03 | 05:00:00 | 11/01/02 | 21:00:55 | | lycos.com/ |
| 01/18/36 | 05:00:00 | 11/01/02 | 21:00:55 | | lycos.com/ |
| 11/02/02 | 21:00:56 | 11/01/02 | 21:00:55 | | lycos.com/ |
| 12/31/36 | 23:59:59 | 11/01/02 | 21:00:52 | | hb.lycos.com/ |
| 06/22/09 | 01:00:00 | 10/22/02 | 19:32:12 | | mediaplex.com/ |
| 06/22/09 | 01:00:00 | 10/22/02 | 19:32:12 | | mediaplex.com/ |
| 10/21/12 | 23:23:36 | 11/01/02 | 21:00:50 | | trafficmp.com/ |
| 11/01/03 | 21:00:46 | | | | trafficmp.com/ |
| 11/01/03 | 21:00:46 | | | | trafficmp.com/ |
| 11/01/03 | 21:00:46 | | | | trafficmp.com/ |
| 11/01/03 | 21:00:46 | | | | trafficmp.com/ |
| 11/01/03 | 21:00:46 | | | | trafficmp.com/ |
| 01/01/30 | 00:00:00 | 11/01/02 | 21:00:50 | | centrport.net/ |
| 10/20/05 | 23:21:43 | 11/01/02 | 21:01:00 | | doubleclick.net/ |

From left to right, the data is as follows: `expires`, `domain`, `path`, `name`, and `value`. Opera also allows you to selectively allow or refuse cookies from particular Web sites: File → Preferences → Privacy → the Edit Server Filters button → choose how you want to filter cookies from that site from the drop-down list at the top → enter the appropriate Web site in the box at the bottom → click Add.

# Limitations of Cookies

For security reasons, cookies are quite limited in what they can do, how big they can get, and who can access them. According to HTTP, cookies have the following limits:

- ✄ A maximum of 20 cookies can be created for any given `domain`. Any attempt to set more will cause the oldest cookie to be overwritten. (Internet Explorer 3 allows only one cookie per domain.)
- ✄ A given client (browser) can store a maximum of 300 cookies.
- ✄ Each cookie cannot exceed 4KB (4,096 bytes) in size. Cookies in excess of 4KB are usually trimmed to fit; the `name` usually remains intact.
- ✄ Browsers may choose to exceed these limits, but are not required to.

With these limits in mind, let's debunk some common rumors.

**Table 14.1    Cookie Rumors vs. Realities**

| Rumor | Reality |
|---|---|
| Cookies can steal your credit card data.<br><br>Cookies can take a "snapshot" of your hard drive. | Cookies cannot get data from your hard drive. They cannot be used to view the contents of your hard drive, let alone individual files on your hard drive. Security-conscious e-businesses are unlikely to write your credit card data to a cookie because it is well known that a cookie is a text file that can be read by anyone with physical access to your computer. If an e-business did store your credit card number in a cookie, it would likely set the cookie as `secure` so it could be accessed only via a secure connection. |
| Cookies can steal your email address. | Only if you give your email address to a Web site can it write it as a cookie. Cookies cannot access other files on your hard drive, nor preferences set in your browser. |
| Any Web site you visit can read the cookies in your cookie file. | A particular domain name can only retrieve cookie data its servers wrote. So you don't have to worry about one Web business reading data stored as a cookie by another Web business. |
| Cookies spread viruses. | Cookies are text files and normally are not executable. Non-executable text files cannot spread viruses. A file must be executable to spread viruses. Even if somehow a cookie was |

set to be executable, it could not automatically spread a virus; you'd still have to execute it in order for it to do so. This is all theoretical; I've never seen an executable cookie or heard of a virus propagated by a cookie.

# Cookies and Your Privacy

Web cookies were originally developed for consumer and programmer convenience, not to be malicious or to abuse surfers' privacy. A cookie is just a tool. Like any tool it can be used carefully or abused beyond recognition of its original intended purpose. Thus, a few companies not so concerned with consumer privacy have discovered a means of abusing cookies to their own ends. Their mission: learn everything possible about a particular user's surfing habits.

## Common Abuses of Cookies

How do they do it? How do these companies track a user's surfing expeditions? Well, it all starts with a banner ad. Banner ads often reside on third-party servers. When a third-party server is contacted to supply the banner graphic, it checks to see if your browser has one of its cookies. For simplicity, we'll call the server Zspy. If you don't have a Zspy cookie, Zspy assigns one to you. Usually the cookie's name is id and its value is a unique identification number assigned specifically to you. Zspy also takes the time to create an entry in its database for you (how kind), using the ID number it just assigned and recording everything it can about your current session. The information it records could include any or all of the following: your IP address, the time you visited the site, the time you left the site, your clickstream information, the type and version of browser you're using, and your operating system type. **Clickstream information** is data that describe the path taken by a visitor as he browses through a Web site.

Next time you visit a Web site whose banner ads are served up by Zspy, Zspy's server retrieves its cookie, your user ID, and records all information possible about that session. The same is true about the next Web site you visit that uses banner ads from Zspy, and the next, and so on. Pretty soon, Zspy has a pretty good profile of your surfing and buying habits, your likes, your dislikes, etc. This allows Zspy to target advertising especially to you. The more you surf, the more accurate Zspy gets.

The potential for abuse of this practice is scary, especially if you consider what could happen if you visit a site with a lax privacy policy that collects your name, address, phone number, etc. and passes that information along to Zspy as well as the usual session data. This type of spying and abuse of the cookie mechanism was certainly *not* part of the original intent of cookies. But they're being used this way nonetheless.

## New Features in Browsers that Help Protect Your Privacy

Before you give up all faith in cookies because of the abuses of a few companies, let's look at the good news. The type of abuse described above caused a coalition of privacy advocates, the IETF (Internet Engineering Task Force), and the major browser vendors to consider changes to the original cookie protocol. The changes would require browsers, by default, to warn surfers before accepting cookies and to limit or inhibit cookie requests from third-party servers. Most of the cookies set by third-party servers are of the Zspy type.

Of the three major browsers, Opera was the first to introduce cookie-filtering functions (in Opera 4) that allow you to preconfigure which servers or types of servers to automatically accept or reject cookies from or to accept and reject cookies on the fly. Netscape was next (in Netscape 6), also adding support for viewing and deleting individual cookie files. Finally, Internet Explorer added its privacy slider with six preconfigured settings ranging from accept all to block all in Internet Explorer 6.

Privacy is a hot topic, and consumer confidence in companies hinges on respect for consumer privacy. If companies want our business, they must be diligent about ensuring that our privacy is respected. The work done by browser vendors is only a start. To truly protect consumer privacy, a lot more needs to be done. You can do your part by letting the companies you do business with know that.

Now let's get on to what you really started reading this chapter for: baking your own cookies.

# Baking Cookies

## Syntax for Setting a Cookie

```
document.cookie = "cookieName=cookieValue ⟶
    ⟶ [; expires=timeInGMTstring] [; path=pathName] ⟶
    ⟶ [; domain=domainName] [; secure]"
```

The format and order are essential. Optional parameters are listed in brackets.

While the syntax for setting a cookie looks pretty straightforward, one little typo can spoil the whole batch. Since you're likely to want to work with cookies pretty often, let's make use of a tried and true cookie library written by Bill Dortch of hIdaho Design and kindly released to the public domain. I've made a few changes, mostly to variable names to make the code a bit more readable. The logic remains unchanged. Script 14.1 shows this wonderful cookie library.

**Programmer's tip**

Don't reinvent the wheel. Reuse existing code that has already been tried, tested, and debugged whenever you can. Why reinvent, test, and debug over and over again if you don't have to? It's a waste of time and time is money. That's why we've spent so much time in this book on libraries. Libraries are your friends.

*Script 14.1*     *cookieLib.js*

```
1    /* Cookie Library -- "Night of the Living Cookie" Version
2
3       Written by: Bill Dortch, hIdaho Design <bdortch@hidaho.com>
4       The following functions are released to the public domain. */
5
6    /* ********************************************************** */
7
8    /* "Internal" function to return decoded value of a cookie */
9    function getCookieVal (offset) {
10           var endstr = document.cookie.indexOf (";", offset);
11           if (endstr == -1) {
12               endstr = document.cookie.length;
13           }
14            return unescape(document.cookie.substring(offset,
             endstr));
15   }
16
17   /* Function to correct for 2.x Mac date bug. Call this function
18       to fix a date object prior to passing it to SetCookie.
19       IMPORTANT: This function should only be called *once*
20       for any given date object! See example at the end of this
21       document. */
22   function FixCookieDate (date) {
23           var base = new Date(0);
24           var skew = base.getTime();
25           // dawn of (Unix) time - should be 0
26           if (skew > 0) {
27           // except on the Mac - ahead of its time
28                   date.setTime(date.getTime() - skew);
29           }
30   }
31
32   /* Function to return the value of the cookie specified by
33       "name".
34           name - String object containing the cookie name.
35           returns - String object containing the cookie value, or
36           null if the cookie does not exist. */
37   function GetCookie (name) {
38           var temp = name + "=";
39           var tempLen = temp.length;
40           var cookieLen = document.cookie.length;
41           var i = 0;
42           while (i < cookieLen) {
```

```
43              var j = i + tempLen;
44              if (document.cookie.substring(i, j) == temp) {
45                      return getCookieVal(j);
46              }
47              i = document.cookie.indexOf(" ", i) + 1;
48              if (i == 0) break;
49          }
50      return null;
51  }
52
53  /*  Function to create or update a cookie.
54      name - String object containing the cookie name.
55      value - String object containing the cookie value. May
56          contain any valid string characters.
57      [expiresDate] - Date object containing the expiration data
58          of the cookie. If omitted or null, expires the cookie at
59          the end of the current session.
60      [path] - String object indicating the path for which the
61          cookie is valid. If omitted or null, uses the path of the
62          calling document.
63      [domain] - String object indicating the domain for which the
64          cookie is valid. If omitted or null, uses the domain of
65          the calling document.
66      [secure] - Boolean (true/false) value indicating whether
67          cookie transmission requires a secure channel (HTTPS).
68
69      The first two parameters are required. The others, if
70      supplied, must be passed in the order listed above. To
71      omit an unused optional field, use null as a placeholder.
72      For example, to call SetCookie using name, value and path,
73      you would code:
74
75          SetCookie ("myCookieName", "myCookieValue", null, "/");
76
77      Note that trailing omitted parameters do not require a
78      placeholder. To set a secure cookie for path "/myPath",
79      that expires after the current session, you might code:
80
81              SetCookie (myCookieVar, cookieValueVar, null,
82              "/myPath", null, true);
83  */
84  function SetCookie (name,value,expiresDate,path,domain,secure) {
85      document.cookie = name + "=" + escape (value) +
86              ((expiresDate) ? "; expires=" +
87              expiresDate.toGMTString() : "") +
```

```
88              ((path) ? "; path=" + path : "") +
89              ((domain) ? "; domain=" + domain : "") +
90              ((secure) ? "; secure" : "");
91   }
92
93   /* Function to delete a cookie. (Sets expiration date to start
94      of epoch)
95      name -    String object containing the cookie name
96      path -    String object containing the path of the cookie to
97      delete.  This MUST be the same as the path used to create the
98      cookie, or null/omitted if no path was specified when
99      creating the cookie.
100     domain - String object containing the domain of the cookie to
101     delete.  This MUST be the same as the domain used to create
102     the cookie, or null/omitted if no domain was specified when
103     creating the cookie. */
104  function DeleteCookie (name,path,domain) {
105          if (GetCookie(name)) {
106              document.cookie = name + "=" +
107                  ((path) ? "; path=" + path : "") +
108                  ((domain) ? "; domain=" + domain : "") +
109                  "; expires=Thu, 01-Jan-70 00:00:01 GMT";
110          }
111  }
```

The copy of this cookie file on the CD accompanying this book includes all of the author's comments. For brevity, I've removed them from Script 14.1. (Even without the comments, the library still covers 111 lines! With the comments, it is 180 lines.)

Let's now look at each function in the library in turn.

## SetCookie

**Script 14.2     The *SetCookie* Function**

```
1    /* Script 14.2: The SetCookie Function */
2    function SetCookie (name,value,expiresDate,path,domain,secure) {
3         document.cookie = name + "=" + escape (value) +
4             ((expiresDate) ? "; expires=" +
5             expiresDate.toGMTString() : "") +
6             ((path) ? "; path=" + path : "") +
7             ((domain) ? "; domain=" + domain : "") +
8             ((secure) ? "; secure" : "");
9    }
```

This function allows you to create or modify a cookie. Its parameters match up with each cookie ingredient described earlier. All parameters are strings, except `expiresDate`, which is a `Date` object representing the date the cookie should expire.

Notice the `escape` function call on the cookie's value in line 3 of Script 14.2? All special characters in a cookie's value must be ASCII-encoded. The `escape` function performs that process.

Lines 4 through 8 make use of the conditional statement. Each one checks to see if a particular parameter was provided when the function was called. If the parameter was provided, the condition evaluates to `true` and the appropriate text is written to the cookie. If the condition evaluates to `false`, meaning that parameter wasn't provided, no text is added to the cookie string.

### Calculating a Cookie's Expiration Date

Remember, JavaScript stores dates as the number of milliseconds since January 1, 1970, 00:00:00:00. So calculating a cookie's expiration date requires a little math. It's a pretty straightforward calculation.

Basically, we have to convert from milliseconds to days. The formula to calculate 365 days from now is

nowInMs + (365 days * 24 hrs/day * 60 mins/hr * 60 secs/min * 1000 ms/sec)

Your actual code would look like this:

```
var now = new Date()
var expDate = new Date(now.getTime() + (365*24*60*60*1000))
```

To calculate one month from now, replace `365` with `30`. To calculate one week from now, replace it with `7`.

Let's try calling the `SetCookie` function in Script 14.3. We'll attach our cookie library (lines 4 through 6), rather than embed it in the document. Notice that I did not place an HTML comment between the opening and closing <script> tags (lines 4 through 6). That's to remind me *not* to write any code between those tags. I usually run the opening and closing script tags together on the same line, which is even better, so I'm not tempted to write anything there. Unfortunately, they won't fit on a single line in this book.

Lines 10 and 11 of Script 14.3 set the expiration date. In this case, they set it to one year from now. Let's prompt the visitor for his or her name (line 13) so we can write a custom greeting and store that name in a cookie so we can retrieve it on the next visit (line 15). We should set the path such that we can retrieve the visitor's name from anywhere on our Web site (notice the last parameter in the `SetCookie` call).

### Script 14.3  Calling *SetCookie*

```
1   <html>
2   <head>
3   <title>Script 14.3: Calling SetCookie</title>
4   <script language="JavaScript" src="cookieLib.js"
```

```
5    type="text/javascript">
6    </script>
7
8    <script language="JavaScript" type="text/javascript"><!--
9         var now = new Date()
10        var expDate = new Date(now.getTime() +
11            (365*24*60*60*1000))
12
13        var visitorName = prompt("What\'s your name?", "")
14
15        SetCookie("Visitor", visitorName, expDate, "/")
16   //-->
17   </script>
18   </head>
19   <body>
20   <script language="JavaScript" type="text/javascript"><!--
21        document.write("<h1>Greetings, ", visitorName, "</h1>")
22
23   //-->
24   </script>
25   <p>Note: in this script, the visitor's name is coming from the
26   variable in which we stored the result of the prompt.</p>
27   </body>
28   </html>
```

Now let's run the script and see if it worked. Keep in mind that new cookies are written to the hard disk only when the visitor quits the browser. Modified cookies are written out immediately. So to view the cookie, you usually have to close the browser. Then you can examine your cookie file to verify that it worked. Netscape 6+ makes the job easier with its cookie-viewing tool. Not only can you see those cookies already written to the hard drive, you can also see those currently in memory. This makes it possible for you to test session cookies, those that last for only one browser session.

After running the above script in Netscape 6+, open the cookie viewer.

- ✗ From the menu, choose Edit → Preferences.
- ✗ Click on the arrow next to Privacy & Security to show the contents of that section.
- ✗ Click on Cookies.
- ✗ On the right, click on Managed Stored Cookies (the label on this button may vary; yours may be View Stored Cookies).

See Figure 14.5.

***Figure 14.5  Accessing Netscape's Cookie Viewer***

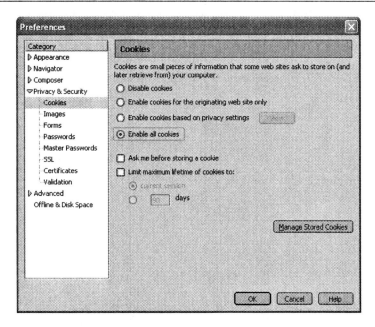

Figure 14.6 shows the cookie viewer itself.

***Figure 14.6  Netscape's Cookie Viewer***

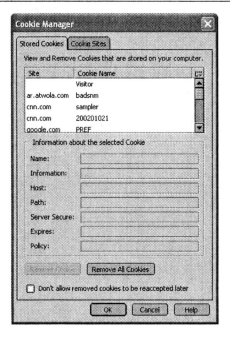

Let's check out our cookie. We ran it offline, so it's right at the top in Figure 14.6 because it doesn't have a domain name associated with it. See the first listing (Visitor)? By clicking on the cookie's name, you can view its details, as shown in Figure 14.7.

**Figure 14.7   *The Visitor Cookie as Viewed in Netscape***

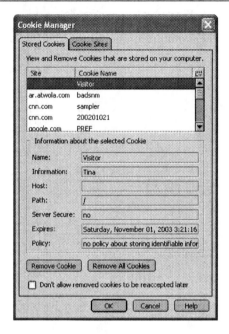

Let's examine each field shown in Figure 14.7.

⚡ **Name** shows the name of the cookie.

⚡ **Information** holds the cookie's `value`.

⚡ **Host** reflects the `domain` for which the cookie is valid.

⚡ **Path** shows the `path` in which the cookie is valid.

⚡ **Server Secure** specifies whether or not a `secure` server is required to access the cookie.

⚡ **Expires** displays the date the cookie `expires`.

All the ingredients are there. In our cookie's case, its `name` is `Visitor`, its `value` is `Tina` or whatever you typed in, its `domain` is not specified because we ran the script offline, the `path` is `/`, it does not require a secure server to be accessed, and it `expires` one year from today.

OK, now we've seen that the `SetCookie` function called in Script 14.3, line 14, worked. Let's try retrieving the cookie we just set like we would normally in Script 14.4.

# Getting a Cookie from the Cookie Jar

To retrieve cookies with JavaScript, you'll again use the `cookie` property of the `document` object. Typically, when retrieved, the `cookie` property returns a string containing every cookie for the current `domain` and `path` as a name-value pair. An equals sign (=) separates each name and corresponding `value`. A semicolon (;) separates pairs. Here's an example:

```
username=Sam; pwd=devan728; visits=5
```

This combining of valid cookies for the current `domain` and `path` into a single string makes retrieving a single cookie `value` a bit of a pain. In order to access the `value` of a particular cookie, you first have to parse the string returned by `document.cookie`. To **parse** means to break it apart into usable chunks.

The `GetCookie` function, shown in Script 14.4, searches the `document.cookie` string and retrieves the `value` of the specific cookie you need, as indicated by the name parameter passed to the function.

### GetCookie

*Script 14.4    The GetCookie Function*

```
1     /* Script 14.4: The GetCookie Function */
2     function getCookieVal (offset) {
3          var endstr = document.cookie.indexOf (";", offset);
4          if (endstr == -1) {
5            endstr = document.cookie.length;
6          }
7          return unescape(document.cookie.substring(offset, endstr));
8     }
9
10    function GetCookie (name) {
11         var temp = name + "=";
12         var tempLen = temp.length;
13         var cookieLen = document.cookie.length;
14         var i = 0;
15         while (i < cookieLen) {
16              var j = i + tempLen;
17              if (document.cookie.substring(i, j) == temp) {
18                   return getCookieVal(j);
19              }
20              i = document.cookie.indexOf(" ", i) + 1;
21              if (i == 0) break;
22         }
23         return null;
24    }
```

The GetCookie function definition begins in line 10. Notice that the only parameter required to call GetCookie is the cookie's name.

Lines 11 through 14 prepare some variables to be used in the search routine in lines 15 through 22. The search routine works through the cookie object, which may contain multiple cookies, cookie by cookie (see lines 15 and 20—individual cookies are separated by a space), looking for a substring (line 17) that matches temp (the name of the cookie being sought with an equals sign appended). When a match is found, getCookieVal is called to retrieve and return the cookie's value.

The getCookieVal function takes one parameter, offset (line 2), an index number specifying where to begin its extraction. getCookieVal first locates the end of the cookie (lines 3 through 6). When more than one cookie is stored in the cookie object, every cookie but the last cookie is terminated with a semicolon. Thus the function first looks for a semicolon, which would signify the end of the cookie. If that is not found, then it is assumed that the cookie sought is the only cookie in the cookie object or is the last cookie in the cookie object, so the length of the cookie object is used as the end point.

Once the end point is determined, the String method substring (line 7) is used to extract the value. The built-in function unescape (line 7) is called to convert the value from ASCII-encoding to the normal ISO Latin-1 character set. Script 14.5 shows an example of calling GetCookie to retrieve the visitor's name (line 9), set on a previous visit, and using it to write a custom greeting (line 26).

**Script 14.5    Calling GetCookie**

```
1    <html>
2    <head>
3    <title>Script 14.5: Calling GetCookie</title>
4    <script language="JavaScript" src="cookieLib.js"
5    type="text/javascript">
6    </script>
7
8    <script language="JavaScript" type="text/javascript"><!--
9         var cookieValue = GetCookie("Visitor")
10
11        if (cookieValue != null) {
12             var visitorName = cookieValue
13        } else {
14             var now = new Date()
15             var expDate = new Date(now.getTime() +
16                 (365*24*60*60*1000))
17             var visitorName = prompt("What\'s your name?", "")
18
19             SetCookie("Visitor", visitorName, expDate, "/")
20        }
21   //-->
```

```
22   </script>
23   </head>
24   <body>
25   <script language="JavaScript" type="text/javascript"><!--
26         document.write("<h1>Greetings, ", visitorName, "</h1>")
27   //-->
28   </script>
29   </body>
30   </html>
```

Notice that if the cookie doesn't exist, then the script prompts the visitor for his name and sets a cookie in anticipation of the next visit (lines 13 through 20).

# Deleting a Cookie

Deleting a cookie is simply a matter of setting its expiration date to some time in the past. By custom, JavaScript programmers often use the Unix date, "Thu, 01-Jan-70 00:00:01 GMT," as the past date to cause the cookie to expire. Early Web servers were run on Unix machines. Even today more Web servers run on some version of Unix than any other operating system, as do the most traffic-intensive Web servers.

**Script 14.6    The *DeleteCookie* Function**

```
1   /* Script 14.6: The DeleteCookie Function */
2   function DeleteCookie (name,path,domain) {
3         if (GetCookie(name)) {
4               document.cookie = name + "=" +
5                     ((path) ? "; path=" + path : "") +
6                     ((domain) ? "; domain=" + domain : "") +
7                     "; expires=Thu, 01-Jan-70 00:00:01 GMT";
8         }
9   }
```

DeleteCookie accepts three parameters: the cookie's name, of course, and optionally, the path and domain name for which it is valid. In order to delete or modify a cookie (we're actually modifying the cookie, giving it an expiration date in the past so it will expire), the name, path, and domain must match exactly. Otherwise, we'll end up creating a new cookie.

Line 3 of Script 14.6 first checks to see if a cookie by the name passed as an argument even exists. If it does, it sets the cookie's expiration date to the Unix date. That's all there is to it.

The browser takes care of actually removing the expired cookie. Script 14.7 shows an example call of DeleteCookie in line 8.

**Script 14.7  Calling `DeleteCookie`**

```
1   <html>
2   <head>
3   <title>Script 14.7: Calling DeleteCookie</title>
4   <script language="JavaScript" src="cookieLib.js"
      type="text/javascript">
5   </script>
6
7   <script language="JavaScript" type="text/javascript"><!--
8       DeleteCookie("Visitor", "/")
9   //-->
10  </script>
11  </head>
12  <body>
13  <p>Note: The visitor cookie should now be deleted.
14  Check your cookie file to verify.</p>
15  </body>
16  </html>
```

Because we never specified a particular domain name when we initially set the `Visitor` cookie, we do not need to specify a domain name now when we call `DeleteCookie` (line 8).

After running the script, let's again use Netscape's Cookie Viewer. This time we'll verify that the `Visitor` cookie no longer exists (Figure 14.8).

**Figure 14.8  No More `Visitor` Cookie**

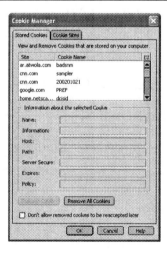

Voilà, it worked! Figure 14.8 shows that the `Visitor` cookie is no more.

## Modifying a Cookie

Modifying a cookie is simply a matter of calling SetCookie again. However, you must make certain that the domain, path, and name arguments passed to the function match the cookie you want to modify exactly. If they don't, you'll end up creating a new cookie.

To demonstrate this, let's create a new cookie, called VisitCount, in Script 14.8. You'll need to run the script several times to see the modification in action.

**Script 14.8    Calling *SetCookie* to Modify an Existing Cookie**

```
1    <html>
2    <head>
3    <title>Script 14.8: Calling SetCookie to Modify
        VisitCount</title>
4    <script language="JavaScript" src="cookieLib.js"
        type="text/javascript">
5    </script>
6
7    <script language="JavaScript" type="text/javascript"><!--
8            var now = new Date()
9            var expDate = new Date(now.getTime() +
            (365*24*60*60*1000))
10
11           if (GetCookie("VisitCount") != null) {
12               var visits = GetCookie("VisitCount")
13                visits++
14                SetCookie("VisitCount", visits, expDate, "/")
15           } else {
16                var visits = 1
17                SetCookie("VisitCount", visits, expDate, "/")
18           }
19   //-->
20   </script>
21   </head>
22   <body>
23   <h1>Greetings!</h1>
24   <script language="JavaScript" type="text/javascript"><!--
25           document.write("Number of visits to this site:
            " + visits)
26   //-->
27   </script>
28   </body>
29   </html>
```

The first time you run the script, your results should resemble Figure 14.9.

**Figure 14.9  Results of First Run of Script 14.8**

The next run should look like Figure 14.10.

**Figure 14.10  Results of Second Run of Script 14.8**

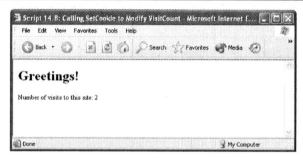

Keep refreshing the page and you'll see VisitCount continue to update. Figure 14.11 shows a view of the cookie in Netscape's Cookie Viewer after eight runs.

**Figure 14.11  VisitCount Cookie after Eight Runs of Script 14.8**

# Detecting If Cookies Are Accepted

Not all browsers and servers support cookies. Some browsers that support cookies have the cookie function turned off and are not accepting them. Before setting a cookie and then relying on it throughout your Web site, it's a good idea to verify whether the browser can or is accepting cookies. Script 14.9 declares a function you can add to your cookie library that does just that.

## cookiesAccepted

*Script 14.9*    *Detecting If Cookies Are Accepted*

```
1    <html>
2    <head>
3    <title>Script 14.9: Detecting If Cookies Are Accepted</title>
4    <script language="JavaScript" src="cookieLib.js"
        type="text/javascript">
5    </script>
6
7    <script language="JavaScript" type="text/javascript"><!--
8          function cookiesAccepted () {
9                var now = new Date()
10               var expDate = new Date(now.getTime() +
                   (1*24*60*60*1000))
11
12               if (document.cookie) {
13                     SetCookie("TestCookie", "Test Value",
                         expDate, "/")
14                     if (GetCookie("TestCookie") != null) {
15                           DeleteCookie("TestCookie", "/")
16                           return true       // cookies accepted
17                     } else {
18                           return false      // cookies not accepted
19                     }
20               } else {
21                     return false            // cookies not accepted
22               }
23         }
24   //-->
25   </script>
26   </head>
27   <body>
28   <h1>Greetings!</h1>
29   <script language="JavaScript" type="text/javascript"><!--
30         document.write("Cookies accepted by this browser? ",
               cookiesAccepted())
```

```
31   //-->
32   </script>
33   </body>
34   </html>
```

The first thing to do is check to see if `document.cookie` is a valid object in the browser (line 12). This is called object detection.

If the browser supports the `cookie` object, verify that the browser can write (line 13) and read (line 14) a cookie. If that's successful, delete the test cookie, for clean-up purposes (line 15), and return `true` (line 16). Otherwise, return `false` (lines 17–19). If the browser doesn't support the `cookie` object, then return `false` (lines 20–22).

Line 30 of Script 14.9 calls the `cookiesAccepted` function for the purpose of testing the function only. Usually, you would call `cookiesAccepted` in an `if` statement whose contents would be your entire cookie routine, like this:

```
if (cookiesAccepted()) {
    // whatever you were planning to do that involved cookies
}
```

Figure 14.12 shows what the results of Script 14.9 would look like in Netscape.

**Figure 14.12    Results of Script 14.9 when Cookies Are Accepted**

To see if the `cookiesAccepted` function works when cookies are disabled or not supported, you'll need to turn off the cookie function in your browser. Then run the script again.

Figure 14.13 shows the results after disabling the cookie function in Internet Explorer.

*Figure 14.13   Results of Script 14.9 when Cookies Are Not Accepted*

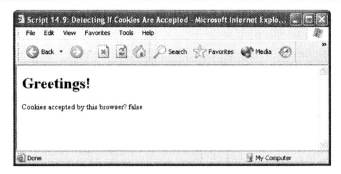

Now that we've covered the basics of baking cookies, let's look at some scripts that make use of cookies.

# Scripts That Leverage Cookies

## Auto Login

One of the most common uses of cookies is to make logging in easier. Many Web sites require that visitors create an account in order to obtain access to special features. Logging in every time can be a chore for the visitor. To make it easier, some sites store the visitor's user name and password as a cookie and complete the login fields automatically on a return visit.

*Script 14.10   Auto Login Feature*

```
1    <html>
2    <head>
3    <title>Script 14.10: Auto Login</title>
4    <script language="JavaScript" src="cookieLib.js"
        type="text/javascript">
5    </script>
6    </head>
7    <body>
8    <h1>Greetings!</h1>
9    <form name="Login" action="" method="post">
10   <table>
11   <tr>
12          <td><b>Username:</b></td>
13          <td><input type="text" name="User" size="15" tabindex="1"
14                   onChange="SetCookie('Username', this.value,
                     expDate, '/')">
15          </td>
16          <td rowspan="2" align="right">
```

```
17                        <input type="submit" value="Login" tabindex="3">
18              </td>
19      </tr>
20      <tr>
21              <td><b>Password:</b></td>
22              <td><input type="password" name="Pass" size="15"
                   tabindex="2"
23                      onChange="SetCookie('Password', this.value, expDate,
                        '/')">
24              </td>
25      </tr>
26      </table>
27      </form>
28      <script language="JavaScript" type="text/javascript"><!--
29              var now = new Date()
30              var expDate = new Date(now.getTime() +
                   (365*24*60*60*1000))
31
32              if (GetCookie("Username") != null) {
33                      document.Login.User.value = GetCookie("Username")
34              }
35              if (GetCookie("Password") != null) {
36                      document.Login.Pass.value = GetCookie("Password")
37              }
38      //-->
39      </script>
40      </body>
41      </html>
```

Notice that the script that automatically completes the form fields (lines 28 through 39) is placed after the HTML form itself. This placement is essential. You cannot access form fields until after they have been created by HTML. Thus, the reason for placing the script that sets the form field values *after* the form.

**side note**

Whenever you elect to allow a site to store your user name and password between visits, keep in mind that anyone else using that computer will be able to automatically log in as well—using the user name and password that you allowed to be stored in a cookie. For that reason, it is a good idea to *never* elect to have your user name and password stored when you're using a public computer. You might also want to take the extra precaution of verifying that no cookies were written when you're done with that Web site.

So how do the `Username` and `Password` cookies get set in the first place? Check out lines 14 and 23. See the onChange event handlers? They set the `Username` and `Password` cookies initially and also modify their values whenever a change is made.

Figure 14.14 shows what Script 14.10 looks like when run after the cookies had been set on a prior visit.

*Figure 14.14   Results of Script 14.10*

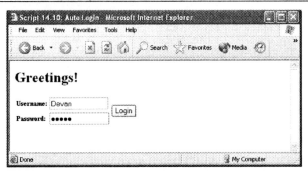

## Storing Visitor Preferences

Another common use of cookies is to store visitor preferences. In the following script, Script 14.11, a pop-up tip is displayed each time the visitor visits the Web site. So as not to continually annoy the visitor with tips he has no desire to see, an option is provided allowing the visitor to disable the pop-up tip on future visits.

*Script 14.11   Pop-up Tip Preferences*

```
1   <html>
2   <head>
3   <title>Script 14.11: Call Pop Up Tips</title>
4   <script language="JavaScript" src="cookieLib.js"
5   type="text/javascript">
6   </script>
7   <script language="JavaScript" src="tipsLib.js"
        type="text/javascript">
8   </script>
9   <script language="JavaScript" src="tips.js"
        type="text/javascript">
10  </script>
11  </head>
12  <body onLoad="popupTip()">
13  <h1>Script 14.11: Call Pop Up Tips</h1>
14  </body>
15  </html>
```

Notice that all Script 14.11 does is call the `popupTip` function when the document loads (line 12) and write a heading to the document (line 13). The three external JavaScript files attached to it do all the work.

&#x2929; **cookieLib.js**—The cookie library we've been working with throughout this chapter. You should know all about its contents by now.

&#x2929; **tipsLib.js**—A new library, shown in Script 14.12, created to handle the job of displaying a random tip on each visit. It contains a function, `getRandom` (lines 3–6), for getting a random number, which is used by `popupTip` (line 41) to choose a random tip from tips.js; the `popupTip` function (lines 15–44), which pops up a window and displays a random tip; and `turnOffTips` (lines 8–13), which sets the `WantTips` cookie to `false` (line 12), causing the document to never display tips again.

&#x2929; **tips.js**—Contains an array of tips to be chosen from randomly (Script 14.13).

Let's look at tipsLib.js (Script 14.12) and tips.js (Script 14.13).

### Script 14.12    Pop-up Tips Library

```
1    // Script 14.12: Pop-up Tips Library of Functions
2
3    function getRandom(maxNum) {
4            var randomNum = Math.floor(Math.random() * maxNum)
5            return randomNum
6    }
7
8    function turnOffTips () {            // requires cookieLib.js
9            var now = new Date()
10           var expDate = new Date(now.getTime() +
               (365*24*60*60*1000))
11           FixCookieDate (expDate)
12           SetCookie ("WantTips", false, expDate, "/")
13    }
14
15    function popupTip () {
16           if (GetCookie("WantTips") == null) {
17                  var startDoc = "<html><head><title>WebWoman\'s
                      Wisdom"
18                  startDoc += "</title></head>"
19                  startDoc += "<body bgcolor=white text=black
                      link=\"#ff3399\" "
20                  startDoc += "vlink=\"#ff3399\" alink=\"#ff3399\">"
21                  var docTitle = "<h2 align=center>WebWoman\'s
                      Wisdom</h2>"
22                  var startP = "<p>"
23                  var endP = "</p>"
24                  var zForm = "<form><table bgcolor=Silver><tr><td>"
```

```
25          zForm += "<input type=Checkbox
              onClick=\"opener.turnOffTips()\"> "
26          zForm += "Do not show tips on next visit.</td>
              </tr></table></form>"
27          var endDoc = "</body></html>"
28
29          if (screen) {
30              topCoord = screen.height/2 - 150 // 1/2 the height
31              leftCoord = screen.width/2 - 200 // 1/2 the width
32          } else {
33              topCoord = 100
34              leftCoord = 150
35          }
36          var features =
              "width=400,height=300,scrollbars,screenX=" +
37              leftCoord + ",screenY=" + topCoord
38          var tipWin = window.open("", "TipWindow", features)
39          tipWin.document.write(startDoc, docTitle, startP,
40                                  tips[getRandom(tips.length)],
41                                  endP, zForm, endDoc)
42          tipWin.focus()
43      }
44  }
```

Look at line 25 of Script 14.12; it shows the text containing the form field, a checkbox, that when checked will call the `turnOffTips` function (lines 8 through 13) and set a `WantTips` cookie to `false` (line 12). Line 16 verifies that `WantTips` does not exist before creating the pop-up window and displaying a tip.

Script 14.13 shows the file that contains the tips. It is just a simple array with text entries (lines 5 through 32).

### Script 14.13   *Tips for Pop-up Tips Program*

```
1   // Script 14.13: Tips for Pop-up Tips Program
2   // WebWoman's Wisdom - JavaScript
3   // Copyright 2002 Tina Spain McDuffie. All rights reserved.
4
5   var tips = new Array()
6   tips[0] = "A History Note. JavaScript was created by Brendan
      Eich "
7   tips[0] += "of Netscape Communications and first released in
      1995 as "
8   tips[0] += "part of Netscape Navigator 2.0."
9
10  tips[1] = "Did you know? Netscape\'s original name for
      Client-Side "
```

```
11   tips[1] += "JavaScript was <i>LiveScript</i>."
12
13   tips[2] = "When scripting for an audience that uses older
        browsers, "
14   tips[2] += "<i>embed</i> all scripts. "
15   tips[2] += "Netscape 2 does not support external JavaScripts."
16
17   tips[3] = "Did you know? The original ECAMAScript, ECMA-262,
        was "
18   tips[3] += "based on Netscape\'s Core JavaScript 1.1."
19
20   tips[4] = "Did you know? JavaScript is an object-based
        scripting "
21   tips[4] += "language developed by Netscape Communications for
        the "
22   tips[4] += "express purpose of making Web pages more dynamic
        and "
23   tips[4] += "interactive."
24
25   tips[5] = "Watch those apostrophes! We\'re so used to using
        them, "
26   tips[5] += "it\'s easy to forget that they\'re special
        characters to JavaScript. "
27   tips[5] += "They\'re used to delimit strings. To use an
        apostrophe, also "
28   tips[5] += "known as a single quote, simply type a backslash
        before the culprit "
29   tips[5] += "to escape its special JavaScript meaning.<br>"
30   tips[5] += "Example: <code>\\\'</code>."
```

Figure 14.15 shows some screen shots of the pop-up tips program in action:

**Figure 14.15  Pop-up Tips Program in Action**

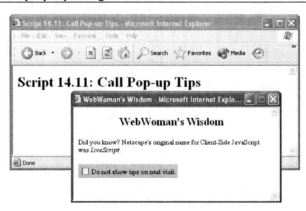

## A Shopping Cart

Here are three fun scripts that together create a small store with a shopping cart.
Script 14.14 creates a small virtual store of products. Visitors may enter a quantity next to
any item and click a button to add the item with the appropriate quantity to their shopping
carts. Script 14.15 displays the contents of the shopping cart, allowing visitors to update the
contents before proceeding to payment processing. Script 14.16 is a shopping cart library
that contains the functions that do all the work.

I suggest you run them and figure out how they work before you start making modifications.

### Script 14.14    *Javabilaya Coffee Shoppe*

```
1    <html>
2    <head>
3    <title>Script 14.14: Javabilaya Coffee Shoppe</title>
4    <style type="text/css" media="all"><!--
5          body {
6                  background-color: #663333;
7                  color: #ffcc99;
8                  background-image: url(images/javaBeans.jpg);
9          }
10         body, table {
11                 font-size: 12pt;
12                 font-family: Arial, Helvetica, sans-serif;
13         }
14   -->
15   </style>
16   <script language="JavaScript" src="cookieLib.js"
        type="text/javascript">
17   </script>
18   <script language="JavaScript" src="shoppingCartLib.js"
        type="text/javascript">
19   </script>
20
21   <script language="JavaScript" type="text/javascript"><!--
22   var now = new Date()
23   var cartExpires = new Date(now.getTime() + (7*24*60*60*1000))
24
25   var coffeeIDs = new Array("BMB", "FV", "GCM", "HK", "JB")
26   var coffees = new Array("Blue Mountain Blast", "French Vanilla",
                           "German Chocolate Mint",
                           "Hawaiian Kona", "JavaBrosia")
29   //-->
30   </script>
31   </head>
```

```
32
33   <body bgcolor="#663333" text="#FFCC99"
        background="images/javaBeans.jpg"
34          onLoad="showCart(document.JavaOrder, coffeeIDs)">
35   <h1>Javabilaya Coffee Shoppe</h1>
36   <p>You can purchase our premium Java beans by the pound. Just
37      enter the quantity you desire below and click Add to Cart.
38      You'll be enjoying a steaming cup of the finest Java in the
39      world before you can say, <i>&quot;Javabilaya.&quot;</i></p>
40   <form name="JavaOrder" method="post" action="">
41      <input type="hidden" name="expDate" value="">
42      <table border="0" cellspacing="5">
43        <tr>
44          <th align="left">Java Beans</th>
45          <th>Quantity</th>
46          <th>Price</th>
47          <th> </th>
48        </tr>
49        <tr>
50          <td>Blue Mountain Blast</td>
51          <td>
52            <input type="text" name="BMBqty" size="7">
53            lbs </td>
54          <td> @ $6 per lb</td>
55          <td>
56            <input type="button" value="Add to Cart"
57            onClick="addToCart(this.form, 'BMB',
              'Blue Mountain Blast', cartExpires)">
58          </td>
59        </tr>
60        <tr>
61          <td>French Vanilla</td>
62          <td>
63            <input type="text" name="FVqty" size="7">
64            lbs </td>
65          <td> @ $7 per lb</td>
66          <td>
67            <input type="button" value="Add to Cart"
68            onClick="addToCart(this.form, 'FV', 'French Vanilla',
                cartExpires)">
69          </td>
70        </tr>
71        <tr>
72          <td>German Chocolate Mint</td>
73          <td>
```

```
 74           <input type="text" name="GCMqty" size="7">
 75           lbs </td>
 76         <td> @ $9 per lb</td>
 77         <td>
 78           <input type="button" value="Add to Cart"
 79           onClick="addToCart(this.form, 'GCM',
                 'German Chocolate Mint', cartExpires)">
 80         </td>
 81       </tr>
 82       <tr>
 83         <td>Hawaiian Kona</td>
 84         <td>
 85           <input type="text" name="HKqty" size="7">
 86           lbs </td>
 87         <td> @ $8 per lb</td>
 88         <td>
 89           <input type="button" value="Add to Cart"
 90           onClick="addToCart(this.form, 'HK', 'Hawaiian Kona',
                 cartExpires)">
 91         </td>
 92       </tr>
 93       <tr>
 94         <td>JavaBrosia (House Blend)</td>
 95         <td>
 96           <input type="text" name="JBqty" size="7">
 97           lbs </td>
 98         <td> @ $5 per lb</td>
 99         <td>
100           <input type="button" value="Add to Cart"
101           onClick="addToCart(this.form, 'JB', 'JavaBrosia',
                 cartExpires)">
102         </td>
103       </tr>
104       <tr align="right">
105         <td colspan=4><br>
106           <br>
107           <input type="button" value="  CHECK OUT   "
108           onClick="checkOut('JavabilayaCart.html')"></td>
109       </tr>
110     </table>
111 </form>
112 </body>
113 </html>
```

When you customize Script 14.14, you need to keep a few things in mind:

✗ The cartExpires date can be modified. In Script 14.14, the cart is set to expire in seven days (line 23). You may want to make the cart stick around a little longer or empty sooner.

✗ You can use whatever ID you want for each item (line 25). I recommend you keep the item ID short and without spaces.

✗ Each quantity field's name must be of the form *itemID*qty (lines 52, 63, 74, 85, and 96), where *itemID* varies with each item. The last part, qty, must be written as is. Do not capitalize it. Several functions in Script 14.16 (showCart, line 11; addToCart, line 16; totalOrder, line 38; and updateQty, line 47) expect it as qty.

✗ The item IDs you set up must be listed in an array (line 25). You can use the array elements in your function calls if you wish. I used the actual item IDs in Script 14.14's function calls to make the connection clear.

✗ You should also create an array of product names (lines 26 to 28). (products in the function definitions, coffees in the implementation.) Product names are longer than item IDs and provide a better, friendlier description of the product. These names are used in the alert boxes (line 21 of Script 14.16) that pop up whenever an item is added to the cart (lines 56–57, 67–68, 78–79, 89–90, and 100–101 of Script 14.14). The alert boxes tell the visitor the product name and the quantity of the item that was added (lines 20 to 26 of Script 14.16).

Figure 14.16 shows what the store looks like with a few selections already made.

**Figure 14.16 Results of Script 14.14**

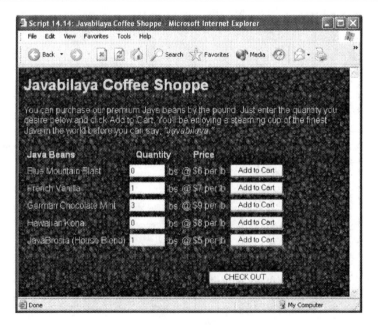

Visitors must click on the appropriate Add to Cart button, or their selections will not be added to the cart. When visitors click the CHECK OUT button, the shopping cart file is opened (Script 14.15).

Now let's look at Script 14.15, which displays the contents of the shopping cart.

### Script 14.15   *Your Javabilaya Shopping Cart*

```
1    <html>
2    <head>
3    <title>Script 14.15: Your Javabilaya Shopping Cart</title>
4    <style type="text/css" media="all"><!--
5          body {
6                  background-color: #663333;
7                  color: #ffcc99;
8                  background-image: url(images/javaBeans.jpg);
9          }
10         body, table {
11                 font-size: 12pt;
12                 font-family: Arial, Helvetica, sans-serif;
13         }
14    -->
15    </style>
16    <script language="JavaScript" src="cookieLib.js"
         type="text/javascript">
17    </script>
18    <script language="JavaScript" src="shoppingCartLib.js"
         type="text/javascript">
19    </script>
20
21    <script language="JavaScript" type="text/javascript"><!--
22    var now = new Date()
23    var cartExpires = new Date(now.getTime() + (7*24*60*60*1000))
24
25    var coffeeIDs = new Array("BMB", "FV", "GCM", "HK", "JB")
26    var coffees = new Array("Blue Mountain Blast", "French Vanilla",
27                            "German Chocolate Mint",
28                            "Hawaiian Kona", "JavaBrosia")
29    var coffeePrices = new Array(6, 7, 9, 8, 5)
30    //-->
31    </script>
32    </head>
33
34    <body bgcolor="#663333" text="#FFCC99"
         background="images/javaBeans.jpg"
```

```
35         onLoad="showCart(document.JavaCart, coffeeIDs);
               totalOrder(document.JavaCart, coffeeIDs, coffeePrices)">
36  <h1>Your Javabilaya Shopping Cart</h1>
37  <form name="JavaCart" method="post" action="">
38    <table border="0">
39      <tr align="left">
40        <td align="left"><b>Java Beans</b></td>
41        <td><b>Quantity</b></td>
42        <td><b>Price</b></td>
43        <td><b>Ext. Price</b></td>
44      </tr>
45      <tr class=odd>
46        <td>Blue Mountain Blast</td>
47        <td>
48          <input type="text" name="BMBqty" size="7"
49                onChange="updateQty(document.JavaCart, 'BMB',
                    coffeeIDs, coffeePrices, cartExpires)">
50          lbs @</td>
51        <td>$6 per lb</td>
52        <td>
53          $<input type="text" name="BMBext" size="11">
54        </td>
55      </tr>
56      <tr class=even>
57        <td>French Vanilla</td>
58        <td>
59          <input type="text" name="FVqty" size="7"
60                onChange="updateQty(document.JavaCart, 'FV',
                    coffeeIDs, coffeePrices, cartExpires)">
61          lbs @</td>
62        <td>$7 per lb</td>
63        <td>
64          $<input type="text" name="FVext" size="11">
65        </td>
66      </tr>
67      <tr class=odd>
68        <td>German Chocolate Mint</td>
69        <td>
70          <input type="text" name="GCMqty" size="7"
71                onChange="updateQty(document.JavaCart, 'GCM',
                    coffeeIDs, coffeePrices, cartExpires)">
72          lbs @</td>
73        <td>$9 per lb</td>
74        <td>
75          $<input type="text" name="GCMext" size="11">
```

```
76          </td>
77        </tr>
78        <tr class=even>
79          <td>Hawaiian Kona</td>
80          <td>
81            <input type="text" name="HKqty" size="7"
82                   onChange="updateQty(document.JavaCart, 'HK',
                        coffeeIDs, coffeePrices, cartExpires)">
83            lbs @</td>
84          <td>$8 per lb</td>
85          <td>
86            $<input type="text" name="HKext" size="11">
87          </td>
88        </tr>
89        <tr class=odd>
90          <td>JavaBrosia (House Blend)</td>
91          <td>
92            <input type="text" name="JBqty" size="7"
93                   onChange="updateQty(document.JavaCart, 'JB',
                        coffeeIDs, coffeePrices, cartExpires)">
94            lbs @</td>
95          <td>$5 per lb</td>
96          <td align="right">
97            $<input type="text" name="JBext" size="11">
98          </td>
99        </tr>
100       <tr>
101         <th colspan=3 align="right"><b>Order Total:</b></th>
102         <th align=left>
103           $<input type="text" name="Total" size="11">
104         </th>
105       </tr>
106     </table>
107     <input type="button" value="Continue Shopping"
108       onClick="continueShopping('JavabilayaStore.html')">
109     <input type="reset" value="Empty Cart"
110       onClick="emptyCart(coffeeIDs)">
111     <input type="button" value="Proceed to Payment Info"
112       onClick="alert('Here you would proceed to PayPal or equiv')">
113 </form>
114 </body>
115 </html>
```

Keep a couple of things in mind when modifying Script 14.15:

☒ Again, the cartExpires date can be modified (line 23). But whatever you set it to, it should match the setting you use in Script 14.14, line 23.

☒ Use the same item IDs (line 25) in this script as in Script 14.14 (line 25) and copy the item IDs array over as well (lines 26 to 28 of Scripts 14.14 and 14.15). In this case it is called coffeeIDs.

☒ Again, each quantity field's name must be of the form *itemID*qty (lines 48, 59, 70, 81, and 92). Several functions in Script 14.16 expect each quantity field name to end with qty (showCart, line 11; addToCart, line 16; totalOrder, line 38; and updateQty, line 47).

☒ Similarly, each extension field's name must be of the form *itemID*ext (lines 53, 64, 75, 86, and 97), where *itemID* varies with each item, but ext is always appended exactly as is. The totalOrder function (lines 32 to 44 of Script 14.16) depends on each extension field name to end with ext (line 40).

☒ The field that will hold the order's total must be named "Total" (line 103 of Script 14.15). The totalOrder function (lines 32 to 44 of Script 14.16) depends on it.

Figure 14.17 shows what the cart looks like.

*Figure 14.17 Results of Script 14.15*

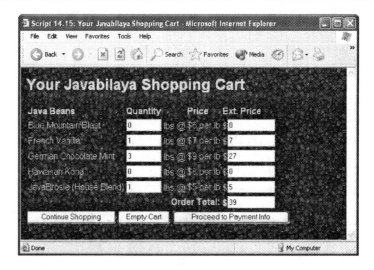

Notice that the selections made in the store have been entered and extended and the entire order totaled in the shopping cart display.

When visitors click on the Continue Shopping button (lines 107–108 of Script 14.15), they are returned to the store, Script 14.14. When they click the Empty Cart button (lines 109–110 of Script 14.15), all form entries are cleared and the cookies holding the quantities selected are deleted.

Clicking on the Proceed to Payment Info button (lines 111–112 of Script 14.15) simply displays an alert right now. When you're ready to put these scripts to work, you can program the button to take the visitor to PayPal or some other payment processor.

Finally, here are the functions that do all of the work.

### Script 14.16: shoppingCartLib.js

```
1    // Script 14.16: Shopping Cart Library
2    // by Tina McDuffie
3
4    function showCart(zForm, productIDs) {
5          var qtyDesired = 0
6          var itemQty = 0
7
8          for (i=0; i<productIDs.length; i++) {
9                qtyDesired = parseInt(GetCookie(productIDs[i]))
10               itemQty = (qtyDesired) ? qtyDesired : 0
11               zForm[productIDs[i] + "qty"].value = itemQty
12         }
13   }
14
15   function addToCart(zForm, itemID, item, expires) {
16     var itemQty = parseInt(zForm[itemID + "qty"].value)
17     if (itemQty != 0) {
18         SetCookie(itemID, itemQty, expires, "/")
19
20         var feedback = (itemQty == 1) ?  "1 pound of " : itemQty +
               " pounds of "
21         feedback += item
22         feedback += (itemQty == 1) ?  " has been " : " have been "
23         feedback += "added to your shopping cart.\n"
24         feedback += "Please click \'Check Out\' when you\'ve
               finished shopping."
25
26         alert(feedback)
27     } else {
28         alert("Please enter a quantity.  Then click Add to Cart.")
29     }
30   }
31
32   function totalOrder(zForm, productIDs, productPrices) {
33         var orderTotal = 0
34         var itemQty = 0
35         var itemExt = 0
36
37         for (i=0; i<productIDs.length; i++) {
```

```
38              itemQty = parseInt(zForm[productIDs[i]+"qty"].value)
39              itemExt = itemQty * productPrices[i]
40              zForm[productIDs[i]+"ext"].value = itemExt
41              orderTotal += itemExt
42              zForm["Total"].value = orderTotal
43          }
44  }
45
46  function updateQty(zForm, itemID, productIDs, productPrices,
        expires) {
47          var itemQty = parseInt(zForm[itemID + "qty"].value)
48          SetCookie(itemID, itemQty, expires, "/")
49          totalOrder(zForm, productIDs, productPrices)
50  }
51
52  function emptyCart(productIDs) {
53          for (i=0; i<productIDs.length; i++) {
54              DeleteCookie(productIDs[i], "/")
55          }
56  }
57
58  function checkOut(cartFile) {
59          location.href = cartFile
60  }
61
62  function continueShopping(storeFile) {
63          location.href = storeFile
64  }
```

I'll leave the rest for you to figure out as an exercise.

## Summary

Cookies provide a means of saving state. Saving state is the preservation of information about the current session between browser sessions. A session begins when a visitor enters a Web site and ends when he leaves it. A browser session begins when the visitor opens his browser and ends when he closes it. While it is also possible to save state with server-side scripting, client-side scripting and cookies are a good method and appropriate to the subject of this textbook.

The term "cookie" is not an acronym and has been used for some time by computer scientists to refer to "an opaque piece of data held by an intermediary." In the case of cookies on the Web, the intermediary is the hard drive on the visitor's computer. The formal name for cookies is "Persistent Client-Side HTTP Objects." They are objects that persist on the client's hard drive and are written and transferred from browser to server and vice versa according to the HTTP protocol.

Cookies have a variety of uses, including, but not limited to saving visitor preferences between visits, storing login information for automatic login on the next visit, storing shopping cart information, and collecting detailed information about your Web surfing habits. While the last may not make you very happy, it is a reality of cookies. Thankfully, the latest browsers now include tools that allow you to pick and choose which cookies you want to accept and to disable the cookie function altogether.

Cookies have six basic ingredients: `name`, which is used to access the stored information; `value`, which is the actual information you desire to store; `expires`, which is a `Date` specifying when a cookie should depart; `path` and `domain`, which specify the path and domain within which a cookie is valid; and `secure`, which indicates whether a secure connection is required to access the cookie. Of these ingredients, only `name` and `value` are required to bake a cookie.

Cookies are stored either in individual cookie files or in one long text file, depending upon the browser. You can view cookie files in a simple text editor. Version 6 of Netscape's browser added a cookie viewer utility, which especially comes in handy for testing the results of scripts that set, modify, or delete cookies.

Cookies do have their limits. According to the HTTP protocol, a maximum of 20 cookies can be generated for any one domain, browsers can store a maximum of 300 cookies, and each cookie may not exceed 4KB in size.

All cookie data for a particular Web page is loaded into the `document.cookie` object when the document loads. While the syntax for setting a cookie seems pretty straightforward,

```
document.cookie = "cookieName=cookieValue ⇢
    ⇢ [; expires=timeInGMTstring] [; path=pathName] ⇢
    ⇢ [; domain=domainName] [; secure]"
```

it's best to use the tried and true cookie functions written by Bill Dortch and released to the public domain. Functions in the library include `SetCookie`, for setting an initial cookie `value` or modifying one already set; `GetCookie`, for retrieving a cookie's `value`; and `DeleteCookie`, for removing a cookie. Another nice function you might want to add to the library, `cookiesAccepted`, checks to see if cookies are supported or are being accepted by a browser. It is useful to check for cookie acceptance before depending on cookie function.

This chapter included several useful scripts that made use of cookies, including scripts for tracking the number of times a visitor has been to a Web page, logging in automatically, storing user preferences, and saving shopping cart selections.

## Review Questions

1. What does it mean to "save state"?
2. What's the difference between a "session" and a "browser session"?
3. Can cookies be generated by other technologies than JavaScript? Explain your answer.

4. What is a cookie?
5. Is "cookie" a new term invented by Netscape? Explain.
6. What is Netscape's formal name for cookies? Explain how each part of the name gives insight into what a cookie is all about.
7. List and describe three well-meaning uses for cookies.
8. List and describe two not-so-well-meaning uses for cookies.
9. List and describe the six cookie ingredients.
10. Which cookie ingredients, if any, are always required to bake a cookie?
11. Where's the cookie jar in Netscape? In Internet Explorer? In Opera?
12. How can you view the cookies in your cookie jar?
13. Do cookies have any limits according to HTTP? If so, what are they?
14. Describe how some companies abuse the cookie function to invade your privacy. How do you feel about that? What can you do about it?
15. What features do the latest browsers have that can assist you in protecting your privacy?
16. What's special about calculating a cookie's expiration date in JavaScript?
17. What does the `cookie` property of the `document` object return when accessed? Be specific.
18. What does it mean to "parse" a cookie?
19. Essentially, how does one delete a cookie?
20. Do all browsers and servers support cookies?
21. Do all browsers accept cookies?
22. What or who determines whether a particular browser accepts cookies or not?
23. Why is it a good idea to verify that cookies are supported and accepted before running a script that uses cookies?

## Exercises

1. Write the code necessary to create an expiration date for a cookie, 14 days from today. You do not have to set the cookie, just create and calculate the expiration date.
2. Write the code necessary to create an expiration date for a cookie, six months from today. You do not have to set the cookie, just create and calculate the expiration date.
3. Run one of the scripts provided in this chapter that sets a cookie in Netscape. Open Netscape's Cookie Viewer and examine the results. Write them down.
4. Run one of the scripts provided in this chapter that sets a cookie in Internet Explorer. Find and view the cookie. Write down the parts you can decipher.
5. Open Opera and set the privacy option to "Display Received Cookies." Run one of the scripts provided in this chapter that sets a cookie. Write down the information that Opera displays when it asks you if you want to accept or reject the cookie.
6. Use Netscape Navigator to visit a Web site that allows you to have your user name and password stored. (As a last resort, run Script 14.10 if you can't find one.) Verify

that your login information was stored by viewing the cookie for yourself using Netscape's Cookie Viewer.

Close Netscape and open Internet Explorer or Opera. Visit the site again. Did the site automatically complete the login information for you? Explain why or why not.

# Scripting Exercises

Create a folder named assignment14 to hold the documents you create during this assignment. Save a copy of your latest toy store documents in a toyStore subfolder.

1. Write a script that saves the date and time in a cookie when a visitor leaves the Web page. (Hint: Think onUnload event handler.)
   a. Feel free to use the functions getCurrentTime and getCurrentDate you wrote in Chapter 10, Scripting Exercise 1.
   b. When the visitor next visits your Web page, display the message "Welcome back. You last visited us " followed by the date and time of her last visit. Write it to the document; don't use an alert.
   c. If it's the visitor's first visit, display the message "Welcome, this is your first visit to our site." Write it to the document; don't use an alert.
   d. Once debugged and tested, add this script to your Toy Store home page.
2. Create a new document named register.html.
   a. Add a pop-up registration form that asks for the visitor's name and an email address the first time he visits the site.
   b. When submitted, store the visitor's name as a cookie and set a cookie named registered to true.
   c. Also create a counter cookie. Every third visit to the page, if the visitor has not yet registered (determined by the registered cookie), pop up the registration window again reminding the visitor of the number of times he has visited the site without registering and encouraging him to register.
   d. If the visitor has registered, greet him by name at the top of the document like this: "Welcome back, Sam. This is visit number 5."
3. Create a new document named password.html.
   a. Add a small form, inside a table with a colored background, in the top right corner of the page. Include two fields, labeled user name and password, and a checkbox labeled "Save password."
   b. If the visitor checks the "Save password" box, save the user name and password as cookies.
   c. Whenever the visitor types a value in the user name field, see if there is a user name cookie. If there is and it matches the user name typed in, complete the password field for the visitor using the password cookie.
4. Create a splash page for a Web site.
   a. Provide two links: "frames" and "no frames."

b. When the visitor clicks on one of the links, store an appropriate value representing that preference in a cookie named `framesPref`, then take the visitor to the appropriate version of the Web site, either framed or non-framed.

c. On the next visit, use the value stored in the `framesPref` cookie to automatically open the appropriate version of the Web site.

5. Create a new document named colorPrefs.html.

a. In a corner of the document, in a table with a background color, provide four checkboxes labeled "Spring," "Summer," "Autumn," and "Winter."

b. When the visitor checks one of the checkboxes, change the document's color scheme (background and text colors) accordingly. You decide on the colors for each season.

c. Set the preference as a cookie and retrieve it and color the document accordingly on the next visit.

6. Change the hard-coded prices listed in the shopping cart to variables, that is, modify the shopping cart provided in Scripts 14.14, 14.15, and 14.16 as follows:

a. Add a `coffeePrices` array to Script 14.14.

b. Use the entries in the `coffeePrices` array to write the appropriate price for each coffee in the form in lines 54, 65, 76, 87, and 98 of Script 14.14.

c. Use the entries in the `coffeePrices` array in Script 14.15 to write the appropriate price for each coffee in the form in lines 51, 62, 73, 84, and 95 of Script 14.15.

7. Create a short form that allows a visitor to customize your home page to her own needs by selecting among several types of content in which she might be interested, including a quote of the day, news, the current date and time, and a tip of the day. Also provide a "none" option.

a. The first time the visitor visits your Web site, pop up a small window to display the form showing the special content choices from which she can choose.

b. Write the visitor's choice(s) in a cookie.

c. In all future visits, use the visitor's preferences, stored in one or more cookies, to provide content customized to that visitor on the home page of your Web site. Some information on the home page of your Web site should be static and delivered to all visitors, regardless of preferences.

d. Provide a link on the home page that allows the visitor to pop up the form again and modify her preferences.

# Project

## Toy Store Shopping Cart

Save a copy of your latest toy store documents in a toyStore subfolder. Using the shopping cart scripts provided in this chapter as a guide, implement your own shopping cart for your Toy Store Web site.

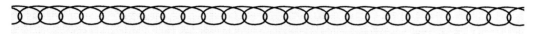

# Dynamic HTML

*That which is static*

*and repetitive is boring.*

*That which is dynamic*

*and random is confus-*

*ing. In between lies art.*

—John A. Locke

**D**ynamic HTML is the animating, hiding, showing, stacking, and formatting of HTML content on the screen using a combination of technologies, specifically Hypertext Markup Language (HTML), Cascading Style Sheets (CSS), and JavaScript. Because DHTML separates a document's structure (HTML) from its presentation (CSS), it makes it easy to change the look and feel of an entire Web site quickly, often by modifying only one document. The most dramatic applications of DHTML use JavaScript to modify stylesheets on the fly in order to create special effects and animations. That's what this chapter is all about.

In this chapter we'll

- define the term Dynamic HTML and look at its major parts, namely HTML, CSS, and JavaScript.
- determine which browsers support DHTML and how they differ in their support.
- see how Cascading Style Sheets work and define and describe the parts of a stylesheet: style rules, selectors, declarations, properties, and values.

✗ revisit the DOM, specifically with an eye toward accessing CSS properties in the three major browsers (Netscape Navigator, Internet Explorer, and Opera).

✗ learn how to work around browser incompatibilities by using object detection.

✗ write scripts to move objects around the screen and to create pull-down menus.

# What Is Dynamic HTML?

**Dynamic HTML (DHTML)**, in its simplest form, is a combination of Hypertext Markup Language (HTML), Cascading Style Sheets (CSS), and JavaScript. HTML provides document structure and context for the information contained in a Web page. CSS provides the details on how to present that information. JavaScript provides the interactivity and dynamism. Let's look at each of these technologies a little more closely.

## HTML

From the earliest days of the Web, **HTML** was only meant to provide structure for a document and context for its content. For example, HTML says, "This text is a heading of level one," with

```
<h1>this text</h1>
```

HTML says, "This is a paragraph," with

```
<p>Blah, blah, blah, blah, blah, blah, blah, blah, blah,
blah, blah, blah, blah, , blah, blah, blah, blah, , blah,
blah, blah, blah, , blah, blah, blah, blah, , blah, blah,
blah, blah, , blah, blah, blah, blah. </p>
```

HTML says, "This is an unordered list," with

```
<ul>
        <li>item one</li>
        <li>item two</li>
        <li>item three</li>
</ul>
```

HTML says, "This is a blockquote," with

```
<blockquote>Any sufficiently advanced technology is
indistinguishable from magic. -Arthur C. Clarke</blockquote>
```

Script 15.1 shows a simple HTML document that uses HTML to specify the structure of the document and to provide context for the content only.

**Script 15.1    HTML: Provides Structure and Context**

```
1    <html>
2    <head>
3    <title>Script 15.1: HTML - Provides Structure and
        Context</title>
```

```
4    </head>
5    <body>
6    <h1>Javabilaya</h1>
7
8    <table id="MainMenu" width="400" border="1" cellpadding="2"
9             bordercolor="#800000"><tr>
10        <td width=100>
11               <a href="beans/index.html">The Beans</a></td>
12        <td width=100>
13               <a href="buzz/index.html">The Buzz</a></td>
14        <td width=100>
15               <a href="catalog/index.html">Catalog</a></td>
16        <td width=100><a href="contactUs/index.html">Contact
            Us</a></td>
17   </tr></table>
18   <br clear=all>
19   <br><br><br><br><br>
20
21   <blockquote>This coffee plunges into the stomach . . . the mind
22      is aroused, and ideas pour forth like the battalions of the
23      Grand Army on the field of battle. . . . Memories charge at
24      full gallop . . . the light cavalry of comparisons deploys
25      itself magnificently; the artillery of logic hurry in with
26      their train of ammunition; flashes of wit pop up like
27      sharp-shooters.       
28      - Honore de Balzac</blockquote>
29
30   <p>Welcome to Javabilaya! We roast our coffee beans daily so
31   your order is always fresh. We know that nothing beats a fresh
32   cup of coffee!</p>
33
34   <p>Here you can learn more about our premium Java beans. We've
35   packed this site with tips and tidbits about your favorite
36   drink: Java. Check out The Buzz and learn how to best store your
37   beans to maintain their flavor, pick up some brewing tips, and
38   explore our recipe section. Soon you'll be brewing Java the gods
39   would envy. You can't help to if you start with our special
40   house blend: JavaBrosia.</p>
41
42   <p>If you thirst for more Java knowledge, The Buzz can also
43   enlighten you on coffee customs and trivia. You can even learn
44   to speak Java! To really quench that Java thirst, browse our
45   catalog and fill your cart with beans that will brew the best
46   Java your tastebuds have ever encountered.</p>
47
```

```
48   <p class="copyright">Copyright Tina McDuffie. All rights
        reserved.
49   <a href="http://www.javascriptconcepts.com/javabilaya/">
50   http://www.javascriptconcepts.com/javabilaya/</a></p>
51
52   </body>
53   </html>
```

Figure 15.1 shows what it looks like when viewed in a browser.

**Figure 15.1    Results of Script 15.1**

Looks pretty plain, huh? That's OK; HTML was never meant to specify how the information contained in its documents should be presented in terms of font styles, margin widths, etc. Stylesheets were intended to take care of those details from the very beginning. The beauty of HTML is that it provides a means for users around the world to share documents, no matter what computer platform they are running or what Web browser they use to view the documents. HTML and the Web have been huge contributors to making this "The Information Age."

As Web authors came to take for granted that information could be shared universally, they, of course, wanted more. They wanted their Web documents to be visually appealing, dynamic, and interactive. Unfortunately, HTML has two major drawbacks:

1. As already mentioned, HTML was only meant to specify the *structure* of a document and the context of the information contained therein. It was never meant to describe presentation details like what font to use and how wide the margins should be.
2. HTML is static. Once an HTML document loads, it cannot change itself.

Enter CSS and JavaScript. CSS solves the presentation problem by providing a means for authors and designers to specify how the browser should present their Web documents. JavaScript solves the static problem by providing a means of modifying an HTML document once it has loaded and responding dynamically to visitor and browser events.

## CSS

**CSS** provides a rich selection of presentation effects that can be applied to all HTML elements, such as color, background, margins, and borders. With CSS, Web developers can set indents on paragraphs, specify a default font for an entire Web site with one line of code, use small caps, assign an image as a bullet for a list item, and accomplish many more things that are impossible with HTML alone.

According to the World Wide Web Consortium (W3C), stylesheets were always envisioned as assigning presentation details to Web documents. It just took the browser vendors a while to catch on and add support for the CSS specification, a long while in Web time. The first real support for CSS came in the 4.0 browsers. The support for CSS has been growing ever since.

To give you an idea of how CSS works, here are some examples of how CSS designates presentation details:

CSS says, "Make the background color of the document white and the text black. Set the margins to 20 pixels and the font to 12-point Arial," with

```
body {
        background-color: white;
        color: black;
        margin: 20px;
        font-size: 12pt;
        font-family: Arial, Helvetica, sans-serif;
}
```

CSS says, "Present headings of level one as bold, centered, purple with a yellow background, and 18-point Times New Roman," with

```
h1 {
        font-weight: bold;
        text-align: center;
        color: purple;
```

```
      background-color: yellow;
      font-size: 18pt;
      font-family: "Times New Roman", Times, Roman, serif;
}
```

CSS says, "Indent the first line of paragraphs by 3 ems," with

```
p {
      text-indent: 3em;
}
```

CSS says, "Make links and visited links blue with a white background. Whenever a link is active or the visitor mouses over a link, display the link with a blue background and white text," with

```
a:link, a:visited {
      color: blue;
      background-color: white;
}
a:active, a:hover {
      background-color: blue;
      color: white;
}
```

The last example shows you how to get a rollover effect without images or JavaScript!

Figure 15.2 shows the same document, shown in Figure 15.1, with the stylesheet in Script 15.2 applied.

*Figure 15.2    Document with Stylesheet Applied*

Another advantage of CSS is that when coded properly, documents degrade gracefully, even in older browsers that do not support stylesheets. You saw a sample in Figure 15.1. The document may have looked plain, but it was totally useable and readable.

Here's the CSS code we placed in the head of the document shown in Figure 15.2 to set the appearance. The rest of the document is the same as Script 15.1.

*Script 15.2    CSS: Designates Presentation Details*

```
1   <head>
2   <title>Script 15.2: CSS - Designates Presentation
    Details</title>
3   <style type="text/css"><!--
4   body {
5         background-color: #663333;   /* dark chocolaty brown */
6         background-image: url(images/javaBeans.jpg);
7         color: #ffffff;              /* white */
8         font-size: 12pt;
9         font-family: "Times New Roman", Times, Roman, serif;
10        margin: 5px 50px;
```

```
11  }
12  a:link, a:visited {
13        color: #800000;              /* dark reddish brown */
14        text-decoration: none;
15        font-size: 10pt;
16        font-family: "Arial Black", sans-serif;
17  }
18  a:active, a:hover {
19        color: #ffcc99;              /* vanilla color */
20        background-color: #800000;   /* dark reddish brown */
21        font-size: 10pt;
22        font-family: "Arial Black", sans-serif;
23  }
24  h1 {
25        float: left;
26        color: #ffcc99;              /* vanilla color */
27        font-weight: bold;
28        font-size: 30pt;
29        font-family: Helvetica, Arial, sans-serif;
30        margin-top: 5px;
31  }
32  table {
33        background-color: #ffcc99;    /* vanilla color */
34        border: #800000;              /* dark reddish brown */
35  }
36  blockquote {
37        font-style: italic;
38        font-size: 11pt;
39        font-family: "Times New Roman", Times, Roman, serif;
40  }
41  div {
42        padding-left: 10px;
43        padding-right: 2px;
44        padding-top: 4px;
45        padding-bottom: 4px;
46        background-color: #ffcc99;    /* vanilla color */
47        border: #800000;              /* dark reddish brown */
48  }
49  #MainMenu {
50        position: absolute;
51        top: 70px;
52        left: 250px;
53  }
54  .copyright {
55        margin-left: 200px;
```

```
56          font-size: small;
57  }
58  .copyright a:link, .copyright a:visited, .copyright a:active {
59          color: #ffcc99;
60          font-family: "Times New Roman", Times, Roman, serif;
61  }
62  .copyright a:hover {
63          font-family: "Times New Roman", Times, Roman, serif;
64  }
65  -->
66  </style>
67  </head>
```

Don't worry if you don't understand the CSS code listed in Script 15.2. We'll explain some of it shortly.

One of the most important things about CSS, especially in terms of pertinence to our discussion in this chapter, is that CSS allows you to position elements absolutely on a Web page, down to the exact pixel. Lines 49–53 of Script 15.2 position the navigation menu at coordinates 250,70. This is known as Cascading StyleSheet Positioning. It was originally an addendum to the first CSS specification, but is now part of the current CSS specification.

Here's an example of how you might position a division on the screen and give it a green background color and a width of 150 pixels:

```
<div id="nav" style="position: absolute; left: 100px; ⟶
⟶ top: 50px; width: 150px; background-color: green;">
     content goes here
</div>
```

Figure 15.3 shows this code in action. In this code, the style rules are written inline with the HTML rather than embedded in the head of the document as in Script 15.2. We'll explain this inline use of CSS in more detail a little later on.

**Figure 15.3    *An Absolutely Positioned Element***

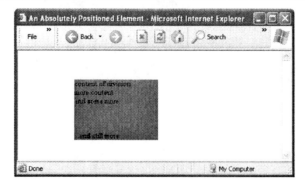

## JavaScript

JavaScript brings dynamism and interactivity to DHTML. You've only to look through this book to get a taste of the cool things that are possible with JavaScript. Not only can it provide interactivity with event handlers, it can also modify document object properties on the fly, pop up windows, and write content dynamically. In the DHTML arena, JavaScript is primarily used to modify stylesheet properties on the fly, after a Web page is loaded, to create animations and special effects.

This use of JavaScript to modify style properties is what we'll concentrate on in this chapter.

# Browser Compatibility Problems with DHTML

Netscape Navigator 4 and Internet Explorer 4 were the first browsers to support DHTML. Unfortunately, they did so using proprietary features and DOM extensions. This forced Web developers desiring to implement DHTML to perform either object detection or browser detection and conditionally write the appropriate code supported by the browser being used.

Although the W3C has specified oodles and oodles of Web technology standards, including HTML, CSS, and the DOM (put them together with a scripting language and you have Dynamic HTML), the browser companies were slow to implement complete support for those standards. The first browser to come close was Netscape's Navigator 6; Opera 6 and IE 6 quickly followed suit.

With each new release, the major browsers support more and more of the standards. Unfortunately, there are still a lot of Web surfers out there using old browsers. If you need to write code that will accommodate the browsers of those lazy updaters, see Appendix F for guidelines and suggestions. In this chapter, we're going to concentrate on the present and future browsers that include support for the W3C's **Document Object Model, Level 2** specification (**DOM2**).

# Understanding CSS

Before we can start applying DHTML, it helps to understand a few more things about stylesheets. We'll start by identifying the parts of a stylesheet, and then show you how to integrate stylesheets into your HTML documents.

## Parts of a Stylesheet

**Stylesheets** are made up of one or more style rules. Each style rule is formed as follows:

```
selector { property: value; }
```

Here's an example of a stylesheet with two style rules.

```
body {
        background-color: #663333; /* dark chocolaty brown */
        background-image: url(images/javaBeans.jpg);
```

```
        color: #ffffff;                         /* white */
        font-size: 12pt;
        font-family: "Times New Roman", Times, Roman, serif;
        margin: 5px 50px;
}
blockquote {
        font-style: italic;
        font-size: 11pt;
        font-family: "Times New Roman", Times, Roman, serif;
}
```

Each **style rule** has two parts: a selector and one or more declarations. The **selector**, usually an HTML element such as body, div, h1, p, or em, specifies to what element(s) the rule applies. The **declaration** specifies what presentation effect to set and how. Declarations are separated by a semicolon.

In the first style rule shown in the stylesheet above, body is the selector, which means that the declarations that follow apply to the whole document, since the whole document, content-wise, is contained within the <body> tag. The <body> tag is an excellent selector for setting a page's default settings such as foreground and background colors and preferred fonts.

In the case of the first style rule, the declarations set the page's background color to a dark chocolaty brown, the background image to javaBeans.jpg, and its foreground or text color to white. The default font is set to 12 point, Times New Roman, with a few substitution options if that font is not available. In order, they are Times, Roman, and serif. Serif is a generic font name and is listed last to allow the browser to substitute a font of that general type as a last resort. Finally, the last declaration in the first style rule sets the top and bottom margins to 5 pixels and the left and right margins to 50 pixels.

Notice the semicolon at the end of each declaration. In CSS, the semicolon is, technically, a statement *separator*, but it's OK to enter one at the end of every line anyway as though it were a statement terminator. In fact, I recommend you get in the habit of ending each declaration with a semicolon. That way you're less likely to leave out one that is critical, between declarations.

> **programmer's tip**
>
> Whenever you use a background image, you should always set a similar background color. That way, if the background image never loads, the visitor can still read the text. If you don't define a background color and the background image doesn't load, then the default background color, often white, will display instead. This could result in an unreadable configuration such as white text on a white background.

Each **declaration** is made up of two parts: a CSS **property** and a **value** to be assigned to that property. A property is a stylistic feature in a document that can be affected. The value associated with a property specifies *how* to affect that stylistic feature. In the case of line 2 of the stylesheet above, the property being affected in the declaration is the background color of the document; how that feature is affected is to be colored dark chocolaty brown.

They say a picture's worth a thousand words, so here's a diagram showing the parts of a stylesheet:

**Figure 15.4     Parts of a Stylesheet**

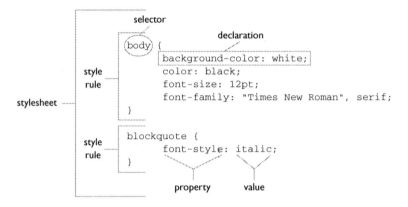

## Types of Selectors

Selectors come in all shapes and sizes. The easiest to understand are **simple selectors**. They apply a style rule to a particular type of HTML element. body, div, h1, p, and em are all simple selectors. For instance, the following rule sets the text color of all paragraphs to green:

```
p { color: green; }
```

**Contextual selectors** are similar to simple selectors in that they usually apply to HTML elements, but HTML elements in the context of HTML elements. Contextual selectors are more specific than simple selectors. For instance, the following rule sets the text color of all emphasized text within a paragraph to red:

```
p em { color: red; }
```

The rest of the text in the paragraph stays the same; only the text inside an <em> tag that itself is inside of a <p> is affected. Text in an <em> tag that is in a <div> will not be affected, and text in an <em> tag just inside the <body> will not be affected by this rule.

The HTML 4 specification added the **class attribute** and made it valid for virtually all HTML elements. It allows authors to classify parts of a document for which there is not already a tag that can provide the necessary context. For instance, you could classify a paragraph of text that contains your copyright notice.

```
<p class="copyright">Copyright Tina McDuffie. All rights
reserved.</p>
```

The advantage of classifying content by its context is that, using a **class selector**, you can then use CSS to apply style rules to the classified content to set stylistic effects. For instance, the following style rule sets the font size to small on all HTML elements whose `class="copyright"`:

```
.copyright { font-size: small; }
```

Notice that in the stylesheet the class name is preceded by a dot to indicate it is a class. A single class can be applied to multiple HTML elements, but each HTML tag can have only one class attribute assigned to it. For instance, you could also assign the copyright class to a division tag:

```
<div class="copyright">Copyright Tina McDuffie. All rights
reserved.</div>
```

The same style rule that uses the `.copyright` selector applies to both the paragraph and division whose `class` attributes are set to `copyright`.

Another type of selector is similar to the class selector. It is the **id selector**. The corresponding `id` attribute was added to the HTML specification to accommodate the need to isolate a single element. While a particular class selector can be applied to multiple HTML elements of the same or various types, a particular ID can be applied to only one HTML element. IDs are primarily used to identify positioned elements.

There are some rules you need to follow when it comes to class and id names. You may not place any spaces or special characters, other than an underscore, in an id or class name. While numbers are allowed, an id or class name cannot begin with a number.

A **positioned element** is any HTML element, usually a division, that has been positioned using the CSS position property. Netscape calls positioned elements **layers**. We'll be working with layers quite a bit in this chapter.

The last selectors that are of any importance to our discussion here are the **anchor pseudo-class selectors**. Ever wonder how a link gets classified as visited or active or just a plain link? The browser does that based on its history list. As there is no HTML element that can differentiate among an unfollowed link, a visited link, an active link, and a link that the mouse is hovering over, CSS introduced the **anchor pseudo-classes**: `a:link`, `a:visited`, `a:active`, and `a:hover`. Notice the colon between the a and the pseudo-class name.

## Connecting CSS Rules to HTML Documents

There are three primary ways of connecting style rules to an HTML document.

1. You can attach an external stylesheet, using the <link> tag in the <head> of the document. **External stylesheets** are plain text documents that have a .css extension. They are the best way to go whenever possible because you can attach the same external stylesheet to multiple documents. If you want to change the look and feel of your site, you change that one document. Here's how you link it to the

document(s) it applies to. Place the <link> tag within the <head> of each document, like this:

```
<head>
    <link rel="stylesheet" href="styles/mainStyle.css"
        type="text/css">
</head>
```

Only style rules and CSS comments can be written in an external stylesheet file. The `rel` attribute specifies how the linked file relates to the document, `href` provides a relative or absolute path to the external stylesheet, and `type` indicates the MIME type of the attached file. Here's what an external stylesheet might look like:

```
/* Main stylesheet for WebWoman Web Site
   Author/Designer: Tina McDuffie
   Last update:                              */
body {
        background-color: white;
        color: black;
        font-family: Arial, Helvetica, sans-serif;
}
a:link {
        color: blue;
}
a:visited {
        color: grey;
}
a:active {
        color: fuchsia;
}
a:hover {
        color: white;
        background-color: blue;
}
```

Notice that there are no HTML tags whatsoever in the document shown above. Do not make the mistake of including <style> tags in an external stylesheet; only stylesheet rules and comments are allowed.

2. You can embed style rules in a <style> tag in the <head> of an HTML document as we saw in Script 15.2. Embedding rules is good when those rules either override rules set in an external stylesheet or when they apply only to the current document.

3. You can write style rules inline with HTML tags. In general, this approach should be avoided whenever possible because it eliminates a lot of the advantages of using

CSS in the first place. However, when it comes to positioning elements and moving them around the screen or performing other special effects with them, inline rules sometimes are the only way that will work. They're also a nice way to test and tweak a style rule before adding it to an external or embedded stylesheet.

To write style rules inline, use the `style` attribute, which can be set on almost all tags you can legally place in the <body> of an HTML document.

```
<div style="position: absolute; top: 20px; left: 100px;">
    content of division tag goes here
</div>
```

Follow it with an equals sign and opening and closing quotation marks. Within the quotation marks, write the style declarations you want to apply to that particular HTML element, separated by semicolons.

In this chapter, we'll primarily be using options 2 and 3. We'll use option 2 to set general styles for documents and we'll use option 3 for absolutely positioned elements. Normally, I would use option 1 to set general style rules, but since we won't be creating a whole Web site, it is easier to embed the rules right into the document to which they apply. Then you can easily see everything that's going on in one script.

Now that we know a little about how stylesheets work, let's see how we can access styles with JavaScript.

## Working with CSS Successfully

*programmer's tip*

Here are some tried and true tips that can help make working with CSS a breeze.

✗ Hide <script> and <style> tag content from older and text-only browsers so your code degrades gracefully with an HTML comment.

✗ When using CSS, stick to pixel units when defining positioning and positive integers when specifying the z-index. Pixels are easier to envision because you're positioning elements on a page that is so many pixels wide by so many pixels high. Keep in mind, however, that many CSS gurus recommend that you use relative units for margins and the like. *Positioning* elements, however, is, in my mind, an absolute science.

✗ Be careful of the order in which you list your content when using CSS. Although CSS will let you position your last bit of content at the top of the page and your first bit at the bottom, be aware that older browsers will simply display the content in the order it is listed in the document. Organize your content so it reads in a meaningful way from the top of the HTML code to the bottom.

✗ When positioning elements with CSS, you'll often have more success if you wrap the element you want to position in a <div> tag, then apply positioning declarations to the <div>. When positioning is directly applied to <img> elements and other tags besides <div>, the positioning often acts unpredictably.

# Accessing Elements According to the W3C's DOM2

The easiest way to access an element in a Web page is to call the
`document.getElementById("objId")` method, which is supported by all DOM2-compliant browsers. Note that it is `Element` singular. This method returns the object with the specified ID. Remember, a particular ID can be used only once, on one, single HTML element. You can use the `document.getElementById("objId")` reference to access or set that object's properties and styles. Keep in mind that the only *style* properties you can access are the ones that were set inline. Those set in an embedded or external stylesheet are accessed differently.

However, you can *set* a style property using the
`document.getElementById("objId")` reference, like this:

```
// in the HTML document, assume this element was created:
// <div id="content">Some text.</div>

document.getElementById("content").style="margin-left:  30px"
```

Cool, huh?

To allow you to access a group of elements by their tag name, the DOM2 specification includes `document.getElementsByTagName("tag")`. Notice the plural `Elements`. `document.getElementsByTagName("tag")` returns an array of all the elements with the designated tag name in the order they appear in the document. You can then use array references to access individual elements. For instance,

```
document.getElementsByTagName("a")
```

returns an array of all of the anchor elements in the document. The code

```
document.getElementsByTagName("a")[0].href
```

returns the `href` attribute of the first anchor tag in the document.

Here's a quick reference to the properties most often used when working with DHTML.

**Table 15.1    DHTML Property Quick Reference**

| Absolutely Positioned Object Property | Property Reference (6.0+ browsers) | Result Type |
|---|---|---|
| background color | `document.getElementById("objId")`<br>`.style.backgroundColor`<br>In OP:<br>`document.getElementById("objId")`<br>`.style.background` | Six-digit hexadecimal number |

| background image | `document.getElementById("objId")`<br>`.style.backgroundImage`<br>In IE: not supported<br>In OP: not supported | URL to image |
|---|---|---|
| border color | `document.getElementById("objId")`<br>`.style.borderColor` | Six-digit hexadecimal number |
| border style | `document.getElementById("objId")`<br>`.style.borderStyle` | String: `solid`, `inset`, `outset`, or `groove` |
| border width | `document.getElementById("objId")`<br>`.style.borderWidth` | String: `n unit` |
| clip | `document.getElementById("objId")`<br>`.style.clip`<br>In OP: not supported | `rect(0px 50px 50px 20px)` `rect(auto auto auto auto)` |
| content | `document.getElementById("objId")`<br>`.innerHTML`[1]<br>In OP: not supported | String |
| height | `document.getElementById("objId")`<br>`.style.height` | String: `n px`<br>In OP, string: `n` |
| left (x-coordinate) | `document.getElementById("objId")`<br>`.style.left` | String: `n px`<br>In OP, string: `n` |
| object | `document.getElementById("objId")` | The object |
| overflow | `document.getElementById("objId")`<br>`.style.overflow`<br>In OP: not supported | `auto`, `hidden`, or `scroll` |
| top (y-coordinate) | `document.getElementById("objId")`<br>`.style.top` | String: `n px`<br>In OP, string: `n` |
| visibility | `document.getElementById("objId")`<br>`.style.visibility` | `hidden`, `visible`, or `inherit` |
| width | `document.getElementById("objId")`<br>`.width` | String: `n px`<br>In OP, string: `n` |

| Other Property | Property Reference (6.0+ browsers) | Result Type |
|---|---|---|
| font color | `document.getElementById("objId")`<br>`.style.color` | Six-digit hexadecimal number |
| set style on an element | `document.getElementById("objId")`<br>`.style = "declaration"` | |
| stylesheet properties | `document.getElementById("objId")`<br>`.style.property` | Depends on property |
| window height | `window.innerHeight`<br>In IE: `window.document.body`<br>`.clientHeight` | Number |
| window width | `window.innerWidth`<br>In IE: `window.document.body`<br>`.clientWidth` | Number |

Replace italicized items appropriately
[1] Not part of W3C standard

There's a lot more to the DOM2 specification, enough to fill an entire book. For our purposes, however, this is all you need to know. Now let's see how it all works together. Let's animate a positioned element.

# Animating a Positioned Element

To get your feet wet, let's start with a simple script that moves a division across the screen. We'll place a picture of a mermaid within the division and have her weave in and out of some Greek columns placed in other divisions on the screen.

## Creating the Divisions with HTML

The first things you need to do are create the divisions and place the pictures in them.

### Script 15.3    Creating the Divisions

```
1    <html>
2    <head>
3    <title>Script 15.3: Creating the Divisions</title>
4    </head>
5    <body bgcolor="#0000FF" background="images/waterBG2.jpg">
6    <div>
7            <img name="Maid" src="images/mermaidSwimming.gif"
8                width="273" height="83" border="0" alt="mermaid">
9    </div>
10   <div>
```

```
11              <img src="images/GreekColumnTransSm.gif" width="76"
12                  height="275" border="0" alt="column">
13  </div>
14  <div>
15              <img src="images/GreekColumnTransSm.gif" width="76"
16                  height="275" border="0" alt="column">
17  </div>
18  <div>
19              <img src="images/GreekColumnTransSm.gif" width="76"
20                  height="275" border="0" alt="column">
21  </div>
22  </body>
23  </html>
```

At this point, the page isn't much to look at. The mermaid and columns appear stacked on top of each other.

*Figure 15.5    Results of Script 15.3*

## Turning the Divisions into Layers with CSS

Now let's turn those static divisions into absolutely positioned elements that you can move around the screen.

**Script 15.4    Positioning the Divisions**

```
1    <html>
2    <head>
3    <title>Script 15.4: Positioning the Divisions</title>
4    </head>
5    <body bgcolor="#0000FF" background="images/waterBG2.jpg">
6    <div id="mermaid"
7     style="position: absolute; top: 150px; left: 0px; z-index: 3;
          width=273">
8          <img name="Maid" src="images/mermaidSwimming.gif"
9                width="273" height="83" border="0" alt="mermaid">
10   </div>
11   <div id="column1"
12     style="position: absolute; top: 30px; left: 100px; z-index: 1">
13          <img src="images/GreekColumnTransSm.gif" width="76"
14                height="275" border="0" alt="column">
15   </div>
16   <div id="column2"
17     style="position: absolute; top: 30px; left: 300px; z-index: 4">
18          <img src="images/GreekColumnTransSm.gif" width="76"
19                height="275" border="0" alt="column">
20   </div>
21   <div id="column3"
22     style="position: absolute; top: 30px; left: 500px; z-index: 2">
23          <img src="images/GreekColumnTransSm.gif" width="76"
24                height="275" border="0" alt="column">
25   </div>
26   </body>
27   </html>
```

Notice the `style` attribute added to each division (lines 7, 12, 17, and 22). These inline style rules set the positioning type as well as the x-, y-, and z-coordinates of the divisions.

The `position` property specifies the type of positioning applied to the selector. Usually, you'll use absolute positioning whenever you want to move, animate, hide, or show a layer dynamically. The `top` property specifies the y-coordinate of the top-left corner of the element being positioned, that is, the number of pixels down from the top edge of the browser window. The `left` property specifies the x-coordinate of the top-left corner of the element being positioned, that is, the number of pixels over from the left edge of the browser window. The `z-index` property specifies the z-coordinate of the element. The higher the `z-index` property, the more on top the element is. Notice that the `mermaid` has a `z-index` of 3 (line 7), while `column1` has a `z-index` of 1 (line 12). With the higher z-index, the `mermaid` will appear on top of `column1` as you can see here in

Figure 15.6. The id attribute added to each division (lines 6, 11, 16, and 21) identifies the divisions so they can be accessed with JavaScript.

***Figure 15.6     Results of Positioning the Divisions in Script 15.4***

Doesn't everything look much better with all of the images positioned?

## Objects, Properties, and Methods Useful for Animating Layers

Now we need to figure out how to access the mermaid layer with JavaScript so you can make her swim across the screen. Fortunately, this is easy with the newest browsers because they all support the DOM2 method `getElementsById("elementId")`. To access the mermaid we would type

```
document.getElementById("mermaid")
```

Next we need to know how to access the mermaid's position (see Table 15.1). The left and top stylesheet properties can tell us that: `style.left` and `style.top`. Each complete reference is

```
document.getElementById("mermaid").style.left
document.getElementById("mermaid").style.top
```

To change their values, type

```
document.getElementById("objectId").style.left = newX + "px"
document.getElementById("objectId").style.top = newY + "px"
```

where `objectId` is the layer's ID, newX is the desired x-coordinate, and newY is the desired new y-coordinate.

## Moving an Object to a Specific Position with JavaScript

Now that we know how to get an object's position, we can write a function to change its position:

```
function moveTo(objectId, newX, newY) {
   if (document.getElementById) {
         document.getElementById(objectId).style.left = newX
         document.getElementById(objectId).style.top = newY
   }
}
```

Notice the `if` statement? That statement is an example of **object detection**, determining if a particular object is supported. The above `if` statement prevents execution of the object movement if the browser doesn't support DOM2's `document.getElementById`. See Appendix F for a more in-depth discussion of object detection and its cousin, browser detection. Appendix F also explains how to use DHTML in older browsers.

## Moving an Object by So Many Pixels with JavaScript

Let's write a function to move an object *by* some number of pixels at a time.

```
function moveBy(objectId, x, y) {
   if (document.getElementById) {
      var left =
         parseInt(document.getElementById(objectId).style.left)
      var top =
         parseInt(document.getElementById(objectId).style.top)
      document.getElementById(objectId).style.left = left + x
      document.getElementById(objectId).style.top = top + y
   }
}
```

The `style.left` and `style.top` properties each return a number followed by a unit of measurement, usually "px" for pixels. Since the `left` and `top` properties are strings, you must convert them to numbers before you can perform any calculations. It's OK to assign numbers to the `left` and `top` properties; JavaScript will assume the measurement is in pixels.

OK, now we have a function that can move an object to a particular position and one that can move it by so many pixels up, down, left, or right. (Use negative numbers to move up or left.) Let's add some form buttons to the document so we can test our functions with different parameters.

### Script 15.5    *Moving the Mermaid Around the Screen*

```
1  <html>
2  <head>
3  <title>Script 15.5 : Moving the Mermaid Around the
     Screen</title>
4  <script language="JavaScript" type="text/javascript"><!--
5  function moveTo(objectId, x, y) {
```

```
 6        if (document.getElementById) {
 7              document.getElementById(objectId).style.left = x
 8              document.getElementById(objectId).style.top = y
 9        }
10  }
11
12  function moveBy(objectId, x, y) {
13        if (document.getElementById) {
14            var left =
               parseInt(document.getElementById(objectId).style.left)
15            var top =
               parseInt(document.getElementById(objectId).style.top)
16            document.getElementById(objectId).style.left = left + x
17            document.getElementById(objectId).style.top = top + y
18        }
19  }
20  //-->
21  </script>
22  </head>
23  <body bgcolor="#0000FF" background="images/waterBG2.jpg">
24  <div id="mermaid"
25   style="position: absolute; top: 150px; left: 0px; z-index: 3;
        width=273;">
26          <img name="Maid" src="images/mermaidSwimming.gif"
27              width="273" height="83" border="0" alt="mermaid">
28  </div>
29  <div id="column1"
30   style="position: absolute; top: 30px; left: 100px;
        z-index: 1;">
31          <img src="images/GreekColumnTransSm.gif" width="76"
32              height="275" border="0" alt="column">
33  </div>
34  <div id="column2"
35   style="position: absolute; top: 30px; left: 300px;
        z-index: 4;">
36          <img src="images/GreekColumnTransSm.gif" width="76"
37              height="275" border="0" alt="column">
38  </div>
39  <div id="column3"
40   style="position: absolute; top: 30px; left: 500px;
        z-index: 2;">
41          <img src="images/GreekColumnTransSm.gif" width="76"
42              height="275" border="0" alt="column">
43  </div>
44  <div align="center"
```

```
45      style="position: absolute; top: 350px; left: 210px;">
46          <form>
47                  <input type="button" value="Up-Left"
48                      onClick="moveBy('mermaid', -10, -10)">
49                  <input type="button" value="UP"
50                      onClick="moveBy('mermaid', 0, -10)">
51                  <input type="button" value="Up-Right"
52                      onClick="moveBy('mermaid', 10, -10)"><br>
53                  <input type="button" value="LEFT "
54                      onClick="moveBy('mermaid', -10, 0)">
55                  <input type="button" value="Center"
56                      onClick="moveTo('mermaid', 190, 130)">
57                  <input type="button" value="RIGHT"
58                      onClick="moveBy('mermaid', 10, 0)"><br>
59                  <input type="button" value="Down-Left"
60                      onClick="moveBy('mermaid', -10, 10)">
61                  <input type="button" value="DOWN"
62                      onClick="moveBy('mermaid', 0, 10)">
63                  <input type="button" value="Down-Right"
64                      onClick="moveBy('mermaid', 10, 10)"><br>
65          </form>
66      </div>
67      </body>
68      </html>
```

Figure 15.7 shows what our document should look like in a browser.

**Figure 15.7    Results of Script 15.5**

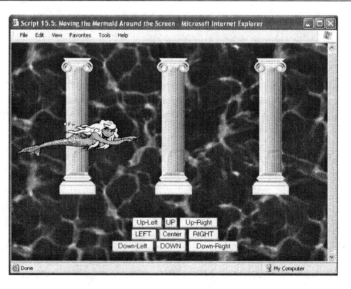

Go ahead and take her for a swim. Click some buttons and watch the mermaid move around the screen.

## Animating an Object

Now that we've got some functions to perform the movement operations, let's see how we can make use of them to perform animations. To animate the mermaid, we need to move her *periodically* and *automatically* a few pixels at a time. The moveBy function we just created and tested should do the trick if we call a setTimeout at the end to recall the function. We'll need to specify an end point and a new starting point once that end point has been reached. This function should do the trick:

```
function animateObj(objectId, startPoint, endPoint) {
    if (document.getElementById) {
        var left =
            parseInt(document.getElementById(objectId).style.left)
        var timeOut = "animateObj(\'" + objectId + "\', " +
                        startPoint + ", " + endPoint + ")"
        if (left < endPoint) {
            document.getElementById(objectId).style.left =
                left + 5
        } else {
            document.getElementById(objectId).style.left =
                startPoint
        }
        setTimeout(timeOut, 2)
    }
}
```

So far so good. Now let's figure out the end point.

## Getting Window Dimensions

Knowing a window's current dimensions can come in handy when you want to position an object in the center of the screen or move it off of the screen.

Netscape added the innerWidth and innerHeight properties to the window object in JavaScript 1.2. Unfortunately, Internet Explorer does not support them. IE does, however, support two similar properties: window.document.body.clientWidth and window.document.body.clientHeight.

Object detection comes in handy to determine which code to use:

```
if(window.innerWidth) {
        // use window.innerWidth property
} else if (window.document.body.clientWidth) {
        // use window.document.body.clientWidth property
}
```

Let's make our mermaid swim to the right and off of the screen completely, then swim back on from the left side. To do this we'll need to perform a calculation: `windowWidth + objWidth`.

```
var swimEnd = 0
var objWidth = 270    // set to width of animated object
if(window.innerWidth) {
        swimEnd = window.innerWidth
} else if (window.document.body.clientWidth) {
        swimEnd = window.document.body.clientWidth
}
swimEnd += objWidth
```

Let's put it all together now and make that mermaid swim by herself!

**Script 15.6    Swimming Mermaid**

```
1    <html>
2    <head>
3    <title>Script 15.6: Swimming Mermaid</title>
4    <script language="JavaScript" type="text/javascript"><!--
5    function moveBy(objectId, x, y) {
6        if (document.getElementById) {
7            var left =
                 parseInt(document.getElementById(objectId).style.left)
8            var top =
                 parseInt(document.getElementById(objectId).style.top)
9            document.getElementById(objectId).style.left = left + x
10           document.getElementById(objectId).style.top = top + y
11        }
12    }
13
14   function animateObj(objectId, startPoint, endPoint) {
15       if (document.getElementById) {
16           var left =
                parseInt(document.getElementById(objectId).style.left)
17           var timeOut = "animateObj(\'" + objectId + "\', " +
18                       startPoint + ", " + endPoint + ")"
19           if (left < endPoint) {
20               document.getElementById(objectId).style.left = left + 5
21           } else {
22               document.getElementById(objectId).style.left =
                    startPoint
23           }
24           setTimeout(timeOut, 2)
25       }
26   }
```

```
27  //-->
28  </script>
29  </head>
30  <body bgcolor="#0000FF" background="images/waterBG2.jpg">
31  <div id="mermaid"
32   style="position: absolute; top: 150px; left: 0px; z-index: 3;
        width=273;">
33        <img name="Maid" src="images/mermaidSwimming.gif"
34            width="273" height="83" border="0" alt="mermaid">
35  </div>
36  <div id="column1"
37   style="position: absolute; top: 30px; left: 100px;
        z-index: 1;">
38        <img src="images/GreekColumnTransSm.gif" width="76"
39            height="275" border="0" alt="column">
40  </div>
41  <div id="column2"
42   style="position: absolute; top: 30px; left: 300px;
        z-index: 4;">
43        <img src="images/GreekColumnTransSm.gif" width="76"
44            height="275" border="0" alt="column">
45  </div>
46  <div id="column3"
47   style="position: absolute; top: 30px; left: 500px;
        z-index: 2;">
48        <img src="images/GreekColumnTransSm.gif" width="76"
49            height="275" border="0" alt="column">
50  </div>
51  <form style="position: absolute; top: 350px; left: 294px;">
52        <input type="button" value="Start Swim"
53            onClick="animateObj('mermaid', -270, swimEnd)">
54  </form>
55  <script language="JavaScript"><!--
56        var swimEnd = 0
57        var objWidth = 270    //set to width of animated object
58        if(window.innerWidth) {
59            swimEnd = window.innerWidth
60        } else if (window.document.body.clientWidth) {
61            swimEnd = window.document.body.clientWidth
62        }
63        swimEnd += objWidth
64  //-->
65  </script>
66  </body>
67  </html>
```

Figure 15.8 shows what the final sea scene created in Script 15.6 looks like.

**Figure 15.8    Swimming Mermaid: Results of Script 15.6**

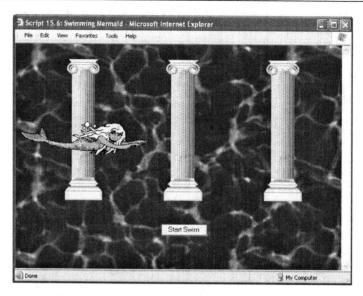

Don't be shy, take her for a swim! Because of the z-index settings, she will swim behind the middle column. Because we set the `endPoint` of her swim to the `windowWidth +` `objWidth` (line 63) she'll swim off the screen, not just till her hands touch the right side. She'll then appear to swim *into* the window from the left, because we set the `startPoint` to a negative number equal to the mermaid's width (line 53).

Now let's look at another popular DHTML task: the pull-down menu.

## Pull-down DHTML Menus

A pull-down Dynamic HTML menu has got to be the most requested DHTML script ever. I can't count the number of students who've asked me for this one. So, because of popular demand, I'll show you how it's done, simply. There are many more complicated pull-down DHTML menu scripts available; "Simply the Best Scripts" (http://www.simplythebest.net/ info/dhtml_menus.html) has quite a few, as does "Dynamic Drive" (http:// www.dynamicdrive.com). After you've mastered the one in this chapter, you might want to try your hand at one of the others.

Let's add a pull-down DHTML menu to the Javabilaya home page shown in Figure 15.2. When a visitor mouses over a menu item that has subcategories, a division is displayed showing those subcategories, like in Figure 15.9.

**Figure 15.9    The Desired Pull-down DHTML Menu**

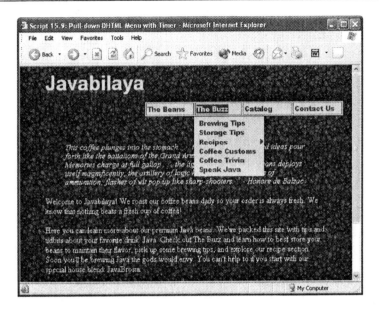

In this pull-down menu script, we'll take the time to make it work in older browsers as well. See Appendix F for a complete cross-browser DHTML reference and discussion.

## Creating and Positioning Divisions for Submenus

The first thing we have to do is create a division for each submenu. Script 15.7 shows the code for the submenu divisions. MainMenu was created with a table; you can see the code for it in Script 15.1, lines 8 through 17. The code for the divisions should be placed right after MainMenu. Give each division an `id` name and position it with a `style` attribute and the appropriate stylesheet declarations.

**Script 15.7    Divisions for Submenus**

```
1    <div id="BeansMenu"
2    style="position: absolute; top: 100px; left: 250px;
        visibility: hidden">
3        <a href="beans/BMB.html">Blue Mountain Blast</a><br>
4        <a href="beans/FV.html">French Vanilla</a><br>
5        <a href="beans/GCM.html">German Chocolate Mint</a><br>
```

```
 6          <a href="beans/HK.html">Hawaiian Kona</a><br>
 7          <a href="beans/JB.html">Javabrosia (House Blend)</a><br>
 8   </div>
 9
10   <div id="BuzzMenu"
11    style="position: absolute; top: 100px; left: 350px;
          visibility: hidden">
12          <a href="buzz/index.html">Brewing Tips</a><br>
13          <a href="buzz/storageTips.html">Storage Tips</a><br>
14          <a href="buzz/recipes/index.html">Recipes</a>
15                  
16              
17          <img src="images/brownArrow.gif" width="6" height="12"
18               border="0" align="bottom" alt="&gt;"><br>
19          <a href="buzz/customs.html">Coffee Customs</a><br>
20          <a href="buzz/trivia.html">Coffee Trivia</a><br>
21          <a href="buzz/glossary.html">Speak Java</a><br>
22   </div>
23
24   <div id="CatalogMenu"
25    style="position: absolute; top: 100px; left: 450px;
          visibility: hidden">
26          <a href="catalog/coffees.html">Coffees</a><br>
27          <a href="catalog/teas.html">Teas</a><br>
28          <a href="catalog/cocoas">Cocoas</a><br>
29          <a href="catalog/equipment/index.html">Equipment</a> 
30          <img src="images/brownArrow.gif" width="6" height="12"
31               border="0" align="bottom" alt="&gt;"><br>
32   </div>
33
34   <div id="RecipesSubmenu"
35    style="position: absolute; top: 136px; left: 488px;
          visibility: hidden">
36          <a href="recipes/french.html">French Kiss</a><br>
37          <a href="recipes/gcmFrapachino.html">GCM
               Frapachino</a><br>
38          <a href="recipes/godsDelight.html">God's Delight</a><br>
39          <a href="recipes/javaBlast.html">Java Blast</a><br>
40          <a href="recipes/konaVolcano.html">Kona Volcano</a><br>
41          <a href="recipes/mochaJoe.html">Mocha Joe</a><br>
42          <a href="recipes/vanillaCloud.html">Vanilla Cloud</a><br>
43   </div>
44
45   <div id="EquipmentSubmenu"
```

```
46    style="position: absolute; top: 155px; left: 554px;
         visibility: hidden">
47        <a href="catalog/equipment/grinders.html">Coffee
            Grinders</a><br>
48        <a href="catalog/equipment/coffeeMakers.html">Coffee
            Makers</a><br>
49        <a href="catalog/equipment/expressoMachines.html">Espresso
            Machines</a><br>
50        <a href="catalog/equipment/cups.html">Java Vessels</a><br>
51    </div>
```

Determining the appropriate coordinates of each submenu requires some guesswork and experimentation. The more you do it, the better you'll become at "guesstimating" pixels.

MainMenu is positioned (lines 51 and 52 of Script 15.2) at the coordinates (250,70). It is a 400-pixel-wide table with each cell's width set to 100. This should make positioning the submenus pretty easy. Because MainMenu's top is positioned at 70 and it's a good guess that the table itself is approximately 25 to 30 pixels high, let's first try 95 (70 + 25) or 100 (70+30) as the value for the top property of the BeansMenu division.

MainMenu's left property was set to 250. Usually, you want the submenu's left edge to line up with the main menu's left edge. That value is easy to determine; in this case, it is 250px, same as that for MainMenu.

OK, now's the time to try it. Set the visibility property for the BeansMenu to visible. See how it looks in your browser. Here's how it looks in IE with the top set to 95:

**side note**

Keep in mind that there's no such thing as one perfect solution for all browsers. Each will look slightly different. I guess all pixels are not created equally in all browsers. The best you can do is get your menu to look decent in all of them and hopefully look the best in the browser most used by your audience. As the browsers continue to improve in their support for W3C standards, this situation should improve as well.

**Figure 15.10  Experimenting to Get the Positioning of Submenus Right**

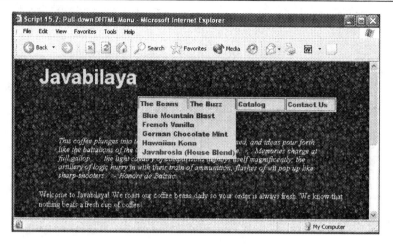

It looks a little high, so try 100. 100 is just perfect, as you can see in Figure 15.9. That's the process: guess, test, and adjust.

## Making a Plan

Let's think a little more about how we want the pull-down menu to work.

1. When the visitor moves the mouse over a MainMenu item that has a submenu, we want to hide any visible submenus, then display the submenu for the current MainMenu item.
2. When the visitor moves the mouse over a submenu item that has its own submenu, then we *don't* want to hide the first submenu, we just want to display that item's submenu.

## Changing an Element's Visibility

First things first, we need to be able to hide and show menus. Sounds like a good time for some functions.

```
function show(elementId) {
    if (document.getElementById) {
        document.getElementById(elementId).style.visibility ⟶
        ⟶ = "visible"
    } else if (document.layers) {
        document.layers[elementId].visibility = "show"
    } else if (document.all) {
        document.all[elementId].style.visibility = "visible"
    }
}
```

```
function hide(elementId) {
    if (document.getElementById) {
        document.getElementById(elementId).style.visibility ⟶
        ⟶ = "hidden"
    } else if (document.layers) {
        document.layers[elementId].visibility = "hide"
    } else if (document.all) {
        document.all[elementId].style.visibility = "hidden"
    }
}
```

These two functions use object detection to execute the appropriate statement to access the `visibility` property in the browser currently being used by the visitor. DHTML browsers compliant with the W3C's DOM2 specification support the `document.getElementById` object. Netscape Navigator 4 and Internet Explorer 4 each support absolutely positioned elements in their own way. NN 4 uses `document.layers[elementId]`, and IE 4 uses `document.all[elementId]`, hence the `else if` statements. If you have no need to support these old browsers, simply remove the two `else if` statements in each function.

To test it, set up two form buttons, one to call the hide function and the other to call the show function.

**Figure 15.11    Testing the `hide` and `show` Functions**

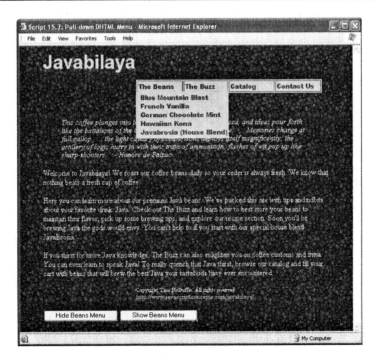

Try it. If you entered everything correctly it should work fine.

According to our plan, sometimes we need to hide all menus and sometimes we don't, so we're going to need to be able to keep track of which menus are active. That way we can easily turn them off. Since we may want to allow even more submenus off of the submenus, an array is in order:

```
var activeMenus = new Array()
```

Make it global; that is, don't declare it within any functions.

Since sometimes we have to hide all of the menus (item 1 of our plan), we ought to write a function to fulfill that task. The `hide` function we wrote earlier can hide only one menu at a time. This function, however, should do the trick.

```
function hideAll() {
    if(activeMenus.length != 0) {
        for (i=activeMenus.length-1; i>=0; i--) {
            hide(activeMenus.pop())
        }
    }
}
```

Now that we have a way to keep track of the IDs of the active menus, we need a function that can pull down (show) a menu according to the needs we identified in our plan. If the visitor rolls over a menu item on the main menu (level 1), then we should hide all menus, otherwise we don't want to hide any menus. Next we should show the appropriate submenu, then we should add the menu's ID to the `activeMenus` array. Here goes:

```
function pullDown(menuId, level) {
    if (level == 1) {
        hideAll()
    }
    show(menuId)
    activeMenus[activeMenus.length] = menuId
}
```

Let's apply it and see if it works. On every menu item that has an associated submenu, set up an onMouseOver event handler to call `pullDown`, like this:

```
<a href="beans/index.html"
    onMouseOver="pullDown('BeansMenu', 1)">The Beans</a>
```

The first argument is the ID of the submenu, the second the menu level. The first level of submenus is level one, the second level two, etc. `MainMenu` is level 0. Now run Script 15.8 from your CD. Figure 15.12 shows what happens when you mouse over Catalog, then Equipment.

### Figure 15.12    Working Pull-down Menu—Sort Of

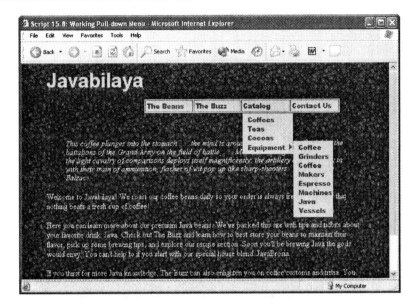

It works. Unfortunately, there's one problem. See if you can discover it.

The problem is that the menu never turns off. It looks like we need to set a timer, whenever we mouse off of an item, to automatically hide all of the menus after a certain period of time has elapsed.

The `setTimeout` window method can do the trick. We'll need to set up a global timer variable so we can clear the timeout as needed, write a function that can be called from an `onMouseout` event handler to start the timer, and modify our `pullDown` function slightly. We can declare the timer global variable right after the declaration of our `activeMenus` array.

```
var timer = null
```

The `startTimer` function should take into account that a timer may already be running, and if so clear it before setting another.

```
function startTimer() {
    if (timer != null) {
        clearTimeout(timer)
    }
    timer = setTimeout("hideAll()", 5000)
}
```

Whenever we mouse over a menu item, we want to show its associated submenu, if it has one. We don't want that submenu disappearing as long as we have the mouse on that menu item, now do we? For that reason, we should clear the timer if it is set whenever we pull down a menu. When we mouse out, we can start the timer again.

```
function pullDown(menuId, level) {
    if (timer != null) {
        clearTimeout(timer)
    }
    if (level == 1) {
        hideAll()
    }
    show(menuId)
    activeMenus[activeMenus.length] = menuId
}
```

OK, now add an onMouseout event handler that calls startTimer to every menu item, like this:

```
<a href="beans/BMB.html"
    onMouseOut="startTimer()">Blue Mountain Blast</a>
```

Here's what the entire pull-down DHTML menu script looks like:

### Script 15.8    Pull-down DHTML Menu with Timer

```
1    <html>
2    <head>
3    <title>Script 15.8: Pull-Down DHTML Menu With Timer</title>
4    <style type="text/css"><!--
5    body {
6            background-color: #663333;   /* dark chocolaty brown */
7            background-image: url(images/javaBeans.jpg);
8            color: #ffffff;                /* white */
9            font-size: 12pt;
10           font-family: "Times New Roman", Times, Roman, serif;
11           margin: 5px 50px;
12   }
13   a:link, a:visited {
14           color: #800000;                /* dark reddish brown */
15           text-decoration: none;
16           font-size: 10pt;
17           font-family: "Arial Black", sans-serif;
18   }
19   a:active, a:hover {
20           color: #ffcc99;                /* vanilla color */
21           background-color: #800000;   /* dark reddish brown */
22           font-size: 10pt;
23           font-family: "Arial Black", sans-serif;
```

```
24  }
25  h1 {
26        float: left;
27        color: #ffcc99;            /* vanilla color */
28        font-weight: bold;
29        font-size: 30pt;
30        font-family: Helvetica, Arial, sans-serif;
31        margin-top: 5px;
32  }
33  table {
34        background-color: #ffcc99;  /* vanilla color */
35        border: #800000;            /* dark reddish brown */
36  }
37  blockquote {
38        font-style: italic;
39        font-size: 11pt;
40        font-family: "Times New Roman", Times, Roman, serif;
41  }
42  div {
43        padding-left: 10px;
44        padding-right: 2px;
45        padding-top: 4px;
46        padding-bottom: 4px;
47        background-color: #ffcc99;  /* vanilla color */
48        border: #800000;            /* dark reddish brown */
49  }
50  #MainMenu {
51        position: absolute;
52        top: 70px;
53        left: 250px;
54  }
55  .copyright {
56        margin-left: 200px;
57        font-size: small;
58  }
59  .copyright a:link, .copyright a:visited, .copyright a:active {
60        color: #ffcc99;
61        font-family: "Times New Roman", Times, Roman, serif;
62  }
63  .copyright a:hover {
64        font-family: "Times New Roman", Times, Roman, serif;
65  }
66  -->
67  </style>
68  <script language="JavaScript" type="text/javascript"><!--
```

```
69  var activeMenus = new Array()
70  var timer = null
71
72  function hide(elementId) {
73    if (document.getElementById) {
74        document.getElementById(elementId).style.visibility =
            "hidden"
75    } else if (document.layers) {
76        document.layers[elementId].visibility = "hide"
77    } else if (document.all) {
78        document.all[elementId].style.visibility = "hidden"
79    }
80  }
81
82  function hideAll() {
83        if(activeMenus.length != 0) {
84            for (i=activeMenus.length-1; i>=0;  i--) {
85                hide(activeMenus.pop())
86            }
87        }
88  }
89
90  function show(elementId) {
91    if (document.getElementById) {
92        document.getElementById(elementId).style.visibility =
            "visible"
93    } else if (document.layers) {
94        document.layers[elementId].visibility = "show"
95    } else if (document.all) {
96        document.all[elementId].style.visibility = "visible"
97        }
98  }
99
100 function startTimer() {
101        if (timer != null) {
102            clearTimeout(timer)
103        }
104        timer = setTimeout("hideAll()", 5000)
105 }
106
107 function pullDown(menuId, level) {
108        if (timer != null) {
109            clearTimeout(timer)
110        }
```

```
111          if (level == 1) {
112              hideAll()
113          }
114          show(menuId)
115          activeMenus[activeMenus.length] = menuId
116 }
117 //-->
118 </script>
119 </head>
120 <body>
121 <h1>Javabilaya</h1>
122
123 <table id="MainMenu" width="400" border="1" cellpadding="2"
124          bordercolor="#800000"><tr>
125        <td width=100>
126              <a href="beans/index.html"
127                onMouseOver="pullDown('BeansMenu', 1)"
128                onMouseOut="startTimer()">The Beans</a></td>
129        <td width=100>
130              <a href="buzz/index.html"
131                onMouseOver="pullDown('BuzzMenu', 1)"
132                onMouseOut="startTimer()">The Buzz</a></td>
133        <td width=100>
134              <a href="catalog/index.html"
135                onMouseOver="pullDown('CatalogMenu', 1)"
136                onMouseOut="startTimer()">Catalog</a></td>
137        <td width=100>
138              <a href="contactUs/index.html"
139                onMouseOut="startTimer()">Contact Us</a></td>
140 </tr></table>
141
142 <div id="BeansMenu"
143  style="position: absolute; top: 100px; left: 250px;
      visibility: hidden">
144        <a href="beans/BMB.html"
145          onMouseOut="startTimer()">Blue Mountain Blast</a><br>
146        <a href="beans/FV.html"
147          onMouseOut="startTimer()">French Vanilla</a><br>
148        <a href="beans/GCM.html"
149          onMouseOut="startTimer()">German Chocolate Mint</a><br>
150        <a href="beans/HK.html"
151          onMouseOut="startTimer()">Hawaiian Kona</a><br>
152        <a href="beans/JB.html"
153          onMouseOut="startTimer()">Javabrosia (House
              Blend)</a><br>
```

```
154  </div>
155
156  <div id="BuzzMenu"
157   style="position: absolute; top: 100px; left: 350px;
         visibility: hidden">
158        <a href="buzz/index.html"
159            onMouseOut="startTimer()">Brewing Tips</a><br>
160        <a href="buzz/storageTips.html"
161            onMouseOut="startTimer()">Storage Tips</a><br>
162        <a href="buzz/recipes/index.html"
163            onMouseOver="pullDown('RecipesSubmenu', 2)"
164            onMouseOut="startTimer()">Recipes</a>
165                  
166             
167         <img src="images/brownArrow.gif" width="6" height="12"
168             border="0" align="bottom" alt="&gt;"><br>
169        <a href="buzz/customs.html"
170            onMouseOut="startTimer()">Coffee Customs</a><br>
171        <a href="buzz/trivia.html"
172            onMouseOut="startTimer()">Coffee Trivia</a><br>
173        <a href="buzz/glossary.html"
174            onMouseOut="startTimer()">Speak Java</a><br>
175  </div>
176
177  <div id="CatalogMenu"
178   style="position: absolute; top: 100px; left: 450px;
         visibility: hidden">
179        <a href="catalog/coffees.html"
180            onMouseOut="startTimer()">Coffees</a><br>
181        <a href="catalog/teas.html"
182            onMouseOut="startTimer()">Teas</a><br>
183        <a href="catalog/cocoas"
184            onMouseOut="startTimer()">Cocoas</a><br>
185        <a href="catalog/equipment/index.html"
186            onMouseOver="pullDown('EquipmentSubmenu', 2)"
187            onMouseOut="startTimer()">Equipment</a> 
188        <img src="images/brownArrow.gif" width="6" height="12"
189             border="0" align="bottom" alt="&gt;"><br>
190  </div>
191
192  <div id="RecipesSubmenu"
193   style="position: absolute; top: 136px; left: 488px;
         visibility: hidden">
194        <a href="recipes/french.html"
195            onMouseOut="startTimer()">French Kiss</a><br>
```

```
196        <a href="recipes/gcmFrapachino.html"
197            onMouseOut="startTimer()">GCM Frapachino</a><br>
198        <a href="recipes/godsDelight.html"
199            onMouseOut="startTimer()">God's Delight</a><br>
200        <a href="recipes/javaBlast.html"
201            onMouseOut="startTimer()">Java Blast</a><br>
202        <a href="recipes/konaVolcano.html"
203            onMouseOut="startTimer()">Kona Volcano</a><br>
204        <a href="recipes/mochaJoe.html"
205            onMouseOut="startTimer()">Mocha Joe</a><br>
206        <a href="recipes/vanillaCloud.html"
207            onMouseOut="startTimer()">Vanilla Cloud</a><br>
208 </div>
209
210 <div id="EquipmentSubmenu"
211  style="position: absolute; top: 155px; left: 554px;
212      visibility: hidden">
212        <a href="catalog/equipment/grinders.html"
213            onMouseOut="startTimer()">Coffee Grinders</a><br>
214        <a href="catalog/equipment/coffeeMakers.html"
215            onMouseOut="startTimer()">Coffee Makers</a><br>
216        <a href="catalog/equipment/expressoMachines.html"
217            onMouseOut="startTimer()">Espresso Machines</a><br>
218        <a href="catalog/equipment/cups.html"
219            onMouseOut="startTimer()">Java Vessels</a><br>
220 </div>
221 <br clear=all>
222 <br><br><br><br><br>
223
224 <blockquote>This coffee plunges into the stomach . . . the mind
225   is aroused, and ideas pour forth like the battalions of the
226   Grand Army on the field of battle. . . . Memories charge at
227   full gallop . . . the light cavalry of comparisons deploys
228   itself magnificently; the artillery of logic hurry in with
229   their train of ammunition; flashes of wit pop up like
230   sharp-shooters.        
231   - Honore de Balzac</blockquote>
232
233 <p>Welcome to Javabilaya! We roast our coffee beans daily so
234 your order is always fresh. We know that nothing beats a fresh
235 cup of coffee!</p>
236
237 <p>Here you can learn more about our premium Java beans. We've
238 packed this site with tips and tidbits about your favorite
239 drink: Java. Check out The Buzz and learn how to best store your
```

```
240 beans to maintain their flavor, pick up some brewing tips, and
241 explore our recipe section. Soon you'll be brewing Java the gods
242 would envy. You can't help to if you start with our special
243 house blend: JavaBrosia.</p>
244
245 <p>If you thirst for more Java knowledge, The Buzz can also
246 enlighten you on coffee customs and trivia. You can even learn
247 to speak Java! To really quench that Java thirst, browse our
248 catalog and fill your cart with beans that will brew the best
249 Java your tastebuds have ever encountered.</p>
250
251 <p class="copyright">Copyright Tina McDuffie. All rights
       reserved.
252 <a href="http://www.javascriptconcepts.com/javabilaya/">
253 http://www.javascriptconcepts.com/javabilaya/</a></p>
254
255 </body>
256 </html>
```

Voilà! Now any open submenus automatically disappear after a few seconds of inactivity.

## Summary

Dynamic HTML is the animating, hiding, showing, stacking, and formatting of HTML content on the screen using a combination of technologies, specifically Hypertext Markup Language (HTML), Cascading Style Sheets (CSS), and JavaScript. Since the earliest days of the Web, HTML was meant to provide the structure of a document and context for the document's content only. It was never meant to designate presentation details. That job was expected to be performed by stylesheets.

CSS provides a rich selection of presentation effects that can be applied to all HTML elements, such as color, background, margins, and borders. With CSS, Web developers can set indents on paragraphs, specify a default font for an entire Web site with one line of code, use small caps, assign an image as a bullet for a list item, and accomplish many more things that are impossible with HTML alone.

JavaScript brings dynamism and interactivity to the DHTML pool. In the DHTML arena, JavaScript is primarily used to modify stylesheet properties on the fly to create animations and special effects.

Before you can access stylesheet properties with JavaScript, it helps to know a little about stylesheets. A stylesheet is made up of one or more style rules. Each style rule is, in turn, made up of a selector and one or more style declarations. A declaration is made up of a stylesheet property to be affected and the value or effect to apply to that property. Selectors come in a variety of flavors, including

✗ simple selectors that apply a style rule to a particular type of HTML element.

✗ contextual selectors that apply a rule to a particular type of HTML element in the context of another.

✗ class selectors that apply rules to HTML elements that have been classified with a class attribute.

✗ ID selectors that apply a rule to an HTML element that has been assigned a unique ID with the id attribute.

✗ anchor pseudo-class selectors that can apply rules to unfollowed links, visited links, active links, and moused over (hover) links.

There are three primary ways to apply style rules to an HTML document: with an external stylesheet, with embedded style rules in the <head> of the document, and inline with HTML using the style attribute on individual HTML elements.

The easiest way to access an element in a Web page is to call the document.getElementById("objId") method, which is supported by all DOM2-compliant browsers. Using that reference, followed by the style property, followed by the name of the property you wish to set, you can easily modify that style property with JavaScript.

To animate an absolutely positioned element, you first create a division with the HTML <div> tag, assign it an ID with the id attribute, and position it with the style attribute and CSS declarations. Once positioned, you can use the moveTo function developed in this chapter to move the object to a particular position on the screen or the moveBy function to move it a few pixels at a time. Using the setTimeout window method you can call moveBy repeatedly to animate the object.

One of the most popular uses of DHTML is to create pull-down menus. To create a pull-down menu, you must first create a division for each submenu, assign each a unique ID, position it, and hide it using the style declaration visibility: hidden. Once positioned and hidden, you can use the hide, show, hideAll, pullDown, and startTimer functions developed in this chapter to implement your pull-down menu.

## Review Questions

1. What is DHTML?
2. What are HTML, CSS, and JavaScript? How does each fit into DHTML, that is, what function(s) does each provide?
3. List and describe five HTML tags that provide structure to a document or context for the document's content.
4. List five presentation effects that you can accomplish with CSS, but cannot accomplish with HTML alone.
5. What were the first browsers to provide any support for DHTML? What was the major problem with their support for DHTML?
6. Do any browsers support the W3C's DOM2 specification? If so, which ones?

7. What was the first browser to provide almost 100% support for the W3C HTML 4, CSS1, and DOM specifications?
8. List and describe the parts of a stylesheet.
9. What's the difference between a property and a value?
10. List and describe the five CSS selectors.
11. Describe the three primary ways by which you can connect style rules to an HTML document. Explain the circumstances in which each is best.
12. Describe the basic steps required to animate an absolutely positioned element.
13. Why is it a good idea to assign an ID to a division you want to position?
14. Can more than one HTML element have the same ID? Why or why not?
15. Which style properties of a positioned element can you modify to change its position?
16. Which style properties of a positioned element can you modify to change its dimensions?
17. What is the proper dot notation to access the width of the current window?
18. Why did we add a timer to the pull-down DHTML menu script?
19. What style property is the key to showing and hiding submenus?
20. What event handlers are used to call the functions that implement a pull-down DHTML menu?

## Exercises

1. Write the appropriate HTML to create sam, an absolutely positioned element at the coordinates (10,35).
2. Write the appropriate dot notation to hide an object whose id="sam". Do not use the hide function developed in this chapter.
3. Write the appropriate dot notation to show an object whose id="sam". Do not use the show function developed in this chapter.
4. Find a blank button image and position five copies of it on the screen. Using more divisions, each with a button's text inside, position the divisions over the blanks to create a set of navigation buttons.
5. Write the appropriate HTML and CSS to create a division at coordinates (30, 100) with a width of 200 pixels, background color yellow, and text color red.

## Scripting Exercises

Create a folder named assignment15 to hold the documents you create during this assignment. Save a copy of your latest toy store documents in a toyStore subfolder.

1. Create a new document named collage.html.
   a. Find several cool images with transparent backgrounds that together create or add to some theme, for instance, balloons, party hats, a birthday cake, etc.
   b. Place each image in a division tag.

    c. Position the divisions on the screen to form an attractive collage. Adjust the z-index of the images as needed to best effect.

    d. Add a script that, after 30 seconds have elapsed, moves one of the objects around the screen in some way. For instance, you might include an image of a cork over a champagne bottle and animate the cork so that it flies up and disappears off the screen. Perform the animation only once.

2. Create a new document named myNavBar.html.

    a. Write the appropriate code to create a navigation bar that is 150 pixels wide and positioned 10 pixels from the right edge of the screen, no matter what the screen's current dimensions.

    b. Give it a yellow background and blue links.

    c. When the visitor hovers over a link, a reverse-text effect should occur. The link color should become yellow and the background color blue.

3. Modify Script 15.8 to use images with rollovers as the main menu.

4. In this chapter we created a vertical pull-down menu. Using the functions in Script 15.8, create a horizontal pull-out menu.

5. Create a new document named rocket.html.

    a. Find pictures of a small rocket and a flame. You'll need to make some additional pictures of the rocket at different angles in a graphics editor.

    b. Write a script to start the rocket (light a flame underneath it), then fly the rocket around the window. After a random period of time, turn the flame off and have the rocket float back down to the bottom of the window.

    c. Provide buttons to launch and reset the rocket.

    d. If your toy store sells rockets, this is a good Web page for it.

6. Add a page to your Toy Store Web site that features a particular toy that moves, such as a ball, an airplane, a car, or a top.

    a. Find at least one picture of the toy, preferably more than one in different positions. For instance you might find a picture of a model airplane and use a graphics editor to make copies of it at different angles: pointing up and left diagonally, up and right diagonally, down and left diagonally, down and right diagonally, straight up, straight down, straight across left, and straight across down.

    b. Write a script that moves the toy quickly across the screen in a random direction every so many seconds, maybe once a minute or every thirty seconds. Experiment. The idea is that every once in while the toy moves into, across, and off of the screen in a random direction while the visitor is reading the document.

# Projects

## Bouncing Ball

Write a script that shows a ball bouncing within the dimensions of the screen. The ball should be able to move up, down, left, right, or diagonally. Whenever the ball encounters the edge of the screen, it should bounce in a random direction.

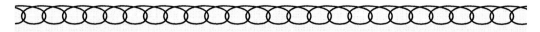

# Creating
# Custom Objects

*I paint objects as I*

*think them, not as I see*

*them.*

—Pablo Picasso

Throughout this book, we've been using objects already predefined by JavaScript. However, one of the coolest things about JavaScript is that it allows you to create your own custom objects and define properties and methods for those objects. Want to add a new property to an existing object? No problem, JavaScript even allows you to extend objects.

In this chapter we'll

- examine why you would want to create a custom object in the first place.
- look again at constructor functions.
- learn how to write constructor functions to define custom objects.
- see how to declare a custom object with the new keyword and the appropriate constructor function.
- examine the prototype property.
- learn how to extend existing objects with custom properties.
- define some methods for custom objects and assign them to the appropriate object.

⚡ extend predefined and custom objects with custom methods using the
   `prototype` property.

⚡ apply the concepts covered in this chapter to automating the creation of the pull-
   down menus shown in the previous chapter.

Ready? Let's get cracking.

# Why Create a Custom Object in the First Place?

Instead of being stuck using only the objects predefined by the JavaScript language, you can
work "outside the box" and create your own objects to suit your own personal programming
needs. Consider custom objects another tool, a powerful one, that you can add to your
programmer's toolbox.

Remember the pull-down menu we created in the previous chapter? To prove to you
just how powerful and useful custom objects can be, we'll use them to automate the menu-
creation process. When we're done, we'll have a complete pull-down menu system. We'll
even make it possible to create *pull-out* menus, as well as the original *pull-down* menus. The
secret will be the custom objects Menu, Submenu, and MenuItem.

Before we tackle the custom objects for a pull-down menu, let's cover the basics of
creating custom objects.

# Creating Custom Objects with Constructor Functions

## Constructor Functions

The best way to create a custom object is to first define a constructor function for that
object. Remember constructor functions? We've used quite a few of the constructor functions built into JavaScript to create arrays,

```
var arrayName = new Array()
```

images,

```
var imageName = new Image()
```

and other objects already defined by the JavaScript language. A **constructor function** tells
the interpreter how to create a particular type of object, including what properties and
methods to assign to it. JavaScript allows you to write your own custom constructor functions that can be used to create custom objects.

These constructor functions look much like any other function. To write a constructor
function, you use the `function` keyword, followed by the name of the function, a set of
parentheses containing any arguments, and a set of braces containing the function's
statements. Here's the general form:

```
function CustomObjectName ([arg1, arg2, arg3, ...argN]) {
       this.property1 = arg1
       this.property2 = arg2
```

```
        this.property3 = arg3
        ...
        this.propertyN = argN
}
```

Sounds like any other function so far, doesn't it? The major differences between regular functions and constructor functions lie in the way you name a constructor function, what its parameters do, and the statements contained within a constructor function.

### Naming Constructor Functions

Traditionally, constructor function names begin with a capital letter. Every constructor function you've called in this book has begun with a capital letter.

Whether you name a constructor function with a capital letter or not has no effect on its ability to do the job. It just makes your code more readable and understandable. Whenever you come across a function definition whose function name begins with a capital letter, you'll automatically think, "That's a constructor function."

### Creating Object Properties

OK, so how are the statements within a constructor function different? Let's look at one and see. The following constructor function defines how to create a student object.

```
function Student(firstName, lastName, id) {
        this.first = firstName
        this.last = lastName
        this.id = id
        this.grade = ""
}
```

Notice how every statement begins with the keyword this? Remember, this always refers to the current object. In the above function definition, this refers to the object that called the constructor function, that is, the object that you are declaring or instantiating when you call the constructor function. Here's an example call of the constructor function Student.

```
var sam = new Student("Sammy", "Sam", 187)
```

When the constructor function Student is called in the above statement, this refers to the variable sam. When you call the constructor function using the keyword new, the function's statements create properties for the object that this refers to, using the arguments firstName, lastName, id, and grade to initialize their corresponding properties. In this case, this refers to sam. Regular functions don't use this like this.

You don't have to create an argument to set a property defined in the constructor function. Notice that the Student object has a grade property that is defined and initialized by the constructor function, but no corresponding argument is listed for it. That's OK.

**Accessing Custom Object Properties**

Accessing the properties of a custom object is the same as accessing the properties of a built-in object. Just use dot notation:

```
objectName.propertyName
```

A custom object works just like a built-in object. For instance, you can access the firstName and id properties of the sam Student object created earlier as

```
document.write("First Name: ", sam.firstName, "<br>")
document.write("ID: ", sam.id, "<br>")
```

The result:

```
First Name: Sammy
ID: 187
```

**Creating Methods for a Custom Object**

One of the benefits of creating custom objects is the ability to define methods that work on or with those custom objects. Recall that methods are functions associated with a particular object. Defining a method for a custom object involves two steps. First, you have to define the method. Then you have to associate it with the object in the object's constructor function. Here's the general form:

```
function CustomMethodName ([arg1, arg2, ... arg3]) {
        // function statements
    }
```

Use the this keyword to make any necessary references to the object to which the method will apply. The last line of the following constructor function shows the general form for associating the method with its object:

```
function CustomObjectName ([arg1, arg2, arg3, ... argN]) {
        this.property1 = arg1
        this.property2 = arg2
        this.property3 = arg3
        ...
        this.propertyN = argN

        this.methodName = CustomMethodName
    }
```

I like to capitalize the first letter of the names of functions that define a custom method. You'll never call that function directly. By capitalizing it, you can easily tell that it has something to do with custom objects. The method name defined in the constructor function can differ. That name, the name of the method you'll actually call with the custom object, should start with a lowercase letter as usual.

Here's a very simple example of a custom method that sets the `grade` property of the `Student` object:

```
function SetGrade(grade) {
      this.grade = grade
}
```

Here's how you associate it with the `Student` object when you first define that object in the constructor function:

```
function Student(firstName, lastName, id) {
      this.first = firstName
      this.last = lastName
      this.id = id
      this.grade = ""

      this.setGrade = SetGrade
}
```

Notice the lack of parentheses after the method name, `setGrade`, and the name of the custom method definition, `SetGrade`. This is appropriate. When associating a custom method definition with an object, you don't list the parameters, only the name of the custom method definition.

Custom methods don't *have* to modify a property of a custom object. They can simply perform some action. The following custom method prompts the visitor to enter a grade and keeps prompting until it receives a valid entry, and then returns the result.

```
function GetGrade() {
      var grade = prompt("Enter a grade:", "")
      grade = toUpperCase(grade)
      while (grade != "A" && grade != "B" && grade != "C" &&
             grade != "D" && grade != "F" && grade != "CR" &&
             grade != "NC" && grade != "I") {
            alert ("Error! Invalid Grade.")
            grade = prompt("Enter a grade:", "")
            grade = toUpperCase(grade)
      }
      return grade
}
```

Here we associate `GetGrade` with the `Student` object when the `Student` constructor function is first defined:

```
function Student(firstName, lastName, id) {
      this.first = firstName
      this.last = lastName
```

```
        this.id = id
        this.grade = ""

        this.setGrade = SetGrade
        this.getGrade = GetGrade
}
```

That wasn't so hard, was it? Notice that in both examples of associating a custom method with an object, we said it would work when you *first* define the constructor function. That's because if, after defining a custom object with a constructor function, you decide you want to add additional properties or methods to that object, you would be *extending* that object. Extending an object requires a different process, which we'll show you shortly.

### Accessing Custom Object Methods

Now that you've added some custom methods to a custom object, how do you access them? Accessing a method of a custom object is the same as accessing a method of a built-in object. Just use dot notation:

```
objectName.methodName([arg1, arg2, ...])
```

Here's how you would call the setGrade method on the Student object named sam that we created earlier:

```
sam.setGrade("A")
```

Here's how you might call the getGrade method:

```
sam.grade = sam.getGrade()
```

or

```
sam.setGrade(sam.getGrade())
```

In object-oriented programming, it's usually considered bad form to set an object's properties directly. Instead, programmers usually create *set* functions for every property they ever want to set. This is an unreasonable and wasteful (memory) requirement for JavaScript. We've been setting JavaScript object properties directly since the beginning. There is certainly no reason to change that habit now. I just wanted you to be aware of the convention.

## Extending an Object

Need more properties than a basic object already has? Or perhaps you'd like to add a method to an already defined object? Whether the object you want to add to is one pre-defined by the JavaScript language or one you defined yourself, you can add additional properties and methods to that object. When you add a property or method to an object, you **extend** that object.

JavaScript allows you to extend a single instantiation of an object or all instances of an object. To extend a single instantiation of an object with a new property, simply use the instantiated object's name followed by a dot and the name of the property you want to add, followed by the value you want to assign to the property, like this:

```
objectName.newPropertyName = someValue
```

To give you a better idea, let's create a new `Student` object named `devan` and add a `status` property to it:

```
var devan = new Student("Devan", "Devlin", 455)
devan.status = "active"
```

The last statement above adds a `status` property to `devan` and initializes it with the value `active`. The `sam` `Student` object created earlier does not get this `status` property, nor will any new `Student` object created later, or earlier for that matter. Only the `devan` instance of the `Student` object acquires the new `status` property.

So what if you wanted to add the `status` property to all `Student` objects, those already in existence as well as any you declare in the future? That's where the `prototype` property comes in handy.

## The prototype Property

The **prototype** property is a built-in property that all JavaScript objects have. It specifies the constructor from which an object was created. When you instantiate an object, custom or built-in, JavaScript assigns a `prototype` property to it behind the scenes, so that you can always access that object's prototype. An object automatically inherits all of the properties of its prototype. So when you modify the prototype, all objects of that object type, already existing or not, will also be modified and get any new properties or methods added to the prototype.

If you want to add a property to all `Student` objects, add it using the `Student` object's `prototype` property like this:

```
Student.prototype.status = ""
```

Notice that empty quotes were assigned to `status`. That's a good default value for `status`, because not all students will have an active status. Whatever value you assign to the new property using the `prototype` becomes the default value assigned to the property whenever a new object is created. In this case, all `Student` objects start with an empty string as their `status` property. If you had assigned `active` in the above statement, all `Student` objects would begin with `status` set to `active`.

You can also extend an object with a new method. Let's create a custom method to display a `Student` object's properties:

```
function DisplayStudent() {
    document.write("Name: ", this.first, " ",
        this.last, "<br>")
```

```
        document.write("ID: ", this.id, "<br>")
        document.write("Grade: ", this.grade, "<br>")
    }
```

Now let's add the `DisplayStudent` method to the `Student` prototype:

```
Student.prototype.display = DisplayStudent
```

To call the `display` method on the `sam` `Student` object, write

```
sam.display()
```

The results:

```
Name: Sammy Sam
ID: 187
Grade: A
```

You can also extend a built-in object with properties and methods using *its* `prototype` property, the same way as demonstrated above for custom objects.

Now let's look at two other ways you can create a custom object.

## Using the Built-in Object Constructor Function

Defining a constructor function seems like overkill when you need only one instance of an object. Fortunately, JavaScript provides another way to create an object: the `new Object()` constructor. Here's an example:

```
var aradia = new Object ()
aradia.name = "Aradia"
aradia.type = "cat"
aradia.gender = "female"
```

If you need multiple instances of an object, it's much more efficient to write a constructor function and use it to create instances of that custom object. For the above example, we'd write a `Pet` constructor function. However, if all you need is one or two, then the `Object` constructor is perhaps a better way to go.

Now let's look at a shortcut for creating a custom object: an object literal.

## Creating a Custom Object Using an Object Literal

Remember array literals? Well, in version 1.2, JavaScript added the ability to create an object using an **object literal**. An object literal is a list of property-value pairs enclosed in braces ({ }). A colon separates each property and its corresponding value; a comma separates adjacent pairs. Here's an example:

```
var sam = {name:"Sam", type:"dog", gender:"male"}
```

This is another good way to create single objects. However, the object constructor technique is still the best way to go when creating multiple instances of an object.

# Using Custom Objects: A Real-World Example

As promised, now that the basics are out of the way, we'll create custom objects to support a pull-down menu system. By using custom objects, we can make the pull-down menu created in the previous chapter a pull-down menu system that is easily customizable. Figure 16.1 shows the same menu with a completely different color scheme. Of course, since this book is in black and white, you won't be able to tell the difference without running the script yourself.

### Figure 16.1: Customizable Pull-down Menu

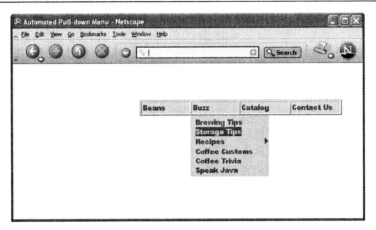

We'll make the system so customizable that you can even choose between the pull-down shown in Figure 16.1 and the pull-out style shown in Figure 16.2.

### Figure 16.2: Customized as Pull-out Menu

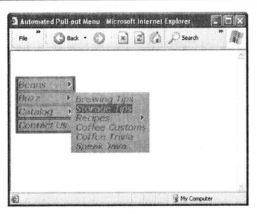

Basically, a pull-down menu is made up of a main menu and one or more submenus. Each menu or submenu is made up of one or more menu items, so those are the custom objects we need to define: `MainMenu`, `Menu`, and `MenuItem`.

Now let's define each one. Let's start with the `MenuItem` object and leave the `MainMenu` until last, since it's the most complicated.

```
function MenuItem(name, url, hasSubmenu, submenuId,
                  submenuLevel, numNbsps) {
    this.name = name
    this.url = url
    this.hasSub = hasSubmenu
    if (hasSubmenu) {
        this.submenuId = submenuId
        this.submenuLevel = submenuLevel
        this.nbsps = numNbsps
    }
}
```

The `MenuItem` object constructor has three required parameters: `name`, `url`, and `hasSubmenu`, which is a Boolean value indicating whether or not the current menu item has a submenu. If a `MenuItem` object has a submenu, the other three parameters must be provided, indicating the submenu's ID, its level in the overall pull-down menu system, and the number of non-breaking spaces that need to be inserted between the `MenuItem` name and the arrow image in the menu so that the arrow lines up on the right side of the menu. The box in the image below shows where the non-breaking spaces will be placed.

### Figure 16.3: Non-Breaking Spaces in Menu Item

Notice that the `if` statement sets only the last three properties if the menu item has a submenu. Now let's look at the constructor function that creates the menus themselves.

```
function Menu(id, x, y) {
    this.id = id
    this.left = x
    this.top = y
    this.items = new Array()

    this.addItem = AddMenuItem
}
```

According to the constructor function above, `Menu` has a property, `items`, that is an `Array` object. The `items` property holds a list of the items to be displayed in the menu. Just like the `document` object can itself have properties that are objects, so too can custom objects have properties that are objects. In this case, the `items` array holds `MenuItem` objects.

Now take a look at the last line of the Menu constructor function. It looks like it associates a custom method with the Menu object that can be used to add an item to the menu. Let's look at the function that is associated with that method:

```
function AddMenuItem(item) {
      this.items[this.items.length] = item
}
```

It's just a short one-liner, but it deserves a close look. Notice the use of the `this` keyword. It refers to the current Menu object. The item passed to the method will be added to the end of the Menu's `items` array.

Ready to look at the `MainMenu` object now? It is, by far, the most complicated.

**Script 16.1    The `MainMenu` Constructor Function**

```
1     function MainMenu(x, y, width, type, bgColor, fgColor,
2                       bgColorHi, fgColorHi, borderSize, borderColor,
3                       cellpadding, cellAlign, font, fontSize,
4                       fontStyle, fontWeight, arrowUrl) {
5           this.left = x
6           this.top = y
7           this.width = width
8           this.type = type                // down or out
9           this.bgColor = bgColor
10          this.fgColor = fgColor
11          this.bgColorHi = bgColorHi
12          this.fgColorHi = fgColorHi
13          this.border = borderSize
14          this.borderColor = borderColor
15          this.padding = cellpadding
16          this.align = cellAlign
17          this.font = font
18          this.fontSize = fontSize
19          this.fontStyle = fontStyle      // plain, italics
20          this.fontWeight = fontWeight    // normal, bold
21          this.arrow = arrowUrl
22          this.items = new Array()
23          this.menus = new Array()
24
25          this.addItem = AddMenuItem
26          this.addMenu = AddMenu
27          this.create = CreateMainMenu
28          this.createSS = CreateStylesheet
29          this.createSubmenus = CreateSubmenus
30    }
```

To allow customization of the menu, the `MainMenu` constructor function has 17 parameters (lines 1 through 4). These allow you to customize the position, width, colors, border settings, padding, text alignment, and font choices for the menu (lines 5 through 20). You can even change the arrow image (line 21).

`MainMenu` has two array properties: `items`, which holds the list of items to be displayed on the main menu, and `menus`, which holds a list of all the `Menu` objects used in the pull-down menu system. The methods that add items and menus to the `MainMenu` object are associated with the object in lines 25 and 26. We've already seen the `AddMenuItem` function, so let's just look at the `AddMenu` function. It is quite similar.

```
function AddMenu(menu) {
    this.menus[this.menus.length] = menu
}
```

As you can see, the `AddMenu` function is quite similar and works the same way as the `AddMenuItem` function, in that it simply adds an object to an array. In this case, `AddMenu` adds a `Menu` object to the menus array of a `MainMenu` object.

The `MainMenu` constructor function lists three more methods: `create`, `createSS`, and `createSubmenus`, which create the `MainMenu`, its stylesheet, and its submenus. Let's look at the functions that define those methods one by one.

**Script 16.2**    *CreateMainMenu Method Definition*

```
1    function CreateMainMenu(type) {
2        document.write("<table width=", this.width, " bgColor=\"",
3            this.bgColor, "\" border=", this.border,
                " cellpadding=",
4            this.padding, " bordercolor=\"", this.borderColor,
5            "\" style=\"position: absolute; left: ", this.left,
6            "px; top: ", this.top, "px;\">")
7        switch (this.type) {
8        case "down":
9            document.write("<tr align=", this.align, ">")
10           for(i=0; i<this.items.length; i++) {
11               document.write("<td width=",
12                   Math.round(this.width/this.items.length),
13                   "><a href=\"", this.items[i].url, "\"")
14               if(this.items[i].hasSub) {
15                   document.write(" onMouseover=\"pullDown(\'",
16                       this.items[i].submenuId, "\', ",
17                       this.items[i].submenuLevel, ")\"")
18               }
19               document.write(" onMouseOut=
                   \"startTimer()\">",
20                   this.items[i].name, "</a></td>")
21           }
```

```
22              document.write("</tr>")
23              break
24      case "out":
25          for(i=0; i<this.items.length; i++) {
26              document.write("<tr align=", this.align, ">")
27              document.write("<td><a href=\"",
                    this.items[i].url, "\"")
28              if(this.items[i].hasSub) {
29                  document.write(" onMouseover=
                        \"pullDown(\'",
30                          this.items[i].submenuId, "\', ",
31                          this.items[i].submenuLevel, ")\"")
32              }
33              document.write(" onMouseOut=
                    \"startTimer()\">",
34                      this.items[i].name, "</a>")
35              if(this.items[i].hasSub) {
36                  for(j=0; j<this.items[i].nbsps; j++) {
37                      document.write(" ")
38                  }
39                  document.write("<img src=\"",
                        this.arrow, "\" ",
40                          "alt=\"&gt;\" align=bottom>")
41              }
42              document.write("</td></tr>")
43          }
44          break
45      }
46      document.write("</table>")
47  }
```

The first thing CreateMainMenu, the definition of the create MainMenu method, does is start a table. It uses some of MainMenu's properties to create a table of the appropriate width, with the appropriate background color, border size, padding, and bordercolor (lines 2 through 4). It then sets the table's style attribute to specify the table's position (lines 5 and 6).

Next, the method determines which type of menu to create, as specified by the MainMenu object's type property (lines 7–47). Using the MainMenu's align property, it sets the appropriate text alignment in the table (line 9 in the down type of menu, line 26 in the out type of menu). Finally, using a for loop, the method writes each item line by line, including the necessary event handlers (lines 10–21 for down type of menu, lines 25–43 for out type of menu); inserts the arrow image and non-breaking spaces as needed; and finishes the table (line 46). The non-breaking spaces and arrow images are needed only in menus that are going to display submenus to the side, not down. That's why the `if` statement (lines 35 to 41) appears only in the "out" case (lines 24–45).

The `CreateSubmenus` method definition, shown in Script 16.3, performs a similar job for each `Menu` object in `MainMenu`'s menus array.

**Script 16.3    *CreateSubmenus* Method Definition**

```
1    function CreateSubmenus() {
2        for(i=0; i<this.menus.length; i++) {
3            document.write("<div id=\"", this.menus[i].id,
4                "\" style=\"position: absolute; left: ",
5                this.menus[i].left, "px; top: ",
                    this.menus[i].top,
6                "px; visibility: hidden;\">")
7            for(j=0; j<this.menus[i].items.length; j++) {
8                document.write("<a href=\"",
9                            this.menus[i].items[j].url, "\"")
10               if(this.menus[i].items[j].hasSub) {
11                   document.write(" onMouseover=
                        \"pullDown(\'",
12                       this.menus[i].items[j].submenuId,
                        "\', ",
13                       this.menus[i].items[j].submenuLevel,
                        ")\"")
14               }
15               document.write(" onMouseOut=
                    \"startTimer()\">",
16                   this.menus[i].items[j].name, "</a>")
17               if(this.menus[i].items[j].hasSub) {
18                   for(k=0; k<this.menus[i].items[j].nbsps;
                        k++) {
19                       document.write(" ")
20                   }
21                   document.write("<img src=\"",
                        this.arrow, "\" ",
22                       "alt=\"&gt;\" align=bottom>")
23               }
24               document.write("<br>")
25           }
26           document.write("</div>")
27       }
28   }
```

The last method definition we need to look at is the `CreateStylesheet` function shown here in Script 16.4.

**Script 16.4     `CreateStylesheet` Method Definition**

```
1    function CreateStylesheet() {
2         document.writeln("<style type=\"text/css\"><!--)
3         document.write("div { padding-left: 10px; ",
4             "padding-right: 2px; padding-top: 4px; ",
5             "padding-bottom: 4px; background-color: ",
6             this.bgColor, "; border: ", this.borderColor, ";}")
7         document.write("a:link, a:visited, a:active, a:hover { ",
8             "text-decoration: none; font-size: ", this.fontSize,
9             "; font-style: ", this.fontStyle, "; font-weight: ",
10            this.fontWeight, "; font-family: ", this.font, ";}")
11        document.write("a:link, a:visited { ",
12            "background-color: ", this.bgColor,
13            "; color: ", this.fgColor, ";}")
14        document.write("a:hover, a:active { ",
15            "background-color: ", this.bgColorHi,
16            "; color: ", this.fgColorHi, ";}")
17        document.writeln(-->")
18        document.writeln("</style>")
19   }
```

As you can see, the `CreateStylesheet` definition for the `createSS MainMenu`
method creates a stylesheet. This method must be called in the <head> of the document.
Rarely do we call functions or methods that write to the document in the <head>. In this
case it is appropriate because we're writing the HTML <style> tag and CSS rules that create
a stylesheet.

All of the functions we defined in the last chapter that make the menu pull down or
pull out have been placed in a library named pullDownMenuLib.js. The constructor
functions and method definitions described in this chapter have been placed in a library
named menuLib.js.

Now all we need to do is create a document that includes those libraries and creates the
actual `MainMenu` and `Menu` objects. Script 16.5 demonstrates how to put it all together.

**Script 16.5     Automated Pull-down Menu System**

```
1    <html>
2    <head>
3    <title>Script 16.5: Automated Pull-down Menu System</title>
4    <script language="JavaScript" src="pullDownMenuLib.js"
5             type="text/javascript"></script>
6    <script language="JavaScript" src="menuLib.js"
7             type="text/javascript"></script>
8
9    <script language="JavaScript" type="text/javascript"><!--
```

```
10  /* This script must go in the head of the document after the
11        script tags that attach the two libraries:
12        pullDownMenuLib.js and menuLib.js. This script should also
13        precede the script that calls createSS.
14        This script defines the name, contents, and positioning of
15        the MainMenu and any submenus. */
16
17  // set up Main Menu
18  var mainMenu = new MainMenu(10, 50, 100, "out", "#cc99ff",
19                       "#0066ff", "#0066ff", "#cc99ff", 1,
20                       "#000080", 2, "left", "\"Verdana\", Arial,
21                       serif", "12pt", "italic", "bold",
22                       "images/purpleArrow.gif")
23  // add items to Main Menu
24  mainMenu.addItem(new MenuItem("Beans", "beans/index.html",
        true, "BeansMenu", 1, 14))
25  mainMenu.addItem(new MenuItem("Buzz", "buzz/index.html",
        true, "BuzzMenu", 1, 17))
26  mainMenu.addItem(new MenuItem("Catalog",
        "catalog/index.html", true, "CatalogMenu", 1, 10))
27  mainMenu.addItem(new MenuItem("Contact Us",
        "contactUs/index.html", false))
28
29  // set up submenus
30  var beansMenu = new Menu("BeansMenu", 118, 50)
31  beansMenu.addItem(new MenuItem("Blue Mountain Blast",
        "beans/BMB.html", false))
32  beansMenu.addItem(new MenuItem("French Vanilla",
        "beans/FV.html", false))
33  beansMenu.addItem(new MenuItem("German Chocolate Mint",
        "beans/GCM.html", false))
34  beansMenu.addItem(new MenuItem("Hawaiian Kona", "beans/HK.html",
        false))
35  beansMenu.addItem(new MenuItem("JavaBrosia (House Blend)",
        "beans/JB.html", false))
36  mainMenu.addMenu(beansMenu)
37
38  var buzzMenu = new Menu("BuzzMenu", 118, 80)
39  buzzMenu.addItem(new MenuItem("Brewing Tips", "buzz/index.html",
        false))
40  buzzMenu.addItem(new MenuItem("Storage Tips",
        "buzz/storageTips.html", false))
41  buzzMenu.addItem(new MenuItem("Recipes",
        "buzz/recipes/index.html", true, "RecipesSubmenu", 2, 20))
```

```
42  buzzMenu.addItem(new MenuItem("Coffee Customs", "buzz/customs",
        false))
43  buzzMenu.addItem(new MenuItem("Coffee Trivia",
        "buzz/trivia.html", false))
44  buzzMenu.addItem(new MenuItem("Speak Java",
        "buzz/glossary.html", false))
45  mainMenu.addMenu(buzzMenu)
46
47  var catalogMenu = new Menu("CatalogMenu", 118, 110)
48  catalogMenu.addItem(new MenuItem("Coffees",
        "catalog/coffees.html", false))
49  catalogMenu.addItem(new MenuItem("Teas", "catalog/teas.html",
        false))
50  catalogMenu.addItem(new MenuItem("Cocoas",
        "catalog/cocoas.html", false))
51  catalogMenu.addItem(new MenuItem("Equipment",
        "catalog/equipment/index.html", true, "EquipmentSubmenu", 2, 2))
52  mainMenu.addMenu(catalogMenu)
53
54  var recipesSubmenu = new Menu("RecipesSubmenu", 255, 110)
55  recipesSubmenu.addItem(new MenuItem("French Kiss",
        "recipes/frenchKiss.html", false))
56  recipesSubmenu.addItem(new MenuItem("GCM Frapachino",
        "recipes/gcmFrapachino.html", false))
57  recipesSubmenu.addItem(new MenuItem("God's Delight",
        "recipes/godsDelight.html", false))
58  recipesSubmenu.addItem(new MenuItem("Java Blast",
        "recipes/javaBlast.html", false))
59  recipesSubmenu.addItem(new MenuItem("Kona Volcano",
        "recipes/konaVolcano.html", false))
60  recipesSubmenu.addItem(new MenuItem("Mocha Joe",
        "recipes/mochaJoe.html", false))
61  recipesSubmenu.addItem(new MenuItem("Vanilla Cloud",
        "recipes/vanillaCloud.html", false))
62  mainMenu.addMenu(recipesSubmenu)
63
64  var equipmentSubmenu = new Menu("EquipmentSubmenu", 223, 158)
65  equipmentSubmenu.addItem(new MenuItem("Coffee Grinders",
        "catalog/equipment/grinders.html", false))
66  equipmentSubmenu.addItem(new MenuItem("Coffee Makers",
        "catalog/equipment/coffeeMakers.html", false))
67  equipmentSubmenu.addItem(new MenuItem("Expresso Machines",
        "catalog/equipment/expressoMachines.html", false))
68  equipmentSubmenu.addItem(new MenuItem("Java Vessels",
        "catalog/equipment/cups.html", false))
```

```
69   mainMenu.addMenu(equipmentSubmenu)
70
71   //-->
72   </script>
73   <script language="JavaScript" type="text/javascript"><!--
74   /* Place this script where you want the stylesheet to be written
75         This should be the last embedded stylesheet in the
76         document so that it has the most importance */
77         mainMenu.createSS()
78   //-->
79   </script>
80   </head>
81   <body>
82
83   <br>
84   <script language="JavaScript" type="text/javascript"><!--
85   /* Place this script where you want the MainMenu and submenus
86         to be created. */
87         mainMenu.create()
88         mainMenu.createSubmenus()
89   //-->
90   </script>
91
92   </body>
93   </html>
```

The libraries pullDownMenuLib.js and menuLib.js are linked to the document in lines 4 through 7.

Lines 18 through 22 call the `MainMenu` constructor function to create the `mainMenu` object. Items are added to the main menu by calling the `addItem` method of `mainMenu` several times (lines 24 through 27). The main menu is written to the document when its `create` method is called in line 87.

In the same fashion, the submenus are created by a call to `mainMenu`'s `createSubmenus` method (line 88). The menu objects themselves are declared in lines 30, 38, 47, 54, and 64. Items are added to each menu by calling each menu's `addItem` method in lines subsequent to each menu declaration. Each menu is then inserted into `mainMenu`'s menus array (lines 36, 45, 52, 62, and 69) by calling `MainMenu`'s `addMenu` method.

Notice that both the `create` and `createSubmenus` methods are called in the `<body>` of the HTML document. This is important, as they write the HTML that creates the table for the main menu and the divisions for the submenus. The `createSS` method, on the other hand, is called in the last `<script>` tag in the `<head>` of the document (line 77). This placement, too, is important, because an embedded stylesheet may be legally placed only in the <head> of an HTML document. These particular placements are essential to the correct functioning of the pull-down menu system.

# Summary

Custom objects are a powerful tool that you can add to your programmer's toolbox. They allow you to customize JavaScript to your own ends, by creating custom objects as well as properties and methods for those objects. You can even extend existing objects.

The best way to create a custom object when you're planning to have multiple instances of that object is to define a constructor function. A constructor function tells JavaScript how to construct an object of that type and declares the properties and methods for that object. Constructor function names should begin with a capital letter to differentiate them from regular functions.

Not all properties of an object must be initialized when the constructor function is called. It's OK to leave some to be set later in your program. Accessing a property of a custom object is no different than accessing the property of a predefined object; simply use dot notation as usual.

It takes two steps to define a custom method for an object. First you must write a function that defines the method. Then you must associate that function with the object in its constructor function. You do not use parentheses or list any function parameters when you associate the function that defines the method with the method name in the object's constructor function. Custom methods are accessed the same way as predefined methods— with the usual dot notation.

After creating a custom object, you can still add more properties and methods to it. You can also add properties and methods to predefined objects.

To add a property to a single instance of an object, simply make an assignment using the instantiated object's name, followed by the name of the property you want to add. If you want to add a property or method to all current instances of an object as well as all future instances of the object, you must use the object's `prototype` property.

The `prototype` property specifies the constructor from which an object was created. To add a property to an object's prototype, use the following form:

```
ObjectName.prototype.newPropertyName = someDefaultValue
```

To add a method, use this form:

```
ObjectName.prototype.newMethodName =
    MethodDefinitionFunctionName
```

There are two other ways to create custom objects besides writing a constructor function. You can use the `Object` constructor function or use an object literal. Both techniques are good for creating only one or two instances of a particular object type. If you need multiple instances of an object, you should write a constructor function.

# Review Questions

1. What good are custom objects anyway?
2. What is a constructor function?
3. How can you differentiate between a constructor function and a regular function?
4. How do you access a property of a custom object?
5. How do you access a method of a custom object?
6. What two steps are involved in creating a custom method? Explain.
7. What does it mean to "extend" an object?
8. How can you add a property to a single instance of an object?
9. What property must you access to add a property or method to all instances of an object as well as all future instances of an object?
10. What is the `prototype` property?
11. Which objects, if any, have a `prototype` property? Why? How do they get it?
12. List and describe three ways of creating a custom object.
13. What does the `Object ()` function do?
14. What is an object literal?
15. Can custom objects and their associated properties and methods help automate some tasks? Explain your answer.

# Exercises

1. Write the appropriate JavaScript statements to create a constructor function for a `Friend` object with the properties `firstName`, `lastName`, `phone`, `birthday` (a date object), and `picture` (an image object).
2. Write the appropriate statements to instantiate two `Friend` objects using the constructor you created in Exercise 1.
3. Write an appropriate statement to extend one of the two `Friend` objects you created in Exercise 2 with a `cellPhone` property.
4. Write an appropriate statement to extend all instances of `Friend`, current and future, with a `cellPhone` property.
5. Write the appropriate JavaScript statements to create a single object named `rose` with two properties: name and `color`.
6. Write a statement to extend the `flower` object with a `type` property.
7. Write a statement to create the object described in Exercises 5 and 6 as an object literal.
8. Write a statement to associate a function named `SetPhone` as a `setPhone` method with the `Friend` object in its constructor function.
9. Write a statement to call the `setPhone` method with one of the `Friend` objects you instantiated in Exercise 2.
10. Write a statement to extend the `Friend` object with a method named `setCellPhone` based on a custom function named `SetCellPhone`.

# Scripting Exercises

Create a folder named assignment16 to hold the documents you create during this assignment.

1. Create a new document named phonebook.html.
    a. Create a custom object named `Student` with the following properties: `firstName`, `lastName`, `phone`, and `email`.
    b. Create a custom method that will display the properties of a `Student` object in an alert box.
    c. Get the names, phone numbers, and email addresses of at least five of your fellow students and instantiate five `Student` objects accordingly.
    d. Add a small form, under the heading "Look Up," to the document, with a text field labeled "Name" and a button labeled "Display Data."
    e. When a name is entered and the Display Data button is clicked, display the information for the student object whose name (variable name) was entered in an alert box. If a `student` object of that name does not exist, display the message "StudentName not found," where StudentName is the name entered in the text box.
2. Create a new document named myPets.html.
    a. Create a custom object named `Pet` with the following properties: `name`, `birthday`, `type`, `breed`, `gender`, `lastShots` (a date object to hold the date the animal last received its shots), and `picture` (an image object).
    b. Create an array of `Pet` objects.
    c. Instantiate a `Pet` object for each pet you currently have. If you don't have any pets right now, instantiate an object for at least two famous pets.
    d. Write a script to write the information for each pet in the array to the document along with the pet's picture.
3. Create a new document named buttonNav.html.
    a. Create a custom object named `WebPage` with the following properties: `name`, `description`, and `url`.
    b. Write a custom method, `makeButton`, that creates a navigation button for the Web page such that when the button is clicked, that document is loaded in the browser.
    c. Create an array of `WebPage` objects. The array should contain at least four elements.
    d. Using a `for` loop and the array of `WebPage` objects, create a set of navigation buttons.
    e. Test and debug your script.
4. Create a new document named books.html.
    a. Create a custom object named `Book` with at least the following properties: `title`, `author`, `isbn`, and `category`. You determine the categories based

on the types of books you like to read. Categories that I read include SciFi, Fantasy, Classic, Spy, Historical, Romance, and General Fiction.

b. Create a custom method that will write information about a book neatly in a table.

c. Create an array of at least 15 Book objects and instantiate the objects according with books on your shelf or books you've read and liked or loved.

d. Write a script to print the books according to category. Use headings for each category, like this:

> Fantasy
>
> info on book
>
> info on book
>
> SciFi
>
> info on book
>
> info on book

5. Create a new document named animation.html.

a. Create a custom object named Sprite.

b. Populate the object with the appropriate properties and methods needed to make Sprite move around the screen. Use the animated mermaid example from the previous chapter as a guide.

# Projects

## Project 1: Shopping Cart Using Custom Objects

Modify the shopping cart script in Chapter 14 to utilize custom objects. At the very least you should have a Product object, but you may want to consider having an OrderForm object and a ShoppingCart object as well.

## Project 2: Tic-Tac-Toe Game Using Custom Objects

Write a modification of the tic-tac-toe game you wrote in Chapter 11 to utilize custom objects.

## Project 3: Planets of Our Solar System

Create a Web site that displays data about the planets in our solar system. Create a Planet object and use instances of the Planet object to store planetary information, including name, position, diameter, and mass, at the very least. You can acquire information about the planets from "The Nine Planets: A Multimedia Tour of the Solar System" located at http://seds.lpl.arizona.edu/nineplanets/nineplanets/nineplanets.html.

You may let the visitor choose a planet from a form, an image map, or a link or prompt the visitor for that information. However the user chooses a planet, the script should call a custom method to write the object's data, including a picture of the planet, in a pop-up window. The content of the pop-up window *must* be generated dynamically.

Once you've got your script working well, dress up your document and make it interesting. Look for pretty pictures of planets and starry backgrounds.

Upload and test your project. Turn in a print-out of your code.

## Project 4: Color Chooser Utility

Modify the color chooser utility you created in Project 3 of Chapter 11 to use custom objects. Upload and test your project. Turn in a print-out of your code.

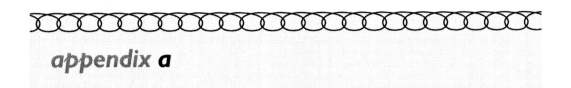

# JavaScript Object and Language Reference

*Warning: Objects in mirror may be closer than they appear.*

## About This Appendix

Objects are divided into two categories: Core JavaScript objects and Client-Side JavaScript objects. The objects in each category are listed in alphabetical order, Core objects first, then Client-Side.

Two columns appear under each Core JavaScript object. The first lists that object's properties, the second its methods.

Three columns appear under each Client-Side and DHTML object. The first column lists its properties, the second its methods, and the third the event handlers that apply to that object. This appendix also includes a cross-browser DHTML reference and a list of basic language conventions.

## Identifying Version Support

You can identify in which JavaScript version each object, property, and method was implemented by its JS superscript. Items with no superscript were included in the original JavaScript 1.0 specification. ECMA Script support is identified by an ES superscript.

# Properties That Are Objects

Many properties are themselves objects. You'll find the properties and methods of those objects under their object names. For instance, the images [] property of the document object is an array of Image objects. These image objects have all of the predefined properties of an image object; you'll find them listed under "Image."

*side note*

ᔕᔕᔕᔕᔕᔕᔕᔕᔕᔕᔕᔕᔕᔕ

This appendix is available as a handy guide: *WebWoman's JavaScript Reference*. Visit http://www.webwomansbooks.com to get yours!

ᔕᔕᔕᔕᔕᔕᔕᔕᔕᔕᔕᔕᔕᔕ

# Recognizing Array Objects

Many objects have arrays among their properties. Array names are usually written in plural form and are always followed by brackets in this listing, for example, images []. You'll find the property and method details for the objects in the arrays under their object names.

# JavaScript Versions

| Core JavaScript Version | ECMA Script Support | Client-Side JavaScript Version | Equivalent JavaScript Version | Browser Support | | | |
|---|---|---|---|---|---|---|---|
| | | | | **NN** | **IE** | **OP** | **MO** |
| 1.0 | | 1.0 | 1.0 | 2.0x | 3.0x | — | — |
| 1.1 | version 1 | 1.1 | 2.0 | 3.0x, | 3.02x* | 3-0x-3.5x* | — |
| 1.2 | | 1.2* | 3.0** | 4.0x-4.05 | 4.0x** | — | — |
| 1.3 | version 2 | 1.3 | 5.0-5.1 | 4.06-4.7x | 5.0x-5.1x* | 4.0x-5.0x | — |
| 1.4 | version 3 | | 5.5 | 5.0 (no release) | 5.5x* | 6.0x | — |
| 1.5 | version 3 | | 5.6 | 6.0x-7.0x+ | 6.0x* | 6.0x | 1.0 |

NN = Netscape Navigator, IE = Microsoft Internet Explorer, OP = Opera, MO = Mozilla
\* Not fully ECMA-262 compliant (current version listed in chart at that level)
\*\* ECMA-262 version 1 compliant

# Accessing Objects with Dot Notation

Most Client-Side JavaScript objects are derived from Web documents and the browser itself. These objects are arranged in hierarchical order. Writing the dot notation for any object is simply a matter of connecting the dots. (Read the diagram in Figure A.1 from left to right.)

✗ Dot notation for current browser window:

```
window
```

✗ For the document contained in the current window:

```
window.document
```

*Figure A. I*      ***Client-Side JavaScript Objects***

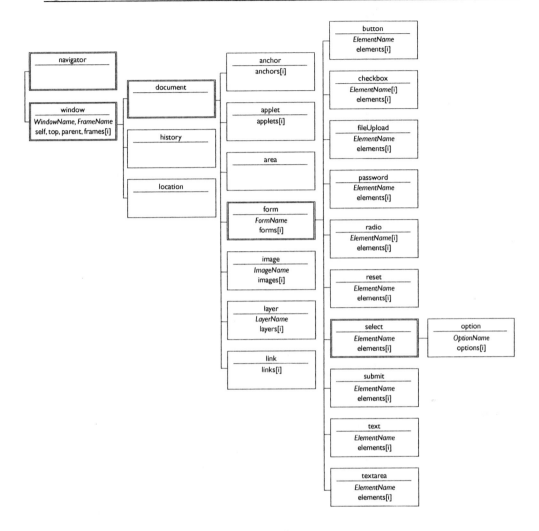

Many objects can be referenced by a name assigned to them in a name attribute with HTML. Here's the dot notation for:

⚔ an image named Sam (using the name attribute):

`window.document.Sam`

⚔ a text box named Email in a form called Order:

`window.document.Order.Email`

Some objects are members of an array and can also be accessed using their array references:

✗ Dot notation for the second image in a document:

```
window.document.images[1]
```

✗ For the third option in a select list that is the fourth element in the first form:

```
window.document.forms[0].elements[3].options[2]
```

To access properties and call methods, simply append the property or method name on to the object reference:

✗ Dot notation for the src property of an image named Devan:

```
window.document.Devan.src
```

✗ Dot notation to call the write method on the document in the window named MapWin:

```
MapWin.document.write()
```

# Core JavaScript Objects

## Array[JS1.1 ES1]

| | |
|---|---|
| index [JS1.2]<br>input [JS1.2]<br>length[JS1.1 ES1]<br>prototype[JS1.1 ES1] | concat(*arrayToAdd, [arrayToAdd2], ...*) [JS1.2 E3]<br>join([*"delimiter"*]) [JS1.1 E1]<br>pop() [JS1.2 E3]<br>push(*element1, ..., elementN*) [JS1.2 E3]<br>reverse() [JS1.1 E1]<br>shift() [JS1.2 E3]<br>slice(*beginIndex, [endIndex]*) [JS1.2 E3]<br>sort([*compareFunction]*) [JS1.1 E1]<br>splice(*startIndex, howMany, [element1,...]*) [JS1.2 E3]<br>toString() [JS1.1 E1]<br>unshift(*element1, ..., elementN*) [JS1.2 E3] |
| new Array(*arrayLength*)<br>new Array(*element0, element1, ..., elementN*)<br>Note: Array indices begin numbering at 0. | |

## Boolean[JS1.1 ES1]

| | |
|---|---|
| prototype[JS1.1 ES1] | toString() [JS1.1 ES1] |
| new Boolean (*value*) | |

## Date[JS1 ES1]

| prototype[JS1.1 ES1] | Date.parse("*dateString*") [ES1] | |
|---|---|---|
| | get [UTC] Date () [JS1.3 E1] | 1–31, day of month |
| | get [UTC] Day () [ES1] | 0–6, day of week |
| | get [UTC] FullYear () [JS1.3 ES1] | four-digit year |
| | get [UTC] Hours () [ES1] | 0–23 |
| | get [UTC] Milliseconds () [JS1.3 ES1] | 0–999 |
| | get [UTC] Minutes () [ES1] | 0–59 |
| | get [UTC] Month () [ES1] | 0–11 |
| | get [UTC] Seconds () [ES1] | 0–59 |
| | getTime () [ES1] | milliseconds since 1/1/70, 00:00:00:00 |
| | getTimezoneOffset () [ES1] | difference between local time and GMT |
| | getYear () [ES1] | dep[JS1.3] use getFullYear () |
| | prototype [JS1.1 ES1] | |
| | set [UTC] Date () [JS1.3 E1] | 1–31, day of month |
| | set [UTC] FullYear () [JS1.3 ES1] | four-digit year |
| | set [UTC] Hours () [ES1] | 0–23 |
| | set [UTC] Milliseconds () [JS1.3 ES1] | 0–999 |
| | set [UTC] Minutes () [ES1] | 0–59 |
| | set [UTC] Month () [ES1] | 0–11 |
| | set [UTC] Seconds () [ES1] | 0–59 |
| | setTime () [ES1] | milliseconds since 1/1/70, 00:00:00:00 |
| | setYear () [ES1] | dep[JS1.3] use getFullYear () |
| | toGMTString () [ES1] | dep [JS1.3] use toUTCString () |
| | toLocaleString () [ES1] | |
| | toString () [JS1.1 ES1] | |
| | toUTCString () [JS1.3 ES1] | |
| | UTC(*year, month, day[, hrs, min, sec, ms]*) [ES1] | milliseconds since 1/1/70, 00:00:00:00 |
| | new Date() | |
| | new Date(*milliseconds*) | |
| | new Date(*dateString*) | |
| | new Date(*year, month, day [, hour, minutes, seconds]*) | |

**side note**

Netscape Navigator 2 cannot handle dates prior to January 1, 1970, and has problems with dates after the year 1999. Navigator 3+ (JavaScript 1.1+) supports all dates, though the value returned by getYear varies in form in some browsers.

## Function [JS1.1 ES1]

| | |
|---|---|
| arguments[] [JS1.1 ES1] dep[JS1.4] * | apply() [JS1.3] |
| arguments.callee [JS1.2] dep[JS1.4] | call() [JS1.3] |
| arguments.caller [JS1.1] dep[JS1.4] | toString() [JS1.1 ES1] |
| arguments.length [JS1.1] dep[JS1.4] * | |
| arity [JS1.2] dep[JS1.4] | |
| length [JS1.1 ES1] | |
| prototype [JS1.1 ES1] | |

```
function functionName (param1, param2, ..., paramN) {
    statements
}
new Function([arg1, arg2 ...,] functionBody)
```
* remains a variable local to the function

## global [JS1.3 ES1]

| | |
|---|---|
| Infinity [JS1.3 ES1] | eval(string) [ES1] |
| NaN [JS1.3 ES1] | isFinite(number) [JS1.3 ES3] |
| undefined [JS1.3 E1] | isNaN(testValue) [JS1.1 E1] |
| | Number(object) [JS1.2 E1] |
| | parseFloat(string) [E1] |
| | parseInt(string, radix) [E1] |
| | String(object) [JS1.2 E1] |
| | toString() [JS1.1 ES1] |

Represents properties and functions not associated with any particular object. In ECMAScript listed under global object.

## Math [JS1 ES1]

| | | |
|---|---|---|
| E [ES1] | e | abs(num) [ES1] |
| LN2 [ES1] | natural log of 2 | acos(num) [ES1] |
| LN10 [ES1] | natural log of 10 | asin(num) [ES1] |
| LOG2E [ES1] | base 2 log of e | atan(num) [ES1] |
| LOG10E [ES1] | base 10 log of e | atan2(y, x) [ES1] |
| PI [ES1] | pi | ceil(num) [ES1] |

| SQRT1_2 [ES1] | square root of 1/2 | cos (*num*) [ES1] |
| SQRT2 [ES1] | square root of 2 | exp (*num*) [ES1] |
| | | floor (*num*) [ES1] |
| | | log (*num*) [ES1] |
| | | max (*num1, num2*) [ES1] |
| | | min (*num1, num2*) [ES1] |
| | | pow (*base, exponent*) [ES1] |
| | | random () [JS1.1 ES1] |
| | | round (*num*) [ES1] |
| | | sin (*num*) [ES1] |
| | | sqrt (*num*) [ES1] |
| | | tan (*num*) [ES1] |

## Number [JS1.1 ES1]

| MAX_VALUE [JS1.1 ES1] | toString () [JS1.1 ES1] |
| MIN_VALUE [JS1.1 ES1] | toExponential (*decDigits*) [JS1.5 ES1] |
| NaN [JS1.1 ES1] | toFixed (*decDigits*) [JS1.5 ES1] |
| NEGATIVE_INFINITY [JS1.1 ES1] | toPrecision (*decDigits*) [JS1.5 ES1] |
| POSITIVE_INFINITY [JS1.1 ES1] | |
| prototype [JS1.1 ES1] | |

new Number (*value*)

## Object [JS1 ES1]

| prototype [JS1.1 ES1] | toString () [JS1.1 ES1] |

new Object ()

## RegExp [JS1.2 ES3]

| $1,...,$9 [JS1.2] | | compile (*pattern[, flags]*) [JS1.2] |
| global [JS1.2 ES3] | | exec ("*string*") [JS1.2 ES3] |
| ignoreCase [JS1.2 ES3] | | test ("*string*") [JS1.2 ES3] |
| input [JS1.2 ES3] | $_ | toString () [JS1.1 ES3] |
| lastIndex [JS1.2 ES3] | | |
| lastMatch [JS1.2] | $& | |
| lastParen [JS1.2] | $+ | |
| leftContext [JS1.2] | $` | |
| multiline [JS1.2 ES3] | $* | |
| prototype [JS1.2] | | |
| rightContext [JS1.2] | $' | |
| source [JS1.2 ES3] | | |

The literal format is used as follows:

    /*pattern*/*flags*

The constructor function is used as follows:

    new RegExp ("*pattern*"[, "*flags*"])

---

## String [JS1] [ES1]

| | |
|---|---|
| length [ES1] | anchor (*name*) |
| prototype [JS1.1] [ES1] | big () |
| | blink () |
| | bold () |
| | charAt (*index*) [ES1] |
| | charCodeAt ([*index*]) [JS1.2] [ES1] |
| | concat (*str2*, ..., *strN*) [JS1.2] [ES3] |
| | fixed () |
| | fontcolor (*color*) |
| | fontsize (*size*) |
| | fromCharCode (*num1*, ...) [JS1.2] [ES2] |
| | indexOf (*searchStr*[, *start*]) [ES1] |
| | italics () |
| | lastIndexOf (*search*[, *start*]) [ES1] |
| | link (*href*) |
| | match (*regexp*) [JS1.2] [ES3] |
| | replace (*regExp, newStr*) [JS1.2] [ES3] |
| | search (*regExp*) [JS1.2] [ES3] |
| | slice (*start, end*) [JS1.2] [ES3] |
| | small () |
| | split ([*delimiter, limit*]) [JS1.1] [ES1] |
| | strike () |
| | sub () |
| | substr (*start*[, *length*]) [JS1.2] |
| | substring (*indexA , indexB*) [ES1] |
| | sup () |
| | toLowerCase () [ES1] |
| | toString () [JS1.1] [ES1] |
| | toUpperCase () [ES1] |

new String (*string*)

Call String methods using string literals, string variables, or string objects.

# Client-Side JavaScript Objects

## Anchor

| | | |
|---|---|---|
| name[JS1.2] | toString() | No event handlers |
| text[JS1.2] | | |
| x[JS1.2] | | |
| y[JS1.2] | | |

document.write(*string*.anchor(*nameAttribute*))

## Area[JS1.1]

| | | |
|---|---|---|
| hash[JS1.1] | handleEvent(*event*)[JS1.2] | onClick= |
| host[JS1.1] | toString()[JS1.1] | onDblClick=[JS1.2] |
| hostname[JS1.1] | | onFocus= |
| href[JS1.1] | | onKeyDown=[JS1.2] |
| pathname[JS1.1] | | onKeyPress=[JS1.2] |
| port[JS1.1] | | onKeyUp=[JS1.2] |
| protocol[JS1.1] | | onMouseDown=[JS1.2] |
| search[JS1.1] | | onMouseOut=[JS1.1] |
| target[JS1.1] | | onMouseOver=[JS1.1] |
| text[JS1.2] | | onMouseUp=[JS1.2] |
| x[JS1.2] | | |
| y[JS1.2] | | |

Area objects are a type of link object and are listed in the links array.

## Button

| | | |
|---|---|---|
| disabled | blur()[JS1.1] | onBlur=[JS1.1] |
| form* | click() | onClick= |
| name | focus()[JS1.1] | onFocus=[JS1.1] |
| type[JS1.1] | handleEvent(*event*)[JS1.2] | onMousedown=[JS1.2] |
| value | toString() | onMouseup=[JS1.2] |

*Refers to button's parent: form.

## Checkbox

| | | |
|---|---|---|
| checked | blur() | onBlur=[JS1.1] |
| defaultChecked | click() | onClick= |
| disabled | focus() | onFocus=[JS1.1] |
| form* | handleEvent(*event*)[JS1.2] | |
| name | toString() | |

| type[JS1.1] | | |
| value | | |

*Refers to checkbox's parent: form.

## document

| alinkColor | captureEvents (*event*) [JS1.2] | onClick= |
| anchors [] | clear () | onDblClick=[JS1.2] |
| applets [] [JS1.1] | close () | onKeyDown= [JS1.2] |
| bgColor | getElementById () [JS1.5] | onKeyPress=[JS1.2] |
| cookie | getElementByName () [JS1.5] | onKeyUp=[JS1.2] |
| domain[JS1.1] | getElementsByTagName () [JS1.5] | onMouseDown=[JS1.2] |
| embeds [] [JS1.1] | getSelection () [JS1.2] | onMouseUp=[JS1.2] |
| fgColor | handleEvent (*event*) [JS1.2] | |
| *formName*[JS1.1] | open ( "*mime*" [, "*replace*" ]) | |
| forms [] [JS1.1] | releaseEvent (*eventType*) [JS1.2] | |
| height[JS1.2] | routeEvent (*event*) [JS1.2] | |
| images [] [JS1.1] | toString () | |
| lastModified | write (*exp1* [, *exp2* ...]) | |
| linkColor | writeln (*exp1* [, *exp2* ...]) | |
| links [] | | |
| location[depJS1.1] | | |
| plugins [] [JS1.1] | | |
| referrer | | |
| title | | |
| URL | | |
| vlinkColor | | |
| width[JS1.2] | | |

## event[JS1.2]

| data[JS1.2] | | |
| height[JS1.2] | | |
| layerX[JS1.2] | | |
| layerY[JS1.2] | | |
| modifiers[JS1.2] | | |
| pageX[JS1.2] | | |
| pageY[JS1.2] | | |
| screenX[JS1.2] | | |
| screenY[JS1.2] | | |
| target[JS1.2] | | |
| type[JS1.2] | | |
| which[JS1.2] | | |

| width[JS1.2] | | |
| x[JS1.2] | | |
| y[JS1.2] | | |

## FileUpload

| disabled | blur() | onBlur=[JS1.1] |
|---|---|---|
| form* | focus() | onChange=[JS1.1] |
| name | handleEvent(*event*)[JS1.2] | onFocus=[JS1.1] |
| type[JS1.1] | select() | |
| value | toString() | |

*Refers to fileUpload's parent: form.

## Form

| action** | handleEvent(*event*)[JS1.2] | onReset=[JS1.1] |
|---|---|---|
| elements[]* | reset()[JS1.1] | onSubmit= |
| encoding | submit() | |
| length | toString() | |
| method** | | |
| name | | |
| target** | | |

*See button, checkbox, fileUpload, hidden, password, radio, reset, select, submit, text, and textarea for element objects.
**May not modify in IE3.

## Frame

| onblur | toString() | onBlur=[JS1.1] |
|---|---|---|
| onfocus | | onFocus=[JS1.1] |
| | | onLoad= |
| | | onMove=[JS1.2] |
| | | onResize=[JS1.2] |
| | | onUnload= |

Every frame is a window object. See window for more information.

## Hidden

| form* | toString() | No event handlers |
|---|---|---|
| name | | |
| type[JS1.1] | | |
| value | | |

*Refers to hidden's parent: form.

## history

| | | |
|---|---|---|
| current[JS1.1] | back() | No event handlers |
| length | forward() | |
| next[JS1.1] | go(*index* \|\| *URL* \|\| *delta*) | |
| previous[JS1.1] | toString() | |

Predefined JavaScript objects accessed through history property of the window object.

## Image[JS1.1]

| | | |
|---|---|---|
| border[JS1.1] | handleEvent()[JS1.2] | onAbort=[JS1.1] |
| complete[JS1.1] | toString()[JS1.1] | onError=[JS1.1] |
| height[JS1.1] | | onKeyDown=[JS1.2] |
| hspace[JS1.1] | | onKeyPress=[JS1.2] |
| lowsrc[JS1.1] | | onKeyUp=[JS1.2] |
| name[JS1.1] | | onLoad=[JS1.1] |
| src[JS1.1] | | |
| vspace[JS1.1] | | |
| width[JS1.1] | | |

new Image ([*width*], [*height*])

## Link

| | | |
|---|---|---|
| hash | handleEvent(*event*)[JS1.2] | onClick= |
| host | toString() | onDblClick=[JS1.2] |
| hostname | | onFocus= |
| href | | onKeyDown=[JS1.2] |
| pathname | | onKeyPress=[JS1.2] |
| port | | onKeyUp=[JS1.2] |
| protocol | | onMouseDown=[JS1.2] |
| search | | onMouseout=[JS1.1] |
| target | | onMouseover= |
| text[JS1.2] | | onMouseUp=[JS1.2] |
| x[JS1.2] | | |
| y[JS1.2] | | |

document.write(*string*.link(*hrefAttribute*))
Each link object is a location object and has the same properties as a location object.

## location

| | | |
|---|---|---|
| hash | assign() | No event handlers |
| host | reload(*forceGet*)[JS1.1] | |
| hostname | replace(*URL*)[JS1.1] | |
| href | toString() | |

| pathname | | |
|---|---|---|
| port | | |
| protocol | | |
| search | | |

## MimeType[JS1.1]

| description[JS1.1] | toString()[JS1.1] | No event handlers |
|---|---|---|
| enabledPlugin[JS1.1] | | |
| suffixes[JS1.1] | | |
| type[JS1.1] | | |

A property of both navigator and plugin objects, indexed by number or type.

## navigator

| appCodeName | javaEnabled()[JS1.1] | No event handlers |
|---|---|---|
| appName | plugins.refresh() | |
| appVersion | preference(prefName[, | |
| language[JS1.2] | newValue])[JS1.2] | |
| mimeTypes[] [JS1.1] | savePreferences()[JS1.2] | |
| platform[JS1.2] | toString() | |
| plugins[] [JS1.1] | | |
| userAgent | | |

## Option

| defaultSelected[JS1.1] | toString() | No event handlers |
|---|---|---|
| index | | |
| length | | |
| selected | | |
| text | | |
| value | | |

See parent object: select.

new Option ([text], [value], [defaultSelected], [selected])

document.FormName.SelectName.options[i] = newOption

## Password

| defaultValue | blur() | onBlur=[JS1.1] |
|---|---|---|
| form* | focus() | onFocus=[JS1.1] |
| name | handleEvent(event)[JS1.2] | |
| type[JS1.1] | select() | |
| value | toString() | |

*Refers to password's parent: form.

## Plugin[JS1.1]

| description[JS1.1] | refresh(true \|\| false)[JS1.1] | No event handlers |
|---|---|---|
| filename[JS1.1] | toString()[JS1.1] | |
| length[JS1.1] | | |
| name[JS1.1] | | |

See parent objects: navigator and document.

Access as navigator.plugins[i] or navigator.plugins[i] [*mimeTypeIndex*].

## Radio

| checked | blur()[JS1.1] | onBlur=[JS1.1] |
|---|---|---|
| defaultChecked | click() | onClick= |
| disabled | focus()[JS1.1] | onFocus=[JS1.1] |
| form* | handleEvent(*event*)[JS1.2] | |
| length | toString() | |
| name | | |
| type[JS1.1] | | |
| value | | |

*Refers to the radio button's parent: form.

## Reset

| disabled | blur()[JS1.1] | onBlur=[JS1.1] |
|---|---|---|
| form* | click() | onClick= |
| name | focus()[JS1.1] | onFocus=[JS1.1] |
| type[JS1.1] | handleEvent(*event*)[JS1.2] | |
| value | toString() | |

*Refers to reset's parent: form.

## screen[JS1.2]

| availHeight[JS1.2] | toString()[JS1.2] | No event handlers |
|---|---|---|
| availLeft[JS1.2] | | |
| availTop[JS1.2] | | |
| availWidth[JS1.2] | | |
| colorDepth[JS1.2] | | |
| height[JS1.2] | | |
| pixelDepth[JS1.2] | | |
| width[JS1.2] | | |

## Select

| | | |
|---|---|---|
| disabled | blur() | onBlur= |
| form* | focus() | onChange= |
| length | handleEvent(*event*)[JS1.2] | onFocus= |
| name | toString() | |
| options[] | | |
| selectedIndex | | |
| type[JS1.1] | | |

See child object: option.
*Refers to select's parent: form.

## Submit

| | | |
|---|---|---|
| disabled | blur()[JS1.1] | onBlur=[JS1.1] |
| form* | click() | onClick= |
| name | focus()[JS1.1] | onFocus=[JS1.1] |
| type[JS1.1] | handleEvent(*event*)[JS1.2] | |
| value | toString() | |

*Refers to submit's parent: form.

## Text

| | | |
|---|---|---|
| defaultValue | blur() | onBlur= |
| disabled | focus() | onChange= |
| form* | handleEvent(*event*)[JS1.2] | onFocus= |
| name | select() | onSelect= |
| type[JS1.1] | toString() | |
| value | | |

*Refers to text box's parent: form.

## Textarea

| | | |
|---|---|---|
| defaultValue | blur() | onBlur= |
| disabled | focus() | onChange= |
| form* | handleEvent(*event*)[JS1.2] | onFocus= |
| name | select() | onKeyDown=[JS1.2] |
| type[JS1.1] | toString() | onKeyPress=[JS1.2] |
| value | | onKeyUp=[JS1.2] |
| | | onSelect= |

*Refers to textarea's parent: form.

## window

| | | |
|---|---|---|
| closed[JS1.1] | alert ( *"message"* ) | onBlur=[JS1.1] |
| crypto[JS1.2] | atob () [JS1.2] | onDragDrop=[JS1.2] |
| defaultStatus | back () [JS1.2] * | onError=[JS1.1] |
| document | blur () [JS1.1] | onFocus=[JS1.1] |
| frames [] | btoa () [JS1.2] | onLoad= |
| history[JS1.1] | captureEvents ( *type* ) [JS1.2] | onMove=[JS1.2] |
| innerHeight[JS1.2] | clearInterval ( *intervalID* ) [JS1.2] | onResize=[JS1.2] |
| innerWidth[JS1.2] | clearTimeout ( *intervalID* ) | onUnload= |
| length | close () | |
| location | confirm ( *"message"* ) | |
| locationbar[JS1.2] | crypto.random ( *numberOfBytes* ) [JS1.2] | |
| menubar[JS1.2] | crypto.signText ( *text. selectionStyle,* | |
| name | *[auth1, ... authN]* ) [JS1.2] | |
| offScreenBuffering[JS1.2] | disableExternalCapture () [JS1.2] | |
| onerror | enableExternalCapture () [JS1.2] | |
| opener[JS1.1] | find ( [ *"str"*, *case, bkwd]* ) [JS1.2] | |
| outerHeight[JS1.2] | focus () [JS1.1] | |
| outerWidth[JS1.2] | forward () [JS1.2] * | |
| pageXOffset[JS1.2] | handleEvent ( *event* ) [JS1.2] | |
| pageYOffset[JS1.2] | home () [JS1.2] | |
| parent | moveBy ( D*x*, D*y* ) [JS1.2] | |
| personalbar[JS1.2] | moveTo ( *x, y* ) [JS1.2] | |
| screenX[JS1.2] | open ( *"URL"*, *"target"*, *"features"* ) | |
| screenY[JS1.2] | print () | |
| scrollbars[JS1.2] | prompt ( *"msg"*, *"defaultValue"* ) | |
| self | releaseEvents ( *type* ) [JS1.2] | |
| status | resizeBy ( D*x*, D*y* ) [JS1.2] | |
| statusbar[JS1.2] | resizeTo ( *width, height* ) [JS1.2] | |
| toolbar[JS1.2] | routeEvent ( *event* ) [JS1.2] | |
| top | scroll ( *x, y* ) [JS1.1] dep[JS1.2] | |
| window | scrollBy ( D*x*, D*y* ) [JS1.2] | |
| | scrollTo ( *x, y* ) [JS1.2] | |
| | setHotKeys ( true \| false ) [JS1.2] | |
| | setInterval ( *function, sec* [, *args* ] ) [JS1.2] | |
| | setResizable () [JS1.2] | |
| | setTimeout ( *function, msec* [, *args* ] ) | |
| | setZOptions ( alwaysRaised \| | |
| | alwaysLowered \| z-lock ) [JS1.2] | |
| | stop () [JS1.2] | |
| | toString () | |

*Not supported by IE; history.back and history.forward can usually substitute for window.back and window.forward for a cross-browser solution.

Setting the following properties or calling the following methods requires UniversalBrowserWrite priviledges: disableExternalCapture()[JS1.2], enableExternalCapture()[JS1.2], screenX[JS1.2], screenY[JS1.2], setHotKeys()[JS1.2], setZOptions()[JS1.2]; visible property of locationbar, menubar, personalbar, scrollbars, statusbar, and toolbar.

### window synonyms

| | |
|---|---|
| opener | window that opened current window |
| parent | parent frameset |
| parent.*frameName* | used to refer to a sibling |
| parent.frames[*i*] | used to refer to a sibling by index number |
| self | current window |
| top | topmost window, outside of all framesets |
| window | current window |

# DHTML Quick Reference

## Hints for Writing Cross-Browser DHTML

1. Use IDs to name your HTML divisions.

   ```
   <div id=MyDiv>...</div>
   ```

2. Use object detection to conditionally write appropriate statements:

   ```
   if (document.getElementById)   // W3C DOM2-compatible
   if (document.layers)           // NN4x
   if (document.all)              // IE4 to 5
   ```

3. General form for setting CSS properties in DOM2-compatble browsers:

   ```
   document.getElementById(id).style.property
   ```

   General form for setting CSS properties in Netscape:

   ```
   document.DivID.property
   ```

   or

   ```
   document.layers["DivID"].property
   ```

   General form for setting CSS properties in IE:

   ```
   DivID.style.property
   ```

   or

   ```
   document.all["DivID"].style.property
   ```

## Cross-Browser DHTML Property Quick Reference

| Layer Property[0] | Property Reference (4.0+ Browsers) | Result Type |
|---|---|---|
| background-color | **NN4:** `document.layers["objId"].bgColor`<br>**IE4:** `document.all["objId"].style`<br>   `.backgroundColor`<br>**OP4:** not supported<br>**OP5+:** `document.getElementById("objId")`<br>   `.style.background`<br>**DOM2:** `document.getElementById("objId")`<br>   `.style.backgroundColor` | six-digit hexadecimal number |
| background-image | **NN4:** `document.layers["objId"].background`<br>**IE4+:** not supported<br>**OP4+:** not supported<br>**DOM2:** `document.getElementById("objId")`<br>   `.style.backgroundImage` | URL to image |
| border color | **DOM2:** `document.getElementById("objId")`<br>   `.style.borderColor` | six-digit hexadecimal number |
| border style | **DOM2:** `document.getElementById("objId")`<br>   `.style.borderStyle` | string:<br>`solid`,<br>`inset`,<br>`outset`, or<br>`groove` |
| border width | **DOM2:** `document.getElementById("objId")`<br>   `.style.borderWidth` | string:<br>*n unit* |
| content | **NN4:** `document.layers["objId"].load("URL",`<br>   *width*`)`<br>**IE4:** `document.all["objId"].innerHTML`<br>**OP4+:** not supported<br>**DOM2:** `document.getElementById("objId")`<br>   `.innerHTML`[1] | string |
| height | **NN4:** not supported<br>**IE4:** `document.all["objId"].style`<br>   `.pixelHeight`<br>**OP4–5:** `document.getElementById("objId")`<br>   `.style.pixelHeight`<br>**DOM2:** `document.getElementById("objId")`<br>   `.style.height` | —<br><br>string: *n* px<br><br>string: *n*<br><br>string: *n* px |

| | | |
|---|---|---|
| left<br>(x-coordinate) | **NN4:** `document.layers["`*objId*`"].left`<br>**IE4:** `document.all["`*objId*`"].style`<br>  `.pixelLeft`<br>**OP4–5:** `document.getElementById`<br>  `("`*objId*`").style.pixelLeft`<br>**DOM2:** `document.getElementById`<br>  `("`*objId*`").style.left` | number<br>string: *n* px<br><br>string: *n*<br><br>string: *n* px |
| object | **NN4:** `document.layers["`*objId*`"]`<br>**IE4:** `document.all["`*objId*`"]`<br>**OP4+:** `document`<br>  `.getElementById("`*objId*`")`<br>**DOM2:** `document`<br>  `.getElementById("`*objId*`")` | object |
| top<br>(y-coordinate) | **NN4:** `document.layers["`*objId*`"].top`<br>**IE4:** `document.all["`*objId*`"].style`<br>  `.pixelTop`<br>**OP4–5:** `document.getElementById`<br>  `("`*objId*`").style.pixelTop`<br>**DOM2:** `document.getElementById`<br>  `("`*objId*`").style.top` | number<br>string: *n* px<br><br>string: *n*<br><br>string: *n* px |
| visibility | **NN4:** `document.layers["`*objId*`"]`<br>  `.visibility`<br>**IE4:** `document.all["`*objId*`"].style`<br>  `.visibility`<br>**OP4+:** `document.getElementById`<br>  `("`*objId*`").visibility`<br>**DOM2:** `document.getElementById`<br>  `("`*objId*`").style.visibility` | hide, show, inherit<br><br>hidden, visible, or<br>  inherit for rest |
| width | **NN4:** not supported<br>**IE4:** `document.all["`*objId*`"].style`<br>  `.pixelWidth`<br>**OP4–5:** `document.getElementById`<br>  `("`*objId*`").style.pixelWidth`<br>**DOM2:** `document.getElementById`<br>  `("`*objId*`").width` | string: *n* px<br>In OP, string: *n* |

| Other Property | Property Reference (4.0+ Browsers) | Result Type |
|---|---|---|
| font color | **NN4:** not supported<br>**IE4:** `document.all["objId"].style.color`<br>**OP4:** not supported<br>**DOM2:** `document.getElementById("objId")`<br>`.style.color` | six-digit hexadecimal number |
| set style on an element | **NN4:** not supported, can only access layer style properties<br>**IE4:** `document.all["objId"].style.property`<br>`= "value"`<br>**OP4:** not supported, can only access layer style properties<br>**DOM2:** `document.getElementById("objId")`<br>`.style = "declaration"` | |
| stylesheet properties | **NN4:** not supported, can only access layer style properties<br>**IE4:** `document.all["objId"].style.property`<br>**OP4:** not supported, can only access layer style properties<br>**DOM2:** `document.getElementById("objId")`<br>`.style.property` | depends on property |
| window height | **NN4:** `window.innerHeight`<br>**IE4:** `window.document.body.clientHeight`<br>**OP4+:** `window.innerHeight`<br>**DOM2:** `window.innerHeight` | number |
| window width | **NN4:** `window.innerWidth`<br>**IE4:** `window.document.body.clientWidth`<br>**OP4+:** `window.innerWidth`<br>**DOM2:** `window.innerWidth` | number |

Replace italicized items appropriately.
[0] layer = an absolutely positioned element, usually a division
[1] not part of W3C standard

# JavaScript Language Reference

## Built-in Functions (aka global object methods)

escape(*"string"*)
eval(*expression*)
isFinite(*number*)[JS1.3]
isNaN(*expression*)[JS1.1]
Number(*object*)[JS1.2]

parseFloat(*"string"*)
parseInt(*"string"*[,*radix*])
String(*value*)[JS1.2]
unescape(*"string"*)

## Control Structures

**Conditional:**        `result = (condition) ? valueIfTrue : valueIfFalse`

**Do...While:**[JS1.2 E3]

```
do {
    statement(s)
}
```

**For:**[E1]

```
for (initialExpression; condition; updateExpression) {
    statement(s)
}
```

**If:**[E1]

```
if (condition) {
    statements if condition is true
}
```

**If...Else:**[E1]

```
if (condition) {
    statement(s) if condition is true
} else {
    statement(s) if condition is false
}
```

**Switch:**[JS1.2 E3]

```
switch (expression) {
    case constantLabel1:
        statement(s)
        [break]
    case constantLabel2:
        statement(s)
        [break]
    ...
    [default:
        statement(s)]
}
```

**While:**[E1]

```
while (condition) {
    statement(s)
}
```

## Creating Custom Objects

```
new Object()

function ObjectName([param1, param2...]) {
    this.property1 = value
    this.property2 = value
```

```
    . . .
    this.method1 = someCustomMethod
}
```

## Data Types

| | |
|---|---|
| boolean | (primitive) |
| number | (primitive) |
| string | (primitive) |
| object | (composite) |
| function | (special) |

## Special Values

| | |
|---|---|
| Infinity | infinity |
| NaN[JS1.1] | not a number |
| null | has no value |
| undefined | is not defined |

## Operators

### Arithmetic

| | | | | |
|---|---|---|---|---|
| + | plus | | % | modulus |
| - | minus | | ++ | increment |
| * | multiply | | -- | decrement |
| / | divide | | -val | negation |

### Assignment

| | | | | |
|---|---|---|---|---|
| = | equals/gets | | *= | multiply by value |
| += | add by value | | /= | divide by value |
| -= | subtract by value | | %= | modulo by value |

### Comparison

| | | | | |
|---|---|---|---|---|
| == | is equal to | | < | is less than |
| != | is not equal to | | <= | is less than or equal to |
| === | is equivalent to | | > | is greater than |
| !=== | is not equivalent to | | >= | is greater than or equal to |

### Logical

| | |
|---|---|
| && | AND |
| \|\| | OR |
| ! | NOT |

### Special

| | |
|---|---|
| delete[JS1.2] | typeof[JS1.1] |
| new | void[JS1.1] |
| this | |

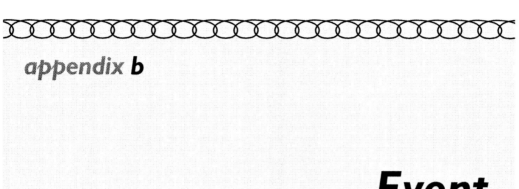

# Event Handlers

E vent handlers handle events generated by the browser or a Web site visitor. This appendix is a list of the event handlers supported by JavaScript. For each event handler, the following information has been provided: the JavaScript objects to which it applies (left column), the corresponding HTML elements to which it applies (right column), and a brief description of when the event handler is invoked.

*Never check for an error condition you don't know how to handle.*

—Anonymous

## onAbort[1.1]

| | |
|---|---|
| Image[1.1] | `<img>`[1.1] |

Invoked when visitor aborts loading an image

## onBlur

| | |
|---|---|
| Button[1.1] | `<input type="button">`[1.1] |
| Checkbox[1.1] | `<input type="checkbox">`[1.1] |
| FileUpload[1.1] | `<input type="file">`[1.1] |
| Frame[1.1] | *must be set with JavaScript* `onblur="statement(s)"` |
| Password[1.1] | `<input type="password">`[1.1] |
| Radio[1.1] | `<input type="radio">`[1.1] |
| Reset[1.1] | `<input type="reset">`[1.1] |
| Select | `<select>` |
| Submit[1.1] | `<input type="submit">`[1.1] |
| Text | `<input type="text">` |
| Textarea | `<textarea>` |
| window[1.1] | `<body>`[1.1] |

Invoked when an element loses focus

## onChange

| | |
|---|---|
| FileUpload[1.1] | `<input type="file">`[1.1] |
| Select | `<select>` |
| Text | `<input type="text">` |
| Textarea | `<textarea>` |

Invoked when an element's value changes between `focus` and `blur`

## onClick

| | |
|---|---|
| Area | `<area href="someURL">` |
| Button | `<input type="button">` |
| Checkbox | `<input type="checkbox">` |
| document | |
| Link | `<a href="someURL">` |
| Radio | `<input type="radio">` |
| Reset | `<input type="reset">` |
| Submit | `<input type="submit">` |

[1.1]Added ability to return `false` to cancel action associated with click event

## onDblClick[1,2]

| | |
|---|---|
| Area[JS1.2] | `<area href="`*someURL*`">`[JS1.2] |
| document[1.2] | `<body>`[1.2] |
| Link[1.2] | `<a href="`*someURL*`">`[1.2] |

Invoked when visitor double-clicks on an element

Not implemented on the Macintosh

Not recognized by Opera

## onDragDrop[1,2]

| |
|---|
| window[1.2] |

Invoked when visitor drags a system item such as a file, shortcut, etc. on to the browser window and drops it

## onError[1.1]

| | |
|---|---|
| Image[1.1] | `<img>` |
| window[1.1] | `<body>` |

To suppress JavaScript error dialogs:

        onError=null
        window.onerror=null

Otherwise use onError=*functionToHandleErrors( )*.

Invoked when a JavaScript syntax or run-time error occurs. For instance, a bad URL in an `<img>` tag or a corrupted image will generate an error event. However, trying to load a file that simply does not exist is a browser error and will not generate an error event.

## onFocus

| | |
|---|---|
| Area | `<area href="`*someURL*`">` |
| Button[1.1] | `<input type="button">`[1.1] |
| Checkbox[1.1] | `<input type="checkbox">`[1.1] |
| FileUpload[1.1] | `<input type="file">`[1.1] |
| Frame[1.1] | `<frame>`[1.1] |
| Link | `<a href="`*someURL*`">` |
| Password[1.1] | `<input type="password">`[1.1] |
| Radio[1.1] | `<input type="radio">`[1.1] |
| Reset[1.1] | `<input type="reset">`[1.1] |
| Select | `<select>` |
| Submit[1.1] | `<input type="submit">`[1.1] |
| Text | `<input type="text">` |
| Textarea | `<textarea>` |
| window[1.1] | `<body>`[1.1] |

Invoked when an element receives focus

## onKeyDown[1,2]

| | |
|---|---|
| Area | |
| document[1,2] | |
| Image[1,2] | |
| Link[1,2] | |
| Textarea[1,2] | |

Invoked when a visitor depresses a key

## onKeyPress[1,2]

| | |
|---|---|
| Area | |
| document[1,2] | |
| Image[1,2] | |
| Link[1,2] | |
| Textarea[1,2] | |

Invoked when a visitor presses and releases a key

## onKeyUp[1,2]

| | |
|---|---|
| Area | |
| document[1,2] | |
| Image[1,2] | |
| Link[1,2] | |
| Textarea[1,2] | |

Invoked when a visitor releases a depressed key

## onLoad

| | |
|---|---|
| Frame | `<frameset>` |
| Image[1,1] | `<img>`[1,1] |
| window | `<body>` |

Invoked when the browser has retrieved all of the content between the <body> tags or all of the frames in a <frameset> tag

## onMouseDown[1,2]

| | |
|---|---|
| Area[1,2] | `<area href="someURL">`[1,2] |
| Button[1,2] | `<input type="button">`[1,2] |
| document[1,2] | |
| Link[1,2] | `<a href="someURL">`[1,2] |

Invoked when a visitor presses a mouse button

## onMouseMove[1,2]

MouseMove is not an event of any object. The programmer must explicitly set it to be associated with a particular object.

Invoked when a visitor moves the mouse

## onMouseOut[1,1]

| Area[1,1] | `<area href="someURL">`[1,1] |
| Link[1,1] | `<a href="someURL">`[1,1] |

Invoked when a visitor moves the mouse off of a link or an area of an image map

## onMouseOver

| Area[1,1] | `<area href="someURL">`[1,1] |
| Link | `<a href="someURL">` |

Invoked when a visitor moves the mouse over a link, area of an image map, or layer

## onMouseUp[1,2]

| Area[1,2] | `<area href="someURL">`[1,2] |
| Button[1,2] | `<input type="button">`[1,2] |
| document[1,2] | |
| Link[1,2] | `<a href="someURL">`[1,2] |

Invoked when a visitor releases a depressed mouse button

## onMove[1,2]

Frame[1,2]
window[1,2]

Invoked when a visitor moves a frame or window

## onReset[1,1]

| Form[1,1] | `<form>`[1,1] |

Invoked when a visitor resets a form by clicking on a reset button or pressing Enter when the reset button has focus or a script calls a form's `reset` method

## onResize[1,2]

Frame[1,2]
window[1,2]

Invoked when a visitor resizes a frame or window

## onSelect

| Text | `<input type="text">` |
| Textarea | `<textarea>` |

Invoked when a visitor or script selects text in a text or textarea form element

## onSubmit

| Form | `<form>` |

Invoked when a visitor submits a form by clicking on a submit button or pressing Enter when the submit button has focus or a script calls a form's `submit` method

## onUnload

| window | `<body>`, `<frameset>` |

Invoked when a new document is requested in the current browser window

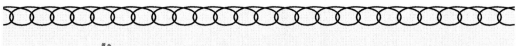

# appendix **c**

# **Reserved Words**

*It is of interest to note that while some dolphins are reported to have learned English—up to fifty words used in correct context—no human being has been reported to have learned dolphinese.*

—Carl Sagan

L ike most programming languages, JavaScript reserves certain words for its own use and future use. These reserved words may *not* be used to name variables, functions, custom objects, properties, and methods. Some of these words have been reserved because they are used by Java. Remember, JavaScript was designed to work and coexist with Java. Some have been reserved because they are part of the ECMAScript language or may eventually be a part of the ECMAScript language.

This appendix contains a list of words reserved by both JavaScript and ECMAScript, as well as a list of unofficially reserved words:

- JavaScript identifiers
- HTML elements and attributes
- CSS properties

For best results, avoid using any of the words cited as variable, object, function, or HTML element names.

# Words Reserved by JavaScript and ECMAScript

| | | |
|---|---|---|
| abstract | final | public |
| boolean | finally | return |
| break | float | short |
| byte | for | static |
| case | function | super |
| catch | goto | switch |
| char | if | synchronized |
| class | implements | this |
| const | import | throw |
| continue | in | throws |
| debugger | instanceof | transient |
| default | int | true |
| delete | interface | try |
| do | long | typeof |
| double | native | var |
| else | new | void |
| enum | null | volatile |
| export | package | while |
| extends | private | with |
| false | protected | |

# Unofficially Reserved Words

The JavaScript language uses many words to identify the properties and methods of core and client-side objects. While these words are not *officially* reserved by JavaScript, you should avoid using them anyway. Don't use them to name variables, arrays, functions, custom objects, or their properties and methods. Don't use them to name HTML elements either. For instance,

```
<form name="form">
```

is very bad form. Try calling the form `orderForm`, `guestbookEntry`, or something else more descriptive and less likely to wreak havoc in your scripts.

Using identifiers already recognized by JavaScript is asking for trouble; the results will always be unpredictable. You should also try to avoid using HTML tag and attribute names since many of them are also the names of JavaScript objects and properties. CSS property names ought to be avoided as well; JavaScript is often used to set stylesheet properties.

The danger list is quite long.

## JavaScript Identifiers

| | | |
|---|---|---|
| abs | charAt | encoding |
| acos | charCode | error |
| action | Checkbox | escape |
| alert | checkbox | eval |
| alinkColor | checked | event |
| anchor | child | exec |
| anchors | clear | exp |
| appCodeName | clearInterval | fgColor |
| applets | clearTimeout | filename |
| apply | click | fileUpload |
| appName | close | find |
| appVersion | closed | fixed |
| arguments | colorDepth | floor |
| arity | compile | focus |
| Array | complete | fontcolor |
| array | concat | fontsize |
| asin | confirm | Form |
| assign | cookie | form |
| atan | cos | forms |
| atan2 | Crypto | forward |
| atob | crypto | Frame |
| availHeight | current | frames |
| availLeft | data | fromCharCode |
| availTop | Date | Function |
| availWidth | date | getDate |
| back | defaultChecked | getDay |
| bgColor | defaultSelected | getElementById |
| big | defaultStatus | getElementByName |
| blink | defaultValue | getElementsByTagName |
| blur | description | getFullYear |
| bold | disabled | getHours |
| border | disableExternalCapture | getMilliseconds |
| btoa | Document | getMinutes |
| Button | document | getSeconds |
| button | domain | getSelection |
| call | E | getTime |
| callee | elements | getTimezoneOffset |
| caller | embeds | getUTCDate |
| captureEvents | enabledPlugin | getUTCDay |
| ceil | enableExternalCapture | getUTCFullYear |

| | | |
|---|---|---|
| getUTCHours | lastModified | Object |
| getUTCMilliseconds | lastParen | object |
| getUTCMinutes | layerX | offScreenBuffering |
| getUTCMonth | layerY | onerror |
| getUTCSeconds | leftContext | open |
| getUTCTime | length | opener |
| getUTCYear | Link | Option |
| getYear | link | option |
| global | linkColor | options |
| go | links | outerHeight |
| handleEvent | LN10 | outerWidth |
| hash | Location | pageX |
| height | location | pageXOffset |
| Hidden | locationbar | pageY |
| hidden | log | pageYOffset |
| History | LOG10E | parent |
| history | LOG2E | parseFloat |
| home | lowsrc | parseInt |
| host | match | Password |
| hostname | Math | password |
| href | math | pathname |
| hspace | max | personalbar |
| ignoreCase | MAX_VALUE | PI |
| Image | menubar | pixelDepth |
| image | method | platform |
| images | mimeType | Plugin |
| index | mimeTypes | plugin |
| indexOf | min | plugins |
| Infinity | MIN_VALUE | pop |
| innerHeight | modifiers | port |
| innerWidth | moveBy | POSITIVE_INFINITY |
| input | moveTo | pow |
| isFinite | multilane | preference |
| isNaN | name | previous |
| italics | NaN | print |
| javaEnabled | Navigator | prompt |
| join | navigator | prototype |
| language | NEGATIVE_INFINITY | push |
| lastIndex | next | Radio |
| lastIndexOf | Number | radio |
| lastMatch | number | random |

| | | |
|---|---|---|
| referrer | setResizable | substring |
| refresh | setSeconds | suffixes |
| RegExp | setTime | sup |
| releaseEvents | setTimeout | taint |
| reload | setUTCDate | tan |
| replace | setUTCDay | target |
| Reset | setUTCFullYear | test |
| reset | setUTCHours | Text |
| resizeBy | setUTCMilliseconds | text |
| resizeTo | setUTCMinutes | Textarea |
| reverse | setUTCMonth | textarea |
| rightContext | setUTCSeconds | title |
| round | setUTCTime | toGMTString |
| routeEvent | setYear | toLocaleString |
| savePreferences | setZOptions | toLowerCase |
| Screen | shift | toolbar |
| screen | signText | top |
| screenX | sin | toString |
| screenY | slice | toUpperCase |
| scroll | small | toUTCString |
| scrollbars | sort | type |
| scrollBy | source | unescape |
| scrollTo | splice | unshift |
| search | split | untaint |
| Select | sqrt | URL |
| select | SQRT1_2 | userAgent |
| selected | SQRT2 | UTC |
| selectedIndex | src | value |
| self | status | vlinkColor |
| setDate | statusbar | vspace |
| setDay | stop | which |
| setFullYear | strike | width |
| setHotKeys | String | Window |
| setHours | string | window |
| setInterval | sub | write |
| setMilliseconds | Submit | writeln |
| setMinutes | submit | x |
| setMonth | substr | y |

## HTML Elements and Attributes

| | | |
|---|---|---|
| a | cols | img |
| accesskey | colspan | input |
| action | controls | ins |
| address | dd | kbd |
| align | del | label |
| alink | direction | language |
| alt | disabled | layer |
| applet | div | leftmargin |
| area | dl | legend |
| autostart | dt | li |
| b | dynsrc | link |
| background | em | loop |
| base | embed | lowsrc |
| basefont | event | map |
| behavior | face | marginheight |
| bgcolor | fieldset | marginwidth |
| bgsound | font | marquee |
| big | for | maxlength |
| blink | form | meta |
| blockquote | frame | method |
| body | frameborder | multiple |
| border | frameset | name |
| bordercolor | framespacing | nobr |
| bordercolordark | h1 | noframes |
| bordercolorlight | h2 | nohref |
| br | h3 | noresize |
| button | h4 | noscript |
| caption | h5 | noshade |
| cellpadding | h6 | nowrap |
| cellspacing | h7 | object |
| center | head | ol |
| charset | height | optgroup |
| checked | hr | option |
| cite | href | p |
| class | hspace | pre |
| clear | html | q |
| code | http-equiv | readonly |
| col | i | rows |
| colgroup | id | rowspan |
| color | iframe | rules |

| | | |
|---|---|---|
| s | strike | thead |
| samp | strong | title |
| script | style | topmargin |
| scrollamount | sub | tr |
| scrolldelay | sup | tt |
| scrolling | table | u |
| select | taborder | ul |
| selected | target | usemap |
| shape | tbody | valign |
| size | td | vlink |
| small | text | vspace |
| span | textarea | wbr |
| src | tfoot | width |
| start | th | |

## CSS Properties

Many CSS properties cannot be used as identifiers in JavaScript because they contain hyphens. However, Netscape's JavaScript Assisted Style Sheets recognizes these properties by eliminating the hyphen and capitalizing the second word. I'd avoid these, too.

| | |
|---|---|
| background | fontSize |
| backgroundAttachment | fontStyle |
| backgroundColor | fontVariant |
| backgroundImage | fontWeight |
| backgroundPosition | height |
| backgroundRepeat | left |
| border | letterSpacing |
| borderBottom | lineHeight |
| borderColor | listStyle |
| borderLeft | listStyleImage |
| borderRight | listStylePosition |
| borderStyle | listStyleType |
| borderTop | margin |
| borderWidth | marginBottom |
| clear | marginLeft |
| clip | marginRight |
| color | marginTop |
| display | overflow |
| float | paddingBottom |
| font | paddingLeft |
| fontFamily | paddingRight |

| | |
|---|---|
| paddingTop | textTransform |
| pixelHeight | top |
| pixelLeft | verticalAlign |
| pixelTop | visibility |
| pixelWidth | whiteSpace |
| position | width |
| textAlignment | wordSpacing |
| textDecoration | zIndex |
| textIndent | |

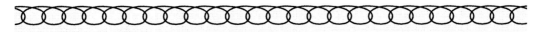

## appendix d

# Debugging
# JavaScript

*As soon as we started programming, we found to our surprise that it wasn't as easy to get programs right as we had thought. Debugging had to be discovered. I can remember the exact instant when I realized that a large part of my life from then on was going to be spent in finding mistakes in my own programs.*

—Maurice Wilkes discovers debugging, 1949

A ll programmers, no matter their experience or the language they use, are bound to make a mistake from time to time. More than one mistake is more likely. These mistakes become errors or *bugs* in your programs. It happens to the best of us, so expect it. While it would be nice if we could simply grab a can of Raid and kill the darn bugs with one spray, debugging programs is not quite that simple. It's not rocket science either. It's sort of an art or skill unto itself that requires the eye of an editor, the logic of a detective, and the persistence of a bulldog.

In this appendix, we'll

- define the terms "bug" and "debugging."
- discuss and describe the four types of errors that can affect your programs: HTML errors, syntax errors, runtime errors, and logic errors.
- see how error messages are our friends.
- list the most common error messages and how to find and remove the bugs they report.
- learn how to clear the browser's memory completely.
- learn how to set variable watch-points with `alert()`.

✗  learn how to use comments to assist with debugging.

✗  use the `javascript:` pseudo-protocol to test code in the location bar.

Let's go squash some bugs.

# What Is Debugging?

In programming terms, a **bug** is an error in a program. **Debugging** is the process of removing bugs from your programs. It is an essential skill all programmers must develop. In general, there are four types of errors you are likely to make when programming in JavaScript:

✗  HTML errors

✗  syntax errors

✗  runtime errors

✗  logic errors

**side note**

Where'd the term "bug" come from anyway?

American engineers have used the term "bug" for over a century to refer to small flaws or defects in machines; in the 1870s, Thomas Edison used the term in connection with electrical circuits. Its first application to computers is credited to pioneer programmer Grace Hopper.

The story goes that on September 9, 1945, at Harvard University, Grace and her associates were working on the granddaddy of modern computers, the Mark II Aiken Relay Calculator. "Things were going badly," Grace said. "There was something wrong in one of the circuits of the long glass-enclosed computer. Finally, someone located the trouble spot and, using ordinary tweezers, removed the problem: a two-inch moth. From then on, when anything went wrong with a computer, we said it had bugs in it." Grace and her associates put out the word that they had "debugged" the machine, thus introducing the term "debugging" a computer program.

The remains of that moth are taped to the page of Hopper's 1945 logbook with the entry: "First actual case of bug being found." The logbook, along with the moth, now resides in the Smithsonian Institute (http://americanhistory.si.edu/csr/comphist/objects/bug.htm).

The focus of this chapter is to teach you how to effectively debug JavaScript scripts. We'll look at each type of error in turn, view some examples, and learn how to fix them without having a debugging utility at our disposal.

# HTML Errors

HTML errors can make errorless JavaScript code go awry. To drive this point home, here's an example of a perfectly formed script that won't work right simply because of an HTML error.

**Script D.1**　　**HTML Error That Bugs a JavaScript Program**

```
1   <html>
2   <head>
3   <title>Script D.1: HTML Error That Bugs a JavaScript
        Program</title>
4   </head>
5   <body>
6   <script language="JavaScript" type="text/javascript><!--
7       document.write("Greetings, Earthlings!")
8   //-->
9   </script>
10  </body>
11  </html>
```

Run it and what do you get?—a blank screen.

**Figure D.1**　　**Results of Script D.1**

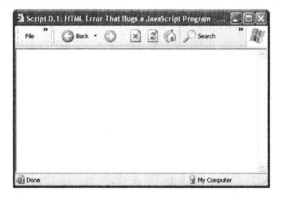

If it weren't for the HTML error in line 6, the script would've written "Greetings, Earth-lings!" to the screen. The first place you're likely to look for an error is in your script, but clearly there is no error present. Line 6 in your HTML code, however, does have an error: a missing closing quotation mark around the value for the type attribute. That's why the script isn't functioning.

We didn't even get an error message! How fair is that?! Rarely will the browser report an error when it's in your HTML. To avoid driving yourself bonkers looking for errors in your programming code where none exist, validate your HTML code before adding scripts to it. Validate it again after you add scripts and more HTML; it can't hurt. Any HTML editor worth its salt has a built-in validator that can help you quickly find and remove any HTML errors that might be present.

In addition to HTML errors, there are three types of scripting errors that you're likely to run into: syntax errors, runtime errors, and logic errors. Let's look at each type in detail.

# Syntax Errors

When you enter code that the JavaScript interpreter does not recognize and, therefore, cannot understand, you create a **syntax error**. It's sort of like asking your friend to "Hand me a crewdriver" when what you meant to say is "Hand me a screwdriver." When you ask for a "crewdriver," your friend has no idea what you're talking about. Similarly, when you commit a syntax error in JavaScript, the browser's interpreter has no idea what you're talking about and usually displays an error message. Here's an example:

### Script D.2    Example of a Syntax Error

```
1    <!DOCTYPE HTML PUBLIC "-//W3C//DTD HTML 4.0 Transitional//EN">
2    <html>
3    <head>
4    <title>Script D.2: Example of a Syntax Error</title>
5    <script language="JavaScript" type="text/javascript"><!--
6        function greetVisitor() {
7            alert("Hello!")
8        }
9    //-->
10   </script>
11   </head>
12   <body onLoad="greetVisitor()">
13
14   </body>
15   </html>
```

Run it in Netscape Navigator and what do you get? A blank screen and no error message. However, if you check the JavaScript Console by typing "javascript:" in the location bar of a Netscape browser, you will see two error messages.

### Figure D.2    Results of Script D.2 in Netscape

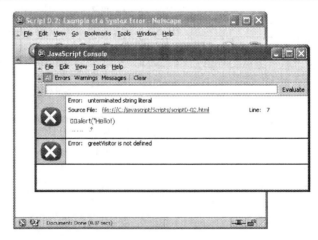

The first error message indicates that there is an unterminated string literal and the second that `greetVisitor` is not defined. The former is the real problem. This is an example of an error message that is telling the truth. As you will learn as you debug scripts on your own, error messages don't always report the *real* error. In this case, the error message is correct: `greetVisitor` isn't defined because an error in the `alert` method call screwed things up. There should be a closing quotation mark after the exclamation point.

**programmer's tip**

**Bookmarking JavaScript Statements**

Using the `javascript:` pseudo-protocol, you can save JavaScript statements as bookmarks and call them at any time to help you examine the results of scripts and assist with debugging. Here's how:

1. Type "javascript: " followed by the statement you'd like to invoke in the location bar.
2. From the Bookmarks menu, choose Add to Bookmarks or File Bookmark. I recommend the latter, then you can file them all in the same folder. I put mine in a bookmark folder named "JavaScript Statements."
3. Now you can access them at any time from your bookmark list, like this:

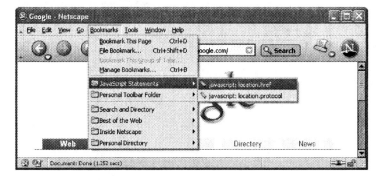

The most common syntax errors usually involve forgetting to type a closing parenthesis or quotation mark. Catching those missing parentheses and quotation marks before they cause you problems is something an editor can do quite well, and is a skill to covet.

## The Eyes of an Editor

Having the eyes of an editor can save you hours of frustration searching for elusive bugs. Once found, you know you can correct them easily; it's finding the darn things in the first place that's difficult. So how do you train your eyes to spot syntax errors quickly? Teach yourself the habit of doing the following whenever you review your code, even as you write it.

**Syntax Error Checklist**

- ✘ Check every opening brace. Is there a matching closing one?
- ✘ Check every opening parenthesis. Is there a closing one?
- ✘ Check every double quotation mark. If it delimits a string, is there a closing one? If it delimits an HTML attribute you're using JavaScript to write out, is it escaped? If it delimits a sentence like "Hand me a screwdriver," escape it and its partner.
- ✘ Check every apostrophe (single quotation mark). Is it escaped? If you're using single quotation marks to delimit a string, verify that there is a closing single quotation mark.
- ✘ Check each function call and verify that its name matches the function's definition name exactly.
- ✘ While you're at it, verify that the arguments used in the function call match the parameters in the function definition in terms of order, data type, and number of arguments.
- ✘ Watch the case on object, property, and method names. Most object, property, and method names in JavaScript begin with a lowercase letter. Only constructor functions and a few core objects, like `Math`, begin with an uppercase letter.
- ✘ Verify that the names of objects in your HTML match the names you use when you try to access those objects and their properties and methods. Watch that case!

## Use Old Navigator Browsers to View Results of `write` Statements

When you're writing a script that generates HTML, it's especially easy to make a mistake; the quotation marks around tag attributes can quickly mess you up. As you escape those quotation marks and other special characters, your code becomes difficult to read; it's enough to drive you buggy. Fortunately, older versions of Netscape Navigator (4.7x and before) can help.

When you view source in an old Netscape Navigator browser, you see the *results* of your `document.write` statements, instead of the `write` statements themselves. This makes it easy to tell if your script is generating the correct HTML statements, stylesheet code, or any other type of string you might be trying to write with a script. Here's an example:

### Script D.3    A Script That Writes Complicated Strings

```
1    <!DOCTYPE HTML PUBLIC "-//W3C//DTD HTML 4.0 Transitional//EN">
2    <html>
3    <head>
4    <title>Script D.3: A Script That Writes Complicated
         Strings</title>
5    <script language="JavaScript" type="text/javascript"><!--
6         var backgroundColor = "#ff8080"
7         var fontColor = "#ffff95"
8         var jb = "JavaBrosia our special House Blend"
9         var jbSpecial = "Buy 2 lbs., get 1 lb FREE!"
10        var hk = "Hawaiian Kona"
```

```
11        var hkSpecial = "FREE Flower Lei with 1 lb. purchase " +
12                        "and a chance to<br>Win a Hawaiian Holiday!"
13   //-->
14   </script>
15   </head>
16   <body>
17   <script language="JavaScript" type="text/javascript"><!--
18        document.writeln("<table width=\"260\" border=\"3\" ",
19                         "cellpadding=\"5\" align=\"right\"" ,
20                         "bordercolor=\"#800000\" bgcolor=\"",
21                         backgroundColor, ">")
22      document.writeln("<tr><td><font color=", fontColor, "\">")
23      document.writeln("<h2>Specials!</h2>")
24      document.writeln("<dl>")
25      document.writeln("<dt><b>", jb, "</b></dt>")
26      document.writeln("<dd>", jbSpecial, "</dd>")
27      document.writeln("<dt><b>", hk, "</b></dt>")
28      document.writeln("<dd>", hkSpecial, "</dd>")
29      document.writeln("<dt><b>Check out our Catalog for new ",
30                       "Gift Packs</b></dt>")
31      document.writeln("<dd><br></dd>")
32      document.writeln("<dt><b>FREE SHIPPING on orders of $25 or ",
33                       "more.</b></dt>")
34      document.writeln("</dl>")
35      document.writeln("</font></td></tr>")
36      document.writeln("</table>)")
37   //-->
38   </script>
39
40   </body>
41   </html>
```

Let's view the result in Netscape Navigator 4.78 or prior so we can view the source code and see our progress. First, let's see how it looks in the browser.

**Figure D.3** **Results of Script D.3 in Netscape Navigator 4.78**

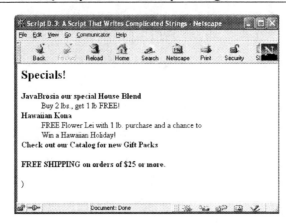

Clearly, something is wrong. The plan was to create a table with a background color to hold the specials and align it on the right. We've got no background color and no right alignment. In fact, our font color isn't working either. So let's view the source code in Netscape Navigator 4.78 or an earlier version and look at the results of our `write` statements.

**Figure D.4** **Write Results of Script D.3**

```
<BASE HREF="file:/C|/javascript/Scripts/">
<!DOCTYPE HTML PUBLIC "-//W3C//DTD HTML 4.0 Transitional//EN">
<html>
<head>
<title>Script D.3: A Script That Writes Complicated Strings</title>
<script language="JavaScript" type="text/javascript">

<!--
        var backgroundColor = "#ff8060"
        var fontColor = "#ffff95"
        var jb = "JavaBrosia our special House Blend"
        var jbSpecial = "Buy 2 lbs., get 1 lb FREE!"
        var hk = "Hawaiian Kona"
        var hkSpecial = "FREE Flower Lei with 1 lb. purchase " +
                               "and a chance to<br>Win a Hawaiian Holiday!"
//-->

</script>
</head>
<body>
<TABLE width="250" border="3" cellpadding="5" align="right"
bordercolor="#800000" hgcolor="#ff8060">
<tr><td><font color=#ffff95">
<H2>Specials!</H2>
<DL>
<DT><B>JavaBrosia our special House Blend</B></DT>
<DD>Buy 2 lbs., get 1 lb FREE!</DD>
<DT><B>Hawaiian Kona</B></DT>
<DD>FREE Flower Lei with 1 lb. purchase and a chance to<BR>Win a Hawaiian Holiday!</DD
<DT><B>Check out our Catalog for new Gift Packs</B></DT>
<DD><BR></DD>
<DT><B>FREE SHIPPING on orders of $25 or more.</B></DT>
</DL>
</FONT></TD></TR>
</TABLE>)



</BODY>
</HTML>
```

Now we can examine the actual strings written by our write line statements. Several errors should be noticeable immediately:

- ✂ There should be a space between the `border` attribute value and the `cellpadding` attribute on the <table> tag.
- ✂ A closing quotation mark is missing on the `bgcolor` attribute.
- ✂ An opening quotation mark is missing on the `color` attribute of the <font> tag.
- ✂ A closing parenthesis follows the closing <table> tag.

Let's correct those errors and see what happens.

***Figure D.5     Results of Script D.3 after Corrections***

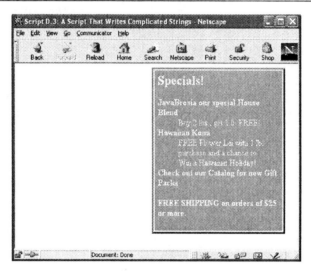

Netscape Navigator 4.78 made finding the errors easy because it showed us the results of our `write` statements, rather than the statements themselves. This was invaluable. I highly recommend that you keep an old version of Netscape Navigator around just for this useful utility. Any pre-version-6 copy will do.

## Try Your Eyes

OK, are you ready to give your eyes a whirl and see what you've learned? Great! What's wrong with the following line of code?

```
<body onLoad="alert('Hello, World!')>
```

Look close.

It's missing a closing quotation mark after the closing parenthesis. How about this one?

```
document.writ("Hello, World!")
```

It should read

```
document.write("Hello, World!")
```

with an *e* on the end of *write*. Here's another:

```
var num = parseFloat(prompt("Enter a number", "")
```

If you don't see it at first, match the parentheses. It needs a closing parenthesis at the end to close the parseFloat function call. One more:

```
document.write("Browser: , Navigator.appName, "<br>")
```

This one has two errors: a closing quote is needed after Browser: to delimit the string and the navigator object should begin with a lowercase letter, not an uppercase letter.

How'd you do? If you caught all five errors, pat yourself on the back; you've got the eyes of an editor. If you didn't do so well, then copy the checklist above and keep it next to you when you're programming until it becomes second nature to look for those errors. Once you're in the habit, you can throw the checklist away; you'll have developed the eyes of an editor.

## Error Messages Are Our Friends

Sometimes error messages can help you locate a syntax error. Let's look at some common error messages and see how they can guide you to find the real culprit.

Run the following script. This time use Internet Explorer.

**Script D.4    *Example of a Syntax Error***

```
1    <!DOCTYPE HTML PUBLIC "-//W3C//DTD HTML 4.0 Transitional//EN">
2    <html>
3    <head>
4    <title>Script D.4: Example of a Syntax Error</title>
5    </head>
6    <body>
7    <script language="JavaScript" type="text/javascript"><!--
8      var num = 2
9      if (isNaN(num) {
10          alert("Invalid number!")
11     } else {
12          alert("Valid number!")
13     }
14    //-->
15    </script>
16    </body>
17    </html>
```

You should receive the following error message in Internet Explorer:

***Figure D.6    Error Message Received in IE in Response to Script D.4***

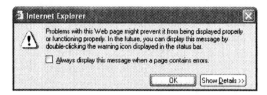

This particular error message isn't any help. You need information more specific to the error encountered by the browser. Click the Show Details button.

***Figure D.7    Error Message Details in IE for Script D.4***

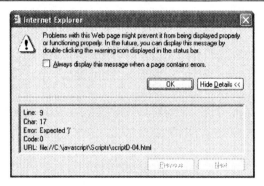

The details tell you the line number and character number where the error occurs and a short error message. In this case line 9, character 17, is the culprit and the error is "Expected ')'."

With this information in hand, you can look at line 9 of your script where indeed there is a missing ) as the error message indicated. This time, the error message reported the correct line number. However, keep in mind that often as not, browsers will report the error on a line above or below the line where the error actually occurs. So if you don't see an error in the line indicated by an error message, look in the general vicinity of that line for an error.

If you didn't receive an error message, you need to turn scripting messages on in your browser.

Let's run Script D.4 again, this time in Opera, so you can see how differently each browser reports the same error.

*side note*

**Turning On or Off Error Messages**

In Internet Explorer: Tools → Internet Options → Advanced → check the box labeled "Display a notification about every script error."

In Opera: File → Preferences → Multimedia → check the box labeled "Report JavaScript Errors."

**Figure D.8     Error Message for Script D.4 in Opera**

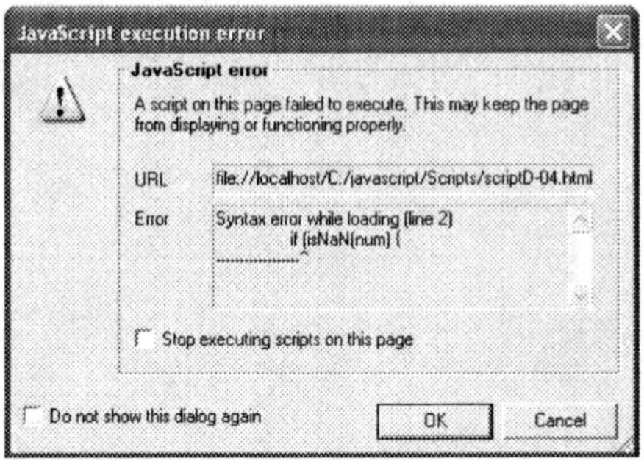

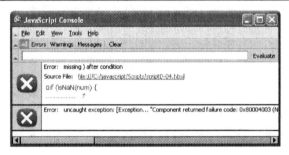

Opera doesn't always give you a line number, but its error messages tend to be less cryptic than Internet Explorer's. For comparisons sake, let's run the script one more time and examine how Netscape Navigator reports the error in the JavaScript Console.

**Figure D.9     Error Message for Script D.4 in Netscape Navigator**

Netscape did the best job of explaining the error in this case. Usually Netscape will also report a line number.

## Common Syntax Error Messages

Now that you've seen how messages about syntax errors are reported in the top three browsers, let's list some other syntax error messages you are likely to encounter along with the likely source of the problem. So you can use this as a reference later, we'll list them in alphabetical order.

**expected identifier**
**missing variable name**
This error occurs when you try to use a reserved word as a variable name, like this (line 6):

**Script D.5     Syntax Error—expected identifier**

```
1    <!DOCTYPE HTML PUBLIC "-//W3C//DTD HTML 4.0 Transitional//EN">
2    <html>
3    <head>
4    <title>Script D.5: Syntax Error - expected identifier</title>
```

```
5    <script language="JavaScript" type="text/javascript"><!--
6         var float = 3.57
7    //-->
8    </script>
9    </head>
10   <body>
11
12   </body>
13   </html>
```

To avoid this type of error, don't use reserved words. For that matter, don't use *any* words already in use by the JavaScript language, whether they're formally reserved or not. See Appendix C for a complete list of words to avoid using as identifiers.

**missing (...**
**missing )...**
We covered this one earlier in Script D.4. It occurs when your parentheses, usually around a condition or a set of function parameters, don't match up. To correct it, match them up, that is, insert the missing parenthesis.

**missing ; after for-loop condition**
**missing ; after for-loop initializer**
**expected ;**
A very common mistake many programmers make is to place commas instead of semicolons between the statements in the initializing line of a for loop, like this (line 12).

### Script D.6    Syntax Error—missing ; after for-loop initializer

```
1    <!DOCTYPE HTML PUBLIC "-//W3C//DTD HTML 4.0 Transitional//EN">
2    <html>
3    <head>
4    <title>Script D.6: Syntax Error - missing ; after for-
5    loop initializer</title>
6    </head>
7    <body>
8    <script language="JavaScript" type="text/javascript"><!--
9         var fruits = new Array("Apple", "Lemon", "Orange",
10                              "Pineapple")
11
12        for(i=0, i<fruits.length, i++) {
13             document.write(i, ". ", fruits[i], "<br>")
14        }
15   //-->
16   </script>
17
```

```
18   </body>
19   </html>
```

Presumably, programmers are used to separating items in a set of parentheses with commas (think function parameters). Regardless of why it happens, to fix it, separate the for loop's initializer, condition, and update statements with semicolons.

**missing { before function body**
**missing } after function body**
**missing } in compound statement**
**expected }**
**expected {**

These errors occur when you forget to delimit the contents of a function or control structure with one or both braces. Here's an example:

**Script D.7    *Syntax Error—missing } after function body***

```
1    <!DOCTYPE HTML PUBLIC "-//W3C//DTD HTML 4.0 Transitional//EN">
2    <html>
3    <head>
4    <title>Script D.7: Syntax Error - missing } after
5    function body</title>
6    <script language="JavaScript" type="text/javascript"><!--
7         function greet() {
8              alert ("Greetings, Earthlings!")
9
10   //-->
11   </script>
12   </head>
13   <body>
14
15   </body>
16   </html>
```

To correct it, insert the necessary brace or braces, in this case, at line 9.

**nested comment**

JavaScript doesn't allow nested comments like this:

```
/* comment /* nested comment */ more comments */
```

While you probably wouldn't normally try to nest a comment, you might accidentally do so when you're commenting out extra code in order to debug a script. Remove the nested comment to correct the error. You can also end the first comment right before the start of the nested comment and start another comment right after the nested comment to correct the error.

### syntax error

This is JavaScript's generic syntax error message. You'll receive it whenever the interpreter can't come up with something more specific. Unfortunately, the generalness of it does make it more difficult to track down. Use the line number reported as a guide and look closely at the lines before and after that line.

### test for equality (==) mistyped as assignment (=)? Assuming equality test

This is another common error: using the equals assignment operator when you really should use the "is equal to" comparison operator. Look closely at line 9 of Script D.8.

*Script D.8      Syntax Error—test for equality mistyped*

```
1    <!DOCTYPE HTML PUBLIC "-//W3C//DTD HTML 4.0 Transitional//EN">
2    <html>
3    <head>
4    <title>Script D.8: Syntax Error - test for equality
        mistyped</title>
5    </head>
6    <body>
7    <script language="JavaScript" type="text/javascript"><!--
8            var num = 1
9            if (num = 2) {
10                alert("Num equals 2!")
11           }
12   //-->
13   </script>
14
15   </body>
16   </html>
```

Line 9 should be

```
if (num == 2)
```

Don't fret, I still do this occasionally and I've been writing JavaScript for a long, long time. It happens.

### unterminated string literal

This error message means that you forgot a closing quotation mark around a string. It may not always report the correct line number, so look at the statements above and below the line reported as well to find the missing quotation mark and insert it. We saw an example of this in Script D.2.

*programmer's tip*

**Clear Your Browser's Memory**

When you're writing scripts or coding HTML, sometimes your browser will keep showing you a cached copy of your document rather than the one with the latest changes. To avoid this, first make certain that your browser is set up to always show you the current document.

In IE: Tools → Internet Options → Settings (Temporary Internet Files) → under "Check for newer versions of stored pages," check "Every visit to the page."

In NN: Edit → Preferences → Advanced → Cache → under "Compare the page in the cache to the page on the network," check "Every time I view the page."

In OP: File → Preferences → Network → History and cache → under "Check modified," check "Always" for documents, images, and other.

Even with these settings, browsers will sometimes refuse to show you the updated document. This is especially true when you're working with frames. You can tell by viewing the source of the document. If it is refusing to show the updated document, the source code will show your old source instead of the updated source. To force your browser to show you the latest document, clear its memory.

In NN: Edit → Preferences → Advanced → Cache → press "Clear Memory Cache."

Usually, clearing the browser's memory is good enough. However, if it's particularly stubborn, you can clear its disk cache, too. That option is usually found in the same place.

# Runtime Errors

Now that we've covered syntax errors in all their gory detail, let's look at runtime errors. Runtime errors occur when the JavaScript interpreter encounters a problem during the execution of a program. This usually happens when the interpreter reads code it can't handle. The code may be perfectly correct, in terms of syntax. If it wasn't, the problem would be a syntax error. However, for some reason the interpreter can't deal with it.

The most common type of runtime error occurs when you try to access an object or variable that doesn't exist. Here's an example.

### Script D.9    Example of a Runtime Error—... is undefined

```
1    <!DOCTYPE HTML PUBLIC "-//W3C//DTD HTML 4.0 Transitional//EN">
2    <html>
3    <head>
4    <title>Script D.9: Example of a Runtime Error - ... is
       undefined</title>
5
6    </head>
7    <body>
8    <script language="JavaScript" type="text/javascript"><!--
9         document.write(greeting)
```

```
10    //-->
11    </script>
12    </body>
13    </html>
```

In this example, `greeting` is a variable that has never been declared, let alone initialized. It is undefined. So the interpreter doesn't know how to handle it and generates an error message.

**Figure D.10    Results of Script D.9**

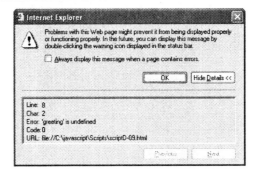

## Eyes of an Editor and Error Messages, Again

Again, the eyes of an editor and error messages can serve you well in sorting out runtime errors. When you receive a message such as "'greeting' is defined," use your editor eyes and look for the following.

### Runtime Error Checklist

- ✗ Has the variable, object, property, or method been declared?
- ✗ Was the variable or property assigned a value before you tried to access it?
- ✗ Was the object created before you tried to access it? Are you sure?
- ✗ Does a function or method with that name really exist? Is it accessible, as written, by the *current* document?
- ✗ Did you name your object the same in your HTML code as the way you're calling it with JavaScript?

## Common Runtime Error Messages

Here's a list of the most common runtime error messages that you're likely to receive along with instructions for correcting them. Again, we've listed them in alphabetical order for easy reference.

**... has no properties**

**... is null or not an object**

This type of error message indicates that you are trying to access the property of an object that doesn't exist or hasn't been created yet. A mistyped hierarchical reference can also generate the error, as in this case:

**Script D.10    Example of a Runtime Error—... has no properties**

```
1    <!DOCTYPE HTML PUBLIC "-//W3C//DTD HTML 4.0 Transitional//EN">
2    <html>
3    <head>
4    <title>Script D.10: Runtime Error - ... has no properties</title>
5    </head>
6    <body>
7    <script language="JavaScript" type="text/javascript"><!--
8          document.write(document.history.go(1))
9    //-->
10   </script>
11   </body>
12   </html>
```

This error occurred because `history` is a property of the `window` object, not the `document` object. To correct it, write

```
document.write(window.history.go(1))
```

Your JavaScript object reference (Appendix A) is a good guide to solving these types of problems.

Here's another example:

**Script D.11    Example of a Runtime Error—... is undefined**

```
1    <!DOCTYPE HTML PUBLIC "-//W3C//DTD HTML 4.0 Transitional//EN">
2    <html>
3    <head>
4    <title>Script D.11: Runtime Error - ... is null or not an
       object</title>
5    </head>
6    <body>
7    <script language="JavaScript" type="text/javascript"><!--
8          document.OrderForm.Total.value = total
9    //-->
10   </script>
11   <form name="OrderForm">
12         ...
13         Total: <input type=text name="Total">
14         ...
```

```
15    </form>
16
17    </body>
18    </html>
```

In this example, you're trying to access a property of a text box that doesn't exist yet. Move the script after the form to correct the problem.

**... is not defined**

**... is undefined**

**... is null or not an object**

These error messages may indicate a misspelling. Any one of them could also mean that you tried to access a variable or object that hadn't been defined. Here's an example:

*Script D.12    Example of a Runtime Error—... is undefined*

```
1     <!DOCTYPE HTML PUBLIC "-//W3C//DTD HTML 4.0 Transitional//EN">
2     <html>
3     <head>
4     <title>Script D.12: Runtime Error - ... is not defined</title>
5     </head>
6     <body>
7     <script language="JavaScript" type="text/javascript"><!--
8          greeting = "Hello, Earthlings!"
9          document.write(greting)
10
11    //-->
12    </script>
13    </body>
14    </html>
```

In this example, the reference to the variable greeting is misspelled as greting in the document's write method call.

**object doesn't support this property or method**

**... has no properties**

This error can occur when you try to call a method on an object that doesn't support that method or when you try to assign a value to an *object* rather than to its value property.

Here's an example of the first:

*Script D.13    Runtime Error—object doesn't support this property or method*

```
1     <!DOCTYPE HTML PUBLIC "-//W3C//DTD HTML 4.0 Transitional//EN">
2     <html>
3     <head>
```

```
4    <title>Script D.13: Run-time Error - object doesn't
5    support this property or method</title>
6    </head>
7    <body>
8    <script language="JavaScript" type="text/javascript"><!--
9         var currLoc = location
10        alert(currLoc.toUpperCase())
11
12   //-->
13   </script>
14   </body>
15   </html>
```

The problem is that location isn't a string, it's an object. To correct the problem, convert it to a string before calling the alert, like this:

```
var currLoc = location.toString()
```

Here's one more example:

**Script D.14     Runtime Error—... has no properties**

```
1    <!DOCTYPE HTML PUBLIC "-//W3C//DTD HTML 4.0 Transitional//EN">
2    <html>
3    <head>
4    <title>Script D.14: Run-time Error - ... has no properties</title>
5    </head>
6    <body>
7    <form name="OrderForm">
8         ...
9         <input type=text name="Total">
10        ...
11   </form>
12
13   <script language="JavaScript" type="text/javascript"><!--
14        document.OrderForm.Total = 150
15   //-->
16   </script>
17   </body>
18   </html>
```

This time the problem was due to attempting to set the Total object itself, instead of its value property.

**out of memory**

This commonly happens when you have too many function calls running at the same time. Scrolling marquee scripts often run out of memory. Endless loops or too many `setTimeouts` can also cause your browser to run out of memory. To correct this problem, simplify your program.

# Logic Errors

When your program functions without error, but does not accomplish what you intended it to accomplish, it has a **logic error**. Logic errors are problems in the design or logic of your program that cause it to produce results other than what you intended. For instance, if you ask your friend to "Hand me a Phillip's screwdriver" when what you really need to do the job is a flat-head screwdriver, then you've committed a logic error.

One very common logic error occurs when you concatenate two strings when what you really intended to do was add the numbers represented by those strings. Errors in logic statements can also produce logic errors. Simply using `&&` when `||` was really called for can result in a logic error. Perhaps you want a `do...while` loop to prompt the visitor for a positive number and keep prompting until she enters a positive number. See Script D.15.

**Script D.15    *Example of a Logic Error—wrong logical operator used***

```
1    <!DOCTYPE HTML PUBLIC "-//W3C//DTD HTML 4.0 Transitional//EN">
2    <html>
3    <head>
4    <title>Script D.15: Example of a Logic Error - wrong
5    logical operator used</title>
6    </head>
7    <body>
8    <script language="JavaScript" type="text/javascript"><!--
9        var num = ""
10       do {
11           num = parseFloat(prompt("Enter a positive number: ", ""))
12           if ( isNaN(num) && num < 0 ) {
13               alert("Error! You did not enter a positive number!")
14           }
15       } while ( isNaN(num) && num < 0 )
16
17       alert("Success! You entered a positive number!")
18   //-->
19   </script>
20   </body>
21   </html>
```

Unfortunately, it doesn't work quite right. For some reason it stops asking after the first try. Look closely at the conditions listed in lines 12 and 15. Think about it. Do they really look right to you?

They shouldn't. Lines 12 and 15 need an || (or) operator, rather than an && (and) operator. Change the operator in those two lines and you've solved the problem.

Another common logic error can arise from accidentally quoting variables. The only way JavaScript can tell the difference between a variable, a number, and a string is that strings are delimited by single or double quotation marks. Should you write the following:

**Script D.16    Example of a Logic Error—quoted variable**

```
1     <!DOCTYPE HTML PUBLIC "-//W3C//DTD HTML 4.0 Transitional//EN">
2     <html>
3     <head>
4     <title>Script D.16: Example of a Logic Error - quoted
        variable</title>
5     </head>
6     <body>
7     <script language="JavaScript" type="text/javascript"><!--
8          var special = "FREE Flower Lei with 1 lb. purchase "
9          document.write("special")
10    //-->
11    </script>
12    </body>
13    </html>
```

you won't receive any error messages. After all, what you did was perfectly legal. Here's the result:

**Figure D.11    Results of Script D.16**

Writing the literal word special is just *not* what you intended to do. What you *intended* was to write the *value* of the variable special. Remove the quotation marks around special and the problem is solved.

## The Logic of a Detective

It often requires the logic of a detective to solve logic errors. Think about what you're trying to accomplish. Does your program do that? Analyze every condition. Does it really do what you want it to do?

Sherlock Holmes would be lost without his magnifying glass. At least, his job would be a lot harder without it. So too, can you benefit from having the right tools to help you solve logic errors in your programs.

### Trace Your Program's Footsteps Using `document.write()` and `alert()`

Sherlock Holmes has been known to follow a suspected culprit step by step as he goes about his business in order to solve a crime. So too can it be beneficial for you to follow your *program's* footsteps line by line and see if they take you where you intended to go. Stepping through a program, live, line by line, is known as **tracing**.

Most debuggers provide a tracing tool. Even if you don't have a debugger, you can still trace your program's footsteps. Simply insert `document.write` or `alert` statements into your program to let you know where you are and what's happening. Here's a very simple example. Notice the `document.write` statements inserted at line 11 and 15.

*Script D.17    Tracing a Program*

```
1     <!DOCTYPE HTML PUBLIC "-//W3C//DTD HTML 4.0 Transitional//EN">
2     <html>
3     <head>
4     <title>Script D.17: Tracing A Program</title>
5     </head>
6     <body>
7     <script language="JavaScript" type="text/javascript"><!--
8          var fruits = new Array("Apple", "Lemon", "Orange",
              "Pineapple")
9
10         for(i=0; i<fruits.length; i++) {
11    document.write("Iteration ", i, "<br>")
12
13              fruits[i] = fruits[i].toLowerCase()
14
15    document.write("fruits", i, " now = ", fruits[i], "<br>")
16         }
17    //-->
18    </script>
19    </body>
20    </html>
```

Notice that the lines used to trace the program's progress have not been indented. This makes it easy to identify them and remove them when you're all done and everything is working as it should.

### Watch Variable and Property Values with `alert()`

It also helps to watch the value of crucial variables or properties as you step through a program. Again, a good debugger will let you set up watch windows to track the progress of a variable. By using strategically placed `alert` statements, you can accomplish the same thing. Just insert an `alert` that displays the variable or property's value at any point in your program where you'd like to check its value.

Good places to set watch-points are before and after function calls to make certain that the value you're trying to pass is making it to its destination and the function is returning a proper value. Here's an example:

### Script D.18    Setting Variable Watch-points

```
1    <!DOCTYPE HTML PUBLIC "-//W3C//DTD HTML 4.0 Transitional//EN">
2    <html>
3    <head>
4    <title>Script D.18: Setting Variable Watchpoints</title>
5    <script language="JavaScript" type="text/javascript"><!--
6         function greet(message) {
7    alert("Received value = " + message)
8              document.write("<h1>", message, "</h1>")
9         }
10   //-->
11   </script>
12   </head>
13   <body>
14   <script language="JavaScript" type="text/javascript"><!--
15        var greeting = "Greetings, Earthlings!"
16   alert("Passed value = " + greeting)
17
18        greet(greeting)
19   //-->
20   </script>
21   </body>
22   </html>
```

In Script D.18, two watch-points have been set: one in line 7 and one in line 16. Again, they have not been indented to make finding and removing them quick and easy.

**Use an Object Inspector**

An object inspector performs the job of Sherlock Holmes' magnifying glass. It illuminates the details of an object. This little program (Script D. 19) allows you to check the current properties of an object quickly and painlessly.

*Script D.19    The Object Inspector*

```
1    <!DOCTYPE HTML PUBLIC "-//W3C//DTD HTML 4.0 Transitional//EN">
2    <html>
3    <head>
4    <title>Script D.19: The Object Inspector</title>
5    <script language="JavaScript" type="text/javascript"><!--
6         function inspect() {
7              obj = eval(prompt("Enter the object", "document"))
8              var report = ""
9              for (i in obj)
10                 report += i + ": " + obj[i] + "\t"
11             alert(report)
12        }
13   //-->
14   </script>
15   </head>
16   <body bgcolor="#FFFFCE" text="Black" link="Fuchsia"
17   vlink="Purple" alink="Red">
18   <h1>Sample Document</h1>
19   <img src="images/img2.jpg" width="145" height="132"
20   border="0" alt="Aradia" align="right">
21   <p>This is my cat Devan, aka "Devil Kitty". He earned
22   that name, by the way!</p>
23
24   <script language="JavaScript" type="text/javascript"><!--
25        inspect()
26
27   //-->
28   </script>
29   </body>
30   </html>
```

The actual object inspector, the `inspect` function, is defined in lines 6 through 12. Line 25 calls `inspect` and prompts you to enter an object name, like this:

**Figure D.12**  **Calling the Object Inspector—inspect( )**

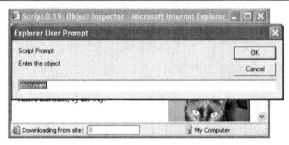

Let's go with the default entry, document, to inspect the document object. Here's what the returned data looks like:

**Figure D.13**  **Results of Inspecting the document Object**

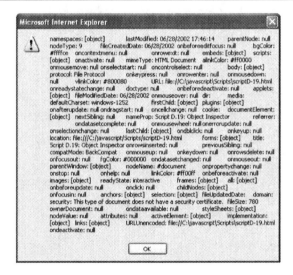

There's a lot of data here, surely more than enough to illuminate the object's details so that you may find and remove the error that is bugging your program. You can modify inspect to show each item on its own line. Just change \t to \n in line 10 of Script D.19.

**Print Form Element Indices and Values**

When debugging forms, especially functions that calculate form totals, it can be helpful to print the index number and value of each form element to get a better idea of the form's physical make-up. Here's the form we want to look at:

## Figure D.14    Sample Form to Examine

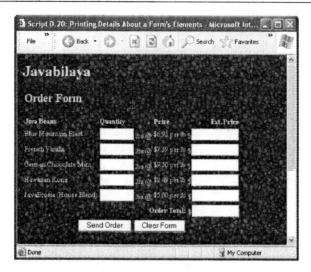

Recognize it? It's the Javabilaya order form we used in Chapter 14. Here's a partial listing of the script that creates the form (lines 9 to 97) and writes out the index number of each form element, the element's name if it has one, and the element's `type` (lines 99 to 104) if it has one. Most of the form details have been left out for succinctness. You'll find the complete script on the CD accompanying this book.

### Script D.20    Printing Details about a Form's Elements

```
1    <html>
2    <head>
3    <title>Script D.20: Printing Details About a Form's
       Elements</title>
4    </head>
5    <body bgcolor="#663333" text="#FFCC99"
6    background="images/javaBeans.jpg">
7    <h1>Javabilaya</h1>
8
9    <form name="OrderForm" method="post" action=""
10        onReset="return confirm('Are you sure you want to
            clear the form?')">
11    <table border="0">
12      <tr>
13      <th align="left"><h2>Order Form</h2></th>
14        <th> </th>
15      </tr>
16      <tr align="left">
17       <th align="left">Java Beans</th>
```

```
18          <th>Quantity</th>
19          <th>Price</th>
20          <th align="right">Ext. Price</th>
21        </tr>
. . .
97  </form>
98  <script language="JavaScript" type="text/javascript"><!--
99       for(i=0; i<document.OrderForm.length; i++) {
100            document.write("<b>", i, ". ",
101                 document.OrderForm.elements[i].name,
102                 " type: ", document.OrderForm.elements[i].type,
103                 "</b><br>")
104          }
105  //-->
106  </script>
107
108  </body>
109  </html>
```

You can modify the script with your own form's name in lines 99 to 104. Don't forget to place it at the end of your document, *after* the form has been defined. Here's what the results look like printed at the end of the document:

**Figure D.15**     *Results of Routine That Displays a Form's Elements Array*

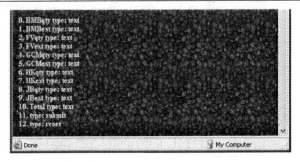

### Watch Out for Reserved Words

Use of words already in use by JavaScript can sometimes create logic errors or cause your program to cease to function. Be careful of using reserved words and any other words used by the JavaScript language. Appendix C contains a detailed list of words to avoid. For instance, `for` is a reserved word; you can't have a variable or function named `for`. Of course, you're probably not very likely to try using `for`. However, `name` is a useful variable name that you may be tempted to use quite often.

By definition, name is not a reserved word. Even so, many objects have a name property. While you may often be able to get away with using name as a variable name or a property name for a custom object, sometimes it'll get you into trouble. You probably won't get an error message. Often the only clue that you're in trouble is that your program doesn't work right and you can't find any other reason for its malfunctioning. The safest course is to avoid all words used by JavaScript and HTML altogether.

# The Persistence of a Bulldog

Sometimes I think programming is 1% inspiration and 99% perspiration. Some problems don't jump out at you immediately—or even eight hours later. In fact, you may go over your code with a fine-tooth comb 20 times and still not find the error. Here are some suggestions that will help you persist in sniffing out a particularly pesky bug.

## Comment Out Unessential Code

Sometimes errors will jump out of the woodworks when you make your program simpler. Comment out all unessential code and try to run the block you're having trouble with. Once you've solved any problems in that section, allow a few more lines in by removing the comments on those lines. Now debug those lines of code. Continue the process until you've got a clean, working program.

## Print It Out

Just like it's easier to spot errors in a printed paper than by reading it on screen, so too is it sometimes easier to spot errors in a printed program. So print out your code and look at the printed page, rather than your flickering screen. Move away from your computer and get comfortable. Sometimes paper and a change of scenery will allow you to see with new eyes and spot errors you missed before.

## Take a Break

Every good detective needs his rest. When you catch your hands reaching up to strangle your monitor's neck in frustration, it's time to take a break. Persistence doesn't mean you have to solve every problem in one session. You just have to keep coming back until the problem is solved. Fresh eyes and a fresh mind will often find a problem in minutes that you've been searching for for hours.

So give yourself a break. Walk away, have a nice cold Dr. Pepper, sleep on it, and come back to it later. The longer you can leave it, the more likely you'll be able to see it with fresh eyes and spot your error immediately. A good night's sleep is even better; it lets your subconscious work on the problem for a while. Given the chance, it will often puzzle the problem out for you and you'll wake up with the answer or ideas for looking into it further. At the very least, you'll have rested your mind and eyes and will be more likely to be able to find and solve problems quickly.

## When All Else Fails, Use Semicolons

Sometimes, when all else fails, placing a semicolon at the end of every statement eliminates a problem. Don't ask me why this works because I don't know. According to the author of the JavaScript language, Brendan Eich, "requiring a semicolon after each statement when a new line would do, [was] out of the question—scripting for most people is about writing short snippets of code, quickly and without fuss." So the JavaScript language does not require the use of semicolons to terminate statements; a simple line break will do.

Still, I've found that sometimes terminating every statement with a semicolon saved the day and left me a little hair to brush in the morning. You could, I suppose, use semicolons all of the time, but why go to all that extra work if you don't have to? They'll just introduce more opportunities for syntax errors whenever you forget one. If Brendan Eich, the creator of JavaScript, didn't think they were necessary, why should you?

# General Tips

Let's wrap up this chapter with some general tips that can help make debugging easier and maybe even help prevent a few errors from creeping into your scripts in the first place.

## Code in Small Blocks

Write scripts in small blocks. Test and debug each block as you go. It's easier to find errors in small blocks of code than in whole pages of code. Test each time you make a modification or addition.

## Install Scripts One at a Time

When adding scripts to a Web document, whether your own or scripts written by someone else, add, test, and debug them one at a time. Don't install another until you get the first one working as desired.

## Make Back-ups

Once you've got a program working perfectly, save that version. Make a copy and add anything new to the copy, leaving the original, working program untouched. Continue to evolve your program in versions. Should something really go awry, you can always go back to the last working version and start from there rather than having to start all over from scratch.

## Be Consistent

Be consistent in naming your variables and functions. In this book, we've followed the following naming conventions:

- ✗ Variable and function names begin with a lowercase letter. The first letter of additional words are capitalized, like this: num1, getNum(), firstName, and visitorsFullName.
- ✗ The first letter of constructor function names are capitalized.
- ✗ The first letter of a function that defines a custom method is capitalized.

> ✄ Constants are written in all caps.
> ✄ Names of objects created in Web documents with HTML are capitalized.

### Write Clean Code

Indent the bodies of functions and control structures to make your code cleaner and easier to read. Then you can easily skim it for starting and ending braces, as well as quickly determine where functions and control structures end. Leave your watch-points and tracing lines unindented so you can find and remove them quickly.

## Summary

Every programmer, no matter his or her experience, makes mistakes while writing code. These mistakes become program errors or bugs. Debugging is the process of removing those bugs. Debugging is an art or skill unto itself that requires the eye of an editor, the logic of a detective, and the persistence of a bulldog.

There are basically four types of errors that can creep into your programs:

1. HTML errors, which generally won't be reported by a browser, but nevertheless can prevent an errorless JavaScript program from functioning or functioning appropriately.
2. Syntax errors, which occur when you enter code that the JavaScript interpreter does not recognize and, therefore, cannot understand.
3. Runtime errors, which occur when the interpreter reads code that it can't handle. The code may be perfectly correct, syntax-wise, but for some reason the interpreter just can't deal with it.
4. Logic errors, which do not generate any error messages whatsoever, but cause your program to produce results other than what you intended.

Training yourself to have the eyes of an editor can help you find and resolve syntax and runtime errors. Use the checklists provided for things you can do to quickly find and remove both syntax and runtime errors and maybe avoid making them in the first place.

Most syntax errors involve missing quotation marks or parentheses. Mistyped words and misspellings can also lead to both syntax and runtime errors. Runtime errors most often occur when an object, property, method, or variable has not been defined at the time that it is accessed. Misspellings can account for some of these.

Error messages can often help you to quickly locate syntax and runtime errors. Keep in mind, however, that interpreters don't always report the exact line on which an error occurs. Sometimes the true error is on a line above or below the reported line. It's a good idea to look in the general vicinity of the line reported.

Common syntax error messages you are likely to encounter include "missing ( . . .," "missing ; after for-loop initializer," "missing { before function body," "nested comment," "syntax error," and "unterminated string literal." Common runtime errors you are likely to see include ". . . has no properties," ". . . is null or not an object," ". . . is undefined," and "object doesn't support this property or method." Each browser may report an error in a slightly different way.

When you're writing a script that generates HTML, a stylesheet, or other long strings, an older version of Netscape Navigator (pre-6.0) can come in handy. Old Navigator browsers display the *results* of document.write statements rather than the statements themselves when you view the source.

Logic errors usually require the logic of a detective to solve. When your program runs without error, but does not do what you intended it to do, then you've got a logic error. Many logic errors occur in incorrectly written conditions, that is, conditions that are functionally correct, but do not perform the test you wanted them to perform. Carefully analyzing each condition or other logic statement in your programs can help you solve logic errors. Other techniques that can help you solve logic errors include tracing through a program, setting watch-points for variables and properties, using an object inspector, printing a list of a form's elements, and avoiding reserved words and other words used by the JavaScript language.

Sometimes it just takes the persistence of a bulldog to completely debug a program. It can help to comment out unessential code, print out the program on paper and review it away from your computer, take a break to refresh yourself, and when all else fails, use semicolons.

In general, you can make your programs easier to debug if you program in small blocks, testing and debugging each block as you go; install scripts one at a time and test before installing another; make back-ups and save working versions of your program as it evolves, be consistent in your naming conventions; and finally, write clean code.

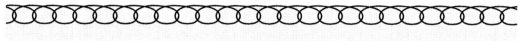

# appendix e

# *Evolution of the Document Object Model*

*Let no one suppose*

*that evolution will ever*

*exempt us from*

*struggles. "You forget,"*

*said the Devil, with a*

*chuckle, "that I have*

*been evolving too."*

—William Ralph Inge

I n the beginning, there was Netscape Navigator 2.0, the first JavaScript-enabled browser. (I just had to start this appendix with "In the beginning . . .") This appendix is all about the evolution of the Document Object Model. It is provided for two reasons:

1. I like to be complete. This appendix will help explain why some things, like rollovers, don't work in the earliest browsers.
2. To help you better appreciate the need for vendor compliance with W3C standards.

With that said, on with the history lesson.

In the beginning, there was Netscape Navigator 2.0, the first JavaScript-enabled browser. Netscape Navigator 2.0 supported the Document Object Model shown in Figure E.1; Netscape called it the "Navigator Object Hierarchy."

**Figure E.1** **Netscape Navigator 2.0 DOM**
**(Navigator Object Hierarchy, JavaScript 1.0)**

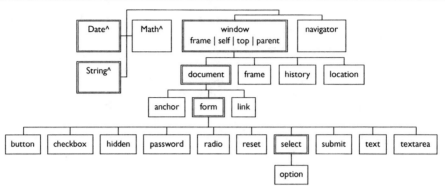

^ Built-in object from Core JavaScript

As you can see, JavaScript 1.0 in Navigator 2 supported only a very limited number of objects, properties, and methods. This is the same DOM adopted by Microsoft in Internet Explorer 3.0. Notice that there is no Image object.

With the release of Navigator 3.0, Netscape expanded its Document Object Model to include images, applets, embeds, plugins, and mimeTypes. It also added two built-in objects to Core JavaScript: Array and Number. Here is the Navigator 3, JavaScript version 1.1, DOM:

**Figure E.2** **Netscape Navigator 3.0 DOM (JavaScript 1.1)**

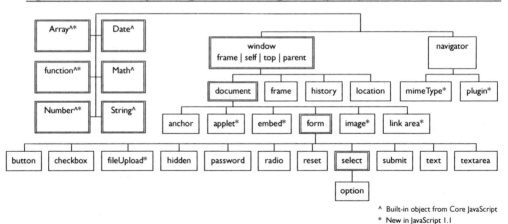

^ Built-in object from Core JavaScript
* New in JavaScript 1.1

Microsoft decided to implement its own version of JavaScript, called "JScript" in Internet Explorer 3.0 for Windows, to compete with Netscape. Although basically compatible with Netscape's JavaScript 1.0, it did have its differences. Macs didn't get JScript until IE3.01 and that version was different from the Windows version. It was just different enough to, of course, make a Web developer's job challenging. JScript version 2 for Windows 95/NT, roughly compatible with JavaScript 1.1, was released with *some* upgraded versions of IE 3.02x. Users had to check the properties on jscript.dll to verify which version they had.

**Figure E.3   Internet Explorer 3.0 DOM**

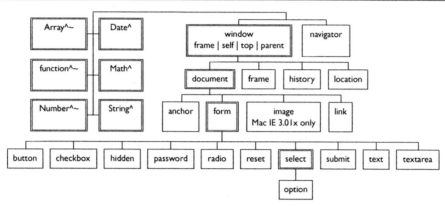

^ Built-in object from Core JavaScript
~ Some versions of IE 3.02x: those with JScript.dll v.2 only, not in NN2

Feeling challenged yet? The good news is that all this mess encouraged the World Wide Web Consortium (W3C), the standards-making body for all things Web, to start work on a Document Model Object Specification. The functionality supported in Netscape Navigator 3 and Internet Explorer 3, if you can figure out exactly what that is, became "DOM Level 0." On October 10, 1997, the W3C published a public working draft of Document Object Model Specification Level 1, a platform- and language-neutral DOM. Netscape, Sun, and Microsoft, among other companies, were principal contributors. While it didn't instantly solve all of the problems, it did provide Web developers with hope. We need hope.

Meanwhile, in 1996, Netscape approached the European Computer Manufacturers Association (ECMA) and began working with them to establish a standard scripting language. The result of that you've already read about: ECMA-262, commonly called ECMAScript. The Opera browser claims compliance with ECMAScript.

When the 4.0 browsers came along and the term "Dynamic HTML" was born, things really got frustrating—er, interesting—for Web developers. Netscape's Navigator 4.0 browser expanded its DOM again (JavaScript 1.2); this time Netscape added visibility access to the location bar, the menu bar, the personal toolbar, the scrollbars, the status bar, and the toolbar and one particularly nice object: the screen object. Microsoft also adopted the screen object in its Internet Explorer 4 release, but contained it in the window object. (Microsoft and Netscape rarely seem

*side note*

DOM Level 1 does not include an event model for HTML documents or a mechanism to access and modify style rules specified with Cascading Style Sheets (CSS).

to do anything the same way.) The `screen` object allows programmers to check the visitor's screen resolution, a very useful and long-desired capability. IE 4.0 shipped with JScript 3.0, which is similar to JavaScript 1.2.

**Figure E.4      Netscape Navigator 4.0 DOM (JavaScript 1.2)**

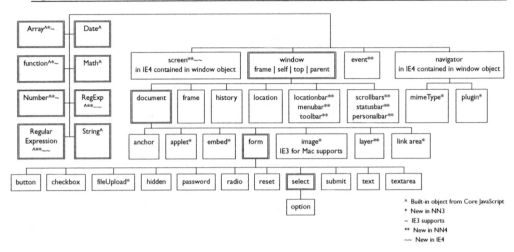

I haven't gotten to the really good part yet. Both browsers claimed complete compliance with the W3C's DOM Level 1. Both further claimed that Web developers could access, modify, or manipulate every object in a Web document including paragraphs and headings. In a way, they were right. We just had to implement that kind of functionality in two completely different ways! In other words, we had to write two separate sets of code and call the appropriate set of code after determining which browser the visitor was using. This meant twice the work. Grrr. Netscape used "JavaScript Assisted Style Sheets" and the Layer tag; Microsoft went with an all-encompassing document.all collection. It's even possible that both 4.0 browsers were fully compliant with DOM1. Like many W3C specifications, DOM1 left a lot of room for interpretation.

**peek ahead**
Appendix F provides all the details you need to implement cross-browser DHTML.

Lack of compliance was splintering the Web and making the job of a Web developer a nightmare. Frustrated with the lack of browser compliance with established W3C standards, groups like the Web Standards Project (WaSP), http://www.webstandards.org, started putting on pressure. In response, both Netscape and Microsoft promised to make their 5.0 browsers fully compliant with existing standards.

Netscape abandoned its 5.0 browser update in favor of completing its 6.0 browser, the first browser that could claim full compliance with the W3C's DOM, HTML 4.0, CSS1, and XML specifications; it was even compliant with ECMA-262, Edition 3, and had some support for CSS2. Microsoft failed to follow through with its promise, so Netscape issued a Standards

Compliance Challenge. (Microsoft came closer to supporting the W3C's CSS1, DOM1, and HTML 4 standards with its IE6 release.) The Web Standards Project (WaSP) and similar groups continued to press the standards issue, thus allowing me to end this long and frustrating description of the DOM's sordid history with a little hope.

> **side note**
>
> DOM Level I does not include mechanisms to access and modify style specified through CSS1. It also does not include an event model for HTML documents.

The W3C's DOM2 specification is being implemented in the latest browsers. Opera 4 was the first browser to begin supporting any of the DOM2 selection methods: `getElementById`, `getElementByName`, and `getElementsByTagName`. Netscape followed suit in Navigator 6. Microsoft also picked up the DOM2 selection methods in its 5.0 browsers. What does this compliance with DOM2 mean? It means it's getting easier to access all elements in a Web document the same way in all browsers. There are just a few minor wrinkles still to be worked out. The 7.0 browsers show real promise.

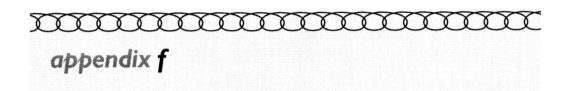

# Cross-Browser Dynamic HTML (XBDHTML)

*Without tolerance, our*

*world turns into hell.*

—Friedrich Dürrenmatt,
"About Tolerance"

Netscape Navigator 4 and Internet Explorer 4 were the first browsers to support DHTML. Unfortunately, they did so using proprietary features and DOM extensions. Opera began supporting some DHTML features in its 4.0 browser as well, taking some object references from DOM2 and borrowing others from both Netscape Navigator and Internet Explorer. If you need to write code that will accommodate these old browsers, then the information in this appendix is for you.

## Browser Compatibility Problems

Although the World Wide Web Consortium (W3C) wrote complete specifications for HTML, CSS, and even the DOM, browser companies have been slow to implement complete support for those standards. The big question is why?

There are several key reasons:

- Standards often leave room for interpretation. Thus vendors often interpret them differently. Case in point: Document Object Model Level 1 (DOM1). Both Netscape and Microsoft claimed that their 4.0 browsers were in complete compliance with the W3C's DOM1 specification. Yet they each implemented its own proprietary DOM that was completely different from the other's!

✄ Standards often include suggestions or recommendations with which vendors are not required to comply.

✄ Standards often permit vendors to add enhancements that are not defined by the standards. *This* the vendors *do* take full advantage of, unfortunately.

✄ The standards definition and ratification process often lags behind the vendors' implementation of the specified functionality.

# How to Work Around the Incompatibilities

## Study the Differences

The first step you can take to adequately work with these incompatibilities is to study how each vendor implements the DOM in relationship to DHTML. This reference will help:

**Table F.1**    ***Cross-Browser DHTML Property Quick Reference***

| Layer Property[0] | Property Reference (4.0+ browsers) | Result Type |
|---|---|---|
| background -color | **NN4:** `document.layers["objId"].bgColor`<br>**IE4:** `document.all["objId"].style`<br>   `.backgroundColor`<br>**OP4:** not supported<br>**OP5+:** `document.getElementById("objId")`<br>   `.style.background`<br>**DOM2:** `document.getElementById("objId")`<br>   `.style.backgroundColor` | six-digit hexadecimal number |
| background -image | **NN4:** `document.layers["objId"]`<br>   `.background`<br>**IE4+:** not supported<br>**OP4+:** not supported<br>**DOM2:** `document.getElementById("objId")`<br>   `.style.backgroundImage` | URL to image |
| border color | **DOM2:** `document.getElementById("objId")`<br>   `.style.borderColor` | six-digit hexadecimal number |
| border style | **DOM2:** `document.getElementById("objId")`<br>   `.style.borderStyle` | string: `solid`, `inset`, `outset`, or `groove` |
| border width | **DOM2:** `document.getElementById("objId")`<br>   `.style.borderWidth` | string: *n unit* |

| content | **NN4:** `document.layers["objId"]` `.load("URL", width)` **IE4:** `document.all["objId"].innerHTML` **OP4+:** not supported **DOM2:** `document.getElementById("objId")` `.innerHTML`[1] | string |
|---|---|---|
| height | **NN4:** not supported **IE4:** `document.all["objId"].style` `.pixelHeight` **OP4–5:** `document.getElementById("objId")` `.style.pixelHeight` **DOM2:** `document.getElementById("objId")` `.style.height` | — string: $n$ px string: $n$ string: $n$ px |
| left (x-coordinate) | **NN4:** `document.layers["objId"].left` **IE4:** `document.all["objId"].style` `.pixelLeft` **OP4–5:** `document.getElementById("objId")` `.style.pixelLeft` **DOM2:** `document.getElementById("objId")` `.style.left` | number string: $n$ px string: $n$ string: $n$ px |
| object | **NN4:** `document.layers["objId"]` **IE4:** `document.all["objId"]` **OP4+:** `document.getElementById("objId")` **DOM2:** `document.getElementById("objId")` | the object |
| top (y-coordinate) | **NN4:** `document.layers["objId"].top` **IE4:** `document.all["objId"].style` `.pixelTop` **OP4–5:** `document.getElementById("objId")` `.style.pixelTop` **DOM2:** `document.getElementById("objId")` `.style.top` | number string: $n$ px string: $n$ string: $n$ px |
| visibility | **NN4:** `document.layers["objId"]` `.visibility` **IE4:** `document.all["objId"].style` `.visibility` **OP4+:** `document.getElementById("objId")` `.visibility` **DOM2:** `document.getElementById("objId")` `.style.visibility` | hide, show, inherit, hidden, visible, or inherit for rest |

| Layer Property[0] | Property Reference (4.0+ browsers) | Result Type |
|---|---|---|
| width | **NN4:** not supported<br>**IE4:** `document.all["objId"].style`<br>    `.pixelWidth`<br>**OP4–5:** `document.getElementById("objId")`<br>    `.style.pixelWidth`<br>**DOM2:** `document.getElementById("objId")`<br>    `.width` | string: *n* px<br>In OP, string: *n* |

| Other Property | Property Reference (4.0+ browsers) | Result Type |
|---|---|---|
| font color | **NN4:** not supported<br>**IE4:** `document.all["objId"].style.color`<br>**OP4:** not supported<br>**DOM2:** `document.getElementById("objId")`<br>    `.style.color` | six-digit<br>hexadecimal<br>number |
| set style on<br>an element | **NN4:** not supported, can only access layer style<br>    properties<br>**IE4:** `document.all["objId"].style`<br>    `.property = "value"`<br>**OP4:** not supported, can only access layer style<br>    properties<br>**DOM2:** `document.getElementById("objId")`<br>    `.style = "declaration"` | |
| stylesheet<br>properties | **NN4:** not supported, can only access layer style<br>    properties<br>**IE4:** `document.all["objId"].style.property`<br>**OP4:** not supported, can only access layer style<br>    properties<br>**DOM2:** `document.getElementById("objId")`<br>    `.style.property` | depends on<br>property |
| window height | **NN4:** `window.innerHeight`<br>**IE4:** `window.document.body.clientHeight`<br>**OP4+:** `window.innerHeight`<br>**DOM2:** `window.innerHeight` | number |
| window width | **NN4:** `window.innerWidth`<br>**IE4:** `window.document.body.clientWidth`<br>**OP4+:** `window.innerWidth`<br>**DOM2:** `window.innerWidth` | number |

Replace italicized items appropriately
[0] layer = an absolutely positioned element, usually a division
[1] not part of W3C standard

## Object Detection and Browser Detection

Before you can apply what you've learned about the browsers' differences regarding DHTML, you first must determine which browser the visitor is using or whether the particular object you want to use is supported. The former is known as **browser detection**, the latter as **object detection**. Once you know that, you can conditionally execute the appropriate code accordingly. This is sometimes called **forking**.

To illustrate one of the browser incompatibilities when it comes to DHTML, the following is the appropriate dot notation to access the `left` property of an absolutely positioned element whose `id="myDiv"` in each browser.

In NN4:

```
document.layers["myDiv"].left
```

In IE4:

```
document.all["myDiv"].style.pixelLeft
```

In OP4 and the DOM2-compatible browsers:

```
document.getElementById("myDiv").style.left
```

Yikes!

The NN4 and IE4 examples use associative index names to index into an array: the `document.layers` array for NN4 and the `document.all` array for IE4. The newer browsers, however, in compliance with the W3C's DOM Level 2 specification, support the `getElementById` method, which makes life much easier. With `getElementById`, there is now a standard way to access layers (absolutely positioned elements). As soon as people stop using the older browsers, our lives as Web developers will be simpler, at least until the browser companies come up with some other proprietary wrench to throw in the works.

# Conditionally Executing Code (Forking)

There are three primary ways to determine which set of code to execute:

1. You can use browser detection to determine which browser the visitor is using.
2. You can use object detection to determine whether an object is supported before trying to execute code associated with that object.
3. You can use a combination of both browser and object detection.

I prefer object detection, primarily because you don't have to update your code every time a new browser is released. Another benefit of object detection is that you don't have to keep track of what objects each browser and version does and does not support. We'll look at both methods, because until people stop using the older browsers, you will occasionally have to use a combination of browser and object detection.

## Object Detection

Object detection simply requires testing to see whether a particular object is supported before executing any code. In many cases you can get by with only three forks in your code:

1. W3C-compliant browsers. Determined by support of getElementById. Generally, NN6+, IE5+, and Opera 4+ fall into this category.
2. NN4x browsers. Determined by support of document.layers.
3. IE4x browsers. Determined by support of document.all. Note that IE5x still supports document.all, so order is important in your code listing.

There are occasions when you may need to have more forks. I think the worst case I ran into had five forks. That's where the combination of browser and object detection comes in handy.

## Browser Detection

To determine which browser the visitor is using, examine the properties of the navigator object.

### Script F.1    *Viewing Navigator Data*

```
1    <html>
2    <head>
3        <title>Script F.1: Viewing Navigator Data</title></head>
4    <body>
5    <script language="JavaScript" type="text/javascript"><!--
6    document.write("<h1>Navigator Data</h1>")
7    document.write("appCodeName: ", navigator.appCodeName, "<br>")
8    document.write("appName: ", navigator.appName, "<br>")
9    document.write("appVersion: ", navigator.appVersion, "<br>")
10   document.write("userAgent: ", navigator.userAgent, "<br>")
11   document.write("platform: ", navigator.platform, "<br>")
12   // -->
13   </script>
14
15   </body>
16   </html>
```

To really see this script in action and get a good idea of what each browser supports, you'll need to run it in several browsers and compare the results. You'll need some old browsers to see the important differences.

## A Combination of Object Detection and Browser Detection

I've found with the latest browsers that you sometimes need to use a combination of browser detection and object detection. It turns out that Opera 4 supports some of the W3C's DOM2, some of IE's proprietary properties and methods, and some of Netscape Navigator's properties and methods. Further, Opera 4's support of some items is inconsistent with Opera 5's. This just adds one more snarl to the mess, making us have to sometimes perform browser detection for Opera 4 as well as the usual three object detections.

OK, now that we have three means of conditionally executing code according to the objects supported by a browser, we can begin to put it all together and support three groups of browsers (NN4, IE4, and W3C-compliant) by object detection with one script. Occasionally, we'll need to use browser detection as well, as explained earlier. Let's begin with accessing the left and top style properties of an absolutely positioned element.

# Getting Layer Coordinates

This script shows you how to get the coordinates of an absolutely positioned element (layer) in all DHTML browsers.

**Script F.2**     *Getting Layer Coordinates—All DHTML Browsers*

```
1    <html>
2    <head><title>Script F.2: Get Coordinates - All DHTML
       Browsers</title></head>
3    <body>
4    <div id="testDiv"
5        style="position:absolute; left:50px; top:20px; width:200px;
           height:100px; background-color:#ff3399; border: none;
           visibility:visible;">
6           Some text, put here for NN4's benefit since it won't create
7           a layer of an empty division.
8    </div>
9
10   <script language="JavaScript" type="text/javascript"><!--
11   if (document.getElementById &&
       navigator.userAgent.indexOf("Opera 4") != -1) {
12      // can't seem to get current coordinates of a layer in Opera 4
13      var myDiv = document.getElementById("testDiv")
14      alert("Opera 4 Coords: " + myDiv.style.pixelLeft + ", " +
           myDiv.style.pixelTop)
15   } else if (document.getElementById) {
16      var myDiv = document.getElementById("testDiv")
17      alert("W3Ccomp Coords: " + myDiv.style.left + ", " +
           myDiv.style.top)
18
19      var x = parseInt(myDiv.style.left)
20      var y = parseInt(myDiv.style.top)
21      alert("W3Ccomp Parsed Coords: " + x + ", " + y)
22   } else if (document.layers) {
23      var myDiv = document.layers["testDiv"]
24      alert("NN4 Coords: " + myDiv.left + ", " + myDiv.top)
```

```
25    } else if (document.all) {
26        var myDiv = document.all["testDiv"]
27        alert("IE4 Coords: " + myDiv.style.pixelLeft + ", " +
          myDiv.style.pixelTop)
28
29        var x = parseInt(myDiv.style.pixelLeft)
30        var y = parseInt(myDiv.style.pixelTop)
31        alert("IE4 Coords: " + x + ", " + y)
32    }
33
34    // -->
35    </script>
36
37    </body>
38    </html>
```

## Moving a Layer

Script F.3 contains the functions moveLayerTo and moveLayerBy. The moveLayerTo function moves a layer to a particular location on the screen; moveLayerBy, which follows, moves a layer by so many pixels. It shifts the layer up, down, left, or right.

### Script F.3    Move Layer Functions—All DHTML Browsers

```
1    <html>
2    <head>
3    <title>Script F.3: Move Layer Functions - All DHTML
     Browsers</title>
4    <script language="JavaScript" type="text/javascript"><!--
5    function moveLayerTo(layerID, newX, newY) {
6    // moves layer directly to a new position
7        if (document.getElementById) {
8            document.getElementById(layerID).style.left = newX
9            document.getElementById(layerID).style.top = newY
10        } else if (document.layers) {
11            document.layers[layerID].moveTo(newX, newY)
12        } else if (document.all) {
13            document.all[layerID].style.pixelLeft = newX
14            document.all[layerID].style.pixelTop = newY
15        }
16    }
17    function moveLayerBy(layerID, xOffset, yOffset) {
18    // moves layer by the specified X-offset and Y-offset
19        if (document.getElementById &&
20            navigator.userAgent.indexOf("Opera 4") != -1) {
```

```
21          // move by not supported in Opera 4
22      } else if (document.getElementById) {
23          var myLayer = document.getElementById(layerID)
24          myLayer.style.left = parseInt(myLayer.style.left) +
              xOffset
25          myLayer.style.top = parseInt(myLayer.style.top) +
              yOffset
26      } else if (document.layers) {
27          document.layers[layerID].moveBy(xOffset, yOffset)
28      } else if (document.all) {
29          var myLayer = document.all[layerID]
30          myLayer.style.pixelLeft =
              parseInt(myLayer.style.pixelLeft) + xOffset
31          myLayer.style.pixelTop =
              parseInt(myLayer.style.pixelTop) + yOffset
32      }
33  }
34  //-->
35  </script>
36  </head>
37  <body>
38  <div id="testDiv"
39      style="position:absolute; left:50px; top:60px; width:200px;
          height:100px; background-color:#ff3399; border: none;
          visibility:visible;">
40      Some text, put here for NN4's benefit since it won't create
41  a layer of an empty division.
42  </div>
43
44  <form>
45      <input type="button" value="Move to 150,220"
46          onClick="moveLayerTo('testDiv', 150,220)">
47      <input type="button" value="Move top n left by 10 "
48          onClick="moveLayerBy('testDiv', 10,10)">
49      <input type="button" value="Move to 0,0"
50          onClick="moveLayerTo('testDiv', 0,0)">
51      <input type="button" value="Move top n left by -10 "
52          onClick="moveLayerBy('testDiv', -10,-10)">
53  </form>
54
55  </body>
56  </html>
```

# Getting the Window Size

Getting the window size is particularly useful if you want to position a window or layer in the center of the screen or move layers around the screen. To do either, the window's dimensions are critical to your calculations. Script F.4 acquires the screen width and height in all DHTML browsers.

**Script F.4**      ***Getting the Window's Dimensions—All DHTML Browsers***

```
1    <html>
2    <head>
3    <title>Script F.4: Getting the Window's Dimensions - All DHTML
4    Browsers</title>
5    <script language="JavaScript" type="text/javascript"><!--
6    function getWindowWidth(zWindow) {
7         if (document.getElementById && !(document.all)) {
8              return zWindow.innerWidth
9         } else if (document.layers) {
10             return zWindow.innerWidth
11        } else if (document.all) {
12             return zWindow.document.body.clientWidth
13        }
14   }
15
16   function getWindowHeight(zWindow) {
17        if (document.getElementById && !(document.all)) {
18             return zWindow.innerHeight
19        } else if (document.layers) {
20             return zWindow.innerHeight
21        } else if (document.all) {
22             return zWindow.document.body.clientHeight
23        }
24   }
25   //-->
26   </script>
27   </head>
28   <body>
29   <div id="testDiv"
30        style="position:absolute; left:50px; top:160px; width:200px;
             height:100px; background-color:#ff3399; border: none;
             visibility:visible;">
31        Some text, put here for NN4's benefit since it won't create
32   a layer of an empty division.
33   </div>
34
35   <form>
```

```
36          <input type="button" value="Display Window Dimensions"
37                  onClick="alert(getWindowWidth(self) + 'x' +
                        getWindowHeight(self))">
38      </form>
39
40      </body>
41      </html>
```

## Resizing a Layer

The following script includes functions for resizing a layer both to a particular size and by a certain number of pixels.

### Script F.5      *Resize Layer Functions—All DHTML Browsers*

```
1    <html>
2    <head>
3    <title>Script F.5: Resize Layer Functions - All DHTML
     Browsers</title>
4    <script language="JavaScript" type="text/javascript"><!--
5    function resizeLayerTo(layerID, newW, newH) {
6    // moves layer directly to a new position
7        if (document.getElementById &&
8            (navigator.userAgent.indexOf("Opera 4") != -1 ||
9            navigator.userAgent.indexOf("Opera 5") != -1)) {
10              document.getElementById(layerID).style.pixelWidth
                    = newW
11              document.getElementById(layerID).style.pixelHeight
                    = newH
12        } else if (document.getElementById) {
13              document.getElementById(layerID).style.width = newW
14              document.getElementById(layerID).style.height = newH
15        } else if (document.layers) {
16              document.layers[layerID].resizeTo(newW, newH)
17        } else if (document.all) {
18              document.all[layerID].style.pixelWidth = newW
19              document.all[layerID].style.pixelHeight = newH
20        }
21    }
22    function resizeLayerBy(layerID, xOffset, yOffset) {
23    // moves layer by the specified X-offset and Y-offset
24        if (document.getElementById &&
25            (navigator.userAgent.indexOf("Opera 4") != -1 ||
26            navigator.userAgent.indexOf("Opera 5") != -1)) {
27              var myLayer = document.getElementById(layerID)
```

```
28          myLayer.style.pixelWidth =
                parseInt(myLayer.style.pixelWidth) + xOffset
29          myLayer.style.pixelHeight =
                parseInt(myLayer.style.pixelHeight) + yOffset
30      } else if (document.getElementById) {
31          var myLayer = document.getElementById(layerID)
32          myLayer.style.width = parseInt(myLayer.style.width)
                + xOffset
33          myLayer.style.height = parseInt(myLayer.style.height)
                + yOffset
34      } else if (document.layers) {
35          document.layers[layerID].resizeBy(xOffset, yOffset)
36      } else if (document.all) {
37          var myLayer = document.all[layerID]
38          myLayer.style.pixelWidth =
                parseInt(myLayer.style.pixelWidth) + xOffset
39          myLayer.style.pixelHeight =
                parseInt(myLayer.style.pixelHeight) + yOffset
40      }
41  }
42  //-->
43  </script>
44  </head>
45  <body>
46  <div id="testDiv"
47      style="position:absolute; left:50px; top:60px; width:200px;
        height:100px; background-color:#ff3399; border: none;
        visibility:visible;">
48        Some text, put here for NN4's benefit since it won't create
49  a layer of an empty division.
50  </div>
51
52  <form>
53      <input type="button" value="Resize to 150,220"
54          onClick="resizeLayerTo('testDiv', 150,220)">
55      <input type="button" value="Resize by 10x10"
56          onClick="resizeLayerBy('testDiv', 10,10)">
57      <input type="button" value="Resize by -10x-10"
58          onClick="resizeLayerBy('testDiv', -10,-10)">
59  </form>
60
61  </body>
62  </html>
```

# Changing Colors and Other Stuff

This script shows how you can change the background color, the background image (when supported), the font color, and even the content (when supported) of an absolutely positioned element.

**Script F.6**  **Layer Functions to Change Color and Other Stuff—All DHTML Browsers**

```
1    <html>
2    <head>
3    <title>Script F.6: Functions to Change Color and Other Stuff - All
4    DHTML Browsers</title>
5    <script language="JavaScript" type="text/javascript"><!--
6    function changeBGcolor(layerID, newColor) {
7         if (document.getElementById &&
8             navigator.userAgent.indexOf("Opera 5") != -1) {
9             // not supported in Opera 4
10            document.getElementById(layerID).style.background =
                  newColor
11        } else if (document.getElementById) {
12                document.getElementById(layerID).style
                     .backgroundColor = newColor
13        } else if (document.layers) {
14            document.layers[layerID].bgColor = newColor
15        } else if (document.all) {
16            document.all[layerID].style.backgroundColor = newColor
17        }
18   }
19
20   function changeFontColor(layerID, newColor) {
21        if (document.getElementById &&
22            navigator.userAgent.indexOf("Opera 5") != -1) {
23            // not supported in Opera 4
24            document.getElementById(layerID).style.color =
                  newColor
25        } else if (document.getElementById) {
26            document.getElementById(layerID).style.color =
                  newColor
27        } else if (document.layers) {
28            // no support
29        } else if (document.all) {
30            document.all[layerID].style.color = newColor
31        }
32   }
33
```

```
34   function changeBGimage(layerID, imgSrc) {
35       if (document.getElementById &&
36           navigator.userAgent.indexOf("Opera") != -1) {
37           // changing the background image not supported in
                Opera
38       } else if (document.getElementById && !document.all) {
39           document.getElementById(layerID).style.backgroundImage
                = imgSrc
40       } else if (document.layers) {
41           document.layers[layerID].background = imgSrc
42       } else if (document.all) {
43           // property unknown or unsupported
44       }
45   }
46
47   function changeContent(elementID, newContent) {
48       if (document.getElementById &&
49           navigator.userAgent.indexOf("Opera") != -1) {
50           // no support in Opera for changing content at this
                time
51       } else if (document.getElementById) {
52           document.getElementById(elementID).innerHTML =
                newContent
53       } else if (document.layers) {
54           // only supported for loading contents of a file into
                a layer
55           // syntax: load(pathNfilename, width)
56           document.layers[elementID].load(newContent, 300)
57       } else if (document.all) {
58           document.all[elementID].innerHTML = newContent
59       }
60   }
61   //-->
62   </script>
63   </head>
64   <body>
65   <div id="testDiv"
66       style="position:absolute; left:50px; top:160px; width:200px;
           height:100px; background-color:#ff3399; border: none;
           visibility:visible;">
67       Some text, put here for NN4's benefit since it won't create
68   a layer of an empty division.
69   </div>
70
71   <form>
```

```
72      <input type="button" value="bgColor to Blue"
73      onClick="changeBGcolor('testDiv', '#0000FF')">
74      <input type="button" value="font color to white"
75      onClick="changeFontColor('testDiv', 'white')">
76      <input type="button" value="cloud background"
77      onClick="changeBGimage('testDiv', 'images/clouds.jpg')">
78      <input type="button" value="Change DIV content"
79      onClick="changeContent('testDiv', 'New Stuff!')">
80      <input type="button" value="Change DIV content NN4 Only"
81      onClick="changeContent('testDiv', 'newLayerContent.html')">
82  </form>
83
84  </body>
85  </html>
```

## Summary

The first browsers to support DHTML did so using proprietary features and DOM extensions. There are many reasons for browser DOM incompatibilities, not least of which is that the standards often leave room for interpretation. For example, both Netscape and Microsoft claimed that their 4.0 browsers were in complete compliance with the W3C's DOM1 specification. Yet they each implemented their own proprietary DOM that was completely different from the other's.

To deal with browser incompatibilities, you must conditionally execute the appropriate code. There are three ways to determine which set of code to execute:

1. You can use browser detection to determine which browser the visitor is using.
2. You can use object detection to determine whether an object is supported before trying to execute code associated with that object.
3. You can use a combination of both browser and object detection.

Object detection is perhaps the best choice, as you don't have to update your code every time a new browser is released. You also don't have to keep track of what objects each browser and version does and does not support. In some cases, you must use both browser and object detection, primarily because of inconsistencies in Opera 4.

This appendix defined functions for performing all of the following DHTML tasks:

- ✗ Getting a layer's coordinates
- ✗ Moving a layer to specified coordinates
- ✗ Moving a layer by so many pixels
- ✗ Acquiring the window's current size
- ✗ Resizing a layer
- ✗ Changing a layer's background color
- ✗ Changing a layer's background image (when supported)

✗ Changing the font color of text within a layer

✗ Changing the content of a layer (when supported)

With these functions in hand, you're on your way to writing DHTML scripts that work in all DHTML-compliant browsers.

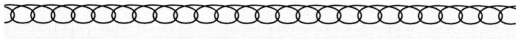

# *Character Sets*

*The measure of a man's real character is what he would do if he knew he would never be found out.*

—Thomas B. Macaulay

T he **ISO 8859-1 (Latin-1) character set** (created by the International Organization for Standardization) represents each character as an eight-bit (one-byte) binary number and supports 256 values. The first 128 values are a direct match of the ASCII character set. While the ISO Latin-1 set was adopted for use on the Internet (MIME) and the Web (HTML and HTTP), it still doesn't come close to covering all of the characters used in the world. Hence the need for Unicode.

**Unicode** is short for Unicode Worldwide Character Standard. It covers the languages of the Americas, Europe, Middle East, Africa, India, Asia, and Pacifica, as well as some historic scripts and technical symbols. Unicode values range from 0 to 65,535. Its first 128 values match the ASCII character set.

This character set listing skips positions 0-31 and 127-159, except for 9, 10, and 13, because ISO 8859-1 does not define displayable characters for those positions. The HTML specification also doesn't allow those positions to be used for display characters, except for 9, 10, and 13, which have been listed in the table.

### ISO 8859-1 (Latin-1) Character Set and
### Unicode Character Set: Basic Latin and Latin-1 Supplement

| Character | Hexadecimal Code | Decimal Code | Name | Description |
|---|---|---|---|---|
| | 09 | 9 | | Tab |
| | 0A | 10 | | New line |
| | 0D | 13 | | Carriage return |
| | 20 | 32 | | Normal space |
| ! | 21 | 33 | | Exclamation mark |
| " | 22 | 34 | quot | Quotation mark |
| # | 23 | 35 | | Hash, pound sign, number sign |
| $ | 24 | 36 | | Dollar sign |
| % | 25 | 37 | | Percent sign |
| & | 26 | 38 | amp | Ampersand |
| ' | 27 | 39 | | Apostrophe |
| ( | 28 | 40 | | Opening parenthesis |
| ) | 29 | 41 | | Closing parenthesis |
| * | 2A | 42 | | Asterisk |
| + | 2B | 43 | | Plus sign |
| , | 2C | 44 | | Comma |
| - | 2D | 45 | | Minus sign, hyphen |
| . | 2E | 46 | | Period, dot, decimal point |
| / | 2F | 47 | | Forward slash |
| 0 | 30 | 48 | | Digit zero |
| 1 | 31 | 49 | | Digit one |
| 2 | 32 | 50 | | Digit two |
| 3 | 33 | 51 | | Digit three |
| 4 | 34 | 52 | | Digit four |
| 5 | 35 | 53 | | Digit five |

| | | | | |
|---|---|---|---|---|
| 6 | 36 | 54 | | Digit six |
| 7 | 37 | 55 | | Digit seven |
| 8 | 38 | 56 | | Digit eight |
| 9 | 39 | 57 | | Digit nine |
| : | 3A | 58 | | Colon |
| ; | 3B | 59 | | Semicolon |
| < | 3C | 60 | lt | Less-than sign |
| = | 3D | 61 | | Equals sign |
| > | 3E | 62 | gt | Greater-than sign |
| ? | 3F | 63 | | Question mark |
| @ | 40 | 64 | | At sign |
| A | 41 | 65 | | Capital letter A |
| B | 42 | 66 | | Capital letter B |
| C | 43 | 67 | | Capital letter C |
| D | 44 | 68 | | Capital letter D |
| E | 45 | 69 | | Capital letter E |
| F | 46 | 70 | | Capital letter F |
| G | 47 | 71 | | Capital letter G |
| H | 48 | 72 | | Capital letter H |
| I | 49 | 73 | | Capital letter I |
| J | 4A | 74 | | Capital letter J |
| K | 4B | 75 | | Capital letter K |
| L | 4C | 76 | | Capital letter L |
| M | 4D | 77 | | Capital letter M |
| N | 4E | 78 | | Capital letter N |
| O | 4F | 79 | | Capital letter O |
| P | 50 | 80 | | Capital letter P |
| Q | 51 | 81 | | Capital letter Q |
| R | 52 | 82 | | Capital letter R |

| Character | Hexadecimal Code | Decimal Code | Name | Description   (continued) |
|---|---|---|---|---|
| S | 53 | 83 | | Capital letter S |
| T | 54 | 84 | | Capital letter T |
| U | 55 | 85 | | Capital letter U |
| V | 56 | 86 | | Capital letter V |
| W | 57 | 87 | | Capital letter W |
| X | 58 | 88 | | Capital letter X |
| Y | 59 | 89 | | Capital letter Y |
| Z | 5A | 90 | | Capital letter Z |
| [ | 5B | 91 | | Opening square bracket |
| \ | 5C | 92 | | Backslash |
| ] | 5D | 93 | | Closing square bracket |
| ∧ | 5E | 94 | | Caret |
| _ | 5F | 95 | | Underscore |
| ' | 60 | 96 | | Grave accent |
| a | 61 | 97 | | Small letter a |
| b | 62 | 98 | | Small letter b |
| c | 63 | 99 | | Small letter c |
| d | 64 | 100 | | Small letter d |
| e | 65 | 101 | | Small letter e |
| f | 66 | 102 | | Small letter f |
| g | 67 | 103 | | Small letter g |
| h | 68 | 104 | | Small letter h |
| i | 69 | 105 | | Small letter i |
| j | 6A | 106 | | Small letter j |
| k | 6B | 107 | | Small letter k |
| l | 6C | 108 | | Small letter l |
| m | 6D | 109 | | Small letter m |
| n | 6E | 110 | | Small letter n |

| | | | | |
|---|---|---|---|---|
| o | 6F | 111 | | Small letter o |
| p | 70 | 112 | | Small letter p |
| q | 71 | 113 | | Small letter q |
| r | 72 | 114 | | Small letter r |
| s | 73 | 115 | | Small letter s |
| t | 74 | 116 | | Small letter t |
| u | 75 | 117 | | Small letter u |
| v | 76 | 118 | | Small letter v |
| w | 77 | 119 | | Small letter w |
| x | 78 | 120 | | Small letter x |
| y | 79 | 121 | | Small letter y |
| z | 7A | 122 | | Small letter z |
| { | 7B | 123 | | Opening brace, left curly bracket |
| \| | 7C | 124 | | Vertical bar |
| } | 7D | 125 | | Closing brace, right curly bracket |
| ~ | 7E | 126 | | Tilde |
| | 7F | 127 | | Unused |
| | A0 | 160 | nbsp | Non-breaking space |
| ¡ | A1 | 161 | iexcl | Inverted exclamation mark |
| ¢ | A2 | 162 | cent | Cent sign |
| £ | A3 | 163 | pound | Pound sign |
| ◇ | A4 | 164 | curren | Currency sign |
| ¥ | A5 | 165 | yen | Yen sign |
| ¦ | A6 | 166 | brvbar | Broken bar |
| § | A7 | 167 | sect | Section sign |
| ¨ | A8 | 168 | uml | Umlaut, dieresis |
| © | A9 | 169 | copy | Copyright sign |

| Character | Hexadecimal Code | Decimal Code | Name | Description  *(continued)* |
|---|---|---|---|---|
| a | AA | 170 | ordf | Feminine ordinal |
| « | AB | 171 | laquo | Left-pointing double angle quotation mark, left-pointing guillemet |
| ¬ | AC | 172 | not | Logical "not" sign |
| - | AD | 173 | shy | Soft hyphen |
| ® | AE | 174 | reg | Registered trademark |
| ¯ | AF | 175 | macr | Spacing macron |
| ° | B0 | 176 | deg | Degree sign |
| ± | B1 | 177 | plusmn | Plus-minus sign |
| ² | B2 | 178 | sup2 | Superscript two |
| ³ | B3 | 179 | sup3 | Superscript three |
| ´ | B4 | 180 | acute | Spacing acute accent |
| μ | B5 | 181 | micro | Micro sign |
| ¶ | B6 | 182 | para | Paragraph sign |
| · | B7 | 183 | middot | Middle dot |
| ¸ | B8 | 184 | cedil | Spacing cedilla |
| ¹ | B9 | 185 | sup1 | Superscript one |
| º | BA | 186 | ordm | Masculine ordinal indicator |
| » | BB | 187 | raquo | Right-pointing double angle quotation mark, right-pointing guillemet |
| ¼ | BC | 188 | frac14 | One quarter |
| ½ | BD | 189 | frac12 | One half |
| ¾ | BE | 190 | frac34 | Three quarters |
| ¿ | BF | 191 | iquest | Inverted question mark |
| À | C0 | 192 | Agrave | Capital letter A with grave |
| Á | C1 | 193 | Aacute | Capital letter A with acute |

| Â | C2 | 194 | Acirc | Capital letter A with circumflex |
|---|---|---|---|---|
| Ã | C3 | 195 | Atilde | Capital letter A with tilde |
| Ä | C4 | 196 | Auml | Capital letter A with umlaut |
| Å | C5 | 197 | Aring | Capital letter A with ring |
| Æ | C6 | 198 | AElig | Capital AE ligature |
| Ç | C7 | 199 | Ccedil | Capital letter C with cedilla |
| È | C8 | 200 | Egrave | Capital letter E with grave |
| É | C9 | 201 | Eacute | Capital letter E with acute |
| Ê | CA | 202 | Ecirc | Capital letter E with circumflex |
| Ë | CB | 203 | Euml | Capital letter E with umlaut |
| Ì | CC | 204 | Igrave | Capital letter I with grave |
| Í | CD | 205 | Iacute | Capital letter I with acute |
| Î | CE | 206 | Icirc | Capital letter I with circumflex |
| Ï | CF | 207 | Iuml | Capital letter I with umlaut |
| Ð | D0 | 208 | ETH | Capital letter ETH |
| Ñ | D1 | 209 | Ntilde | Capital letter N with tilde |
| Ò | D2 | 210 | Ograve | Capital letter O with grave |
| Ó | D3 | 211 | Oacute | Capital letter O with acute |
| Ô | D4 | 212 | Ocirc | Capital letter O with circumflex |
| Õ | D5 | 213 | Otilde | Capital letter O with tilde |
| Ö | D6 | 214 | Ouml | Capital letter O with umlaut |
| × | D7 | 215 | times | Multiplication sign |
| Ø | D8 | 216 | Oslash | Capital letter O with slash |
| Ù | D9 | 217 | Ugrave | Capital letter U with grave |
| Ú | DA | 218 | Uacute | Capital letter U with acute |

| Character | Hexadecimal Code | Decimal Code | Name | Description  (continued) |
|---|---|---|---|---|
| Û | DB | 219 | Ucirc | Capital letter U with circumflex |
| Ü | DC | 220 | Uuml | Capital letter U with umlaut |
| Ý | DD | 221 | Yacute | Capital letter Y with acute |
| Þ | DE | 222 | THORN | Capital letter THORN |
| ß | DF | 223 | szlig | Small letter sharp s |
| à | E0 | 224 | agrave | Small letter a with grave |
| á | E1 | 225 | aacute | Small letter a with acute |
| â | E2 | 226 | acirc | Small letter a with circumflex |
| ã | E3 | 227 | atilde | Small letter a with tilde |
| ä | E4 | 228 | auml | Small letter a with umlaut |
| å | E5 | 229 | aring | Small letter a with ring |
| æ | E6 | 230 | aelig | Small letter ae ligature |
| ç | E7 | 231 | ccedil | Small letter c with cedilla |
| è | E8 | 232 | egrave | Small letter e with grave |
| é | E9 | 233 | eacute | Small letter e with acute |
| ê | EA | 234 | ecirc | Small letter e with circumflex |
| ë | EB | 235 | euml | Small letter e with umlaut |
| ì | EC | 236 | igrave | Small letter i with grave |
| í | ED | 237 | iacute | Small letter i with acute |
| î | EE | 238 | icirc | Small letter i with circumflex |
| ï | EF | 239 | iuml | Small letter i with umlaut |
| ð | F0 | 240 | eth | Small eth |
| ñ | F1 | 241 | ntilde | Small letter n with tilde |
| ò | F2 | 242 | ograve | Small letter o with grave |
| ó | F3 | 243 | oacute | Small letter o with acute |

| ô | F4 | 244 | ocirc | Small letter o with circumflex |
|---|---|---|---|---|
| õ | F5 | 245 | otilde | Small letter o with tilde |
| ö | F6 | 246 | ouml | Small letter o with umlaut |
| ÷ | F7 | 247 | divide | Division sign |
| ø | F8 | 248 | oslash | Small letter o with slash |
| ù | F9 | 249 | ugrave | Small letter u with grave |
| ú | FA | 250 | uacute | Small letter u with acute |
| û | FB | 251 | ucirc | Small letter u with circumflex |
| ü | FC | 252 | uuml | Small letter u with umlaut |
| ý | FD | 253 | yacute | Small letter y with acute |
| þ | FE | 254 | thorn | Small letter thorn |
| ÿ | FF | 255 | yuml | Small letter y with umlaut |

Sources:

✗ "C0 Controls and Basic Latin Range: 0000-007F." Excerpt from the character code tables and list of character names for the Unicode standard, version 3.0., by Unicode, Inc. URL: http://www.unicode.org/charts/PDF/U0000.pdf

✗ "C1 Controls and Latin-1 Supplement Range: 0080-00FF." Excerpt from the character code tables and list of character names for the Unicode standard, version 3.0., by Unicode, Inc. URL: http://www.unicode.org/charts/PDF/U0080.pdf

✗ "ISO 8859-1 character set overview" by Web Design Group. URL: http://www.htmlhelp.com/reference/charset/

# *Glossary*

**\b** A JavaScript escape sequence that inserts a backspace.

**\r** A JavaScript escape sequence that inserts a carriage return.

**\"** A JavaScript escape sequence that inserts a double quotation mark.

**\f** A JavaScript escape sequence that inserts a form feed.

**\n** A JavaScript escape sequence that inserts a new line.

**\'** A JavaScript escape sequence that inserts a single quotation mark or apostrophe.

**\t** A JavaScript escape sequence that inserts a tab.

**+** Add. A mathematical operator that adds two numbers together. When applied to one or more strings, it acts as the concatenation operator.

**+=** Add by value. An assignment operator that adds the right numeric operand to the left numeric operand and assigns the result to the left operand. It becomes "concatenate by value" if applied to one or more strings.

**&&** AND. A logical binary operator that returns `true` only if both operands are true. Otherwise it returns `false`.

**+** Concatenate. A string operator that concatenates the second operand to the end of the first. If applied to two numbers, it becomes the addition operator and adds the two operands.

**+=** Concatenate by value. An assignment operator that concatenates the string on the left to the end of the string on the right and assigns the result to the left operand. If one of the operands is a number, it is automatically converted to a string.

**--** Decrement. Can be placed either before (pre-decrement) or after (post-decrement) an operator is performed and subtracts 1 from the operand. Pre-decrement decrements the operand by 1 and then performs the evaluation. Post-decrement evaluates the operand's current value and then decrements it by 1.

**/**  Divide. The division operator. This arithmetic operator divides the first operand by the second and returns the result. JavaScript automatically converts numeric strings to numbers. If one or both operands are non-numeric strings, then NaN is returned.

**/=**  Divide by value. This assignment operator divides the left operand by the right and assigns the result to the left operand. JavaScript automatically converts numeric strings to numbers to perform the operation. If one or both of the operands is a non-numeric string, the left operand is set to NaN.

**==**  Equal to. A comparison operator that compares two values and returns false if they are not equal and true if they are. If one operand is a number, JavaScript automatically converts the other operand to a number to perform the comparison. For example, 9 == "9" returns true.

**=**  Equals or gets. An assignment operator that assigns the result of the expression on the right to the variable on the left.

**===**  Equivalent to. A comparison operator that returns true if the two operands are both equal to each other and of the same data type; otherwise returns false. For example, 8 === "8" returns false.

**>**  Greater than. A comparison operator that returns true if the left operand is greater than the right. JavaScript automatically converts numeric strings to numbers to perform the comparison.

**>=**  Greater than or equal to. A comparison operator that returns true if the left operand is greater than or equal to the right. JavaScript automatically converts numeric strings to numbers to perform the comparison.

**++**  Increment. Can be placed either before (pre-increment) or after (post-increment) an operator. If before (pre-), the operand is incremented and then evaluated. If after (post-), the operand is first evaluated and then incremented.

**<**  Less than. A comparison operator that compares two operands and returns true if the left operand is less than the right. Numeric strings are automatically converted to numbers for the comparison.

**<=**  Less than or equal to. A comparison operator that compares two operands and returns true if the left operand is less than or equal to the right. Numeric strings are automatically converted to numbers for the comparison.

**:**  Line label. Primarily used in switch statements to label a case and continue a program execution at the matching case line label.

**\***  Multiply. The multiplication operator. This arithmetic operator multiplies the first operand by the second and returns the result. If one or both operands is a numeric string, JavaScript automatically converts the string to a number in order to perform the operation. If it is used on one or more strings that cannot be converted to a number, it returns NaN.

**\*=**  Multiply by value. An assignment operator that multiplies the left operand by the right and assigns the result to the left operand. JavaScript automatically converts numeric strings.

**%**  Modulus. The remainder operator. A mathematical operator that divides the first number, the dividend, by the second number, the divisor, and returns the remainder.

**%**  Modulus by value. An assignment operator, modulus by value treats the operand on the left of the operator as the dividend and the operand on the right as the divisor. It then performs integer division and assigns the result to the left operand.

**–**  Negation operator. Written as -n, where n is the value negated.

**!**  NOT . A logical operator that turns a true Boolean value into a false value and vice versa.

**!=** Not equal to. A comparison operator that compares two values and returns `true` if they are not equal to each other and `false` if they are. If one operand is a number, JavaScript automatically converts the other operand to a number to perform the comparison. For example, 7 ! = "7" returns `false`.

**!==** Not equivalent to. A comparison operator that compares two values and returns `true` if they are not equal to each other or not of the same data type. If the two values are of the same data type and equal to each other, !== returns `false`.

**||** OR. A logical operator that returns `true` if one or both operands evaluate to `true`; it returns `false` only if both operands evaluate to `false`.

**–** Subtract. When applied to numbers or numeric strings, the subtraction operator subtracts the second number from the first and returns the results. JavaScript converts numeric strings automatically and then performs the subtraction. If used on non-numeric strings, that is, strings that cannot be converted to numbers, it returns `NaN`.

**–=** Subtract by value. An assignment operator that subtracts the right operand from the left and assigns the result to the left operand. JavaScript automatically converts numeric strings to numbers to perform the operation.

**abort** An event that occurs when a visitor stops loading an image, perhaps by following a link or clicking on the Stop button.

**action attribute** An attribute of a <form> tag that specifies the URL to take action when the form is submitted.

**active image** An input tag whose type = image. It allows the programmer to use an image in place of a submit button.

**Active Server Pages** A server-side programming technology by Microsoft.

**alert dialog** A dialog box launched by calling a `window` object's `alert` method. It displays a message.

**Anchor object** A property of the document created with the <a> tag by assigning it a `name` attribute.

**anchor pseudo-class selectors** CSS selectors that can differentiate among an unfollowed link, a visited link, an active link, and a link that the mouse is hovering over.

**anchor pseudo-classes** `a:link`, `a:visited`, `a:active`, and `a:hover`. They can be used as CSS selectors to apply style rules to unfollowed links, visited links, active links, and moused-over links, respectively.

**Apache** A Web server software package originally for Unix-based machines. Today Apache comes in versions for both Unix and Windows.

**applet** Small Java program that can run in a Web page using the <applet> tag.

**Area object** A property of the `document` object created by any areas in an image map using the <area> tag.

**argument** Also known as a function parameter, a data value or data reference that can be passed to a function for it to work on or use.

**arithmetic operators** Also known as mathematical operators. These are the operators that perform mathematical computations.

**array** A collection of data values, usually of the same data type. Individual elements of an array are referenced by the array's name followed by a positive integer in square brackets. Indexing begins at 0. For example, `student [0]` accesses the value of the first element in the array. An array's `length` property returns the number of items in the array.

**Array ( )**   A built-in constructor function that, when called with the new operator, creates an array object. For example, var *arrayName*=new Array ( ).

**array literal**   A list of zero or more expressions enclosed in brackets ( [ ] ). Each expression represents an array element.

**Array object**   An object of type Array, usually created with the Array ( ) constructor.

**ASCII (American Standard Code for Information Interchange)**   A character set that represents each alphabetic, numeric, or special character as a seven-bit binary. In the ASCII character set, only 128 characters are defined.

**ASP**   See *Active Server Pages.*

**assignment operators**   Those operators that assign a value to a variable, object, or property.

**assignment statement**   An operation that assigns a value to a variable. The most often used assignment operator is = (equals).

**associative array**   An array indexed by a word, rather than by an ordinal number.

**base target**   Defines the default target for a Web document's links. It overrides _self, the default target.

**batch validation**   A validation routine that is performed all at once when a form is submitted.

**blur**   An event that occurs when a visitor or a script removes focus from an element that has focus.

**Boolean**   A truth value. It specifies whether something is true or false. There are only two possible Boolean values: true and false. Boolean is a primitive data type.

**break**   Usually used in loops and switch statements. It immediately ends execution of the current control structure and continues execution of the first line after the control structure.

**Brendan Eich**   Creator of the JavaScript language.

**browser**   A program that allows users to view Web sites and access other services on the Internet.

**browser detection**   The process of determining which browser the visitor is using.

**browser session**   Begins when the user opens the browser and ends when the browser is closed.

**built-in functions**   Those functions predefined by the JavaScript language.

**button**   A clickable or pressable display element created with the HTML <input> tag by setting the tag's type property to button. It is often used in conjunction with JavaScript to create navigation buttons or execute JavaScript functions.

**Button object**   A property of the form object created by an <input> tag in the document whose type attribute equals button.

**byte code**   A computer object code that is processed by a program's virtual machine, usually the Java virtual machine. The virtual machine converts each basic instruction into specific instructions that the computer's processor can understand.

**call a function**   To invoke execution of a function by referencing its name, followed by any required or optional parameters in parentheses.

**Cascading Style Sheet Positioning**   An addition to CSS1 that allows Web developers to position HTML elements on the screen, set their z-coordinate, and make those elements visible or invisible.

**Cascading Style Sheets**   A technology that allows Web developers to specify the presentation details of a Web document. It provides a rich selection of presentation effects that can be applied to all HTML elements, such as color, background, margins, and borders.

**case insensitive** Indicates that capitalization does not make a difference in the content of the writing, e.g., `bgcolor` is the same as `bgColor`.

**case sensitive** Indicates that capitalization does matter, e.g., `bgColor` is not the same as `bgcolor`.

**case statement** Used in the switch control structure. Statements in a particular case execute when the switch value matches the code label.

**ccTLD** Country code top-level domain. It is a top-level domain name, usually two letters long, that belongs to a particular country. For instance, .us = United States, .fr = France, .it = Italy, etc.

**CGI scripting** The process of writing CGI scripts.

**CGI scripts** Often written in Perl, Practical Extraction and Report Language, CGI scripts are programs that run server-side and are capable of interacting with other applications and server resources. CGI scripts can be written in any language that supports the Common Gateway Interface protocol, including Perl, Java, C++, and Tcl.

**change** An event that occurs when a `blur` event occurs and the value of a form field has changed from the value it had when it first received focus.

**check digit** A digit added to a number that helps validate the authenticity of the number.

**checkbox** Allows the visitor to check any or all of the values that apply in a group of responses.

**checkbox object** A property of the `form` object created by any HTML <input> tags whose `type = "checkbox"`.

**`class` attribute** An attribute that can be added to almost all HTML elements in the HTML 4 specification that allows programmers to classify one or more HTML elements and to provide context that cannot be otherwise provided by an existing HTML tag. CSS rules can then be applied to elements of a particular class.

**class selector** Used to apply style rules to the content classified with a `class` attribute.

**click** An event that occurs when the visitor clicks with a mouse on a link or form element or presses the Enter key when a link or form element has focus.

**click-stream information** Data that describes the path taken by a visitor as he or she browses through a Web site.

**client** In a client-server relationship, the computer or program that is making a request of a server.

**client-pull** A dynamic document mechanism whereby a Web page contains a directive, usually in a <meta> tag, that re-requests a page after a defined amount of time, e.g., every seven seconds.

**client-side form validation** A validation routine whose processing is performed by the client machine. This makes the process fast and responsive. If the visitor has turned off JavaScript support in the browser, the form validation cannot be run, which could result in invalid or missing data.

**Client-Side JavaScript (CSJS)** Extends the JavaScript core language to provide access to browser and Web document objects via the Document Object Model (DOM) supported by a particular browser. Client-Side JavaScript is, by far, the most popular form of JavaScript.

**client-side script** A script whose processing and execution is performed by the client's machine.

**color-coding** A feature of many text editors that enables a programmer to differentiate between different types of text within an HTML document. For instance, commented-on lines may appear in gray.

**comment** A short description within a JavaScript script or HTML file that does not change the outcome of the document.

**Common Gateway Interface (CGI)** A protocol that specifies the details of passing data between a client and a server or a server and other programs and vice versa.

**comparison operators** Those operators that compare two values or expressions and return a Boolean value indicating the truth of the comparison.

**compile** Translate a program into machine code and store it for later execution. When the compiled program is run, it executes immediately without further need of interpretation. This makes the program both fast and responsive.

**composite data type** A data type that is made up of a combination of data, usually of various types, e.g., an object is a composite data type.

**condition** An expression that evaluates to a Boolean value, either `true` or `false`. Most control structures rely on a condition to operate.

**conditional statement** Evaluates an expression and returns one of two values depending on whether the result is true or false. If the condition evaluates to `true`, the conditional statement returns the first value; if the condition evaluates to `false`, it returns the second value.

**confirm dialog** A dialog box launched by a window's `confirm` method that presents the visitor with a message and two choices, OK and Cancel. If OK is pressed, `confirm` returns `true`; if Cancel is pressed, `confirm` returns `false`.

**constant** A symbolic name that represents a value that does not change during a program's execution.

**constructor** An object-oriented programming term that refers to a function or method that specifies how to create and initialize an object.

**constructor function** A function that tells the interpreter how to create a particular type of object, including what properties and methods to assign to it. Constructor function names usually begin with a capital letter.

**contextual selectors** Similar to simple selectors in that they usually apply to HTML elements, but HTML elements in the context of another HTML element. Contextual selectors are more specific than simple selectors. For instance, em indicates emphasized text that is, itself, within a paragraph.

**`continue` statement** Used in `for`, `while`, and `do...while` loops to skip execution of the remaining iteration and continue executing at the next iteration.

**control structure** Allows the programmer to control the flow of programs and make them capable of reacting dynamically to a variety of conditions.

**cookie** A computer science term that is used to describe an opaque piece of data held by an intermediary. In the case of cookies on the Web, the intermediary is the hard drive on the visitor's computer.

**Core JavaScript** The basic JavaScript language. It includes the language's basic rules, data types, and control structures. ECMAScript is modeled after Core JavaScript.

**Cross-Browser Dynamic HTML** Scripts that utilize DHTML and work in all DHTML-capable browsers.

**cross-platform** Describes the ability to run on a variety of operating systems and computer types.

**CSS** See *Cascading Style Sheets.*

**CSSP** See *Cascading Style Sheet Positioning.*

**custom object** An object defined by a programmer and not already built into the JavaScript programming language.

**Date ()**   A built-in constructor function that, when called with the new operator, creates a Date object.

**Date object**   A Core JavaScript object that holds a date in terms of the number of milliseconds since 0:00:00 January 1, 1970.

**debugger**   A program that helps a programmer find and eradicate bugs in a computer program.

**debugging**   Finding and eliminating coding errors in a script or program.

**declaration**   Part of a stylesheet rule, made up of two parts: a CSS property and a value that specifies what presentation effect to set and how.

**declare**   Tell the computer to set aside space in memory to hold the value of a variable or an object.

**declare a variable**   Use the var keyword to instruct the computer to set aside space in memory for a value and give that space in memory a symbolic name or label that the programmer can use to refer to that variable during program execution.

**delete operator**   A special operator that allows a programmer to completely remove an element from memory. It applies only to arrays and objects.

**dense array**   An array that is initialized or filled at declaration.

**design phase**   The Web development phase during which a plan is created about how to solve the problem, answer the needs, and reach the goals determined during the requirements analysis phase.

**DHTML**   See *Dynamic HTML.*

**dialog box**   Small pop-up boxes that display a message and allow the visitor to respond in some way. JavaScript supports three dialogs that programmers can generate as needed: alert, confirm, and prompt.

**do...while**   A control structure whose contents always execute at least once because the condition is not tested until after the statement block. This is called a post test.

**document object**   A property of a window object indicating the current HTML document loaded therein.

**Document Object Model (DOM)**   A template built into a browser that specifies all of the objects and properties in a Web document that the browser can identify, access, and manipulate, plus all of the methods you can perform with or on those objects. The Document Object Model represents possibilities. The W3C has also written a DOM specification that describes all of the objects, properties, and methods a browser should support in order to be compliant with that specification.

**Document Object Model, Level 2**   The second DOM specification written by the W3C. DOM2 is more specific than its predecessor in terms of specifying appropriate references to document objects by tag names, IDs, etc.

**DOM**   See *Document Object Model.*

**DOM2**   See *Document Object Model, Level 2.*

**dot notation**   A JavaScript entry used to refer to an object's properties and methods.

**Dreamweaver**   A WYSIWYG (what you see is what you get) text editor by Macromedia. Dreamweaver is quickly becoming the standard WYSIWYG tool for Web developers.

**Dynamic HTML (DHTML)**   A combination of Hypertext Markup Language (HTML), Cascading Style Sheets (CSS), and JavaScript used to create animations and special effects in an HTML document.

**dynamically typed**   A programming language is said to be dynamically typed when the data type of its variables can change on the fly.

**ECMA**   The European Computer Manufacturers Association.

**ECMAScript**   The European Computer Manufacturers Association's cross-platform scripting language standard for the Internet, also called ECMA-262. Version 1 of the standard was based on Netscape's Core JavaScript 1.1. ECMA released version 3 in December of 1999.

**elements**   A property of a `form` object that represents an array of all `form` elements contained in the form.

**Emacs**   Short for *editing macros*. Emacs is a Unix-based text editor created by Richard Stallman at MIT using the LISP programming language. It is primarily used for writing programs and scripts and has more built-in commands than vi. It is not a simple program by any means—it is more complicated and slower than vi—but it has more capabilities. It can even start a compiler and handle email from within the editor.

**error**   An event that is rarely handled. It's associated with both images and windows and occurs when a JavaScript syntax or runtime error is encountered.

**escape**   To preface a character with a backslash (\) in order to escape its special meaning to JavaScript and treat it as a literal. For example, \" causes a quotation mark to be treated as a literal rather than as a delimiter for a string. Also, to give a normal character special meaning in JavaScript. For example, \n inserts a new line character.

**event handlers**   The mechanisms that allow programmers to capture and respond to an event with a scripting language.

**event model**   Specifies the user and browser supported by a particular browser.

**events**   Occurrences generated by a Web browser, such as loading a document, or by a visitor, such as moving the mouse or clicking a button.

**expression**   Any valid set of literals, variables, operators, and expressions that evaluates to a single value. The resulting single value can be a number, string, Boolean, or special value (`null`, `undefined`, or `NaN`).

**expression evaluation**   The process of determining the value of an expression.

**extend**   To add a property or method to an object.

**Extensible Markup Language (XML)**   A flexible language for creating common information formats and sharing them on the Web. XML is a subset of SGML that is simpler and easier to use. XML was recommended by the W3C. Its goal is to enable generic SGML to be served, received, and processed on the Web as is now possible with HTML. It is a self-describing language, that is, XML not only provides data, it describes that data as well.

**external links**   Links that request documents outside of the current site.

**external stylesheet**   A plain text document that has a .css extension and contains style rules.

**flags**   A special character placed after the closing slash (/) of a regular expression to modify the function of any method that uses that regular expression. There are three flags: g (global match), which instructs a method to check for all instances of the regular expression in the string; i (ignore case), which instructs a method to ignore case; and m (match over multiple lines), which instructs a method to do as its name implies. Flags can be used in any combination to suit your needs.

**floating point**   An integer, positive or negative, that has a decimal.

**focus**   An event that occurs when the visitor or a script gives focus to a window, frame, form element, or link.

**for loop**  A control structure whose contents execute a set number of times depending on an initializer that sets up the starting value of the loop counter, a condition that specifies when to stop execution of the loop, and an update statement that updates the value of the loop counter between iterations.

**forking**  The process of executing the appropriate code according to a particular condition.

**form**  An HTML display element that can gather or display data in various formats.

**form elements**  Form fields and controls.

**Form object**  A property of the document object created by an HTML <form> tag that usually contains various form fields and controls.

**form validation**  The process of checking the data entered into a form to make certain that all required data has been provided and that the data submitted is of the proper format or length.

**frame**  A subset of a window.

**frameset**  An HTML element that allows a programmer to break a window up into multiple frames arranged by either rows or columns.

**framing**  The process of loading someone else's Web document or frameset within your own frameset. Also, when someone else loads your Web documents or frameset within their own frameset.

**FTP client**  A program used to access an FTP server in order to upload, download, view, rename, or delete files. Sophisticated FTP clients can even set file permissions and perform other useful actions.

**function**  A series of JavaScript statements, usually defined at the beginning of a JavaScript program, whose execution is deferred until the function is called. A particular function may be called many times during the execution of a program.

**Function object**  A core JavaScript object that allows every defined function or method to be accessed as an object with associated properties.

**function parameter**  Also known as an argument, a data value or data reference that can be passed to the function for it to work on or use.

**generic top-level domain (gTLD)**  A top-level domain name. Currently there are 13: .com, .org, .net, .edu, .mil, .gov, .biz, .name, .pro, .info, .museum, .aero, and .logo.

**get method**  One way that form data can be sent. This method appends form data to the end of the URL specified in the action attribute of the <form> tag.

**global variable**  Any variable defined outside of a function.

**gTLD**  See *generic top-level domain.*

**hidden**  A form element that has a name and holds a text value but does not appear in the browser window as part of the form. It is hidden from the visitor's view.

**Hidden object**  A property of a form element representing an HTML <input> element whose type = "hidden".

**History object**  An object representing the browser's history list.

**HomeSite**  A full-featured HTML editor by Macromedia. (Originally by Allaire, then Macromedia bought the company.)

**HTML**  See *Hypertext Markup Language.*

**Hypertext Markup Language**   A markup language meant to provide structure for a document and context for its content. It is the language used to create Web documents.

**id selector**   Used primarily to identify positioned elements. The id attribute was added to the HTML specification to accommodate the need to isolate a single element. While a particular class selector can be applied to multiple HTML elements of the same or various types, a particular id can be applied to only one HTML element.

**if**   A control structure that tells the script to perform an action or set of actions only if a particular condition is true.

**if...else**   A control structure that instructs the script to perform one of two actions, or sets of actions, depending on some condition. If the condition evaluates to true, the first set of statements contained in the if block are executed, otherwise, the second set of statements, contained in the else block, are executed.

**IIS**   Internet Information Server. A Web server software created by Microsoft.

**Image ()**   A built-in constructor function that, when called with the new operator, creates an Image object.

**Image object**   A property of the document object that represents an image displayed in the document with an <img> tag. An Image object can also be preloaded in memory using the Image constructor function to declare the object and then assigning the Image object's src property a value.

**image rollover**   An effect that changes an image's src property in order to display a different image in response to some user event, such as the visitor moving the mouse over an image link.

**image submit button**   Created with the <input> tag by setting its type property to image. When a form is submitted with an image submit button, the coordinates clicked on in the image are sent as well.

**implementation phase**   The Web development phase during which the actual coding is performed, writing JavaScript and HTML as necessary and testing and debugging along the way.

**index**   An array element's index is its numbered position in the array, beginning with zero.

**initialize**   To assign a variable a default or starting value.

**instance**   A particular occurrence of a object.

**instance hierarchy**   A hierarchical listing in the browser's memory of all objects created as the document is read and interpreted by the browser.

**integer**   A whole number with no decimal.

**internationalized domain names**   Domain names in 39 different character sets for over 350 languages that have been proposed by Network Solutions for adoption by ICAAN.

**Internet Explorer**   A Web browser created by Microsoft.

**Internet Information Server**   See *IIS*.

**interpret**   To translate a program's statements, line by line, into machine code, which can be understood by a particular type of computer, before executing the program, every time the program is run.

**isNaN ()**   A built-in function that returns true if the parameter is not a number and false if it is a number.

**ISO 8859-1 (Latin-1) character set**   A character set by the International Organization for Standardization that represents each character as an eight-bit (one byte) binary number and supports 256 values. The first 128 values are a direct match of the ASCII character set. The ISO 8859 character sets have been adopted for use on the Internet (MIME) and the Web (HTML and HTTP).

**Java**   A full-fledged, object-oriented programming language created by Sun Microsystems.

**JavaScript**   An object-based programming language created by Brendan Eich of Netscape Communications to enhance Web documents with interactivity and dynamism.

**Jscript**   Microsoft's version of JavaScript.

**layer**   A proprietary object in Netscape Navigator browsers that represents an absolutely positioned element created with the proprietary <layer> tag or CSS. In DHTML terms, layer has come to mean an absolutely positioned element created with CSS rules and HTML.

**lexicographical**   Describes an alphabetical ordering of elements, as in a dictionary or telephone book, by comparing them *as strings*. For instance, `"50"` comes before `"6"`.

**library**   A group of reusable functions, usually related to each other in some way.

**line numbers**   An important tool found in the best text editors. Error messages usually report the line number on which the error occurred. Being able to quickly locate that line in your text editor is an invaluable feature.

**Link object**   A property of the `document` object created by any <a> tag with an `href` attribute.

**Linux**   A Unix-based operating system created by Linus Torvalds and associates at the University of Helsinki in Finland. They also made use of system components developed by members of the Free Software Foundation for the GNU project.

**literal**   Any value that can be expressed verbatim; a fixed value taken in its basic sense, exactly as written.

**load**   An event that occurs for a document when the browser has retrieved all of the content between the <body> tags of a document or all of the frames within a <frameset> tag. A load event occurs on an image when the image is displayed.

**local variables**   Variables defined inside of a function, using the `var` keyword.

**Location object**   An object representing the current document's location (URL).

**logical operators**   Also known as Boolean operators, those operators that take Boolean values as operands and return a Boolean value indicating the truth of the relationship.

**loop**   A control structure that iterates. See *for loop*, `while` *loop*, and `do...while`.

**loosely typed**   A language is loosely typed when it is not necessary to declare the type of data that will be stored in a variable before you use it.

**LUHN formula**   Created by a group of mathematicians in the 1960s. It is a simple algorithm that uses a check digit to validate the authenticity of a number. Major credit card companies quickly utilized this public-domain algorithm to validate credit card numbers.

**machine code**   Programming instructions understandable by a particular type of computer.

**magic target names**   Special target names recognized by HTML. They are `_blank`, `_parent`, `_top`, and `_self`.

**mailto URL**   A URL that starts a message to an email address.

**Math object**   A built-in object whose properties are mostly mathematical constants such as PI and whose methods perform mathematical computations.

**metacharacter** A character or character combination that is used to specify a pattern, a modifier, or how to process the characters that follow it. For instance, the backslash character indicates that the character that follows it should be treated in a special way: \n means treat it as a new line, \" means treat it as a literal quotation mark, and \' means treat it as a literal single quote or apostrophe.

**method** A function associated with a particular object that defines an action that can be performed with or on that object.

**method attribute** An attribute of the <form> tag that specifies how form data is sent.

**MIME** See multipurpose Internet mail extensions.

**mimeType object** A property of both the Navigator and the Plug-in objects. Each mimeType object represents a MIME type supported by a particular browser.

**modulus 10** The algorithm preferred by most major credit card companies, also known as the LUHN formula.

**mouseOut** An event that occurs when the mouse is moved off of a link or other document object.

**mouseOver** An event that occurs when the mouse is moved over a link or other document object.

**multi-line comment** An inactive programming statement that gives in-depth information about the script. Slash star (/*) begins a multi-line comment and (*/) ends it.

**multipurpose Internet mail extensions** Defines the generic and specific file type of a file with a particular extension. For example, a file with an .htm or .html extension has a MIME type of text/html, which means its generic type is a text file and its more specific type is a Hypertext Markup Language file.

**NaN** Special JavaScript value that means "not a number."

**navigator object** An object that represents the Web browser itself.

**Netscape Navigator** A Web browser by Netscape Communications. It was the first Windows-compatible Web browser on the market.

**Netscape Navigator 2** The first Web browser to support JavaScript.

**Netscape Navigator 6** The first Web browser to have 99%+ support for W3C specifications, including HTML 4, CSS1, and DOM2.

**new operator** A special operator that, when used in conjunction with a constructor function, creates a new object of the type indicated by the constructor.

**null** A special value meaning no value.

**number** A primitive data type; any numeric value, be it a floating-point number (float) such as 4.17 or −32.518 or a whole number (integer) such as −55 or 187.

**Number object** A core JavaScript object representing any numeric value.

**object** A composite data type that is composed of zero or more pieces of data, each of which may be of a different basic data type. An item or thing with attributes or properties that describe it and make it unique. An object also has methods, which are actions you can perform with or on the object.

**object detection** The process of determining if a particular object is supported.

**object wrappers** A JavaScript process that causes a variable to temporarily become an appropriate object for the duration of a method call; then the "object" is discarded from memory.

**object-based** Describes a programming language that is based on objects but lacks the intricacies of a true object-oriented language. JavaScript is an object-based language.

**object-oriented programming** More complicated than object-based, object-oriented programs, like those created with Java, create reusable software objects that can be included in other programs.

**onAbort** A rarely used event handler that can be attached only to an image. It is invoked when the visitor stops the loading of an image.

**onBlur** An event handler that is invoked when a blur event occurs. It is often used to erase the hint shown by an onFocus event handler.

**onChange** An event handler that is invoked when a change event occurs. It is often used to perform calculations or to validate field contents whenever a field's value has changed.

**onFocus** An event handler that is invoked when a focus event occurs. It is often used to display a hint for a form field entry in the status bar.

**onLoad** An event handler that is invoked when a load event occurs. It is often used to display alert messages, pop up windows, and call image preload functions or other document-preparation routines.

**onSubmit** An event handler that can be implemented only on a form when it is submitted. It is most often used to call form-validation routines.

**onUnload** An event handler that is invoked when an unload event occurs. It is often used to display messages or pop up a window when a visitor or the browser requests a new page in the same browser window.

**Opera** A Web browser that began life in 1994 as a research project for the national phone company in Norway and is now considered to be the third most popular Web browser in use today.

**operators** The workers in expressions, either unary or binary.

**option** A possible selection in a select list.

**Option object** A property of a select list that indicates an option created with the <option> tag.

**parallel arrays** Two or more arrays whose elements are related to each other by their respective positions.

**parse** To break apart into usable chunks.

**parseFloat ()** A built-in JavaScript function that converts a string to a floating-point number.

**parseInt ()** A built-in JavaScript function that converts a string to an integer.

**password** A form element that is essentially like a text box in its appearance and attributes; however, it displays asterisks instead of letters or numbers, so no one can read what is being typed. It is created with the <input> tag by setting its type attribute to password.

**Password object** A property of a form object that represents an HTML password element created with an <input> tag whose type = password.

**Perl** See *Practical Extraction and Report Language*.

**Persistent Client-Side HTTP Object** Netscape's formal name for a browser cookie.

**PHP** Originally an acronym for personal home page, it now means hypertext preprocessor. It is a server-side technology that preprocesses hypertext documents and can process forms and perform other server-side programming activities.

**Pico** An acronym for *pine composer*. Pico is a display-oriented text editor developed from the Unix Emacs editor for use with the pine email system. It is primarily used for writing scripts, short notes, and email messages and features paragraph justification, cut-and-paste, and a spelling checker. Unlike most other Unix text editors, Pico was designed for the sake of "simplicity in editing." It is also available as a separate, stand-alone program.

**plug-in**  A program that adds capabilities to a Web browser. Some examples are Shockwave, Flash, QuickTime, RealAudio, RealVideo, and Windows Media Player.

**Plug-in object**  An object that represents a particular plug-in supported by a Web browser. Each Plug-in object contains an array of the mimeType supported by that plug-in.

**pop-up window**  A small window that appears to display contents on top of the current browser window.

**positioned element**  Any HTML element, usually a division, that has been positioned using the CSS position property.

**post method**  Causes form data to be sent separately from the actual call to the URL specified in the form's action attribute. Because the form data is sent under separate cover, there is no limit to the amount of data that can be sent.

**Practical Extraction and Report Language**  Originally created by Larry Wall as a scripting language to extract data and write reports. Because of its prevalence on Unix servers, the first to support Web server software, it was quickly adopted by Web developers for writing server-side CGI programs.

**preloading**  The process of creating an image object in the <head> of the document and assigning a URL to its src property, causing the browser to request the image from the server, thus making it available in memory for use in a rollover, slideshow, or other effect.

**primitive data types**  The three basic data types supported by JavaScript: number, string, and Boolean.

**prompt dialog**  A dialog box invoked by a call to a window's prompt method that presents the visitor with a message for a text entry field in order to gather data.

**properties**  Attributes that describe a particular object.

**prototype**  A built-in property that all JavaScript objects have. It specifies the constructor from which an object was created.

**radio button**  A type of form input element that allows a visitor to select only one response from a set.

**Radio object**  A property of a form object that represents a radio button created with an <input> tag by setting the type attribute to radio. All radio buttons in a set must have the same name for the radio button set to function correctly.

**real-time validation**  A validation routine that is performed real-time upon completion of a field entry. The visitor is alerted as soon as an error is made.

**recursion**  When a function or method calls itself into use. It can do so once or more than once.

**RegExp object**  An object that represents a regular expression.

**regular expression**  A pattern, usually delimited by slashes (/) and defined with a combination of characters and metacharacters. It is used as a matching device against strings in various RegExp and String methods.

**regular expression literal**  Any regular expression. It is a series of characters and metacharacters, delimited by slashes (/) and followed by optional flags, that represents a pattern.

**requirements analysis phase**  The Web development phase during which the project's requirements and goals are specified and determined.

**reset**  An event associated only with forms. It occurs when the contents of a form are cleared. Both visitors and scripts can generate a reset event.

**reset button**   A form element that, when activated, causes the contents of the form to clear, or reset. It is created with the <input> tag by setting the `type` to `reset`.

**Reset object**   A property of a `form` object representing a reset button created with HTML.

**return**   A special keyword in JavaScript that causes execution to return to the caller. It may return a value as well.

**saving state**   The process of preserving information about the current session as the user browses through documents on the site.

**screen object**   An object that represents the current computer screen.

**script**   A small program usually written in a special-purpose language like JavaScript or Perl.

**script development process**   A four-step process that takes a programmer from the conception of a program through the final product.

**scripting language**   A programming language that is generally easy to learn, easy to use, excellent for small routines and applications, and developed to serve a particular purpose.

**search and replace tools**   Utilities found in text editors that help programmers find and replace text in a document. The best editors support regular expressions as well.

**select**   An event that occurs when a visitor or script selects text in the document or a form field.

**select list**   A pull-down menu form element that provides a means of listing a lot of data in a very small space. It is created with the HTML <select> tag and a series of option tags.

**Select object**   A property of a `form` element that represents an HTML select list.

**selector**   Usually an HTML element such as body, div, h1, p, or em that specifies to what element(s) a particular CSS rule applies.

**server**   In a client-server relationship, the computer that answers requests or serves up data.

**server-push**   A technology by which a server sends a requested document while maintaining the connection and, after some period of time, delivers more data. The server has total control over when and how often data is sent.

**server-side form validation**   A form validation routine performed by the server that requires some type of server-side scripting. It is typically slower and less responsive than client-side validation. The major advantage is that the browser need not support client-side scripting or have it turned on in order for the form to be validated. The drawback is that it increases the load on the server, leaving it less free to handle other requests quickly.

**Server-Side JavaScript (SSJS)**   A Netscape server-side technology that uses JavaScript to provide access to databases, etc.

**server-side program**   A script that executes on the Web server using the resources and computing power of that computer. Server-side programs are more demanding on a server than client-side programs.

**server-side script**   See *server-side program*.

**session**   Begins when a user enters a Web site and ends when the user leaves the Web site.

**session cookie**   A cookie that will expire at the end of the browser session when the Web browser it was set in closes. It is also known as a transient cookie. See *cookie* for more details.

**SGML**   See *Standard Generalized Markup Language*.

**Simple Mail Transfer Protocol (SMTP)**   A protocol used to send email.

**simple selector**  Applies a style rule to a particular type of HTML element. body, div, h1, p, and em are all simple selectors.

**single-line comment**  Can be used to describe what each line of code is doing and to clarify new variables as they are introduced. It is designated by two forward slash marks (//). A single-line comment must reside entirely on one line.

**SMTP**  See *Simple Mail Transfer Protocol*.

**SMTP server**  A server that sends email messages using SMTP.

**special operators**  Operators that are used for different purposes and include `conditional`, `instanceof`, `in`, `delete`, `void`, `new`, `this`, `typeof`, and `comma` operators.

**splash page**  A Web page that shows a graphic or runs a Flash animation, then automatically takes the visitor on to the main Web site.

**Standard Generalized Markup Language**  A standard for specifying a document markup language or text set, also known as a document type definition (DTD). It is not actually a markup language itself, but rather a description of how to create one. HTML is an example of an SGML-based language.

**statement**  Any set of declarations, method calls, function calls, and expressions that performs some action.

**static frame**  A frame whose contents do not change after the frameset is loaded.

**status bar**  The bar across the bottom of a browser that informs the visitor about the current action. In Opera the status bar can be moved to different locations.

**string**  Any combination or *string* of letters, numbers, punctuation, etc. A string is always delimited by quotation marks. JavaScript allows the use of either double quotes or single quotes for delimiting strings. `String` is a primitive data type.

**string literal**  Any string; a series of characters delimited by quotation marks.

**String method**  A function that can be performed on strings, string objects, and string literals.

**String object**  An object representing a string.

**string operators**  Those operators that work on strings. There are only two: + and +=.

**strongly typed**  A programming language is said to be strongly typed when variables and their type must be declared before they can be used.

**style rule**  Describes one or more presentation instructions to apply to a particular selector. A style rule is made up of a selector and one or more declarations.

**stylesheet**  Lists presentation rules for an HTML document. A stylesheet is made up of one or more style rules.

**submit**  An event that occurs when a visitor or a script submits a form.

**submit button**  A form element that, when pressed, causes the form in which it resides to be submitted to the URL specified in the `action` attribute of the <form> tag.

**Submit object**  A property of a `form` object that represents an HTML submit button in that form.

**Sun Microsystems**  The creators of Java, the cross-platform programming language.

**support and maintenance phase**  The Web development phase that commences once a project is complete. During this phase the project is monitored and fixed as needed.

**switch**  A control structure that attempts to match a single value against multiple cases, transferring execution to the appropriately labeled case (the one that matches).

**switch statement**   See *switch*.

**syntax**   The special combination of words and symbols used by and recognized by a programming language to write and read programming commands.

**target attribute**   Specifies into which window or frame to load the document specified in the href attribute of a link.

**text box**   A form element that allows visitors to enter a single-line text entry. It is created with the <input> tag by setting the type attribute to text.

**Text object**   A property of a form representing an HTML text box.

**textarea**   A form element that is a multi-line text box, often with a scrollbar down the right side. It is created with the HTML <textarea> tag.

**Textarea object**   A property of a form representing an HTML textarea.

**this operator**   A special operator that always refers to the current object, wherever this happens to be.

**top-level domain (TLD)**   Either a generic or country code top-level domain name.

**toString()**   A built-in JavaScript function that converts object values or number literals into string literals.

**transient cookie**   See *session cookie*.

**typeof operator**   A special operator that returns the data type of the parameter provided to it as a string, for example, "number", "string", "Boolean", "object", or "undefined".

**unassigned**   Describes a variable that has not yet been given a value.

**undefined**   A special value indicating that a variable or object has not been declared or that it has been declared but not yet assigned a value.

**Unicode**   Unicode Worldwide Character Standard. It is a character set that covers the languages of the Americas, Europe, Middle East, Africa, India, Asia, and Pacifica, as well as some historic scripts and technical symbols. Unicode values range from 0 to 65,535. Its first 128 values match the ASCII character set and its first 256 match the ISO 8859-1 (Latin-1) character set.

**unload**   An event that occurs when the browser or visitor requests a new document in the current browser window.

**URL-encoding**   The format used by the browser when sending data to the server and vice versa. Any time you send data from the client to the server or vice versa, it must be URL-encoded. That's a requirement of HTTP. With JavaScript, there are three cases when you will likely need to send a string to the server: when sending form data, when writing a cookie, and when requesting a URL.

**validate**   To verify that some piece of data is correct in terms of value or format.

**variable**   A symbolic name that represents a value that can, and likely will, change during a program's execution. Physically, it is a storage place in memory that can be accessed using a symbolic name that is chosen by the programmer when the variable is declared.

**vi**   Pronounced by saying each letter ("vee-aye"), a popular text editor widely used on Unix-based systems. Like Pico and Emacs, vi is primarily used for writing scripts, short notes, and email messages. Control is primarily by keyboard rather than the combination of keyboard and mouse usually seen in Windows and Macintosh text editors. It was invented before Emacs, another Unix-based text editor. Almost all Unix systems have a copy of vi installed. Its wide availability and succinct interface make it extremely useful for people who work on a computer all day.

**visitor** A person who views a Web site with a Web browser.

**W3C** See *World Wide Web Consortium.*

**Web browser** A program used to view Web sites and to access other types of content on the Internet.

**Web client** A Web browser.

**Web development process** A phased process by which Web sites are created.

**Web server** Either a machine that runs Web server software to provide access to Web pages or the software that performs that function.

**while loop** A loop control structure that continues executing a set of statements as long as some condition is true or until that condition is false.

**window** A browser window in which Web documents can be viewed.

**window object** An object that represents a browser window.

**Windows** An operating system with a graphical user interface, created by Microsoft.

**with** A control structure that allows the programmer to avoid typing the entire formal address of each and every property or method in a group of statements that all deal with the same object again and again.

**World Wide Web Consortium** The maker of all Web specifications.

**XBDHTML** See *Cross-Browser Dynamic HTML.*

**XHTML** A markup language specification by the W3C that is supposed to act as a bridge for Web developers between the user-friendly, forgiving HTML and the strict, unforgiving syntax of XML.

**XML** See *Extensible Markup Language.*

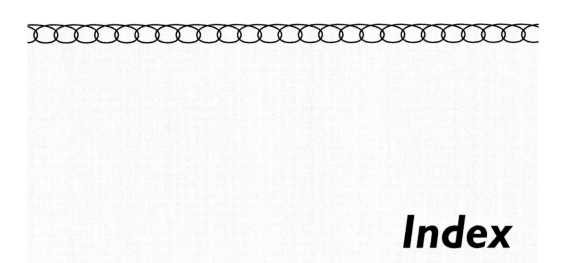

# Index

# Other Titles from Franklin, Beedle & Associates

To order these books and find out more about Franklin, Beedle & Associates, visit us online at **www.fbeedle.com**.

## The Internet & the World Wide Web

Internet & Web Essentials: What You Need to Know (isbn 1-887902-40-6)
Learning to Use the Internet & the World Wide Web (isbn 1-887902-78-3)
Searching & Researching on the Internet & the World Wide Web: Third Edition
    (isbn 1-887902-71-6)
Web Design & Development Using XHTML (isbn 1-887902-57-0)
The Web Page Workbook: Second Edition (isbn 1-887902-45-7)

## Computer Science

ASP: Learning by Example (isbn 1-887902-68-6)
Basic Java Programming: A Laboratory Approach (isbn 1-887902-67-8)
Computing Fundamentals with C++: Object-Oriented Programming & Design: Second
    Edition (isbn 1-887902-36-8)
Computing Fundamentals with Java (isbn 1-887902-47-3)
Data Structures with Java: A Laboratory Approach (isbn 1-887902-70-8)
DHTML: Learning by Example (isbn 1-887902-83-X)
Fundamentals of Secure Computing Systems (isbn 1-887902-66-X)—*Upcoming*
Guide to Persuasive Programming (isbn 1-887902-65-1)
Modern Programming Languages: A Practical Introduction (isbn 1-887902-76-7)
Prelude to Patterns in Computer Science Using Java: Beta Edition (isbn 1-887902-55-4)
XML: Learning by Example (isbn 1-887902-80-5)

## Operating Systems

Linux eTudes (isbn 1-887902-62-7)

Linux User's Guide: Using the Command Line & GNOME with Red Hat Linux
(isbn 1-887902-50-3)

Understanding Practical Unix (isbn 1-887902-53-8)

Windows 95: Concepts & Examples (isbn 1-887902-00-7)

Windows 98: Concepts & Examples (isbn 1-887902-37-6)

Windows 2000 Professional Command Line (isbn 1-887902-79-1)

Windows 2000 Professional: Concepts & Examples (isbn 1-887902-51-1)

Windows Millennium Edition: Concepts & Examples (isbn 1-887902-49-X)

Windows User's Guide to DOS: Using the Command Line in Windows 95/98
(isbn 1-887902-42-2)

Windows User's Guide to DOS: Using the Command Line in Windows 2000 Professional
(isbn 1-887902-72-4)

Windows User's Guide to DOS: Using the Command Line in Windows Millennium Edition
(isbn 1-887902-64-3)

Windows XP Command Line (isbn 1-887902-82-1)

Windows XP: Concepts & Examples (isbn 1-887902-81-3)

## Software Applications

Access 97 for Windows: Concepts & Examples (isbn 1-887902-29-5)

Excel 97 for Windows: Concepts & Examples (isbn 1-887902-25-2)

Microsoft Office 97 Professional: A Mastery Approach (isbn 1-887902-24-4)

## Professional Reference & Technology in Education

The Dictionary of Computing & Digital Media Terms & Acronyms (isbn 1-887902-38-4)

The Dictionary of Multimedia (isbn 1-887902-14-7)

Technology Tools in the Social Studies Curriculum (isbn 1-887902-06-6)